ANIMOSITY, THE BIBLE, AND US

Society of Biblical Literature

Global Perspectives on Biblical Scholarship

Number 12

ANIMOSITY, THE BIBLE, AND US:
SOME EUROPEAN, NORTH AMERICAN,
AND SOUTH AFRICAN PERSPECTIVES

ANIMOSITY, THE BIBLE, AND US

SOME EUROPEAN, NORTH AMERICAN, AND SOUTH AFRICAN PERSPECTIVES

Edited by
John T. Fitzgerald,
Fika J. van Rensburg,
and
Herrie F. van Rooy

Society of Biblical Literature
Atlanta

ANIMOSITY, THE BIBLE, AND US: SOME EUROPEAN, NORTH AMERICAN, AND SOUTH AFRICAN PERSPECTIVES

Copyright © 2009 by the Society of Biblical Literature

All rights reserved. No part of this work may be reproduced or transmitted in any form or by any means, electronic or mechanical, including photocopying and recording, or by means of any information storage or retrieval system, except as may be expressly permitted by the 1976 Copyright Act or in writing from the publisher. Requests for permission should be addressed in writing to the Rights and Permissions Office, Society of Biblical Literature, 825 Houston Mill Road, Atlanta, GA 30329 USA.

Library of Congress Cataloging-in-Publication Data

Society of Biblical Literature. International Meeting (2004 : Gröningen, Germany).
    Animosity, the Bible, and us : some European, North American, and South African perspectives / edited by John T. Fitzgerald, Fika J. van Rensburg, and Herrie F. van Rooy.
        p. cm. — (Society of Biblical Literature global perspectives on biblical scholarship ; no. 12)
    "This collection of essays is the result of a three-year research project launched in 2004 by the School of Biblical Studies and Bible Languages at North-West University in Potchefstroom, South Africa ... this project was pursued at the 2004 International Meeting of the Society of Biblical Literature in Groningen and at meetings of the European Association of Biblical Studies from 2004 to 2006"—Pref.
    Includes bibliographical references and indexes.
    ISBN 978-1-58983-401-9 (pbk. : alk. paper)
    1. Violence—Biblical teaching—Congresses. 2. Hostility (Psychology)—Biblical teaching—Congresses. I. Fitzgerald, John T., 1948- II. Van Rensburg, Fika, 1951- III. Rooy, Herrie F. van. IV. European Association of Biblical Studies. V. Title.
    BS680.V55S63 2004
    220.8'3036—dc22   2009026564

            17 16 15 14 13 12 11 10 09   5 4 3 2 1
    Printed in the United States of America on acid-free, recycled paper conforming to ANSI/NISO Z39.48-1992 (R1997) and ISO 9706:1994 standards for paper permanence.

Contents

Preface
  John T. Fitzgerald vii

Abbreviations xi

War and Violence in the Old Testament World: Various Views
  Eben Scheffler 1

The World's First Murder: Violence and Justice in Genesis 4:1–16
  Eric Peels 19

The Enemies in the Headings of the Psalms: A Comparison of
Jewish and Christian Interpretation
  Herrie F. van Rooy 41

Disputes about the Calendar in Jewish Apocalyptic Literature and
Its Basis
  Marius Nel 59

Animosity in Targumic Literature
  Eveline van Staalduine-Sulman 87

Domestic Violence in the Ancient World: Preliminary Considerations
and the Problem of Wife-Beating
  John T. Fitzgerald 101

Animosity against Jewish and Pagan Magic in the Acts of the Apostles
  Rainer G. H. Reuter 123

Paul and the Others: Insiders, Outsiders, and Animosity
  Jeremy Punt 137

Switching Universes: Moving from a Cosmology of Fear and
Animosity to One of Reconciliation in Colossians
  J. J. Fritz Krüger 153

Useless Commandment: Animosity toward the Earlier Covenant in Hebrews
    Outi Leppä 177

No Retaliation! An Ethical Analysis of the Exhortation in 1 Peter 3:9 Not to Repay Evil with Evil
    Fika J. van Rensburg 199

Animosity in the Johannine Epistles: A Difference in the Interpretation of a Shared Tradition
    Dirk G. van der Merwe 231

Hostility against the Wealth of Babylon: Revelation 17:1–19:10
    Paul B. Decock 263

Animosity and (Voluntary) Martyrdom: The Power of the Powerless
    Henk Bakker 287

Assessment—Animosity, the Bible, and Us: A Few Tentative Remarks
    Herrie F. van Rooy 299

Bibliography 301

Contributors 331

Index of Ancient Authors and Texts 335

Index of Modern Scholars 356

Preface

Animosity is a perennial problem that has plagued every form of interpersonal and international relationship from the dawn of human existence. The histories of all peoples have shown, time and again, that any kind of deep-seated bitterness rarely remains dormant for a great length of time. On the contrary, it seethes and simmers beneath the surface, festering like a wound. At any moment, with or without provocation, it is liable to break out into the open, manifesting itself in all kinds of hostile words and hateful acts. Although animosity is hardly a new problem in today's world, it is, unfortunately, a prevalent one, and modern technology has raised its potential consequences to a frightening level.

The term itself appears to have entered the English language in the fifteenth century, when the French noun *animosité* was Anglicized as "animosity." The French word was not a new coinage but simply derived from the postclassical Latin term *animositas*. The latter is used by the Vulgate to render the Greek word θυμός (*thymos*) in both 2 Cor 12:20 and Heb 11:27 (see also Sir 31:30 LXX = 31:40 Vulg.). As that translation already suggests, the ancient world was well aware of the link between anger and animosity, and several of the essays included in this volume provide further evidence of this linkage.

This collection of essays is the result of a three-year research project launched in 2004 by the School of Biblical Studies and Ancient Languages at North-West University in Potchefstroom, South Africa. Because animosity is a global problem, this endeavor was designed from the outset as an international effort, with contributors from three different continents offering perspectives on the subject of "Animosity, the Bible, and Us." Under the leadership of my co-editors, Fika J. van Rensburg and Herrie F. van Rooy, this project was pursued at the 2004 International Meeting of the Society of Biblical Literature in Groningen and at meetings of the European Association of Biblical Studies from 2004 to 2006. Participants presented papers on a wide variety of topics, some dealing with the Bible and others with different aspects of animosity in the ancient Near East and the Greek and Roman worlds. Some gave considerable attention to the hermeneutical implications of their findings; others left it to readers to draw the implications for themselves. For reasons of space, not all contributions could be included in this volume. Those that were selected for inclusion have been revised and updated for publication. Five contributors are from Europe (three from the Netherlands and one each from Finland and Russia), one is from North America (the United States), and eight are from Africa (from various universities in South Africa).

The original goal of the project was to examine the biblical text to see how it understands and presents the phenomenon of animosity and to glean any insights that it might offer to help us address this problem. At the same time, we knew from the outset that the Bible itself and how it has been used have sometimes contributed to the problem of animosity. Ours is not the first generation to be troubled by various things that we read—or do not read—in Scripture. To give but one example, after the Egyptians have drowned in the Sea of Reeds, the Israelites, led by Moses and Miriam, sing a song to Yahweh celebrating his triumph and their deliverance (Exod 15). This is a perfectly natural human response, especially after the harsh oppression the Israelites suffered at the hands of the Egyptians. Yet some later rabbis, troubled by the moral problem of singing and dancing festively when there has been a grievous loss of human life, asked: Is this also God's response? To address this issue, some created a midrash in which God had a dialogue with his angels, who wanted to join in the singing of the Israelites' song. In this connection, Rabbi Yohanan not only declared that the Holy One "does not rejoice at the downfall of the wicked" but also has God rebuke the angels and shame them into silence by saying, "My creatures are drowning in the sea, yet you wish to sing a song?"[1]

The volume comprises fourteen essays. We begin with Eben Scheffler's examination of the phenomenon of war and violence within the context of the ancient Near East, then turn to the Hebrew Bible and the Jewish traditions connected with it, within the context of ancient Israel and the ancient Near East. Eric Peels discusses Cain's killing of Abel, the Bible's first case of homicide. This is followed by the essay of Herrie van Rooy, who gives attention to the Psalter and the many occasions on which a psalmist makes reference to

---

1. I cite the form of the statement as it appears in b. Meg. 10b; the translation is that of Jacob Neusner, *Bavli Tractate Megillah* (vol. 10 of *The Talmud of Babylonia: An Academic Commentary*; Atlanta: Scholars Press, 1995), 49, slightly modified and with the brackets removed. A similar version of the saying appears in Midrash Rabbah on Exod 23:7: "When the angels desired to chant Song before God on that night when Israel crossed the Sea, the Holy One, blessed be He, prevented them, saying, 'My legions are in distress, and you wish to utter Song before Me?'" (trans. S. M. Lehrman in H. Freedman and M. Simon, eds., *Midrash Rabbah* [3rd ed.; 10 vols.; London: Soncino, 1983], 3:285).

his enemies. Later tradition tried to identify these enemies, and van Rooy compares and contrasts the Jewish and Christian interpretations of the enemies as they are reflected in the headings to the psalms.

During the Hasmonean and Roman periods of Jewish history, numerous debates involved the Jerusalem temple. One of these centered on the calendar to be used for the observance of holy days and festivals, and more than a few individuals were alarmed by the prospect of a Jewish high priest, using the wrong calendar, entering the adytum of the sanctuary on a day that was not the true Yom Kippur. The essay by Marius Nel examines this controversy, giving particular attention to the differences among the competing calendars. His essay is followed by that of Eveline van Staalduine-Sulman, who examines animosity in Targumic literature, comparing its depiction of certain instances of enmity and hostility with that of the Hebrew Bible. As is the case with modern cinematic depictions of biblical characters and scenes, the Targumim change the picture of acrimonious relationships in revealing ways.

Following my discussion of the problem of domestic violence in the ancient world, we turn to early Christian literature outside the Gospels. We begin this section of the volume with Rainer Reuter's discussion of three episodes involving magic in the Acts of the Apostles. The next two essays deal with quite different issues in the Pauline corpus. Jeremy Punt discusses Paul's penchant for using insider/outsider terminology and the potential for animosity engendered by this kind of language. Fritz Krüger explores the prospects for our dealing effectively with the problem of animosity by examining the cosmological narrative embedded in Colossians, comparing it and its worldview with two other such narratives.

Outi Leppä discusses Hebrews and its author's extensive use of the rhetorical technique of comparison (*synkrisis*) to exalt Christ at the expense of the people and institutions connected with the former covenant, and she argues that this "word of exhortation" (Heb 13:22) is not only disparaging but also generates feelings of animosity. In the next essay, Fika J. van Rensburg examines a quite different problem, that of abused Christians who are encouraged by the author of 1 Peter not to retaliate by repaying evil for evil (1 Pet 3:9). Yet another situation involving animosity surfaces in the Johannine Epistles, where there is open hostility between different groups of Christian believers, each refusing to extend hospitality to the other group. This acrimonious situation is discussed by Dirk van der Merwe.

Apocalyptic literature frequently offers a vision of the future in which the suffering righteous are vindicated and their oppressors punished. The book of Revelation is typical in that regard, with the seer John giving us a vision of the downfall of "Babylon." Paul Decock discusses this Christian animus toward Rome, giving special attention to how various interpreters have understood this animosity and its function. The final essay is that of Henk Bakker, who looks at martyrdom in the early church. He gives particular attention to the phenomenon of voluntary martyrdom, arguing that it was and still can be "the power of the powerless" in confronting open aggression. The volume is brought to a close by Herrie van Rooy's assessment of this research project. He notes its contributions and limitations, and he expresses the hope that this volume may be a stimulus to future studies in this important area of research and reflection.

John T. Fitzgerald

Abbreviations

AB	Anchor Bible
ABD	*Anchor Bible Dictionary*. Edited by David Noel Freedman. 6 vols. New York: Doubleday, 1992.
ANTC	Abingdon New Testament Commentaries
AJP	*American Journal of Philology*
AJSR	*Association for Jewish Studies Review*
ANET	*Ancient Near Eastern Texts Relating to the Old Testament*. Edited by James B. Pritchard. 3rd ed. Princeton: Princeton University Press, 1969.
ANF	*The Ante-Nicene Fathers: Translations of the Writings of the Fathers Down to A.D. 325*. Edited by Alexander Roberts and James Donaldson. 10 vols. 1885–87. Repr., Peabody, Mass.: Hendrickson, 1994.
ArBib	The Aramaic Bible
BAGD	Bauer, Walter, William F. Arndt, F. Wilbur Gingrich, and Frederick W. Danker. *A Greek-English Lexicon of the New Testament and Other Early Christian Literature*. 2nd ed. Chicago: University of Chicago Press, 1979.
BAR	*Biblical Archeology Review*
BDAG	Bauer, Walter, Frederick W. Danker, William F. Arndt, and F. Wilbur Gingrich. *A Greek-English Lexicon of the New Testament and Other Early Christian Literature*. 3rd ed. Chicago: University of Chicago Press, 2000.
BETL	Bibliotheca ephemeridum theologicarum lovaniensium
BHS	*Biblia Hebraica Stuttgartensia*. Edited by Karl Elliger and Willhelm Rudolph. Stuttgart: Deutsche Bibelgesellschaft, 1983.
Bib	*Biblica*
BibInt	*Biblical Interpretation*
BJRLM	*Bulletin of the John Rylands Library of Manchester*
BJS	Brown Judaic Studies
BKAT	Biblischer Kommentar Altes Testaments
BN	*Biblische Notizen*

BNTC	Black's New Testament Commentaries
BTB	*Biblical Theology Bulletin*
BZAW	Beihefte zur Zeitschrift für die alttestamentliche Wissenschaft
CBQ	*Catholic Biblical Quarterly*
CBQMS	Catholic Biblical Quarterly Monograph Series
CQ	*Communication Quarterly*
CRINT	Compendia rerum Iudaicarum ad Novum Testamentum
CurBR	*Currents in Biblical Research*
DDD	*Dictionary of Deities and Demons in the Bible*. Edited by Karel van der Toorn, Bob Becking, and Pieter W. van der Horst. Leiden: Brill, 1995.
DNP	*Der neue Pauly: Enzyklopädie der Antike*. Edited by Hubert Cancik and Helmuth Schneider. Stuttgart: Metzler, 1996–.
EABS	European Association of Biblical Studies
EAJS	European Association of Jewish Studies
ET	English translation
FAT	Forschungen zum Alten Testament
FB	Forschung zur Bibel
FC	Fathers of the Church
FCNTECW	Feminist Companion to the New Testament and Early Christian Writings
FOTL	Forms of the Old Testament Literature
FRLANT	Forschungen zur Religion und Literatur des Alten und Neuen Testaments
HDR	Harvard Dissertations in Religion
HKAT	Handkommentar zum Alten Testament
HNT	Handbuch zum Neuen Testament
HTKNT	Herders theologischer Kommentar zum Neuen Testament
HTR	*Harvard Theological Review*
HUCA	*Hebrew Union College Annual*
HvTSt	*Hervormde teologiese studies*
ICC	International Critical Commentary
Int	*Interpretation*
ITC	International Theological Commentary
JAB	*Journal for the Aramaic Bible*
JBL	*Journal of Biblical Literature*
JECS	*Journal of Early Christian Studies*
JETS	*Journal of the Evangelical Theological Society*
JJS	*Journal of Jewish Studies*
JNSL	*Journal of Northwest Semitic Languages*
JPS	Jewish Publication Society

JRS	*Journal of Roman Studies*
JSJ	*Journal for the Study of Judaism in the Persian, Hellenistic and Roman Periods*
JSNT	*Journal for the Study of the New Testament*
JSNTSup	Journal for the Study of the New Testament Supplement Series
JSOT	*Journal for the Study of the Old Testament*
JSOTSup	Journal for the Study of the Old Testament Supplement Series
JSP	*Journal for the Study of the Pseudepigrapha*
JSPSup	Journal for the Study of the Pseudepigrapha Supplement Series
JTS	*Journal of Theological Studies*
KEK	Kritisch-exegetischer Kommentar
KV	Korte Verklaring der Heilige Schrift
LN	*Greek-English Lexicon of the New Testament: Based on Semantic Domains*. Edited by J. P. Louw and Eugene A. Nida. 2nd ed. New York: United Bible Societies, 1989.
LCBI	Literary Currents in Biblical Interpretation
LCL	Loeb Classical Library
LEC	Library of Early Christianity
LNTS	Library of New Testament Studies
NAC	New American Commentary
NCB	New Century Bible
Neot	*Neotestamentica*
NGTT	*Nederduitse gereformeerde teologiese tydskrif*
NICNT	New international Commentary on the New Testament
NICOT	New International Commentary on the Old Testament
NIDOTTE	*New International Dictionary of Old Testament Theology and Exegesis*. Edited by Willem A. VanGemeren. 5 vols. Grand Rapids: Zondervan, 1997.
NLT	New Living Translation
NovT	*Novum Testamentum*
NovTSup	Supplements to Novum Testamentum
NRSV	New Revised Standard Version
NTD	Das Neue Testament Deutsch
NTS	*New Testament Studies*
OBT	Overtures to Biblical Theology
OCD	*The Oxford Classical Dictionary*. Edited by Simon Hornblower and Antony Spawforth. 3rd ed. Oxford: Oxford University Press, 1996.
OTE	Old Testament Essays

ÖTK	Ökumenischer Taschenbuch-Kommentar
OTL	Old Testament Library
OTP	*The Old Testament Pseudepigrapha*. Edited by James H. Charlesworth. 2 vols. New York: Doubleday, 1983–85.
OtSt	Oudtestamentische Studiën
OtSt	*Oudtestamentische Studiën*
OTWSA	*Ou-Testamentiese Werkgemeenskap van Suid-Afrika*
PGM	*Papyri graecae magicae: Die griechischen Zauberpapyri*. Edited by Karl Preisendanz. 2 vols. in 6 parts. Leipzig: Teubner, 1928–31.
PW	*Paulys Real-Encyklopädie der classischen Altertumswissenschaft*. New edition by Georg Wissowa and Wilhelm Kroll. 50 vols. in 84 parts. Stuttgart: Metzler and Druckenmüller, 1894–1980.
RevQ	*Revue de Qumran*
RGG	*Religion in Geschichte und Gegenwart*. Edited by Kurt Galling. 7 vols. 3rd ed. Tübingen: Mohr Siebeck, 1957–65.
RHR	*Revue de l'histoire des religions*
RNT	Regensburger Neues Testament
RSV	Revised Standard Version
SAIS	Studies in Aramaic Interpretation of Scripture
SBLDS	Society of Biblical Literature Dissertation Series
SBLEJL	Society of Biblical Literature Early Judaism and Its Literature
SBLSBS	Society of Biblical Literature Sources for Biblical Study
SBLSymS	Society of Biblical Literature Symposium Series
SBLWGRW	Society of Biblical Literature Writings from the Greco-Roman World
SBM	Stuttgarter biblische Monographien
SBS	Stuttgarter Bibelstudien
SBT	Studies in Biblical Theology
SCHNT	Studia ad corpus hellenisticum Novi Testamenti
SJLA	Studies in Judaism in Late Antiquity
SJT	*Scottish Journal of Theology*
SNTSMS	Society for New Testament Studies Monograph Series
SPCK	Society for Promoting Christian Knowledge
SSJC	Sources for the Study of Jewish Culture
STDJ	Studies on the Texts of the Desert of Judah
SVTP	Studia in Veteris Testamenti pseudepigraphica
TAPS	Transactions of the American Philosophical Society
TDNT	*Theological Dictionary of the New Testament*. Edited by Gerhard Kittel and Gerhard Friedrich. Translated by Geoffrey W.

	Bromiley. 10 vols. Grand Rapids: Eerdmans, 1964–76.
Tg.	Targum
Tg. Jon.	Targum Jonathan (to the Prophets)
Tg. Neof.	Targum Neofiti (to the Torah)
Tg. Ps.-J.	Targum Pseudo-Jonathan (to the Torah)
THKNT	Theologischer Handkommentar zum Neuen Testament
TNTC	Tyndale New Testament Commentaries
ThWAT	*Theologisches Wörterbuch zum Alten Testament*. Edited by G. Johannes Botterweck and Helmer Ringgren. Stuttgart: Kohlhammer, 1970–.
VT	*Vetus Testamentum*
VTSup	Supplements to Vetus Testamentum
WBC	Word Biblical Commentary
WMANT	Wissenschaftliche Monographien zum Alten und Neuen Testament
WUNT	Wissenschaftliche Untersuchungen zum Neuen Testament
ZAW	*Zeitschrift für die alttestamentliche Wissenschaft*
ZBK	Zürcher Bibelkommentar
ZBNT	Zürcher Bibelkommentare Neues Testament
ZNW	*Zeitschrift für die neutestamentliche Wissenschaft*

WAR AND VIOLENCE IN THE OLD TESTAMENT WORLD: VARIOUS VIEWS

Eben Scheffler

1. INTRODUCTION

The title of the paper is two-pronged. It deals with the variety (and contrary) views of violence in the Old Testament world, as well as the variety of scholarly viewpoints on this matter. Various forms of violence existed in the Old Testament world, including interpersonal physical assault and murder (e.g., Cain and Abel,[1] Moses and the Egyptian, violent coups d'état), rape (e.g., Dinah and the gang rape in Judg 19), psychological violence (e.g., giving false witness to the neighbor), the death penalty,[2] and, of course, war. Without denying the importance of these various forms (which all deserve in-depth investigation),[3] in this paper I have confined myself to the issue of war for a twofold reason: because it produces death and suffering on such a large scale; and because it is the only form of violence that is still sanctioned and even religiously justified by most societies in the world. The option of pacifism is not only seldom tolerated in human societies; in most societies it is even detested and punished.

In his short overview on war and violence in the Old Testament world, Kraus reflects on what can be called the general view on violence and war as far as the Old Testament is concerned.[4] This general view is essentially

---

1. See the contribution of Eric Peels in this volume.
2. See Francis Klopper, "Doodstraf in Ou-Testamentiese Perspektief" (M.A. thesis, University of Port Elizabeth, 1988).
3. See Susan Niditch, *War in the Hebrew Bible* (New York: Oxford University Press, 1993); and Peet van Dyk, "Violence and the Old Testament," *OTE* 16 (2003): 96–112.
4. Hans-Joachim Kraus, "Krieg im AT," *RGG* 4:64–65.

monolithic and "marcionitic"[5] in nature, regarding war and violence not only as part and parcel of the Old Testament message, but also actually characteristic of it.

The features of this "general view" are the following: Yahweh Sebaot (probably but not definitely meaning "Yahweh of the armies") is a warrior god (Exod 12:41; 15:3), and the ark is the palladium of his presence in Israel's war (1 Sam 4:3). Yahweh himself wages the wars, which are actually *his* wars (Exod 14:4; Deut 1:30; Josh 10:14; Num 21:14). The occupation of the land is depicted by the book of Joshua as a laudable military victory.[6]

It became an accepted view that there existed (particularly in the "theocratic" period of the Judges) an institution of "holy war" (following von Rad)[7] where war was totally sanctified and justified and where there existed a complete overlap between Israel's needs and Yahweh's will.

The need for military stability is the cause of the monarchy, explaining the conflict between Samuel and the people over whether or not there should be kings. The idea that Yahweh *alone* provides victory in war now seems to be abandoned. Kings like Saul and David are essentially military leaders, the latter even waging imperialistic wars, whereas, although Solomon did not wage any wars, his kingdom was also based on military strength (1 Kgs 10:26). David and Solomon also had personal bodyguards. The king still consults Yahweh (2 Sam 8:14), and the wars are to an extent still interpreted as Yahweh's wars (1 Sam 18:17). During the monarchy, Israel became part and parcel of the political and military conflicts of the ancient Near East (involving especially Egypt, Syria, Assyria, Babylonia, and Persia) with its coalitions and intrigues (see, e.g., Isa 18:1; 30:1; 31:1).[8]

Even the prophetic advice to King Ahaz (Isa 7:4), for example, is not interpreted by Kraus as a criticism of war but as defense of the tradition of holy war in which God finally acts (Isa 31:4; Pss 44; 60; Zech 4:6).[9]

---

5. The classic treatment of Marcion's views is that of Adolf von Harnack, *Marcion: Das Evangelium vom fremden Gott* (Darmstadt: Wissenschaftliche Buchgesellschaft, 1960). For a brief discussion, see John Bright, *The Authority of the Old Testament* (Grand Rapids: Baker, 1975), 60–79.

6. See Kraus, "Krieg im AT," 64–65.

7. Gerard von Rad, *Der Heilige Krieg im alten Israel* (Zürich: Theologischer Verlag, 1951); ET: *Holy War in Ancient Israel* (trans. and ed. Marva J. Dawn; Grand Rapids: Eerdmans, 1991).

8. Eben H. Scheffler, *Politics in Ancient Israel* (Pretoria: Biblia, 2001), 88–166.

9. Kraus, "Krieg im AT," 65.

Even the eschatological future is interpreted in terms of war. On the *yom Yahweh* the military power of Yahweh will subjugate the Gentile nations and bring an end to all arrogant worldly power (Ezek 30; Isa 13; 34; Zeph 1:7).

It is my contention that this one-sided, monolithic perspective on war in the Old Testament world is essentially false and based on a confessional view of Israel's traditions and scriptures as authoritative and holy in themselves, and therefore demanding a unified interpretation. This situation not only jeopardizes any attempt to eradicate war in the modern world where the Old Testament still exerts authority in world Christianity, but to my mind violates the essential nature of the Old Testament itself. The Old Testament (as I hope to illustrate) does not reflect a unified view on war and violence at all, but rather a diversity of perspectives and an inner dialogue between different views.

Rather than providing a military history of ancient Israel,[10] discussing all its wars (such a discussion would in any case be too voluminous), in what follows I attempt to provide a glimpse into the diversity of views on war and its complexities. To my mind this must be done undauntedly and fearlessly if one wants to proceed to what I can only call "preliminary thoughts on a hermeneutical reflection" on the issue of war and violence in view of its ultimate eradication. Before I attempt the latter, I therefore first pay attention to the religious sanctification of war in the Old Testament world, the romantic and heroic view of war, the criticism of war, the basic nonviolent stance of the Old Testament, and instances of proactive intervention or pacifism. References are also made to the ancient Near Eastern world to show that ancient Israel was not in all dimensions unique as far as its reflection on and appropriation of war is concerned.

2. The Religious Sanctification and Justification of War in the Old Testament

Von Rad's view that presupposes the existence of an institution of holy war in ancient Israel became universally accepted among Old Testament scholars during the latter half of the previous century. Although the term "holy war" does not exist in Hebrew (as *polemos ieros* and *jihad* exist in Greek and Arabic), the characteristics of this phenomenon can be deduced from various pieces of information scattered in the texts. These characteristics (that sanctify and justify a war effort), are (in short) the following: (1) the war starts

---

10. For a short overview, see Roland de Vaux, *Ancient Israel: Its Life and Institutions* (trans. John McHugh; London: Darton, Longman & Todd, 1961), 247–50.

with a trumpet call (Judg 6:34); (2) the army is called "people of Yahweh" (Judg 5:11, 13; 20:2); (3) the soldiers are consecrated before going into battle (Deut 23:9; Josh 3:5; 1 Sam 21:6); (4) sacrifices are offered to Yahweh before the battle (1 Sam 7:9; 13:9); (5) the priests or prophets consult Yahweh on the outcome (Judg 20:23, 27; 1 Sam 7:9; 1 Kgs 22); (6) the holy oracle ("Yahweh has given into your hands") contains Yahweh's answer that ensures victory (Josh 2:24; 6:2); (7) the fearlessness of the people is ensured (by Yahweh's oracle and sending home those who fear, Judg 4:14; Deut 20); (8) fear and the divine terror fall on the enemy (Exod 15:14; 23:27), often involving natural phenomena as well; (9) the final divine ban of the enemy (*herem*) ensures that the enemy is totally eradicated (Josh 6:18; 1 Sam 15) and "sacrificed" to God. The fact that no booty may be taken (except in foreign wars; see Deut 20) is an indication that the war belongs to Yahweh.

These elements were not always present in all the wars in Israel's history. During the period of the monarchy, the king (and not Yahweh) is often portrayed as leading the people in battle. Ordinary politics come into play, as can be gleaned from the summary of the imperialistic wars of David in 2 Sam 8. Nevertheless, Yahweh is still seen as the one who "made David victorious everywhere" (2 Sam 8:14).

When differences surfaced on the justification of a war, prophetic opposition (especially in the case of Isaiah), instead of condemning the wars directly, would ironically appeal to Yahweh's intervention as in a holy war. Isaiah's advice to Ahaz is that the king must be quiet and still and Yahweh alone will ensure victory and scatter the enemy (Isa 7; 30:15–16). However, this appeal to the holy war was only partial, since the latter definitely involved the participation of the people themselves (contra Isa 30:15–16).[11]

According to Zimmerli[12] the term "holy war" is perhaps a misnomer, and the term "Yahweh's war" (see the *sefer milchamot Yahweh* referred to in Num 21:14) should rather be used. Besides the fact that this view allows for the possibility that not everything that comes from Yahweh is automatically holy, the features mentioned by von Rad are all present and the religious nature of war prevalent.

In de Vaux's view, ancient Israel's idea of "holy war" differs from the *jihad* of the Islamic world, since it is not waged to spread the faith among the

---

11. Although "holy war" and prophetic "pacifism" seem to represent opposite views on war in the Old Testament, there seems to be an "ironic" similarity: Yahweh's action, participation, or intervention.

12. Walther Zimmerli, *Die Weltlichkeit des Alten Testaments* (Göttingen: Vandenhoeck & Ruprecht, 1971); ET: *The Old Testament and the World* (trans. John J. Scullion; Atlanta: John Knox, 1976).

nations but functions to ensure the existence of Israel as a nation.[13] It is not clear why de Vaux emphasizes this distinction. If, however, it is done to justify ancient Israel's holy wars, while rejecting the *jihad*, to my mind it is hardly convincing.

The fact is that in ancient Israel generally, no distinction was made between sacred and secular reality, especially when life and death issues were at stake. As occasionally occurs in all human societies and especially in the ancient Near East of the first three millennia B.C.E., war was a reality in the life of ancient Israel. The national gods of the ancient Near East were all involved in their wars. An example close to ancient Israel illustrates this. On the famous Moabite Stone from Diban in Jordan, King Mesha receives his order to wage war against Israel from his god Chemosh, to whom he also attributes his victory.

> And Chemosh said to me, "Go and take Nebo from Israel." So I went by night and fought against it from the break of dawn until noon, taking it and slaying it all, seven thousand men, boys, women, girls and maid-servants, for I had devoted them for the destruction for Ashtar-Chemosh.... Chemosh drove him out before me....[14]

As in the case of ancient Israel, the god here also gives the instruction that the war should take place, he gives the victory, and the enemy becomes the victim of a ban that makes the people of Nebo a sacrifice to the god of King Mesha.

Israel therefore seems not to have decided to make war and then rationally and theologically reflected on whether the war was justified or not. Everything seems to have occurred simultaneously. The war itself was experienced as a religious act from start to finish and as such represented the ultimate example of any form of *ius in bello*.

3. The Romantic and Heroic View of War

One way to ensure that ordinary people (who normally are expected to refrain from killing) do on occasion engage in war is to portray war as something that God expects (as in a holy war). Another way is to glorify it. The participants of war are glorified and praised for their courage and valor. Probably at an early age children in ancient Israel were told stories about Israel's

---

13. De Vaux, *Ancient Israel*.
14. Translation adapted from *ANET*, 320–21; for a translation and discussion, see Eben H. Scheffler, *Fascinating Discoveries from the Biblical World* (Pretoria: Biblia, 2000), 86–89.

leaders, which were not only entertaining but also ensured that, when the day for duty eventually arrived, they would comply. The story of David and Goliath (1 Sam 17) probably had such a function. David, even in his youth, displayed great courage in fighting the giant. Trusting in God, he succeeded. The same holds true in the case of Gideon (Judg 6), where the emphasis is placed on the bravery of a few men rather than large numbers. During the time of the judges, Deborah and Samson (Judg 4–5; 13–15) also played this role, despite all the violence involved. In the latter stories it is as if the explicit portrayal of extreme violence serves the ideology of the text. No one entertained by these stories dares to doubt that the war effort is justified. It can even be enjoyed.

In the ancient Near East, the praise of kings and leaders who were brave men who defeated many nations has the function of making subjects proud of their history and traditions and want to identify with these traditions. From Egyptian history we know that Merneptah was not such a successful militarist, but the stela that bears his name (or the so-called Israel Stela) reports the following:

> Great rejoicing has risen in Egypt
> jubilation has issued from the towns of Egypt
> they recount the victories
> which Merneptah wrought in Libya
> how beloved he is, the victorious ruler
> how exalted is the king among the gods
> how fortunate he is, the master of command…
>
> The princes lie prostrate begging for peace
> not one lifts his head among the Nine Bows
> destruction for Libya; Hatti is pacified
> Canaan is plundered with every evil
> Ashkelon is taken, Gezer is captured
> Yanoam is made nonexistent
> Israel lies desolate, its seed is no more
> Hurru has become a widow of Egypt
> All the lands in their entirety are at peace
> All the nomads have been curbed by King Merneptah.[15]

---

15. Translation adapted from *ANET*, 376–78; for a discussion of the stela, see Scheffler, *Fascinating Discoveries*, 82–85.

The deeds of the king are exaggerated and glorified and written on a stela (a monument about 3 meters high and 1.5 meters wide) where everybody can see and read it.

The same function is served by the two-meter-high Black Obelisk of King Shalmaneser III, who ruled Assyria from 858 to 824, found by Layard in Nimrud. The obelisk's four sides have five rows of sculptured reliefs containing scenes of tribute-bearing with captions above the panels in cuneiform referring to the contents of the depictions. For the student of the Old Testament, the second row of reliefs is of particular importance. The first panel shows King Jehu (who ruled northern Israel 842–814 B.C.E.) or his emissary prostrating himself before the king of Assyria with his forehead to the ground, possibly in the process of kissing the king's feet. Above the king's head is a winged symbol of the Assyrian god Ashur protecting and affirming him. Behind Jehu are four Assyrians followed by thirteen Israelite tribute-bearers. The superscription above the panel reads: "Tribute of Jehu, son of Omri. Silver, gold, a golden bowl, golden beaker, golden goblets, pitchers of gold, tin, staves for the hand of the king, javelins, I received from him."[16] There is no mention in the Bible that Jehu paid tribute to the Assyrian king. This should be interpreted in view of the fact that the Bible itself also tends to glorify (some of) Israel's kings. The Bible does not portray Jehu anywhere as being submissive. On the contrary, he is depicted as a harsh and mighty king who brutally killed Omri's descendants to usurp the throne and wipe out all Baal worshipers (2 Kgs 9:14–10:36).

The contrast between Jehu's submissiveness according to the Black Obelisk and the author of the biblical text demonstrates the bias of political propaganda, even in ancient times. In all likelihood the Black Obelisk of Shalmaneser III exaggerated Jehu's subservience, since, during the ninth century, there does not seem to have been any full-scale war between Assyria and Israel in which the Assyrians subjugated the Israelites. On the other hand, Jehu could indeed have paid tribute to Shalmaneser (whether as a result of war or not), appeasing him with the view to prevent (further) war. This, therefore, he did not have recorded in his official annals, since it would have minimized his own "powerful heroic image" in the eyes of his Israelite subjects.

Apart from the famous Lachish reliefs celebrating the victory of the Assyrian king, Sennacherib, over the southern Judean city of Lachish,[17] a

---

16. For the translation above and a discussion of the Black Obelisk, see Scheffler, *Fascinating Discoveries*, 36–41; see also *ANET*, 281.

17. For an elaborate discussion, see David Ussishkin, *The Conquest of Lachish by Sennacherib* (Tel Aviv: Institute of Archaeology of Tel Aviv University, 1982); for a briefer one, see Coenie Scheepers, "Lachish—City in the Shephelah," in Coenie Scheepers and Eben H

similar example involving an Assyrian and Israelite king reflecting two perspectives on history, is that of the Assyrian Annals of King Sennacherib (705–681) as inscribed on the Taylor prism[18] and the biblical text involving King Hezekiah. Sennacherib boasted:

> But as for Hezekiah, the Jew, who did not bow in submission to my yoke, I laid siege to forty-six of his fortified cities and innumerable smaller villages in their vicinity. I besieged and conquered them by stamping down earth-ramps and then by bringing up battering rams, by the attack of foot soldiers, by breaches, tunneling and sapper works. I drove out 200,000 people, young and old, male and female, countless horses, mules, donkeys, camels, large and small cattle, which I considered as booty. He [= Hezekiah] himself I made a prisoner in Jerusalem, his royal city, like a bird in a cage.

Hezekiah begged for deliverance with Isaiah the prophet. Isaiah responded (2 Kgs 19:32–34):

> This is what Yahweh said about the Assyrian emperor: "He will not enter this city or shoot a single arrow against it. No soldiers with shields will come to the city, and no siege-mounds will be built round it. He will go back by the same road he came, without entering the city. I Yahweh have spoken. I will defend this city and protect it, for the sake of the promise I made to my servant David."

The text of 2 Kgs 19:35 proceeds:

> That night an angel of Yahweh went to the Assyrian camp and killed 185,000 soldiers. At dawn the next day, there they lay, all dead! Then the Assyrian emperor Sennacherib withdrew and returned to Nineveh.... two of his sons ... killed him.

In Hezekiah's case, the honor for the victory was given to Yahweh. This, however, did not mean that the Israelite kings were not honored or glorified. An earlier probably pre-Deuteronomistic pro-Saul narrative[19] praised

---

Scheffler, *From Dan to Beersheba: An Archaeological Tour through Ancient Israel* (Pretoria: Biblia, 2000), 214–71.

18. Translation and discussion in Scheffler, *Fascinating Discoveries*, 90–92; see also *ANET*, 287–88.

19. See Eben H. Scheffler "Saving Saul from the Deuteronomist," in *Past, Present and Future: The Deuteronomistic History and the Prophets* (ed. Johannes C. de Moor and Herrie F. van Rooy; OtSt 44; Leiden: Brill, 2000), 263–71; Willem S. Boshoff, Eben H. Scheffler, and Izak Spangenberg, *Ancient Israelite Literature in Context* (Pretoria: Protea, 2000), 82–83.

the (militarily) successful reign even of Saul, mentioning that "wherever he fought, he was victorious. He fought heroically and defeated even the people of Amalek, saving Israel from all attacks." David's lament for Saul and Jonathan (in all likelihood the women's lament attributed to David) praises their bravery and valor (2 Sam 1:23–25):

> Saul and Jonathan, so wonderful and dear;
> together in life, together in death;
> swifter than eagles, stronger than lions …
> the brave soldiers have fallen.

If Saul is glorified, David the more. After all, the former has killed thousands, and the latter tens of thousands. Second Samuel 8:1–16 (see also 1 Chr 18:1–17) not only summarizes David's extensive military victories but also mentions that he made sure that his people were always treated fairly and justly (2 Sam 8:15). When Absalom planned rebellion, he was reminded of David's reputation by Hushai (2 Sam 17:8): "You know that your father David and his men are hard fighters and that they are as fierce as a mother bear robbed of her cubs. Your father is an experienced soldier and does not stay with his men at night" (see also Judg 6:12; 1 Sam 14:22; 16:18; 23:22; 24:9). One can even say that the whole story about David as recorded in the two Samuel books is a glorification of David, and even more so the version of the Chronicler.

Comparing some instances of the romanticizing of war in ancient Israel with instances in the ancient Near East serves the function of illustrating that the views about war in ancient Israel were not unique but integrate well with attitudes toward war that were cherished in the ancient world. What were unique are instances of digressing views, which, although perhaps not so dominant, reflect a different kind of thinking about war. These now require our attention.

4. Criticism of War

So much for ancient Israel's positive attitudes to war. With the prophetic movement, a situation established itself in ancient Israel where the king alone did not have the final say in political matters. At least other voices that could come into conflict with the king were also heard. This meant that critical thinking about war started to develop and that a war was not automatically justified.

An example of such a conflict of opinion is recorded in 1 Kgs 22, when Micaiah ben Imlah warned Ahab (contrary to the advice of about four hundred court prophets who promised Ahab victory): "I can see the army of Israel scattered over the hills like sheep without a shepherd. And Yahweh said, 'These men have no leader; let them go home in peace'" (1 Kgs 22:17). Of course, Ahab was furious and threw Micaiah into prison, but this did not prevent Ahab from dying on the battlefield.[20]

We have already referred to the prophet Isaiah, who serves as a second example. His calls to Ahaz and Hezekiah to be quiet and still, to wait for Yahweh to provide security for Israel, have even been interpreted as a form of quietism.[21] A typical expression of his views is found in Isa 30:15-17, where the people are called to trust quietly in Yahweh in order to be strong and secure, instead of trusting in fast horses. His vision for peace is "messianically" expressed in Isa 9:1-7, describing how Yahweh will defeat the nation that oppressed and exploited his people, "when the boots of the invading army and all their bloodstained clothing will be destroyed by fire," when the future king will reign as a "prince of peace" (see also Isa 2:2-4). As we have already indicated, he seemed to revive the views of the ancient holy war where Yahweh brings the ultimate victory (as in the case of Hezekiah versus Sennacherib, referred to above). Although Isaiah was also a court prophet basically rooted in Zion theology, having direct access to the king, he was interpreted by later historians as being trustworthy and vindicated in his criticism of the king. The fact that Ahaz eventually did not engage in the Syro-Ephraimitic war[22] by offering tribute to Assyria and calling for their help meant that the southern kingdom lasted a hundred years longer than the north.

A third example: the prophet Jeremiah's criticism of King Zedekiah's war effort against the Babylonians toward the end of the sixth century represents yet another perspective, differing from that of Isaiah. It is all the more significant since Zedekiah was involved in a defensive war (which is usually more easily justified). According to Jeremiah, Nebuchadnezzar's onslaught on Jerusalem should be interpreted as a chastisement for the injustices that prevailed within Jerusalem (2 Kgs 23:27; 24:3, 20; Jer 4:3, 6; 21:5; 34:22). Contrary to Isaiah, there cannot be any mention of quietism in Jeremiah's thought, since Yahweh has sided with the enemy. Which view seems the more radical, Isaiah's or Jeremiah's, is of course a matter of perspective. What is more important is that Jeremiah introduced a kind of holistic thinking into

---

20. For a moving discussion of the incident, see Ferdinand E. Deist, *Die noodlottige Band: Kerk en Staat in Oud-Israel* (Kaapstad: Tafelberg, 1975), 60-61.

21. See Lambertus A. Snijders, *Jesaja Deel I* (Nijkerk: Callenbach, 1969), 94-96; James A. Loader, "Was Isaiah a Quietist?" *OTWSA* 22-23 (1979-80): 130-42.

22. See Scheffler, *Politics in Ancient Israel*, 120-21; James Maxwell Miller and John H. Hayes, *A History of Ancient Israel and Judah* (Philadelphia: Westminster, 1986), 329.

the contemporary debate on the justification of war. Whether to go to war or not should not be seen in isolation: the people cannot practice social injustice and idolatry among themselves and then expect Yahweh's blessing in war. Inner reflection and self-criticism are needed, even repentance (of course on a social level, not to be confused with individual piety). According to Jeremiah, the Judeans cannot even rely on the fact that the temple is traditionally Yahweh's abode (contrary to Isaiah's Zion theology), since Yahweh will allow it to be destroyed (Jer 7). According to de Vaux, "it is impossible to imagine anything more opposed to the ancient ideology of the holy war."[23]

Another interesting aspect of critical thinking about war in the Old Testament is that there are examples where the war efforts initially seemed to have been justified but were criticized later, as time went on. These examples relate to David, Solomon, and Jehu.

As far as *David* is concerned, we have already referred to the fact that he was not only hailed as a war hero in ancient Israel but that his ("imperialistic") war efforts had been regarded as a success by the Deuteronomist because "Yahweh made him victorious everywhere" (2 Sam 8). The Chronicler (who generally reflects a pro-David stance), although retaining the just-quoted phrase (1 Chr 18:6, 18), also had another perspective on David's wars. He pictures a David who reflected on the bloodshed and wars he had been involved in during his lifetime, saying to Solomon: "But the word of Yahweh came to me, saying, 'You have shed much blood and have waged great wars; you shall not build a house to my name, because you have shed so much blood in my sight on the earth'" (1 Chr 22:8). This critical view provided by the Chronicler correlates with the fact that the content of 1 Sam 17 (the glorification of David in the David-Goliath story) is absent from his narrative (1 Chr 20:4–8 mentions only that David's *men* were involved in battles against Philistine giants). In this connection the Chronicler's criticism of David's taking a military census can also be mentioned (1 Chr 21).

As far as *Solomon* is concerned, I have already noted that he (although involved in a blood purge after usurping the throne; see 1 Kgs 2) was not involved in many wars (except for some minor skirmishes).[24] He did, however, rely on a large military strength (at least partially created by forced labor) to maintain the political power that he inherited from David (see the references to fortified cities, horses, and chariots in 1 Kgs 9:15–22). The criticism of a large military build-up that emanates from Deut 17:16, although not explicitly mentioned, most surely (see also the warning against many

---

23. De Vaux, *Ancient Israel*, 265.
24. See Scheffler, *Politics in Ancient Israel*, 82–83.

wives and riches in verse 17) had Solomon in mind: "The king is not to have a large number of horses for his army and is not to send people to Egypt to buy horses." By inserting this reference in Deut 17 during exilic times, the larger Deuteronomistic narrative therefore portrays a Solomon who transgressed the precepts of Mosaic law.[25]

The bloodshed in which *Jehu ben Nimsi* (who ruled the northern kingdom from 843 to 816) was involved after being proclaimed king by the army is vividly portrayed in 2 Kgs 9–10.[26] He assassinated his predecessor Jehoram and killed the latter's brother-in-law Ahaziah and Queen Jezebel in the most violent manner, as well as all the sons of Ahab and Ahaziah, after which he destroyed the Baal temple and cult. He was a type of Constantine figure whose violent actions were overlooked because he brought about the triumph of Yahwism. Second Kings 10:30 seems to condone his actions: "And Yahweh said to Jehu, 'Because you have done well in carrying out what is right in my eyes, and have done to the house of Ahab according to all that was in my heart, your sons of the fourth generation shall sit on the throne of Israel.'" Directly opposed to this view is Yahweh's instruction to the prophet Hosea (1:4) to name his child Jezreel: "Call his name Jezreel; for yet a little while, and I will punish the house of Jehu for the blood of Jezreel, and I will put an end to the kingdom of the house of Israel. And on that day, I will break the bow of Israel in the valley of Jezreel." Is this Yahweh changing his mind or human beings ascribing their own views to Yahweh?[27]

5. Loving the Enemy as Proactive Intervention in Ancient Israel

The fact that the sixth commandment (Exod 20:13) states that "thou shall not kill" indicates that (as in all cultures) a basic nonviolent stance was part and parcel of ancient Israel's worldview. In fact, the story of Cain and Abel (Gen 4:1–16) can be read as an etiological story that endeavored to explain why human beings kill one another despite their yearning for peace.[28] This wrestling with the problem of violence, already present in ancient Israel, is to my

---

25. On Solomon, see Eben H. Scheffler, "Die nie al te wyse Salomo," *HvTSt* 60 (2004): 769–89.

26. See Scheffler, *Politics in Ancient Israel*, 101–2; Miller and Hayes, *History of Ancient Israel*, 284–98.

27. For a discussion of the perspective of the book Hosea on violence and contra violence, see the useful study of Eckart Otto, *Krieg und Frieden in der Hebräischen Bibel und im Alten Orient: Aspekte für eine Friedensordnung in der Moderne* (Stuttgart: Kolhammer, 1999), 76–86.

28. See also the essay of Peels in this volume.

mind important, since it militates against present-day closed ethical systems (which can be labeled dogmatic ethics) that seem to have final answers as far as the justification of war is concerned.[29]

In this respect, the issue should be pressed even further, especially in view of the misuse of the Old Testament in the justification of war. Because the notion to "love one's enemy" (implying not passivity but proactive interventions or concrete acts of love that counter and eradicate hatred) is so closely related to Jesus of Nazareth (especially Matt 5:43–44, contra Luke's version), the idea of love for the enemy is often regarded as being absent in the Old Testament (an impression created by Marcion's views). A comparison between Matt 5:43–44 and the text that the Matthaean Jesus seemed to have quoted (Lev 19:17–18) ironically reveals a contrary result:

> You have heard that it was said, "You shall love your neighbor and hate your enemy." But I say to you, Love your enemies and pray for those who persecute you. (Matt 5:43–44)

> You shall not hate your brother in your heart, but you shall reason with your neighbor, lest you bear sin because of him. You shall not take vengeance or bear any grudge against the sons of your own people, but you shall love your neighbor as yourself: I am Yahweh. (Lev 19:18)

Although the Leviticus text is confined to "the sons of your own people," it does not contain the phrase "hate your enemy" (as in the Matthaean text). If neighborly love is therefore extended to include people of other nations, the enemy should be loved, even on that level. In the New Testament such a "crossing of boundaries" specifically occurs in the parable of the Good Samaritan. However, scholars studying the Lukan parable have long noted that the parable is a "creative re-interpretation"[30] of the incident reported in 2 Chr 28:12–15, where the people of Samaria also showed mercy toward the people of Judah (clearly being a case of loving one's enemy), across national boundaries. The actions of the four (northern) Israelites toward their Judean prisoners (a war situation is therefore presupposed!) have remarkable resemblances to what is narrated in the Lukan parable:

> So the armed men left the captives and the spoil before the princes and all the assembly. And the men who have been mentioned by name rose and

---

29. E.g., Helmut Thielecke, *Ethik des Politischen* (Tübingen: Mohr Siebeck, 1958).

30. See Eben H. Scheffler, *Suffering in Luke's Gospel* (Zürich: Theolgischer Verlag, 1993), 81. On the Good Samaritan, see Eben H. Scheffler, "Die Kommunikasie van die Gelykenis van die Barmhartige Samaritaan in Konteks," *HvTSt* 57 (2001): 318–43.

took the captives, and with the spoil they clothed all that were naked among them; they clothed them, gave them sandals, provided them with food and drink, and anointed them; and carrying all the feeble among them on asses, they brought them to their kinsfolk at Jericho, the city of palm trees. Then they returned to Samaria. (2 Chr 28:14–15)

Although few and far between, other Old Testament texts also report on proactive deeds that form the opposite pole of violence: Exod 23:4–5, 9 (helping your enemy's donkey and not ill-treating a foreigner, confined to the compatriot in Deut 22:1–4); Isa 2:4 (hammering swords and spears into ploughs and pruning-knives, par. Mic 4:3, contra Joel 3:10); and Prov 25:21–22 (giving your enemy food and drink) can be mentioned (see also the debate on the pacifism in the Priestly Document[31] and the inclusive perspective in Numbers[32]).

These "suppressed voices" in the Old Testament need to be raised, to cause the "Scheitern" of the one-sided "marcionitic" perspective of violence in the Old Testament.

6. Conclusion: Some Hermeneutical Considerations

The issue of war and violence is too serious a matter to warrant a mere phenomenological "scientific" discussion. In what follows I will merely (by making statements that need further reflection) indicate what needs to be addressed by biblical scholars if they in any way aspire to help toward eradicating war in a (post)modern world.

(1) A fundamentalist view of the Bible as the "Word of God"[33] that contains a unified and monolithic view on war and violence should be exposed.

---

31. Oral communication by Ed Noort and Horst Seebass during a seminar at the Colloquim Biblicum Lovaniense, Louvain, August 2006. See also Niditch, *War in the Hebrew Bible*, 152–53; Van Dyk, "Violence and the Old Testament," 106–7.

32. See the unpublished paper by Reinhard Achenbach, "Das Heiligkeitsgesetz und die sakralen Ordnungen des Numeribuches," read at the Colloquium Biblicum Lovaniense in Louvain, August 2006, and his *Die Vollendung der Tora: Studien zur Redaktionsgeschichte des Numeribuches im Kontext von Hexateuch und Pentateuch* (Wiesbaden: Harrassowitz, 2003).

33. To my mind the idea of the Bible as the "Word of God" can only be entertained if it functions as a metaphor for the fact that humans, by reading it, strive to find the will of God for their own lives. However, as such it is an unfortunate metaphor that in the past has given rise to much misunderstanding. Respect for the Bible demands that it should be interpreted according to its diverse and complex nature. On these issues, see Don Cupitt, *The Sea of Faith: Christianity in Change* (London: BBC, 1984), 78–112.

The conflicting views on violence encountered in the Old Testament world cannot be confined and systematized into a clearly uniform "biblical" view on violence that could function as a prescriptive norm for Christians today. The Bible should be exegeted according to its true nature: *various* books that contain a *kaleidoscopic diversity* of different and even contrary views on war and violence that dialogue with one another. Such an approach would facilitate tolerance.

(2) The Bible should be studied in its *Weltbezogenheit*, in other words, the reality of mundane life with all its complexities fully recognized (involving individual emotional feelings of love and hatred and physical and social material needs). The views encountered in the Old Testament are products of the historical circumstances in which the texts originated and correlate with the needs of a particular community at a certain stage in history. Any banning of the Bible to an exclusive spiritual or religious sphere should at all costs be avoided, as well as any retreat into political apathy or quietism.[34] As such the issue of war and violence should be fully recognized as part of the *conditio humana*, especially in the sense of its *predicament*.

(3) By studying the various views in their diversity, an effort should be made to understand the human *dynamic* and psychology behind war and violence.[35] Since the Old Testament contains so many divergent texts on war and violence, it can function as a "gold mine of information." Comparisons could be made between the dynamics behind ancient conflicts and those of the present-day world.

(4) In particular, due attention should be given to the "suppressed voices" that condemn violence and advocate love for the enemy as proactive inter-

---

34. Referring (among others) to Ps 23:5, Walther Zimmerli, *Die Weltlichkeit des Alten Testaments* (Göttingen: Vandenhoeck & Ruprecht, 1971), 70, remarks: "Der Feind und die Verwundbarkeit durch den Feind sind im alttestamentlichen Glauben immer wieder eine volle Wirklichkeit" ["The enemy and vulnerability through the enemy are always a conscious reality in the Old Testament faith"]. See also J. Patout Burns, ed., *War and Its Discontents: Pacifism and Quietism in the Abrahamic Traditions* (Washington, D.C.: Georgetown University Press, 1996).

35. Although today his answer to this question may not be regarded as sufficient in terms of the complexities of present-day conflicts, the author of the letter of James in the New Testament explicitly reflected on the psychological reasons for war and violence: "What causes wars, and what causes fighting among you? Is it not your passions that are at war in your members? You desire and do not have, so you kill. And you covet and cannot obtain; so you fight and wage war. You do not have, because you do not ask. You ask and do not receive, because you ask wrongly, to spend it on your passions" (Jas 4:1–3 RSV).

vention.³⁶ This includes an in-depth study of the concept of *shalom* in the Bible as the intended "reality for which God created the world."³⁷

(5) Biblical scholars should challenge and dialogue with *systematic theologians* (especially ethicists), who in the past have used the Bible to create the concept of a "justified war," more often than not misusing the Bible in the process. Ethicists should rather be encouraged to reflect on war and violence in view of its eradication and not its justification. In an involved way biblical scholars should facilitate such debates and reflections.

(6) Biblical scholars should call for and actively engage in an *interdisciplinary debate* with philosophers, representatives of other religions, political scientists, biologists, sociologists, and psychologists on war and violence with a view to its eradication.³⁸

(7) A special debate with the discipline of *psychology* is called for. In her book on war in the Hebrew Bible, Niditch³⁹ argued that different attitudes on war may be representative of the internal psychological struggle within individuals as they grapple with the internal conflict between compassion and enmity. Of special importance here is the psychology of Sigmund Freud, who distinguished between the *eros* and *Thanatos* instincts in humans. A debate on this issue took place between Freud and Einstein in the 1930s⁴⁰ but should take place today between biblical scholars and psychologists.

(8) Biblical scholars should read and appropriate the literary and philosophical works of *great minds* in human history that have dealt with the issue of violence and peace. I have in mind, in particular, the work of Kant (*Zum ewigen Frieden*), Ghandi (*My Experiments with Truth*), Einstein (*Über den*

---

36. Otto (*Krieg und Frieden*, 76–151) discusses Hosea, Deuteronomy, Psalms, and Isaiah in this regard.

37. Paul D. Hanson, "War and Peace in the Hebrew Bible," *Int* 38 (1984): 341. See Van Dyk, "Violence and the Old Testament," 109–10. See also Gillis Gerleman, "*slm*, genug haben," *ThWAT* 2:919–35 and the literature mentioned there.

38. See the challenging book by Deepak Chopra, *Peace Is the Way: Bringing War and Violence to an End* (London: Rider, 2005); Cornel W. du Toit, ed., *Violence, Truth and Prophetic Silence* (Pretoria: Research Institute for Theology and Religion, Unisa, 1999); M. B. Ramose, "Wisdom in War and Peace," in *After September 11: Globalisation, War and Peace* (ed. Cornel W. du Toit and G. J. A Lubbe; Pretoria: Research Institute for Theology and Religion, Unisa, 2002), 151–78. For the challenging views of an "atheistic" biologist, see Richard Dawkins, *The God Delusion* (London: Bantam, 2006).

39. Niditch, *War in the Hebrew Bible*, 155; Van Dyk, "Violence and the Old Testament," 105.

40. This correspondence was originally published under the title *Warum Krieg?* before the Second World War and forms part of Albert Einstein, *Über den Frieden: Weltordnung oder Weltuntergang* (Neu Isenburg: Melzer, 2004), 204–20.

Frieden), Hemingway (*A Farewell to Arms*), Albert Schweitzer (speech when receiving the Nobel price for peace), and Hermann Hesse (various novels).[41]

(9) Mainstream *churches* (Roman Catholic as well as Protestant) should be challenged to internalize new results in biblical scholarship (the Old Testament and especially the historical Jesus) as far as war and violence is concerned and to change their present stance. In particular, the voices of women, children, and older people (who have experienced the futility of war) should be listened to,[42] as well as nonmainstream churches that propagate a nonviolent stance.[43] Wherever war occurs in the world, it should be opposed by the church (whether at the local or ecumenical level). The church should be challenged to confess that it has taken the wrong stance since the age of Constantine. Especially where the Muslim world is concerned, the church should confess that the crusades of the twelfth century were wrong. Political leaders should be constantly questioned by the church. Without abandoning its ministry to soldiers, churches should be challenged to abandon their participation in the compromising system of chaplaincy.[44]

(10) All forms of *glorification* or simulation of violence in education, on television, Internet, computer games, ordinary toys, and so forth should be opposed, as well as the sport of boxing and American wrestling. The history of wars should be studied in terms of their tragedies and not only their supposed historical significance in terms of politics or heroism. From an early age, children should be encouraged to learn that "cowards" are the real heroes.

---

41. See also Hermann Hesse, *Lektüre für Minuten I* (Frankfurt am Main: Suhrkamp, 1971), 9–36; idem, *Lektüre für Minuten: Neue Folge* (Frankfurt am Main: Suhrkamp, 1976), 9–41.

42. See in this regard Bryan Perrett, *The Taste of Battle: Front Line Action 1914–1991* (London: Cassel, 2000); Michael Moore, *Will They Ever Trust Us Again? Letters from the War Zone* (London: Penguin, 2004).

43. See Clarence Bauman, *Gewaltlosigkeit im Täufertum: Eine Untersuchung zur theologischen Ethik des oberdeutschen Täufertums der Reformationszeit* (Leiden: Brill, 1968); John H. Yoder, *The Politics of Jesus* (Grand Rapids: Eerdmans, 1972).

44. I say this having being compelled to serve as a chaplain in the South African navy in 1979. Although it was in many ways an enriching experience, in hindsight I regret it. Since chaplains are compelled to wear the uniform of the army to which they minister, churches providing chaplains are extremely naïve with regard to their co-option for the cause of the country waging war. It is unimaginable that chaplains would be allowed to minister in an army among the troops if they refused to wear the uniform and questioned the justification of the war effort.

The World's First Murder: Violence and Justice in Genesis 4:1-16

Eric Peels

1. Introduction

For the average user of the Bible, it is quite a disconcerting experience to discover that the most prominent anthropological theme in the Old Testament is that of violence.[1] This fact implies a special task for the exegesis and biblical theology of the Old Testament, now more than ever before. In our modern society, the theme of violence is at the center of attention with regard to political, social, and religious issues. In a relatively short period of time, the humanities have made the relation between religion and violence into an exciting object of research,[2] while sometimes media and public opinion quickly draw parallels between monotheism and intolerance, religious belief and outrage. Understandably, in recent times there has been a renewed interest in the work and thought of Marcion.[3]

How does the Old Testament deal with violence? Of course, a response to this question will also concern both the morality and the image of God as we find them in the Old Testament and are, therefore, of the utmost theological importance. In this article, I will apply this issue to Gen 4:1-16, the well-

---

1. "No other human activity or experience is mentioned so frequently (as the act of violence), neither the world of labor and economy, nor that of family and sexuality, nor that of the experience of nature and of human knowledge," thus Raymund Schwager, *Brauchen wir einen Sündenbock? Gewalt und Erlösung in den biblischen Schriften* (München: Kösel, 1978), 58 (my trans.).

2. See also the literature mentioned in Jean-Pierre Wils, *Sacraal geweld* (Assen: Van Gorcum, 2004).

3. See the recently published dissertation by Ph. L. Krijger, *De tragiek van de schepping: Het geding rondom Marcion in de Nederlandse theologie van de twintigste eeuw* (Zoetermeer: Boekencentrum, 2005).

known story of Cain and Abel. Given the fact that it is in this passage that we read about the initial occurrence of violence, it may be vital to our understanding of the theme of violence in the Old Testament.[4] After the expulsion from the garden of Eden and from God's direct presence, man shows himself to be potentially violent. Immediately this violence takes the worst form possible, that of fratricide.[5] Death enters creation. Especially in the dialogues between God and Cain, violence, with both its roots and its branches, is brought into the limelight in such a way that this pericope as a whole gets a paradigmatic function. In my analysis of this passage, I focus on the question of what it tells us about the image of God: What, according to the author of Gen 4, is God's attitude toward human violence?

In what follows, I first sketch the contours of the specific place, nature, and structure of Gen 4:1–16. Then I move through the text in order to sketch an outline of exegesis. Related to this, special attention is paid to the question of what the meaning of Cain's mark is. The exegesis results in an ethical and theological evaluation of the theme of violence within this pericope. Finally, the conclusions drawn on this basis will be put under scrutiny by asking the question of whether God himself is in some sense the initiator of the spiral of violence that we find in Gen 4: Does this chapter present us with the image of an arbitrary God?

2. Genesis 4 and Primeval History

Genesis 4 not only contains the *first* description of the phenomenon of human violence in the Old Testament; this chapter also offers an *exemplary* description of it. The latter fact is strongly related to the place of Gen 4 in its literary and canonical contexts. The present form of the book of Genesis has been structured into a whole by means of a repeated genealogical formula: "these are the generations [תלדות] of…." This formula occurs eleven times[6] and is, except for one instance, always followed by the genitive of the progenitor, which itself is followed by a genealogy or a narrative account. The only excep-

---

4. Mark H. McEntire, *The Blood of Abel: The Violent Plot in the Hebrew Bible* (Macon, Ga.: Mercer University Press, 1999), 18.

5. "This familiar story and its sequel in the descendants of Cain illustrate the accumulating disorder within human society, starting at the very place where love and support should be strongest—between brothers," thus Christopher Wright, *Old Testament Ethics for the People of God* (Downers Grove, Ill.: InterVarsity Press, 2004), 215–16.

6. Gen 2:4; 5:1; 6:9; 10:1; 11:10, 27; 25:12, 19; 36:1, 9; 37:2. See the discussions on this formula in Benno Jacob, *Das Buch Genesis* (Berlin: Schocken, 1934; repr., Stuttgart: Calwer, 2000), 71–79; and Karel Deurloo, *Genesis* (Kampen: Kok, 1998), 9–15.

tion is 2:4: "These are the generations of the heavens and the earth." Although the unusual phrasing provides a link to the introduction as found in 1:1–2:3, the formula here, as elsewhere, should be read as the heading of the section that follows.[7]

In between the story of the creation of heaven and earth in Gen 1 and the narrative of the development of humankind in Gen 5 and the succeeding chapters, Gen 2–4 is an editorial unit with its own superscript and its own intention. The actual genealogy of Adam with the תלדות-formula only starts in 5:1, but preceding that, the biblical author offers something like a theological anthropology in the separate section 2:4–4:26 under the תלדות of heaven and earth (2:4). Here the basic relational patterns are described: between man and God, man and his fellow man, man and the earth. In the first generation after the creation of man (Gen 2) there is a rift between man and God (Gen 3), while in the second generation there is a rift between man and his fellow man (Gen 4). Down to the smallest detail, Gen 3 and 4 are geared to one another: structurally, thematically, literally, and idiomatically.[8] Westermann, on the basis of this parallelism, has correctly pointed out that these two chapters should not only be read *after* one another but also *alongside* one another.[9] Genesis 4, however, is more than just the social reverse of the religious fall of Gen 3, since a clear progression in sin and alienation (from God) becomes manifest.[10]

Genesis 2:4–4:26 deals with some of the big questions of humanity: life and death, labor, sexuality and violence, strength and weakness. Family history and world history blend into one another, while in this narrative on the beginning of human culture, the prototypes are also seen as archetypes. In these textual units the author is describing real individuals from the primeval past whose actions are significant for all humanity. These stories describe patterns of behavior into which every person is likely to lapse, and they stand as warnings to all who are tempted to disregard God's laws.[11] That is why Gen

---

7. Gordon J. Wenham, *Genesis 1–15* (WBC 1; Waco, Tex.: Word, 1987), 55ff.

8. On this topic, see also Alan J. Hauser, "Linguistic and Thematic Links between Genesis 4:1–16 and Genesis 2–3," *JETS* 23 (1980), 297–305; Lothar Ruppert, *Gen 1,11–11,26* (vol. 1 of *Genesis: Ein kritischer und theologischer Kommentar*; FB 70; Würzburg: Echter, 1992), 5–6; and Wenham, *Genesis 1–15*, 99–100.

9. Claus Westermann, *Theologie des Alten Testaments in Grundzügen* (Göttingen: Vandenhoeck & Ruprecht, 1978), 75; idem, *Genesis 1–11* (BKAT; Neukirchen-Vluyn: Neukirchener, 1974), 431–33; see also Karel Deurloo, *De mens als raadsel en geheim: Verhalende antropologie in Genesis 2–4* (Baarn: Ten Have, 1988), 100–101.

10. See Gerhard von Rad, *Die Theologie der geschichtlichen Überlieferungen Israels* (vol. 1 of *Theologie des Alten Testaments*; Munich: Kaiser, 1961), 157–64.

11. See Wenham, *Genesis 1–15*, 117; Walther Zimmerli, *Grundriss der alttestamentlichen Theologie* (Stuttgart: Kohlhammer, 1978), 148. Incidentally, Brevard Childs rightly

4 is not just about the particularity of outrage. It is about the universality of violence as well.

3. Nature and Structure of Genesis 4:1-16

In almost every academic work on Gen 4:1-16 one comes across the remark that it is a tantalizing story because so much has been left unsaid. The overall plot is pretty clear, but the lacunae in the story give rise to all sorts of detailed questions and speculation: Why does Cain take the initiative to bring a sacrifice to God? Why is his sacrifice not accepted? How does he know this? What does he say to his brother? Why does he kill his brother? Of whom is he afraid? And so on. The *Wirkungsgeschichte* of Gen 4 offers a colorful palette of explanations starting with the *versiones*, which try to fill the lacunae and get rid of obscurities.[12]

In an earlier stage of biblical studies, in order to explain the incongruities of the text much attention was paid to the reconstruction of the supposed *Vorlagen* with universal narrative motifs such as fratricidal struggle, the rivalry between the profession of shepherd and farmer, and the tension between cultivated land and nomadism. For a long time the view of Bernhard Stade and Julius Wellhausen was predominant. They explained Gen 4 as an etiology of the Kenites, with Cain as ancestor. This line of *kollektiv-stammesgeschichtliche* explanation has been judged to be inadequate, especially since the voluminous commentaries of Umberto Cassuto (1961-64) and Claus Westermann (1974), and scholars have preferred the *individual-urgeschichtliche* explanation.[13] It is with good reason that the modern, literary-synchronic analysis

---

says: "However, the canonical structure of the composition guards against dissolving the narrative into ontological concerns to which the story only functions as illustration" (*Introduction to the Old Testament as Scripture* [London: SCM, 1979], 158).

12. Ricardo J. Quinones, *The Changes of Cain: Violence and The Lost Brother in Cain and Abel Literature* (Princeton: Princeton University Press, 1991); Louis Goosen, *Van Abraham tot Zacharia: Thema's uit het Oude Testament in religie, beeldende kunst, literatuur, muziek en theater* (Nijmegen: SUN, 1990), 153-58; Rochus Zuurmond, "Het oordeel over Kain in de oud-joodse traditie," *Amsterdamse cahiers voor exegese en Bijbelse theologie* 3 (1982): 107-17.

13. Exceptions to this are, e.g., Walter Dietrich, "'Wo ist dein Bruder?' Zu Tradition und Intention von Genesis 4," in *Beiträge zur Alttestamentlichen Theologie: Festschrift für Walther Zimmerli zum 70. Geburtstag* (ed. by Herbert Donner, Robert Hanhart, and Rudolf Smend; Göttingen: Vandenhoeck & Ruprecht, 1977), 94-111; and Horst Seebass, *Urgeschichte (1,1-11,26)* (vol. 1 of *Genesis*; Neukirchen-Vluyn: Neukirchener, 1996), 143-64.

decides in favor of the original unity of the text.¹⁴ This makes a coherent explanation possible, although questions will remain, both because of the elliptic writing style¹⁵ and because of the occurrence of exegetical cruces (e.g., in vv. 1 and 7).

Genesis 4 shows a clear internal coherence via the mention of community, pregnancy, and birth in verses 1, 17, and 25, the *reprise* of verse 15 in verse 24, and the *inclusio* of the invocation of the name of Yahweh in verses 1 and 26. At the same time, the pericope of verses 1–16 makes one neat unit with its own plot, starting with the mention of Cain's rise "with Yahweh" (v. 1) and ending with his downfall "out of Yahweh's presence" (v. 16). The text itself consists of an alternation of narrative and dialogue: 1–5, introduction; 6–7, first dialogue; 8, outrage; 9–15a, second dialogue; 15b–16, closing. It is remarkable that the narrative is concise while the main emphasis is on the dialogues.¹⁶

4. Reading of the Text

4.1. First Scene: Introduction and Oblation (Gen 4:1–5)

The first verse of Gen 4 relates this chapter to the previous one. When Eve gives birth to Cain, her expression of joy,¹⁷ "I have brought forth a man"

---

14. See, e.g., Kenneth A. Mathews, *Genesis 1–11* (NAC; Nashville: Broadman & Holman, 2001), 260–64. Certainly this does not exclude the possibility of an ancient narrative tradition with a more complete version of the story of Cain and Abel. Thus Umberto Cassuto, *From Adam to Noah: Genesis I–VI 8* (vol. 1 of *A Commentary on the Book of Genesis*; Jerusalem: Magnes, 1961), 183–84.

15. Donald E. Gowan's remark is characteristic: "[The story] has been told with care and skill in the concise, highly selective way that was typical of Hebrew story telling, although this may be one of the more extreme examples of selectivity" (*From Eden to Babel: A Commentary on the Book of Genesis 1–11* [ITC; Grand Rapids: Eerdmans, 1988], 63).

16. "We must conclude that the focal point is to be sought in the spoken and not in the narrative portion…. the doctrines the Torah wished to inculcate here are not comprised in the *episodes* it relates, but in *the words of the Lord* that it connects therewith," says Cassuto rightly (*From Eden to Babel*, 183–84). See also Ellen van Wolde, "The Story of Cain and Abel: A Narrative Study," *JSOT* 52 (1991): 36: "The causes underlying the murder and the consequences that follow it are more central to this story than the murder itself."

17. Compare 2:23. The explanation of Eve's words in v. 1 as a proud shout of triumph ("As Yahweh did, I have created a man") is less plausible, since in that case one would expect a different preposition, but also because anywhere else the verb קנה with the meaning "to create" has God as the subject; see Edward Lipiński, "קנה," *ThWAT* 7:63–71. Among the proponents of this explanation are Cassuto, *From Eden to Babel*, 201–2; Westermann, *Genesis 1–11*, 395–96.

(איש), is telling: it concerns the second generation of humankind,[18] which outside the garden of Eden will have to start a new way of life. Although expelled by God, man is not without God: Eve boasts of the fact that she brought forth Cain "with" (את) Yahweh. There is uncertainty with regard to the exact meaning of this preposition in this context,[19] but it seems to be true that it expresses a positive thought: Yahweh, as the giver of fertility, makes life possible despite the threat of death (see 2:17). Via the popular-etymological punning with the verb קנה (to bring forth, create), it is suggested that Cain (*qayin*) is a creature in relation to Yahweh.[20]

The presentation of Cain and Abel in the first section of Gen 4 is telling: Cain as the first, accompanied by the shout of joy of his mother, who puts him in relation to the blessing of Yahweh; Abel comes without any shout of joy as the second child and, even before we hear his name, is typified as Cain's brother (v. 2). Cain as the first and oldest follows in the footsteps of his father: he becomes a farmer, whereas Abel becomes a shepherd (see 3:17–19, 23). The name Abel (הבל) means "breath," "nullity," "vapor"[21]—he only figures as the counterpart, the weak rival who hardly develops his own story. Cain plays the leading part, whereas Abel's role is only a supporting one and fading away.

It is Cain's initiative (v. 3) to bring an offering (מנחה) to God. In this he is followed by his brother (v. 4). The offering itself has to do with their respective professions, although Abel's offering is described in a more elaborate way than Cain's.[22] The divine response is described in a very concise way: Yahweh looks with favor on Abel and his offering, but on Cain and his offering he does not look with favor (v. 5).[23] The word order switches the attention from the offering to the person—it will concern Cain himself. The question of how

---

18. Nowhere else in the Old Testament is a newborn child called איש.
19. See further the overview of different opinions in Westermann, *Genesis 1–11*, 396–97.
20. See Deurloo, *Genesis*, 58. The historical etymology of the name Cain is uncertain: "smith," "javelin," "metalworker"; see Bob Becking, "Cain קין," *DDD*, 343–44.
21. Bob Becking, "Abel הבל," *DDD*, 3–4.
22. Neither the reason nor the background of this practice of offering is mentioned. Strictly speaking, this story is not yet about the bringing of sacrifices but about the bringing of gifts. However, the description of the gifts is modeled after the sacrificial terminology that can be found in later times (see also §7 below).
23. The verb שעה ("to pay attention to") is not specific enough to conclude that Cain is condemned; it only shows that God prefers Abel's offering, as Deurloo rightly claims (*Genesis*, 59; idem, *De mens als raadsel en geheim*, 105–6; idem, *Kain en Abel: Onderzoek naar exegetische methode inzake een 'kleine literaire eenheid' in de Tenakh* [Amsterdam: Ten Have, 1967], 101–2). The word "sin" can only be found further on in the text (v. 7).

both brothers know about Yahweh's response is neither asked nor answered. Immediately the text focuses on the person of Cain. He becomes very angry (חרה מאד), which is also visible from the outside: his face fell (v. 5b; see also Jer 3:12). This kind of anger is often a prelude to homicidal acts.[24]

4.2. First Dialogue (Gen 4:6–7)

The first dialogue starts in 4:6–7 with a few questions by Yahweh to Cain.[25] Yahweh, who did not accept Cain's offering, did not forsake Cain. The cause of this intervention is given in verse 5b: the great anger of Cain. Apparently, Yahweh knows about Cain's inner motives and feelings and puts them in the light of doing good or not doing good (יטב). Unfortunately, verse 7 is notorious for being cryptic both in its syntactical and exegetical respects, and therefore its explanation is but tentative.

The least difficult is verse 7a: over against the "falling" (נפל) of the face, God places the "lifting up" (נשׂא) of the face. Cain has no reason to feed his great anger if he does good. In this way, albeit implicitly, Cain's behavior is characterized as not good; he has taken the wrong path. Therefore, Yahweh warns him not to continue on this path. The reason for God's warning can be found in the danger of "sin," which is about to spread like wildfire (v. 7b). For the first time in the Old Testament the word "sin" (חטאת)[26] is used and this at a crucial moment, when a distortion of interpersonal relations could lead to violence.

It is not entirely clear in which way the passage deals with the theme of sin. Most exegetes interpret the text as a reference to the threatening power of sin, which almost demonically tries to ensnare Cain completely in its power.[27] Or does the text contain the idea that for Cain, his brother Abel is the "door"

---

24. See also Gen 34:7; 1 Sam 18:8; Neh 4:1. Given, among other things, these parallels, the interpretation of נפל פנים as an indication of a despondency must be rejected, contra Mayer I. Gruber, "Was Cain Angry or Depressed?" *BAR* 6.6 (1980): 35–36; and Victor P. Hamilton, *The Book of Genesis: Chapters 1–17* (NICOT; Grand Rapids: Eerdmans, 1990), 224.

25. The same thing happens in the second dialogue (4:9–15a). With respect to the rhetorical function of the questions, see Kenneth M. Craig, "Questions outside Eden (Genesis 4.1–16): Yahweh, Cain and Their Rhetorical Interchange," *JSOT* 86 (1999): 107–28.

26. The view that this passage is not about the notion of sin but rather about an offering of purification is not very plausible. See Joaquim Azevedo, "At the Door of Paradise: A Contextual Interpretation of Gen 4:7," *BN* 100 (1999): 45–59, who translates v. 7b as follows: "a purification-offering [a male sacrificial animal] lies down at the door [of Paradise]."

27. See Westermann, *Genesis 1–11*, 407–10; Wenham, *Genesis 1–15*, 106.

in the sense of the "entrance to" or "cause of" sin?[28] Or should we interpret the expression in such a way that Cain himself is lying at the door of sin, if he does not do what is right?[29] Still another opinion is that the participle רבץ offers a further explanation of the "sin": "there is at the door sin, (namely,) being on the lurk."[30] With regard to the end of verse 7 as well, there are several divergent views, although most exegetes agree that this phrase is about the "concupiscence" of the power of sin, which Cain has to master. Another explanation takes into account the parallelism between 4:7b and 3:16 and claims that it has to do with the orientation of Abel on Cain and Cain's vocation as firstborn to reoccupy his leading position with respect to his younger brother.[31]

For our analysis the meaning of this dialogue is not unclear—despite these exegetical uncertainties. The roots of the violence that comes to the surface in what follows are already being exposed: the anger that contains a whole world of emotions, the break off of communication ("fallen face"), the consequence of not doing what is right. The evil that Cain could perform, if he continues on the same path, is not his "fate," but a power of sin—which he must master, and apparently also can prevent. The way in which Yahweh is introduced is telling: he intervenes and gives Cain free choice; he appeals to Cain and warns him. It is evident that the tenor of this dialogue is that God wants to prevent man from giving in to the evil of violence.

4.3. Second Scene: The Deed (Gen 4:8)

It will strike the reader that the first dialogue is broken off: Cain does not give an answer. When he speaks, he speaks to his brother Abel (v. 8). The text does not tell us what Cain said to Abel.[32] Some exegetes make this need into a virtue by claiming that this silence is telling, testifying to the negation of the

---

28. So Bernd Janowski, "Jenseits von Eden: Gen 4,1–16 und die nichtpriesterliche Urgeschichte," in *Die Dämonen Demons: Die Dämonologie der israelitisch-jüdischen und frühchristlichen Literatur im Kontext ihrer Umwelt* (ed. Armin Lange, Hermann Lichtenberger, and Diethard Römheld; Tübingen: Mohr Siebeck, 2003), 137–59. He translates v. 7b as follows: "and if you do not let it be/do not act rightly, he settles himself down as an (opening) occasion to a false step" (my trans. of the German).

29. This is Deurloo's contention; see *Kain en Abel*, 103–7; idem, *Genesis*, 59–60.

30. This view is defended by van Wolde, "The Story of Cain and Abel," 31ff.

31. Thus, e.g., Deurloo, *Kain en Abel*, 108–12; idem, *Genesis*, 60; Janowski, "Jenseits von Eden," 149.

32. For the addition "Let us go out to the field" by the *versiones*, see the text-critical apparatus of *BHS*. Too ingenious is the view of P. Tamarkin Reis, "What Cain Said: A Note on Genesis 4.8," *JSOT* 27 (2002): 107–13, who interprets the syntaxis of v. 8 as a taunting

existence of the other as an equal, as a brother.[33] Whether or not that is true, it is certainly true that in a very concise way this passage tells us how man, who for the very first time in history is given the choice between good and evil (see 2:17; 3:5, 22), chooses in favor of evil. A further explanation is absent. The succinctness of this text, which is at the center of the whole pericope, displays something of the eruptive and irrational aspects of violence. Both the fact that the deed occurs in "the field" (see Deut 22:25) and the wording of Cain's "attacking" (קום; see Deut 19:11) his brother indicate a fully conscious deed. Cain is the first murderer in human history.

4.4. SECOND DIALOGUE (GEN 4:9–15A)

The second dialogue is shaped in the form of a lawsuit: examination and denial, accusation and charge, curse and punishment.[34] This whole passage is characterized by a judicial coloration. Yahweh appears as judge, who makes a stand for those who have lost their voice. The person who ended the life of his brother has to deal not only with his brother but with Yahweh as well. God calls Cain to account, but Cain resolutely dismisses responsibility for his brother Abel (v. 9). Cain's reply shows that in the wake of violence, other phenomena that dissolve society arise: the lie ("I do not know") and the cheeky denial of care for one's brother ("Am I my brother's keeper?"). However, the murder committed in secret cannot remain hidden: even if Abel is permanently silenced, his blood calls out (v. 10). This blood is crying (צעק: the "Zeter ruf") to Yahweh for retribution for the crime committed. It is not necessarily the notion of blood feud that is at issue here. Rather, and more generally, it is the judicious action of Yahweh that is at issue.[35] In verse 10 a thought can be found that occurs frequently in the Old Testament: Yahweh as protector of what is weak and insignificant and as a judge who takes up the cudgels for the victims.[36]

---

remark of Cain about Abel (e.g., against his parents) and who in this way relates v. 8 to v. 7: the "door" at which sin is crouching is that of the mouth, the tongue.

33. Van Wolde, "The Story of Cain and Abel," 35: "It can be seen as pointing ahead to the actual elimination of the other"; see also McEntire, *Blood of Abel*, 23. According to Craig, "Questions outside Eden," 118, the author creates tension on purpose by not giving the content of the discussion between Cain and Abel.

34. See Walter Brueggemann, *Genesis* (Interpretation; Atlanta: John Knox, 1982), 60; Westermann, *Theologie des Alten Testaments*, 104.

35. See Eric Peels, *The Vengeance of God: The Meaning of the Root NQM and the Function of the NQM-Texts in the Context of Divine Revelation in the Old Testament* (OtSt 31; Leiden: Brill, 1995), 67–69.

36. See Wenham, *Genesis 1–15*, 107; Peels, *Vengeance of God*, 290–92.

When in verses 11–12 the judge passes judgment on Cain and punishes him, this happens in the form of a curse in which the אדמה-motif, which is highly important in Gen 2–4, is clearly incorporated. Whereas in Gen 3 the earth is cursed for the sake of man, in Gen 4 man is cursed out of the earth: Cain will no longer receive anything from the earth, which has received the blood of his brother.[37] In one day Cain becomes "Gottlos—Heimatlos—Brotlos" (H. Frey). Cain will be a perpetual vagrant and vagabond (נָע וָנָד, v. 12) in the land נוֹד (v. 16). Whoever kills his brother will have to live without any brothers. In the background of these words we find the phenomenon of the "Friedloslegung," the expulsion from the family that was the fate in tribal societies of those who murdered close relatives.[38] By violence a man is turned into a beggar, and the bonds, which give joy, meaning, and purpose to life, are broken.

Now, for the first time, in verses 13–14 we hear Cain lamenting his distress. There is no condition worse than that of the outcast (see Job 15:22–23; 18:18–21; 30:3–8). Apart from any social affiliation and without any form of protection, he is destined to live alone, like an outlaw. At his death no one would shed a tear, and even if he were to be murdered nobody would bat an eye. When in verse 14 Cain relates his punishment, we hear the words of 3:24 echoed: Yahweh expelled (גרש) man from the garden of Eden, but Cain is expelled even further. The translation of verse 13 has evoked much discussion. Because of the ambivalent semantic value of the word עון, the expression used by Cain, נשא עון (literally: to carry iniquity/punishment), can mean both "my iniquity is too great to be forgiven" and "my punishment is too great to bear."[39] The former translation could lead to the conclusion that Cain finally confesses his guilt, thus implicitly displaying regret. Although in Hebrew the notions of guilt and punishment are hardly separated, most exegetes rightly think that the latter translation is the better one: nowhere in the story can a suggestion of confession, repentance, or forgiveness be found.[40] In verse 14 Cain laments only the weight of his punishment. We can conclude that verse

---

37. Hermann Gunkel, *Genesis* (HKAT; Göttingen: Vandenhoeck & Ruprecht, 1902), 39: "Cain cultivated the field, he harvested the fruits of the field, he gave the field fraternal blood as a drink; but from the field the blood is accusing him; hence the field denies him its fruit; therefore he is banished from the field" (my trans.). See also Deurloo, *Kain en Abel*, 119ff.; Frank A. Spina, "The 'Ground' for Cain's Rejection (Gen 4): ʾadāmāh in the Context of Gen 1–11," *ZAW* 104 (1992): 317–32, who both study this motif extensively.

38. On this issue, see Peels, *Vengeance of God*, 68 n. 81; Wenham, *Genesis 1–15*, 108.

39. See Klaus Koch, "עון," *ThWAT* 5:1165 and also the discussion in commentaries.

40. See, e.g., Gowan, *From Eden to Babel*, 51; Mathews, *Genesis 1–11*, 276; Hamilton, *The Book of Genesis*, 233; Westermann, *Genesis 1–11*, 420.

13 does not contain a trace of remorse but of self-pity and resentment. Cain's answer is not a request, but a complaint and a protest. The murderer is afraid of being murdered.

God has the last word in this dialogue: "Then Yahweh said to him: 'Indeed, whoever kills Cain: sevenfold shall he be avenged!' "[41] These words form a solemn general verdict[42] and bring about an unexpected turn in the story: even he who commits fratricide is put under divine protection. The vengeance for Cain's death shall be sevenfold: a full number that functions to demonstrate heightened intensity.[43] Cain's life is guaranteed "sevenfold," that is to say, completely.[44]

4.5. Third Scene: The End (Gen 4:15b–16)

The divine promise of judicial protection is confirmed to Cain in an almost sacramental manner by means of a mark. I deal with this mark in more detail in §5 below. In verse 16 the end of the story is told: Cain leaves, away from the countenance of Yahweh. The story started with the "falling" of Cain's countenance (v. 5), a conscious break in communication, which, via the act of violence, ends in a life far away from God's countenance. The farmer has become a beggar: without parents, without a brother, without land, without God. Violence also affects one's own identity. The judgment of Yahweh is exer-

---

41. For this translation, see Peels, *Vengeance of God*, 62.

42. V. 15a "is a determination or stipulation, which is formally shaped in an exact analogy to the apodictic sentences of jurisdiction" (Westermann, *Genesis 1–11*, 423–24 [my trans.]); see also Gerhard Liedke, *Gestalt und Bezeichnung alttestamentlicher Rechtssätze: Eine formgeschichtlich-terminologische Studie* (WMANT 39; Neukirchen-Vluyn: Neukirchener, 1971), 124 and 143. The apodosis gives the juridical result that would take place if the boundaries mentioned in the participial protasis are not heeded. The juridical character of v. 15a is confirmed by the seal with an official sign (and recognizable as such). In this way v. 15 forms a fitting conclusion to the whole section of vv. 9–16, in which the juridical action of God is described in the hearing (vv. 9–10), verdict (vv. 11–15), and driving away (v. 16). See also Nahum M. Sarna, *Genesis* (JPS Torah Commentary; Philadelphia: Jewish Publication Society, 1989), 35.

43. See also Ps 12:7; Prov 6:31; Dan 3:19; and especially Ps 79:12 (cf. v. 10).

44. We have to reject the idea that this verse contains the phrase by which seven members of the murderer's clan must suffer for Cain's murder—an explanation that is related to the older etymological exegesis. E. Otto, "שבע," *ThWAT* 7:1014: "With the motif of sevenfold revenge, Gen 4:15 is surely not 'a primitive text' full of uncontrolled vengeance but expresses the all-embracing protection of life by the general prevention brought about by divine sanction" (my trans.). The Targum and later rabbinical literature interpret the "sevenfold" as a suspension of the judgment on Cain up to the seventh generation—so that afterwards he could in fact be killed (see Jacob, *Das Buch Genesis*, 146).

cised instantaneously: now Cain is נָד (v. 12) in the land נוֹד (v. 16). This land is further qualified by the words "east of Eden," the same clause as in 2:24. The man who chooses violence is getting further and further away from God.[45]

5. The Mark of Cain (Gen 4:15b)

Perhaps the most surprising element in the whole pericope 4:1–16 is that the murderer, who was just punished by God with a severe curse, receives the promise of God's protection. Yahweh wants to be the keeper of the man who did not want to be his brother's keeper. Every biblical scholar agrees that it is obvious that the mark of Cain, in opposition to the meaning that is often given to it in popular speech, does not refer to a shameful stigma. In the context of Gen 4, the mark is obviously something that deters potential attackers and, therefore, offers protection. But this might be the only point of consensus among the exegetes. There are an enormous variety of different opinions as to what the mark exactly was.[46]

Most exegetes suppose that the mark (אוֹת) has been put on Cain himself (שִׂים ל) by Yahweh, while they point to parallels in Exod 12:13 (the blood on the doorposts), Ezek 9:4 (marks on the foreheads of those who reject Jerusalem's gruesome deeds), and Rev 7:9 (the servants of God have marks on their foreheads; see 14:9, the mark of the beast on one's forehead or one's hand). With regard to this mark, there are two different exegetical paths along which one could proceed: the collective or the individual explanation. The collective explanation, which was predominant in the older research, saw Cain as ancestor of the Kenites or as a representative of nomadic life. In this way the mark of Cain could be explained as a tribal sign of the Kenites, which marks its bearers as worshipers of Yahweh. Sometimes this was even further explained: the mark of Cain was the first character of the name of God, printed on one's forehead, or it was the professional mark of smiths. Less specific is the thought that it was a tattoo as a distinguishing mark of a nomadic tribe.[47] Nowadays, these sorts of interpretations have been almost entirely abandoned, given the

---

45. See Robert Gordon, *Holy Land, Holy City: Sacred Geography and the Interpretation of the Bible* (Carlisle: Paternoster, 2004), 20–24. See also Manfred Görg, "Kain und das 'Land Nod,'" *BN* 71 (1994): 5–12.

46. Thus Wenham: "The nature of Cain's sign or mark has been the subject of endless inconclusive speculation" (*Genesis 1–15*, 109). See also the digression by Westermann, *Genesis 1–11*, 424–27; Deurloo, *Kain en Abel*, 24–49; Ruth Mellinkoff, *The Mark of Cain* (Berkeley and Los Angeles: University of California Press, 1981).

47. A recent variant of this is the suggestion that it was some sort of standard (see Ps 74:4) that Cain himself could erect (Seebass, *Urgeschichte*, 159).

fact that most exegetes have turned to the individual explanation of the story of Cain. Many suggestions have been made along this line in order to identify Cain's mark: leprosy, a horn on the forehead, a black skin, a wild appearance, a brand mark in the face, a tattoo, a specific hairstyle, and so on. The Jewish tradition that explained the "mark" of Cain as a dog who would accompany Cain and keep away the enemies is quite inventive.[48] Still another explanation is that Cain's mark is his own name, because of the sound combination of קין and יֻקַּם (he will be avenged).[49]

A totally different line of explanation is offered in the idea that at issue is not a mark *on* Cain (a "Schutzzeichen") but rather a mark *for* Cain (a "Beglaubigungszeichen"). Yahweh has given Cain a special sign of revelation in order to confirm his promise of judicial protection, for example a thunderclap—comparable to the function of the rainbow in Gen 9:16. This explanation has failed to gain approval because the context of the mark of Cain is too explicit about its function as deterrence of potential enemies.

The conclusion is inevitable: the question as to what the precise content and form of the sign of Cain were has never gotten a satisfactory answer. Neither is this question really relevant, given the narrative economy of this tightly set up elliptic story. What is significantly more important is the question of what was the real intention of giving this sign to Cain. On this point as well, there are two divergent exegetical paths.

On the one hand, there are exegetes who assert that the sign of Cain meant a sharpening or increasing of his punishment.[50] Cain will have to pay the full price of his punishment. By this mark Yahweh wants to prevent a premature interference in the execution of the punishment: a premature death would cut short his sentence. The problem with this explanation is that the way in which verse 15 is connected to the previous verse is insufficiently taken into account. Cain complains of his dire fate, culminating in the decree that as an outlaw he can now be slaughtered by anyone. The mark that Yahweh gives him is a response to this. The structural parallelism with Gen 3 as well points in a different direction: in 3:21 we read how Yahweh, after the condemnation and cursing of man but still before his expulsion (גרשׁ), makes clothes for

---

48. "In any case, a worthwhile interpretation," says Jacob, *Das Buch Genesis*, 146 (my trans.).

49. See the view of P. A. H. de Boer, quoted by Wenham, *Genesis 1–15*, 109.

50. See, e.g., Otto Procksch, *Die Genesis* (Leipzig: Deichert, 1913), 48: "It is precisely this sevenfold protection of the committer of fratricide that entails the most severe punishment: the cursed life is absolutely worthless but nonetheless inviolable" (my trans.). See also Josef Scharbert, *Genesis 1–11* (Würzburg: Echter, 1983), 68.

him. This suggests that the mark of Cain after his condemnation and cursing, but before his expulsion, has a positive function. But what is it?

The second line of explanation interprets God's giving the mark to Cain as a reduction of sentence. This is often coupled to an interpretation of verse 13 as a token of Cain's repentance or at least a confession of guilt—that is why Yahweh comes to Cain with his protection.[51] As we have seen, there is not much to say in favor of this exegesis; on closer investigation verses 13–14 instead show a hardening on the part of Cain.[52] However, this certainly does not exclude the possibility that in verse 15 Yahweh, with his mark for Cain, aims at a reduction of punishment in order to grant Cain life. Is this a sign of grace for Cain? On this point theological considerations often loom enormously, and sometimes a Pauline doctrine of justification is read into the text: Gen 4:15 would be the first signal of the *iustificatio impii*. It is principally von Rad who, with his salvation-historical view on the development of sin and forgiveness in Gen 1–11, has contributed to this line of thought.[53] Golka, however, rightly questions the idea: no such thing as a pardon of Cain comes into play.[54]

Even if we had to speak of grace, it would be "common grace" rather than particular mercy for Cain. There is no conflict between the curse upon Cain's life and the avenging of Cain's death. The mark of Cain in verse 15 implies neither intensification nor reduction of the punishment. In conjunction with Cain's words in verse 14 (not a prayer but a lament), verse 15 addresses nothing other than protection from death. The strength of the punishment is unmitigated. The punished murderer will have to live his life far away from God, but still not inaccessible to him. In this context the meaning of the judicial protection by the mark of Cain will be this: that by this mark Yahweh puts a stop to the downward spiral of violence. The increasing violence of Gen 4:1–16 threatens to escalate and carry others away. Yahweh, however, puts limits to the spirit of violence: look to the mark of Cain! Von Rad formulates

---

51. See, e.g., Jacob, *Das Buch Genesis*, 144: "Because of Cain's remorse, he is pardoned for the time being" (my trans.).

52. See the explanation in §4.4 above.

53. Von Rad, *Theologie der geschichtlichen Überlieferungen Israels*; see also idem, *Das erste Buch Mose: Genesis* (ATD; Göttingen: Vandenhoeck & Ruprecht, 1972), 117; Horst Dietrich Preuss, *Israels Weg mit JHWH* (vol. 2 of *Theologie des Alten Testaments*; Stuttgart: Kohlhammer, 1992), 185, 283.

54. Friedemann W. Golka, "Keine Gnade für Kain," in *Werden und Wirken des Alten Testaments: Festschrift für Claus Westermann zum 70. Geburtstag* (ed. by Rainer Albertz et al.; Göttingen: Vandenhoeck & Ruprecht; Neukirchen-Vluyn: Neukirchener, 1980), 58–73.

this in a splendid way: "Here an organizing and protecting divine will manifests itself. The murderous spirit, which broke out in Cain, must be prevented from spreading out in increasingly wider circles, and the punishment, which God inflicted on Cain, shall not be the occasion of an ever growing brutalization among people."[55] Even in the midst of God's just judgment of human sin, he intervenes to save people from the worst possible consequences they might bring upon themselves.

The rest of Gen 4 displays, however, with utter clarity the proliferating nature of violence despite the threat of divine counterviolence. It is obvious that in Cain's offspring the restriction of violence by Yahweh is violated. With a direct allusion to God's words on his judicial protection of Cain (v. 15), Lamech proclaims an unlimited *conservatio sui* in a world full of violence (v. 24): evil overflows its banks.

In the meanwhile it has become clear that Yahweh is a God who, in taking up the cudgels for the victims of evil, taking judicious action toward those who commit crimes, and promising to execute sevenfold avengement to potential murderers, is himself engaged in this story—this story in which sin and injustice threaten to dominate life. For that purpose, Yahweh can threaten with violence or even use violence, in order to restrict evil. For the first time in the history of humankind, Gen 4 expresses both the possibility and the existence of counterviolence in the service of justice.

6. Violence and Justice: A Theological Evaluation

On the basis of the preceding exegetical analysis we can now draw a few conclusions with respect to the evaluation of the theme of violence and its implications for the image of God in Gen 4:1–16.

The biblical story of Cain and Abel reflects a deep understanding of morality, both in the rejection of violence and in the accentuation of the care for one's fellow human. In this chapter there is no trace of some sort of exaltation of violence, as we find this elsewhere in the literature of the ancient Near

---

55. Von Rad, *Das erste Buch Mose: Genesis*, 80 (my trans.); Mathews, *Genesis 1–11*, 278. See also André Kabasele Mukenge, "Relecture de Gn 4,1–16 dans le contexte africain," in *Lectures et relectures de la Bible: Festschrift P.-M. Bogaert* (ed. André Wénin and Jean-Marie Auwers; Leuven: Leuven University Press; Peeters, 1999), 427: "Now we understand that God, by resolutely protecting Cain from human vengeance, aims at avoiding the chain reaction that could have been released by the assassination of Abel. The intention of the mark of Cain seems to be the instruction that society should accommodate the murderer without tolerating the crime. Cain is still under verdict, but he is not turned over to the people's revenge" (my trans.).

East.[56] Rather, the mechanisms of violence are unmasked and denounced in both an ethical and a theological manner. Genesis 4 offers fundamental insights into the nature, roots, and consequences of violence.

Of utmost importance in this passage is the direct connection between violence and "sin" (חטאת v. 5; עון v. 13), a term that here, remarkably enough, is used for the first time in the Bible. Violence is sketched as the product and manifestation of the power of evil. Man is not defenseless against this phenomenon; he has to recognize the threat and resist it (v. 7b). However, the fact that the first man on earth—as soon as the human race starts to develop itself outside of the garden of Eden—commits a violent crime is telling. Apparently, this belongs to the potential of man who became disobedient toward his God. His knowledge of good and evil brings him little good: as soon as he is given a free choice (v. 7a), he falls short by choosing evil. From the beginning, he is inclined not to listen to God, not to give account (v. 6) of his deeds, but rather to resort to violence (v. 8). According to its own nature, violence is the denial of and an attack on solidarity; fratricide is the archetype of all violence. At the same time, there is a deeper dimension: violence against one's brother cannot be disposed of as a merely interpersonal event; it has to do with God himself, the Creator of life (vv. 1, 9–10). Therefore, violence can never have the last word (v. 10), because it makes man worthy of punishment. The offender is personally called to account for his deeds (vv. 9–10). Violence tends toward expansion and escalation: in the wake of the outrage we find the lie, impudence, and rejection of responsibility for another person (v. 9), self-pity, protest against God (vv. 13–14), and finally the possibility of a new murder (vv. 14–15; see also v. 24). Where violence overflows its banks and escalates, only the counterviolence of God can hold back the consequences (v. 15).

In the biblical narrative, the roots of human violence are localized on the breeding ground of turbid emotions. It does not make much sense to try to find deeper psychological reasons for violence: jealousy, wounded pride, and so on. Violence against one's brother flows from great anger and malice, which break off communication (v. 5b). This hazardous attitude is characterized as not-doing-right (v. 6). Related to this are the eruptive and irrational aspects of violence—it strikes with suddenness and intensity (v. 8). Violence is literally sense-less.

In the same unveiling way this pericope tells us about the fatal consequences of violence. Violence disturbs all relations that make life good and

---

56. See Klaas Smelik, *Een tijd van oorlog, een tijd van vrede: Bezetting en bevrijding in de Bijbel* (Zoetermeer: Boekencentrum, 2005).

worthwhile: with God, with one's fellow man, with the earth, with oneself. Violence brings man wholly into a process of alienation and isolation. Life with violence is a life under the curse. Violence against the life of one's fellow man turns against the inflictor himself, because the God who created life guards it and acts as judge. Not violence, but justice will have the last word. By violence the bond with one's fellow man is broken (v. 9). He who hands himself over to violence looses the bond with God as well (vv. 14, 16). The violent man violates his relation to creation itself; the earth will no longer be a source of life and joy for him (v. 12). The offender himself is also changed by his violence: equilibrium and safety disappear; the life of this man becomes a flight (vv. 12–16). By violence a process of hardening and loneliness sets in (vv. 9, 14). The way of disobedience toward God (vv. 6–7), giving in to sin (v. 8) and refusing to take up one's responsibility (v. 9), is in every regard a dead-end road.

In Gen 4 violence is sketched as thwarting the good plan of God's creation. However, at the same time in Gen 4 a countermovement becomes visible. Where man chooses in favor of death, God stands up in favor of life; over violence God places justice. The story of Cain offers us profound insights not only on the mechanisms of human violence but also on God's attitude toward it. We can point at least to the following four elements.

First, the very telling dialogue in verses 6–7. Yahweh acts as a *pastor* who knows exactly what is in the heart of man. By his questions he seeks to awaken Cain and to warn him of what threatens to happen. Obviously, the intention of this dialogue is that God wants to direct man in the good direction in order to prevent violence. Second, after the murder God calls the inflictor to account for his deeds, in which he acts with the function of the *iudex supremus*. The evil cannot remain hidden; God stands up for the victims of violence. This God is the last hope for all helpless and silenced people in a world where the powers of sin, violence, and death prevail. He is a judge who holds people responsible for their deeds. Third, God unmasks the lies of the inflictor and pronounces judgment on the evil of the violence. He thereby restores the boundary that was consciously violated by man: the creature does not have the right to lay violent hands on the life of his fellow man. Fourth, God holds back the consequences of violence by acting as the *protector*—even of the inflictor himself. God's last word is not the curse but a mark that he gives to him who killed his brother. The spirit of murder, which permeates the human race, is stopped by a boundary that God has placed.

7. An Ambiguous God in Genesis 4?

The question can be asked whether the image of God as *pastor*, *iudex*, and *protector* as sketched in the previous sections is not too positively colored and whether Gen 4:1–16 does not reveal another, darker, line too. In this passage, do we not encounter a God who is essentially unpredictable and in the end starts the spiral of violence, or is at least partly responsible for it? In the *belles lettres* of Romanticism, some people pleaded in Cain's defense and argued for his rehabilitation.[57] Does he not have good reasons to be angry? He is the firstborn (v. 1), he spontaneously takes the initiative to bring a gift (v. 3), nothing indicates that his sacrifice was somehow inferior to that of Abel (v. 4), and still he is passed over. When Yahweh later punishes Cain's violence, he does so rightly, but is not God himself involved in this as well, since by his selective preference in favor of Abel's sacrifice he gave rise to Cain's animosity? Referring to God's sovereign election (Westermann, Zimmerli, and von Rad) does not solve this question but makes it even more pressing.[58] Brueggemann goes somewhat further when he claims that the traditional explanation of Genesis is too harsh with regard to Cain and smooths over too much with respect to Yahweh: "The trouble comes not from Cain, but from Yahweh, the strange God of Israel. Inexplicably, Yahweh chooses—accepts and rejects.... Essential to the plot is the capricious freedom of Yahweh."[59]

Much depends on the right interpretation of Gen 4:3–5, which is the passage on the offerings. The text itself does not give a straightforward explanation of the fact that God "looks with favor" on the offering of Abel but does not look with favor on Cain's offering. Why is the offering of Cain not accepted? In general, three different answers have been given to this question.[60]

The starting point of the first explanation is the very fact of the absence of an explicit motivation of God's choice itself. Westermann is the most prominent representative of this way of thinking. According to him, in this regard we cannot but talk about God's inscrutability. This story reflects the reality of

---

57. As do Coleridge, Byron, and Baudelaire; see www.torah.org/projects/genesis/topic1.html.

58. Golka, "Keine Gnade für Kain," 62; G. G. de Kruijf, "Give Place unto Wrath!" in *Christian Faith and Violence* (ed. Dirk van Keulen and Martien Brinkman; 2 vols.; Studies in Reformed Theology 11; Zoetermeer: Meinema, 2006), 2:116.

59. Brueggemann, *Genesis*, 56. In his *Theology of the Old Testament: Testimony, Dispute, Advocacy* (Minneapolis: Fortress, 1997), Brueggemann elaborates the theme of ambiguity in the Old Testament image of God with a clear preference for words such as "odd," "unstable," "unreliable," "capricious," "irascible," "irrational," "abusive," etc. See also McEntire, *Blood of Abel*, 29–30; Ronald S. Hendel, "When Gods Act Immorally," in *Approaches to the Bible: The Best of Bible Review* (ed. Harvey Minkoff; 2 vols.; Washington, D.C.: Biblical Archeology Society, 1995), 2:16–25, 310–11.

60. The view of Gunkel (*Genesis*, 37) that the reason is to be found in God's preference of shepherds to farmers hardly deserves serious attention, given Gen 2:15.

life with the experience of sometimes-inexplicable blessings or misfortunes, acceptance and rejection. "Therefore, it must remain inexplicable why God accepts Abel's sacrifice and rejects Cain's. And this, so the narrator wants to make clear, is one of the decisive motifs of a conflict, wherever brothers live together."[61] One is also often alerted to the fact that in Gen 4, for the first time, a motif occurs that will play a major role in the book of Genesis: the election of the youngest above the oldest (Ishmael–Isaac; Esau–Jacob, Joseph–Judah, etc.),[62] and indeed this motif can play a part here: Yahweh breaks through the human patterns of priority and hierarchy and acts over against the "number one," Cain, in favor of the weaker Abel (*hebel*). However, this cannot entirely explain the rejection of Cain's gift. In Gen 4 the youngest plays merely a supporting role and soon disappears from the story, which is certainly not the case in all other instances of the divine election of the youngest.

A second explanation seeks to find the motive in the nature of the gifts themselves. An ancient view is that a blood sacrifice would be more pleasing to God than an offering of grain.[63] In the light of the Old Testament legislation with regard to sacrifices, it is hard to consider this as decisive. Another idea that has been put forward is the view that Cain's gift is not accepted by God because it was taken from the soil (אדמה), while the earth was cursed by God shortly before (3:17).[64]

A third explanation finds the reason for the rejection of Cain's offering in the attitude of the person who brings the sacrifice. Without wanting to explain too much, I think that this view does more justice to the text than the others. I offer four arguments in favor of this view. (1) There is clearly incongruence in the description of the gifts. In the case of Abel's offering there is a detailed description of how he brings the best of the best: the "firstborn" (בכרות) and the fat portions. Cain does not bring the בכרים, but only some of the "fruits" (פרי) of the soil. Read through the eyes of a Jewish reader, this is an undeniable indication.[65]

---

61. Westermann, *Genesis 1–11*, 405 (my trans.).
62. Such, for instance, can be seen in Deurloo, *Kain en Abel*, 101; Van Wolde, "The Story of Cain and Abel," 29. See also Everett Fox, "Stalking the Younger Brother: Some Models For Understanding A Biblical Motif," *JSOT* 60 (1993): 45–68.
63. Jacob, *Das Buch Genesis*, 137.
64. This is defended extensively by Gary A. Herion, "Why God Rejected Cain's Offering: The Obvious Answer," in *Fortunate the Eyes That See: Essays in Honor of David Noel Freedman in Celebration of His Seventieth Birthday* (ed. Astrid B. Beck et al.; Grand Rapids: Eerdmans, 1995), 52–65; Spina, "The 'Ground' for Cain's Rejection."
65. Thus Craig, "Questions outside Eden," 111–12; Hamilton, *The Book of Genesis*, 223.

(2) In the context of the pericope the full focus is on the progressive hardening of Cain.⁶⁶ The difficult verse 7 as well seems to imply that from the very beginning Cain's behavior was not right. It is not mere coincidence that both times in the wording of God's (not) "looking in favor upon" in verses 4 and 5, the person is mentioned before the offering.

(3) An investigation into the motif of the rejection of the offering, both in the Old Testament and in Israel's *Umwelt*, brings to light that the proper attitude and obedience of the person who brings the offering is of crucial importance in deciding whether or not the offering is accepted.⁶⁷

(4) A broader reading in the context of Gen 2–11 also sustains this explanation. Von Rad and others rightly speak of "a development to the completely Titanic" in this part of Genesis.⁶⁸ The author of these chapters has been a person, according to Vriezen, "who fully measured the depth of sinfulness of the human heart and who has given expression to his spiritual conviction that the human race is depraved."⁶⁹ With humanity it goes from bad to worse, and the suggestion of Gen 4 is that it is especially in the first representative of a new generation, a new אדם, that this comes to light.⁷⁰

Read in this way, Gen 4 fits seamlessly in the structure of the book of Genesis. Not a capricious and inscrutable God, but rather man himself is responsible for the thrust to violence that corrupts creation and brings a curse on man. It is man who willingly and knowingly forces the bursting of the dike. At the same time, Gen 4 recounts of Yahweh, who does not hand his world and humankind over to the powers of sin and violence: he warns, stands up for victims, brings a stop to those who commit violence, and summons them; he punishes and restricts violence.

---

66. See also Allen P. Ross, *Creation and Blessing: A Guide to the Study and Exposition of the Book of Genesis* (Grand Rapids: Baker, 1988), 156.

67. See Johannes de Moor, "The Sacrifice Which Is an Abomination to the Lord," in *Loven en geloven: Opstellen van Collega's en Medewerkers aangeboden aan Prof. Dr. Nic. H. Ridderbos* (ed. H. M. van Es et al.; Amsterdam: Bolland, 1975), 211–26, an essay that has insufficiently been taken into account. He claims: "According to the Yahwistic author of Gen. 4 the personal attitude of the sacrificer has been decisive from the beginning of the sacrificial cult" (223).

68. Von Rad, *Theologie der geschichtlichen Überlieferungen Israels*, 164 (my trans.). Wenham, *Genesis 1–15*, li: "The opening chapters of Genesis describe an avalanche of sin that gradually engulfs mankind."

69. Th. C. Vriezen, *Hoofdlijnen der Theologie van het Oude Testament* (Wageningen: Veenman en Zonen, 1974), 449: "die de diepte der zondigheid van het mensenhart volkomen heeft gepeild, en in de hele oerhistorie uitdrukking heeft gegeven aan zijn geestelijke overtuiging van de verdorvenheid van het menselijke geslacht."

70. See the reception of Gen 4 in Heb 11:4; Jude 11; and 1 John 3:11–12.

In Gen 4 we find for the first time in the Old Testament sin and violence, with the consequent alienation from life and the beginning of death. This is the introduction of a religious book that to a bewildering extent is full of stories and texts of violence and offers insight into a world full of evil and animosity. From a hermeneutical and theological perspective, it is worth noting that in the final canonical redaction of the Old Testament, Gen 4 has received this key position as the narrative overture of what the reader can expect in what follows. In this passage it becomes clear not only what is alive in the heart of humans but also what is alive in the heart of God. The reader of the Old Testament comes across things that are puzzling and sometimes even horrible, stories in which one can encounter the inscrutability and incomprehensibility of the works of Yahweh in this world. But it is already indicated at the outset by the positioning of Gen 4 that in this world God places his justice over against violence, as an advocate of victims and a judge of perpetrators, a judge who at the same time is also a pastor, in order to save this world from chaos.

The Enemies in the Headings of the Psalms: A Comparison of Jewish and Christian Interpretation

Herrie F. van Rooy

1. The Enemies in the Hebrew Psalter

Enemies are mentioned very frequently in the Psalms. One can indeed say that the majority of the psalms refers to enemies.[1] The issue of animosity is not a minor theme in the Psalter. It is central to the message of the Psalms.[2] The question of who the enemies were is frequently related to different kinds of psalms and different kinds of authors of the different psalms. Although psalms were written by individuals, each individual might have acted in an individual capacity or on behalf of some group. In some cases it is clear that the individual was a king or a leader. In other instances this individual might have spoken on behalf of a larger group.[3] References to enemies occur in a wide variety of psalms, including individual (e.g., 5; 6; 7; 9; 10; 13; 22; 27) and communal (44; 74; 79; 80; 83) laments and royal psalms.[4] In his discussion Anderson distinguishes the same three groups of psalms: those with a subject in the plural ("we"), those with a subject in the singular ("I"), and a third group in which the "I" is clearly a king.[5] There appears to be consensus that a consideration of the enemies in the Psalms, approached from the perspective of form criticism, leads to a distinction between different types of

---

1. Nicolaas H. Ridderbos, *De Psalmen I* (KV; Kampen: Kok, 1962), 27.
2. Erich Zenger, *Ein Gott der Rache? Feindpsalmen verstehen* (Freiburg: Herder, 1998), 26.
3. Ridderbos, *Psalmen I*, 28.
4. Marvin E. Tate, *Psalms 51–100* (WBC 20; Waco, Tex.: Word, 1990), 60.
5. George W. Anderson, "Enemies and Evildoers in the Book of Psalms," *BJRL* 48 (1965–66): 19. See also John W. Rogerson, "The Enemy in the Old Testament," in *Understanding Poets and Prophets: Essays in Honour of George Wishart Anderson* (ed. A. Graeme Auld; JSOTSup 152; Sheffield: Sheffield Academic Press, 1993), 286.

psalms, such as the threefold distinction mentioned above.[6] The enemies of Israel can then be seen in the royal psalms and the prayers of the community in particular.[7]

The issue of the enemies is an old problem that has received a great deal of attention through the years. Back in 1921 Sigmund Mowinckel called it an old problem.[8] Before the time of Mowinckel and since his time, many scholars have grappled with this problem, and they will probably continue to do so. Mowinckel said that the main question is whether the enemies are external enemies, such as Gentiles and foreign rulers, or internal enemies, such as apostate and unfaithful Jews.[9] He said that most scholars accept both kinds of enemies. He distinguished between laments of the community and individual laments. In laments of the community the enemies were external enemies, the enemies of the nation, such as neighboring countries.[10] In the individual laments, however, his research pointed in the direction that the enemies were sorcerers.[11]

This latter view of Mowinckel is related to the fact that in many of the psalms talking about enemies, the author is ill.[12] One can ask what was first, the illness or the enemies. Did the enemies act because the author was ill, or did he become ill as a result of their enmity?[13] Ridderbos emphasizes the importance given to the words of the enemies.[14] When the words of the enemies are emphasized, he thinks that they are not foreigners. A very common view distinguishes between the enemies on account of the different kinds of psalms. The enemies in the communal laments are generally regarded as foreigners,[15] while the situation is not that clear with regard to individual laments. Perhaps different options should be kept in mind when one considers the individual laments.[16]

---

6. See Hans-Joachim Kraus, *Theologie der Psalmen* (3rd ed.; Neukirchen-Vluyn: Neukirchener, 2003), 156.
7. Ibid., 156.
8. Sigmund Mowinckel, *Awän und die individuellen Klagepsalmen* (vol. 1 of *Psalmenstudien*; Christiana: Dybwad, 1921), 76.
9. Mowinckel, *Awän und die individuellen Klagepsalmen*, 76.
10. Ibid.
11. Ibid., 77.
12. See Ridderbos, *Psalmen I*, 28.
13. See ibid., 29.
14. Ibid., 31–32.
15. See also Tate, *Psalms 51–100*, 61.
16. See ibid., 62.

Puukko is of the opinion that in the majority of instances the enemies are internal enemies, not foreign enemies.[17] In most of the cases the enemy is a member of the poet's own people.[18] He dates these enemies to the postexilic Jewish community,[19] but his article does not take notice of nor respond to the important work that Birkeland had done already before World War II.

Following a major publication in 1933, Birkeland's important work on the enemies in the Psalms culminated in a final publication in 1955.[20] He regards the enemies in the individual laments as being the same as the enemies in the other groups of psalms, namely, the enemies of the nation, such as the Gentiles.[21] He refers to the two views existing before his own publication of 1933.[22] Some scholars regarded the enemies of the individual as a faction in late Judaism that was hostile to the pious Jews (one of the views referred to by Mowinckel in 1921), while Mowinckel regarded them as sorcerers. His own view is that there is in principle no difference between individual and collective psalms of lament with regard to the enemies. It is indeed true that individuals had enemies among their own people, but these enemies are usually not mentioned in the Psalms, with Ps 127:5 as perhaps the only exception.[23]

Ridderbos took a view different from Birkeland and Mowinckel before him. He says many psalms presuppose a situation like the situation of David when he was persecuted by Saul, during the revolt of Absalom, or when he was opposed by Sheba or Adonijah.[24] Ridderbos refers to Pss 3; 5; 7; 11; 12; 14; 17; 18; 26; 28; 31, 34; 40; and many more. Psalms such as 6; 38; 39; and 41 refer to animosity from the side of his own people, stirred up by the illness of the king or leader. In Pss 10; 12; 14; and 37 the evildoers are Israelites oppressing the helpless, the poor, and so forth. In Pss 20; 21; 33; and 35 the enemies are foreigners.

---

17. A. Filemon Puukko, "Die Feind in den alttestamentliche Psalmen," *OtSt* 8 (1950): 48.
18. Ibid., 56.
19. Ibid., 48.
20. Harris Birkeland, *The Evildoers in the Book of Psalms* (Avhandliger utgitt ar Det Norske Videnskaps-Akademi i Oslo. II. Hist.-Filos. Klasse. 1955. No. 2, Oslo: Dybwad, 1955).
21. Ibid., 9.
22. Ibid., 10.
23. Ibid., 46.
24. Ridderbos, *Psalmen I*, 32.

Brongers published an important study on the psalms of vengeance in 1963.[25] In communal laments he sees the enemies as foreign enemies, including Pss 44; 74; 79; and 133. In these psalms the people are remonstrating to God about the injustices done to them by other nations, and they petition him to act.[26] In communal laments the motivation for the psalm is the same in every instance. Foreign armies entered the land of Israel and defeated the people of God. These psalms begin with an exposition of the affliction of the people. This is followed by their cry for help, then usually a statement of the actions of vengeance they are hoping for. The psalm then concludes with an expression of trust and thanks.[27] In individual laments[28] the same pattern appears. The distress is stated, help is asked for, and the vengeance is detailed.[29] Brongers agrees with the view that it is difficult to identify the enemies in the individual laments.[30] He refers to the different theories in this regard, such as the theories of Mowinckel (sorcerers), Birkeland (national enemies), the myth and ritual school (chaos powers), Eerdmans (the enemies of the Hasidim), and Puukko (a variety of private and public enemies).[31] He states that in the individual laments two kinds of people are introduced: people who are ill and people who are unjustly accused. The cry for vengeance belongs to the second group, as in Pss 5; 7; 9–10; 17; 31; 109; 140; 141; and 143.[32] When interpreting these psalms, one must keep in mind that this kind of psalm was not a typical Israelite phenomenon, that the psalmist did not seek personal vengeance, and that the purpose of the call for punishment was the victory of justice and the justification and acknowledgement of the living God.[33] The believers crying to God wanted to see justice being done in this world.[34]

Anderson sees the enemies in the psalms with "we" and with a king as subject as foreign enemies.[35] With regard to the psalms with "I" as subject, he refers to the many opinions as well.[36] Anderson's view is that one should

---

25. Hendrik A. Brongers, "Die Rache- und Fluchpsalmen im Alten Testament," in *Studies on Psalms* (ed. P. A. H. de Boer; OtSt 13; Leiden: Brill, 1963), 21–42.

26. Ibid., 21.

27. Ibid., 24–25.

28. He lists the following psalms: 5; 7; 9–10; 12; 17; 21; 31; 35; 40; 54–56; 58; 59; 69; 70; 94; 109; 139; 140; and 142 (ibid., 22).

29. Ibid., 6.

30. Ibid., 27.

31. Ibid., 27–28.

32. Ibid., 28.

33. Ibid., 32–33.

34. Ibid., 42.

35. Anderson, "Enemies and Evildoers," 19.

36. Ibid., 20–26.

not look for one single answer to all the problems.[37] One should rather leave room for a range of interpretations, including national enemies, illness of a leader or individual, slander, and a variety of cultic acts and situations.[38]

The idea that the enemies of the community and the king must be identified with foreign enemies has gained almost general acceptance.[39] The enemies of the king are the nations waging war against the people of God or their kings and rulers. The background for this is the universal rule of the king in Jerusalem, which is linked to the universal rule of God.[40] The same is true of the enemies in communal laments. The people's enemies became the enemies of God.[41] The enemies of the individual are primarily people, but this human picture of the enemy can be transcended to make the enemy the image of evil.[42] They are mainly the impious and the persecutors of the individual.[43]

Keel makes a very important contribution to the study of the enemies of the individual. He regards it as a problem that the main question normally dealt with in studies on this subject is the problem of the identification of the enemies. Keel is more concerned about the way in which the enemies are pictured in the literature and this picture is then related to their way of life.[44] He emphasizes the individual's bond to the community in Israel, leading to a mistrust of foreigners. On the other hand, he accepts that, within the community, rivalry can lead to animosity as well.[45] Changes in the community, such as the institution of the monarchy, however, lead to alienation within the community.[46] In the description of enemies, the main purpose of a poet is to ask Yahweh to intercede on his or her behalf.[47] Because of this, the psalms are not reports of events but express the sorrows and fears of the poet.[48] These remarks of Keel are very important, because they emphasize the importance of reading the descriptions of the enemies in the Psalms not as

---

37. Ibid., 28.
38. Ibid., 29.
39. See, e.g., Hans-Joachim Kraus, *Psalm 1–59* (vol. 1. of *Psalmen*; 5th ed.; BKAT 15.1; Neukirchen-Vluyn: Neukirchener, 1978), 112; idem, *Theologie der Psalmen*, 157.
40. Kraus, *Theologie der Psalmen*, 157.
41. Ibid., 159.
42. Kraus, *Psalm 1–59*, 115–16; Kraus, *Theologie der Psalmen*, 168.
43. Kraus, *Theologie der Psalmen*, 161.
44. Othmar Keel, *Feinde und Gottesleugner: Studien zum Image der Widersacher in den Individualpsalmen* (SBM 7; Stuttgart: Verlag Katholisches Bibelwerk, 1969), 34.
45. Ibid., 90.
46. Ibid., 90–91.
47. Ibid., 92.
48. Ibid., 91.

factual but rather as programmatic. They present a picture, a portrait, of the enemies. This portrait is not realistic but rather impressionistic. In picturing the enemies, the Psalms distinguish two kinds of enemies. The one group can be regarded as adversaries, like those indicated by the word אויב. The other group can be described on the moral level as evildoers, the רשעים.[49] In the Psalms the poets saw their enemies in relation to Yahweh, asking him to act on their behalf.[50] In this way the enemies became identified with evildoers.

The enemies are usually not identified explicitly in the Psalms.[51] Psalm 2 is a good example of this. This psalm has to do with a threat to the ruler in Jerusalem, a ruler chosen by God.[52] The psalm does not make clear who the kings and rulers were who opposed the anointed one of God, but it makes clear that their opposition would be futile.[53] Rogerson states that this psalm must be read against the background of a Zion theology, building on the idea of the universal rule of the God of Israel.[54] The king in Jerusalem was too insignificant in the eyes of the major powers of that time to cause them real concern, but the psalm sees this king as a sign of hope.[55] In some instances the enemies may be explicitly identified, as in Ps 137. This psalm mentions Edom and Babylon, but this is the exception, not the rule.

It is often the case that scholars judge very negatively the way in which the Psalms treat the enemies. A clear example of this is Anderson's view: "The imprecations of the Psalmists have sometimes been condemned with a ferocity and intolerance similar to those of which they are themselves accused, often, it may be supposed, without any awareness that the identity of the enemies and the evildoers and the nature of their activity raise any problem whatsoever."[56] Such treatment of the enemies in the Psalms does not differ from what one could read in the remainder of the Old Testament. Deuteronomy 20:10–14 can be quoted as an example of the brutal treatment of enemies.[57] For many the solution to the problem of the enemies in the Psalms is either to ignore or to correct the statements by the authors of the relevant psalms about vengeance on their enemies.[58]

---

49. Ibid., 129.
50. Ibid., 217.
51. Tate, *Psalms 51–100*, 61.
52. Rogerson, "The Enemy in the Old Testament," 286.
53. Ibid., 287.
54. Ibid.
55. Ibid., 287–88.
56. Anderson, "Enemies and Evildoers," 18.
57. See Rogerson, "The Enemy in the Old Testament," 285.
58. Zenger, *Ein Gott der Rache*, 43.

Just as in the New Testament, however, believers in the time of the Old Testament were supposed to love their enemies (Lev 19:17–8; Exod 23:4–5). The poet of a psalm may have hated his oppressors, but God hates oppression.[59] We should not see a dogma of retribution behind these psalms, something that was rejected by the New Testament.[60] The laments of the individual must be seen against the background of a plea for justice. The enemies of the individual did him injustice. In this way, their actions questioned the place of justice in this world. The prime concern of the plea in an individual lament is the cry for justice to be done.[61] The author of a psalm is praying about his suffering because of the injustices done to him.[62] If one accepts this, the enemy of the individual is not necessarily a foreigner.[63] The author of a lament is, however, confronting God with the mystery of evil in this world.[64] Rogerson prefers to define the enemies not in social terms, such as the alien or outsider, but in moral terms, as those, internal or external to the community, who seek to undermine God's justice.[65] In this way Rogerson links the problem of animosity to the desire for universal justice, which can serve as a guideline in our time as well.

This discussion shows that the issues regarding the enemies have not been resolved to the satisfaction of all concerned. The findings of form-critical research are still valid, and the differences between individual and communal laments, as well as royal psalms, must be kept in mind. It would probably be best to keep an open mind for more than one possibility. In many instances the enemies are indeed foreigners, but in some instances internal enemies are also possible. In the majority of the instances the enemies are not explicitly identified.

2. The Enemies in the Headings of the Hebrew Psalms

The headings of the psalms have been ignored in research for many years, but in the recent past they started receiving more attention. The kind of attention they have been receiving, however, differs substantially from the way in which they had been used in the distant past, especially with the weight given to the historical reliability of the information contained in the headings of the

---

59. Peter C. Craigie, *Psalms 1–50* (WBC 19; Waco, Tex.: Word, 1982), 41.
60. Brongers, "Die Rache- und Fluchpsalmen," 41.
61. Rogerson, "The Enemy in the Old Testament," 289–90.
62. Zenger, *Ein Gott der Rache*, 133.
63. Rogerson, "The Enemy in the Old Testament," 290.
64. Zenger, *Ein Gott der Rache*, 133.
65. Rogerson, "The Enemy in the Old Testament," 293.

psalms. Much of the information in the headings was linked to the issue of authorship of the psalms.[66]

The rabbis regarded all the psalms as coming from David, even those that did not have headings referring to David. A psalm such as Ps 137 was then seen as prophetic about the Babylonian exile.[67] Delitzsch is a good example of an older exegete who took the historical references in some of the headings of the psalms seriously in the process of interpreting a psalm. With regard to Ps 3, he argues that many of the psalms date from the time when David was persecuted by Saul, although only Pss 3 and 63 can be dated to the time of Absalom.[68] He does not regard the fact that the psalm itself does not make a direct reference to Absalom as a problem in linking the psalm to the time of his rebellion. Psalm 7 dates from the time when David was persecuted by Saul. If one reads 1 Sam 24–26, it will be quite clear that this psalm contains many references to that time in the life of David.[69] The same is true of Ps 54. The reference to Doeg in the heading links the psalm to the time when David was persecuted by Saul.[70]

This kind of approach to the headings of the psalms was abandoned not long after the time of Delitzsch, although half a century later Tur-Sinai still had a high regard for the historical information in the headings.[71] He did not accept the cultic setting of the psalms but rather saw them as songs borrowed from the historical books. However, this view did not receive much support.[72] Already in 1906 Briggs wrote that the headings "give evidence of the different stages in the editing and use of the Pss.; and not of their authorship, date, or character of the originals."[73] The headings, therefore, represent several editorial stages, and this process was continued in the Septuagint and Peshitta,

---

66. Not all the headings contain historical infomation. Erhard S. Gerstenberger (*Psalms, Part 2, and Lamentations* [FOTL 15; Grand Rapids: Eerdmans, 2001], 536) distinguishes four kinds of information: musical-technical information; possible authors; genre classifications; and historical settings.

67. Horst D. Preuss, "Die Psalmenüberschriften in Targum and Midrasch," *ZAW* 71 (1959): 49–50.

68. Franz Delitzsch, *Biblische Kommentar über die Psalmen* (Leipzig: Dörffling & Franke, 1894), 79. In the German edition of 1894 that I used, he refers to the time of Solomon, but that is probably an error.

69. Ibid., 100.

70. Ibid., 378.

71. N. Harry Tur-Sinai, "The Literary Character of the Psalms," *OtSt* 8 (1950): 264–65.

72. Brevard S. Childs. "Psalm Titles and Midrashic Exegesis," *JSS* 16 (1971): 137.

73. Charles A. Briggs, *The Book of Psalms* (2 vols.; ICC; Edinburgh: T&T Clark, 1906–7), 1:lviii.

according to Briggs.⁷⁴ He refers to the thirteen psalms that contain historical references to David. The statements in these headings depend on the narratives in Samuel and are later than the Deuteronomic redaction.⁷⁵ He regards these thirteen psalms as a small collection on their own, part of what he called the Psalter of David from the late Persian period.⁷⁶ As an example of his views on the headings, he says that the heading of Ps 3 refers to an event in the life of David that fits the experiences of the poet of the psalm.⁷⁷ Anderson also regards the headings as later additions and links them to the understanding of these psalms by postexilic Jewish exegetes.⁷⁸

This kind of approach is common today. Kraus, for example, argues that the heading of Ps 3 links this psalm to a specific situation in the life of David, as in 2 Sam 15–18.⁷⁹ The contents of the psalm make it clear that this link is wrong. The poet of Ps 3 does not flee like David, and there is no sign of David's mourning over Absalom.⁸⁰ The author of the heading tries to situate the psalm in a historical situation to aid the understanding of the psalm. The heading can be regarded as a witness to a first interpretation of this psalm. However, there is no general consensus on this issue. Dahood, for example, argues that the historical significance of these allusions to events in the life of David is still a matter of dispute.⁸¹ Millard offers a long discussion of the contents of Ps 3 and the correspondence between this psalm and the events recorded in Samuel.⁸² He considers it a possibility that the whole of Ps 3 may be seen as a midrash on the life of David.⁸³

A very important study that had a significant influence on current scholarship with regard to research on the headings was published by Childs in 1971.⁸⁴ Although he accepts that the headings did not have reliable information about the genuine historical setting of a given psalm, they provided a setting that became normative for the canonical situation. Because of this,

---

74. Ibid., 1:lviii.
75. Ibid., 1:lxiii.
76. Ibid., 1:lxi, lxiii.
77. Ibid., 1:25.
78. Arnold A. Anderson, *The Book of Psalms* (2 vols.; NCB; London: Oliphants, 1972), 1:51.
79. Kraus, *Psalm 1–59*, 160.
80. Anderson, *The Book of Psalms*, 1:70.
81. Mitchell Dahood, *Psalms: Introduction, Translation, and Notes* (3 vols.; AB 16–17A; Garden City, N.Y.: Doubleday, 1966–70), 1:13–14.
82. Matthias Millard, *Die Komposition des Psalters: Ein formgeschichtliche Ansatz* (FAT 9; Tübingen: Mohr Siebeck, 1994), 128–31.
83. Ibid., 131.
84. Childs, "Psalm Titles and Midrashic Exegesis," 137.

they are very important for the history of exegesis. He conducts a form-critical study of the thirteen headings containing historical information. With the exception of Pss 7 and 18, they all have a fixed form, with the infinitive construction following on the preposition ב in a noun clause, followed by a subordinate clause with a finite verb.[85] According to this, Ps 7 does not contain a historical reference, while Ps 18, with its heading, was taken from 2 Sam 22.[86] He summarizes his findings as follows: "The Psalm titles do not appear to reflect independent historical tradition but are the result of an exegetical activity which derived its material from within the text itself."[87] Following this, he surveys the different titles with historical information to see if he can determine the nature of this exegetical process. In this regard he concludes that general parallels between the situation described by the psalm and incidents in the life of David may be the most important factor in this process.[88] He dates these headings later than the Chronicler and before Qumran.[89] The titles come from a pietistic circle of Jews and unlock David's inner life for the reader.[90]

Petersen concurs largely with Childs. He finds it striking that eleven of the thirteen psalms with historical headings are laments.[91] The authors of these headings regarded David as the prime example of a person who had reason to compose laments. He had many enemies, from outside, such as the Philistines, and from within, such as Saul, Sheba, and Absalom, but he was able to escape from them or to achieve victory over them.[92]

A new tendency in Psalms study is to give more attention to the editing of the Psalter as a whole than was common in the time when form-critical studies dominated.[93] In this more recent approach the headings of the psalms are considered anew, especially in relation to what the headings may reveal about the editing of the Psalter as a whole. Two good examples of this approach are the works of Wilson and Millard.[94] They are interested in the redaction of the Psalter as a whole and treat the headings of the psalms within this context.

---

85. Ibid., 138.
86. Ibid., 138–39.
87. Ibid., 143.
88. Ibid., 147.
89. Ibid., 148.
90. Ibid., 149.
91. David L. Petersen, "Portraits of David: Canonical and Otherwise," *Int* 40 (1986): 139–40.
92. Ibid., 140.
93. See, e.g., James L. Mays, "The David of the Psalms," *Int* 40 (1986): 143–44.
94. Gerald H. Wilson, *The Editing of the Hebrew Psalter* (SBLDS 76; Chico, Calif.: Scholars Press, 1985); Millard, *Die Komposition des Psalters*. See also J. Clinton McCann,

Wilson is of the opinion that the addition of headings with historical information and the situating of the specific psalm in a certain historical context obscure the original cultic matrix of the psalm. This has the effect of shifting the function of that psalm to a more personal level. This personalization of these psalms through the headings would then impact on other psalms without these kinds of headings as well.[95] Connecting a psalm to a specific event through a heading is not based on any actual historical continuity but should be regarded as operating on a literary level.[96] The link is related to the exegesis of the psalm. Wilson views the persons responsible for the addition of these headings as a circle of pietistic Jews.[97] The effect of the addition of the headings has been to provide individuals with a hermeneutical key to use the psalms within their individual contexts.[98] The same view with regard to the headings as separating the psalms from the cult is stated by Zenger.[99] The headings with their references to the life of David pictures David as part of the laity. This closer link of the Psalter to David makes the Psalms a noncultic book of examples.[100] Millard also emphasizes the importance of the headings of the psalms for the study of the composition of the Psalter as a whole.[101]

Wilson says further that the tendency to link the psalms to David to a greater extent than in the Hebrew Psalter is even more evident in the manuscripts from Qumran, the Septuagint, and the Peshitta. Preuss made a study of the headings of the psalms in the Targum and Midrash. The Targum did not add any headings to those in the Hebrew Psalter; the Septuagint added twelve headings to the Hebrew, while the Peshitta has headings for all the psalms.[102] In his description of the headings in the Peshitta, he refers to two kinds of remarks in the headings of the Peshitta. The first part of the heading gave a description of the original situation, while the second part was directed at the Christian reader. From this remark it is clear that he used an edition like the one of Lee[103] and not any of the original manuscripts. He published this study

---

ed., *The Shape and Shaping of the Psalter* (JSOTSup 159; Sheffield: Sheffield Academic Press, 1993).

95. Wilson, *Editing of the Hebrew Psalter*, 143.
96. See ibid., 172.
97. See ibid. and the remark of Childs above.
98. See Wilson, *Editing of the Hebrew Psalter*, 173.
99. Erich Zenger, "Psalmenforschung nach Hermann Gunkel und Sigmund Mowinckel," in *Congress Volume: Oslo, 1998* (ed. André Lemaire and Magne Sæbø; VTSup 80; Leiden: Brill, 2000), 431.
100. Zenger, "Psalmenforschung," 431: "einer nicht-kultischen Rolendictung."
101. Millard, *Die Komposition des Psalters*, 27.
102. Preuss, "Die Psalmenüberschriften in Targum and Midrasch," 44.
103. Samuel Lee, *Vetus Testamentum Syriace* (London: Bible Society, 1823).

before the publication of the edition of Bloemendaal[104] of the headings of the East Syrian church and did not know of the differences between different traditions contained in manuscripts of the Peshitta. For the Targums, however, David remained the sole author of the Psalms, under divine inspiration.[105] As far as the Septuagint is concerned, one must be careful not to conclude, as Wilson does, that the tendency to link more psalms to David is more evident in the Septuagint. Pietersma cautioned that one must not take the edition of Rahlfs[106] as representing the Old Greek of the Psalter in every instance. In his study of David in the Greek Psalms, he indicated that some of the Davidic additions in the Greek must not be regarded as part of the Old Greek. He is of the opinion that Rahlfs was too inclusive in his approach, including some of the additions to the Hebrew Psalms as part of the Old Greek, disregarding important aspects of the translation technique in the Greek Psalter.[107] Most of the additions only add the name of David. Psalms 92; 95; and 96 add more information, but Pietersma makes it quite clear that the translation technique points in the direction that these additions were not part of the Old Greek.[108] In the end, Pietersma is convinced that the differences between the Hebrew and the Old Greek are smaller than one would think when looking at the text published by Rahlfs. It would, however, still mean that the tendency to link more psalms to David occurred in the process of the transmission of the Greek Psalter. In a previous study the headings of the manuscripts from Qumran were treated in detail.[109] Without repeating all of the detail of that analysis, it became clear that in the majority of instances the headings from the Dead Sea Scrolls agree with the Masoretic Text. Only in the case of Pss 33; 104; and probably 93 some of the evidence agrees with the Septuagint. These instances and some of the unique readings may indicate something of a tendency to ascribe more psalms to David than in the Masoretic Text, but the extent of this tendency is not very great, and it is mostly restricted to psalms from books 4 and 5 of the Psalter.[110]

---

104. Willem Bloemendaal, *The Headings of the Psalms in the East Syrian Church* (Leiden: Brill, 1960).

105. See Mays, "The David of the Psalms," 145.

106. Alfred Rahlfs, *Psalmi cum Odis* (3rd ed.; Vetus Testamentum Graecum 10; Göttingen: Vandenhoeck & Ruprecht, 1979).

107. Albert Pietersma, "David in the Greek Psalter," *VT* 30 (1980): 214.

108. Ibid., 221.

109. Herrie F. van Rooy, "The Headings of the Psalms in the Dead Sea Scrolls," *JNSL* 28 (2002): 127–41.

110. See ibid., 138–40.

In a study of the picture of David in the Psalter, Ballhorn made a number of interesting remarks on the headings with historical references.[111] He says that the majority of the psalms with historical headings are individual laments, with the exception of Pss 18; 30; and 34. One has to know the history of David to understand the references. It is indeed so that the events referred to cannot be regarded as climax points in the life of David. In the headings we meet David as the endangered individual, not as a royal figure. David is pictured as the person who can express his emotions in a song under such conditions. Because he is not pictured as a king, but as a person in peril, he invites identification with him. In this way the headings link the metaphorical language of the Psalms with concrete life-situations. The life-situations are mostly of the same type in the relevant psalms. David is seen as somebody in need who is delivered by the Lord.[112] He trusted the Lord, prayed to him, and was delivered. In this way the headings are used not to give real historical information but to relate the psalms to the lives of people who have also known threats and enemies.[113] David is held up as an example to be followed by believers.

The fact that only David is referred to in the psalms with historical heading is an indication of the regard in which the people responsible for these headings held David. He was seen not only as the author of the psalms but also as the perfect example for believers of a later generation. The way in which David is pictured in Chronicles was an example for the later authors of the headings. David was responsible for the institution of the cult, and he was also the one to whom the psalms were ascribed. His life, his trials and tribulations became paradigmatic for believers of a later generation. His experiences, on a personal level, are not so different from the experiences of believers from other times. In this way his songs became their songs, and his words were used to sing about their experiences and to pray to God to come to their assistance as well.

3. The Enemies in the East Syrian Psalm Headings

The study of the headings in the different traditions contained in manuscripts of the Peshitta is an important subject on its own, and it cannot be dealt with here in detail. The Peshitta did not retain the headings of the Masoretic Text. Some manuscripts have no headings at all, while four groups of head-

---

111. Egbert Ballhorn, "'Um deines Knechtes David willen' (Ps 132,1): Die Gestalt Davids im Psalter," *BN* 76 (1995): 23–24.
112. See Mays, "The David of the Psalms," 151.
113. Ibid., 152.

ings can be distinguished among the manuscripts and editions that do have headings.[114] These groups include the headings in the East Syrian Church, headings of Western origin related to the headings in the Codex Ambrosianus, the headings in the editions of Sionita and Lee and in the polyglots, and a mixed group. The headings of the second group may, in some way, be related to the commentary on the Psalms by Daniel of Salach.[115] This group is not as consistent as the first group, with much more variation in the headings.[116]

There are a number of references to enemies in the headings of the second group, as can be seen from the heading to Ps 3 in the Codex Ambrosianus: "Spoken by David when he fled from his son Absalom." In some instances the headings may differ substantially, as can be seen from a number of headings for Ps 143:

- Codex Ambrosianus: Spoken by David when he spoke to the Aramaeans who came to him on account of King Hadadezer.
- 9t2: Spoken by David about the prayer of the Maccabees in the time of their distress.[117]
- 9t3: Spoken by David when Saul sought to kill him.

Reference is made to enemies in all these headings.

The variation that appears in some of the manuscripts from the Western tradition does not occur in the headings of the East Syrian Church. References to enemies occur in many of the headings. The enemies are not only enemies from the life and time of David, but represent enemies from a more extended period in the history of Israel, from the time of David up to the time of the Maccabees, even extending to the time of the New Testament. Some examples from a number of psalms may illustrate this.

- Ps 16: He declares what words the children of Israel ought to employ because of their salvation and on account of the slaughter of their enemies surrounding them.

---

114. See Bloemendaal, *Headings of the Psalms*, 2–3.

115. See Sebastian P. Brock, *Catalogue of Syriac Fragments (New Finds) in the Library of the Monastery of Saint Catherine, Mount Sinai* (Athens: Mount Sinai Foundation, 1995), xxi.

116. See Herrie F. van Rooy, "The Headings of the Psalms in the Two Syriac Versions of the Commentary of Athanasius," *OTE* 17 (2004): 660–61.

117. The notation used for the different Syriac manuscripts is the one developed for the critical edition of the Peshitta of the Old Testament in Leiden. See Peshitta Institute, *List of Old Testament Peshitta Manuscripts (Preliminary Issue)* (Leiden: Brill, 1961).

- Ps 2: He prophesies about the things that were done by the Jews during the Passion of our Lord, and he reminds us of his human nature as well.
- Ps 3: Spoken by David when he was pursued by Absalom.
- Ps 22: Spoken by David instead of a prayer when he was pursued by Absalom.
- Ps 11: When David was pursued by Saul and (some) of his people counseled him to flee before him.
- Ps 17: Prayer of David when he was pursued by Saul.
- Ps 14: About the impiety and presumption of Sennacherib and the Rabshakeh and about the punishment they received.
- Ps 20: Prayer for Hezekiah when he was delivered from the Assyrians.
- Ps 21: He points out about Hezekiah after he was delivered from the Assyrians and was delivered from his sickness.
- Ps 44: Request of the Maccabees when they were compelled by Antiochus to sacrifice to the idols.
- Ps 47: He points out the victory and the triumph of the house of the Maccabees in the war.

These examples show something of the variety of the headings in the manuscripts of the East Syrian Church. In the case of the Hebrew headings, all the headings with historical references dealt with the life of David. In the examples quoted above, there are still references to the time of persecution by Saul and Absalom, but there are also references to Hezekiah and the Maccabees. Psalms 2; 8; 45; and 110 even have headings that link these psalms to Jesus. Not all the headings refer to enemies, but many do.

The following enemies are named in the different headings.[118]

- Absalom: Pss 3; 22; 70
- Ahithophel: Ps 7
- Surrounding nations in time of David: Ps 9
- Saul: Pss 11; 17; 36; 39; 64
- Saul, slanderers, and treacherous people: Ps 139
- Aramaeans in the time of David: Ps 35
- Sennacherib and/or the Rabshakeh and/or the Assyrians: Pss 14; 15; 20; 21; 27; 29; 48; 52; 53; 54; 75; 77; 86; 87; 91; 92
- Damascenes and house of Ephraim: Ps 46

---

118. For an edition of the headings, see Bloemendaal, *Headings of the Psalms*.

- Evil men and friends in the time of Hezekiah: Pss 28; 41
- Babylonians during the time of exile: Ps 123
- Surrounding nations or enemies after the return from exile: Pss 117; 124; 126; 149
- Antiochus: Pss 44; 62; 83
- Antiochus and Demeter: Ps 79
- Kinsmen of Onias: Ps 55
- Evil surrounding the Maccabees: Ps 56; 74
- Enemies of Maccabees, including nations, kinsmen, and strangers: Pss 57; 58; 69; 109; 143
- The Jews: Ps 2
- Rich among people: Ps 10
- Enemies surrounding them: Ps 16

The headings are connected to the following periods in the history of Israel: David, Hezekiah, the Babylonian exile and shortly thereafter, the Maccabees, and the New Testament. Only Pss 10 and 16 are not connected to a specific point in the people's history.

The different headings do not all contain the same kind of information. A number of examples of headings have been quoted above. They illustrate the variety of information contained in the headings.

In many instances the headings contain information about the time of composition or of the time prophesied above, as in Pss 2 and 3. This information might include information about the punishment the enemies received, as in Ps 14. Many of the headings say that the psalm was composed as a prayer, a request, or a thanksgiving in certain circumstances, as in Pss 22 and 44. The prayer could be for deliverance (Ps 56) or for the punishment of the enemies (Ps 109). Some of the headings contain an instruction regarding the use of the psalm, as in Ps 16.

It is well known that the interpretation behind the headings of the East Syrian Church is the exegesis of Theodore of Mopsuestia.[119] The important manuscript 12t4 has a number of headings for each psalm, including one explicitly identified as the heading of Theodore. The headings ascribed to Theodore in this manuscript are the headings found in the manuscripts of East Syrian origin. Theodore's commentary on the Psalms had a short introduction for each psalm. These headings are related to the introductions of Theodore.[120]

---

119. See ibid., 4–12.

120. See Herrie F. van Rooy, *Studies on the Syriac Apocryphal Psalms* (Journal of Semitic Studies Supplement Series 7; London: Oxford University Press, 1999), 21–25.

The commentary of Theodore on the first eighty psalms was published by Devreesse.[121] One example from this commentary will illustrate the relationship between the commentary and the headings. The commentary on Ps 2 starts with the following remark: "In secundo psalmo beatus Dauid profetans narrat omnia quae a Iudeis passionis dominicae impleta sunt tempore" ("In the second psalm the blessed David, while prophesying, tells of all the things done by the Jews at the time of the passion of our Lord").[122] That this agrees with the first part of the East Syrian heading of Ps 2 is quite clear ("He prophesies about the things that were done by the Jews during the passion of our Lord").

The East Syrian headings reflect the exegesis of Theodore, who rejected the headings of the Hebrew Psalter and substituted them with his own summaries in his commentary. They refer to a much larger part of the history of Israel than the headings of the Hebrew Psalter. In these headings David is pictured as a prophet prophesying about events still in the future. The enemies come from different times. Some of the enemies of David are mentioned again, such as Saul and Absalom. In some instances the enemies are rulers, such as Sennacherib or Antiochus. Foreign nations are mentioned, such as the Aramaeans, Assyrians, and Babylonians. The enemies also include friends and other members of the poet's own people.

The picture of the enemies in the East Syrian Psalter is much broader than that in the Hebrew Psalter. They come from many different times and countries. The headings reflect prayers for deliverance as well as thanksgiving for deliverance brought about by the Lord. Whereas the Hebrew headings testify to a personalization of the Psalms, the East Syrian headings tell of the universal rule of the Lord and his dealings with enemies from within and without. The faithful can pray to him, as David did, with the certainty that he will bring about deliverance from all kinds of evil forces. Rulers and peoples are subject to the rule of God.

4. Conclusion

This study has only scratched the surface of the study of the enemies in Syriac Psalters. The West Syrian headings are still to be published, and their relationship to Syrian exegesis is still to be determined. The East Syrian headings

---

121. Robert Devreesse, *Le Commentaire de Théodore de Mopsueste sur les Psaumes (I–LXXX)* (Studi e Testi 93; Cittádel Vaticana: Biblioteca Apostolica Vaticana, 1939). Recently a new translation of this commentary was published by Robert C. Hill, *Theodore of Mopsuestia: Commentary on Psalms 1–81* (SBLWGRW 5; Atlanta: Society of Biblical Literature, 2006).

122. Devreesse, *Le Commentaire de Théodore de Mopsueste*, 7.

linked up with the exegesis of Theodore. They do not focus as much on the person of David but see him as a prophet telling about and praying for deliverance for God's people through the ages.

Disputes about the Calendar in Jewish Apocalyptic Literature and Its Basis

Marius Nel

1. Introduction

Systemic analysis of apocalyptic literature of the fourth to the second centuries B.C.E. suggests that the groups responsible for the Enochian and Qumran literature, although distinct social groups, were all part of the same trajectory of thought.[1] Ancient authors and orators such as Pliny the Elder, Dio of Prusa, and Philo apply the name "Essene" to this movement.[2] What does the movement consist of?

Apocalyptic texts are dramatic narratives that originate in times of crisis when a group of people in the community become dissatisfied with the status quo or an aspect thereof and start fighting it or respond by withdrawing from the community. Apocalyptic groups yearn for a new order, a new world, and in their writings they find new rest and meaning.[3] The writings compensate for what they (as yet) do not have. The authors believe "that their own lives and the life of the community were part of the ongoing struggle between good and evil, that God had revealed to them the approaching end of the struggle,

---

1. Gabriel Boccaccini, "Response: Texts, Intellectual Movements, and Social Groups," in *Enoch and Qumran Origins: New Light on a Forgotten Connection* (ed. Gabriel Boccaccini; Grand Rapids: Eerdmans, 2005), 423.

2. The Dead Sea sect has been identified with the Essenes, whom Josephus describes as one of the three main Jewish groups around the turn of the era, along with the Pharisees and Sadducees. This issue is discussed more extensively in note 93.

3. James R. Davila ("The Animal Apocalypse and Daniel," in Boccaccini, *Enoch and Qumran Origins*, 36) warns that the term *apocalyptic* has become overloaded, useless, and harmful, a motley collection of aspects of prophetic, sapiential, and recycled royal theologies. I think that it is still justified to use the term *apocalyptic*, but then cautiously, and that Davila's warning is timely, that researchers should focus on concrete phenomena rather that synthetic constructs of dubious value such as apocalyptic.

that they were preparing themselves for an active participation in the final climax, and even that they were already living somehow in the final phase."[4]

In studying apocalyptic texts from this period, as part of Second Temple literature, a methodological question surfaces: How does one move from "texts" to "people" and from "communities of texts" to "communities of people"? In the words of Nickelsburg, "texts are historical artefacts, created in time and space, by real human beings."[5] Ancient documents are the equivalent of ruins in archaeology, showing that a family of books indicates a family of people who handed them down.[6] Books do not introduce readers to "intellectual phenomena" but to the lives and behavior of people. The historian's task is to take note of the plurality of philosophies and many voices in texts representing social groups in which the texts emerged and which change people.[7] Intellectual movements and social groups do exist behind and intertwined in texts, even though they are hard to detect.

Scholars today recognize the presence of an intellectual tradition since the period before the Maccabean revolt that was at odds with the priestly establishment in Jerusalem, usually called Enochic Judaism, the result of the politico-theological fervor of a social entity, the Enoch group, and that both Essene and Qumran origins are largely hidden in the Enoch literature.[8]

It is necessary to make a clear methodological distinction between intellectual movements and social groups in order to reconstruct the history of Jewish thought. The different parts of 1 Enoch, Jubilees, the Temple Scroll, the Halakhic Letter, and the Testaments of the Twelve Patriarchs are the product of a large intellectual movement, even though each set of documents was the product of a single social group. Thus the Enoch group and the Qumran group were components of the same intellectual trend.[9]

---

4. Florentino García Martínez, "Apocalypticism in the Dead Sea Scrolls," in *The Continuum History of Apocalypticism* (ed. Bernard J. McGinn, John J. Collins, and Stephen J. Stein; New York, London: Continuum, 2003), 89.

5. George W. E. Nickelsburg, *1 Enoch: A Commentary on the Book of 1 Enoch, Chapters 1–36; 81–108* (Hermeneia, Minneapolis: Fortress, 2001), 2.

6. Helge S. Kvanvig, "Jubilees—Read as a Narrative," in Boccaccini, *Enoch and Qumran Origins*, 81.

7. Eugenio Garin, "Osservazioni preliminari a una storia della filosofia," *Fiornale Critico Della Filosofia Italiana* 38 (1959): 1–55.

8. Boccaccini, "Response," 417.

9. Not every part of the writings produced by this movement is apocalyptic if taken on its own, but its inclusion in a text with definite apocalyptic intention changes the way it should be read, in my opinion. Compare, for instance, the stories in Dan 1–6, which are not apocalyptic in intent but which should be read against the background of the rest of the book, with its clear apocalyptic intent. See also John J. Collins, "From Prophecy to

David Hellholm describes the function of apocalypses as "intended for a group in crisis with the purpose of exhortation and/or consolation, by divine authority."[10] The appeal for divine intervention is necessitated because the world is believed to be in the grip of hostile powers.

In this essay a single aspect in different documents, the use of calendrical data to determine dates for religious feasts, will be discussed with the aim of distinguishing between different social groups and their unique purposes and identifying undercurrents of animosity existing between the groups.[11]

2. Apocalyptic Literature of the Fourth to the Second Centuries B.C.E.

The book of 1 Enoch is a collection of traditions and writings composed between the fourth century B.C.E. and the turn of the era, primarily in the name of Enoch, the son of Jared, mentioned only once in the Hebrew Bible, in Gen 5:21–24.[12]

The book is extant only in a Geʿez (ancient Ethiopic) translation[13] of a Greek translation of the Aramaic originals that are attested by manuscript

---

Apocalypticism: The Expectation of the End," in McGinn, Collins, and Stein, *The Continuum History of Apocalypticism*, 77.

10. David Hellholm, "The Problem of Apocalyptic Genre and the Apocalypse of John," *Semeia* 36 (1986): 13–64.

11. Frank M. Cross (*The Ancient Library at Qumrân and Modern Biblical Studies* [rev. ed.; Garden City, N.Y.: Doubleday, 1961], 77 n. 35a) is of the opinion that "preoccupation with calendrical observation," a feature of apocalypses, forms part of the mythological imagery and astrological motives of the ancient Near East.

12. Although Enoch's and Daniel's books have long been separated by their different "canonical" status, they are nearly contemporary, being dated during the years of the Maccabean revolt, and they share the same literary genre (apocalypse) and the same worldview (apocalypticism) and substantially address the same questions (Gabriele Boccaccini, "The Covenantal Theology of the Apocalyptic Book of Daniel," in Boccaccini, *Enoch and Qumran Origins*, 39). The Old Greek translation, dating from the third century B.C.E., makes significant departures from the Hebrew text in Gen 5:21–24: (1) it twice replaces "Enoch pleased God" (vv. 22, 24) for "Enoch walked with God"; (2) it has "he was not found" instead of "he was not" (v. 24); (3) it has "God removed him" in place of "God took him" (v. 24); and (4) in place of the Hebrew stating that Enoch walks with the *ʾelohim* but being taken by *ʾelohim*, the Greek in all cases renders with *the God*. James C. VanderKam (*Enoch: A Man for All Generations* [Columbia: University of South Carolina Press, 1995], 15) thinks this is due to spiritualizing tendencies in the LXX.

13. The Ethiopic church accepted 1 Enoch as part of its canon, but it was not included in the canon of Scripture due to Rabbi Judah the Prince, who compiled the Mishnah, and Jerome, who considered the book apocryphal. Augustine as well as the compiler of the

fragments from Qumran.[14] The corpus is supposed to be revelations given to Enoch, seventh after Adam,[15] and transmitted to his son Methuselah for the benefit of the righteous living in the end times. Enoch is introduced in the first book of the Tanak as a man who "walked continuously with God [or the godly beings]; then he was no more, for God took him" (Gen 5:23–24). Enoch lived for 365 years (Gen 5:23).[16] The subjects discussed are the nature of the created structure of the cosmos and the origins, nature, consequences, and final judgment of evil and sin. Enoch is variously pictured as seer, sage, scribe, priest (or mediator), and eschatological judge. "To the biblical scholar and to

---

Apostolic Constitutions did not consider the work canonical. See R. H. Charles, *The Book of Enoch or 1 Enoch* (Oxford: Clarendon, 1912), xci–xcii.

14. After the Ethiopic version was "rediscovered" by James Bruce in 1773, Richard Laurence edited (*Libri Enoch prophetae versio aethiopica* [Oxford: Typis Academicis, 1838]) and translated it (*The Book of Enoch the Prophet* [Oxford: Parker, 1821; 2nd ed., 1833; 3rd ed., 1838). See also August Dillmann, *Liber Henoch aethiopice* (Leipzig: Vogel, 1851); idem, *Das Buch Henoch übersetzt und erklärt* (Leipzig: Vogel, 1853); Johannes Paul Gotthilf Flemming, *Das Buch Henoch* (Leipzig: Hinrichs, 1902). At the turn of the twentieth century, the text was located in the broader context of Jewish apocalyptic literature in R. H. Charles, *The Book of Enoch Translated from Professor Dillmann's Ethiopic Text Emended and Revised, Edited with Introduction, Notes, Appendices, and Indices* (Oxford: Clarendon, 1893); idem, *The Ethiopic Version of the Book of Enoch* (Oxford: Clarendon, 1906); idem, *The Book of Enoch, or 1 Enoch, Translated from the Editor's Ethiopic Version, and Edited with the Introduction, Notes, and Indexes of the First Edition Wholly Recast, Enlarged, and Rewritten* (Oxford: Clarendon, 1912); idem, *The Book of Enoch* (London: SPCK, 1917). The publication of the Qumran fragments are in J. T. Milik, *The Books of Enoch: Aramaic Fragments of Qumrân, Cave 4* (Oxford: Clarendon, 1976). A new English translation was published in E. Isaac, "1 (Ethiopic Apocalypse of) Enoch," *OTP* 1:5–89. Collections also appeared in Italy (1981), Spain (1984), Germany (1984), England (1984), and France (1987). Two new translations of 1 Enoch have recently been published: Daniel Olson, *Enoch: A New Translation* (North Richland Hills, Tex.: BIBAL, 2004); George W. E. Nickelsburg and James C. VanderKam, *The Book of Enoch* (Minneapolis: Fortress, 2004).

15. This position is significant in the Hebrew Bible. The Septuagint does not mention this fact.

16. The length of his life stimulated reflections on God's calendar. It suggested a solar calendar, not a lunar (James H. Charlesworth, "The Books of 1 Enoch or 1 Enoch Matters: New Paradigms for Understanding Pre-70 Judaism," in Boccaccini, *Enoch and Qumran Origins*, 443). James C. VanderKam ("Response: Jubilees and Enoch," in Boccaccini, *Enoch and Qumran Origins*, 166) emphasizes that the correct calendar is not simply a convenient means of organizing time but is a necessity to ensure that holidays will not fall on the Sabbath and allows a coordination of heavenly and earthly worship. Milik (*The Books of Enoch*, 8–9) refers to the Hellenistic Jewish historian Eupolemos, whose *History of the Jews* was completed in 158 B.C.E. and who describes Enoch as the inventor of astrology, contrary to the Greeks' claim that Atlas invented it.

the student of Jewish and Christian theology *1 Enoch* is the most important Jewish work written between 200 BC and 100 AD."[17]

The book of 1 Enoch is governed by two myths. The primary myth is derived from Gen 5 and its supposed Mesopotamian sources, that Enoch undertook journeys to the heavenly throne room and through the cosmos, and describes the wisdom he acquired in the revelations given during these excursions. The second myth concerns a primordial heavenly revolt with evil consequences for the human race. The prevailing assumption is that human beings are accountable for their conduct as well as their response to the revelations given in the book.[18]

The oldest part of the book is the Book of the Heavenly Luminaries, or the Astronomical Book (1 En. 72–82), stemming from the third century B.C.E.[19] Enoch recounts to Methuselah his journey through the heavens and over the earth during which Uriel, the angel in charge of the luminaries, interpreted what Enoch was seeing (76:14; 79:1). The movement of the stars is described in order to establish the true calendar, which was a major cause of sectarian division in ancient Judaism.[20] The book of Enoch is the first extra-

---

17. Charles, *The Book of Enoch Translated*, vi. See also the comment of Charlesworth: "In my judgment the book of Enoch seems, in some ways, even to be more important than Daniel. ... they are the most important and creative collection of documents produced in second temple Judaism. The collection's cohesiveness, complex thought, development of earlier traditions, and sheer mass distinguish it from all other compositions of the time. The corpus is important because it is full of brilliant insights and reflections, is one of the major apocalypses ever written, and ultimately, in the final composition or book, elevates Enoch as Son of Man" ("Summary and Conclusions," 440–41).

18. George W. E. Nickelsburg, "Enoch, First Book of," *ABD* 1:490–91.

19. Matthew Black (*The Book of Enoch or 1 Enoch: A New English Edition with Commentary and Textual Notes* [SVTP 7; Leiden: Brill, 1985], 387) is of the opinion that it dates from the Persian period. VanderKam (*Enoch: A Man for All Generations*, 17) states that most scholars accept a third-century date, although there is room for debate about it. The primary argument in favor of a time of composition no later than the third century arises from one of the four copies of the Astronomical Book found among the Dead Sea Scrolls. Milik (*The Books of Enoch*, 7, 273–74) dates its script to the end of the third or the beginning of the second century. Since this manuscript is probably not the original, the paleographical dating suggests that the book was written at an earlier time.

20. Collins, "From Prophecy to Apocalypticism," 69. The introductory verse of the Astronomical Book supplies details for understanding the book: "The book of the Motion of the Luminaries of the Heaven, how each of them stands in relation to their number, to their powers and their times, of their names and their origins and their months, as the holy angel Uriel, who is their leader, showed to me when he was with me. And he showed to me their whole description as they are, and for the years of the World to eternity, until the creation will be made anew to last forever" (72:1, as translated by Otto Neugebauer in

biblical documentation for Enoch and includes far more information than the scanty reference in Gen 5:21–24 to Enoch. Its eleven chapters assume to reproduce and explain the data given in Gen 5, but they virtually explode one aspect of it, the reference that Enoch lived for the unusual number of 365 years.[21] Chapters 72–82 then present extended heavenly revelations concerning astronomical matters related to the length of the year and assert that all these revelations were disclosed to Enoch by an angel. Most scholars accept that more material existed when the Priestly writer wrote Gen 5, material that the editor chose not to use but was utilized by the author of 1 Enoch, or else that major developments occurred between the sixth and third centuries.[22]

The Book of the Watchers (1 En. 1–36) dates from the second half of the third century but refers back to traditions stemming from the fourth century. As an introduction to the book, it describes Enoch as a righteous man who saw heavenly visions interpreted by angels and now transmitted as a blessing to "the righteous chosen" living in the end time of eschatological judgment. Later additions to 1 Enoch are Enoch's Two Dream Visions (1 En. 83–90); two pieces of Testamentary Narrative (1 En. 81:1–82:3; 91); the Epistle of Enoch (1 En. 92–105) schematizing human history from the days of Enoch to the eschaton; an account of Noah's birth (1 En. 106–107); another book of Enoch (1 En. 108) of uncertain origin and date; the Book of Parables (or Similitudes) (1 En. 37–71), the longest of the books and containing three parables dating from the last half of the first century B.C.E. or the first three quarters of the first century C.E.;[23] and the Book of Giants, which is not part of the Ethiopic

---

Black, *The Book of Enoch*; see also 74:2 and 75:3). Uriel's name translates as "God of light," a suitable name for a figure who reveals the motion of light and is the leader of the heavenly luminaries but who is not mentioned by the Old Testament (VanderKam, *The Book of Enoch*, 18). The angel did not dictate the revelation but showed it to Enoch while taking him on a tour of the heavens so that his teaching is reinforced by firsthand acquaintance.

21. This relatively short life span in relation to the other preflood figures stands in direct contrast to Enoch's father, Methuselah, who reached the highest age. Enoch is given a year in which three (or seven) angels return him to his house with the task to inform Methuselah and his children what has been revealed to Enoch, an attempt to align the chronology of the Astronomical Book with Gen 5 in 1 En. 81:5–10. Enoch was 364 when he returned to his family, a suggestive age for the man to whom the workings of the 364-day calendar have been disclosed. Gen 5:22's reference to the *'elohim* is understood by the author of 1 Enoch as "angels."

22. VanderKam, *Enoch: A Man for All Generations*, 17.

23. The Similitudes are presented as a heavenly vision of Enoch, but their content is most notably indebted to the book of Daniel. They are not found among the Dead Sea Scrolls and were the work of a different sect.

version but is represented in fragments of six copies of the work among the Qumran Aramaic fragments and dating from the early first century B.C.E.

All the major sections of 1 Enoch are represented among the Qumran Aramaic manuscripts, with the exception of the Parables and chapters 83–84 and 108. Researchers conclude that the indication is that all component parts, including the Parables, were composed in Aramaic.

Literary genres represented in 1 Enoch as a forerunner of the Targum and Midrash with its rewriting of biblical narrative are apocalypse (1 En. 17–36; 81:1–82:3; 85–90; 91:11–17; 93:1–10; 108), as well as testament and testimony.

An important development in 1 Enoch from biblical literature is the dualism of the phenomenal world as a reflection of a hidden world whose complex realities can only be known if they are revealed.[24] Revealed knowledge of the hidden world of luminaries is necessary for right conduct, also in the cult. Correct calendrical practice thus played an enormous role in the exposition of the Enochic Torah in order to ensure that the phenomenal world is in line with the hidden world.

Another part of the dualism is that a significant part of the evils in this world can be attributed to a hidden demonic world. Human beings are responsible for their own actions, but the Enochic traditions refer to an angelic rebellion that took place in the heavenly realm and the primordial past.

A last part of the dualism lies in the remedy given by the authors for the present world in a hidden future when divine judgment will usher in a new age, when the Creator's original intention with the earth will be realized and evil eradicated. In this way the two contradictory concepts of human responsibility and human victimization coexist between absolute determinism and absolute antideterminism. "The Enochic corpus explains the origin and presence of sin and evil on earth in two ways: (1) sin and evil are the function of a primordial heavenly revolt whose results continue to victimize the human race; (2) responsibility for sin and evil lies with the human beings who transgress God's law."[25]

These writings were created and transmitted from the fourth to the first centuries B.C.E. in Jewish circles that are otherwise unknown but probably were continued in a way in the early Qumran circles, as indicated by the presence of many Enoch manuscripts at Qumran and the allusion to this literature in Qumran sectarian documents, as well as a substantial number of similari-

---

24. Collins ("From Prophecy to Apocalypticism," 70) ascribes this dualism to Zoroastrian influences.
25. Nickelsburg, *1 Enoch*, 46.

ties between 1 Enoch and various sectarian texts.[26] One of these similarities is important for the argument in this article, a common solar calendar.

In the last two decades, the most important development in Enochic studies is that "the emphasis has shifted from the study of the Enoch texts to the study of the intellectual and sociological characteristics of the group behind such literature."[27] Consensus among researchers is that the texts in 1 Enoch were the core of a distinctive movement of thought in Second Temple Judaism.[28] The boundaries of this movement overlapped yet did not coincide with the broader corpus of Jewish apocalypses, some of which might have belonged to different, and even opposite, parties.[29] Enochic Judaism is described as a nonconformist, anti-Zadokite, priestly movement of dissent, active in Israel since the late Persian or early Hellenistic period, with neither the temple nor

---

26. Qumran quickly lost its interest in Enoch literature. The last quotation of Enoch is in the Damascus Document, which originated at a very early stage in the community's life. The Qumran community's theology was dualistic and predeterministic, while Enoch maintained that evil originated not with God's permission but as a result of a rebellious conspiracy hatched behind God's back (myth of the fallen angels). See James H. Charlesworth, "The Origins and Subsequent History of the Authors of the Dead Sea Scrolls: Four Transitional Phases among the Qumran Essenes," *RevQ* 10 (1980): 227; John J. Collins, *Apocalypticism in the Dead Sea Scrolls* (London: Routledge, 1997), 35–36; Gabriele Boccaccini, *Beyond the Essene Hypothesis: The Parting of the Ways between Qumran and Enochic Judaism* (Grand Rapids: Eerdmans, 1998), 129–31.

27. Gabriele Boccaccini, "The Rediscovery of Enochic Judaism and the Enoch Seminar," in *The Origins of Enochic Judaism* (ed. Gabriele Boccaccini; Turin: Zamorani, 2002), 9. Contemporary research in 1 Enoch is a collective enterprise, with Florentino García Martínez, Michael Knibb, Klaus Koch, Helve Kvanvig, and Loren Stuckenbruck in Europe; John J. Collins, James Charlesworth, Martha Himmelfarb, Lawrence Schiffman, David Suter, and James C. VanderKam in the United States; Devorah Dimant, Hanan Eshel, Ithamar Gruenwald, and Michael Stone in Israel.

28. For a discussion of the many Judaisms of the Second Temple period, compare Paolo Sacchi, *History of the Second Temple Period* (JSOTSup 285; Sheffield: Sheffield Academic Press, 2000); Lester L. Grabbe, *Judaic Religion in Second Temple Judaism* (London: Routledge, 2000); Gabriele Boccaccini, *Roots of Rabbinic Judaism: An Intellectual History, from Ezekiel to Daniel* (Grand Rapids: Eerdmans, 2002); George W. E. Nickelsburg, *Ancient Judaism and Christian Origins: Diversity, Continuity, and Transformation* (Minneapolis: Fortress, 2003).

29. Gabriele Boccaccinni, "Introduction: From the Enoch Literature to Enochic Judaism," in Boccaccinni, *Enoch and Qumran Origins*, 3–4. For the contribution of 1 Enoch to the broader development of apocalypticism in the Second Temple period, compare James C. VanderKam, *Enoch and the Growth of an Apocalyptic Tradition* (CBQMS 16; Washington, D.C.: Catholic Biblical Association of America, 1984); John J. Collins, *The Apocalyptic Imagination: An Introduction to the Jewish Matrix of Christianity* (New York: Crossroad, 1984).

the *torah* at the center but a unique concept of the origin of evil that made the "fallen angels" or "sons of God" (in Gen 6:1–4) ultimately responsible for the spread of evil and impurity on earth.[30] "The myths assert, deterministically on the one hand, that human beings are less the perpetrators than the victims of sin, which had its origin in the divine realm. On the other hand, they maintain that sin and evil originated not with God's permission, but as the result of a rebellious conspiracy that was hatched behind God's back."[31] If either of these extremes were emphasized, the Enochic system would collapse into condemnation of God as the unmerciful source of evil or as the unjust scourge of innocent creatures.[32]

Nickelsburg's work led to insights regarding the sociology of the Enoch group. "[T]he 108 chapters of 1 Enoch provide little explicit information about an Enochic community.... some textual evidence points in the direction of a community or group. Collective terms like 'the righteous, the chosen, and the holy' indicate a consciousness of community."[33] The strongest evidence for this is that the Enochic literature developed in stages, over three centuries, from a core narrative about the Watchers. Channels of transmission are supposed for this evolving tradition, and the texts themselves indicate a process of developing composition in the name of Enoch.[34] One can thus speak of "a community or communities who believed that their possession of the divinely given wisdom contained in the Enochic texts constituted them as the eschatological community of the chosen, who are awaiting the judgment and the consummation of the end time."[35] What this movement was called or what it called itself is not known, but "Enochic Judaism" seems appropriate and satisfactory as a modern label.[36]

The Enochic authors might have been "scribes," and "it is possible, though not altogether certain, that at least some of the authors of the Enoch literature were also priests, indeed, disaffected members of the Jerusalem priesthood."[37] Enochic traditions possibly originated in Upper Galilee.[38]

---

30. Boccaccini, "Introduction," 6.
31. Nickelsburg, *1 Enoch*, 47.
32. Boccaccini, "Introduction," 5.
33. Nickelsburg, *1 Enoch*, 46.
34. Ibid.
35. Ibid., 64.
36. Boccaccini, "Introduction," 5.
37. Nickelsburg, *1 Enoch*, 67; Gabriele Boccaccini, "The Priestly Opposition: Enochic Judaism," in idem, *Roots of Rabbinic Judaism*, 89–103.
38. Nickelsburg, *1 Enoch*, 119, 238–47; David Suter, "Why Galilee? Galilean Regionalism in the Interpretation of *1 En.* 6–16," *Henoch* 25 (2003): 167–212.

The Enochic party was not a closed conventicle but had manifestly a large influence and generated a broader movement of thought focused on the idea of the demonic origin of evil, as can be seen in the citations and allusions to 1 Enoch in Second Temple Jewish documents such as Jubilees, the Testament of Moses, the Testament of Simeon (5:4), the Testament of Levi (10:5; 14:1; 16:1), the Testament of Dan (5:6), the Testament of Jude (18:1), the Testament of Zebulon (3:4), the Testament of Naphtali (4:1), the Testament of Benjamin (9:1), the Testament of Reuben (5:1–6), 2 Baruch, the Life of Adam and Eve, 2 Enoch, the Apocalypse of Abraham, 4 Ezra, and Barnabas (4:3; 16:5–6).[39] Enochic Judaism also shaped emergent Christianity, with the Letter of Jude mentioning the writings of Enoch as part of Scripture, a view supported by many church fathers, while becoming increasingly alien to Jewish traditions trying to consolidate their religion after the destruction of Jerusalem in 70 c.e.[40]

3. Calendar In Apocalyptic Traditions

3.1. Solar Calendar in the Astronomical Book of Enoch

The Astronomical Book (1 En. 72–82) originated during the third century b.c.e. and deals with "those who fail to reckon the four intercalary days in the [solar] year..., not with those who use the moon in their calendrical calculations."[41] The question is: What is the view of the Ethiopian Enoch tradition about the two solar calendars that existed and led to conflict?[42]

---

39. For further references, see Charlesworth, "The Books of 1 Enoch or 1 Enoch Matters," 442.

40. Nickelsburg, *1 Enoch*, 1. Examples of references in the church fathers to 1 Enoch are Justin Martyr (*Apologia breviore*), Irenaeus (*Haer.* 4), Tertullian (*De idolatria*), Clement of Alexandria (*Eclogae propheticae*; *Stromata*), and Origen (*Commentarium in Ioannem*; *Contra Celsum*); specific references are found in Richard Laurence, *The Book of Enoch the Prophet* (2nd ed.; Oxford: Parker, 1833), xv–xvii; Johann A. Fabricius, *Codex pseudepigraphus veteris testementi* (2 vols.; Hamburg: Christoph, 1722), 1:60–99; Charles, *The Book of Enoch*, lxx–xcv.

41. James C. VanderKam, "2 Maccabees 6:7a and Calendrical Change in Jerusalem," *JSJ* 12 (1981): 57. Collins writes: "The Astronomical Book ... does not make an issue of the festivals and does not polemicize against the 354-day calendar. Instead it attacks a 360-day calendar that fails to include the four additional days (75:1–2; 82:4–6), although we do not know that such a calendar was ever used in Judaism" (*The Apocalyptic Imagination*, 61).

42. A major problem is the shape of the original 1 Enoch because we have so little of it and because only a limited amount of material from the various stages of its subsequent textual journey have survived. The author wrote in Aramaic, as proved by the discovery

The angel Uriel, guide of all the lights in the firmament, reveals to Enoch the unchanging calendar of the universe, "the nature of the years of the world unto eternity, till the new creation which abides forever is created" (72:1). The sun moves through the six eastern gates of the heavens to the six western gates and back again, so that the years consist of 364 days. The structure of this calendar corresponds to the one used at Qumran, as well as with the first-century C.E. 2 Enoch.[43] The sun takes 42 days to get out of the first gate, 35 days to get out of the second, third, fourth, and fifth gates, and 42 days out of the sixth gate, before going in reverse order (2 En. 13:3–4), giving a total of 364 days.[44]

The Astronomical Book explains the contents of the astronomical revelations claimed for Enoch:

> ▶ A solar year of 364 days, divided into four seasons with 91 days each and twelve months, with eight having 30 days each and the third, sixth, ninth, and twelfth having 31 days each. The sun in its annual course rises from six gates in the east and sets in six gates in the west. The variation of daylight and darkness during the days at the solstices is 2:1. The chief error in regard to the calendar is that people forget to add the 4 days.[45]

---

of four Aramaic copies of the Astronomical Book in Qumran Cave 4. From the Aramaic version only small fragments exist. A copy of the Aramaic text was translated into Greek, of which only a few scraps have survived. From Greek it was rendered into Ethiopic, in which the complete work is preserved, but it is rather different from what is known of the Aramaic original (VanderKam, *Enoch: A Man for All Generations*, 20).

43. The Qumran community accepted a solar calendar of 364 days by which the festivals were dated. A series of calendrical works were found in Cave 4, relating to the zodiac, to the calculation of feast days, and the courses of the priests, enabling scholars to relate it to the Enoch calendar (Cross, *The Ancient Library at Qumrân*, 46). At the same time, they also accepted a lunar calendar and synchronized it with the solar arrangement. In this respect it agreed with the Astronomical Book of Enoch but not with Jubilees, which rejects a lunar calendar. Evidence in the texts from Qumran suggests that the group's distinctive solar calendar was a cause of friction with other Jews and was a factor in their decision to separate from them (James C. VanderKam, *An Introduction to Early Judaism* [Grand Rapids: Eerdmans, 2001], 156). Because they followed a 364-day calendar, the Qumranites would have celebrated their holidays almost always at different times than did the rest of the nation.

44. See VanderKam, *Enoch: A Man for All Generations*, 23–24, for charts showing the movements of, respectively, the sun and moon through the six gates, according to the Astronomical Book, as adapted from Neugebauer in Black, *The Book of Enoch or 1 Enoch*.

45. See Neugebauer in Black, *The Book of Enoch or 1 Enoch*, 393–94.

- A lunar year of 354 days. The movements of the moon and sun are correlated, but 10 extra days are needed to bring the lunar year into harmony with the solar year (354 + 10 = 364). Six of the lunar months have 30 days, and six have 29. The lunar surface is dark before the new moon and has a fourteenth of its surface lighted for each day of its waxing; it loses a fourteenth for each day of its waning. The cycle of the moon is a seventh of that of the sun.
- The writer does not evaluate solar and lunar calendars. He simply presents schematic accounts of both, using numbered months (he never names them) and correlates them. He does not even bring them into a Jewish cultic context of festival cycles or the rotations of priestly groups within the calendar. No reference to the Sabbath is made in the Astronomical Book.

What is important for the author is that the revealed laws will be operative until the new creation. All of the laws are revealed by an angel, and nature is governed and run by angels on behalf of God (80:1).[46]

The writer emphasizes that the astronomical description of the years corresponds to the real structure of the months, with the year consisting of four seasons, each having two 30-day months and one 31-day month, and each season having thirteen weeks.

What is unique to the 1 En. 72 calendar is the role played by the equinoxes and solstices, at the end of each season, resulting in each third, sixth, ninth, and twelfth month being a day longer (72:14, 20, 26, 32). The spring equinox marks the end of the year (72:32). The book does not give any indication how the calendar is adjusted for the astronomical year of 365 and a quarter days while still being based on the Sabbath calendar. Such a mechanism is necessary for a calendar based on equinoxes and solstices.

In 1 En. 73–74 the cycle of the moon's twelve lunar months of 354 days is compared to the twelve solar months of the sun calendar, in an ideal year

---

46. VanderKam (*Enoch: A Man for All Generations*, 25) states that Enoch's tour has reminded scholars of the guided tour experienced by Ezekiel (Ezek 40–48). Milik (*The Books of Enoch*, 273) reports that the thirty-six fragments that remain from the first Qumran manuscript "contain only the 'synchronistic calendar', i.e. the writer's synchronizing of the movements of the sun and moon." Milik proposes that the original Astronomical Book started with an introductory chapter, such as 1 En. 72, and that the next item was this synchronistic calendar. That calendar originally took the full form it has in the Qumran manuscripts, including a schematic account of the relative positions of sun and moon throughout an entire year, not the highly truncated shape it now has in the Ethiopic version.

where the sun and new moon appear together at the beginning of the first month. Here the year consists of 360 days, and the solar year is only six days longer than the lunar year (74:11). But then it is added that "when it is completed, it turns out to be 364 days" (74:11–12), and the difference is always ten days a year (74:13–17). Each month has thirty days, as if the four 31-day months do not figure. And the text continues that additional times are necessary to complete the year, with four additional days, which are like the leaders of the captains of a thousand who do not leave their fixed stations according to the reckoning of the year. These four days are not counted in the reckoning of the year (75:1). "On this account, people err in them" if they do not acknowledge that "the year is completed scrupulously in 364 fixed stations of the cosmos" (75:2). The text contradicts itself here and confuses the modern reader. This revelation is authorized by Uriel himself, which the God of glory has appointed forever over all the lights of the heavens, in the heaven and in the world (75:3). Isaac thinks this section is "meaningless" because of its contradicting detail about the calendar.[47] Sacchi explains that the text reflects two clearly different layers, an older tradition representing a 360-day calendar and a more recent calendar consisting of 364 days, with the last as the more correct calendar.[48] But rather, what is happening in the text is that the four equinoxes and solstices are not discussed but are reckoned into the calendar for a year. In the old solar calendar the solstices and equinoxes are not days but special times causing the division of the seasons, while the Astronomical Book counts these times as separate days. Thus the calendar that the book of Enoch wishes to change was not based on a 360-day nonsabbatical year but on a 360+4-day sabbatical calendar consisting of twelve months with thirty days each, and with four intercalary times between the seasons.

If seen from this perspective, the Astronomical Book is logical, because the difference between the twelve solar months and the twelve lunar months is six "days" over a year, while 2 Enoch stresses that the solar year needs four additional times counted as years. In this way the difference between the solar and lunar year is ten "days," with the error if the solstices and equinoxes are not counted as "days."

This is confirmed when 2 En. 82 sums up 2 En. 72–75 and announces, "blessed are those who walk in the street of righteousness and have no sin like the sinners in the computation of the days in which the sun goes its course in the sky" (82:4). Further, 2 En. 82:4 explains how the 360+4-day calendar

---

47. Isaac, "1 (Ethiopic Apocalypse of) Enoch," 1:5–89.
48. Paolo Sacchi, "The Two Calendars of the Book of Astronomy," in idem, *Jewish Apocalyptic and Its History* (trans. William J. Short; JSPSup 20; Sheffield: Sheffield Academic Press, 1997), 135.

works, with the solar months consisting of thirty days, together with four additional times, which divides the year into four parts of seasons. The text reaffirms (as in 2 En. 75:2) that the solstices and equinoxes are not additional times but real days, as explained by Uriel (82:5–8).

The Astronomical Book targets neither the lunar calendar consisting of 354 days nor the Mesopotamian calendar consisting of 360 days, but another solar calendar consisting also of 360+4 days that recognizes the existence of intercalary times between seasons but does not reckon them as "days of the months." The dispute is not about the length of the solar calendar, which is in any case 364 days, and it is not about the sabbatical structure of the solar calendar, which is fifty-two weeks in every case, but about the nature of the year: whether or not the equinoxes and solstices are counted as days of the year or are considered as merely "divisions of the year."

3.2. Solar Calendar in the Book of Daniel

Daniel 7:25 mentions: "He will defy the Most High and wear down the holy people of the Most High. He will try to change their sacred festivals and laws [ויסבר להשניה זמנין ודת], and they will be placed under his control for a time, times, and half a time" (NLT). The text refers to Antiochus IV Epiphanes' Hellenization program in Jerusalem and his forced changes of the Zadokite solar-based calendar to the Hellenistic lunar-based calendar, to suppress Jewish rebellion.[49]

Which calendar did the book of Daniel use? The implication is that it used the Zadokite solar calendar, but nothing whatsoever is mentioned in the book of a change to the lunar calendar or the antiquity of the solar calendar, popular themes in Jewish documents from this period. Perhaps the chronological references in Daniel are purposefully obscure because the writer does not want his/her readers to know which calendar he or she is using.[50] Daniel 9:27 refers to a "half-week" (וחצי השבוע); 7:25 and 12:7 to "a time, times, and a

---

49. Annie Jaubert, "Le calendrier des Jubilés et de la secte de Qumrân: Ses origenes bibliques," *VT* (1953): 250–64; James C. VanderKam, "The Origin, Character, and Early History of the 364-Day Calendar: A Reassessment of Jaubert's Hypotheses," *CBQ* 41 (1979): 390–411; idem, "2 Maccabees 6:7a," 52–74; idem, *Calendars in the Dead Sea Scrolls* (London: Routledge, 1998).

50. John J. Collins, "The Meaning of 'The End' in the Book of Daniel," in *Of Scribes and Scrolls: Studies on the Hebrew Bible, Intertestamental Judaism and Christian Origins* (ed. Harold W. Attridge, John J. Collins, and Thomas H. Tobin; Lanham, Md.: University Press of America, 1990); idem, *Seers, Sybils and Sages in Hellenistic-Roman Judaism* (JSJSup 54; Leiden: Brill, 1997).

half" (עד־עדן ועדנין ופלג עדן), referring to symbolical times; while 8:14 refers to "two thousand and three hundred days" (ערב בקר אלפים ושלש מאות). These numbers are different from those mentioned in Dan 12:11–12.

None of these numbers support the solar or lunar calendar, but researchers cite three reasons why the book of Daniel probably used the sun calendar.[51] The first consideration is the remark in Dan 6:8(7), 13(12) that suggests that "thirty days" (ומין תלתין) refer to some kind of standard period. This period is the standard length of a month according to the solar calendar. The thirty-day period mentioned here in Dan 6, however, does not refer necessarily to a month but could be any arbitrary period decided upon by the counselors, or it may refer to a month according to the Mesopotamian calendar, without any connection to the Jerusalem temple calendar.

A second consideration refers to the only date mentioned in the book, the "twenty-fourth day of the first month" (בום עשרים וארבעה לחדש) in Dan 10:4. The practice to date events with the counting of the months is typical in Priestly literature after the Babylonian exile, and most researchers accept that the sun calendar is used here. In any case, 24 Nisan does not have any meaning in the moon calendar, while the twenty-fourth day of the first month in the sun calendar refers to a Friday, the day before the Sabbath and in Jaubert's view the ideal time for a vision.[52] Daniel 10:4 thus proves that the writer knew the Sabbath calendar of the Second Temple period. The Sabbath calendar divided the year into fifty-two weeks in order that a specific day would fall on the same day each year, in order to regulate religious feasts.

Lastly, in Dan 12:1–2 the difference between 1,290 days and 1,335 days is forty-five days. This number is senseless unless the month consists of thirty days, referring to a month and a half. The implication is that the author uses a calendar in which the months are not reckoned according to the moon, with its succession of months of thirty and twenty-nine days. Daniel 12:5–13 gives "half a week" (v. 7), "1,290 days" (v. 11), and "1,335 days" (v. 12) as a series, and the implication is that the same relation exists between half a week and 1,290 days. According to the calendar consisting of 364 days used in Jubilees and at Qumran, three and a half years consist of 1,274 days. When sixteen are added, one gets to 1,290, and an addition of forty-five brings one to 1,335. But these additions are meaningless. Why does Daniel refer to "half a week"?

The only text that enlarges on these numbers is the book of Revelation, where the time of persecution is forty-two months: Rev 11:2; 13:5 (1,260

---

51. Gabriele Boccaccini, "The Solar Calendars of Daniel and Enoch," in *The Book of Daniel: Composition and Reception* (ed. John J. Collins and Peter W. Flint; 2 vols.; Boston: Brill, 2001), 2:312.

52. Jaubert, "Le calendrier des Jubilés," 262.

days—11:3; 12:6; or "a time, times, and an half"—12:14). According to Revelation's reckoning it is clear that Daniel uses the sun calendar in which a year consists of twelve months of thirty days each, giving a total of 360 days a year.[53]

When one accepts that Daniel used the solar calendar, the three references in Dan 12 make sense. "Half a week," or three and a half years, consists of 1,260 days, with the addition of a month of thirty days adding up to 1,290 days, with the addition of a further month and a half adding up to 1,335 days. This led to the argument of Marti and Beckwith that Daniel uses the Mesopotamian calendar of 360 days, and the numbers added in Dan 12:11–12 are the addition of intercalary months.[54] The Jews knew this calendar, as can be seen from the flood narrative, where the period from "the seventeenth of the second month" to "the seventeenth of the seventh month" adds up to 150 days, consisting of five months of thirty days each (Gen 7:11, 24; 8:3–4).

The calendar used in the early Second Temple period was based on the movements of the sun calendar, with the result that every day of the year occurs on the same day of the week for each year, which was not the case in the Mesopotamian calendar.[55] The chronological reference in Dan 10:4 also makes sense only when "the twenty-fourth day of the first month" refers to a Friday, as is the case in the Sabbath calendar used in the temple. But how could it be possible for Daniel to use a 360-day calendar as well as a calendar based on the Sabbath?

The confusing way in which the book of Daniel repeats dates in the last chapter has been the subject of repeated research since Gunkel in 1895 formulated the theory that additions were made to the text to justify the "delay of the end" and to encourage believers when salvation did not occur.[56] This hypothesis is not supported by any textual variants or versions, and Porteous is correct in asking how urgent corrections could have been added to a book that had recently been issued, with the information being updated within less

---

53. Boccaccini ("The Covenantal Theology," 43) emphasizes the role of the number four as the number for punishments: God repeats the curses in Leviticus (26:18, 21, 23–24, 27–28) four times; the seventy weeks are divided into four subdivisions (7 + 62 + half a week + half a week); the iniquitous king persecuted the people four times; and there are four kingdoms.

54. Karl Marti, *Das Buch Daniel* (HKAT 18; Tübingen: Mohr Siebeck, 1901); Roger T. Beckwith, "The Earliest Enoch Literature and Its Calendar: Marks of Their Origin, Date and Motivation," *RevQ* 10 (1981): 365–403.

55. Annie Jaubert, "Le calendrier des Jubilés et les jours liturgiques de la semaine," *VT* 7 (1957): 35–61.

56. Hermann Gunkel, *Schöpfung und Chaos in Urzeit und Endzeit* (Göttingen: Vandenhoeck & Ruprecht, 1895).

than forty-five days.⁵⁷ "That both vv. 11–12 should be permitted to remain in the text is sufficient commentary on this rather unadroit explanation."⁵⁸ There is no good reason to talk of later additions.⁵⁹ Chronological indications rather show skillful planning, with references to Antiochus's persecution consequently indicated as "half a week of years" (Dan 9:27) or "a time, times and a half" (Dan 7:25; 12:7). In the frame around Dan 9, different chronological indications occur, with "2,300 evenings and mornings" (Dan 8:14) and "1,290" or "1,335 days" (Dan 12:11–12). It is clear that the author(s) expected that something important was going to happen before and immediately after the foretold death of Antiochus.⁶⁰

Why are two different numbers given side by side? The second figure is probably given after the first number of days had passed. The phenomenon of recalculation is well-known in later apocalyptic movements.⁶¹ Daniel is also not certain what will happen when the number of days has passed, or else does not give any indication of what he is thinking. The days are calculated from the time that the temple was desecrated and the cult disrupted, and the expected "end" might refer to the restoration of that cult. This is the implication of Dan 8:14. But according to 1 Macc 1:54; 4:52–54, Judas purified the temple three years to the day after its pollution. Both dates in Dan 12 thus point to a date after that restoration. The last date (Dan 12:12) was at least added after the purification of the temple. Another consideration is that the numbers in Dan 12:11–12 follow the prophecy of the victory of Michael and the resurrection of the dead, and Daniel is given the assurance in Dan 12:13 that he will rise from his rest, at the end of days. "The end" is then the time when the archangel Michael intervenes and the resurrection takes place, at the time indicated by later tradition as the end of the world.⁶²

---

57. Norman W. Porteous, *Daniel: A Commentary* (OTL; Philadelphia: Westminster, 1979), 172.

58. Robert A. Anderson, *Signs and Wonders: A Commentary on the Book of Daniel* (Edinburgh: Handsel; Grand Rapids: Eerdmans, 1984), 153.

59. Boccaccini, "The Solar Calendars of Daniel and Enoch," 321.

60. Collins says, "This is in fact the only instance in an ancient Jewish apocalypse of an attempt to calculate the exact number of days" ("From Prophecy to Apocalypticism," 75). Compare it with the words in the commentary on Habakkuk from the Dead Sea Scrolls (col. 7): "God told Habakkuk to write what was going to happen to the last generation, but he did not let him know the end of the age."

61. Leon Festinger, Henry W. Riecken, and Stanley Schachter, *When Prophecy Fails: A Social and Psychological Study of a Modern Group That Predicted the Destruction of the World* (New York: Harper, 1956), 12–23.

62. Collins, "From Prophecy to Apocalypticism," 76.

Collins argues that Dan 8 focuses primarily on the restoration of the temple cult, while Dan 10–12 describes the end in terms of the resurrection of the dead.[63] Daniel does not consider the temple impure, as Enoch does, and Dan 8 predicts that the offerings in the temple would be restored, implying that the temple cult is legitimate. Daniel also rejects the Enochian doctrine that the sins of angels have deprived humans of their freedom and responsibility and distinguishes between the judgment of individuals and collective Israel, causing the lengthening and synchronizing of chronological indications in Dan 12. The judgment of the nations (Dan 7) and the judgment of individuals (Dan 12) do not occur synchronically.

The extra thirty and forty-five days added to the end of the seventy-year weeks cannot be intercalary months, but how the 360+4–day calendar added intercalary days is unknown.[64]

The "2,300 evenings and mornings" (Dan 8) are too precise to be symbolic, and LaCocque reckons that it refers to an actual period counted after the events.[65] According to Daniel's calculation, the fall equinox of 167 B.C.E. is in the middle of the last week of years, when Antiochus started his persecution of the Jews. From this date, 2,300 evenings and mornings should be counted.[66] When 1,150 days are reckoned to this, one gets to the twenty-seventh day of the first month of 164–163. The Megillat Ta'anit, a list of lucky days composed between the two Jewish Wars, calls the twenty-seventh day of the eighth month an important day.[67] This date could refer to something hap-

---

63. Collins, "The Meaning of 'The End,'" 163.

64. For the Sabbath calendar to agree with the astronomical calendar, thirty-five days have to be added over a twenty-eight-year period. Perhaps this was done by adding a week after each Sabbath cycle and two weeks extra after every twenty-eight-year cycle. Or the Jubilee year of Lev 25:8–17 was seen as an intercalatory period time of forty-nine days to be added after every Jubilee of forty-nine years, as suggested by S. Zeitlin, "Notes relatives au calendrier juif," *Revue de études juives* (1930): 349–54. The problem is, however, that the Jubilee year is never again after the Babylonian exile celebrated according to the rabbinical tradition. The primary task of the Zadokite calendar was to ensure that the feasts were celebrated on the correct dates, and for that reason it was based on the Sabbath calendar, and only weeks of seven days could be added to a Sabbath calendar. Dan 12:11–12 uses the cultic calendar and adds one month, the month of *pesach*, to get 1,290 days. To this is added forty-five days to reach the third month, in the Zadokite calendar "the month of the oath" (2 Chr 15:10–15; Jubilees). The feast of Shevu'ot is on the fifteenth of the third month, the feast of the renewal of the covenant, an ideal time for the final judgment.

65. André LaCocque, *The Book of Daniel* (Atlanta: John Knox, 1979), 250.

66. Compare 1 En. 72, which also refers to "mornings," not "days."

67. "On the twenty seventh thereof [i.e., Heshvan, the eighth month] they began again to bring the offerings of fine flour upon the altar."

pening during the Feast of Hanukkah in the time of the Hasmoneans. First and Second Maccabees use the lunar calendar so that their twenty-fifth day of Kislev, the ninth month, refers to the twenty-seventh of the eighth month of the Zadokite solar calendar, with the effect that Daniel and the books of Maccabees probably refer to the same event.[68] Josephus (*Ant.* 12.320) agrees with the book of Maccabees' chronology and takes the day of the rededication of the temple as the fulfillment of the "three and a half years" predicted by Daniel (1.32).

Daniel expected that the end of the final week would be later, during the spring equinox of 163 B.C.E. He predicted that Antiochus would lead a successful campaign against Egypt that did not take place and is vague about the time and circumstances of Antiochus's death, implying that the book of Daniel originated in its present form shortly after the cessation of the daily sacrifices. Thus the only real predictions of the book were not realized, but that is no problem because in apocalyptic literature predictions usually are not realized.[69]

3.3. Zadokite and Enochic Calendar and Jubilees

The book of Jubilees assigns, just as Enoch's calendar, the four additional times to days. After the Maccabean rebellion new developments occur in Enoch Judaism,[70] and Jubilees uses the same 364-day calendar as the Astronomical Book, with the solstices and equinoxes having no independent interest. The first days of each season are emphasized as "the days of remembrance … in the four parts of the year … on the first of the first month and on the first of the fourth month and on the first of the seventh month and on the first of the tenth month" (Jub. 6:23). Noah was the first to celebrate these days as feasts for eternal generations (6:24). And in the heavenly tablets it is described that these days should be celebrated forever (6:28–29), implying that God has decreed it. In the Jubilees calendar these days replaced the four additional times of the 364-day calendar by parting the year into four periods of thirteen weeks each (6:29), with the result that the completed year exists of fifty-two weeks of 364 days (6:31–32). In the Astronomical Book this function was fulfilled by the solstices and equinoxes (1 En. 72:32).

---

68. VanderKam, "2 Maccabees 6:7a," 52–74.

69. Boccaccini, "The Solar Calendars of Daniel and Enoch," 325. "It is in the nature of apocalyptic eschatology that it cannot be fully realized in this life. Even when the hopes could be realized in principle, they most often failed to materialize.…While it can never deliver on its promises, it continues to speak eloquently to the hearts of those who would otherwise have no hope at all" (Collins, "From Prophecy to Apocalypticism," 86).

70. Boccaccini, *Beyond the Essene Hypothesis*, 86–98.

The more ancient rendering of the calendar can be seen in Jub. 29:16, where Isaac sends all kinds of food to his mother Rebecca four times a year—between the appointed times of the months, between plowing and reaping, between fall and the rainy season, and between winter and spring. The four appointed times "between the seasons" are no longer part of the 364-day calendar. Jubilees 5:17 calculates the period of the flood according to the 360+4–day calendar where the intercalary times are not reckoned as "days," when it explains that the water stayed on the earth for five months, that is, 150 days. According to the Enoch-calendar, five months consist of 152 days.

The earliest researchers of the Astronomical Book realized that these texts use a Sabbath calendar with twelve unchangeable months of thirty days each with four intercalary days between the seasons, a solar calendar where the two solstices and two equinoxes are not reckoned in the months, but are counted as additional, extramonthly days.[71]

The Dead Sea Scrolls confirm the existence and antiquity of the solar calendar and shed more light on its structure and meaning.[72] The calendar used at Qumran counts the four additional times as days in the third, sixth, ninth, and twelfth months without explaining that it developed from a more ancient Sabbath calendar where these times were not reckoned as days. The redactor of the Astronomical Book, working while the Zadokite high priests ruled over the temple, knew about the new developments in the calendar and describes it as an error (1 En. 75:2; 82:5). The 360+4–day calendar predates the Astronomical Book and was authoritative in the third century. This calendar was used by the Zadokite house and regulated by temple practice, not the 364-day calendar of the Enochic tradition.[73]

At the time Jubilees was written down, the conflict existing between the Zadokite and Enochic calendars was forgotten. Now a new conflict arose, where the new lunar calendar replaced the solar calendar of the Second Temple, described by Jub. 6:32–38 as the calendar of the heathen. Antiochus

---

71. Benjamin Wisner Bacon, "Chronology of the Account of the Flood in P: A Contribution to the History of the Jewish Calendar," *Hebraica* 8 (1891–92): 79–88; idem, "The Calendar of Enoch and Jubilees," *Hebraica* 8 (1891–92): 124–31; Julius Morgenstern, "The Three Calendars of Ancient Israel," *HUCA* 1 (1924): 13–78.

72. Cross (*The Ancient Library at Qumrân*, 76) emphasizes that the Essenes did in fact institute and practice an independent calendar of feasts. Annie Jaubert ("La date de la dernière Cène," *RHR* 146 [1954]: 140–73) was the first to argue that the Gospel accounts are best understood if Jesus celebrated his Last Supper on the date of the Passover in the Essene (and old religious) calendar, while his crucifixion took place on the eve of the official Jewish Passover.

73. Boccaccini, *The Solar Calendar*, 319–20.

IV established the new calendar to introduce his Hellenization process within the Jerusalem temple.

The difference between the Zadokite and Enochic calendar was theoretical, with both based on the Sabbath week with the result that the order of feasts never changed.[74] The introduction of the lunar calendar was, however, a "temple-quake."[75] Now it became impossible to celebrate the feasts at the appointed times. Onias III died at the beginning of the Maccabean revolt, and Onias IV fled to Egypt, with the result that the Zadokites lost all influence. The Enochic movement tried to restore the Zadokite calendar and maximize their influence. The newly established Hasmonean high priesthood was not interested in accepting Enochic leadership and rejected all Zadokite institutions. The Enochic movement lost its influence, which led to the emergence of the Essene community as organized opposition and an alternative to the Jerusalem temple leadership.

4. Context of the Enochic Movement

What is the sociological context in which the Enochic revelations were received and that led to the dispute about calendars, showing patterns of animosity between groups in the social organization of pre-Maccabean Judea? Collins is of the opinion that the Astronomical Book does not seem to have been generated by a conflict within the Jerusalem temple. "It is difficult to see how the authors of this book could have functioned in a temple regulated by a lunar calendar." His solution is to suggest that the Astronomical Book was composed in the eastern Diaspora, where actual use of the temple was not an immediate issue.[76] Collins does not provide reasons for his argument that the Enoch literature does not presuppose conflict within the Jerusalem establishment, and I think that it is probable that the literature originated from such a conflict.

Judea was ruled by Seleucid Syria as a part of the province of Coele-Syria, with the high priest and his fellow priests acting as imperial agents and local leaders.[77] High-priestly rule led to rivalry, with Joseph the Tobiad gaining the right at one stage to collect imperial taxes for the Ptolemaic rulers of Egypt,

---

74. "[E]very sabbath, month, year, and likewise every feast, was determined by the name of a priestly family; in other words they were under the 'sign', 'ôt,' of such a family" (Milik, *The Books of Enoch*, 62).

75. Boccaccini, *The Solar Calendar*, 320.

76. Collins, *The Apocalyptic Imagination*, 73.

77. Patrick Tiller, "The Sociological Context of the Dream Visions of Daniel and 1 Enoch," in Boccaccini, *Enoch and Qumran Origins*, 23.

as reported by Josephus. In the second century, when the Syrian Antiochus IV ruled over Judea, high-priestly rule was recognized, as can be seen by the plots and counterplots to obtain the position. The high priest presided over a *gerousia*, a council of elders, but no more is known about the functioning or powers of this council.

The Syrian rulers supported the high priest with military might, but the high priest also had his own soldiers, if the information provided in 2 Macc 4:40 and Josephus (*Ant.* 12.239–240) is correct. The book of Sirach provides a picture of the political-social structure of Seleucid Syria, even though it is clearly biased in its description. The picture is of an orderly society with the high priest ruling and sages such as Ben Sira serving as teachers of the people, along with advisers, judges, diplomats, and other positions. This is confirmed by Antiochus III's decree as preserved by Josephus (*Ant.* 12.138–144), which describes Jerusalem as the center of the temple state led by a council of elders, with priests, scribes, and temple singers forming the privileged aristocracy.[78]

This portrait of Judea as a harmonious society does not reflect the whole situation. Seleucid rule was characterized by the establishment of competing authorities, each reporting directly to the king. In this way the king polarized Judean society to the benefit of defusing the rebellious attitude for which the Judean population has become famous. In this way Antiochus III appointed the *gerousia* as the most important factor in the Jerusalem hierarchy, while Antiochus IV negotiated exclusively with the high priest. Provincial officials reported directly to the king and not to some local chief, as illustrated by the Scythopolis Inscription.[79]

Sages/scribes were members of the privileged aristocracy created by the imperial rule and dependent on it for their position and stature in society.[80] They were loyal to their patrons, and when the patrons had conflicting interests, the loyalties of the sages/scribes would also conflict. The context of sages/scribes forms the social setting in which 1 Enoch (as well as the dream visions of the book of Daniel) were produced. The visions themselves do not give clear evidence of the social location of their setting, but some hints are available. For instance, the Animal Apocalypse places itself within a group of elect Judeans around the beginning of the second century B.C.E. This group

---

78. James E. Taylor, "Seleucid Rule in Palestine" (Ph.D. diss., Duke University, 1979), 170.

79. The inscription was found by Y. H. Landau in 1966, and it is discussed extensively in Taylor, "Seleucid Rule in Palestine," 108–68. The inscription is a record of correspondence with the Syrian king concerning disputes between agents of the empire.

80. Tiller, "The Sociological Context," 24.

developed their own version of piety in clear distinction from the corrupt temple, and with time they engaged in armed resistance to established religion in Jerusalem.[81] The differences between the books of Sirach (especially book 5) and 1 Enoch show that Ben Sira and the sages responsible for 1 Enoch were in conscious opposition to each other, with Ben Sira advocating the high-priestly rule.[82] The authors are pictured in both books as sages and teachers, but each in another tradition and representing another ideology. The Enochic sages oppose high-priestly rule in the strongest terms and wish to change the structure prescribed by Antiochus III.[83]

What kind of community produced the Enochic literature? The question depends on whether 1 Enoch was inscribed performances of oral tradition or whether it originated directly as writings. If an oral tradition existed before it was penned down, political and ethnic groupings linked to villages or larger populations can probably be considered as sociologically identifiable communities with boundaries and rules of their own, like the community associated with the Qumran documents.[84]

The Enochic literature itself does not give evidence for such a community, and the idea formed when reading the revelations is rather that it was produced by an aggregate of individuals with similar interests, without an organized social structure with defined boundaries and constraints. "We should not think that 1 En. 92–105 is the product of a movement or group any more than we would understand the text of Sirach as testimony to Ben Sira heading a social movement."[85] Neither Ben Sira nor Enoch made

---

81. Patrick A. Tiller, *A Commentary on the Animal Apocalypse of 1 Enoch* (SBLEJL 4; Atlanta: Scholars Press, 1993), 109–26.

82. Benjamin G. Wright III, "Fear the Lord and Honor the Priest: Ben Sira as Defender of the Jerusalem Priesthood," in *The Book of Ben Sira in Modern Research: Proceedings of the First International Ben Sira Conference* (ed. Pancratius C. Beentjes; BZAW 255; Berlin: de Gruyter, 1997), 189–222.

83. Collins ("From Prophecy to Apocalypticism," 80) describes the part played by the apocalypses of Daniel and Enoch in causing turmoil leading to the Maccabean revolt. Josephus is probably quoting Dan 7 when he writes about the Jewish Revolt of 66–70 C.E. and claims that "what more than all else incited them to the war was an ambiguous oracle, likewise found in their sacred scriptures, to the effect that at that time one from their country would become ruler of the world" (*J.W.* 6.312).

84. "A consensus seems to be emerging that we can talk about a community or group of Jews behind the books of Enoch. The degree to which the texts allow us to reconstruct the sociology of such a group and groups will always remain problematic" (Charlesworth, "The Books of Enoch or 1 Enoch Matters," 448).

85. Richard A. Horsley, "Social Relations and Social Conflict in the *Epistle of Enoch*," in *For a Later Generation: The Transformation of Tradition in Israel, Early Judaism, and*

an exclusive claim to election or advise their readers to withdraw from the larger society.

The wise function as teachers for others who are not among the wise, and their teaching is based on revealed wisdom, as implied in the Animal Apocalypse.[86] To what extent these teachers succeeded in gaining followers is unknown, and we do not know whether any social groups formed in adherence to the teachings of Enoch. Grabbe warns that there is no necessary connection between apocalypses and apocalyptic communities.[87] What is probable is that the sages or teachers who produced the Enochic literature were members of a larger social group and that their teachings reflected the ideals of the group, making them the spokespersons.[88]

What is the relation between the different interpretations of the solar calendar in terms of sociological contexts, and what does it reflect of Judean society of the third and second centuries B.C.E.?

5. Worldviews and Milieus of Conflict and Animosity

What has become evident is that different movements existed within the Jewish religion and political world, leading to patterns of division and animosity. On the one hand, the temple hierarchy existed, and on the other hand, opponents of the hierarchy.[89]

The producers of visionary literature understood themselves to function as teachers and sages and are connected to wisdom literature.[90] The question is: Do we encounter one apocalyptic movement or a multiplicity of small

---

Early Christianity (ed. Randal A. Argall, Beverly Bow, and Rodney Alan Werline; Harrisburg, Pa.: Trinity Press International, 2000), 115.

86. George W. E. Nickelsburg, "The Epistle of Enoch and the Qumran Literature," *JJS* 33 (1982): 333–48.

87. Lester L. Grabbe, "The Social Setting of Jewish Apocalypticism," *JSP* 4 (1989): 27–47.

88. Tiller, "The Sociological Context," 26.

89. James C. VanderKam and Peter Flint (*The Meaning of the Dead Sea Scrolls* [New York: HarperSanFrancisco, 2002], 275) mention three major Jewish groups or factions in the later Second Temple period: Pharisees with whom the Zealots agreed almost entirely; Sadducees; and Essenes. Presumably there were more groups, but Josephus limits himself in naming these three groups.

90. Jonathan Z. Smith, *Map Is Not Territory: Studies in the History of Religions* (SJLA 23; Leiden: Brill, 1978), 74; Collins, *The Apocalyptic Imagination*, 30; Grabbe, "The Social Setting of Jewish Apocalypticism," 27–47.

conventicle-like apocalyptic groups?[91] Apparently, the authors of apocalyptic texts such as 1 Enoch and Jubilees understood themselves as part of elect groups.[92]

Traditionally, the same group, the Hasidim, was held responsible for the Enochic, Danielic, and Jubilees apocalypses, which was identified with the so-called new covenant and which formed the parent group of the Essenes.[93]

---

91. John J. Collins, "Pseudepigraphy and Group Formation in Second Temple Judaism," in *Pseudepigraphic Perspectives: The Apocrypha and Pseudepigrapha in Light of the Dead Sea Scrolls* (ed. Esther G. Chazon and Michael E. Stone; STDJ 31; Leiden: Brill, 1999), 43–58.

92. They share a common worldview. "Apocalypticism is a worldview that is indebted to ancient Near Eastern myths and to Hebrew prophecy, but which arose in response to the new challenges of the Hellenistic and Roman periods. The essential ingredients of this worldview are a reliance on supernatural revelation, over and above received tradition and human reasoning; a sense that human affairs are determined to a great degree by supernatural agents; and the belief that human life is subject to divine judgment, culminating in reward or punishment after death" (Collins, "From Prophecy to Apocalypticism," 85).

93. Martin Hengel, *Judaism and Hellenism: Studies in Their Encounter in Palestine during the Early Hellenistic Period* (2 vols.; Philadelphia: Fortress, 1974), 1:175–180; Collins, "Pseudepigraphy and Group Formation," 44. What the relation is between the Essenes and Qumran has been the topic of much discussion. The Groningen Hypothesis, put forward by Florentino García Martínez in 1988, accepts without reservation the two major tenets of the Essene hypothesis: that the ruins of Qumran were of a religious community who owned the scrolls and authored part of them; and that that community was an Essene community. The Qumranites split off, according to this hypothesis, from a mainstream Jewish movement, the Essene *hairesis*, which had its ideological roots in the pre-Maccabean Palestinian apocalyptic tradition, during the high priesthood of John Hyrcanus (134–104 B.C.E.). Philo (*Prob.* 75) and Josephus (*Ant.* 18.21) explain that the Essenes were a large and populous movement of at least 4,000 adult members, while Qumran's ruins attest to only around 150 people living in the harsh desert environment. If Qumran was indeed an Essene community, all the Essenes obviously did not stay at Qumran. What is the relation between Qumran and the rest of the Essene movement? Either the community at Qumran was simply one of the many Essene communities existing in Israel in the late Second Temple period, or it was a leading group, perhaps the headquarters of the group, or it was a splinter, marginal group (Gabriele Boccaccini, "Qumran: The Headquarters of the Essenes or a Marginal Splinter Group," in Boccaccini, *Enoch and Qumran Origins*, 303–4). Boccaccini agrees with Nickelsburg that the Enoch literature provides evidence of at least a major stream of thought and a major group that originated long before Qumran and played an important role in Qumran origins and that the Qumran community was a derivative of or successor to the community or communities that authored and transmitted the Enochic texts. Something happened that separated the Enoch and Qumran groups. With time, Qumran lost its interest in Enoch literature, nurturing its own deterministic and dualistic worldview, over against Enoch's assertion that evil originated not with God's permission but as the result of a rebellion hatched behind God's back. The conclusion is

Collins differs from this viewpoint and shows that more differences than parallels can be found in descriptions of groups in the Enochic and Danielic apocalypses.[94] But the self-designations of authors and tradents of the apocalypses in question are different, and so is their attitude toward the Mosaic *torah*. In Enochic literature, involvement in politics has a military component, while Daniel is pacifist. Further, pseudepigraphy is absent in the Essene texts from Qumran, while it is abundant in Enochic and Danielite literature.[95] Thus Collins argues for a multiplicity of small conventicle-like apocalyptic groups.[96]

How did these groups relate to each other? Did some groups share a common worldview?[97] Almost no sociological data has been preserved, and the answer can only be based upon an analysis of the imagery and visionary techniques employed by the different apocalypses.[98] Lange comes to the conclusion that Danielic and Enochic conventicles share an apocalyptic worldview, and from their shared interpretation of allegoric dreams he places the domain of this conventicle among the sages. Next to the wisdom influence there also exists a prophetic influence on apocalypticism.

Jubilees is from the same period as Daniel and some parts of Enoch, like the Book of Dream Visions and the Book of Giants. It is not an apocalypse but rewritten Bible.[99] It comes from a priestly background, as can be seen from its discussion of Sabbath laws, the sacred calendar, properly celebrated festivals, sacrificial regulations, the prohibition of consuming blood, circum-

---

that Qumran is not representative of the entire Essene movement and Essene theology and way of life and that the terms "Essene" and "Qumran" are not interchangeable. Qumran's believers were not ordinary Essenes but rather outcasts within their own movement (Boccaccini, "Qumran," 308–9; Nickelsburg, *1 Enoch*, 57, 65). Raymond F. Surburg (*Introduction to the Intertestamental Period* [St. Louis: Concordia, 1975], 60) concurs with this view.

94. Collins, "Pseudepigraphy and Group Formation," 44–49, 55–58. Boccaccini agrees: "The two apocalyptic writings could not be the product of the same group, as their ideologies were divergent if not opposite" ("The Covenantal Theology," 39).

95. "There was a precedent for pseudonymity in Jewish tradition: the book of Deuteronomy was ascribed to Moses, although it was promulgated by King Josiah in 621 B.C.E. and probably took its present form during the Babylonian Exile" (Collins, "From Prophecy to Apocalypticism," 68).

96. John J. Collins, "Pseudepigraphy and Group Formation," 55–58.

97. Lange prefers to speak of "milieu" in place of Collins's "worldview," without clarifying what he means with the term; see Armin Lange, "Dream Visions and Apocalyptic Milieus," in Boccaccini, *Enoch and Qumran Origins*, 28–31.

98. Ibid.

99. Ibid., 32.

cision, and the avoidance of impurity and uncleanness.[100] Jubilees does not share the same apocalyptic milieu as Daniel and Enoch, as can be seen from the different use of the calendar. The priestly circles in which Jubilees originated have less interest in sapiential and prophetic traditions.

However, Collins warns against the tendency to easily polarize the different groups that were active in the third to first centuries B.C.E. No evidence of intense polemic exists between the Enochic and Danielic tradition, as later found in the Dead Sea Scrolls between sectarian groups. At least some of the Enochic writings share with Daniel the same common enemy, the Seleucid king. They also share beliefs about the way the world functions, assuming that human life is influenced by angelic and demonic forces, that history runs a predetermined course, and that it will be interrupted by divine intervention, to be followed by a universal judgment and the transformation of the elect.[101] The common elements in the two books include shared beliefs and symbols, which finds expression in a shared literary genre. Does this require a common social milieu? Evidence is inadequate to answer the question, and we do not know whether the authors or tradents associated in any way with each other. Both writings became part of the Essene library, implying that they were not regarded as incompatible with each other.[102]

6. Synthesis

From the discussion of the use of calendars, the conclusion is that respective apocalyptic books have nuances showing patterns of difference with other groups. These differences are in many cases not incompatible because the books share symbolism, ideas, and literary techniques that distinguish them from other books. While the books of Enoch and Daniel each had distinctive emphases, they were not engaged in ideological warfare with each other but rather with the temple hierarchy and Seleucid menace, which was brought to

---

100. James C. VanderKam, "Jubilees, Book of," *ABD* 3:1030–32.

101. John J. Collins, "Response: The Apocalyptic Worldview of Daniel," in Boccaccini, *Enoch and Qumran Origins*, 59–66.

102. Ibid., 65. García Martínez concurs with this view: "It is my contention that all these strands of thought are interwoven in the thought on the origin of evil that we find in the Dead Sea Scrolls, and that all of them contribute in some way to shape the new solution they gave to the problem. It is clear that the Scrolls know the myth as it is presented in the *Book of the Watchers*. Not only have several copies of the composition appeared in Cave 4, but the story itself is used in some other Qumran compositions such as 4Q180, a *pesher* on the periods, in which Asael plays a leading role.... Similarly, *Jubilees* has had a deep influence in the thought of the community" ("Apocalypticism in the Dead Sea Scrolls," 93).

a crisis point with the Hellenization process introduced by Antiochus Epiphanes IV.[103]

---

103. Collins, "Response," 66.

ANIMOSITY IN TARGUMIC LITERATURE

Eveline van Staalduine-Sulman

1. INTRODUCTION

Two centuries before the beginning of the Common Era, Jewish leaders began to translate the Hebrew Bible. Alongside Greek, Aramaic became more and more the vernacular among Jews. Hebrew functioned less as the daily language and received the status of holy language. Aramaic translations were made to study the Word of God, as well as to explain this Word in the synagogues to the ordinary people. The earliest complete translation of a biblical book is the Targum of Job, found in the Qumran caves. But as far as we know now, the official Targums of the Torah and the Prophets saw the light from the second century C.E. onwards.[1]

Of course, Targum Jonathan to the Prophets (Joshua, Judges, Samuel, Kings, Isaiah, Jeremiah, Ezekiel and the twelve Minor Prophets) is a translation of the biblical text, and as such it contains many thoughts about animosity drawn from the biblical authors. But like every other translation of the Bible, Targum Jonathan to the Prophets betrays the presuppositions of its translators, which appear "in the conjunction of the added material and that which replicates the Biblical text. For what happens is that the added scenes place their meaning onto the Biblical material. While the biblically accurate scenes help authorize the added ones, the added scenes provide the context within which the Biblical scenes have meaning."[2] By studying these conjunctions one can trace a kind of targumic theology, although it will never be a systematic

---

1. Willem F. Smelik, *The Targum of Judges* (OtSt 36; Leiden: Brill, 1996), starts with an excellent survey of the history and purposes of Targumic literature.
2. Paul V. M. Flesher and Robert Torry, "Filming Jesus: Between Authority and Heresy," *SBL Forum*, online: http://www.sbl-site.org/Article.aspx?ArticleId=226.

one.[3] What emerge are some aspects of the targumic theology of violence and animosity, especially around the figure of King David. This might function as a mirror for our own theology and make us wonder if the targumic approach is the right one for achieving peace and reconciliation.

2. Warfare in Targum Jonathan

Reading the Targum of Samuel, one can easily conclude that the targumists had no problem at all with violence and warfare. Whereas Ulfila at about the same time refused to translate the book into Gothic because of its violence,[4] Targum Jonathan not only translates the book but also adds new violent scenes to it.

Living in the Roman world, targumists modernized Scripture by adding Roman habits. Some were innocent, such as the custom of clients and servants of paying a daily visit to their patron and asking him about his welfare.[5] This is replacing the Hebrew phrase that some men presented gifts to the new king Saul.

1 Sam 10:27 NRSV	Tg. Jon. 1 Sam 10:27
They despised him and brought him no present.	They despised him and did not ask about his well-being.

Other Roman customs were less innocent, such as dragging prisoners of war through the streets. Whereas the Hebrew text suggests that the Ammonites were punished by severe forced labor, Targum Jonathan intimates that David behaved like a Roman conqueror.

---

3. See, e.g., Étan Levine, *The Aramaic Version of the Bible: Contents and Context* (BZAW 174; Berlin: de Gruyter, 1988).

4. According to Philostorgius, *Church History* 2.5, Ulfila did not translate the books of Kings (i.e., Samuel and Kings), because these contained stories of wars, and his people loved war; see Joseph Bidez, *Philostorgius Kirchengeschichte* (Leipzig: Hinrich, 1913), 18; Philip R. Amidon, trans., *Philostorgius: Church History* (SBLWGRW 23; Atlanta; Society of Biblical Literature, 2007), 21. Philostorgius wrote his book around 440 C.E. It is transmitted to us via the works of Photius; see Hendrik Anthonie van Bakel, "Het Credo van Wulfila," in idem, *Circa Sacra: Historische Studiën* (Haarlem: Willink, 1935), 86–113.

5. Leivy Smolar and Moses Aberbach, *Studies in Targum Jonathan to the Prophets* (New York: Ktav, 1978), 100; followed by Daniel J. Harrington and Anthony J. Saldarini, *Targum Jonathan of the Former Prophets: Introduction, Translation and Notes* (ArBib 10; Edinburgh: T&T Clark, 1987), 120 n. 43.

2 Sam 12:31b NRSV	Tg. Jon. 2 Sam 12:31b
… and sent them to the brickworks.	… and dragged them through the streets.

And this is only one phrase from 2 Sam 12:31. The entire verse is exegetically and ethically difficult. Several modern commentators are pleased to see possibilities within the text for avoiding a most cruel execution of the Ammonites.[6] Most ancient versions, however, do not hesitate to translate the assumed cruelties in this verse. David sawed the Ammonites into pieces or killed them with butchers' knives. Targum Jonathan is similar: "and sawed them with saws and iron picks and iron axes." Josephus summarizes it with the words "tortured them and put them to death" (Josephus, *Ant.* 7.161).

Although the Targumim deviate from the Hebrew text in order to picture biblical heroes in the most righteous possible way, they did not feel the urge to "correct" texts concerning warfare. On the contrary, King David was a hero, especially in warfare. In the Targumic version of his last words (Tg. Jon. 2 Sam 23:1–8) the earthly King David functions as a model for the coming Messiah: he is said to be "prepared with sets of armor, going out as the champion, and victorious in battle. He wields his spear against eight hundred slain in one time."[7] Only in a much later version of this song is King David depicted as a rabbi and musician, whose heroism lies in the art of singing and in explaining the Torah (Tg. 1 Chr 11:11).[8]

3. Animosity in Targum Jonathan

When we look at animosity and hatred on a more personal level in Targum Jonathan, we see a slightly different approach. The Hebrew text of Samuel is in itself cautious about David as an enemy or hater. Targum Jonathan is even more careful, depicting him as a noble and gentle person. David had enemies, but he himself hated no one. Only King Saul spoke of him in that manner to his daughter Michal: "Why have you deceived me thus, and let my enemy go, so that he has escaped?" (1 Sam 19:17). David's animosity only existed in Saul's mind.

---

6. See Eveline van Staalduine-Sulman, *The Targum of Samuel* (SAIS 1; Leiden: Brill, 2002), 557–58.

7. This is an apocalyptic view of the Messiah: he uses violence, but his people can quietly wait for redemption.

8. See further Eveline van Staalduine-Sulman, "Reward and Punishment in the Messianic Age (Targ. 2 Sam. 23.1–8)," *JAB* 1 (1999): 273–96.

When David made plans to conquer Jerusalem, the Jebusites mocked David with the words, "You will never enter this place. Even the blind and the lame will turn you back" (2 Sam 5:6). David's reaction in the Hebrew text is ambiguous. The Ketiv states that these blind and lame people hated David's soul, but the Qere writes that these people were hated by David's soul.[9] Targum Jonathan avoids both forms of hatred and states that David removed[10] these people from the city, a clean and religious act, because the Targum interprets the blind and the lame as a metaphor for sinners.[11] Personal hate is avoided; David is turned into a just and pious king.

2 Sam 5:8	Tg. Jon. 2 Sam 5:8
Ketiv: the lame and the blind, who hate David's soul	And David's soul rejected the sinners and the guilty.
Qere: the lame and the blind, who are hated by David's soul	

This absence of hatred is not only found in the exemplary King David; it is derived from the targumic image of God. God's holiness and transcendence is stressed so much in targumic literature that a direct contact between God and humankind is always avoided, even a contact of enmity or hatred. No one is God's enemy; there are only enemies of God's people (1 Sam 25:28; 30:26; 2 Sam 12:14).

These two lines of argument—David is no enemy; no one is God's enemy—converge in Tg. Jon. 1 Sam 28:16. Saul forced the woman of Endor to summon up the spirit of Samuel. When it arrived, it questioned Saul, and one of the questions was, "Why, then, do you ask me, since the Lord has turned from you and become your enemy?" The Hebrew text clearly states that God has become Saul's enemy. Targum Jonathan could not maintain that idea and

---

9. There are quite a few verses in the Hebrew Bible that have standardized marginal notes. These notes prescribe that the text is written (Ketiv) in a certain way but is to be read (Qere) differently. Reverence for the original text forbade that the Hebrew text was altered.

10. Although the verb can also mean "to spurn," pointing to human emotions, it is striking that Targum Jonathan chose not to use "to hate" but the verb that is used for God's rejection of King Saul (see 1 Sam 15:23, 26; 16:1, 7; 18:12; 28:15, 16), a translation of less-emotional Hebrew verbs.

11. On the basis of Isa 42:18–19 and other texts, see Alberdina Houtman, "Sin and Illness in the Targum of the Prophets," in *Purity and Holiness: The Heritage of Leviticus* (ed. Marcel J. H. M. Poorthuis and Joshua Schwartz; Leiden: Brill, 1999), 195–206, esp. 204. See further van Staalduine-Sulman, *The Targum of Samuel*, 507–12.

supposed that the animosity was between Saul and David, not between Saul and God. On the other hand, David could not be depicted as Saul's enemy, because he was a just and pious person, knowing no hatred against the anointed of the Lord. So Targum Jonathan had to come up with a different solution and chose a text in which Saul was said to be the enemy:

1 Sam 28:16 NRSV	Tg. Jon. 1 Sam 28:16
since the Lord has turned from you and become your enemy?	since the Memra of the Lord has rejected you and is in the aid of the man whose enemy you are?

4. A Provisional Conclusion

Whereas the Hebrew text speaks rather freely of God's feelings, both good feelings and bad feelings, Targum Jonathan attempts to confine these texts to God's actions. God is a just and righteous judge. He is not led by feelings, only by the righteous stipulations of his law.[12] Consequently, the distance between God and humans is enlarged. Therefore, the combination of God and animosity is denied in the Targum and replaced by animosity between humans.[13]

In the Hebrew text of the narratives concerning David, there is hardly any animosity on David's side. Almost all the animosity comes from Saul's side, and it is Saul who considers David an enemy. Targum Jonathan recognized this pattern and even enhanced it in its translation: David is just and pious, and therefore he does not know hatred. The targumic David is, in this respect, a true follower of his targumic God. Consequently, the distance between this biblical hero and his adversaries is enlarged, too.

At first sight, this kind of theology seems a step toward reconciliation. No one is God's enemy; God is no one's enemy. David knows no animosity or hatred. The other side of the picture, however, shows a line of holiness. God is holy, beyond any direct contact with humankind. And David is one of the righteous heroes, following in God's footprints. The result is a kind of polarization between good and bad, between the heroes and the villains.

---

12. This may have arisen from Stoic influences on the Jewish religion; see Katie Maguire, "Hellenism and the Jewish Afterlife," online: http://classes.maxwell.syr.edu/his301-001/hellenistic_effects_on_judaic_li.htm.

13. Targum Onqelos treats the combination of God and hatred less restrictively. Humans can hate God (e.g., Exod 20:5; Deut 7:10) and can think that God hates them (Deut 1:27).

5. Polarization

Polarization between good and bad is one of the motifs behind the Aramaic translations. Targum Jonathan achieves it primarily by depicting the biblical heroes as examples of faith.[14] One specimen will suffice to illustrate this motive. Several people in the books of Samuel are called "dead dog" or "flea" to illustrate their humbleness or to call them names. In most cases these nicknames are replaced by more common expressions, such as "a weakling" and "a common fellow" (see 1 Sam 24:14; 26:20; 2 Sam 3:8; 9:8). In one verse, however, the expression "dead dog" is maintained by Targum Jonathan, because it is used for Shimei, the opponent of David, who should be depicted as a villain.

1 Sam 24:14 NRSV—David	Tg. Jon. 1 Sam 24:14
After whom has the king of Israel come out?	After whom has the king of Israel come out?
Whom do you pursue? A dead dog! A single flea!	Whom do you pursue? A weak person! One common man!
2 Sam 16:9 NRSV—Shimei	Tg. Jon. 2 Sam 16:9
Why should this dead dog curse my lord the king?	Why should this dead dog curse my lord the king?

This is one side of the picture—praising the heroes—resulting in a group of people who are very special, called the righteous.[15] These righteous people find favor with God and will eventually experience God's love and mercy, while God's anger and doom fall upon the other side, the wicked ones. Targum Jonathan even tends to soften harsh prophetic words and to emphasize prophetic words of consolation.[16]

---

14. See Daniel Patte, *Early Jewish Hermeneutic in Palestine* (SBLDS 22; Missoula, Mont.: Scholars Press, 1975), 78. The list in Heb 11 is similarly adjusted to contemporary traditions. The biblical heroes are all depicted as examples.

15. E.g., Tg. Jon. 1 Sam 2:8–9; 2 Sam 22:29; 23:4. Several separate manuscripts add the word "righteous" to certain people to give them the status of "worthy to rise to eternal life," such as Abraham, Manoah, Samson, Moses, and Aaron; see van Staalduine-Sulman, *The Targum of Samuel*, 154.

16. Alberdina Houtman, "Doom and Promise in the Targum of Isaiah," *JJS* 49 (1998): 17–23, esp. 23.

The other side of polarization, humbling the nonheroes, is not often found in the official Targumim, Onqelos, and Jonathan. It is to be found in separate manuscripts, in additions and expansions in the margins, and in the so-called popular Palestinian Targumim to the Pentateuch. The designation "popular" does not mean that they are written by laymen nor that they deviate from the official Jewish exegesis. On the contrary, many midrashic explanations found their way into the Palestinian translations. The popular Targumim should rather be compared to our popular genre of biblical films. They are often the result of long historical and exegetical research, but they contain many elements that make them popular in the sense of "easily accessible": extra historical and exegetical data; modernizing elements; and, last but not least, scenes that complement and complete the biblical narrative.[17]

Let us take a closer look at the other side of polarization, the humbling of the nonheroes. One of the rare occurrences of this present in the official Targum is the Song of Hannah, where the fall of Rome is predicted.

1 Sam 2:5 NRSV	Tg. Jon. 1 Sam 2:5
but she who has many children is forlorn.	and Rome which is filled with a mass of peoples, her armies will cease to be. She will be desolate and destroyed.

Some manuscripts expand the theme on their own and state that Rome will be destroyed, because she is "guilty."[18]

1 Sam 2:5 NRSV	MSS Tg. Jon. 1 Sam 2:5[19]
but she who has many children is forlorn.	and *guilty* Rome which is filled with a mass of peoples, her armies will cease to be. She will be desolate and destroyed.

More material on humbling the nonheroes is found in the so-called Tosefta-Targumim, that is, additional fragments mostly found in the margins of Western manuscripts. These fragments do not follow the fairly literal trans-

---

17. Flesher and Torry, "Filming Jesus."
18. Van Staalduine-Sulman, *The Targum of Samuel*, 211 n. 164. A similar addition is made by some manuscripts in 2 Sam 22:9, where Pharaoh is called wicked; see ibid., 647 n. 1217.
19. MS Add. 26879, British Museum, London; Codex Reuchlin, Badische Landesbibliotek, Karlsruhe; MS Or. Fol. 1–4 of the Staatsbibliothek, Berlin; *Prophetae priores*, Leiria 1494.

lational style of the official Targumim but expand on their subject as long as they deem necessary.[20] The content of these fragments is usually based on Jewish midrashic exegesis.

A fine example is Goliath, who is the opponent of David and the people of Israel in the Hebrew text of 1 Sam 17, but is turned into an archvillain in the Toseftot. In one of the most important manuscripts, Codex Reuchlin, a fragment in the margin of 17:4 states that Goliath is a descendant of Samson, hence his strength, and Orpah, hence his unfaithfulness and his animosity against David, the descendant of Ruth. Several manuscripts quote a poem in the margin of verse 8 in which Goliath is boasting that he killed Hophni and Phinehas, the sons of Eli, and that he was the one who captured the ark and brought it into the temple of his god Dagon.[21] Codex Reuchlin stresses in the margin of verse 16 that Goliath not only did his blaspheming for forty days but that he did it precisely at the time of the continual offering.[22] Two other manuscripts add to verse 39 that he was killed by a stone, since he blasphemed, quoting the Torah instruction that whoever blasphemes must be stoned to death (Lev 24:14–16).[23] Altogether, Goliath's reputation was inversely proportional to David's.

Many more examples can be mentioned, but the richest source for villains is the corpus of Palestinian Targumim. It is in accordance with the books of Kings that Ahab is described as the enemy of the prophet Elijah, although the place, Targum Pseudo-Jonathan to Deut 33:11, is quite surprising.

---

20. An almost complete survey of Tosefta-Targumim in Targum Jonathan is given by Rimon Kasher, *Toseftot of the Targum to the Prophets* (SSJC 2; Jerusalem: World Union of Jewish Studies, 1996).

21. There are three versions of this boasting. A very short one is attested in Codex Reuchlin. The Sefardi version is the most poetical and is attested in MS p. 116, Montefiore Library, Jews' College, London; *Prophetae priores*, Leiria 1494; MS Kennicott 5 [85], Bodleian Library, Oxford; MS 1, Salamanca. The Ashkenazi version is attested in MS Add. 26879, British Museum, London; MS El. f.6, Universitätsbibliotek, Jena; *Biblica Rabbinica*, Bomberg, Venice 1515–1517; MS Or. 1471, British Museum, London.

22. See also Alberdina Houtman and Eveline van Staalduine-Sulman, "Joden, christenen en hun Targum," in *Joden, christenen en hun Schrift: Een bundel opstellen aangeboden bij het afscheid van C.J. den Heyer* (ed. C. Houtman and L. J. Lietaert Peerbolte; Baarn: Ten Have, 2001), 147–60, esp. 158–60.

23. MS p. 116, Montefiore Library, Jews' College, London; *Prophetae priores*, Leiria 1494.

Deut 33:11 NRSV
Bless, O Lord, his substance,
and accept the work of his hands.

Crush the loins of his adversaries,
of those that hate him.

Tg. Ps.-J. Deut 33:11
Bless, O Lord, the possessions of …
and accept with good will the sacrifice
from the hand of Elijah, the priest, who
offered up at Mount Carmel.
Break the loins of Ahab, his enemy,
and the joint of the false prophets who
arose against him.[24]

The polarization is already present in the Hebrew text of the verse. Pseudo-Jonathan makes it specific by adding the names of Elijah and Ahab, supported by the elaborate description of the enmity between Elijah and King Ahab in the books of Kings.[25]

Less polarization is present in the Hebrew text when it comes to Jacob and Esau. Yet for apologetic reasons Esau is depicted as a nonbeliever, denying the resurrection, a villain sinning on the day of Abraham's death in Targum Pseudo-Jonathan. It attributed to Jacob, however, the virtue of comforting his grieving father.[26]

Gen 25:29 NRSV
Once when Jacob was cooking a stew,

Esau came in from the field,
and he was famished.

Tg. Ps.-J. Gen 25:29
The day Abraham died,
Jacob boiled dishes of lentils
and went to comfort his father.

Esau came from the country,
and he was exhausted,
because he had committed five transgressions that day:

he had practiced idolatry,
he had shed innocent blood,

---

24. Translation from Ernest G. Clarke, *Targum Pseudo-Jonathan: Deuteronomy* (ArBib 5B; Edinburgh: T&T Clark, 1998), 99–100.

25. See also Luis Díez Merino, "Exculpación-Inculpación: Principio de exegesis Targúmica desconocido en la hermenéutica judia oficial," in *III Simposio Bíblico Español (I Luso–Espanhol)* (ed. J. Carreira das Neves et al.; Valencia-Lisboa: Fundación Bíblica Española, 1991), 441–76, esp. 472.

26. Targum Pseudo-Jonathan to Gen 25:29, explained and provided with its midrashic parallels in Herman Sysling, *Techiyyat ha-Metim: De opstanding van de doden in de Palestijnse Targumim op de Pentateuch en overeenkomstige tradities in de klassieke rabbijnse bronnen* (Zutphen: Terra, 1991), 105–36.

> he had gone in to a betrothed maiden,
> he had denied the life of the world to come,
> and he had despised the birthright.[27]

For the targumists, Esau was not only a person in the past; he represented Edom, and, in the days of the Roman Empire, he represented Rome. The guilt of Rome and the animosity between the Roman conquerors and the Jewish people are integrated into the narrative of Esau and Jacob. The same animosity is also the background to a marginal addition in Targum Neofiti to Gen 25:27:[28]

Gen 25:27 NRSV	Tg. Neof. Gen 25:27
When the boys grew up, Esau was a skilful hunter, a man of the field,	And the young men grew and Esau was a man of thighs of bronze, because he had bronze in his left thigh, likened to a sword which served him as a distinctive sign of a robber lord; he went out to rob the passers-by and those that came back, and because of this did his father bless him, saying: And you shall live by your sword.

---

27. Translation from Michael Maher, *Targum Pseudo-Jonathan: Genesis* (ArBib 1B; Edinburgh: T&T Clark, 1992), 90.

28. See also C. T. R. Hayward, "A Portrait of the Wicked Esau in the Targum of Codex Neofiti 1," in *The Aramaic Bible: Targums in Their Historical Context* (ed. D. R. G. Beattie and Martin J. McNamara; JSOTSup 166; Sheffield: JSOT Press, 1994), 291–309, esp. 307, although there are other influences visible apart from the identification of Esau with Rome; Luis Díez Merino, "Translation of Proper Names: A Targumic Method of Hermeneutics in Targum Esther," in *Targum and Scripture: Studies in Aramaic Translations and Interpretation in Memory of Ernest G. Clarke* (ed. Paul V. M. Flesher; SAIS 2; Leiden: Brill, 2002), 203–23, esp. 207.

| while Jacob was a quiet man, dwelling in tents. | Jacob was a man perfect in good work,[29] sitting and assisting at the schoolhouse[30] of Shem and of Eber, seeking instruction from before the Lord.[31] |

A final example: Jacob's uncle Laban was a shrewd and deceiving person in the Hebrew text of Genesis, but no worse than Jacob himself. He is, however, not highly valued in midrashic literature. Whereas the Hebrew text of Gen 29:13 says that Laban embraces Jacob to greet him, Gen. Rab. 70:13 suggests that this embracing was done in order to find out whether Jacob carried some money under his clothes. This explanation found its way into the Samaritan Targum, which does not translate "embrace" but "body-searched."[32]

6. Conclusions

Targumic literature translated biblical war scenes without any embarrassment. It even stressed and enlarged the cruelties committed by biblical heroes, such as the harsh persecution of the Ammonites and the dragging of the war prisoners through the streets by King David.

Animosity on a personal level is translated with some caution. Targum Jonathan gives the same general picture as the Hebrew text, but there are two exceptions due to the abundant reverence for God and his people. First, there is no animosity from and toward God: no one is God's enemy; God is no one's enemy. All animosity is placed on the human level. But second, the human

---

29. This side of the polarization is also found in Tg. Jon. 2 Sam 22:26–27, where Abraham is said to be loyal, Isaac to be perfect, and Jacob to have walked in purity.

30. This virtue of Jacob, visiting the *beth hamidrash*, is also inserted in Targum Onqelos and Pseudo-Jonathan. See Bernard Grossfeld, *Targum Neofiti 1: An Exegetical Commentary to Genesis* (New York: Sepher-Hermon, 2000), 188–89.

31. Translation from Alejandro Díez Macho, *Neophyti 1: Targum Palestinense MS de la Biblioteca Vaticana*, Tomo 1: Génesis (Madrid: Consejo Superior de Investigaciones Científicas, 1968), 563 n. 1.

32. Díez Merino, "Translation of Proper Names," 203–23, esp. 207. Targum Pseudo-Jonathan depicts Laban as an idolator (Tg. Ps.-J. Gen 24:31, based on Gen 31:19, 30, 34) and as a person trying to poison Eliezer the servant of Abraham (Tg. Ps.-J. Gen 24:33); see C. T. R. Hayward, "Inconsistencies and Contradictions in Targum Pseudo-Jonathan: The Case of Eliezer and Nimrod," *JSS* 37 (1992): 31–55, who gives indications that these targumic stories are part of the early traditions in Pseudo-Jonathan.

level is divided into two sections: the section of the biblical heroes, the righteous, the pious; and the section of the nonheroes, the wicked, and the sinners. Reading in the Targum of Samuel one encounters a righteous King David, a model of the pious Jew, obeying the Torah.[33] He was not called names, he did not know hatred and animosity, and he was more than a common man.

At first sight, it sounds sympathetic to avoid animosity between God and humans, but religious animosity returns indirectly. God's people and God's king are depicted in such a holy and reverent way that enmity against them is synonymous with blasphemy. Being David's enemy is just as evil as being God's enemy, and obstructing David's kingdom is the same as obstructing God. Any war against Israel is interpreted as being a religious war, and religious fanaticism (e.g., zealotism) is also involved. There is a similar line of thought behind 9/11 and March 11.[34]

This reverence has led to polarization between heroes and nonheroes in the popular versions of the targumic literature. Israel, the archfathers, the prophets, the pious kings, all function as models of faith. Their opponents, sympathetic or not in the Hebrew text, are models of heresy, wickedness, and sin. The gap between God and humans in the Hebrew Bible is now replaced by a gap between God and his people, on the one hand, and the other nations, on the other hand.[35] This is an apologetic or didactic way to strengthen the identity of the readers and to justify their own religious system.[36] This is best

---

33. Except in the case of Bathsheba, which was not to be read and translated in the synagogue.

34. This is most probably due to the warlike conditions during the period of origin of the Targumim. A comparison between the book of Jubilees and the Targumim shows "changing relationships between the Jews and their neighbours." Reading the Targumim one must say that "the peaceful coexistence is seen as a thing of the past, the warlike conditions gradually taking over and terminating that peaceful period" (Roger Syrén, "Ishmael and Esau in the Book of *Jubilees* and Targum Pseudo-Jonathan," in Beattie and McNamara, *The Aramaic Bible*, 310–15, esp. 314).

35. The latter gap is expressed by Paul in Eph 2:14 with the words "dividing wall of hostility."

36. See Sysling, *Techiyyat ha-Metim*, 265. This can be explained as opposition to the Greco-Roman world (Pekka Lindqvist, "Golden Calf in the First Century" [paper read at the seventh congress of EAJS, 21–25 July 2002, Amsterdam]), especially when we realize that the Targum to the Prophets originated in a period of suppression by the Roman Empire, after the two Jewish revolts. Elisabeth Schüssler Fiorenza ("Paul and the Politics of Interpretation," in *Paul and Politics: Ekklesia, Israel, Imperium, Interpretation: Essays in Honor of Krister Stendahl* [ed. Richard A. Horsley; Harrisburg, Pa.: Trinity Press International, 2000], 40–57) calls this "the politics of othering."

done by demonizing the other and by denying his or her right to exist.[37] Narrowing the gap, or even reconciliation, is not the issue in targumic literature. That can better be achieved by showing the human, that is, the limited and sinful side, of the biblical heroes—and of ourselves.

A final remark: in targumic literature the feelings of God and his people are restricted and often even discounted. The positive side of this feature seems to be to safeguard God's objective righteousness and fairness. The negative side, however, is a lack of warmth and mercy toward outsiders. This leads me to the paradoxical conclusion that discounting feelings of hostility results in a greater animosity.

---

37. According to Schüssler Fiorenza, "systems and discourses of marginalization, vilification, and dehumanization" ("Paul and the Politics of Interpretation," 45).

Domestic Violence in the Ancient World: Preliminary Considerations and the Problem of Wife-Beating

John T. Fitzgerald

1. Introduction

Domestic violence is a grim reality for all modern societies, a problem that is as pervasive as it is pernicious.[1] No country, no religion, no ethnic group is exempt from this malady, for people of every age, economic status, educational level, occupation, race, sexual orientation, and social class are affected by this global epidemic. The problem is so severe that it threatens the very fabric of our society, and how we deal with it will affect the future of our communal existence. Statistics on domestic violence vary, not only because nations differ in how accurately they report instances of family violence, but also in how they define it.[2] The United States, for example, does not even have a uniform definition of domestic violence. Some states limit domestic violence to cases in which the perpetrator and victim are current or former spouses, or are indi-

---

1. This essay is a considerably revised version of a paper presented in July 2004 at the European Association for Biblical Studies meeting in Groningen, Netherlands. Subsequent versions were presented in South Africa in 2006 at the University of Johannesburg, the University of KwaZulu-Natal, and the University of Stellenbosch. Research on this paper was completed during my time as a Visiting Research Scholar at the School of Biblical Studies and Ancient Languages, North-West University, Potchefstroom, South Africa. I am greatly indebted to Professor Thomas K. Hubbard of the Classics Department, University of Texas at Austin, for his many helpful insights and suggestions in regard to this undertaking. I am, of course, solely responsible for the errors and inadequacies of this treatment.

2. The lack of a uniform definition is also evident in the different ways in which the fields of social services, medicine, and law define domestic violence. See *Pathfinder on Domestic Violence in the United States* (New York: Center on Crime, Communities & Culture, 1997), 6–7.

viduals who presently occupy the same residence or once did so, or are people who have a child in common. But other states, in addition to these three categories, include instances of violence involving individuals who have a current or former dating relationship, even if they have never resided together.[3] It will be immediately obvious that the focus of such definitions is the adult couple in their relationship to each other, and that is indeed the modern domestic relationship most susceptible to instances of violence. According to almost all surveys and estimates, at least one in every three or four women around the world has been or will be the victim of violence during her lifetime.[4] That at least one-fourth and possibly more than one-third of all women will be or already have been beaten, sexually assaulted, or otherwise abused is a chilling statistic and one that should be totally unacceptable to any civilized society.[5] The human cost is, of course, incalculable, but even on economic grounds alone, domestic violence is a problem that cannot be ignored.[6]

Yet violence within the family is not limited to adult partners who have or have had a sexually intimate relationship. As is well known, adult members of some households abuse children both physically and sexually, and they

---

3. This description of the differences in state domestic violence laws in the United States is based on the "National Facts" synopsis of its "Domestic Violence Facts." The synopsis was compiled by the Public Policy Office of the National Coalition against Domestic Violence and is available online at http://www.ncadv.org/files/DomesticViolenceFactSheet (National).pdf.

4. Statistics regarding domestic violence, especially against women, are readily available on many websites, such as those of the National Coalition against Domestic Violence (http://www.ncadv.org) and the Family Violence Prevention Fund (http://endabuse.org). For domestic violence as a global problem, see Randal W. Summers and Allan M. Hoffmann, eds., *Domestic Violence: A Global View* (Westport, Conn.: Greenwood, 2002).

5. Physical assaults by women against men, especially wives against husbands, constitute another form of domestic violence, the prevalence of which remains vigorously contested. Compare Philip W. Cook, *Abused Men: The Hidden Side of Domestic Violence* (Westport, Conn.: Praeger, 1997); Murray A. Straus, "Women's Violence toward Men Is a Serious Social Problem"; and Donileen R. Loseke and Demie Kurz, "Men's Violence toward Women Is the Serious Social Problem," the latter two both in *Current Controversies on Family Violence* (ed. Donileen R. Loseke, Richard J. Gelles, and Mary M. Cavanaugh; 2nd ed.; Thousand Oaks, Calif.: Sage, 2005), 55–77 (Straus), 79–95 (Loseke and Kurz).

6. Michael A. Bedke in the foreword to the American Bar Association Commission on Domestic Violence's *A Guide for Employers: Domestic Violence in the Workplace* (Washington, D.C.: American Bar Association, 1999), 3, notes that domestic violence costs "U.S. companies an estimated four to five billion dollars per year in absenteeism, employee turnover, reduced productivity, higher health insurance premiums, and the like." When that figure is recalculated for inflation and extended globally, it immediately becomes clear how massive and costly the problem is.

also are violent toward other adults residing in the same household, especially the elderly. In a similar way, younger members of the household occasionally abuse older members, and such instances of abuse are not always acts of retaliation against those who have abused them. Nor are siblings exceptions to this phenomenon, especially when instances of sibling rivalry develop into acts of aggression and violence. Finally, even household pets are not immune to this social epidemic, for many instances of cruelty toward animals occur within the household.

Given the severity of the problem of domestic violence in the modern world, it is surprising that very little scholarly attention has been given to the history of such violence, especially in the ancient world.[7] Classicists have given some attention to the problem, but not as much as one might have anticipated.[8] Biblical scholars, for their part, are increasingly interested in the general subject of violence, with the events of 11 September 2001 creating a new context for that accelerating interest.[9] Yet biblical scholars, especially

---

7. Specialists in various fields of the humanities, including scholars of religion, have investigated the problem in other periods; see, for instance, Eve Salisbury, Georgiana Donavin, and Merrall Llewelyn Price, eds., *Domestic Violence in Medieval Texts* (Gainesville: University of Florida Press, 2002); and Ann Taves, ed., *Religion and Domestic Violence in Early New England: The Memoirs of Abigail Abbot Bailey* (Religion in North America; Bloomington: Indiana University Press, 1989).

8. On the general topic of violence in Greece and Rome, see esp. Andrew Lintott, *Violence, Civil Strife and Revolution in the Classical City: 750–330 BC* (London: Croom Helm, 1982); idem, *Violence in Republican Rome* (2nd ed.; Oxford: Oxford University Press, 1999). For Christian religious violence against pagan temples and holy sites during the reign of Theodosius I (379–395 C.E.), see Thomas Sizgorich, "'Not Easily Were Stones Joined by the Strongest Bonds Pulled Asunder': Religious Violence and Imperial Order in the Later Roman World," *JECS* 15 (2007): 75–101.

9. See, e.g., Phyllis Trible, *Texts of Terror: Literary-Feminist Readings of Biblical Narratives* (OBT 13; Philadelphia: Fortress, 1984); Mark H. McEntire, *The Blood of Abel: The Violent Plot in the Hebrew Bible* (Macon, Ga.: Mercer University Press, 1999); François Bovon, "The Child and the Beast: Fighting Violence in Ancient Christianity," *HTR* 92 (1999): 369–92; Jack Nelson-Pallmeyer, *Is Religion Killing Us? Violence in the Bible and the Quran* (Harrisburg, Pa.: Trinity Press International, 2003); Jonneke Bekkenkamp and Yvonne Sherwood, eds., *Sanctified Aggression: Legacies of Biblical and Post-biblical Vocabularies of Violence* (JSOTSup 400; Bible in the Twenty-First Century 3; London: T&T Clark, 2003); JoAnn Hackett, "Violence and Women's Lives in the Book of Judges," *Int* 58 (2004): 356–64; Todd Penner and Caroline Vander Stichele, "Gendering Violence: Patterns of Power and Constructs of Masculinity in the Acts of the Apostles," in *A Feminist Companion to the Acts of the Apostles* (ed. Amy-Jill Levine; FCNTECW 9; London: T&T Clark, 2004), 193–209; Shelly Matthews and E. Leigh Gibson, eds., *Violence in the New Testament* (London: T&T Clark, 2005). On the more general subject of homicide in ancient Near

those who deal primarily with the New Testament and other early Christian literature, have paid little or no attention to domestic violence as such. The most important work relevant to this topic has been done by scholars of the Hebrew Bible, especially feminist scholars such as Renita Weems and Athalya Brenner, who have focused on depictions of violence against women in the Hebrew Bible,[10] and Andreas Michel, who has written on violence against children.[11] Despite the presence of such treatments, it is striking that even studies on ancient families have not usually focused on family violence.[12]

Therefore, there is much to be done on the problem of domestic violence in the ancient world. This essay is extremely limited in its scope and represents no more than my initial, exploratory efforts in what I expect to be an extended research project. Three major parts comprise this essay. In the first part, I discuss the meaning of the term "domestic violence," identifying the scope of the phenomenon, indicating some of the difficulties in defining domestic violence in the ancient world, and noting some key differences between the modern and ancient understandings of the problem.[13] In the second part, I focus on the phenomenon of spousal abuse in the form

---

Eastern law and the biblical text, see now Pamela Barmash, *Homicide in the Biblical World* (New York: Cambridge University Press, 2005).

10. Renita J. Weems, *Battered Love: Marriage, Sex, and Violence in the Hebrew Prophets* (OBT; Minneapolis: Fortress, 1995); and Athalya Brenner, "Some Reflections on Violence against Women and the Image of the Hebrew God: The Prophetic Books Revisited," in *On the Cutting Edge: The Study of Women in Biblical Worlds: Essays in Honor of Elisabeth Schüssler Fiorenza* (ed. Jane Schaberg, Alice Bach, and Esther Fuchs; New York: Continuum, 2003), 69–81.

11. Andreas Michel, *Gott und Gewalt gegen Kinder im Alten Testament* (FAT 37; Tübingen: Mohr Siebeck, 2003). For the New Testament and children, see now Peter Balla, *The Child-Parent Relationship in the New Testament and Its Environment* (WUNT 155; Tübingen: Mohr Siebeck, 2003).

12. For studies of the family in the ancient world, see Suzanne Dixon, *The Roman Family* (Baltimore: Johns Hopkins University Press, 1992); Shaye J. D. Cohen, ed., *The Jewish Family in Antiquity* (BJS 289; Atlanta: Scholars Press, 1993); Leo G. Perdue, Joseph Blenkinsopp, John J. Collins, and Carol Meyers, *Families in Ancient Israel* (The Family, Religion, and Culture; Louisville: Westminster John Knox, 1997); Sarah B. Pomeroy, *Families in Classical and Hellenistic Greece: Representations and Realities* (Oxford: Clarendon, 1997); Carolyn Osiek and David L. Balch, *Families in the New Testament World* (The Family, Religion, and Culture; Louisville: Westminster John Knox, 1997); and idem, eds., *Early Christian Families in Context: An Interdisciplinary Dialogue* (Religion, Marriage, and Family; Grand Rapids: Eerdmans, 2003).

13. We should recall that "domestic violence" is a relatively recent concept in the modern world, though the phenomenon of violence involving household members has long been noted.

of wife-beating. In terms of the materials that will be considered, I confine myself to evidence derived from the Greek and Roman worlds. In the third part, I note how the mythological traditions of both the ancient Hebrews and Greeks reflect an awareness of the problem of familial discord and domestic violence. Although the evidence used in this essay is highly fragmentary, it suggests that domestic violence not only begins in the ancient world but was already a troublesome problem in that world.

2. Preliminary Considerations

Let me begin this section of my essay with two caveats. First, it would be a mistake to infer from my focus in this essay that all ancient families were characterized by domestic violence or that expressions of familial concord and harmony were lacking. That is certainly not the case, and ancient documents and inscriptions contain frequent expressions of affection for various members of the family.[14] But domestic violence was part of ancient societies, just as it is part of modern societies, and some of these expressions of familial concord belie the actual situation, which was anything but harmonious.[15] Indeed, it is the prevalence of domestic violence in the Greco-Roman world that evokes such works as Plutarch's *On Parental Affection* and *On Brotherly Love* and provides the larger context in which those works and the exhortations that they contain need to be understood.[16] My essay is intended as an initial inquiry into this sinister side of life in certain households.

---

14. For affective bonds among various members of the Roman family, see the index in Judith P. Hallett, *Fathers and Daughters in Roman Society: Women and the Elite Family* (Princeton: Princeton University Press, 1984), 413.

15. Augustine, for example, says that his mother Monica had expressed the desire to be buried with her husband Patricius because they had lived together "very harmoniously" (*valde concorditer*: *Conf.* 9.11.28). Yet Augustine's depiction of their relationship in *Conf.* 9.9.19 shows the marriage, which was marked by Patricius's infidelity and anger, to have been far from ideal, at least until Patricius's conversion (9.9.22).

16. For a similar judgment about the relationship of expressions of conjugal concord to social reality, see Brent D. Shaw, "The Family in Late Antiquity: The Experience of Augustine," *Past and Present* 115 (1987): 3–51, esp. 32 n. 122: "Expressions included in the epitaphs of lower-order populations of the Latin west commonly include stereotypical phrases that husbands lived with their wives *sine/ullo-a/querella, discordia, iniuria, animi laesione, crimine, stomacho, iracundia, bile, maledictu* ["without any complaint, discord, injury, mental wound, accusation, vexation, wrath, anger, abusive language"], and so on. Though conventional, these negative sentiments would hardly be worth repeating in formulaic fashion if assumptions about real conditions to the opposite were not equally pervasive."

Second, ancient households were more comprehensive than modern nuclear families. Household slaves (οἰκέται), for example, were viewed as members of the household and were often the victims of domestic violence and occasionally were themselves guilty of such conduct. Indeed, violence toward slaves appears to have been the most prevalent form of domestic violence in the ancient world, though that assessment is necessarily restricted to households that were sufficiently affluent to include slaves.[17] Although slaves are no longer present in the households of modern families, any study of ancient domestic violence must pay special attention to the abuse of household slaves, and elsewhere I have made this form of domestic abuse the subject of a separate treatment.[18]

By "domestic violence," I mean principally the physical violence that typically takes place in the *domus* or οἶκος ("house") and among members of the *domus* or οἶκος ("household"). That is, I use the term to refer primarily to the physical abuse that one member of the household inflicts on another household member, with that violence usually but not always taking place within the house itself. I am thus excluding from my purview purely verbal abuse by one member of the household against another. Just as early Christians suffered persecution that was both physical and verbal, so did members of ancient Greek and Roman households. Verbal violence can be just as devastating, if not emotionally more so, than physical violence, as anyone who has been the recipient of a fierce tongue-lashing can attest. Indeed, as Ben Sira noted long ago, "The blow of a whip raises a welt, but a blow of the tongue crushes the bones" (28:17 NRSV). Nevertheless, as a means of limiting the scope of my inquiry, I am excluding from the outset instances of verbal assault unless they are accompanied by physical abuse, or threaten bodily harm, or recall instances of previous assaults. Verbal threats of physical abuse did play a significant role in ancient households, and I give attention to that aspect of domestic violence later in this essay.

---

17. On the torture of slaves in classical Athens, see esp. Virginia J. Hunter, *Policing Athens: Social Control in the Attic Lawsuits, 420-320 B. C.* (Princeton: Princeton University Press, 1994), 89–94. Later philosophical treatises on anger clearly depict slaves as the primary victims of household rage. See, e.g., Seneca, *Ira* 2.25.1–4; 3.5.4; Plutarch, *Cohib. ira* 459a; 459d; 459f–460a; 460c; 460f; 461b–c; 462a; 462e; 463a–b.

18. John T. Fitzgerald, "Early Christian Missionary Practice and Pagan Reaction: 1 Peter and Domestic Violence against Slaves and Wives," in *Renewing Tradition: Studies in Honor of James W. Thompson* (ed. Mark W. Hamilton, Thomas H. Olbricht, and Jeffrey Peterson; Princeton Theological Monograph Series; Eugene, Ore.: Pickwick, 2007), 24–44. For the sexual abuse of female slaves, see Carolyn Osiek, "Female Slaves, *Porneia*, and the Limits of Obedience," in Balch and Osiek, *Early Christian Families in Context*, 255–74.

But excluding pure verbal abuse from the inquiry does not do much to limit the scope of the investigation. As in the modern world, the most serious ancient instances of domestic violence were homicides. These included instances of patricide (the killing of one's father), matricide (the killing of one's mother), uxoricide (the killing of one's wife), mariticide (the killing of one's husband),[19] fratricide (the killing of one's brother), sororicide (the killing of one's sister), infanticide (the killing of a child), and parricide (the killing of any near relative). At this point in my investigation, I do not yet have any idea as to the frequency of domestic violence homicides and thus no idea as to how they might relate statistically to our modern situation. At the same time, the contemporary situation is perhaps suggestive. According to statistics compiled by the National Coalition against Violence, in the state of Alabama in 2004, 12 percent of all homicides were the result of domestic violence. Yet most cases of domestic violence in Alabama that year did not lead to death. In that same year, Alabama had 1,969 cases of aggravated domestic assault and 26,599 cases of simple domestic assault. The latter constituted 34 percent of all simple assaults that year. In Alabama in 2004, therefore, slightly more than one-third of all simple assaults were instances of domestic violence.[20] These figures are probably, but by no means certainly, suggestive of reality in both the modern and ancient world as a whole. That is, the vast majority of instances of domestic violence, both now and then, are likely to be instances of simple assault, resulting in blackened eyes, busted lips, and so forth. In some instances, perhaps a tenth or more, the violence will escalate, resulting in cases of aggravated assault and more severe injuries. Most of these assaults, however, will not result in death. Given the differences in modern and ancient medicine, however, the mortality rate in instances of aggravated assault is likely to be much higher for the ancient world than for the modern one.

It is important in this connection to note that not all victims of violence in the home were members of the household. Friends of the family were sometimes victims,[21] and so also were adulterers. The situation that typically

---

19. For the theme of mariticide in ancient Jewish literature, with a focus on the superstition that the husbands of certain women are fated to die, see esp. Mordechai A. Friedman, "Tamar, A Symbol of Life: The 'Killer Wife' Superstition in the Bible and Jewish Tradition," *AJSR* 15 (1990): 23–61.

20. The statistics are available online at http://www.ncadv.org/files/Alabama.pdf.

21. Instances of rage and violence against friends are mentioned by moralists in their discussions on anger, and the house would have been one of the settings in which these occurred. See, e.g., Plutarch, *Cohib. ira* 455b; 455d; 455f; 460e–f; 462a; 464a. Confrontations with enemies also took place within the house; see, e.g., Demosthenes, *Mid.* (= *Or.*

evoked violence against the latter was when the husband caught his wife in bed with another man and attacked him, either injuring or killing him. This circumstance was addressed explicitly by Athenian law, which even granted the right of immediate execution to a man who found his wife in bed with another man.[22] Augustus addressed this same situation in legislation that regulated marriage and adultery, and these laws gave a husband the right to kill his wife's seducer if he caught him in the act in his own home, whether the seducer were a pimp, gladiator, criminal, freedman, or slave.[23] Similar laws existed in many cities,[24] and such laws point to a major difference between the ancient world and the modern one. Whereas the husband's killing of a man who had violated his marriage-bed was often a legally sanctioned act of violence in antiquity, in the modern world it is a homicide for which the killer is typically arrested and prosecuted by the state.

As the differing perspectives on the husband and the man caught in adultery indicate, modern and ancient understandings of domestic violence do not always coincide. Two further examples may be helpful in this regard. First, ancient laws sometimes permitted parents, under certain circumstances, to kill their children, either directly or indirectly. In early imperial Rome, the second section of the Julian Laws passed by Augustus in 18 B.C.E. permitted a father to kill his daughter on the spot if he found her in bed with a man other than her husband. He could do so whether he caught her in his own home or in that of his son-in-law.[25] For most people today, the father's killing of

---

21) 78–79, where the orator accuses Meidias and his brother of bursting into their house and verbally abusing him, his mother, his sister, and the rest of his family.

22. See Lysias, *Or.* 1.30–31. Euphiletus appeals to this law, which is attributed to Dracon or Solon, to justify his killing of Eratosthenes, whom he found in bed with his wife.

23. The Augustan laws dealing with marriage and adultery are the Julian Laws of 18 B.C.E. and the Papia-Poppaean Laws of 9 C.E.; for these laws, see the *Acta Divi Augusti* (Rome: Ex officina typographica R. Academiae italicae, 1945), esp. 113–16, 123, 126. The husband's authority to kill the seducer is restricted to incidents that happen within his own house, not those of his father-in-law. In addition to authorizing the husband to kill his wife's seducer, it obligates him to divorce his wife without delay. If he fails to act against his wife and her lover, he is to be regarded as a pimp and punished accordingly. See also Pseudo-Seneca, *Oct.* 728–739, where Poppaea has a vision in which she sees Nero bury his sword in her husband's throat, though it is disputed whether her former husband Crispinus or her current husband, Nero himself, is meant.

24. See Xenophon, *Hier.* 3.3; and Chariton, *Chaer.* 1.4.10.

25. The consequences for the seduced daughter are thus more severe than for the seduced wife, who was divorced rather than killed. The Julian Laws also permitted the father to kill his daughter's seducer. See note 23 above.

his daughter would be an act of domestic violence, but in imperial Rome it was a legally sanctioned deed and an expression of the father's absolute control over the lives of his children.[26] There are numerous references to this and other legally sanctioned acts of violence against children in declamations and rhetorical treatises from the Roman imperial period,[27] though it is difficult to know to what extent these oratorical works reflect social reality.[28] In any case, for the purposes of this essay, I shall not focus on instances of domestic vio-

---

26. According to Dionysius of Halicarnassus (*Ant. rom.* 2.26–27), Romulus "gave virtually full power to the father over his son, even during his whole life, whether he thought proper to imprison him, to scourge him, to put him in chains and keep him at work in the fields, or to put him to death. ... [Romulus] even gave leave to the father to make a profit by selling his son as often as three times, thereby giving greater power to the father over his son than to the master over his slaves." In a similar way, Roman fathers had the legal right to expose their newborn children; see Jo-Ann Shelton, *As the Romans Did: A Sourcebook in Roman Social History* (2nd ed.; New York: Oxford University Press, 1998), 17. How often Roman fathers exercised these rights is impossible to quantify statistically, but instances of fathers killing or having their adult sons put to death were relatively rare (see, e.g., Dionysius of Halicarnassus, *Ant. rom.* 2.26.6). For a discussion of this notorious *vitae necisque potestas* ("power of life and death"), see esp. William V. Harris, "The Roman Father's Power of Life and Death," in *Studies in Roman Law in Memory of A. Arthur Schiller* (ed. Roger. S. Bagnall and William V. Harris; Columbia Studies in the Classical Tradition 13; Leiden: Brill, 1986), 81–95, and compare Deut 21:18–21.

27. To take only one example, Pseudo-Hermogenes' *On Invention* treats the following three instances of family violence: (1) a father kills his son for suspected incest, with the mother dying of shock (95, 125, 136–37, 163 Rabe); (2) a father kills all three of his sons and asks to be supported at public expense because he has no living son to support him (155–56 Rabe); and (3) a mother kills her son when he deserts his military post (99–100 Rabe). Pseudo-Hermogenes also refers to an instance of fratricide mentioned by Herodotus (425 Rabe). The treatise also deals with the following situations involving the family: (1) parents sell their children into slavery in order to pay tribute (108 Rabe); (2) a father commits suicide after his son refuses to support him, using the sword that his son had given him to earn his own keep as a mercenary (96 Rabe); and (3) a father commits adultery with his son's wife (206, 210 Rabe). The treatise as edited by Hugo Rabe is now available in an English translation by George A. Kennedy, *Invention and Method: Two Rhetorical Treatises from the Hermogenic Corpus* (SBLWGRW 15; Atlanta: Society of Biblical Literature, 2005).

28. Note esp. the complaint of Tacitus regarding classrooms exercises: "The subject matter is far removed from reality and, in addition, the style of delivery used is sheer declamation. And thus it happens that problems which are rarely or never at all debated in the Forum—such as 'The Reward for the Tyrant-Killer' or 'The Alternatives of the Raped Woman' or 'The Remedy for the Plague' or 'A Mother's Incest' or other problems debated every day in the rhetor's school—are discussed and described by students in grandiose language" (*Dial.* 35, trans. Shelton, *As the Romans Did*, 118).

lence homicide, whether legally sanctioned or not, but deal with less severe cases.

A second significant difference in regard to what constitutes domestic violence in the ancient and modern worlds is seen in the antithetical attitudes of ancient parents and many modern ones toward corporal punishment. Although numerous parents in the contemporary world continue to use corporal punishment to discipline their children, many modern parents view it as abusive and criticize their peers who employ this method.[29] In the ancient world, by contrast, there was little or no debate at all. Corporal punishment was not only ubiquitous but even regarded as a sign of love. Parents who failed to administer corporal punishment were viewed as negligent and criticized by their peers for being poor disciplinarians.[30]

Other differences could be mentioned, but these should suffice to indicate that modern perspectives on what constitutes domestic violence are not always the same as those found in the ancient world. And there can be little doubt that the refusal to define certain actions as a form of violence is what allowed them to continue for so long and, as far as the corporal punishment of children is concerned, still to be endorsed and practiced in various parts of society today. One particularly atrocious form of domestic violence that still occurs today, though almost universally condemned, is wife-beating. The second part of this essay examines the phenomenon of wife-beating in the ancient Greek and Roman worlds as well as some of the attitudes toward this atrocity.[31]

---

29. Compare the differing viewpoints of John Rosemond, "Proper Socialization Requires Powerful Love and Equally Powerful Discipline," and Murray A. Straus, "Children Should Never, Ever, Be Spanked No Matter What the Circumstances," in Loseke, Gelles, and Cavanaugh, *Current Controversies on Family Violence*, 131–36 (Rosemond), 137–57 (Straus).

30. See John J. Pilch, "'Beat His Ribs While He Is Young' (Sir 30:12): A Window on the Mediterranean World," *BTB* 23 (1993): 101–13; and John T. Fitzgerald, "Proverbs 3:11–12, Hebrews 12:5–6, and the Tradition of Corporal Punishment," in *Scripture and Traditions: Essays on Early Judaism and Christianity in Honor of Carl R. Holladay* (ed. P. Gray and G. R. O'Day; NovTSup 129; Leiden: Brill, 2008), 291–317.

31. For reasons of space, I do not include here a discussion of Jewish instances of wife-beating. The latter has been treated by Naomi Graetz, *Silence Is Deadly: Judaism Confronts Wifebeating* (Northvale, N.J.: Aronson, 1998). See also her "Rejection: A Rabbinic Response to Wife Beating," in *Gender and Judaism: The Transformation of Tradition* (ed. Tamar M. Rudavsky; New York: New York University Press, 1995), 13–23 (on the issue of wife-beating in the *responsa* literature from 600 C.E. to the modern period); and Abraham J. Twerski, *The Shame Borne in Silence: Spouse Abuse in the Jewish Community* (Pittsburgh: Mirkov, 1996), esp. 43–79.

3. WIFE-BEATING

To illustrate wife-beating, I shall begin by using two passages that are separated by nearly a thousand years. One text is written in Greek, the other in Latin. Taken together, they suggest that not much changed in the treatment of some wives during these thousand years.

The first passage appears in fragment 7 of the Greek iambic poet Semonides of Amorgos, whose date is disputed but who probably flourished in the late sixth century B.C.E.[32] In this fragment of 118 lines, Semonides "expounds the thesis that different types of women were created from different animals and have their qualities."[33] To be precise, he delineates ten types of women, seven of which are made from animals, one from an insect, and two from matter.[34] The animals from which women are made are, respectively, the sow, the vixen (she-fox), the bitch (she-dog), the ass, the weasel (polecat), the mare, and the monkey. One type of woman is made from the bee, and two more types are made from the earth and the sea, respectively.[35] Semonides' general view is stated conspicuously in the final section of the poem: "the

---

32. Although Semonides is typically assigned to the mid-seventh century (so, e.g., by M. L. West, "Semonides," *OCD*, 1383), Thomas K. Hubbard argues convincingly for a late sixth-century date; see his "Elemental Psychology and the Date of Semonides of Amorgos," *AJP* 115 (1994): 175–97.

33. West, "Semonides," 1383. For notes and commentaries on the poem, see David A. Campbell, *Greek Lyric Poetry: A Selection of Early Greek Lyric, Elegiac and Iambic Poetry* (London: Macmillan, 1967), 187–91; Hugh Lloyd-Jones, *Females of the Species: Semonides on Women* (London: Duckworth, 1975), 63–92; Ezio Pellizer and Gennaro Tedeschi, eds., *Semonides: Testimonia et Fragmenta* (Lyricorum Graecorum quae exstant 9; Rome: Edizioni dell'Ateneo, 1990), 119–55; and Martin Steinrück, *Regards sur la femme: Analyse rythmique et interprétation de Sémonide fr. 7 Pellizer-Tedeschi* (Biblioteca di quaderni urbinati di cultura classica 6; Rome: Gruppo Editoriale Internazionale, 1994).

34. The relationship of Semonides frg. 7 and Phocylides frg. 2, which has women derive from four animals (bitch, bee, sow, and mare) is disputed. Those who make Semonides a younger contemporary of Archilochus (seventh century) typically view Phocylides (sixth century) as dependent on Semonides; see, e.g., Campbell, *Greek Lyric Poetry*, 184, 187. Douglas E. Gerber (*Greek Elegiac Poetry: From the Seventh to the Fifth Centuries BC* [LCL 258; Cambridge: Harvard University Press, 1999], 393) is more cautious; although conceding that Phocylides is "perhaps" influenced by Semonides, he also thinks that "both could be drawing on a common tradition." I follow Hubbard, "Elemental Psychology," 193–94, in thinking that Semonides' poem most likely owes its inspiration to Phocylides.

35. The poem was known during the Greco-Roman period and was quoted by both Athenaeus (fl. 200 C.E.) in *Deipn.* 5.179d and Aelian (165/170–230/235 C.E.) in *Nat. an.* 16.24.

greatest plague that Zeus has created is this—women" (96–97).[36] A man who dwells "with a woman never goes through a whole day in good spirits. … And whenever a man seems to be especially enjoying himself in his home, either through divine dispensation or the kindness of men, she finds fault and puts on her helmet for battle" (100, 104–105). The only exception to the rule in this "tirade on women"[37] is the Bee-Wife: "The one who gets her is lucky, since on her alone blame does not settle. … Such women are the best and the most sensible whom Zeus bestows as a favor on men" (83–84, 92–93).

On the other hand, of the ten types, the one from the monkey "is absolutely the worst plague that Zeus has given to men" (71–72). Yet it is not she but the Dog-Wife with her constant yapping that is subjected to domestic violence:

> Another [woman is made][38] from a bitch, ill-tempered, her mother all over again.[39] She wants to hear everything and to know everything, and peering and prowling everywhere she yaps even if she sees no one. *A man can't stop her with threats, nor even if in anger* [χολωθεὶς] *he should knock out her teeth with a stone* [λίθῳ], nor can he by speaking to her soothingly, not even if she happens to be sitting among guests, but she constantly keeps up her yapping which nothing can be done about. (12–20, emphasis added)

As is generally recognized, the poem is mostly satire,[40] with its disparaging comments about women reflecting an attitude that was not uncommon

---

36. All translations of Semonides are those of Douglas E. Gerber, ed. and trans., *Greek Iambic Poetry: From the Seventh to the Fifth Centuries BC* (LCL 259; Cambridge: Harvard University Press, 1999), occasionally modified.

37. The phrase is that of Campbell, *Greek Lyric Poetry*, 184.

38. The rest of the poem makes it clear that God (Zeus) is the one who "sets" or "places" (line 7: ἔθηκ') the soul from the animal into the woman (lines 1, 72, 96). Hubbard, "Elemental Psychology," 189–90, sees here the influence of the Pythagorean doctrine of the transmigration of souls between human bodies and animal bodies.

39. The meaning of the last two words of line 12 (λιτοργόν, αὐτομήτορα) is uncertain, and thus they are variously interpreted; see Campbell, *Greek Lyric Poetry*, 187–88; Lloyd-Jones, *Females of the Species*, 40, 67–68 ("vicious, own daughter of her mother"); Pellizer and Tedeschi, *Semonides*, 97, 123–24 ("ed è ribalda come la madre sua"). Steinrück (*Regards sur la femme*, 8) gives two translations: "L'autre de la chienne méchante, la fille de sa mere," and "L'autre de la chienne méchante, étant elle-même mere." He prefers (29) the latter, viewing αὐτομήτορα as suggestive of a paronomasia (κύων—κυῶν) whereby the dog becomes mother and produces an unceasing flow of words. Compare the rendering of M. L. West, *Greek Lyric Poetry* (Oxford: Clarendon, 1993), 17: "a slut, that by herself gets pregnant."

40. Lloyd-Jones, *Females of the Species*, 22.

in archaic Greek literature.[41] The poem was "designed as a conventional entertainment" and "should be compared to routine jokes about mothers-in-law in the more vulgar kind of modern comedy."[42] Inasmuch as satire and crude humor usually have some grounding in social reality, Semonides may be offering us a glimpse into archaic Greek family life in the last quarter of the sixth century B.C.E. But the light that it sheds is not direct but somewhat refracted.

Although it is certainly credible that an archaic Greek husband may on occasion have knocked out one or more of his wife's teeth, it is highly unlikely that he would have done so using a rock or stone. It is much more likely that he would have used his fist, a piece of wood, a pot, or some other kitchen utensil. The image of the stone derives from a different social reality, namely, that one uses stones to scare off a threatening dog.[43] Inasmuch as the woman here is the Dog-Wife, her husband's use of a stone is precisely what we would expect in the context of the poem. Whereas the stone is thus a literary adaptation designed to meet the needs of the poem, other aspects of the poem, especially the basic sequence of events involving the husband and wife, are quite likely grounded in actual archaic occurrences.[44] In any event, the poem's irritated husband first attempts to silence his wife with threats, and when that does not work, he angrily resorts to physical violence by knocking out her teeth. In striking her mouth, he is attacking the source of the Dog-Wife's incessant "barking."

This same basic pattern—irritation, verbal threat, anger, and physical violence—recurs again and again in numerous texts throughout history, though occasionally the abusive husband omits the threats and simply starts hitting. It appears, for example, in the second passage that merits our attention in regard to wife-beating, namely, Augustine's *Confessions*, which were published about 397 C.E. The passage provides a remarkable glimpse into life in

---

41. West, *Greek Lyric Poetry*, xi, rightly noting, "The theme of women as a plague appeared in other iambographers too." For another archaic Greek denunciation of women, see Hesiod, *Theog.* 589–602.

42. West, *Greek Lyric Poetry*, xi.

43. See, e.g., Homer, *Ody.* 14.29–38: when Odysseus approached the lodge of the swineherd Eumaeus, the latter's dogs began to snarl and "rushed upon him with loud barking" (14.30). When the swineherd saw that Odysseus would soon be mauled and torn limb from limb by the fierce watchdogs (14.32, 37–38), he "called aloud to the dogs, and drove them this way and that with a shower of stones" (14.35–36), saving Odysseus from harm (trans. Murray, LCL).

44. For the idea of knocking out the teeth of a filthy wretch who talks glibly, "like an old kitchen-wife," see Homer, *Ody.* 18.26–29.

Augustine's own childhood home and that of others in the town (Thagaste)[45] in which he grew up. And it shows the strategy that one Christian woman—his mother Monica (= Monnica)—adopted in order to avoid becoming the victim of domestic violence at the hands of her pagan husband Patricius:

> When she [= Monica] reached marriageable age, she was given to a man [named Patricius] and *served [servivit]* him as her lord *[domino]*. She tried to win him for you [= Lord God], speaking to him of you by her virtues through which you made her beautiful, so that her husband loved, respected, and admired her. She bore with his infidelities and never had any quarrel with her husband on this account. For she looked forward to your mercy coming upon him, in hope that, as he came to believe in you, he might become chaste. Furthermore, he was exceptional both for his kindness and for his quick temper [*ira fervidus*]. *She knew that an angry [irato] husband should not be opposed, not merely by anything she did, but even by a word.* Once she saw that he had become calm and quiet, and that the occasion was opportune, she would explain the reason for her action, in case perhaps he had reacted without sufficient consideration. *Indeed, many wives married to gentler [mansuetiores] husbands bore the marks of blows and suffered disfigurement to their faces.* In conversation together they used to complain about their husband's behavior. *Monica,* speaking as if in jest but offering serious advice, used *to blame their tongues.* She would say that since the day when they heard the so-called matrimonial contract [*tabulas ... matrimoniales*] read out to them, they should reckon them to be legally binding documents [*instrumenta*] by which *they had become slaves [ancillae]. She thought they should remember their condition and not proudly withstand their masters [dominos]. The wives were astounded, knowing what a violent [ferocem] husband she had to put up with. Yet it was unheard of, nor was there ever a mark to show, that Patricius had beaten his wife or that a domestic quarrel had caused dissension between them for even a single day.* In intimate talk the wives would ask her the reason. She told them of her plan which I have just mentioned. Those who followed her advice found by experience that

---

45. Thagaste (modern Souk Ahras in Algeria) was a municipality in Numidia at the time of Augustine's birth in 354, about 60 miles to the south of Hippo Regius, where he later served as bishop. For brief treatments of the little that is known of Augustine's birthplace, see Claude Lepelley, *Les cités de l'Afrique romaine au bas-empire* (2 vols.; Paris: Études Augustiniennes, 1979–81), esp. 2:175–84; Allan D. Fitzgerald, "Thagaste," in *Augustine through the Ages: An Encyclopedia* (ed. Allan D. Fitzgerald; Grand Rapids: Eerdmans, 1999), 824–25; and John J. O'Meara, *The Young Augustine: The Growth of St. Augustine's Mind Up to His Conversion* (2nd ed.; New York: Alba House, 2001), 1–14.

they were grateful for it. Those who did not follow her way were treated as subordinate and maltreated. (*Conf.* 9.9.19)⁴⁶

As previously indicated, the same basic pattern appears here as in Semonides' satirical poem. The husband becomes irritated by something that his wife says or does, and that anger increases if she opposes him, until he lashes out and strikes her on the face, sometimes causing a permanent disfigurement. Monica's solution was to adopt a servile manner,⁴⁷ neither criticizing her husband for his philandering ways nor withstanding him when he was irate. Only when he was calm and the moment was right, when there was less risk that he might again erupt in rage, would she venture to explain the words or deeds that had made him angry in the first place. Her strategy was effective in the sense that she was not brutalized in the way that some of the women in her social circle were, yet it came at a high price—the functional loss of her status as a free woman. "The language of domination applied to marriage here evokes … the institution of slavery: the marriage contract [*tabulas matrimoniales*] is equated with the purchase deed [*instrumenta*] of slavery, and wives were to understand that they had been made 'slave women' [*ancillae factae essent*] to their 'masters' [*dominos*]."⁴⁸ Consequently, inasmuch as "the *tabellae matrimoniales* … were the tools by which they [= the wives] had voluntarily been made slaves [*ancillae factae*], so they ought not to show uppityness to their masters [*superbire adversus dominos non oportere*]."⁴⁹ Needless to say, although Monica's strategy may have been necessary as a temporary coping or survival mechanism, it hardly commends itself to most people today as a viable option for any woman in a long-term relationship.⁵⁰

---

46. The translation, slightly modified and with emphases added, is that of Henry Chadwick, *Saint Augustine: Confessions* (New York: Oxford University Press, 1991), 168–69.

47. Silence and deference are typical servile traits, for as one slave says to another, "I, too, am a slave and have not the right to speak freely" (Chariton, *Chaer.* 2.7.3, trans. Goold, LCL). Because frankness of speech (παρρησία) was grounded in freedom, slaves did not possess it; see David E. Fredrickson, "Παρρησία in the Pauline Epistles," in *Friendship, Flattery, and Frankness of Speech* (ed. John T. Fitzgerald; NovTSup 82; Leiden: Brill, 1996), 165–66.

48. Patricia Clark, "Women, Slaves, and the Hierarchies of Domestic Violence: The Family of St. Augustine," in *Women and Slaves in Greco-Roman Culture: Differential Equations* (ed. Sandra R. Joshel and Sheila Murnaghan; London: Routledge, 1998), 109–29, esp. 114.

49. Shaw, "Family in Late Antiquity," 32.

50. I have referred to this strategy as Monica's, but it must be remembered that this is Augustine's depiction of his mother's strategy, not that of Monica herself.

4. Domestic Violence and Ancient Mythology

Although we in the modern world do not always agree with our ancient counterparts on what constitutes domestic violence, we share their recognition that household conflict and the violence frequently associated with it are evils that disrupt and often dissolve families. We also agree with them that it is a problem that has plagued families from the beginning of human history. The problem of domestic violence is reflected in the mythological traditions of both the ancient Hebrews and Greeks, though in strikingly different ways. In ancient Israel, the Yahwist indicated his awareness of the problem by placing the story of Cain and Abel immediately after his account of the fall.[51] Domestic violence in the form of fratricide is thus the first concrete manifestation of life in a fallen world (Gen 4:1–16). As the rest of Genesis makes clear, the problem does not end with the primeval period but continues to afflict all human communities, even the descendants of Abraham. Thus Esau threatens to kill his brother Jacob (27:41–42), and some of Joseph's brothers suggest slaying him (37:20). Consequently, fratricide emerges as the form of domestic violence most likely to threaten the concord of ancient Hebrew families.[52] At the same time, Genesis shows how the ancestors of ancient Israel attempted to find ways to resolve family conflicts in nonviolent ways.[53] These stories are vivid theo-

---

51. In attributing the fall (Gen 3:1–24) and the story of Cain and Abel (4:1–16) to the Yahwist, I am following conventional source analysis of Gen 1–11, which ascribes Gen 2:4b–4:26 to the Yahwist. As is well known, the date and even the existence of the Yahwist are currently being vigorously discussed by scholars of the Hebrew Bible (see, e.g., Thomas B. Dozeman and Konrad Schmid, eds., *A Farewell to the Yahwist? The Composition of the Pentateuch in Recent European Interpretation* [SBLSymS 34; Atlanta: Society of Biblical Literature, 2006]), but it is beyond the scope of this essay to address this issue. Suffice it to note that Joseph Blenkinsopp has recently assigned traditional Yahwist or J material in Gen 1–11 to a putative postexilic, non-Priestly source that was added to Priestly (P) material to form the primeval history. See his "A Post-exilic Lay Source in Genesis 1–11," in *Abschied vom Jahwisten: Die Komposition des Hexateuch in der jüngsten Diskussion* (ed. Jan Christian Gertz, Konrad Schmid, and Markus Witte; BZAW 315; Berlin: de Gruyter, 2002), 49–61.

52. Greek brothers also had severe conflicts with each other from an early period, as Hesiod's complaints about his brother Perses in his *Works and Days* makes clear. Such conflicts are also reflected in Greek mythological traditions, such as those that concern Eteocles and Polyneices, the sons of Oedipus (see esp. Aeschylus, *Seven against Thebes*). The best known attempt by a moralist to encourage brotherly affection is Plutarch's *On Brotherly Love*; for a discussion of this work, see Hans Dieter Betz, "De Fraterno Amore (Moralia 478A – 492D)," in *Plutarch's Ethical Writings and Early Christian Literature* (ed. Hans Dieter Betz; SCHNT 4; Leiden: Brill, 1978), 231–63.

53. See esp. David L. Petersen, "Genesis and Family Values," *JBL* 124 (2005): 5–23.

logical reminders that family violence is part and parcel of life in a fallen world and that no community, group, or nation is immune from the threat it poses.

Greek myth differs significantly from the account provided in Genesis. It does so by placing the strife and violence within the divine realm, thus giving us a portrait of divine domestic violence. Thus in Hesiod's *Theogony*, the story of the genesis of the divine is marked by hostility and violence within the divine family. Sky (Ouranos) hates his children from the time that they are born (155–156) and causes Earth (Gaia) pain by refusing to allow any more children to see the light of day by emerging from her (156–159). But she conspires with their son Kronos, who castrates his father with a jagged sickle (178–181). Once Kronos attains supremacy, however, he turns out to be no better than Sky, for he gobbles down his own children just as soon as they are born (459–460). He is eventually dethroned by his son Zeus, whom Kronos did not succeed in consuming at birth, and he is violently expelled to Tartaros (717–733). Hesiod's origin of the gods is thus a story of intergenerational family conflict between father and son and of collusion between mother and son. As Richard Caldwell has suggestively argued, the Greek theogonic succession myths can be read as psycho-history, as the struggles and strategies of human families projected onto the universe.[54] The Hesiodic myths are much more than those projections, but they are at least that much.

In a similar way, S. Douglas Olson has argued that important aspects of Homer's depiction of the Olympian gods are grounded in the realities of Greek family life in the eighth to fourth centuries B.C.E. and reflect its psychological structure.[55] Of particular interest in this regard is the way in which Hera's relationship with Zeus is depicted in the *Iliad*.[56] On three different occasions he threatens her with physical violence. The first time, when she is seeking to thwart Thetis's request that Zeus favor the Trojans, he tells her, "Now go sit down. Be quiet now. Obey my orders, for the gods, however

---

54. Richard Caldwell, *The Origin of the Gods: A Psychoanalytical Study of Greek Theogonic Myth* (New York: Oxford University Press, 1989). For another attempt to use psychoanalysis to examine intergenerational issues in ancient Greek myth, see Bennett Simon, *Tragic Drama and the Family: Psychoanalytic Studies from Aeschylus to Beckett* (New Haven: Yale University Press, 1988), esp. 1–102. See also Philip E. Slater, *The Glory of Hera: Greek Mythology and the Greek Family* (Boston: Beacon, 1968).

55. S. Douglas Olson, "The Return of the Father," in idem, *Blood and Iron: Stories and Storytelling in Homer's Odyssey* (Mnemosyne; Leiden: Brill, 1995), 161–83. I wish to thank Professor Olson (Department of Classical and Near Eastern Studies, University of Minnesota) for providing me with the bibliographical reference to his essay.

56. On the divine couple, see Carl [Karl] Kerényi, *Zeus and Hera: Archetypal Image of Father, Husband, and Wife* (Bollingen Series 65/5; Princeton: Princeton University Press, 1975).

many Olympus holds, are powerless to protect you when I come to throttle you with my irresistible hands" (1.565–567).[57] The second instance is when Zeus has Iris deliver the following threat to Hera and his daughter Athena as they are on their way to intervene in battle on the Achaeans' behalf: "He'll maim your racers for you, right beneath their yokes, and you two goddesses, he'll hurl you from your chariot, smash your car, and not once in the course of ten slow wheeling years will you heal the wounds his lightning bolt rips open" (8.415–419). The third and final threat of physical violence occurs after Hera has deceived Zeus and persuaded Poseidon to enter the fray on the Achaeans' behalf. Awakening from his sleep to find Hector vomiting blood, he turns to his wife and issues the following threat: "I wouldn't be surprised, my Queen, if you were the first to reap the pernicious whirlwind you have sown—I'll whip you stroke on stroke" (15.16–17).

These are threats that Hera must take seriously because, on some previous occasion, as her husband by way of intimidation reminds her after his third word of warning, Zeus had made good on his threats and physically tortured Hera by hanging her up with chains wrapped around her hands and with anvils on her feet (15.18–21). Apparently it was also on that occasion when Hera's son Hephaestus tried to intervene and stop the abuse, only to suffer violence himself when Zeus grabbed him by the foot and hurled him from Mount Olympus down to Lemnos (1.590–594; see also 15.22–24). That may have been the occasion when Hephaestus became lame.[58] Other sons (Hypnos = Sleep) and daughters (Ate = Ruin) suffer or almost suffer similar fates (14.256–261: Hypnos; 19.126–131: Ate), and Zeus issues various threats to other children in his divine household, such as Athena (8.415–420), with whom he is even angrier than is he with Hera (8.406–408, 420–424). Indeed, Zeus makes clear to all his children at a family meeting that none of them, either individually or collectively, can overcome him (8.1–27). Threats and violence are thus the means that Zeus uses to control his divine family,

---

57. Translations of the *Iliad* are those of Robert Fagles, *Homer, The Iliad* (New York: Penguin, 1990), occasionally modified.

58. The *Iliad* contains two contradictory accounts of Hephaestus being hurled from Olympus. In the first, Zeus hurls him (1.590–594), whereas in the second it is Hera herself (18.394–399) who throws him down into the sea in an apparent attempt to conceal the fact that she had given birth to a lame child. Although Hephaestus's lameness is not explicitly mentioned in conjunction with the first account, the latter was likely etiological and functioned to explain how the god of fire had become lame. For this understanding of the first version of the myth, see Timothy Gantz, *Early Greek Myth: A Guide to Literary and Artistic Sources* (Baltimore: Johns Hopkins University Press, 1993), 75; and Simon Pulleyn, *Homer, Iliad, Book One* (New York: Oxford University Press, 2000), 270–71.

especially his wife, and to retain his preeminent place in his patriarchal household.[59] This is "household management" at its worst, for it is nothing other than domestic terrorism.

Indeed, Katerina Synodinou has argued that there is "an ascending scale in [Zeus's] threats corresponding to the effectiveness of Hera's schemes. … Corresponding to the ascending scale of Zeus's terrorism is Hera's response to it; the more formidable the menaces she is confronted with, the more submissive she becomes." Ultimately, "she is reduced to no less than an instrument of Zeus; she becomes his servant." And she does so because "a paralyzing fear of Zeus or rather of Zeus's violence is the pervasive characteristic of the divine couple's relationship."[60]

The result of such domestic threats and physical violence is the woman's silence and servility. In that respect, Hera the great goddess and Monica the Christian wife are no different. Both are victims who are forced to reckon with the real possibility that their husband's anger may turn his threats into reality, and they both become servile to avoid that dire fate.

Texts not only reflect social reality but also help shape it. That is especially true for texts such as those associated with Homer, who exerted an immense and unparalleled influence on subsequent Greek thought. Homer's depiction of domestic violence was clearly controversial in later times, with critics lambasting him for such scenes as the "binding of Hera" and the "throwing down of Hephaestus." Others defended Homer by either allegorizing these texts[61] or maintaining that they were paradigmatic for human domestic relations. The allegorists explicitly or implicitly conceded that such depictions of household violence were impious,[62] whereas some scholiasts and commentators adopted a far more troubling interpretation. They regarded Zeus's treatment of Hera as paradigmatic for the way in which husbands should treat their wives. To give only one example, the scholia on Zeus's initial threat of physical violence note with approval that Zeus here shows how you should treat women. They

---

59. Zeus is hardly unique is invoking his superior strength as a means of exercising control over others. Hera herself does so to Artemis in *Il.* 21.479–488.

60. Katerina Synodinou, "The Threats of Physical Abuse of Hera by Zeus in the Iliad," *Wiener Studien* 100 (1987): 13–22, esp. 15 and 17.

61. See, e.g., the way in which Heraclitus allegorizes these scenes in an attempt to defend Homer against criticism (see *Hom. Prob.* 25.12 and 40.1–12 for the binding of Hera, *Hom. Prob.* 26.1–16 for the throwing down of Hephaestus).

62. Heraclitus's comment on the "conspiracy against Zeus" (Homer, *Il.* 1.399–406) is typical of his perspective as a whole: "There is only one remedy for this impiety: to show that the myth is an allegory" (*Hom. Prob.* 22.1). The translation is that of Donald A. Russell and David Konstan, ed. and trans., *Heraclitus: Homeric Problems* (SBLWGRW 14; Atlanta: Society of Biblical Literature, 2005), 41.

compare Hector's exhortation in 6.490: "Go therefore back to our house, and take up your own work" and add: "Zeus now beats her off with words but at other times he also chastises her in action, *the poet maybe teaching that a woman would be something unbearable if not dealt with disdainfully.*"[63]

5. Final Comments and Conclusions

The results of this initial probe are far from conclusive, but they are suggestive for what more detailed research may uncover. The evidence examined here suggests that ancient families, like our own, were often battle fronts rather than centers of refuge. The primary victims of domestic terrorism were household slaves whose words or deeds had angered their masters, both male and female, and who had to pay for their offenses with their bodies (Demosthenes, *Andr.* [= *Or.* 22].55). Wives were also frequently victims, and to survive physically they were often forced to become servile in their attitudes and actions. One of the major deterrents to wife-beating was the wife's birth family, to which the husband would have to answer if he either battered his wife or abused her in other ways. And the more geographically proximate the wife's family, the greater the deterrence the spouse's family would likely have posed. Having a father-in-law and/or brothers-in-law living practically next door was not a setting that was conducive to spousal abuse, especially if the in-laws happened to be bigger, stronger, and more numerous than the abusive husband. Hera's plight was that no one, either individually or collectively, was sufficiently powerful to save her from Zeus.[64] Hephaestus had tried once to do so, but to no avail. So, recognizing his own impotence, he can only regretfully advise her, "Patience, mother! Grieved as you are, bear up, or as precious as you are [to me], I will have to see you beaten right before my eyes" (*Il.* 1.586–588).

---

63. Gertrud Lindberg, "Hera in Homer to Ancient and Modern Eyes: The Nagging Wife, the Evil Seductress, or the Forceful Goddess in the Struggle for Power?" in *Greek and Latin Studies in Memory of Cajus Fabricius* (ed. Sven-Tage Teodorsson; Göteborg: Acta Universitatis Gothoburgensis, 1990), 65–80, here 70 (emphasis added).

64. The attempt by Hera, Poseidon, and Athena to put Zeus in chains failed when Thetis summoned Briareus to come to his aid (*Il.* 1.399–406). For discussion of this strange story, which is probably a Homeric creation rather than a traditional myth, see Pulleyn, *Iliad I*, 222–25. For treatments of this infamous story by later allegorists, see Cornutus, *Theol.* 17 (= Carl Lang, ed., *Cornuti theologiae graecae compendium* [Bibliotheca scriptorum Graecorum et Romanorum Teubneriana; Leipzig: Teubner, 1881], 27); and Heraclitus, *Hom. Prob.* 21–25.

Limitations of space preclude any treatment here of domestic violence within the sphere of early Christianity. As the story of Monica shows, wife-beating was a common phenomenon in Augustine's home town, and there is no reason to think that Thagaste was in any way exceptional in this regard. John Chrysostom was well aware of the problem of domestic violence, even in Christian homes, and tried to deal with it pastorally.[65] In addressing this issue, he was not dealing with a new and recent problem for Christians but with one that stretches back to the first century.[66] Sadly, it remains a problem today for all communities of faith as well as the world at large.

---

65. Joy A. Schroeder, "John Chrysostom's Critique of Spousal Violence," *JECS* 12 (2004): 413–42.

66. Although not usually recognized, Monica's strategy is an instantiation of the counsel given wives in 1 Peter, a writing that is directly concerned with the domestic abuse of both household servants and wives (1 Pet 2:18–3:6). See n. 18 above.

Animosity against Jewish and Pagan Magic in the Acts of the Apostles

Rainer G. H. Reuter

1. Preliminary Remark

When the first Harry Potter books were published in Germany, they were not undisputed in Protestant congregations. The discussion was not so much about the literary qualities of the stories but around the main theme in those books: magic. In certain conservative Protestant circles, people advised not to buy or read those books, since they were said to deal with dangerous matters.

The discussion started anew when the first Harry Potter film came to German cinemas. The fact that the whole story is fictional did not play any role in that argument. Readers of the book and spectators of the film formed two camps. One camp consisted of people who felt animosity toward those films and books, because they thought that both media were dealing with perilous if not satanic things. The other camp consisted of those who had no problem at all with the subject and saw these stories as what they were meant to be—as entertainment.

If the conservative camp of Harry Potter enemies was fighting with a straw man of satanic magic in a children's fiction book, in the book of Acts the early Christian missionaries actually had to fight "real" contemporary magic. Two camps can be seen there as well, except that the camps were formed from opponents and supporters of magic, and it was—according to Luke's depiction—the supporters of magic who were on the aggressive side fighting against Christianity. On their turn the missionaries reacted to such hostility, but without any concrete acts of animosity in the sense of committing acts of violence. In these conflicts Christian missionaries are always depicted as superior to the magicians against whom they struggle. Luke's message in all these stories is rather clear: magic cannot compete with the practice of Christian faith.

With this message, the author of the Lukan works shows clearly his animosity against Jewish and pagan magic.[1] It may be interesting to study how it is worked out in those stories.

2. Christians and Magic in Luke Acts

2.1. Philip and Peter versus Simon the Magician (Acts 8:4–25)

Luke's first story in Acts dealing with magic contrasts the Christian missionaries Philip and Peter with the magician Simon. In this story, Luke first of all[2] depicts Philip's missionary success (Acts 8:5–8). Philip, one of the seven from Acts 6:5, came to a Samarian town, most probably Samaria itself,[3] preaching Christ (8:5). His ministry there gained much attention by the Samaritan

---

1. Since "there is no generally accepted definition of magic in Greco-Roman culture" (Everett Ferguson, *Backgrounds of Early Christianity* [3rd ed.; Grand Rapids: Eerdmans, 2003], 227), my own definition needs to be given here. When I talk in this paper about magic, I take it as a deliberate human action to influence the environment with the help of supernatural powers by applying certain formula and actions (see Ferguson, *Backgrounds of Early Christianity*, 229). The author of the Lukan works labels Simon the magician and Bar Jesus/Elymas as magicians by using the terms μάγοι (Acts 13:6, 8), μαγεία (8:11), and μαγεύων (8:9). The magicians in Acts 19 are described as a type of ἐξορκιστής who is doing his deeds with the help of spells (19:13). All these men are similar in that they do their acts deliberately and use their power in a controlled way. This is different from the female slave in Acts 16:16, who is said to be possessed by a πνεῦμα πύθωνα that leads to certain mantic effects (μαντεύομαι). Obviously, she does not do this deliberately and is not in control of her actions, nor does she use spells. Obviously driven by some spirit, she follows Paul and his travel companions, proclaiming that they are servants of the highest God and teaching a way of salvation. The author of Acts seems to understand this as a pitiable gift that is used by the slave's masters to make money (16:19). If anyone, it is only the masters who could be reckoned as magicians, but Luke depicts them mainly as greedy for profit. Therefore, this story will not be taken into account here.

2. The structure of the story is well-depicted by Dietrich Alex Koch, "Geistbesitz und Wundermacht: Erwägungen zur Tradition und zur lukanischen Redaktion in Act 8,5–25," *ZNW* 77 (1986): 67. We have two larger sections: Acts 8:5–13, focusing on the work of Philip; and 8:14–25, focusing on the work of Peter and John in Samaria. The first section has two smaller parts: 8:5–8, giving a general overview of Philip's activities; and 8:9–13, narrating the founding of the Samarian congregation. The second section has three subsections: 8:14–17, on the apostles' gift of the spirit; 8:18–24, on the conflict with Simon; and 8:25, a concluding verse about the apostles' mission in Samaria.

3. See Jacob Jervell, *Die Apostelgeschichte* (KEK 3; Göttingen: Vandenhoeck & Ruprecht, 1998), 260.

crowds (8:6), especially because of the healings and exorcisms he practiced. This "interest" preceded the later conversion.[4]

In the following part of the story, Philip's opposite is introduced, Simon the magician. His actions are described as μαγεύων (8:9) and as μαγεία (8:11).[5] Simon's magic is depicted as very effective, as the Samaritans fully bought into it (8:10: ἀπὸ μικροῦ ἕως μεγάλου) before Philip arrived there.[6] The author himself gives a reason for this situation in a short commentary: Simon has been in Samaria for a long time (ἱκανῷ χρόνῳ),[7] and with his magic he had cast his spell over the people.

According to Acts 8:9, Simon called himself "a great one" (λέγων εἶναί τινα ἑαυτὸν μέγαν), while the Samaritans according to Acts 8:10 called him "the power of God" (δύναμις τοῦ θεοῦ), which is also called "the Great" (ἡ καλουμένη μεγάλη). If we compare these claims with those rejected by Paul in Act 14:11-12, it becomes rather clear that Luke depicts Simon as "exalt[ing] himself in a most damning and contemptible way."[8] If these statements really report historical facts, Simon obviously has understood himself to be a kind of incarnation of the highest deity[9] or at least as an instrument of heavenly power. However, Luke mainly emphasizes Simon's role as a miracle worker and magician, though he does not explicitly explain what exactly this magic was and which concrete deeds Simon did.

---

4. See Charles K. Barrett, *A Critical and Exegetical Commentary on the Acts of the Apostles* (2 vols.; ICC 34; Edinburgh: T&T Clark, 1994-98), 1:403; in contrast to Jervell, *Apostelgeschichte*, 260, who takes this interest already as an act of conversion. But since conversions are explicitly mentioned only in v. 12 (see Barrett, *Critical and Exegetical Commentary*, 1:404), the "joy" in 8:8 also must be interpreted as joy about the healings and not as joy about salvation, as Jervell takes it.

5. According to Charles K. Barrett ("Light on the Holy Spirit from Simon Magus [Acts 8,4-25]," in *Les Actes des Apôtres: Traditions, rédaction, théologie* [ed. Jacob Kremer; BETL 48; Leuven: Leuven University Press 1979], 291), Luke understands such a man as follows: "The magus makes money by trafficking in the supernatural." See also Barrett, *Critical and Exegetical Commentary*, 1:406.

6. With regard to the wording, see Acts 26:22. The phrase is taken over from the LXX. See also Gen 19:11; 1 Sam 5:9; 30:2, 19; 2 Kgs 23:2; 25:26; Jdt 13:4, 13; 1 Macc 5:45; Isa 22:5, 24; Jer 6:13; 38:34; 49:1, 8; 51:12; Barn. 1:4.

7. In the New Testament this expression occurs only in the Lukan works: Luke 8:27; 20:9; 23:8; Acts 8:11; 14:3; 27:9.

8. See Susan R. Garrett, *The Demise of the Devil: Magic and Demonic in Luke's Writings* (Minneapolis: Fortress. 1989), 67.

9. See Jervell, *Apostelgeschichte*, 261 n. 799; Jürgen Roloff, *Die Apostelgeschichte* (2nd ed.; NTD 5; Göttingen: Vandenhoeck & Ruprecht, 1988), 134; and Hans Conzelmann, *Die Apostelgeschichte* (2nd ed.; HNT 7; Tübingen: Mohr Siebeck, 1972), 60, referring to Justin Martyr (*Apol.* 1.26.3) and Irenaeus (*Haer.* 1.23.1).

After introducing the two main figures of this story, Luke brings them together in Acts 8:12–13. Already in 8:12, where Simon is not mentioned at all, Luke built up a contrast between these two persons. Simon's long-lasting magical activity (8:11), which only caused a certain interest, is contrasted there by the immediate and complete conversion of the Samaritans—only by Philip's preaching.[10] Concerning its content, this preaching is characterized as about "the rule of God and the name of Jesus Christ" (περὶ τῆς βασιλείας τοῦ θεοῦ καὶ τοῦ ὀνόματος Ἰησοῦ Χριστοῦ). What Philip preaches is according to Luke so convincing that not only all men and women wanted to become Christians (8:12),[11] but also Simon himself came to faith and was baptized (8:13a). By telling this, Luke clearly emphasizes the superiority of Christian proclamation over magical practices[12] and also the superiority of the Christian missionaries over Simon himself.

In the following verses, Luke no longers mentions Simon as a miracle worker or magician, although he seems to give hints that Simon had not given up all thoughts about magic. Luke comments on Simon's baptism briefly in 8:13 by mentioning that Simon started following Philip because he saw the great signs and miracles Philip did and that he was excited about them (8:13b: θεωρῶν τε σημεῖα καὶ δυνάμεις μεγάλας γινομένας ἐξίστατο). Luke most probably wants to express that Simon took Philip's signs and miracles as a more effective and powerful magic than he himself had once practiced. If this is right, Luke seems to suggest that Simon began to follow Philip only because he wanted to discover *his* magic.[13] According to the antecedent context (Acts 8:6–7), we have to interpret Philip's powerful deeds as exorcisms and healings.[14]

As we can see in this story, Simon and Philip are directly contrasted by the author of Acts, and this contrast has the goal of depicting the superiority of Philip over the magician Simon.[15] This becomes evident when we briefly look at the author's commentary in Acts 8:13. There two words are taken up

---

10. See Barrett, *Critical and Exegetical Commentary*, 1:408.

11. See Acts 8:14: Samaria accepted the word of God. Luke obviously thinks here of a more or less complete conversion of the Samaritans to Christianity.

12. See, e.g., Charles S. C. Williams, *A Commentary on the Acts of the Apostles* (Harper's New Testament Commentaries; New York: Harper, 1957), 116; Conzelmann, *Apostelgeschichte*, 61; Garrett, *Demise of the Devil*, 69; and Jervell, *Apostelgeschichte*, 262.

13. So, among others, Roloff, *Apostelgeschichte*, 135; and especially Garrett, *Demise of the Devil*, 69: "The reader is thereby encouraged to conclude that, although Simon did believe Philip, his motives for conversion were wrong."

14. See Barrett, *Critical and Exegetical Commentary*, 1:409.

15. See the overview in Gerd Lüdemann, *Das frühe Christentum nach den Traditionen der Apostelgeschichte: Ein Kommentar* (Göttingen: Vandenhoeck & Ruprecht, 1987), 101.

that appeared before in Simon's characterization in Acts 8:9–11, and they are taken up for the purpose of contrast. According to Acts 8:9–10, Simon was "a great one" or "the great power of God" (δύναμις τοῦ θεοῦ ἡ καλουμένη μεγάλη). In Acts 8:13b it is now Philip who practices *great* signs and *powerful* miracles (σημεῖα καὶ δυνάμεις μεγάλας). This wording is surely not accidental, since Luke normally uses the phrase "signs and deeds" (σημεῖα καὶ τέρατα).[16] The lexeme δύναμις is applied to miraculous deeds only in Acts 2:22, where it is added to the phrase "signs and deeds" in order to characterize the miracles of Jesus. Also the use of the adjective μέγας is hardly accidental, since it is seldom applied to miracles in the Lukan works. In Acts 6:8 the author uses it with regard to Stephen, who did "great wonders and signs" (τέρατα καὶ σημεῖα μεγάλα). By using in his commentary in Acts 8:13b the exact words he used earlier to describe Simon, Luke obviously contrasts Philip's deeds initiated by the Holy Spirit with the magical actions of Simon. But the superiority of the Christian gospel to magic is also depicted in the fact that wonders and miracles attracted not only the Samarian people, as it was the case with Simon also, but now even the "great" magician himself. The use of the verb ἐξίστημι in verses 11 and 13 is caused by a clear intention of outbidding. Christian preaching, attested by signs, is superior to magic, since it moves the people faster, obviously because it is more convincing.

Continuing the story (8:14–17), Luke writes about how the Samaritans received the Holy Spirit through two apostles sent from Jerusalem, Peter and John. The gift of the Spirit was imparted by prayers (8:15) and laying hands on a person (8:17). Exactly at this stage Simon is mentioned again. He seems to be even more astonished by what the Jerusalem apostles did than he was before by Philip's deeds. He is so impressed that he wants to buy this gift of giving the Spirit (8:18–19)—probably in order to use it commercially.[17] Luke may well suggest that Simon sees the gift of giving the Spirit as a unique form of magic.[18] Simon's wish, then, was to have the same authority (ἐξουσία) as the apostles had and to be able to provide for the reception of the Spirit according to his own will (8:19b: ἵνα ᾧ ἐὰν ἐπιθῶ τὰς χεῖρας λαμβάνῃ πνεῦμα ἅγιον). This wish was interpreted by Peter as an act of wickedness.[19]

---

16. The combination of the lexemes σημεῖα and τέρατα occurs in Acts 2:22, 43; 4:30; 5:12; 6:8; 7:36; 14:3; 15:12.

17. See Garrett, *Demise of the Devil*, 70; Barrett, *Critical and Exegetical Commentary*, 1:413.

18. See Ernst Haenchen, *Die Apostelgeschichte* (7th ed.; KEK 3; Göttingen: Vandenhoeck & Ruprecht, 1977), 295; Roloff, *Apostelgeschichte*, 136.

19. See 8:22: μετανόησον οὖν ἀπὸ τῆς κακίας σου ταύτης.

Having uttered this wish, Simon was addressed by Peter as someone serving Satan[20] and then was threatened with a formula similar to a curse (8:20).[21] According to it, he was to be excluded from every share in the word of God (8:21)[22] if he did not repent (8:22).[23] Threatened in this way, Simon begged the apostles for intercession to stop the curse (8:24).[24] Again the author of Acts here clearly underlines the superiority of the apostles,[25] so Simon's repentance is presupposed though not narrated.[26] Whether Simon finally repented or not is obviously not a matter of interest for this narrative.

This raises a question about what function this narrative might have. The story clearly invites the reader to observe, on the one hand, the difference between Christian miracles and the magic of the Jewish or pagan environment[27] and, on the other hand, the opposition of God's power and demonic magic.[28] To do this, Luke constructs a direct opposition between the main figures on both sides: Philip and Peter on the one side and Simon on the other. The apostles have the authority to give the gift of the Spirit, the power of God (Luke 24:49; Acts 1:8), while Simon falsely claimed to be the power of God. But they are depicted as even more powerful. The apostles also have the

---

20. See Garrett, *Demise of the Devil*, 71–72.

21. Haenchen, *Apostelgeschichte*, 295, referring to Otto Bauernfeind, *Die Apostelgeschichte* (THKNT 5; Leipzig: Deichert, 1939), 127. The phrases may be derived from the Greek Old Testament, since a similar one is used in Dan 2:5 Theod. See also Garrett, *Demise of the Devil*, 70; Barrett, *Critical and Exegetical Commentary*, 1:414.

22. According to Haenchen (*Apostelgeschichte*, 295) and Roloff (*Apostelgeschichte*, 136), this is a formula expressing excommunication, but in the present context it clearly functions as a formula of condemnation. See also Jervell, *Apostelgeschichte*, 265.

23. According to Conzelmann (*Apostelgeschichte*, 62), this sentence is directed to the reader and functions as a general instruction concerning magic.

24. According to Gustav Stählin (*Die Apostelgeschichte* [7th ed.; NTD 5, Göttingen: Vandenhoeck & Ruprecht, 1980], 125), Luke's depiction indicates that Simon still thinks in categories of magic. He takes the apostles' prayer for a "magic prayer" (Zaubergebet) and does not beg for forgiveness but begs to avert the damage announced by Peter: "It is the fear of the stronger magician and the more powerful magic."

25. See Hans-Josef Klauck, *Magie und Heidentum in der Apostelgeschichte des Lukas* (SBS 167; Stuttgart: Katholisches Bibelwerk, 1996), 34. See also Jervell, *Apostelgeschichte*, 266, who states that Simon begs for the apostles' prayer because it is stronger than his own.

26. See Jervell, *Apostelgeschichte*, 266; Barrett, *Critical and Exegetical Commentary*, 1:418. Manuscript D and the middle-Egyptian tradition obviously understood it in that way and added that Simon regretted and associated himself with the apostles.

27. See Gerhard Schneider, *Die Apostelgeschichte* (2 vols.; HTKNT 5.1–2; Freiburg: Herder, 1980–82), 1:484; and Conzelmann, *Apostelgeschichte*, 62.

28. See Haenchen, *Apostelgeschichte*, 298; Conzelmann, *Apostelgeschichte*, 62.

power to punish and condemn the great magician, a power Simon could not oppose with anything.

By underlining the superiority of Christian preachers in this way, Luke clearly expresses the inferiority of magic, and by depicting Simon "as a satanic figure,"[29] Luke even says a bit more. He rates magic as dangerous and those who practice it as enemies of God.

2.2. Paul versus Bar Jesus/Elymas (Acts 13:4–12)

Similar to the narrative about the conflict between Philip and Simon, Luke also narrates about a clash between Paul and a magician. Luke places this story in the frame of the so-called first missionary journey, where Paul— here still under the name Saul—together with Barnabas is an ambassador of the congregation in Antioch. Their first stop on this journey is the island of Cyprus (Acts 13:4–12). According to the Lukan depiction, Saul and Barnabas first worked in the city of Salamis (13:5), then they continued, preaching[30] through the whole island (13:6a), and finally reached Paphos, where the headquarters of the governor were located.

In Paphos Paul had to struggle against a miracle worker with the name Bar Jesus (13:6). Luke himself calls him a magician (μάγος) and additionally a Jewish[31] false prophet. By this addition, on the one hand, the negative connotation of the word μάγος[32] is clearly emphasized. On the other hand, this expression produces a direct contrast between Bar Jesus and Saul, since Saul is in Acts 13:1 himself called prophet.[33] This contrast is even stronger, since Bar Jesus is depicted as a person not serving God but the devil,[34] while Saul is chosen and sent by the Holy Spirit (Act 13:2). In Acts 13:8, the magician

---

29. See Garrett, *Demise of the Devil*, 75.
30. See Barrett, *Critical and Exegetical Commentary*, 1:612.
31. The art of Jewish magicians was famous. See Kirsopp Lake and Henry J. Cadbury, *English Translation and Commentary* (vol. 4 of *The Acts of the Apostles*, part 1 of *The Beginnings of Christianity*; ed. F. J. Foakes Jackson and Kirsopp Lake; London: McMillan, 1933), 143, referring to Pliny, *Nat.* 30.2.
32. This connotation exists already in the early Greek language. See Arthur Darby Nock, "Paul and the Magus," in *Additional Notes to the Commentary* (vol. 5 of *The Acts of the Apostles*, part 1 of *The Beginnings of Christianity*; ed. F. J. Foakes Jackson and Kirsopp Lake; London: McMillan, 1933), 165–66, 181–82; Gerhard Delling, "μάγος, μαγεία, μαγεύω," *TDNT* 4:356–59; Conzelmann, *Apostelgeschichte*, 81.
33. This contrast is correctly emphasized by Stählin, *Apostelgeschichte*, 176. See also Barrett, *Critical and Exegetical Commentary*, 1:613.
34. For detail, see Garrett, *Demise of the Devil*, 80–81; see also Acts 13, esp. v. 10.

is said to bear also the Greek name Elymas,[35] which is according to Luke the translation of the word "magician."[36]

Although Luke does not tell us exactly what kind of magical practices Bar Jesus/Elymas performed, the expression "false prophet" points to a mantic activity.[37] Bar Jesus is said to be permanently in the entourage[38] of the proconsul (ἀνθύπατος) Sergius Paulus (13:7a), most probably as a paid astrologer of the court,[39] who at the same time claims to know the magic formula to banish the force of fate.[40] Exactly at the moment Sergius Paulus showed interest in Paul's and Barnabas's preaching, Elymas turned against the Christian missionaries—most probably in order not to lose his influence on the governor. Different from Simon in Acts 8, Elymas exercised active resistance in trying to turn away the governor from Christian faith (13:8: ἀνθίστατο δὲ αὐτοῖς..., ζητῶν διαστρέψαι τὸν ἀνθύπατον ἀπὸ τῆς πίστεως).

In the following miracle of punishment, Paul—this name is introduced in Acts 13:9—took the lead.[41] He addressed the magician directly as "son of the devil" (υἱὲ διαβόλου),[42] sentenced him, and spoke the words that caused the punishment.[43] Paul's look mentioned in 13:9 most probably should be regarded as a part of the act of miracle working,[44] as is the cry "the hand of

---

35. According to Diodorus Siculus 20.17.1, this is a Libyan name. See Conzelmann, *Apostelgeschichte*, 81.

36. See, e.g., Haenchen, *Apostelgeschichte*, 383; Lüdemann, *Apostelgeschichte*, 155; Klauck, *Magie und Heidentum*, 63; Jervell, *Apostelgeschichte*, 346. Barrett (*Critical and Exegetical Commentary*, 1:616) takes this "translation" simply as a Lukan mistake.

37. See Barrett, "Light on the Holy Spirit," 289: "he has been deceitfully claiming prophetic powers and making money out of them."

38. See Haenchen, *Apostelgeschichte*, 382; Jervell, *Apostelgeschichte*, 346.

39. See Barrett, "Light on the Holy Spirit," 289.

40. Haenchen, *Apostelgeschichte*, 382; Barrett, "Light on the Holy Spirit," 289. A similar figure is the Jewish magician Atomos, being part of the entourage of the procurator Felix (see Josephus, *Ant.* 20.142), or Trasyllus the astrologer of Tiberius (see Nock, "Paul and the Magus," 183).

41. This is correctly emphasized by Henry J. Cadbury, *The Making of Luke-Acts* (London: SPCK, 1968), 225; Barrett, *Critical and Exegetical Commentary*, 1:616.

42. This is most probably a conscious contrast to the magician's name Bar Jesus (= son of Jesus).

43. This announcement can be understood entirely as a curse. See Haenchen, *Apostelgeschichte*, 385; Conzelmann, *Apostelgeschichte*, 82; Barrett, *Critical and Exegetical Commentary*, 1:617.

44. See Gottfried Schille, *Die Apostelgeschichte des Lukas* (THKNT 5; Berlin: Evangelische Verlagsanstalt, 1983), 288, referring to Acts 3:4; see also Alfons Weiser, *Die Apostelgeschichte* (2 vols.; ÖTK 5.1–2; Gütersloh: Mohn; Würzburg: Echter, 1985), 2:318, referring to Philostratus, *Vit. Ap.* 4.20.

the Lord is against you," which is an Old Testament formula of curse.⁴⁵ The punishment itself followed immediately (13:11b: παραχρῆμα), and the magician was left helpless. Although the punishment was meant to be only for a while, this does not mean that it was only a call to repentance.⁴⁶ The miracle was a powerful act showing the consequences that resistance against "the ways of the Lord"⁴⁷ had.

At the end of the story, Luke briefly notes that the proconsul became a believer (v. 12). This happened, according to Luke, "after he had seen the miracle" (τότε ἰδὼν ὁ ἀνθύπατος τὸ γεγονὸς ἐπίστευσεν).⁴⁸ The proconsul was now impressed by the Christian doctrine (ἐπὶ τῇ διδαχῇ τοῦ κυρίου). This final remark provides a close connection between the miracle of punishment and Christian doctrine. It points out a clear difference between a miracle of the Lord and non-Christian magical acts.⁴⁹ Christian miracles underline and confirm Christian preaching, while the magician does his magical acts on behalf of himself.

As happened in Acts 8, Luke also in this story depicts the superiority of Christian missionaries over non-Christian magicians. The magician was unable to prevent the proconsul from turning to the Christian faith,⁵⁰ and he was also unable to protect himself from the punishment brought upon him. All in all, Luke presents this magician as a person serving Satan and resisting God's ways. On the other hand, Paul, as well as Philip and Peter in Acts 8, is depicted as a powerful man who, being empowered by God, is able to fight against such satanic magic.⁵¹

Compared to Acts 8, the resistance of the magician is clearly increased, and because of that also the response of the Christian missionaries. It may well be that this is a literary technique. It enables the author to show the reader that fighting against contemporary magic is not at all a peripheral or harmless matter but a fight against evil, which is connected to the fading rule of Satan. At the same time, the author offers the clear message that evil and magic are going to be defeated by Christ and his power.⁵²

---

45. Schille, *Apostelgeschichte*, 288–89, referring to 1 Sam 7:13. However, it should be noted that the wording of LXX 1 Sam 12:15 is closer to the wording in Acts.
46. So Roloff, *Apostelgeschichte*, 199. According to Barrett (*Critical and Exegetical Commentary*, 1:617), it was meant to *lead* to repentence.
47. See Acts 13:10: οὐ παύσῃ διαστρέφων τὰς ὁδοὺς τοῦ κυρίου τὰς εὐθείας.
48. See Barrett, *Critical and Exegetical Commentary*, 1:618.
49. See Lüdemann, *Apostelgeschichte*, 156; Stählin, *Apostelgeschichte*, 178.
50. See Williams, *Commentary on the Acts of the Apostles*, 156.
51. See ibid.
52. See Conzelmann, *Apostelgeschichte*, 81–82.

2.3. The Danger of Magic (Acts 19:11–20)

The third and last story dealing with magicians we find in Acts 19:11–20. This passage is a literary composition consisting of three parts.[53] In this section Acts 19:11–12 has the function of an exposition[54] to the burlesque following in 19:13–17, while 19:18–20 is a kind of epilogue depicting the reaction of the Ephesians to the event narrated in 19:13–17.

In the exposition of the story, Paul is depicted as a successful instrument[55] of God's power (19:11). He radiates so much of this heavenly power that even clothes he had worn on his skin[56] caused healings.[57] Although Luke's description in Acts 19:12 strongly verges on magic,[58] the author leaves no doubt that it is God himself who caused these healings.[59] Paul did not do these miracles on his own or in his own authority, but only as an instrument by which God's power became perceptible. This is, according to Luke, the crucial difference

---

53. This is correctly emphasized by Roloff, *Apostelgeschichte*, 285.
54. See Conzelmann, *Apostelgeschichte*, 120.
55. The phrase διὰ τῶν χειρῶν does not indicate a magic touch with the aim of establishing a flow of power (so, among others, Schille, *Apostelgeschichte*, 379, referring to Lake and Cadbury, *English Translation and Commentary*, 239) but simply says that this person is a kind of medium through whom God acts (see Garrett, *Demise of the Devil*, 66; Jervell, *Apostelgeschichte*, 481; Barrett, *Critical and Exegetical Commentary*, 2:907). The phrase is taken over from the LXX (see Gen 30:35; 32:17; 39:4, 22–23; 49:24; Lev 10:11; Josh 17:4; 1 Kgs 10:13; 2 Kgs 14:27; 1 Chr 11:3; 24:19; 26:28; 29:5, 8; 2 Chr 7:6; 13:8; 23:18; 24:11; 26:11; 28:5; 31:15; 34:14; 35:4, 6; Jdt 13:14; 1 Macc 5:62; Wis 12:6; Jer 30:4; Ezek 27:21; 30:10; 37:19; 38:17) and is one of Luke's favorite phrases, occurring in the plural as well as the singular form (Acts 2:23; 5:12, 7:25; 11:30; 14:3; 15:23; 19:11, 26; in the rest of the New Testament only in Mark 6:2). In this phrase the noun "hand" functions as *pars pro toto* for the whole person (see Walter Bauer, Barbara Aland, and Kurt Aland, *Griechisch-deutsches Wörterbuch zu den Schriften des Neuen Testaments und der frühchristlichen Literatur* [6th ed.; Berlin: de Gruyter 1988], 1755).
56. It is not exactly clear what kinds of clothes are meant here. The lexeme σιμικίνθιον is a Latin loanword (*semicictium*) that usually designates an apron worn by workers (Bauer, Aland, and Aland, *Griechisch-deutsches*, 1501), while σουδάριον, also a Latin loanword (*sudarium*), comes nearer to our handkerchief (Bauer, Aland, and Aland, *Griechisch-deutsches*, 1517).
57. A similar motif is Peter's healing shadow in Acts 5:15. See also Luke 8:44, where the permanently menstruating woman (different from Mark 5:27) does not touch Jesus' garment but only the edge or a tassel.
58. This is correctly emphasized by Walter Schmithals, *Die Apostelgeschichte des Lukas* (ZBK 3.2; Zürich: Theologischer Verlag Zürich, 1982), 176.
59. See Klauck, *Magie und Heidentum*, 113; Jervell, *Apostelgeschichte*, 481.

between Christian missionaries and Jewish or pagan magicians.[60] At the same time, these verses function as a contrasting foil[61] to the following narrative in which magicians try to use the name of Jesus as part of an incantation.

As in the preceding stories dealing with the confrontation between the Christian message and ancient magic, in Acts 19 it is again Jewish men who make use of magic. Luke depicts them as traveling miracle workers (19:13: τινες ... τῶν περιερχομένων Ἰουδαίων) who professionally practiced exorcisms.[62] Obviously, they were so impressed by Paul's success in healing that they tried by themselves to use the name of Jesus to cause similar effects.[63] As in the Simon story, Christian miracles are mistaken as magic.[64] The exorcists used the name of Jesus as part of an incantation that Luke reports in Acts 19:13: ὁρκίζω ὑμᾶς τὸν Ἰησοῦν ὃν Παῦλος κηρύσσει.[65] This incantation is reminiscent of an utterance of demons that is reported in Mark 5:7 and that was linguistically changed by Luke in the parallel verse Luke 8:29.

---

60. So correctly Roloff, *Apostelgeschichte*, 285.

61. So, among others, Conzelmann, *Apostelgeschichte*, 120; Roloff, *Apostelgeschichte*, 286; Jervell, *Apostelgeschichte*, 481.

62. See Barrett, "Light on the Holy Spirit," 290; idem, *Critical and Exegetical Commentary*, 2:908. With regard to the practice of Jewish exorcism, see Matt 12:27 par. Luke 11:19. First of all, Solomon was regarded as a mighty banisher of demons (see the overview by Hermann L. Strack and Paul Billerbeck, *Exkurse zu einzelnen Stellen des Neuen Testaments: Abhandlungen zur Neutestamentlichen Theologie und Archäologie* [vol 4. of *Kommentar zum Neuen Testament aus Talmud und Midrasch*; 2nd ed.; 2 vols.; Munich: Beck, 1966], 1:533–34). Josephus traces back the entire ability for exorcism to the fact that God gave this knowledge to Solomon (*Ant.* 8.45). In accordance with this knowledge, Solomon composed certain incantation formulas that were said to be so effective that the demons did not return (with regard to this motif, see Matt 12:43–45 par. Luke 11:24–26). According to Josephus, this Solomonian art of exorcism was still practiced during his time, and he tells of an exorcism performed in the time of Vespasian by a certain Eleazar (*Ant.* 8.46). A special ring that was said to have kept a piece of a root of a certain plant mentioned by Solomon functioned as the remedy. The ring was held under the nose of the suffering person, which pulled the demon out of the person's nose. Only after this procedure were certain Solomonian incantations applied. Their function was to banish the evil spirit and to prohibit his return (Josephus, *Ant.* 8.47). See also Justin Martyr, *Dial.* 85.

63. See Garrett, *Demise of the Devil*, 92; Jervell, *Apostelgeschichte*, 482. They tried to imitate Paul. Often quoted as a parallel is a formula known from *PGM* 4:3019–20: "Ich beschwöre dich bei Jesus, dem Gott der Hebräer" ("I adjure you by Jesus, the God of the Hebrews"). See, among others, Schille, *Apostelgeschichte*, 379; Klauck, *Magie und Heidentum*, 114–15.

64. See Garrett, *Demise of the Devil*, 92.

65. The plural form is (against Schille, *Apostelgeschichte*, 379) not "clumsy" at all, since Acts 19:13 is a summarizing sentence, obviously referring back to the evil spirits (plural!) mentioned before.

Later, in Acts 19:14, the Jewish magicians are described as sons of a certain Skeuas, who is characterized as belonging to the priestly aristocracy.[66] The short note that this is a group of seven people creates a strong contrast to Paul, who in 19:12 is acting alone and not consciously.[67] Again the Christian missionary is depicted as a superior figure. This is also shown by the incantation used by the magicians, which alone by its wording makes a very weak impression, since it does not manage without the name of Paul.[68] The sons of Skeuas do not charm simply "by Jesus" but "by the Jesus whom Paul proclaims."[69]

The reaction of the unsuccessfully charmed demon reported in Acts 19:15 shows the complete weakness of these would-be exorcists. The demon well knows the name of Jesus used here as a magic spell. He even knows[70] Paul, who in the name of Jesus drives out demons, but the sons of Skeuas are not people who have any kind of authority.[71] The following verse underlines the absolute inability of these people. Instead of leaving the possessed person, the demon causes him to set upon the would-be exorcists and to overpower them although they were in a sevenfold majority. They were so weak that they could only flee, hurt and naked (19:16).

The story told in Acts 19:13–17—even if it originally was a profane burlesque[72]—is in the present context by no means a narrative that is meant for entertainment only or serving some religious interests.[73] On the contrary, it shows that magic is something dangerous. It also serves to depict again the superiority of the Christian faith over any form of magic,[74] even over magic that uses the name of Jesus as part of the incantation formulas. According to

---

66. See Barrett, *Critical and Exegetical Commentary*, 2:909. This man was by no means a high priest. His name is most probably a Greek form of the Latin name Skaevas (see, among others, Roloff, *Apostelgeschichte*, 286). According to Williams (*Commentary on the Acts of the Apostles*, 222), this Skeuas could have been a Jewish renegade who functioned as a priest at one of the Ephesian cults.

67. See Klauck, *Magie und Heidentum*, 115.

68. See, among others, Haenchen, *Apostelgeschichte*, 542.

69. This differs from the practice of the exorcist mentioned in Luke 9:49–50 (par. Mark 9:38–41), who banished demons in the name of Jesus (ἐν τῷ ὀνόματί σου).

70. That the different verbs indicate a difference in rank is clearly seen by Roloff, *Apostelgeschichte*, 286.

71. See Klauck, *Magie und Heidentum*, 115; Garrett, *Demise of the Devil*, 93; Jervell, *Apostelgeschichte*, 483; and Barrett, *Critical and Exegetical Commentary*, 2:910.

72. So, among others, Schille, *Apostelgeschichte*, 379.

73. See, e.g., Martin Dibelius, *Aufsätze zur Apostelgeschichte* (5th ed.; FRLANT 42; Göttingen: Vandenhoeck & Ruprecht, 1968), 23.

74. See, among others, Weiser, *Apostelgeschichte*, 532.

Luke, the name of Jesus is effective only when it is used by Christians[75] and in a nonmagical way, that is, not as a spell. Christian faith and magical practice exclude each other.

This becomes absolutely clear in the subsequent verses, Acts 19:18–20, which are not part of the burlesque itself. These verses show the impact the failed attempt of exorcism had on the Ephesian environment. As such, they are the striking finale of the sons of Skeuas episode.[76] According to Acts 19:17, the whole incident became well known among all the inhabitants of Ephesus, not only among the Jews but also among the Greeks. The consequence was on the one hand fear, on the other hand praise of Jesus' name. From this general reaction Luke distinguishes in Acts 19:18 a special reaction of those Ephesians who had come to faith. They confessed that they had been involved in those magical acts[77] for which the town was well known.[78] This confession was a public act of repentance, which is underlined by the burning of the magic books.[79] Burning those books is depicted as a voluntary act done by the people themselves. It was neither done nor triggered by the apostles.[80] The value of these books was, according to Luke, 50,000 denarii of silver.[81] Most probably the sum is mentioned here to show, on the one hand, how widespread magic was among the inhabitants of Ephesus[82] and, on the other hand, how great Paul's success has been.[83]

---

75. See Schille, *Apostelgeschichte*, 380. See also Weiser, *Apostelgeschichte*, 532; Barrett, *Critical and Exegetical Commentary*, 2:912.

76. This is correctly emphasized by Roloff, *Apostelgeschichte*, 285.

77. See Barrett, *Critical and Exegetical Commentary*, 2:912.

78. In antiquity, Ephesus was well-known for magical practice. Almost proverbial is the expression *ephesia grammata* for magic spells. The expression refers to words written on the statue of the Ephesinian Artemis. This string of meaningless words was used for exorcisms and protection. See Fritz Graf, "Ephesia Grammata," *DNP* 3:1076–77.

79. Concerning the magical books, see Lake and Cadbury, *English Translation and Commentary*, 243. Most probably Luke is thinking of collections of spells and charms similar to the later collections of "magical papyri" from the second to the sixth centuries. See Ferguson, *Backgrounds of Early Christianity*, 231; Barrett, *Critical and Exegetical Commentary*, 2:913.

80. See Klauck, *Magie und Heidentum*, 117. In this respect it differs from Augustus's burning of two thousand mantic books (see Suetonius, *Aug.* 31.3).

81. This is the Vulgate reading, but more probably one should think of Cappadocian drachms. See Marius Reiser, "Numismatik und Neues Testament," *Bib* 81 (2000): 477; Barrett, *Critical and Exegetical Commentary*, 2:913.

82. See Jervell, *Apostelgeschichte*, 484.

83. Schneider, *Apostelgeschichte*, 271.

As in the narratives analyzed before, here again a strong competition between the Christian faith and ancient magic can be observed, and again Christian faith and practice is depicted as superior to magic.

3. Conclusion

All the stories analyzed show a clear contrast between the Christian faith and ancient magic. Although the deeds of the Christian missionaries at first glimpse seem to have much in common with deeds of magic, there are, according to Luke, several big differences: (1) while the magician acts independently, the Christian miracle worker is an instrument of God; (2) while magic acts stand for themselves and are used in a commercial way, Christian miracles are closely connected to Christian preaching, which is noncommercial; and (3) while magicians use magic means such as spells, Christian missionaries pray.

In all three stories Luke also depicts magic as a dangerous thing, since it is incompatible with the ways of God. Magicians either want to use the gifts of God for their own purposes[84]—Simon as well as the sons of Skeuas—or become aggressive against Christian doctrine. Animosity from the Christian side is depicted as a reaction to initial abuse or aggression, a difference from the contemporary Harry Potter fighters, for example. In none of these stories do Christians show a violent animosity against magical acts or against people practicing magic. According to Luke, the Christian message is so convincing that people who in former times practiced magic renounce it voluntarily.

Different from our contemporary fighters against "magic," Luke did not need to forbid explicitly the use of magic in Christian circles. Maybe he trusted more in the power of the word of God than modern fighters against magic do?

---

84. We may also think here of the female slave's masters in Acts 16:16, 19 (see n. 1 above).

Paul and the Others: Insiders, Outsiders, and Animosity

Jeremy Punt

1. Introduction: New Testament Ambivalence

The New Testament has often been seen as a useful ally against violence, rallied for a *broadly* defined vision of peace, which includes calls for relieving poverty and other human needs. When Director-General of UNESCO Mayor argues that "first we must live, and give meaning to life. Eliminating violence: that is our resolve. Poverty, ignorance, discrimination and exclusion are forms of violence, which can cause—although they can never justify—aggression, the use of force and fratricidal conflict,"[1] the New Testament has been found to readily provide resources with which to address such concerns: Jesus' inaugural speech (Luke 4), and Paul's concern with both poverty (2 Cor 9–10) and economic independence.[2] In fact, people get excited about the potential of the New Testament documents to offer scriptural parameters for a rhetoric of praxis designed to challenge, invert and do away with barriers defined along racial, ethnic, and various other lines.[3]

Within the New Testament it is the Pauline letters in particular that promote a *new identity*, accompanied by a new ethos and worldview. These documents create the possibility for a complete reversal of the social location and standing of the Other, becoming part of the Christian family, a brother or sister[4]—one of "us"! The advocacy of a new identity involved more than

---

1. Federico Mayor, "The Human Right to Peace," *Bulletin* 4 (1997): 1–2.

2. See Amos Jones Jr., *Paul's Message of Freedom: What Does It Mean to the Black Church?* (Valley Forge, Pa.: Judson, 1984).

3. See recently Miroslav Volf, *Exclusion and Embrace: A Theological Exploration of Identity, Otherness, and Reconciliation* (Nashville: Abingdon, 1996).

4. A growing consensus agrees that Paul's letters were not so much aimed at persuading their receivers about justification by faith (as opposed to works-righteousness),

a new consciousness, and the New Testament, although the documents of a faith community, can be claimed as a partner in the global search for peace and human rights, given its contribution to common human values.

On the other hand and amid enduring ambiguities, the New Testament can be seen to tolerate violence and, even worse, at times promote and incite animosity if not violence. The violent element is related to various socio-historical and theological factors, determined by interests of communities, ideologies, and others. The reluctance to deal with the entanglement of the New Testament in violence may be appreciated; both, however, require investigation. Could the reluctance be related to the New Testament's strong calls for peace, which are more easily explained within theological perimeters and are more palatable than its malevolent tenor? Could it be that the New Testament's ambivalent attitude on both peace and violence is simply subsumed in a rather facile, spiritualized notion of peace? With such questions in the background, the focus here is on the toleration and promotion of violence in the New Testament and how to deal with such difficult texts.

Paul's expectations regarding the new identity of believers in Christ would prove particularly troublesome to some Jews and contribute to animosity between them and Paul and between them and Pauline communities. Ironically, Pauline-initiated communities would attract people from different walks of life, only to be met by Paul's appeals to close ranks around the newly formed communities. While new initiates were welcomed, certain situations led Paul to advise the exclusion of some on the grounds of internal differences. Those who were unwilling to join the Pauline communities were castigated and vilified, at times in harsh language. Paul's advocacy of a new identity was evidently closely connected to his vision of a new community and the resultant new identity within such a community.[5] The other side of

---

or at the salvation of the Gentiles, but rather at forging one unified community consisting of believers from among Jews and Gentiles; see, e.g., Nils A. Dahl, *Studies in Paul: Theology for the Early Christian Mission* (Minneapolis: Augsburg, 1977), 20; Alan F. Segal, "Response: Some Aspects of Conversion and Identity Formation in the Christian Community of Paul's Time," in *Paul and Politics: Ekklesia, Israel, Imperium, Interpretation: Essays in Honor of Krister Stendahl* (ed. Richard A. Horsley; Harrisburg, Pa.: Trinity Press International, 2000), 188.

5. Dieter Georgi (*Theocracy in Paul's Praxis and Theology* [trans. David E. Green; Minneapolis: Fortress, 1991], 52ff.) refers to "the corporate identity of Christ"; for the "fundamental emphasis on community in Paul's thought," see also Richard B. Hays, *The Moral Vision of the New Testament: A Contemporary Introduction to New Testament Ethics* (San Francisco: HarperSanFrancisco, 1996), 32–36. Luther H. Martin ("The Anti-individualistic Ideology of Hellenistic Culture," *Numen* 41 [1994]: 117–40) questions the supposed individualist character of Hellenism. It is interesting to note how much of the original Pau-

this position was, in a word, animosity directed toward those who either disregarded or rejected the vision of the new identity described by Paul.

This contribution considers the problem of outsiders in the Pauline documents in particular and the broader setting of Paul's politics of difference, or politics of othering.[6] The focus is on the strong oppositional categories invoked to describe people and how these contribute to animosity and violent statements.[7]

2. Subtle Violence: The Insider-Outsider Mentality

Given the claims and counterclaims about identity, the voices of Paul and others in the New Testament cannot be posited as simply and generally exclusive or hostile, as much as sweeping demands about the New Testament's promotion of inclusivity fail to convince. The insider-outsider mentality in the New Testament is a complex matter, revolving largely around matters of identity, but it was influenced also by social, political, economic, and other concerns. Besides those who are defined as outsiders from the outset, there are those who, although they at some stage became insiders, over the course of time and for various reasons became outsiders again.[8] The New Testament shows how certain lines of demarcation are broken through, if not broken down, but at the same time provides evidence of reinforcing other divisions. Paul's own position illustrates how he wielded the yardstick for aspirant insiders and considered certain beliefs and actions as appropriate for belonging to the community and for maintaining community solidarity.[9]

---

line emphasis was retained in the Eastern church: "In the Eastern church, the problem of the relation of faith to works has never had such a central position. In the East, Christians regard Paul as a saint, a mystic and a martyr. As to his theology, his *image of the church as the body of Christ* was more important than his doctrine of justification" (Dahl, *Studies in Paul*, 20, emphasis added).

6. Elisabeth Schüssler Fiorenza, "Paul and the Politics of Interpretation," in Horsley, *Paul and Politics*, 40–57.

7. In the subtext of this study, a thorny issue that keeps surfacing is how it happened that the traditional notion of Paul as an advocate for inclusion and tolerance almost obliterated another angle, his politics of exclusion and othering.

8. Some of the strongest warnings in this regard are probably found in Hebrews.

9. Segal reckons that Paul saw the terms of commitment and choice more rigidly than many other contemporary Jews; as a recent convert, he considered no middle positions: "In any event Paul's polarized sense of choices available marks him as a Pharisee.... Paul retains his preconversion superiority to those who do not keep the law as the Pharisees do" (Segal, "Response," 186–87). See also Elizabeth A. Castelli, *Imitating Paul: A Discourse of*

Discussing the insider-outsider mentality requires full consideration of first-century identity, but in the interest of space, a few remarks have to suffice. The strong sense of identity and continuous efforts to maintain and also elaborate notions of identity necessarily required procedures of demarcation as much as processes of identification. The erection of borders between people, the construction of "us" and "them," the selves and the others, was within the first-century, agonistic society not seen as complementary as the New Testament documents attest. Opposites did not attract as in today's cliché but led to competition and, at times, called forth hostilities, which was understandable in the first-century Mediterranean world, where violence was part of everyday life,[10] the extent of which emerges clearly even from a brief analysis of the New Testament vocabulary.[11]

2.1. COMMUNITIES, INSIDERS, AND OUTSIDERS: US AND THEM

Given the volatile and fragile nature of identity in the changing first-century environment, defining communal identity was a precarious undertaking. The difficulties and dangers are evident in, for example, nonretaliation, a topic appearing often if differently in early Jewish and Christian writings. An important distinction in exhortations on nonretaliation relates to two broadly different contexts, intracommunal conflict and persecution, and external oppression of the community. In the case of the former, the concern is generally with reconciliation and harmony, and with the other, longing for God's vengeance becomes the motivational argument. And in intracommunal conflict, the definition of the community is sometimes more specific than in other instances, where even other friends or neighbors are included.[12]

Power (LCBI; Louisville: Westminster John Knox, 1991), who finds in Paul's frequent calls for imitation a (warped) discourse of power.

10. See Pieter J. J. Botha, "Submission and Violence: Exploring Gender Relations in the First-Century World," *Neot* 34 (2000): 1–38.

11. The vocabulary for violence is varied, including physical human violence, the cosmic struggle between good and evil, and (metaphorically) the Christian's life of service to God as a spiritual battle; however, military terms dominate, indicative of the military environment of the day (Michel R. Desjardins, *Peace, Violence and the New Testament* [Biblical Seminar 46; Sheffield: Sheffield Academic Press, 1997], 63–64). On the other hand, the failure to address social justice issues and an emphasis on "peace" that does not allow for resistance against physical oppression can also be considered violence (Desjardins, *Peace, Violence and the New Testament*, 34).

12. Where interpersonal conflict and nonlitigious offenses are concerned, nonretaliation was seen as forgiveness, love, and good deeds aimed at reconciliation. In some texts, reconciliation is restricted by "sharp socio-economic divisions, moral elitism or personal

Despite the difficulties involved in such identity-processes, and regardless of the community's ability to maintain beliefs or the level at which these are posed as normative, the identification of self and others was part of being a faith community built around core beliefs. Such beliefs generally exude and even encourage a certain ethical practice. In the Hebrew Bible, with its strong monotheistic stance and theocratic setting, the people of Israel not only identified themselves accordingly but conversely and by default identified other people in contrast to such claims and ideals.[13] This was the case in early Christianity, too, with—at times diverse!—beliefs centering around Jesus Christ, accompanied by the promotion of a strong ethos in the nascent Christian communities. Traces of inclusivity related to the universal impact of Jesus Christ are found in the New Testament, with religious ritual and entrance requirements that could have posed barriers for new recruits at times trimmed down. At the same time, the New Testament also attests to the identification and allocation of people into groups, undergirding such practices and their accompanying claims with both religious fervor and argument.

Absolute claims inevitably lead to rigid categories, as much as strong boundaries have a way of calling out for their own protection and for the custody of those on the inside. The New Testament authors, explicitly or otherwise, claimed a particular way to gain God's favor as described and prescribed by them. Dissent is outlawed, except for inconsequential matters, and compromise is not warranted, especially in a world dominated by the struggle between evil and good forces. The grouping of humanity in camps necessarily entailed (mutual) exclusion and, depending on control over power and ideology, also marginalization.

This "we-they perspective" is found in all the major corpuses in various contexts in the New Testament. In the Gospels it is the strong anti-Judaic tone that surfaces repeatedly, revealing two strata of the Jesus story. On the one level, it is a relatively simple story of Jesus that is primary, but amid the reinterpretation of the events, which took place after his death, the story about him is told with the communities' concerns in mind. The Fourth Gospel expresses anger against Jews who became the symbol for all who rejected God (John 5:16; 8:57–59; 18:12; 19:10), in a context where the early followers of Christ dreaded the Jewish authorities for fear of exclusion and the

---

enmities," whereas in other documents nonretaliation applies regardless, to the extent that some even included Gentiles "in the horizon of application" (Gordon M. Zerbe, *Non-retaliation in Early Jewish and New Testament Texts: Ethical Themes in Social Contexts* [JSPSup 13; Sheffield: JSOT Press, 1993], 219–94).

13. The accuracy and legitimacy of such claims regarding self as well as others is a discussion reserved for another time.

might of the Roman Empire to annihilate whole communities for dissent.[14] Echoes of the concern with the insiders and outsiders are heard throughout the associated Johannine writings,[15] invoking categories of the saved and the damned.[16]

Other binary opposites are found throughout the New Testament corpus, often playing on religious or spiritual distinctions and employing symbolic language, such as to be free or enslaved, children of the light or children of the darkness, the faithful or the apostates, those on the narrow or those on the broad way, the wheat or the chaff, the sheep or the goats, the strong or the weak. Some opposites invoked sentiments that entail going beyond religious categories for explaining the force of the contrast and even the original identity-concerns, and might be related to categories of privilege and marginalization, wealth and poverty, and other sociopolitical configurations.

2.2. Self and Other in Paul

In the Pauline letters, communities are encouraged to develop a sense of belonging, and in this regard familial and affectionate terms (e.g., 1 Thess 2:7–8) are often found, and the body metaphor (Rom 12:3–5; 1 Cor 10–12; etc) is of specific significance in his letters.[17] The baptismal discourse (Gal 3:27–28; 1 Cor 12:12–13; see the later tradition, Col 3:9–11) underscores the notion that a community of people with the same focus is established through their commitment to Christ. A case can be made for Paul's advocacy of the inclusivity of the reign of God and its earthly manifestations, as seen, for example, in Rom 1:14 and 13:1–14. But on the other hand, Paul generally made such

---

14. The Johannine writings provide interesting parallels: the Fourth Gospel begins with a (negative) reference to the insiders, καὶ οἱ ἴδιοι αὐτὸν οὐ παρέλαβον (John 1:11: "and his own [people] did not receive him"), that sets the tone for the rest of the Gospel with its exclusionist tendency.

15. See Tina Pippin, *Death and Desire: The Rhetoric of Gender in the Apocalypse of John* (LCBI; Louisville: Westminster John Knox, 1992), 55–56, about the boundaries of the new-covenant group in Rev 21 and 22: "The boundary of the redeemed sets up a system of opposites expressed as insider and outsider, Christian and non-Christian, and fornicators and virgins. There is no room for dissent and no place for women's power and women's voices."

16. On insiders and outsiders in 2 and 3 John, see Judith Lieu, *The Second and Third Epistles of John: History and Background* (Studies of the New Testament and Its World; Edinburgh: T&T Clark, 1986), 125–65, esp. 145–48.

17. In the subsequent Pauline tradition, the body metaphor is altered in Colossians and Ephesians, with Jesus Christ now portrayed as the head of the body, while Christians make up the rest of the body (Col 1:18; Eph 1:22; 4:15).

inclusiveness dependent on the communities' assent to his visions, understandings, and praxis so that people in the Pauline community had access to spiritual information and knowledge not available to others.

This ambiguity emerges clearly in Galatians with Paul's explanation of the covenant, which is exclusive by nature, presupposing insiders and outsiders. The reference to "Jerusalem above" (Gal 4:26) entails divine origin, but not necessarily "an invisible people, to whom all races belong in their diversity, who receive the logic of faith as the founding principle of their practices, attitudes, and relations in their own particular world."[18] The choice is not for or against Jews, for or against Gentiles, but an inclusive choice for all people[19]—but such inclusion is according to the requirements of Paul's understanding.

Insiders are positioned against outsiders, reminding insiders of hostile people who threaten them and increasing the degree of hostility, as can be seen in the vice catalogues (e.g., 1 Cor 6:9–11) and the frequent virulent attacks on opponents.[20] In the New Testament, the adjectival adverb ἔξω ("outside") is used a total of 63 times, six instances of which it is substantiated, and in five[21] of these it expresses the notion of the outsiders, those outside the community, the people not part of the in-group—the others. Probably not without significance, the substantiated use of the adverb ἔξω occurs, with one exception (Mark 4:11), in the Pauline tradition only (1 Cor 5:12, 13; 1 Thess 4:12; see also Col 4:5).

In some of Paul's letters (esp. Galatians and Philippians) it becomes only too clear how inclusivity turns into sharp exclusion, when those threatening the fiber of the community or the veracity of Paul's expressed convictions and commitments are vilified and marginalized. Those who reject the Christian message fall into a different category of human beings and are accused of the vilest acts.[22] To claim that Paul eschewed any particular ethnic identity[23]

---

18. James D. G. Dunn, *The Epistle to the Galatians* (BNTC; Peabody, Mass.: Hendrickson, 1993), 249.

19. See Eung Chun Park, *Either Jew or Gentile: Paul's Unfolding Theology of Inclusivity* (Louisville: Westminster John Knox, 2003).

20. At times conflicts provide the context and requirement to define identity, e.g., Paul in Galatia (see Nicholas H. Taylor, "Conflict as Context for Defining Identity: A Study of Apostleship in the Galatian and Corinthian Letters," *HvTSt* 59 [2003]: 915–45).

21. In the other instance, ὁ ἔξω refers to corporeality, the external or outer side of being human, as opposed to the inner being, ὁ ἔσω (2 Cor 4:16).

22. In the later New Testament traditions, the intensity of the animosity increases, as illustrated well by the accusations leveled against the "ungodly" one of Jude.

23. "[S]ometimes Paul's opponents must be Christians as well as, presumably, Jews. I would include in that category gentile Christians who had already been circumcised, making them Jews for all intents and purposes" (Segal, "Response," 186).

in favor of an all-inclusive community of the Lord fails to deal with the evidence, which suggests that it is often not ethnic identity as such that is cause for exclusion but rather the position people assumed.[24] "[Paul] initiates a discourse that in many cases validates sameness, that condemns certain kinds of difference and by means of silence renders others unthinkable, that promotes community cohesion by self-discipline and outright self-denial."[25]

As in other New Testament writings, moderating features are present amid Paul's politics of othering. In his letters the boundary line is generally not fixed, since the missionary drive allowed for the outsider to be seen as a potential insider. Pauline attempts to break through some insider-outsider, us-them molds are arguably found in celebrated texts such as Gal 3:28 and other baptismal formulae. Calls for inclusivity, for tolerance and respect, and for difference are found in Rom 12:3–8 (esp. 4–5); 1:14;[26] 15:7–13.[27] A niggling question is whether such calls are limited to the intracommunal situation, restricted to the different groups or factions inside the early Christian church. And although as a rule the New Testament does not portray Christians as violent toward the outsiders, exceptions to the rule do appear. More fundamentally, and even when granting the differences of the first-century context at many levels, a basic problem still persists in the lack of respect for another person's right to exist and be different in that existence.

3. Paul, a Politics of Othering, and Animosity

The New Testament's saturation with language of identification renders images, processes, and structures of claiming and disavowing identity, of tracing insiders and allocating status, pointing to outsiders and marginalizing them or appealing for their marginalization. These faith communities of the first century rarely indulged the concern for diversity, flexibility, and being

---

24. The claims that "Paul's mission implies an alternative vision of the path toward global reconciliation. It runs neither through Roman propaganda and imperial rule nor through conversion to a single ethnic identity or theological orientation" and that "Since God's grace is equally available to all, no claim of superiority remains valid and therewith the basis for every kind of imperialism has been removed" (Robert Jewett, "Response: Exegetical Support from Romans and Other Letters," in Horsley, *Paul and Politics*, 71) may be accurate on one level but do not address the broader picture, where the Pauline notion of identity rules the day.

25. Sandra Hack Polaski, *Paul and the Discourse of Power* (Gender, Culture, Theory 8; Sheffield: Sheffield Academic Press, 1999).

26. Jewett, "Response," 62–65.

27. See also ibid., 69–71.

open-ended, at least not in its twenty-first-century, postmodern format.[28] In an imperialist context of oppression and want such as the first-century Mediterranean world, often accompanied by dispossession and persecution, communities of faith were more readily attuned to identify the foreigner and especially the opponent!

Claims regarding the identity and status of the self and others vis-à-vis the community were expressed in numerous ways, according to the style of the particular New Testament author, the issue at hand, the nature of the community, relevance to the message conveyed, and so on. There was no one particular, agreed-upon way of expressing notions of belonging and dissociation, rendering, for example, the Pauline sibling language, the Johannine letters' emphasis on "my (little) children," among others. However, tracing a single word (such as ἀδελφοί) or phrase (such as οἱ ἴδιοι) through the New Testament writings leads to limited and even incomplete pictures. Since words and phrases—and their particular usage—are reflective and representative of one tradition, the contributions of other New Testament traditions are then often marginalized or even excluded.

A strong focus on postulating and describing, establishing and maintaining identity inevitably required the construction of perimeters and borders. The purpose of borders was to provide a social location for the insiders, as much as it was to fend off outsiders whether or not they challenged the insiders and their sense of identity. Even without the benefit of Girard's scapegoat theory,[29] it is possible to understand how keeping the outsiders at bay even to the extent of their elimination is considered vital in an intentional community, especially in its early days of formulating a new, or different, at least, sense of identity.

3.1. POLITICS OF OTHERING: AN OBFUSCATING DISCOURSE OF POWER

A politics and rhetoric of othering deals with ideological justification and can in its more well-known forms be traced back to the "classic undemocratic discourses" of Plato and Aristotle, even if they were later refined and continued by the post-Enlightenment philosophers such as Locke, Hobbes,

---

28. Even today, the notion of human diversity as a "great resource, which is underpinned—this is our strength—by universal cultural values that must be passed on from the cradle to the grave" (Mayor, "The Human Right to Peace," 2) often remains idealist.
29. Charles Selengut, *Sacred Fury: Understanding Religious Violence* (Walnut Creek, Calif.: AltaMira, 2003).

Rousseau, and Hegel.[30] The Greek *polis* of times before the New Testament already reflects the patterns of identification and domination, marginalization and exclusion.[31] In its patriarchal context, the city-state embodied political-philosophical values in accordance with an andro-social understanding of democracy. Political and social power was the province of elite, propertied men, excluding not only slave men and women but also free-born propertied women, poor men and women, and, of course, barbarian (i.e., not Greek) men and women. For such sociopolitical arrangements, in view of the Sophist belief that all people are equal by nature, ideological justification was found in the articulation of dualisms[32] and the notions of natural superiority and inferiority of some people.[33] The politics of othering does not intend to describe the generic person but generalizes the imperial standard as the universal subject,[34] a practice that has through the centuries become the norm in hegemonic and colonialist discourse.

Once the hierarchy is established and legitimated, mechanisms of control are put in place within systems of domination and subordination, and an authenticating discourse is adopted to obscure these practices by claiming them as natural or (divinely) ordained.[35] These are the dynamics of a politics of othering. The identification of the discourse of power in the Pauline letters is a first step in uncovering the disempowerment of others and those on the margins of the Pauline communities, in particular.[36]

---

30. "Not just religious studies but all modern theories of political and moral life are shot through with the politics of othering, that is, with ideologies of sexism, colonialism and racism, the systems and discourses of marginalization, vilification, and dehumanization" (Schüssler Fiorenza, "Paul and the Politics of Interpretation," 45).

31. E.g., the distinction between the public and private realms of life leaves the civic public inhabited by an "impartial and universal point of view of normative reason" and the private with its emphasis on the family seen as the domain of women and thus of "the body, affectivity and desire" (ibid.).

32. Such as human-animal, male-female, slave-free, native-alien (ibid., 46). For the stratified society, see, e.g., Wayne A. Meeks, *The Moral World of the First Christians* (LEC; Louisville: Westminster John Knox, 1986), 32–38.

33. It was predominantly about the assertion of the inferiority of slaves and (freeborn) women as the targets of the ideological constructs on the inferiority of these groups and the concomitant need to treat them accordingly.

34. Schüssler Fiorenza, "Paul and the Politics of Interpretation," 46.

35. Dorothy Smith calls these "relationships of ruling" (cited in Schüssler Fiorenza, "Paul and the Politics of Interpretation," 46).

36. Polaski, *Paul and the Discourse of Power*, 136.

3.2. Othering in the Pauline Texts: The Opponents

The politics and rhetoric of othering found in the Pauline discourse is situated primarily in two particular ways of establishing and treating counter-identity: assimilating the differences of the other to the same (but, of course, an inferior version), and vilifying and idealizing difference as otherness.[37] Claims to identity and exclusion from identity and resulting structures of domination and subordination are substantiated through an appeal to naturalized differences, as embodied in a perceived or even revealed *natural* order. Only through recognizing such appeals to be part of a historical political process rather than absolutist revelation or universal, transcultural natural order can the process of dismantling a politics of othering begin.

A politics of othering is predominantly a rhetoric of legitimization, constructing a discourse replete with cause, development, and effect, by means of which certain people or groups of people are identified contra the selves and are thus considered as deserving of exclusion, marginalization, vilification, and, at times, brutalization. The strongest invectives originating from his politics of othering are possibly reserved for Paul's strongly worded opposition to the opponents in Galatians, Philippians, and 2 Corinthians (10–13). The politics of othering is, however, not reserved for opponents only, whether inside or outside the Pauline communities, but also includes strategies of marginalization and silencing where variously defined groups in- and outside these communities are the targets of the Pauline controls.

A prominent strategy on Paul's side is the gendering of his discourse, often claiming himself as the *father* of the communities and the one who will present the community as *bride* to her husband (e.g., 2 Cor 11:2–3). The negative overtones in gendering the community relate to the narrative of the seduction of Eve. Such a symbolic construct of gender dualism at once coheres in and undermines the other dualistic oppositions insofar as it casts all speaking subjects (Paul, the opponents, contemporary interpreters, and so on) as masculine and construe their audience (the Corinthian community, Judaism, contemporary readers, etc.) in feminine terms as passive, immature, and gullible.[38]

---

37. Schüssler Fiorenza, "Paul and the Politics of Interpretation," 45ff.
38. Ibid., 47. Paul's references to himself in feminine terms (e.g., Gal 4:19) did not destabilize the gendering of his discourse.

3.3. The Legacy: Pauline Interpreters

Both the canonical texts and the history of their interpretation[39] are implicated in the Pauline politics of othering. "This Western 'politics of identity' and 'rhetorics of othering' establishes identity either by comparison to the other as an inferior 'same' or by emphasizing and stereotyping difference as the otherness of the other."[40] These differences are taken by the powerful as legitimate warrant to control and rule, and they portray the differences to the powerless as either natural or divinely ordained sanction for submissiveness and subordination. Theological as well as sociological angles on the disputes recalled in the Pauline letters accord Paul's voice pride of place, dismissing the positions of the opponents of Paul as either heretical challenges to orthodoxy or sectarian deviance.[41]

The nature of discourse complete with its many binaries in Paul's letters is too often constructed as a series of dualistic religious, cultural and political discords such as "orthodoxy-heresy, apostle-community, honor-shame, mission-propaganda, and theology of the cross-libertine enthusiasm," whereas they amount to no more than "theological arguments over meaning and interpretation." In the end, the first elements of such binaries are privileged, claiming them for Paul, the early Christian church, or even for Christianity today. "Such interpretive dualistic oppositions muddle and play down the linking and connecting terms such as 'audience, community, gospel' by subsuming them under either pole of the opposition rather than seeing them as a possibility for overcoming the argumentative dualism constructed by Paul."[42]

3.4. Remaining Ambiguities

The need to investigate Pauline rhetorics and politics of meaning is clearly important. Similarly, not to valorize and reinscribe a (Pauline) rhetoric and politics of othering is an abiding concern. This requires biblical interpreters to avoid a hermeneutics of identification with Paul as a "master-voice" in the New Testament, through an investigation of the politics of meaning in

---

39. Pauline interpretation is faulted in particular for two illegitimate processes of identification that lead to a hegemonic politics of interpretation: "malestream" interpreters identify themselves with (the letters of) Paul and assume Paul to be identical with the communities he addressed (ibid., 44).
40. Ibid., 46.
41. Ibid., 46–47.
42. Ibid., 47.

contemporary interpretation and by holding on to an appropriate ethics of interpretation!

The ambiguity of insider-outsider rhetoric in Paul is not collapsed by Schüssler Fiorenza's comments about Paul's use of a politics of othering as imperialist device, even if her comments are probably most appropriate for describing the history and legacy of Pauline interpretation. How is it, for example, decided whether the hegemonic claims attributed to Paul cannot more readily be ascribed to his opponents, who often apparently operated in service of the imperial or religious center against the Pauline groups who at the time were found on the periphery rather than in the center?[43] On a different level, is the decision about whether Paul might be interpreted as having positively or negatively contributed toward an equitable sociopolitical environment, given his social and temporal location, ultimately a discussion about Pauline motives or about our contemporary political concerns?

Is it fair and accurate to slam attempts to "understand" Pauline calls for submissiveness as nothing less than acquiescing to domination, to claim that such attempts only make them (more) palatable and therefore acceptable? Is it an ethical reading to transpose the political sensitivities of today—a longing for egalitarian communities with democratic participation—onto Pauline texts, effectively exercising hegemonic control from a position of hermeneutical privilege based on the shaky ground of political correctness?[44] In short, is the ambiguity of the Pauline texts dealt with accurately and responsibly when stark categories are employed by which all interpretations of Paul's letters are vanquished that do not render either a liberation-focused Paul or ἐκκλησία or a contra-Paul reading?

4. Conclusion: Religion, Otherness/Sameness, and Violence

Such questions remain important, since religion, identity, and insider-outsider notions are today often implicated in animosity and armed conflicts across the

---

43. Jewett "Response," 60.

44. For example, Schüssler Fiorenza ("Paul and the Politics of Interpretation," 48–53) argues against Horsley's reading of 1 Corinthians as a challenge to the social values and dominant relations of the Greco-Roman Empire, claiming that the "self-understanding" of the ἐκκλησία is rather to be privileged. She similarly challenges Neil Elliott's ("Paul and the Politics of Empire: Problems and Prospects," in Horsley, *Paul and Politics*, 17–39) account of the apparent advocacy of voluntary subordination in Rom 13 as the lesser of two evils—the other being political annihilation!—questioning both the *accuracy* of Paul's representation of the historical contexts or the rhetorical situations as well as the *adequacy* of his "theoethical" responses.

world. As the history of the Inquisition and other more recent religious-based programs have shown, "belief in one's own absolute religious truth leads to intolerance and dissonance which calls forth violent means to destroy religious dissent."[45] The enemy within, the dissenters found inside one's own religious tradition, are very often the first to come face to face with religious violence, in a context where guilt can play an instructive role ("they deserved what they got"; "they were looking for it"; etc). Paul's anger, in Galatians but also elsewhere, is not so much directed at the opponents or not as harshly as toward the erstwhile faithful, the new converts who have departed from the way of the community.[46] It appears that the danger of "otherness within" was a greater cause for concern than the threat from (those) outside the community.

The existence of powerful social structures in the (post)modern world challenges established identities, also those which are religious in nature.[47] "Globalisation carries with it a danger of uniformity and increases the temptation to turn inwards and take refuge in all kinds of convictions—religious, ideological, cultural, or nationalistic."[48] The interesting paradox inherent to *globalization* is that as much as it challenges and changes existing inherited particularist cultures and identities, it also contributes to the invention and reinforcing of some cultures and identities as a measure of establishing control over systemic power.[49] Amid the real or perceived threat that globalization poses to local identities, religion can often become the last sanctuary within

---

45. Selengut, *Sacred Fury*, 84

46. See Luke Timothy Johnson, *The Writings of the New Testament: An Interpretation* (Minneapolis: Fortress, 1986).

47. In our postmodern times, a politics of location that allows for a "fluid, shifting, and generally context-dependent" view of identity is called for. Rather than some essential category, identity depends on location, which again is determined by "facts of blood" (social, personal, and familial alignments) and "facts of bread" (national, economic, and political matters), elements that are often at violent odds with one another (Mary Ann Tolbert, "Afterwords: The Politics and Poetics of Location," in *Social Location and Biblical Interpretation in the United States* (vol. 1 of *Reading from This Place*; ed. Fernando F. Segovia and Mary Ann Tolbert; Minneapolis: Fortress, 1995), 305ff.

48. Mayor, "The Human Right to Peace," 2.

49. On the abuse of multiculturalism in order to maintain a new form of monoculturalism, see Elizabeth A. Povinelli, "The State of Shame: Australian Multiculturalism and the Crisis of Indigenous Citizenship," *Critical Inquiry* 24 (1998): 574ff.; on the contribution of multiculturalism in Britain to "the reinforcement of centralized state power and the aestheticization of moral identities," see Talal Asad, *Genealogies of Religion: Discipline and Reasons of Power in Christianity and Islam* (Baltimore: Johns Hopkins University Press, 1993), esp. 266; on seeing multiculturalism as an excuse for imposing capitalism, see Slavoj Žižek, "Multiculturalism, Or, the Cultural Logic of Multinational Capitalism," *New Left Review* 225 (1997): 28–51.

which a particular identity is fostered.⁵⁰ Such religiously justified consciousness often proves more recalcitrant to accepting change and adjustments and can even lead to societal conflict when the actions and aims of such communities clash with those of broader society.

Today still, an ecclesiocentric theology creates problems in relating to religious pluralism—the saved community against the unsaved world⁵¹—and, depending on the boundaries of the ἐκκλησία, potentially also among different faith communities.⁵² The problem is foremost, however, with the formulation of identity (consciousness) and the construction of community (boundaries). Marginalized groups can claim their detrimental status as both an indication of their special status before God and as a warrant for venting anger and violence on their opponents and the rest of society in general.⁵³ Groups who feel exposed, ignored, abandoned, and humiliated, and thus having to deal with frustrated expectations, are fertile feeding grounds for dissent, anger, and violence.⁵⁴ Assuming a special status with God, they believe they are endowed with unique rights to punish their victimizers and perpetrators to gain their rightful place in society and to undo their position as a persecuted and stigmatized community.⁵⁵

---

50. More ominously, "[v]arious kinds of cultural 'cleansings' demand of us *to place identity and otherness at the center of theological reflection* on social realities" (Volf, *Exclusion and Embrace*, 17, emphasis original).

51. S. Wesley Ariarajah, *The Bible and People of Other Faiths* (Risk Book Series; Geneva: World Council of Churches, 1985).

52. The danger is always there that the insider-outsider rhetoric will mutate into the call for holy war, "the earliest and most elemental expression of religious violence" (Selengut, *Sacred Fury*, 17).

53. *Multiculturalism* often equals tension and conflict, especially where "identity with itself" is found, as is the case with the identity of modern Europe with its history of colonization, oppression, and destruction of cultures and imposition of its religion "all in the name of its identity with itself" (Volf, *Exclusion and Embrace*, 17). This resulted in a totalizing, absolutizing self-identity, therefore exclusivist and oppressive and often violent toward the other.

54. Selengut, *Sacred Fury*, 85.

55. The link between normative writings (Scripture) and a sense of identity, or "enscripturalised identity," entails self-definition but also the identification of the other through the interpretation and appropriation of the biblical texts. Identities of the self and other are often also textually enscribed. The relation between hermeneutical processes of identity and othering and social identity and othering is worth noting, especially against the background of a pragmatist or interpersonal hermeneutic: hermeneutical and social "otherness" are interrelated. See Jeremy Punt, "Enscripturalised Identity: Scripture and Identity in Christian Communities," *NGTT* 43 (2002): 83–93.

Animosity and even conflict is generated by the insider-outsider mentality. "Until interpreters uncover the complex dynamics of power, until communities of faith acknowledge the hidden structures that quietly oppress, Paul's writings will remain blunt instruments in the hands of those who would reinscribe their denial of difference."[56] A particular threat is the discovery of otherness within, especially in the Christian tradition that is for a large part a scriptural community,[57] given the role of the Bible as its foundational document.[58] Otherness in Christianity is often expressed in "biblical" terms, and the Bible and its interpretation is still found useful for identifying the others and for legitimating violence against them.[59] It is therefore important to account for the insider-outsider rhetoric found in the New Testament and the potential of such rhetoric to fuel animosity.[60]

---

56. Polaski, *Paul and the Discourse of Power*, 136.

57. Christianity is largely a "scriptural community" rather than a textual community; the latter is "defined by shared devotion … to an authoritative text or set of texts," which constitutes the community's worldviews and regulates the community's life. In a textual community, the texts form a "superstructure of agreed meaning, the textual foundation of behavior having been entirely internalized," defining the center of the community and as well as its periphery (William S. Green, "Otherness Within: Towards a Theory of Difference in Rabbinic Judaism," in *To See Ourselves as Others See Us: Christians, Jews, "Others" in Late Antiquity* [ed. Jacob Neusner, Ernest S. Frerichs, and Caroline McCracken-Flesher; Chico, Calif.: Scholars Press, 1985], 53–54, 68). In a "scriptural community" the emphasis shifts to Scripture, which is often, but not exclusively, inscribed textually: the "textual" aspect is incidental to the scriptural, the "foundational" tradition. See Jeremy Punt, "Peace, Conflict and Religion in South Africa: Biblical Problems, Possibilities and Prospects," *Missionalia* 27 (1999): 263–98.

58. Green, "Otherness Within," 49–69.

59. Scriptural communities, like textual communities, are fragile, in the sense that the "ultimacy, primacy, and constitutive character" of the community's sense of Scripture can be corrupted or diminished. In scriptural communities, too, "[t]he most threatening kind of otherness, [is] the otherness within" (ibid., 69).

60. Another version of the discussion of Paul's politics of difference, with particular focus on identity perspectives, can be found in Jeremy Punt, "A Politics of Difference in the New Testament: Identity and the Others in Paul," in *The New Testament Interpreted: Essays in Honour of Bernard C. Lategan* (ed. C. Breytenbach, J. C. Thom, and J. Punt; NovTSup 124; Leiden: Brill, 2006), 199–225. Valuable insights in David G. Horrell, *Solidarity and Difference: A Contemporary Reading of Paul's Ethics* (London: T&T Clark, 2005), 133–65, 204–45, 246–72, on Paul and the others became available to me only after this essay was already completed.

Switching Universes: Moving from a Cosmology of Fear and Animosity to One of Reconciliation in Colossians

J. J. Fritz Krüger

1. Introduction

Living in a world where various manifestations of deep-seated animosity are constantly present in all aspects of life, both public and private, presents one with the question of how to bring about change. On a daily basis, we are confronted with reports of hostility and war, of fights and divisions, of resistance and struggle, of rebellion and rioting, of persecution and attack, of conquering crusades and revenge-seeking actions.[1] As often as we are confronted by these things, we also experience the desperate futility of trying to speak out against it, because it seems as if mere words are powerless in the face of such basic animosity. More often than not, Christians' attempts to work change, to find peace and reconciliation, amount to prescriptions, exasperated injunctions, legalistic diatribes, or fundamentalist reiteration of biblical texts[2]—attempts that themselves betray a fundamental animosity toward the non-Christian world. Needless to say, the effects are almost always disappointing—nothing really changes, except perhaps for still deeper mutual animosity between Christians and non-Christians.

In this essay I argue that an alternative strategy for understanding and dealing with animosity in our world is called for, one that makes use

---

1. The outline of subdomains within domain 39, "Hostility, Strife," in the Greek-English lexicon of Louw and Nida (LN, 492), presents a useful overview of the various possible categories of animosity—at least semantically speaking. Its concrete manifestations are infinitely and frighteningly varied.

2. See Willi Marxsen, *New Testament Foundations for Ethics* (Minneapolis: Fortress, 1993), 184.

of worldview and cosmological narratives. Because worldviews generate, prescribe, and maintain ethical systems on the basis of fundamental metaphysical matrices,[3] these metaphysical matrices—in the form of cosmological narratives—should be our point of departure. Without discussing underlying metaphysical matrices, meaningful discussion or understanding of ethics is very difficult. The letter to the Colossians will be used as the demonstrating text for the purpose of this essay, and the underlying metaphysical matrix that will be dealt with is that of cosmic alienation.

A few basic presuppositions should be stated at the outset. These concern the hermeneutics underlying the argument of this paper: (1) cosmological material in the Bible is consistently theocentric or christocentric: God (or God-in-Christ) is the acting agent central in all history, and history serves to reveal God and/or Christ, so that history itself becomes epiphany;[4] (2) although contemporary (nonbiblical) history is not as clearly understandable as epiphany, I believe that present-day history is still the theater where the same God-in-Christ is active on the stage; he is the God who is actively and dynamically taking all things with him to the eschatological moment of fulfillment; (3) because the Christ-centered cosmological narrative of Colossians is regarded as authoritative divine revelation, this narrative is also authoritative for our contemporary world: if Christ is indeed the living κύριος τῶν παντῶν, he is this also of the world we live in today—by the same means, namely, his blood shed on the cross (Col 1:20); and (4) I believe that it is meaningless to discuss the problem of animosity in our time without taking as a point of departure the above principles: *without* them, we are drifting in the wind; *with* them, we are free to address the issues of our own times with a powerful, biblical appeal that is more than a mere example of how one author dealt with similar problems in the remote past of the ancient world.

---

3. See Clifford Geertz, *The Interpretation of Cultures* (London: Hutchinson, 1973), 90, 108; J. W. Bowker, "Cosmology, Religion and Society," *Zygon* 25 (1990): 9; Walter T. Wilson, *The Hope of Glory: Education and Exhortation in the Epistle to the Colossians* (NovTSup 88; Leiden: Brill, 1997), 104.

4. See Eduard Schweizer, "Das hellenistische Weltbild als Produkt der Weltangst," in *Neotestamentica: Deutsche und englische Aufsätze 1951–1963* (ed. Eduard Schweizer; Zürich: Zwingli, 1963), 15.

2. Worldview and Cosmological Narrative

2.1. Definitions

According to Wilson,[5] *worldview* can be defined as follows:

> [A worldview] is a person's comprehensive and pre-reflective understanding of reality, an integrating framework of fundamental considerations which gives context, direction and meaning to life in light of one's ultimate commitments. This is a particular way of looking at the world, of integrating different provinces of knowledge and experience into a symbolic totality, a symbolic universe. … In adopting the elements of a worldview cognitively and normatively, individuals are able to "locate" themselves; all of history and the entire biography of the individual are seen as events occurring in this world.

Worldview becomes *cosmology* as soon as it is raised from the pretheoretical level to that of critical consciousness, as soon as there is conscious reflection on it and conscious use of its metaphysical categories to talk about and reflect on the meaning and value of life.[6] Furthermore, *cosmology* can be understood as a worldview articulated in the form of a narrative (in this instance, then, *cosmology* equals *cosmological narrative*): all worldviews by nature contain a narrative element.[7]

Cosmic alienation occurs where people experience "worldview dissonance"—where their internalized model of the world they live in and which prescribes both their own identity and their mode of existence no longer fits their lived experience. This could be the result of rapid social change, political upheaval, religious conversion, or traumatic experiences—any of which have the power to rearrange the foundations of our worldviews like a strong earthquake would rearrange the structure of the tectonic plates on which we build our cities and live our lives. The result is invariably fear, bewilderment, a pro-

---

5. Wilson, *The Hope of Glory*, 100; see also Albert M. Wolters, *Creation Regained: A Biblical Basis for a Reformational Worldview* (Grand Rapids: Eerdmans, 1985), 1–2; W. Andrew Hoffecker, "Preface: Perspective and Method in Building a World View," in *God, Man and Knowledge* (vol. 1 of *Building a Christian World View*; ed. W. Andrew Hoffecker; Phillipsburg: Presbyterian & Reformed, 1986), ix–x.

6. See Robert A. Oden, "Cosmogony, Cosmology," *ABD* 1:1162.

7. Wilson, *The Hope of Glory*, 190; with reference to N. T. Wright, *The New Testament and the People of God* (vol. 1 of *Christian Origins and the Question of God*; Minneapolis: Fortress, 1992).

found *Angst* that is reflected in morality, community, religion, and almost all other aspects of human life.⁸

In the case of a letter such as Colossians, a narrative substructure can be found underlying the epistolary surface structure of the letter, not necessarily coinciding with the epistolary structure of the letter in all details,⁹ but nevertheless providing the necessary convincing power for the paraenetic teaching of the letter, thus constituting a *normative* or *controlling narrative*. In the case of Colossians, the question would simply be: What is the true story of Christ (as controlling narrative over and against other possible narratives), and what difference does this story make to how we live?¹⁰ Abstracting the controlling narrative reveals the driving motives behind ethical injunctions, without which the injunctions often appear both meaningless and powerless. For the sake of relevant contemporary application of the ethical injunctions found in a letter such as Colossians, it is therefore essential to follow the detour of uncovering the controlling cosmological narrative of the letter.

A last set of definitions is necessary. A typical cosmological narrative will in most cases follow a clear scheme of three distinct moments:

(1) An *initial sequence* introducing the protagonist of the narrative and identifying the basic problem to be overcome. No closure is presented during this sequence; it merely sets the action of the topical sequences in motion. Very often, this element recalls the past and explains the origins of reality (cosmogony) as well as the causes of the various crises in the present.

(2) *Topical sequences* presenting the main action of the narrative in relation to the solution of the main problem by the protagonist. These sequences often relate lived reality in the present in a comprehensive way.

(3) A *final sequence* presenting the solution to the problem introduced in the initial sequence, thereby presenting closure. Often this is a projected,

---

8. See Schweizer, "Das hellenistische Weltbild"; Wilson, *The Hope of Glory*, 3.

9. Norman R. Petersen, *Rediscovering Paul: Philemon and the Sociology of Paul's Narrative World* (Philadelphia: Fortress, 1978), 43–55.

10. In general, research on Colossians fails to recognize (or simply denies) the centrality of the Christ narrative in this letter; see Craig A. Evans, "The Colossian Mystics," *Bib* 63 (1982): 203; Fred O. Francis, "The Background of *Embateuein* (Col 2:18) in Legal Papyri and Oracle Inscriptions," in *Conflict at Colossae: A Problem in the Interpretation of Early Christianity Illustrated by Selected Modern Studies* (ed. Fred O. Francis and Wayne A. Meeks; SBLSBS 4; Missoula, Mont.: Scholars Press, 1975), 204. The vast majority of studies on Colossians focus on the so-called "problem" of the "heresy" of Colossians, which results in a philosophical rather than a christological discussion of the letter. Similarly, in ethical discussion, the imperatives of the last two chapters are often quoted naïvely, which again misses the point that the letter is a unique revelation of Jesus Christ as κύριος τῶν πάντων.

teleological future vision (eschatology). The initial and final sequences are often similar in content and structure, which implies that, should one be missing, its approximate (re)construction should be possible on the basis of the other.[11]

2.2. Cosmology and Power

All cosmological structures focus primarily on the absolute source(s) of power in the universe.[12] For the sake of their salvation and prosperity, people should know who is in control of their destiny—which power or god is angry and in need of pacification or which one is benevolent and should be maintained in this state of benevolence. In a universe where metaphysical powers or gods are often seen as being at war, it is a critical question who will win the war, because tipping the balance of cosmic power will have a profound effect on the lives of people. Marriage, pregnancy, agriculture, health, life and death, war, peace, and prosperity are all directly influenced by the cosmic balance of power. The vital question is, therefore, almost always: Where is the source of absolute power, and how can it be influenced or manipulated to the advantage of people (either as communities or as individuals)?

Interestingly enough, this latter question contains a strange contradiction often found in religious myths: although it is acknowledged that metaphysical powers are in control of people's lives, it is also accepted that people are able to manipulate or control these metaphysical powers (by means of magic, sorcery, rites, etc.)—which begs the question of who exactly is in possession of absolute power. The contradiction is not unexpected, though: it reflects a profound humanism and a schizoid cosmology in which, despite all protestations to the contrary, people place themselves in the supreme position—they are at the same time both victims and masters of cosmic powers, and their own destiny and well-being constitutes the highest teleological goal of history. Perhaps this constitutes the most fertile breeding ground for animosity yet: every other person who is like me constitutes a threat to my own destiny and well-being, my own control of supreme power, which is why I must do everything in my power to subdue, dominate, control, or destroy others.

Collins states that the era of Roman Hellenism was characterized by a revaluation of those cosmological beliefs fundamental to a stable society, on

---

11. Wilson, *The Hope of Glory*, 205–8.
12. Robert Doran, *Birth of a Worldview: Early Christianity in Its Jewish and Pagan Context* (Boulder, Colo.: Westview, 1995), 6; see also Clinton E. Arnold, *Ephesians, Power and Magic: The Concept of Power in Ephesians in the Light of Its Historical Setting* (SNTSMS 63; Cambridge: Cambridge University Press, 1989), 34–35.

the basis of a general experience of cosmic alienation and historical incongruence.[13] This resulted in deeply felt existential uncertainty and profound ethical changes, as well as reorientation to sources of cosmic power. Often, this kind of uncertainty also gives rise to animosity in its many concrete forms, because somebody or something else (1) is hindering one's own exercise of power, or (2) does not want to submit willingly to one's own power, or (3) makes one powerless by means of absolute domination.

2.3. Cosmologies in Conflict

In a pluralistic society, the cosmologies of different religious groups will often come in contact and conflict with each other.[14] Each group will have its own explanatory cosmogony and teleology, and the resulting conflict can only be resolved in one of three ways: (1) one or both groups close themselves off in radical, conservative self-preservation, with an attitude of overt hostility toward all those outside their own group; (2) one of the groups communicates its own views with strong missionary fervor, often inviting the hostility of the other group(s); (3) one of the groups converts totally to the opposing group's viewpoints, thus dissolving all previously existing reasons for conflict.

Something like this process of cosmologies in conflict is also evident in Colossians, where a Christ-centered cosmology is contrasted with one or more alternative cosmologies. This is also exactly what happens in ethical discussions on the many faces of animosity in our society today: more than merely a clash of relative moral viewpoints, it is rather a clash of cosmologies, or better still, a clash of universes. The discussion will gain in both clarity and effectiveness once this is accepted and the discussion itself is transferred to this level.

2.4. The Function of Cosmology

According to the scientific consensus of the late twentieth century,[15] based primarily on the work of Eliade,[16] cosmological speculation arises in times of great dislocation, when human existence becomes trapped in a web of dis-

---

13. John J. Collins, "Cosmos and Salvation: Jewish Wisdom and Apocalyptic in the Hellenistic Age," *HR* 17 (1977): 141.

14. Luke Timothy Johnson, *The Writings of the New Testament: An Interpretation* (Minneapolis: Fortress, 1999), 14.

15. See Oden, "Cosmogony, Cosmology," 1170–71.

16. Mircea Eliade, *Cosmos and History: The Myth of the Eternal Return* (trans. Willard R. Trask; Princeton: Princeton University Press, 1965).

cordant experiences. Such experiences create the suspicion that human life in the cosmos knows no real order or meaning, no emotional structure and no moral coherence—in short, cosmic alienation. It is especially the result of a feeling of being at the mercy of a power or powers that people do not know and cannot control.

Traumatic discordant experiences often cause people to raise their pretheoretical worldview to the critical conscious level, with cosmological reflection as a result. Cosmological explanations (most often in the form of myths) do not serve to rationalize away discordant experiences but to assign meaning to them in order to make them bearable. Every cosmology has this function: it seeks to match lived experience (whether actual or intended) to cosmic reality. Paraenetic literature is a method par excellence to help people to abstract and master their worldview, so that they can stay on course and live with integrity.[17] In this sense, almost all cosmological narratives have an ethically prescriptive or paraenetic goal and also a community shaping or social function: they present symbolic worlds as systems of shared meaning enabling people to live together.[18]

In order for meaningful ethical discussions to become a possibility, representatives of opposing groups will have to become aware of both their own and their opponents' cosmological narratives and conduct their discussions at this level. Changed behavior will only be the result of adopting a different cosmology, or in terms of the title of this essay, of *switching universes*, as every cosmology (and thus every distinct symbolic universe) has its own distinct and fitting corresponding life practice.[19]

3. Alternative Cosmologies in Colossians

3.1. A Clash of Universes

It is now time to turn to the letter to the Colossians and to explore the issues of worldview and cosmology outlined above. First of all, again, a short hermeneutical excursion is called for.

In recent years, research on Colossians has been effectively reduced to the problem of the identity of the so-called "philosophy" referred to in Col

---

17. Wilson, *The Hope of Glory*, 183.
18. Johnson, *The Writings of the New Testament*, 12; see also Bowker, "Cosmology, Religion and Society," 7; Wilson, *The Hope of Glory*, 192.
19. Bowker, "Cosmology, Religion and Society," 18–19.

2:8.[20] However, despite many attempts at identifying the opponents of Paul in Colossians, there is still no conclusive certainty on the matter, only rampant (albeit sophisticated) speculation. It is my contention that, in order to be able to understand the letter, it is not necessary to identify the opponents conclusively. Not only are there more issues at stake in the letter, but the debate on the identity of the opponents also serves to draw the focus away from the central revelation of Jesus Christ.

Van Riessen has reminded us of the vitality of religious (or rather pseudo-religious philosophical) discussion in the era of Roman Hellenism.[21] Popular folk religion, as a cosmological narrative seeking to provide identity, meaning, and purpose in a time of radical cosmic alienation,[22] was extremely tenacious, and it was characterized, at least from the perspective of the philosophers, by irrational superstition (or δεισιδαιμονία). Most of the major philosophical schools of the time—including the Stoics and the Epicureans—were out to denounce popular folk religion and to provide their own rational alternatives. The Jewish communities and intellectuals of the time were also actively taking part in the debate, often presenting the Jewish faith and Scriptures as the best philosophy available on the market (see Col 2:8), far superior to anything the Greeks or Romans could offer. One such "school" was that of the Jewish apocalyptic mystics.[23]

One possibility of what could have happened at Colossae is the following: the Christians at Colossae and certain Jewish apocalyptic mystics, who were presenting their views as rational and convincing philosophy, came in conflict because of two factors: the missionary zeal of the Christians (see Col 4:5–6); and the Christians' appropriation of a significant part of Jewish religious heritage: the Scriptures and messianic rhetoric.

However, for a clear understanding of the christological revelation in Colossians, and for the sake of modern contextualization of this letter, it must be recognized that, although the letter seems to answer to some form of

---

20. See Harold W. Attridge, "On Becoming an Angel: Rival Baptismal Theologies at Colossae," in *Religious Propaganda and Missionary Competition in the New Testament World: Essays Honouring Dieter Georgi* (ed. Lukas Bormann, Kelly Del Tredici, and Angela Standhartinger; Leiden: Brill, 1994), 482; Angela Standhartinger, *Studien zur Entstehungsgeschichte und Intention des Kolosserbriefs* (NovTSup 94; Leiden: Brill, 1999), 2; Wilson, *The Hope of Glory*, 34–35.

21. Hendrik van Riessen, *Wijsbegeerte* (Kampen: Kok, 1970), 56.

22. Schweizer, "Das hellenistische Weltbild," 15–27.

23. For thorough discussion of this school and convincing arguments linking them to Colossians, see Thomas J. Sappington, *Revelation and Redemption at Colossae* (JSNTSup 53; Sheffield: JSOT Press, 1991); and J. H. Roberts, "Jewish Mystical Experience in the Early Christian Era as Background to Understanding Colossians," *Neot* 32 (1998): 161–89.

Jewish apocalyptic mysticism (which is impossible to identify conclusively), this Jewish "philosophy" was itself part of the wider intellectual debate concerning the supposed superstition of popular pagan[24] folk religion, which was, in its turn, an attempt at making sense of the experience of cosmic alienation at the time (specifically, in the first century C.E.). The most direct thrust of the revelation content of Colossians should be located at this level: it presents the cosmic lordship of Jesus Christ as God's answer to cosmic alienation, in direct contrast to the answers presented by Jewish mystics, Hellenistic philosophers, and pagan folk religion. From the opening salutation of the letter (Col 1:1–3), the message is clear: it is a message of grace and peace from Jesus Christ to his holy ones in Colossae. They are the ones who have crossed over from the dominion of darkness into the kingdom of the beloved Son (1:13), the only kingdom where this grace and peace is possible. It represents a journey that is fundamentally a switch of universes: leaving behind one universe characterized by dark powers of animosity and fear and moving into another universe of gracious reconciliation through the blood of Jesus Christ on the cross.

Effective contextualization of Colossians will consist of seeking out the varied faces of modern cosmic alienation, including its ethical manifestations, and presenting the cosmological controlling narrative of Colossians as a powerful redemptive answer.

In what follows, I will attempt to outline briefly the popular pagan, Jewish apocalyptic-mystic and Christ-centered cosmological narratives relevant to the understanding of Colossians. Following that, I will demonstrate the ethical importance of this "clash of universes" in terms of the contrast between animosity and reconciliation as central ethical motifs.

3.2. The Alternative Cosmological Narratives of Colossians in Outline

The popular pagan, Jewish apocalyptic mystic and Christ-centered cosmological narratives will be presented in table-form below, in order to facilitate comparative reading. The following factors are relevant to the construction of these narratives. (1) The popular pagan cosmological narrative can only be described approximately, because the religious diversity of the first century was so great that nothing more than the greatest common denominator can be described. In this sense, the proposed construction is only one among

---

24. The term *pagan* is not used here in a derogatory sense but in line with accepted scholarly practice, which distinguishes between Jewish, Christian, and pagan religious beliefs in the time of Roman Hellenism.

many possible constructions and also admittedly biased toward astral religion.

(2) No one exemplary text or collection of texts is available on the basis of which the popular pagan cosmological narrative can be constructed. Even a careful researcher such as Arnold has to rely on fragments of documents and inscriptions to compile an approximate description of popular pagan thought. Instead, a synthesis of scholarly overviews,[25] regarded as the accepted interpretation of the scholarly community of our times, is used for the construction of this narrative.

(3) The resulting cosmological narrative will in various respects differ markedly from the available literary and philosophical sources from first-century Roman Hellenism, precisely because it represents the religious sentiments of the illiterate, unsophisticated masses, not often represented in the literary and philosophical canon of the time.

(4) The Jewish apocalyptic mystic cosmological narrative is based largely on the text of 1 Enoch,[26] as a typical example of early Jewish mysticism.[27]

(5) The Christ-centered cosmological narrative is constructed on the basis of the text of Colossians.

(6) The topical sequences of the Christ-centered narrative in Colossians can be divided into three parts: the fundamental part concerning the cross and resurrection; a universal-cosmic part; a human-ecclesiological part. This

---

25. Clinton E. Arnold, *The Colossian Syncretism: The Interface between Christianity and Folk Belief at Colossae* (Tübingen: Mohr Siebeck, 1995); idem, *Ephesians, Power and Magic*; J. L. de Villiers, "Philosophical Trends in the Graeco-Roman World," in *The New Testament Environment* (vol. 2 of *Guide to the New Testament*; ed. Andrie B. du Toit; Halfway House: Orion, 1998), 169–90; idem, "Religious Life," in de Villiers, *The New Testament Environment*, 191–214; Eric R. Dodds, *Pagan and Christian in an Age of Anxiety* (Cambridge: Cambridge University Press, 1965), 6–36; Everett Ferguson, *Backgrounds of Early Christianity* (Grand Rapids: Eerdmans, 1987), 132–253; Frederick C. Grant, *Roman Hellenism and the New Testament* (Edinburgh: Oliver & Boyd, 1962), 4–74; Johnson, *The Writings of the New Testament*, 25–35; Helmut Koester, *History, Culture and Religion of the Hellenistic Age* (New York: de Gruyter, 1995), 137–96, 219–32, 338–64; Eduard Lohse, *The New Testament Environment* (Nashville: Abingdon, 1976), 222–51; Schweizer, "Das hellenistische Weltbild."

26. The translation and chapter divisions of R. H. Charles, *The Apocrypha and Pseudepigrapha of the Old Testament* (Oxford: Clarendon, 1913), have been used for the purposes of this essay. Although 1 Enoch is itself a very complex document and may even present competing cosmological ideas within one document, it would probably have been read as one document by ancient readers. Despite the difficulties mentioned, it still serves the purpose of constructing an exemplary cosmological narrative.

27. Gershom G. Scholem, *Major Trends in Jewish Mysticism* (New York: Schocken, 1964), 40–43.

latter part is indeed cosmological, although it may not at first glance seem to be. Christ's victory over the powers (Col 2:14–15) is not only an eschatological moment but should also be understood as a new cosmogonic moment, resulting in the new αἰών and the church (as body of Christ) as the new κόσμος.[28]

Popular Pagan Cosmological Narrative	Jewish Apocalyptic Mystic Cosmological Narrative	Christ-Centered Cosmological Narrative (Colossians)
	Initial Sequence	
• The protagonist of the narrative is the human person. • The origin of humankind is the planetary-astral sphere beyond the moon, with the soul having its origins in the spheres furthest removed from earth, where the divine is represented in its purest form. • The cosmos exists of a mixture of spiritual-divine and material elements, graded from pure divine spirit down	• Enoch, in his role as cosmic figure transcending his mere humanity, is the primary protagonist of the narrative.[29] • Although 1 Enoch contains no explicit cosmogonic narrative, it could perhaps be accepted that, in line with Jewish tradition, Gen 1–2 should be regarded as the implied cosmogony. The following points, however, represent fragments of secondary cosmogonic material.	• The cosmogonic element in this narrative is radically Christ-centered, echoing the language of Prov 8:22–32 and Wis 6–9. It makes clear that, from creation to the eschatological fulfillment, the existence and historical acts of God and Christ take precedence over all other historical actions: there is no cosmogonic dualism. All things outside of God and Christ belong to the created order

---

28. See Eduard Schweizer, "σῶμα." *TDNT* 7:1035; W. C. Vergeer, "ΣΚΙΑ and ΣΩΜΑ: The Strategy of Contextualization in Colossians 2:17: A Contribution to the Quest for a Legitimate Contextual Theology Today," *Neot* 28 (1994): 382. It could, however, be argued that this re-creation of the world in the form of the church is in itself already an eschatological theme in the broader sense, so that new cosmogony and eschatology should not be separated too strictly.

29. In the narrative of 1 Enoch, there are many potential candidates for the role of the protagonist: God himself; the good angels (Michael, Uriel, Gabriel); and Enoch. However, Enoch is portrayed in various visions as the messenger of cosmic order and the dominion of God; he is also the messenger of judgment (see 13:1–11) who eventually merges with the messianic Son of Man (70:17), who restores order and peace in his role as eschatological judge of the universe.

- to pure matter—the latter being inferior in all senses to the spiritual-divine.

- The problem presents itself as the human spirit being removed or banished from the planetary-astral spheres through some fault or transgression and then being united with the material body in the earthly sphere.

- Trapped in the material body and its impure passions, as well as the necessity of physical survival, the spirit is unable to return to its origins. This would require purely spiritual activity, made impossible by the passions and needs of the body.

- Return to the planetary-astral spheres is further blocked by demons and the planetary powers or gods

- From the narrative about the fall of the angels (1 En. 7–8; 68:1–6) can be deduced that God had originally created the angels as a separate class of created beings: heavenly and spiritual; intended to serve God, people, and creation in general ;and able to commune with people.

- Initially, there is a strict law-bound order and stability to the processes of nature and the heavenly bodies (3:1–3; 17–18; 32–35). This order is destroyed by the fall (transgression of the law) of people and the angels (79:3–9),[30] resulting in their expulsion from the presence of God.

- Cosmic order is based on the faithfulness of God (68:19–26) and was given in the hands of angels (see also Uriel as angel in charge of and are fundamentally subject to Christ.

- The cosmogonic sub-narrative can be found in the hymn of Col 1:15–20 and can be described in the following way:

- Jesus Christ is the image (εἰκών) of the invisible God (1:15), which means that he not only *reveals* God but that he also *represents* God in the full extent of his creation and government of all things, as well as in his work of grace.[31] It is in this sense that God lives in him in bodily form in fullness (1:19; 2:9).

- Jesus Christ is called the *firstborn* over all creation (πρωτότοκος πάσης κτίσεως, 1:15), which means not only that he existed before all things (1:17) but also that he has author-

---

30. This makes possible the deduction that obedience to the law in true righteousness is not merely a matter of personal holiness but is necessary in order to maintain the cosmic order. The idea is supported by mystic interpretation of the Torah, according to which the Torah is more than merely a legal code but rather a living organism and incarnation of divine wisdom, providing the "skeleton" for created order (see Scholem, *Major Trends in Jewish Mysticism*, 14). The individual *mitzvot* of the Torah then become, in their execution, sacramental acts of cosmic importance, maintaining the cosmic order of creation. Scholem (*Major Trends in Jewish Mysticism*, 30) links this to the magic-mechanical worldview of Hellenism where a ritual act, executed within a magic context, effects the whole cosmic structure (see Sappington, *Revelation and Redemption at Colossae*, 57).

31. Herman N. Ridderbos, *Aan de Kolossenzen* (Commentaar op het Nieuwe Testament; Kampen: Kok, 1960), 135.

- who guard the entrance to the divine spheres.
- On earth, in their bodily existence, people are the powerless object of all kinds of demonic and cosmic powers out to destroy them. Their daily existence is marked by positive and negative events that can be ascribed to fate (εἱμαρμένη) as expressed in the blind determinism of planetary and astral powers.
- Their existence is further marked by constant change and mortality: nothing ever remains the same, and everything must perish.
- All of the above causes a fearful and insecure existence where people perceive themselves to be strangers in their earthly and bodily existence: both their bodies and the cosmic powers keep them from enjoying the fullness they would have enjoyed in the divine spheres.
- People become essentially without identity (civil, national, and religious) and find themselves drifting in a cosmopolitan universal world without borders.

- the movement of the sun, moon, and seasons, with the fate of people closely related to these movements [63–74]. Obedience to calendar stipulations becomes one of the primary marks of righteousness, with cosmic order as such being at stake [72–82].)
- The Son of Man is initially a hidden figure in his preexistence (61:10) but seems to have played some role in safeguarding righteousness and wisdom, and therefore cosmic harmony and peace (48:1–5).
- The implied cosmogony of Gen 1–2 should probably be supplemented by material from the Wisdom of Solomon (see Wis 6–9): it is Wisdom, as pure and holy emanation of the power and glory of God, who provides structure for the universe. Wisdom, as image of God, is the immanent presence of a transcendent God in creation.
- The problem Enoch, as protagonist, is presented with is that of the suffering of the righteous in difficult

ity over all things: all things are created *in*, *through*, and *unto* him (ἐν αὐτῷ ... δι' αὐτοῦ ... εἰς αὐτόν, 1:16). God subjects all things to Christ and determines that all things will find their fulfillment in Christ alone. Christ himself provides the point of integration of all diversity in the created realm, ensuring that the *cosmos* does not sink into *chaos* (see 1:17: καὶ τὰ πάντα ἐν αὐτῷ συνέστηκεν).

- The "all things" (τὰ πάντα) mentioned repeatedly from 1:15 includes the evil powers in the series of θρόνοι, κυριότητες, ἀρχαὶ, ἐξουσίαι (1:16) and their spheres of influence—despite what they later became.
- The problem in this narrative must be constructed from implied references and could be described in the following way:
- Some kind of rebellion must have occurred, turning the powers of 1:16 against God and Christ and away from their initial position "unto Christ," so that they were now in need

- Death itself presents itself to some as the great nothing—the ultimate annulment of existence and the final proof of the meaninglessness of human existence. For others, it is the doorway to an afterlife where the gods repay them for their deeds on earth, by way of either reward or punishment.

- times (see 1:1)—people who complain to God because he is apparently not doing anything to help them (9:3–14).

- The problem was caused by the fall of some of the great angels who took people with them in their fall.

- of subjection and reconciliation (1:20; 2:15).

- The estrangement of the powers led to the estrangement of people, so that they too became enemies of God (see ἀπαλλοτριόομαι in 2:21).

- This had ethical consequences, resulting in evil works (2:21) being unholy, imperfect, and full of blemishes (1:22; see also 3:5–9).

- People now lived in the power of darkness (1:13), ruled by death (1:18; 2:13), being under the judgment of God (3:6) with a damning written code against them (see χειρόγραφον in 2:14).

- In a useless attempt to change their circumstances, they live in subjection to manmade laws and traditions (2:8, 20, 22–23).

- The protagonist of this narrative is Jesus Christ.

Topical Sequences

- The first solution to people's problem is that they must find power to resist or manipulate the cosmic powers.

- The topical sequences begin with the announcement of God's impending judgment over sinful people and the angels, with

(1) The cross and resurrection

- God wants (1:19, εὐδόκησεν) to reconcile the estranged

There are three possibilities for doing this:

- Astrology, sorcery, divination, and mantic prophecy enable them to know beforehand what fate has in store for them, thus enabling them to live in such a way that they experience minimal disruption and disappointment.

- They can also turn to magic, aimed at obtaining and using occult power in order to manipulate the cosmic powers in such a way that their personal experiences become more bearable.

- They could take part in the cult of a god or goddess with greater power than the planetary or astral powers (see Artemis of Ephesus). Syncretism presented endless possibilities.

- Rigid asceticism, aimed at denying the body and everything physical as far as possible, was another way of winning the benevolence of the cosmic powers.

the promise that Enoch and his descendants would be spared. In this way, God intended to bring new life to creation (10:4–5, 10–18).

- Although there is no explicit reference to any ascetic preparation for Enoch's visions, his eternal righteousness is emphasized (70:17), while his soul is also freed from his body (70:13). His own (ascetic) holiness and righteousness (in terms of the Mosaic covenant and the law) should therefore be regarded as implied.[32]

- First, Enoch is sent by God to announce judgment to the fallen angels (12:5–7), without any chance of redemption (13:1–14:5).

- After this, Enoch experiences a heavenly journey (14:8 et seq.) during which he sees two houses. The second house is God's dwelling place, where he sits in unapproachable glory on his throne. Neither angels nor people can look at or approach God. Enoch is a witness

cosmic powers together with the rest of creation to himself through Jesus Christ (1:20), and he sends his Son to accomplish this.

- Jesus sheds his blood on the cross, dies, and is resurrected (1:20; 2:14; 1:18).

- His blood works forgiveness for sin (1:14, 22) and cancels the written code with its regulations that are fundamentally hostile to people (2:14, χειρόγραφον).

- This is the revelation of Jesus Christ as people's hope of glory (1:27).

- On the basis of his resurrection from death, Jesus is exalted to the position of ruler (πρωτεύων) over all things (1:18; 3:1).

(2) The universal-cosmic part

- Because of the above, the rulers and authorities, together with the rest of the cosmic τὰ πάντα, have been conquered, disarmed, and made subject to Christ (2:15).

---

32. If it is accepted that Enoch, in his role as messianic figure, is also intended to be an example to and teacher for the righteous ones, his righteousness and the stripping of his body has clear ethical implications for these people.

- In order to make the experience of loneliness, loss of identity, and estrangement more bearable, there was also the option to join cultic societies, the mysteries, or one of the philosophical schools.

- Within the context of popular cosmology, there was no answer to the problems of constant change or mortality.

- of the heavenly liturgy (39:12) and takes part in the glorification of God (70:9–15).

- Despite the inapproachability of God, Enoch is eventually called to approach (14:24–25), having apparently passed the test of absolute holiness (14:23). He receives revelations concerning the fate of the fallen angels and evil spirits, about the cosmic order, and about the coming eschatological judgment/redemption (17:1–18:12; 33–35; 41; 59).

- Enoch describes his visions as secrets that have been revealed to him alone: he received mystical revelations concerning wisdom as the way to eternal life (19:3; 37:1–2). He becomes the Chosen One and the Hidden One (messianic titles) who alone can reveal God's wisdom to people, so that the righteous ones can live. Enoch, as messianic wisdom teacher, thus becomes the agent of eternal life or salvation.[33]

(3) The human-ecclesiological part

- As the ruler of all things, Jesus Christ is the head of the church, his body (1:18, ἡ κεφαλὴ τοῦ σώματος τῆς ἐκκλησίας).

- To this communion of head and body, God elects, calls, and sanctifies people who have previously been estranged from him (3:12, 15; 1:2), because of the events of the cross and resurrection and the cancellation of the χειρόγραφον.

- People become part of this new community of holy ones and of the people of God *when* they are brought from the dominion of darkness into the kingdom of the beloved Son (1:13–14), *by* hearing and believing the gospel of the cross-events. *Baptism* is the visible event accompanying the transition (2:11–13).

- The new mode of existence in the church as body of Christ is one of mutual support, unity, and growth (2:19), a

---

33. According to this narrative, salvation becomes a matter of mystical insight into the wisdom of God, for which personal holiness (as defined by the Torah) is both the prerequisite and the required result. Some measure of ascetic practice is therefore required.

fellowship of love (2:2; 3:12–15) without sinful divisions (3:11).

- In this community, people are comforted (2:2) because they share in the fullness of God (2:9–10), which means that they are free from the feared influence of the powers and authorities who have been disarmed by Christ (2:15).

- In this community, people persevere in the power of Christ (1:11).

- In this community, people are made new according to the pattern of God-in-Christ by putting on the new person (3:10). They now both know and do the will of God (1:9–10) in new styles of relating to others (3:12–15), in social responsibility (3:18–4:1), guided by the Word who lives in them in full richness (3:16).

- They are thankful (3:16–17).

- The prayerfully seek opportunities to proclaim the gospel (4:2–6).

- This new body-existence is a hidden existence until the time

The Final Sequence

- The final sequence of this narrative is in a sense atypical and open, because it presents no solution to the problem introduced in the initial sequence. In terms of the problem-narrative, there is no means to return to the astral origins of the soul. There was always the hope of divine empowerment, and thus salvation, but this was only available to a select few and not to the masses. Even the philosophers could not present a way out of the grip of fate; they could merely suggest ways to make life here and now more bearable.

- In the end, death changes cosmic alienation into permanent exile.

- The end begins with the powerful appearance of God (55:1; 58), the revelation of the Son of Man, and the resurrection of the dead (1:2; 61:10; 50:1; 60:11).

- The execution of the eschatological fulfillment is in the hands of the messianic Chosen One, who will change the appearance of heaven and earth and give people peace and blessings (45:3–5), especially by judging sinners (48:3). The righteous ones will join in this judgment of sinners (38:5).

- The messianic figure (Enoch himself, 70:17) has been hidden until now but will be revealed in the end, when he will also reveal all hidden treasures of righteousness, wisdom, and eternal life (46:2; 61:10; 68:38).

- The result of the judgment is restored peace and righteousness (10:21–22), cosmic harmony (10:23–24),

of the eschatological fulfillment (3:3)—*real, yet not fully revealed*.

- Jesus Christ is revealed in glory when he returns (3:4).

- The faithful, who have remained grounded in hope and held on to the Head (1:28; 2:19), are revealed with him in glory (3:4), so that what has been hidden until now is revealed (see 3:3).

- Christ presents these faithful ones to God as holy and without blemish (1:22, 28).

- God lets them enter into their inheritance, the hope of glory, which has been kept for them in heaven (1:12; 3:24; 1:5, 27).

- The unrighteous, who did not hold on to the Head (2:19), are placed under the judgment and wrath of God (3:6) and receive their own unrighteousness as inheritance (3:25).

- Thus peace is restored to creation: all estrangement has been reconciled, except for that estrangement which has become all nations worshiping God (10:26). Heavenly life is portrayed as life in the light of the sun (56:3, 5) as opposed to life in darkness on earth, in which the Chosen One clothes with life the righteous whose names are written in the book of life (46:3; 61:18).

- God himself now reigns on earth, and his children share in his endless goodness (24:1–11; 27–31).

- The fallen angels, evil spirits, and all who followed them are kept in the depths of the earth in eternal punishment (25–26). Those who had power through their evil deeds are now stripped of all power by the messianic Chosen One and are judged by those who have been oppressed by them (46:3–4; 36:4–5; 52–53).

- Only now is there a perfect manifestation of the communion of the saints (38:2–3; 52:6–7) under the wings of God. Power now belongs to them as their eternal inheritance (39:8).

permanent under the judgment of God in Christ.

3.3. The New Universe Revealed in Christ

The question now remains: What are the key differences in the universe presented by Christ? What difference do they make to our power-consciousness and therefore to our way of living and relating?

First of all, it is important to emphasize the role of Jesus Christ as *the only primary cosmic protagonist* from cosmogony to eschatological fulfillment. No other historical agents can ever take this primary position in the lives of those who are in fellowship with Jesus Christ. Because of the motif of the subjection of the powers to Christ, the driving force of fear and hence the need for self-preservation (which is at the root of animosity) is removed.

As cosmic protagonist, Christ is immutable, constant, stable, good, and powerful, presenting real hope to people in the grip of uncertainty, mutability, mortality, and fate. Furthermore, Christ is *personal*, as opposed to the *impersonal* powers or abstract fate. He makes the love, grace, and fullness of God present with and within people. He is also *historically human*, his incarnation representing an act of divine solidarity with people in their cosmic estrangement, thus bridging the gap between God and people as well as ending their isolation and loneliness.

In a universe where Christ is the cosmic protagonist, the world is never the theater only of evil or of the powers that are in rebellion against God. God is always active and present in the Son, who is the embodiment of his love and his will to reconcile all things to himself. God never retreats in the face of evil or of the powers but remains constant and present in the lives of those he calls his children.

Also, it is important to notice that, in the Christ-centered cosmological narrative, the *soteriological responsibility* to "fix" things is never in the hands of people. Hence, people are freed from the terrible necessity of seeking, using, or manipulating power (whether personal or cosmic) in order to guarantee their own well-being.

In the Christ-centered cosmological narrative of Colossians, the importance of the cosmic powers is underplayed, while the *personal sin and responsibility of people* is emphasized. Fallen people face the wrath of God, not of the powers or the astral gods. The powers themselves are in need of reconciliation with God, and in the center of the cosmos-wide act of divine reconciliation stands humankind. In the fellowship with Christ, there is a clear shift away from the question of the cosmic power balance, hence also a relaxation in power consciousness and abolition of any need to obtain or manipulate power to one's own advantage. In the end, only the power of Christ is important, but it is not a power that is available in the first place to vindicate the oppressed. It is significant that, in the Jewish apocalyptic mystic narrative, human attainment of cosmic power is still in focus, probably through an acute experience of powerlessness and marginalization. In a sense, the inherent animosity between the powerful and the weak has been transferred to the messianic figure, who becomes the agent of judgment for the powerless and oppressed. This cosmological narrative therefore offers no real alternative: it still operates on a model of vengeance and enmity—only the agents have changed. It can offer no real peace and reconciliation, only a postponed (eschatological) showdown between oppressor and oppressed. The Christ-centered narrative is very different in this regard: it no longer contains any element of vengeance but actively calls for reconciliation also with one's enemies (see Col 3:5–17). What is important here is not power awarded to the faithful in divine retribution but rather a powerful Christ who strengthens, sanctifies, and perfects the saints.

In contrast to the Jewish apocalyptic mystic narrative, in the Christ-centered narrative the stage for cosmic reconciliation is not the *eschatological future* but the lived-in *present*. In a sense, the present is already eschatological, because of the events of the cross and the resurrection of Jesus. Every personal conversion today is a reenactment and continued actualization of the cosmic reconciliation wrought by Christ. Baptism itself becomes an event of cosmic importance, representing the cosmic migration from the domain of darkness to the kingdom of the beloved Son.

The sphere within which the reality of the new universe (which is accessible only in fellowship with Christ) is experienced is *the church as the body of Christ*. The church is the preliminary manifestation of the new creation, where neither powers nor the law plays a role. No extraordinary power games, no manipulation of cosmic power, no mystical access to the mysteries of cosmic power, no purely future-directed expectation of a better world, no zealous asceticism have any place in this new universe. Relationships in this sphere are no longer characterized by divisions, fear, estrangement, abuse, animosity, enmity, hopelessness, or mutual manipulation but are governed by the will of God (motivated by love and reconciliation), by a search for the honor of Christ, and by a positive missionary attitude to those who do not yet share in Christ as the hope of glory.

4. Animosity versus Reconciliation: A Switch of Universes and Ethics

Although the whole text of Colossians is rich in material that can be exploited for the purpose of ethics, only the small passage of Col 3:5–17 will be discussed. Not only is this more manageable in terms of an essay such as this, but the passage is also one of the clearest with regard to the ethical implications of the Christ-centered cosmological narrative.

The third chapter of the letter begins with the injunction to set one's mind on the things above (τὰ ἄνω φρονεῖτε, 3:2), referring to the wonderful reality of the glorified and victorious Christ as ruler of all things—the key motif of the cosmological narrative of Colossians. This constitutes a command to live one's life as a perpetual *sursum corda* to the glorified Christ. In practice, it amounts to the following: (1) putting to death the earthly members (3:5, Νεκρώσατε οὖν τὰ μέλη τὰ ἐπὶ τῆς γῆς); (2) putting off a whole plethora of sins (3:8, νυνὶ δὲ ἀπόθεσθε καὶ ὑμεῖς τὰ πάντα); (3) putting on the new self (3:10, καὶ ἐνδυσάμενοι τὸν νέον τὸν ἀνακαινούμενον); (4) clothing oneself with new virtues (3:12, ἐνδύσασθε οὖν...). These commands, taken as a whole, amount to the command to execute the cosmos-wide Christ-event (into which one is included in baptism) in one's own life, especially the reconciling, peace-working, and sanctifying death and resurrection of Christ (see 1:18, 20–22; 2:11–13; 3:1–4). This is the practical manifestation of life as constant *sursum corda* to the glorified Christ, who is the ruler of all things.

The references to putting to death, putting off, putting on, and clothing oneself are all terms of baptism,[34] linking the salvation in Christ as cosmic event to ethical implications. What is given here is not a mere "Do not do this but do this!" but is much rather an injunction to walk in Christ (2:6), the protagonist of the cosmological narrative of Colossians.

The first catalogue of sins (3:5), listing sexual immorality, impurity, lust, evil desires, and greed, does not at first glance betray the presence of animosity. However, closer inspection reveals that these are all sins that destroy human fellowship. Sexual immorality transforms people into objects of lust and evil desires. Neither greed nor impurity holds others in honor or serves them in selfless love; both rather operate on the basis of profound selfishness to the exclusion of the interests of others. The second catalogue of sins (3:8–9) lists the so-called sins of the tongue, where the underlying animosity is clearly visible. Anger, rage, malice, slander, filthy language, and lies serve to create suspicion and estrangement between people, destroy relationships and even lives. It also betrays the same profound selfishness and self-serving attitude as the first catalogue of sins mentioned above.

Uitman identifies these sins as characteristic of societies in transition, anywhere and at any time: rapid social change creates cosmic alienation, causing loneliness and isolation of the individual, with profound selfishness and self-assertion as well as a basic animosity toward others.[35] Colossians 3:7

---

34. Lohse, *The New Testament Environment*, 147.

35. J. E. Uitman, *De brief van Paulus aan de Colossenzen* (De prediking van het Nieuwe Testament; Nijkerk: Callenbach, 1972), 80–81.

identifies this as the lifestyle of the unconverted[36]—those who are still in the dominion of darkness, who live as cosmic exiles, and who have not made the switch to the universe where Christ is Lord of all.

In the place of these sins, life in the new universe of Christ is motivated by the *peace* of Christ that reigns in the hearts of the converted (3:15, καὶ ἡ εἰρήνη τοῦ Χριστοῦ βραβευέτω ἐν ταῖς καρδίαις ὑμῶν). The peace of Christ that reigns in the heart of people causes their whole existence, in all its facets and concrete manifestations, to be in the grip of the reconciliation with God in Christ. Lohse remarks that this peace of Christ becomes the sphere in which the converted live—especially within the social circles of the church as body of Christ.[37] The peace of Christ is in this sense *the expression of a new cosmic order* that came into existence in the Christ-events, focused in the church as the center of the lordship of Christ. This becomes the determining motif in the lives of Christians, and not fear of any cosmic powers, nor the fears of a cosmic stranger, nor fear of the wrath of God that awaits those who break the numerous laws of the ascetics.

The above becomes even clearer when one considers that the *new person* the converted are to put on is none other than Christ himself (see Rom 13:14): believers stand before God clothed with Christ, in a new corporate identity. The practical consequences of this are spelled out in the virtue list of 3:12–14. One of the key virtues here is the willingness to forgive, which is not only motivated by the forgiveness received in Christ but also reflects and proclaims his forgiveness (see 3:17). It is important to note that all the virtues mentioned here—compassion, kindness, humility, gentleness, patience, forgiveness, love (the perfecting virtue), and peace—are fellowship-creating virtues, in contrast to the fellowship-destroying sins mentioned earlier.

Of special importance is 3:11, where we see the complete equality of all in the fellowship of Christ: none of the old status-categories of Hellenistic society are maintained in the fellowship of the church.[38] The walls of superiority and inferiority (and thus of mutual animosity) on grounds of ethnicity, culture, language, or social issues no longer exist in the church. Even people who were not regarded as human beings and who were regarded as revolting (the slaves) received a place in the new community. In the body of Christ, where he is Lord of all, there is only one determining reality: the Christ with whom all are clothed and the body of Christ to which they all belong and to which they have all been called equally. In this way the fellowship of the church

---

36. Περιεπατήσατέ ποτε; Margaret Y. MacDonald, *Colossians and Ephesians* (Sacra Pagina 17; Collegeville, Minn.: Liturgical Press, 2000), 136.

37. Lohse, *The New Testament Environment*, 150.

38. See MacDonald, *Colossians and Ephesians*, 138–39.

becomes a home to all those who have become strangers in a world they can no longer call home. The church as the body of Christ becomes a community of hope and liberation, because the hope-filled expectation of the return of Christ and the liberation from sin in fellowship with Christ receive practical and concrete actualization in the interpersonal and intercultural relationships within the church. In this way, the church becomes an exemplary (almost sacramental) community, pointing to the fullness of redemption in Christ at his return.

None of these ethical injunctions would make any real sense without the foundations of the cosmological narrative of Colossians. They would have no persuasive power or authority without the driving force of the story of cosmic reconciliation in Christ, and especially not without the context of the cosmic migration or switch of universes (expressed in baptism) the converted undergo when they hear and believe the gospel of Jesus Christ, the Lord of all.

5. Conclusion

Ethical discussions that do no more than to set injunction against injunction rarely do more than to preach to the converted or to bother those who do not want to hear. It also reduces Christian ethics to hard and loveless legalism and asceticism, which hold little attraction for hurting, despairing people. However, when ethical discussions are conducted within the context of cosmological narratives, meaningful discussions become a possibility. Not only does it create the opportunity to plumb the depths of people's despair when they find themselves in an unrecognizable and frightening world, thus making possible real understanding of the way they live their lives and of their attitudes to others (often characterized by profound animosity that finds expression in many subtle ways of self-preservation and self-assertion), but it also offers the opportunity to share the gospel of Jesus Christ in a way that addresses the deepest hurts and insecurities of people. Christian ethics can then be explained as an expression of the peace of Christ—a peace that is not merely some esoteric hippie mantra but is actually nothing less than the new cosmic order of the universe where Christ is Lord of all through the reconciliation he accomplished through his death and resurrection. The lives of Christians then become an invitation to consider emigration, to make a switch of universes, from the dominion of darkness to the kingdom of the beloved Son.

USELESS COMMANDMENT: ANIMOSITY TOWARD THE EARLIER COVENANT IN HEBREWS

Outi Leppä

1. PRELIMINARY REMARKS

It is typical of Hebrews to present comparative arguments that contrast Christ and his significance to persons and institutions of the earlier covenant based on the agreement between Moses and God. Christ is shown to be superior to the angels (1:13–14), Moses (3:1–6), Aaron (5:1–10), and the Levitical priests (7:1–28). His sacrifice is superior to those of the old sanctuary (9:1–14), and the covenant based on his work is better than the first one (8:7–13; 9:15–22; 12:24).[1]

The origin of Hebrews is a mystery. It was included in the Pauline corpus in its earliest known form P[46]. Yet on the basis of stylistic and theological differences between Paul's undisputed letters and Hebrews, there is a wide consensus of scholarship that Paul did not write the text. Furthermore, Hebrews cannot be clearly identified with any known writer.[2] The genre of Hebrews is also ambiguous. It has a concluding section typical of an ancient letter but no epistolary opening. However, the text seems to be rather a

---

1. See, among others, Harold W. Attridge, "Hebrews, Epistle to the," *ABD* 3:97–105, esp. 99.

2. Similarly William Lane, *Hebrews 1–8* (WBC 47A; Dallas: Word, 1991), xlix; Craig R. Koester, *Hebrews: A New Translation with Introduction and Commentary* (AB 36; New York: Doubleday, 2001), 42–46; Floyd V. Filson, *'Yesterday': A Study of Hebrews in the Light of Chapter 13* (SBT 2/4; London: SCM, 1967), 9–12; Attridge, "Hebrews, Epistle to the," 3:97; Harold W. Attridge, *The Epistle to the Hebrews: A Commentary on the Epistle to the Hebrews* (Hermeneia; Philadelphia: Fortress, 1989), 1–6; Barnabas Lindars, *The Theology of the Letter to the Hebrews* (New Testament Theology; Cambridge: Cambridge University Press, 1991), 15–17. Contra Victor C. Pfitzner, *Hebrews* (ANTC; Nashville: Abingdon, 1997), 25–26, who states that nothing excludes the authorship of Apollos.

"sermon in epistolary form" than a real letter.³ The author himself defines his work as "a word of exhortation" (Heb 13:22). The text is full of expositions of the Scriptures, including several quotations of and allusions to the Old Testament. The text is based on Ps 110 in particular. Therefore, the text seems to be composed like a Jewish homiletical midrash. The writer presents his own interpretation of the sacred text trying to find its true meaning.⁴ In the same way as the origin of Hebrews, its addressee is unclear. Since the author employs the Old Testament very often, scholars generally suggest that the text is addressed to Jewish Christian believers.⁵ The writer's wide knowledge of the Old Testament also indicates that the author was a converted Jew.⁶

Although the juxtaposition between Christ's covenant and the Mosaic covenant is the most distinctive characteristic of Hebrews, scholars often tend to emphasize that the book is not hateful toward Judaism. They contend that the purpose of the author is to prove the distinctiveness of Christ only, not to disparage Moses or the Levitical system.⁷ Sometimes it is also highlighted

---

3. Pfitzner, *Hebrews*, 20, who also suggests that the text was likely meant to be read in gatherings of the congregation. See Attridge, "Hebrews, Epistle to the," 3:98, who calls Hebrews a "homily"; Gerd Schunack, *Der Hebräerbrief* (ZBNT 14; Zürich: Theologische Verlag, 2002), 13, who considers it a homiletic tractate ("homiletische Traktat"); Siegfried Schulz, *Die Mitte der Schrift: Der Frühkatholizismus im Neuen Testament als Herausforderung an den Protestantismus* (Stuttgart: Kreuz, 1976), 257: "eine schriftlich abgefasste Predigt." Contra Lindars, *Theology of the Letter*, 6–7, who emphasizes that Hebrews should be defined as a letter since it is aimed to people from afar.

4. George Wesley Buchanan, *To the Hebrews: Translation, Commentary and Conclusions* (AB 36; Garden City, N.Y.: Doubleday, 1972), xix–xxii.

5. Walter Edward Brooks, "The Perpetuity of Christ's Sacrifice in the Epistle to the Hebrews," *JBL* 89 (1970): 205–14, esp. 205; Lane, *Hebrews 1–8*, liv–lv; Helmut Koester, "'Outside the Camp': Hebrews 13.9–14," *HTR* 55 (1962): 299–315, esp. 299–303; Filson, 'Yesterday', 61–66; Susanne Lehne, *The New Covenant in Hebrews* (JSNTSup 44; Sheffield: JSOT Press, 1990), 16; John Dunnill, *Covenant and Sacrifice in the Letter to the Hebrews* (SNTSMS 75; Cambridge: Cambridge University Press, 1992), 22. Cf. Pfitzner, *Hebrews*, 28, who interprets that the congregation being addressed included mostly Jewish Christians but on the basis of Heb 2:3 assumes that it also included Gentile Christians. Differently, Attridge ("Hebrews, Epistle to the," 3:97–98) points out that the writer's acquaintance with the Old Testament indicates a Jewish Christian author only.

6. See Attridge, "Hebrews, Epistle to the," 3:97–98.

7. See Pfitzner, *Hebrews*, 29 and 72: "The argument of Hebrews is thus not anti-Jewish, but is designated to prove the distinctiveness of Christian faith and worship for a group of Jewish Christians"; Hugh Montefiore, *A Commentary on the Epistle to the Hebrews* (BNTC; London: Black, 1964), 71: "It is noteworthy that our author never attempts in any way to denigrate Moses." See also Koester, *Hebrews*, 248; David A. deSilva, "Despising Shame: A Cultural-Anthropological Investigation of the Epistle to the Hebrews," *JBL* 113 (1994):

that the author of Hebrews only emphasizes that Christ is "better" than Moses and that his covenant is "better" than the earlier one.[8] However, when the author of Hebrews compares Christ with Moses and Aaron in order to exalt him, he has to argue that these people, who were highly appreciated in Jewish circles, were inferior to Christ, which makes it likely that at the same time that the author exalts Christ he has to, at least occasionally, disparage those who were exalted in Judaism. It was a standard technique of ancient writers to make comparisons in order to give honor upon some persons and disgrace upon others.[9] However, the extensive use of this method to exalt Christ and boast the author's own generation of early Christians at the expense of the persons and institutions connected with the earlier covenant gives us a reason to assume that the style of Hebrews is not always fair to Judaism. The purpose of this essay is to investigate the animosity appearing in the descriptions of the Mosaic covenant and the Levitical system in Hebrews as well as to call attention to the attempts of scholars to diminish or ignore the animosity in their interpretations.

2. Moses as Being Inferior to Christ

Hebrews 3:1–6 highlights that both Jesus and Moses were trustworthy to God. The text quotes Num 12:7–8, which emphasizes Moses' trustworthiness as the servant of God.[10] Moreover, the influence of the Nathan oracle (2 Sam 7:14; 1 Chr 17:11–14) is likely.[11] In Jewish tradition, Num 12:7 was generally employed to show the fidelity and authority of Moses as well as his superior-

---

439–61, esp. 447; Norman A. Beck, *Mature Christianity in the 21st Century: The Recognition and Repudiation of the Anti-Jewish Polemic in the New Testament* (rev. ed.; Shared Ground among Jews and Christians 5; New York: Crossroad, 1994), 314–17.

8. See Montefiore, *A Commentary on the Epistle*, 71; Pfitzner, *Hebrews*, 41.

9. Carol J. Schlueter, *Filling Up the Measure: Polemical Hyperbole in 1 Thessalonians 2.14–16* (JSNTSup 98; Sheffield: JSOT Press, 1994), 75, 79; Lauri Thurén, "Hey Jude! Asking for the Original Situation and Message of a Catholic Epistle," *NTS* 43 (1997): 451–65, esp. 458; Andrie B. du Toit, "Vilification as a Pragmatic Device in Early Christian Epistolography," *Bib* 75 (1994): 403–12, esp. 411–12.

10. Buchanan, *To the Hebrews*, 56; Pfitzner, *Hebrews*, 72.

11. Mary Rose D'Angelo, *Moses in the Letter to the Hebrews* (SBLDS 42; Missoula, Mont.: Scholars Press, 1976), 70–76; Sverre Aalen, "'Reign' and 'House' in the Kingdom of God. Supplement: 'Kingdom' and 'House' in Pre-Christian Judaism," *NTS* 8 (1961): 215–40, esp. 236; Philip Edgcumbe Hughes, *A Commentary on the Epistle to the Hebrews* (Grand Rapids: Eerdmans, 1977), 130, 137; Lane, *Hebrews 1–8*, 72, 76.

ity over the angels.¹² However, the author of Hebrews emphasizes that Jesus as a high priest and as an apostle is worthy of more glory than Moses in the same way as "the builder of the house has more honor than the house itself" (v. 3). The author employs here a common ancient thought that the one who constructs is greater than his construction (see Philo, *Plant*. 68).¹³ "House" refers to the "house of Israel," which Moses belonged to and served.¹⁴ In contrast, Jesus, as an apostle and Son of God, belonged to the builder. Though apostolic Christology also occurs in other early Christian writings, Heb 3:2 is the only case where Jesus is directly called an apostle. As a representative of God, Christ thus has the same authority as God, who sent him.¹⁵ Though the comparison between Moses and Jesus starts from the likeness between them—both are described as faithful to God—from the beginning, the author's purpose is clearly to show Jesus' superiority. As a heavenly figure, he is a priori superior to Moses, who is an earthly person, and thus his glory overshadows that of Moses.¹⁶

Numbers 12:7-8 highlights that God spoke with Moses "mouth to mouth" (στόμα κατὰ στόμα) and that Moses "saw the glory of the Lord" (τὴν δόξαν κυρίου εἶδεν). Moses was thus generally highly praised in Judaism (see Philo, *Leg*. 2.67; 3.228). Though Heb 3:5 seems to cite the term "servant" (θεράπων) from Num 12:7, the comparison between Jesus as a representative of God contrasted to Moses as God's servant is rather more dismissive than a fair description of a highly appreciated Jewish prophet. Furthermore, Moses has a very utilitarian role in the text. He testified "to the things that would be spoken later," not in his but in Christ's time (Heb 3:5). Therefore, at the same time that the author of Hebrews exalts Christ, he also disparages Moses.¹⁷

---

12. Pfitzner, *Hebrews*, 72, following D'Angelo, *Moses in the Letter*, 95–149. For Jewish interpretations of Num 12:7, see D'Angelo, *Moses in the Letter*, 95–149; Hermann L. Strack and Paul Billerbeck, *Die Briefe des Neuen Testaments und die Offenbarung Johannis* (vol. 3 of *Kommentar zum Neuen Testament aus Talmud und Midrasch*; 8th ed.; Munich: Beck, 1985), 683; Buchanan, *To the Hebrews*, 56–57.

13. Montefiore, *A Commentary on the Epistle*, 72; James Moffatt, *A Critical and Exegetical Commentary on the Epistle to the Hebrews* (ICC; Edinburgh: Clark, 1986), 42; Koester, *Hebrews*, 251. Philo, *Plant*. 68: "he that has gained possession is better than the possession, and he that has made than that which he has made" (ὁ κτησάμενος τὸ κτῆμα τοῦ κτήματος ἀμείνων καὶ τὸ πεποιηκὸς τοῦ γεγονότος).

14. Lehne, *The New Covenant in Hebrews*, 29; Buchanan, *To the Hebrews*, 57.

15. Buchanan, *To the Hebrews*, 55–57.

16. Lehne, *The New Covenant in Hebrews*, 22–23.

17. Similarly Buchanan, *To the Hebrews*, 59; see also 57. Cf. Dunnill, *Covenant and Sacrifice*, 168–69, who highlights that the praise of Moses is invalidated by associating him as a failed leader and mediator of an insufficient covenant. Contra Pfitzner, *Hebrews*, 72:

Scholars often try to neglect or diminish the inequitable setting of the comparison. Lane highlights that, in the same way as in the Jewish tradition, in Heb 3:5 Moses is seen as a honored servant of God (Exod 4:10; 14:31; Num 11:11; Deut 3:24; Josh 1:2; 1 Chr 16:40).[18] In addition, deSilva emphasizes the respect Moses is given in Hebrews: "Rather than giving a polemic against Moses, the author relies on the high esteem Moses enjoyed."[19] Montefiore and Craig R. Koester neglect the unfair comparison by emphasizing that the author of Hebrews does not recall Moses' unfaithfulness mentioned in Num 20:12.[20] In addition, Koester points out that the author does not contrast Moses' fading splendor with Christ's abiding glory, which Paul refers to in 2 Cor 3:7–11.[21] These interpretations, which are based on *argumentum e silentio*, as well as those that emphasize that Hebrews describes Moses as a highly esteemed person, seem to be attempts to diminish the fact that Moses, a honored prophet in Judaism, is disparaged in the text. Scholars want to censor the animosity toward Judaism in the New Testament.[22]

Besides the comparison between Jesus and Moses in Heb 3:1–6, the use of the word "mediator" (μεσίτης) in Hebrews highlights the superiority of Christ compared to Moses. It is remarkable that the noun "mediator" is always connected to Christ and the new covenant (Heb 8:6; 9:15; 12:24),[23] while in contemporary Jewish literature Moses had the role of the mediator between God and his people (see As. Mos. 1:14; Philo, *Mos.* 2.166).[24] In Hebrews, the role of Moses is thus given to Christ. Moses loses his position that he had in Judaism as the mediator between God and his people and as a prophet in his own right. Instead, Moses is described as a servant whose only duty was to prepare the way for Christ. Therefore, the figure of Moses in Heb 3:1–6 is in sharp contrast to the position he had in Judaism. Accordingly, when Hebrews highlights the distinctiveness of Christ compared to the position of Moses, Moses is dismissed. It is yet noteworthy that Moses is not always blamed in Hebrews. Hebrews 11:23–29 praises the faith of Moses and Jesus quite equally,

---

"The rhetorical technique of comparison is again adopted to exalt Christ, not to denigrate his counterpart."

18. Lane, *Hebrews 1–8*, 78.

19. See deSilva, "Despising Shame," 447.

20. Montefiore, *A Commentary on the Epistle*, 71; Koester, *Hebrews*, 248. See also Lane, *Hebrews 1–8*, 80.

21. Koester, *Hebrews*, 248.

22. See Luke Timothy Johnson, "The New Testament's Anti-Jewish Slander and the Conventions of Ancient Polemic," *JBL* 108 (1989): 419–41, esp. 421.

23. Lane, *Hebrews 1–8*, 208, calls attention to this detail.

24. Hughes, *Commentary on the Epistle*, 296.

although this passage also emphasizes that Jesus is the perfector of faith and Moses was only his forerunner.[25]

In Heb 3:1, 6 it is emphasized that Jesus is the high priest of "*our confession*" and that "*we are his house if we hold firm the confidence.*" Since in Heb 3:1–6 Christ and Moses are contrasted, "our confession" in Heb 3:1 is the belief in Christ, which is contrasted to the doctrine associated with Moses.[26] "His house" in Heb 3:6 must refer to "God's house," where Christ is faithful as a son. It does not seem likely that the author has in mind two houses, God's house and Christ's house side by side.[27] These "we" references include a self-conscious notion that the doctrine that the author represents is the correct one. In order to highlight the issue, the author uses an insider-outsider dichotomy and describes those who do not share the opinion as outsiders. They are objectified, and their teachings are marginalized.[28] However, it is not clear who the insiders and who the outsiders are. Those of the readers who follow the doctrine that the author represents and hold fast to the confidence evidently belong to the insiders,[29] but all Christian believers as such do not seem to have a permanent position as insiders.[30] Yet it is not clear whether the author regards a wider group of Christians as insiders.[31] Furthermore, in spite of the strong juxtaposition between Moses and Jesus and the disparagement toward Moses in Heb 3:1–6, it is also not self-evident that the author excludes all Jews from the house of God and thus makes

---

25. Attridge, *Hebrews*, 341–43. See also Pfitzner, *Hebrews*, 164–65.

26. See Moffatt, *Critical and Exegetical Commentary*, 41.

27. Ibid., 42; Jürgen Roloff, *Die Kirche im Neuen Testament* (Grundrisse zum Neuen Testament 10; Das Neue Testament Deutsch, Ergänzungsreihe 10; Göttingen: Vandenhoeck & Ruprecht, 1993), 284–85.

28. For the insider-outsider dichotomy, see Pamela Thimmes, "Women Reading Women in the Apocalypse: Reading Scenario 1, the Letter to Thyatira (Rev. 2.18–29)," *CurBR* 2 (2003): 128–44, esp. 133–136; Elisabeth Schüssler Fiorenza, "Paul and the Politics of Interpretation," in *Paul and Politics: Ekklesia, Israel, Imperium, Interpretation: Essays in Honor of Krister Stendahl* (ed. Richard A. Horsley; Harrisburg, Pa.: Trinity Press International, 2000), 45; Outi Leppä, "Animosity in Early Christian Debates about the Jewish Food Rules" (paper presented at the EABS Annual Meeting, Dresden, 8 August 2005), 11–16.

29. See Lane, *Hebrews 1–8*, 79; Koester, *Hebrews*, 252–53; see also Buchanan, *To the Hebrews*, 58.

30. Similarly Montefiore, *A Commentary on the Epistle*, 73.

31. The following scholars seem to represent the view that the author has a wider group of Christians in mind: deSilva, "Despising Shame," 458; Montefiore, *A Commentary on the Epistle*, 73; Hughes, *Commentary on the Epistle*, 158.

them outsiders.³² I shall return to the division between insiders and outsiders in section 5.

3. Israelites as Unable to Benefit from God's Promises

Hebrews 4:2 describes how both the Israelites and "we" were evangelized (εὐηγγελισμένοι) in the same way. Though the word *gospel* (εὐαγγέλιον) does not appear in Hebrews, the author seems to assume an equivalence between the promise (ἐπαγγελία) given to the exodus generation and the gospel preached to his own contemporaries.³³ However, the author emphasizes that the hearing of the gospel did not benefit (οὐκ ὠφέλησεν) the Israelites since it was not united by faith. The original form of the Greek text is uncertain, and thus it is unclear how the gospel and faith should have been united in the time of exodus. In any case, the main point of the text is the contrast between the Israelites and the author's generation. The promise was given to the Israelites, but because of unbelief they missed heeding the gospel. In contrast, the author's generation represents those "who have believed" (Heb 4:3).³⁴

Hebrews 3–4 is a psalm midrash. The author gives his explanation of the rest of God promised in Ps 95:11.³⁵ In Heb 4:1–3 the author reminds his readers about the promise of entering that rest, which is still "unfulfilled" (καταλειπομένης), and exhorts that no one should fail to reach it. The previous chapter already begins the argumentation by describing the disobedience, rebelliousness, sinfulness, and lack of belief of the exodus generation. On the one hand, the author wants to prove that the Israelites were unable to reach that rest because of their sinfulness in order to show that the promise is still "unfulfilled" and thus available to him and his readers.³⁶ On the other hand, the author intends to emphasize that time is irrelevant for the fulfillment of God's promises, and thus the door is still open; the "today" referred

---

32. Roloff (*Die Kirche im Neuen Testament*, 283–85) rejects the alternative that the Jews could be excluded from God's house by interpreting that according to Hebrews both Jews and Christians work together in the house of God. Yet his interpretation neglects entirely the unfair attitude toward Moses in Heb 3:1–6.

33. Attridge, *Hebrews*, 124–25; Hughes, *Commentary on the Epistle*, 156. See also Lehne, *The New Covenant in Hebrews*, 47.

34. See Attridge, *Hebrews*, 125–26; Koester, *Hebrews*, 269–70; Pfitzner, *Hebrews*, 80; Buchanan, *To the Hebrews*, 70–71.

35. Attridge, *Hebrews*, 123–24; Pfitzner, *Hebrews*, 79.

36. This is highlighted by Buchanan, *To the Hebrews*, 68, 70; Attridge, *Hebrews*, 123–24; Pfitzner, *Hebrews*, 79.

to in Ps 95:7 is today (see Heb 3:7; 4:7).[37] Accordingly, there is a sharp contrast between the generations: the exodus generation was unable to receive the gospel because of their lack of faith, and thus God in his anger swore that they would not enter his rest, while the writer's generation has been able to adopt the gospel and to believe, and so his rest is available to them.[38]

The description of the exodus generation as representatives of unbelief in Heb 3:7–19, which in Heb 4:1–3 reaches its peak in the sharp contrast between the belief of the author's generation and such unbelief of the exodus generation that even influenced God's anger, does not do justice to the Israelites. It is remarkable, however, that Jews themselves also used the exodus generation as an example of unbelief, which influenced God's anger (see Pss 78; 95). The author of Hebrews employs the same weapon in order to highlight the belief of his own generation. He stereotypically describes the exodus generation as nothing but bad: no positive characteristic is connected to them.[39]

It is noteworthy that in Heb 3–4 the author uses many techniques typical of ancient writers to vilify his opponents. He mentions disreputable persons from the past in order to abuse persons of his own time and to emphasize the contrast between good addressees and bad opponents. The same technique is used by John the Seer, who in Rev 2:14, 20 associates his opponents with Balaam and Jezebel,[40] and by the author of Jude, who enumerates several disreputable persons from the Israelites' history (Jude 5–11).[41] It is also a standard stereotyped charge in Jewish and Gentile traditions to emphasize that the Jews displease God (see 1 Thess 2:14–16).[42] Furthermore, the author of Hebrews passes a judgment-threat on his opponents when emphasizing that God swore that the exodus generation would not enter his rest but that only

---

37. Hughes, *Commentary on the Epistle*, 155; and Montefiore, *A Commentary on the Epistle*, 83–84, emphasize this aspect.

38. See Montefiore, *A Commentary on the Epistle*, 83–84; Hughes, *Commentary on the Epistle*, 158.

39. See du Toit's definition of stereotyped vilificatory language: "In those instances where the vilificatory language has become stereotyped … the historical element has disappeared. The references to the opposition are not intended to characterize them otherwise than that they are in fact opposition and should be strongly rejected" ("Vilification as a Pragmatic Device," 411, following Johnson, "Anti-Jewish Slander," 429–30, 433, 441).

40. For the rhetorical technique employed in Rev 2:14, 20, see Leppä, "Animosity in Early Christian Debates," 11–16; David E. Aune, *Revelation 1–5* (WBC 52A; Dallas: Word, 1997), 185–86; du Toit, "Vilification as a Pragmatic Device," 410. Du Toit presents, besides Rev 2, 2 Pet 2:15 and Jude 11 as examples of associating opponents with dubious historical characters.

41. For the method used in Jude, see Thurén, "Hey Jude," 461–62.

42. Schlueter, *Filling Up the Measure*, 100.

those of author's generation who believe in Christ are able to reach it. This method is used also in 2 Cor 11:15; Gal 5:10; 2 Pet 2:3–22; 3:16; Jude 4–16; and 2 Clem. 10:5.[43] Moreover, the author defends his argumentation by referring to the authority of God and projecting his animosity onto God: it is not his but God's anger that judges the Israelites. The habit of projecting the hostility onto God, who will punish, also occurs in other early Christian writings (see Matt 3:7; Luke 3:7; Rom 1:18; 2:5, 8; 12:19; 1 Thess 4:8).[44] As in the comparison between Christ and Moses, the author again uses an insider-outsider dichotomy. While the writer with his readers are those "who have believed" and are able to reach God's rest, his opponents are objectified as outsiders. Although the author of Hebrews picks examples of disreputable persons from the Israelites' history, it is not necessary to assume that he opposes the Jews of his own time. He does not identify his adversaries but only makes the distinction between those "who have believed" and those who have not and are thus outsiders.[45]

4. LEVITICAL PRIESTHOOD AS BASED ON THE LAW OF A FLESHLY COMMANDMENT

Hebrews 7:11–28 is an exposition on Ps 110:4: "You are a priest forever according to the order of Melchizedek," which is quoted in Heb 7:17. The passage describes Christ's priesthood as superior to that of Levitical priests, emphasizing that it is based on "the order of Melchizedek" and that it lasts "forever."[46] The author highlights that Jesus was not from the tribe of Levi but descended from Judah, and thus, like Melchizedek, he did not come from priestly stock.[47] In addition, the writer refers to the detail that Moses

---

43. Referring to 2 Cor 11:15; Gal 5:10; 2 Pet 2:3–22; 3:16; Jude 4–16; and 2 Clem. 10:5, du Toit ("Vilification as a Pragmatic Device," 410) suggests that the passing of the judgment-threat on one's opponents was one commonplace technique of vilification of the early Christian letter writers.

44. See William V. Harris, *Restraining Rage: The Ideology of Anger Control in Classical Antiquity* (Cambridge: Harvard University Press, 2001), 394–95; Schlueter, *Filling Up the Measure*, 89–90.

45. It is also remarkable that, although Ignatius in *Phld.* 6:1 and *Magn.* 8:1 explicitly warns about Judaism (Ἰουδαϊσμός), he likely has in mind some Judaizing form of Christianity; see William R. Schoedel, "Ignatius, Epistles of," *ABD* 3:383–87, esp. 385.

46. Similarly, Pfitzner states that the author puts his central emphasis on these two details (*Hebrews*, 109). See also Michael C. Astour, "Melchizedek (Person)," *ABD* 4:684–86, esp. 686; Hughes, *Commentary on the Epistle*, 264.

47. Pfitzner, *Hebrews*, 110; Attridge, *Hebrews*, 199; Brooks, "Perpetuity of Christ's Sacrifice," 205–6. As Dunnill (*Covenant and Sacrifice*, 167) emphasizes, the role of

said nothing about priests from that tribe (Heb 7:14). On that grounds, the author concludes that Christ's priesthood is based on the order of Melchizedek and highlights that Christ did not come to the priesthood "through the law of a fleshly commandment" (κατὰ νόμον ἐντολῆς σαρκίνης),[48] as did the Levites, but "through the power of an indestructible life" (κατὰ δύναμιν ζωῆς ἀκαταλύτου; Heb 7:16). According to Israel's tradition, there was only one priesthood, that of the physical descendants of the tribe of Levi. Therefore, the author of Hebrews makes a contrast with the generally accepted tradition and develops it.[49] Besides referring to the genealogical requirements of the Levitical priesthood, the adjective σάρκινος, "fleshly, composed of flesh," has pejorative nuances. It includes the connotation of corruptibility[50] and likely foreshadows the critique of the law in Heb 9:9–10, 13, which regards the law as concerning external and physical issues only.[51]

Accordingly, in contrast to Christ's eternal and heavenly status, the author presents the Levitical priesthood as based on a fleshly and earthly system, which even seems to be inwardly corrupt. The critical attitude toward the Levitical priesthood in Hebrews is exceptional compared to contemporary Jewish writers. Philo presents the Levitical priesthood as "that perfect priesthood, by which mortality is commended to and recognized by God, whether it be through burn-offering or peace-offering or repentance of sins" (*Sacr.* 132). Even after the destruction of the temple, Josephus wrote about Levitical priests in a very appreciative tone.[52] Therefore, while Jewish writers accepted the Levitical system as given by God, Hebrews reserves the heavenly and eternal status for Christ. The reference to inward corruption resembles the rhetorical method of ancient philosophers of blaming their opponents for having the appearance of virtue but yet being inwardly corrupt.[53] Accordingly, the description of the Levitical priesthood in Hebrews is abusive. In addition, the author of Hebrews again uses the insider-outsider dichotomy. He presents Christ as a high priest with the characteristics "holy, blameless, undefiled, and

---

Melchizedek is to show that, like him, Christ is an "anomalous" figure who contravenes the system.

48. Translation from Buchanan, *To the Hebrews*, 87.

49. Koester, *Hebrews*, 359.

50. Eduard Schweizer, "σάρξ, σαρκικός, σάρκινος," *TDNT* 7:98–151, esp. 102. Buchanan (*To the Hebrews*, 125) interprets the term as indicating that the Levitical priesthood included issues that were ethically bad.

51. Attridge, *Hebrews*, 202.

52. *Ag. Ap.* 2.184–188; see Koester, *Hebrews*, 358–59.

53. Johnson ("Anti-Jewish Slander," 430) calls attention to the use of this kind of method in Aelius Aristides, *Platonic Discourses* 307.10.

separated from sinners," which recalls the Levitical purity rules,[54] and emphasizes that he and his readers are "we" who have such a perfect priest, while the opponents are outsiders, who have "other high priests" (Heb 7:26–27).

In Heb 7 the author bases his argumentation on his own interpretation of Ps 110, which he presents as a new declaration from God.[55] After abusing the Levitical system, in Heb 7:17–18 the author concludes his argumentation by strongly criticizing the law itself. "The earlier commandment" has been abrogated since it was weak and useless (ἀνωφελές) and "the law made nothing perfect." Furthermore, Heb 7:12 interprets that the change in the priesthood has influenced the change of the law. The critique of the Jewish law in Hebrews is very radical since Jews considered the law as the perfect representation of God's will.[56] Rabbinic texts present different interpretations about the law but do not contend that the law itself has been changed.[57] The attitude toward the law in Hebrews is also more radical than that of Paul in Rom 7:14, where the functioning of the law is criticized but the law itself is considered spiritual.[58] When the author of Hebrews disparages the Levitical sacrificial system and its powerlessness to cleanse, he invalidates its ability to sanctify and enable people to approach God.[59] In fact, he overrules the whole law by stating that it has been changed and abrogated. It is also noteworthy that the author of Hebrews leaves the law completely out of the new system: there is no room for a "new" or "better" law in the new covenant.[60] Therefore, the old law is totally rejected in Hebrews.[61]

Some scholars apologetically attempt to soften Hebrews' radical attitude toward the Levitical sacrificial system and the Mosaic law. Referring to Rom 7:12, 14, Hughes interprets that according to Heb 7 the law itself is not deficient but the sinful people who are not able to fulfill the law. By harmonizing

---

54. Buchanan, *To the Hebrews*, 87; Attridge, *Hebrews*, 212–13.
55. See Pfitzner, *Hebrews*, 110.
56. Montefiore, *A Commentary on the Epistle*, 124.
57. Koester, *Hebrews*, 360, esp. n. 239.
58. Attridge, *Hebrews*, 204–5.
59. Similarly Montefiore, *A Commentary on the Epistle*, 124; Brooks, "Perpetuity of Christ's Sacrifice," 213; Lane, *Hebrews 1–8*, 180, 185; Lindars, *Theology of the Letter*, 86–87.
60. Lehne, *The New Covenant in Hebrews*, 27, 99.
61. See Attridge, *Hebrews*, 203, who points out that the abrogation of the law "does not point to its relative inferiority, but to a fundamental disability deriving from its essential 'fleshiness,' which proverbially entails weakness"; Heikki Räisänen, *Paul and the Law* (Philadelphia: Fortress, 1986), 154: "The writer [of Hebrews] is very clear in his rejection of the old law as being weak in nature. Consistently enough, it is the *law* itself that is σάρκινος in this writing (7:16)."

Heb 7 with Rom 7, Hughes thus neglects Hebrews' radical attitude toward the law.[62] In the same way, Beck harmonizes Heb 7 with Rom 7:6 as well as with 2 Cor 3:6–7 and suggests that the law made nothing perfect because of men's weaknesses as high priests.[63] Furthermore, Craig Koester seeks to diminish the critique by emphasizing that the author "does not casually reject the Law," since he bases his interpretation on the issue that Scripture itself mentions the priesthood of Melchizedek.[64] However, as Koester himself admits, the author of Hebrews is in contrast with the tradition of the Levitical priesthood being generally appreciated as the only correct one in Judaism. Furthermore, the author connects Christ with Melchizedek quite intentionally and randomly. The start of the argumentation in Heb 7:11 already reveals that perfection is reserved for Christ only (see Heb 2:10; 5:9).[65] The purpose of the author seems to be to demonstrate the distinctiveness of Christ, that his new priesthood is based on "the power of an indestructible life," which indicates that Christ's life is glorious and eternal (see Heb 2:10). In order to highlight the contrast, he has to show that Christ's priesthood is due to a different foundation than the Levitical system. Therefore, probably inspired by contemporary speculations,[66] he bases his argument on the priesthood of Melchizedek.[67] As Attridge points out, "the rationale for Christ's High-Priestly status becomes

---

62. Hughes, *Commentary on the Epistle*, 265.

63. Beck, *Mature Christianity*, 316–17. Contra Luz, Räisänen, Attridge, and Johnson, who have criticized this kind of harmonizing and censoring interpretation that neglects the purpose of Hebrews. Attridge emphasizes that the point in Hebrews "is not that the Law is useless if not kept, as Paul argues in Rom 2:25" (*Hebrews*, 203 n. 77). Räisänen (*Paul and the Law*, 155), following Ulrich Luz ("Der alte und der neue Bund bei Paulus und im Hebräerbrief," *EvT* 27 [1967]: 318–36, esp. 329), criticizes such interpretations that suggest that according to Hebrews only sinful people are blamed, not the earlier covenant itself. Furthermore, Räisänen (*Paul and the Law*, 208) highlights that according to Hebrews the Old Testament law has been abolished, and thus the stance of Hebrews toward the law is more radical than that of Paul. Johnson ("Anti-Jewish Slander," 421 n. 5) criticizes Beck by stating that the attitudes that offend our emotions are systematically censored in Beck's *Mature Christianity*.

64. Koester, *Hebrews*, 359. See also Schulz, *Die Mitte der Schrift*, 262, who argues that Hebrews spiritualizes the Old Testament law and limits it to social and moral regulations.

65. See Pfitzner, *Hebrews*, 109.

66. Attridge, *Hebrews*, 187.

67. See Attridge, *Hebrews*, 187: "Ultimately he [the author] is concerned not so much with Melchizedek as with Christ, and what he says of the former is influenced heavily by what he firmly believes of the latter." Montefiore describes the purpose of the passage thus: "Paul wished to show that the Law had been abrogated" (*A Commentary on the Epistle*, 123).

the basis for an indictment of the Levitical priesthood and the religious system of which, in our author's eyes, it was the heart."[68]

Accordingly, the main purpose of Heb 7 is to demonstrate the superiority of Christ's priesthood compared to the Levitical one. In order to achieve his goal, the writer abuses the Levitical priesthood by defining it as fleshly, which refers to corruptibility, and by invalidating its ability to sanctify and enable people to serve God. Furthermore, the author rejects the whole Mosaic law by highlighting its abrogation. This is a strong attack on the Jewish sacrificial system and the law: the author of Hebrews marginalizes Jewish teaching and the whole religious system.[69]

5. The Levitical Sanctuary: A Shadowy Copy Made by Hand

Hebrews 8:1–2 describes Christ as a high priest ministering in the sanctuary that is "the true tent/tabernacle" (ἡ σκηνὴ ἡ ἀληθινή) that the Lord has set up, "not any mortal" (οὐκ ἄνθρωπος). The adjective "true" does not seem to be here the opposite of "false," but it emphasizes what is heavenly, eternally valid, and abiding in contrast to what is earthly, temporary, and transient (see Heb 9:1).[70] The author employs a general Jewish idea of heavenly sanctuary, which is an archetype for earthly temples. A similar notion occurs in Heb 10:1, where the cultic regulations of the older sanctuary are considered as "only a shadow of the good things to come," and in Heb 8:5, which calls the earthly sanctuary "a sketch and shadow of the heavenly one."[71] The contrast between a shadow and the heavenly one resembles Platonic distinctions, which are also used by Philo, although any direct connection between Philo and Hebrews is not evident.[72] However, perhaps better than Platonic philosophical thinking, the contrast between the earthly and the heavenly sanctuary recalls a characteristic Near Eastern notion of the relationship between earthly objects and their heavenly prototypes.[73] In any case, the emphasis that the Levite priests served

---

68. Attridge, *Hebrews*, 199.
69. See Attridge, *Hebrews*, 394, who highlights that, when the author of Hebrews in 4:2; 7:18; and 13:9 considers the Israelites to be totally unable to adopt the gospel, he in fact blames the old cult in its entirety for being useless.
70. See Koester, *Hebrews*, 376; Pfitzner, *Hebrews*, 118; Lane, *Hebrews 1–8*, 205–6.
71. For the Jewish notion of a heavenly temple, see Koester, *Hebrews*, 376; Attridge, *Hebrews*, 217, 219, 222–24; Pfitzner, *Hebrews*, 118–19.
72. Lincoln D. Hurst, *The Epistle to the Hebrews: Its Background of Thought* (SNTSMS 65; Cambridge: Cambridge University Press, 1990), 8–42.
73. See Buchanan, *To the Hebrews*, 134–37; Lane, *Hebrews 1–8*, 207–8, who follow Ronald Williamson, "Platonism and Hebrews," *SJT* 16 (1963): 415–24.

in a sanctuary that was only a shadowy copy of the true sanctuary of Christ clearly emphasizes the inferiority of the earthly temples and their sacrifices.[74] There is an ontological difference between the heavenly temple and its earthly prototype.[75] The description of "a shadow of the good things to come" in Heb 10:1 resembles the way in which the author of Colossians labels the teaching being confronted as "only a shadow of what is to come," which is the opposite of the correct teaching of Christ (Col 2:16–17).[76] Furthermore, the emphasis in Heb 8:1–2 that the true sanctuary has not been set up by any mortal, human person (οὐκ ἄνθρωπος) has pejorative connotations. It was typical of Judaism to denounce the wrong kind of religious practices as human inventions. In Isa 29:13 it is stressed that a personal knowledge of God is essential to the Israelites, not only a worship "that is human commands and teachings" (my translation, διδάσκοντες ἐντάλματα ἀνθρώπων καὶ διδασκαλίας). Mark 7:7 and its parallel Matt 15:9 follow the tradition and label Pharisaic tradition concerning food laws as nothing but "human commands and teachings." Furthermore, Col 2:22 uses the same phraseology in order to condemn the legalistic teaching being opposed.[77] Accordingly, when Heb 8:1–2 intends to prove the distinctiveness of Christ and his sanctuary as heavenly, at the same time it dismisses the Levitical system as being an earthly, human invention only. In the same way as in Heb 3:1, 6 and 7:26–27, in 8:1 is a self-conscious notion that "*we have* such a high priest," which suggests the privilege of special Christian ownership[78] and objectifies those who do not represent the same teaching as the author as the "other," as an outsider.

Hebrews 9:11, 24 uses phraseology very similar to Heb 8:1–2 when highlighting the significance of Christ's sanctuary compared to the Levitical one. Hebrews 9:11 describes that, when Christ came as a high priest, he came "through the greater and perfect tent not made by hand" (διὰ τῆς μείζονος καὶ τελειοτέρας σκηνῆς οὐ χειροποιήτου). In addition, Heb 9:24 emphasizes

---

74. Similarly Attridge, *Hebrews*, 219. See also Dunnill, *Covenant and Sacrifice*, 169.

75. Luz, "Der alte und der neue Bund," 330.

76. For the relationships between Col 2:16–17 and Heb 10:1, see Outi Leppä, *The Making of Colossians: A Study on the Formation and Purpose of a Deutero-Pauline Letter* (Publications of the Finnish Exegetical Society 86; Helsinki: Finnish Exegetical Society; Göttingen: Vandenhoeck & Ruprecht, 2003), 142, 145.

77. See Eduard Lohse, *Colossians and Philemon: A Commentary on the Epistles to the Colossians and to Philemon* (trans. William R. Poehlmann and Robert J. Karris; Hermeneia; Philadelphia: Fortress, 1971), 124; Peter T. O'Brien, *Colossians, Philemon* (WBC 44; Waco, Tex.: Word, 1982), 151. For the relationships between Isa 29:13, Col 2:22, and Mark 7:7, see Leppä, *Making of Colossians*, 151–52, 258–59.

78. Lehne, *The New Covenant in Hebrews*, 104. See also Hughes, *Commentary on the Epistle*, 281.

that Christ did not enter into a sanctuary that was made by hand and was "a mere copy of the true one" (ἀντίτυπον τῶν ἀληθινῶν). In both cases the author again strongly highlights the superiority of Christ's sanctuary compared to that of the Levitical one. Hebrews 9:24 includes the same idea as 10:1: the Levitical sacrifices were only a prototype, a shadow, of Christ's sacrifice.[79] The notion that the sanctuary of Christ is "not made by hand" indicates in Heb 9:11 implicitly that the earlier sanctuary was made by hand, but Heb 9:24 states the issue directly.[80]

The juxtaposition between the earthly and heavenly sanctuary in Heb 9:11, 24 greatly resembles the way that Paul, in 2 Cor 5:1, describes our human body as "the earthly house of our tabernacle" (ἡ ἐπίγειος ἡμῶν οἰκία τοῦ σκήνους),[81] which is contrasted to our eternal heavenly body, "a house not made by hand" (οἰκία ἀχειροποίητος). In 2 Cor 5:1 Paul implicitly denigrates the earthly body, which is made by hand.[82] In addition, in Col 2:11, where Christian baptism is highlighted as a circumcision not made by hand, the circumcision not made by hand is clearly considered as much better than the one made by hand. Therefore, the negative attitude toward issues made by hand in 2 Cor 5:1 and Col 2:11 indicates that the emphasis that the Levitical sanctuary was made by hand has pejorative connotations in Heb 9:11, 24.[83] It is worth noting that the formulation "made by hand" was generally used for idols in the LXX (see Lev 26:1, 30; Isa 2:18; 10:11; 19:1; 21:9; Dan 5:4, 23; Jdt 8:18; Wis 14:8).[84] Opposition to the temple was characteristic of early Jewish Christianity, and one of the central points of the criticism was that the temple was hand-made (see Mark 14:58; Matt 26:61; Acts 7:42–50).[85] The notion that God does not live in buildings made by humans also occurs in the LXX,

---

79. Cf. the use of ἀντίτυπος in 1 Pet 3:21.

80. See Jack T. Sanders, *Schismatics, Sectarians, Dissidents, Deviants: The First One Hundred Years of Jewish-Christian Relations* (London: SCM, 1993), 96.

81. English translation from Alfred Plummer, *A Critical and Exegetical Commentary on the Second Epistle of St. Paul to the Corinthians* (ICC; Edinburgh: T&T Clark, 1915), 141. Although σκῆνος generally means "body" in ancient Greek literature, it is interesting that Paul uses a temple metaphor similar to Hebrews. For the use of σκῆνος, see Margaret E. Thrall, *A Critical and Exegetical Commentary on the Second Epistle to the Corinthians* (2 vols.; ICC; Edinburgh: T&T Clark, 1994), 1:357–58.

82. Fredrik Lindgård, *Paul's Line of Thought in 2 Corinthians 4:16–5:10* (WUNT 2/189; Tübingen: Mohr Siebeck, 2005), 148–49. See also Sanders, *Schismatics, Sectarians, Dissidents, Deviants*, 96.

83. Similarly, Koester (*Hebrews*, 377, 409–10) suggests that the term χειροποίητος has pejorative connotation in Heb 9:11, 24.

84. Koester, *Hebrews*, 409–10, also calls attention to the issue.

85. Sanders, *Schismatics, Sectarians, Dissidents, Deviants*, 96, 292, following Gerd

for example, in Isa 66:1–2. Quoting this passage, Acts 7:42–50 criticizes the Jerusalem temple for being "made by hand" (χειροποίητος). It is more noteworthy yet that Acts 17:24 uses the phrase "made by hand" about the pagan, idolatrous sanctuary. Therefore, I consider it possible that also in Heb 9:11, 24 the expression "made by hand" could include the notion that the Levitical sanctuary is even idolatrous, which would be a serious accusation against the Jewish religious system.[86]

6. The First Covenant as Obsolete

Hebrews 8:8–12 quotes Jer 31:31–34 (38:31–34 LXX), where God promises to establish a new covenant (διαθήκη καινή) between God and the Israelites, since they did not continue in his covenant (Heb 8:8–9). The author refers to a superior covenant already in Heb 7:22, but now he justifies his idea through the citation of the Scriptures.[87] The text from Jeremiah is quoted to show that the first covenant could not have been faultless, since there was a need for a second one (Heb 8:7). On the basis of God's own word in the Scriptures, the author suggests that God himself, through Jeremiah, desired a new covenant.[88] The introduction to the quotation in Heb 8:8, "God finds fault with them when he says," interprets that God himself faulted the first covenant.[89] After the citation, in Heb 8:13, the author draws the conclusion that in speak-

---

Theissen, *Sociology of Early Palestinian Christianity* (trans. John Bowden; Philadelphia: Fortress, 1978), 52–58.

86. See Buchanan, *To the Hebrews*, 153. Contra Koester, *Hebrews*, 409–10, who emphasizes that "made by hand" cannot indicate that Levitical sacrifices were idolatrous, since according to Heb 8:5 Moses built the sanctuary by God's command.

87. Koester, *Hebrews*, 388–89.

88. Montefiore, *A Commentary on the Epistle*, 140; Koester, *Hebrews*, 385; Hughes, *Commentary on the Epistle*, 298–99.

89. The textual evidence is quite evenly divided between the accusative αὐτούς (ℵ* A D* I K P Ψ etc.) and the dative αὐτοῖς (P⁴⁶ ℵ² B D² etc.). Therefore, some commentators who prefer the dative αὐτοῖς consider the pronoun as the object of the verb λέγει "says" and emphasize the detail that God finds fault with the first covenant, not with the people only (see Hughes, *Commentary on the Epistle*, 298–99; Lane, *Hebrews 1–8*, 202). However, the connection between the verb λέγει and the pronoun αὐτός is unlikely, since Hebrews generally introduces biblical citations with the verb λέγει without any object (see Heb 2:6, 12; 3:7, 15; 4:3, 7; 6:14; 9:20; 10:5, 15; 12:5, 26; Koester, *Hebrews*, 385). It is also noteworthy that scholars who do not maintain the connection between λέγει and αὐτός usually interpret Heb 8:8 to mean that, besides people, God also finds fault with the entire covenant; see Koester, *Hebrews*, 385–86. See also Räisänen, *Paul and the Law*, 154, 155 n. 129.

ing about "a new covenant" God has judged the earlier covenant as "obsolete" (πεπαλαίωκεν). God himself has thus canceled the validity of the earlier covenant.⁹⁰

Although in Jer 31 God is unsatisfied with the Israelites and refers to the need for a new covenant, the sharp critique of the earlier covenant is not the point in Jeremiah's oracle. By interpreting that God finds fault in the Mosaic covenant and by defining "old" as the opposite of "new," which indicates obsolescence, the author of Hebrews emphasizes the negative side of the prophecy.⁹¹ Referring to the authority of the Scriptures and God, the author thus disparages the covenant between God and Moses in order to show that the covenant in Christ is superior to the earlier one.⁹² Furthermore, as in Heb 4, the author projects his animosity onto God: it is God who was unsatisfied with the Israelites and canceled the covenant between God and Moses.

In the same way as the author intentionally used the priesthood of Melchizedek from Ps 110 as the basis for the superiority of Christ's priesthood compared to that of the Levites in Heb 7, in Heb 8 he uses Jer 31 in order to argue for the superiority of the new covenant in contrast to the old one. Already in Heb 8:6, before the quotation from Jer 31, the covenant mediated by Jesus is defined as a better covenant based on better promises than the earlier one. The verb νομοθετέω "enact" is used in Heb 7:11 of the inauguration of the old covenant in the same way as Paul employs the noun νομοθεσία about the giving of the law to the Israelites in Rom 9:4. In contrast, in Heb 7:8 the verb νομοθετέω is reserved for the new covenant of Christ, which has replaced the first agreement. The contrast between the law and the promise in Heb 8:6 resembles Gal 3:21. Yet the author of Hebrews criticizes the old covenant more radically than Paul does. While Paul denies strict juxtaposition

---

90. Heinrich Seesemann, "πάλαι, παλαιός, παλαιότης, παλαιόω," *TDNT* 5:717–20, esp. 720; Lane, *Hebrews 1–8*, 210; Hughes, *Commentary on the Epistle*, 302. See also Heikki Räisänen, *Jesus, Paul and Torah: Collected Essays* (trans. David E. Orton; JSNTSup 43; Sheffield: JSOT Press, 1992), 247: "The law of the old covenant as a whole receives the stamp of the 'blameworthy.'"

91. Lehne, *The New Covenant in Hebrews*, 30–31; Koester, *Hebrews*, 389. See also Windisch, cited by Räisänen, *Jesus, Paul and Torah*, 247: "The author takes from the rich content of the text only the one idea that the promise of the new διαθήκη makes the old one obsolete."

92. See Lehne, *The New Covenant in Hebrews*, 53: "He chooses to quote Jeremiah's prophecy twice, but then develops the NC [new covenant] theme largely independently of his proof-text."

between the law and the promise, the author of Hebrews connects the law with the cult that he dismisses.[93]

Accordingly, in Heb 8:6–13 the author intends to demonstrate that the covenant between God and Israelites was faulty, obsolete, canceled, and replaced by a better one. On the basis of the authority of the Scriptures and God, the author disparages the covenant between God and Moses in order to show that the new covenant in Christ is superior to the earlier one.

7. Concluding Remarks

The previous examples have shown that in Hebrews the comparison between Christ and his significance to people and institutions of the earlier covenant is often dismissive and even hateful to Judaism. It is not fair to describe Moses, a highly praised prophet in Judaism, as a servant of God in contrast to Christ, who as the Son of God has the same authority as God. In this description Moses loses his position not only as the mediator between God and his people but also as an honored prophet in his own right. Instead, he is described as a servant whose only duty was to prepare the way to Christ. The figure of Moses given in Hebrews is thus in sharp contrast to the position he had in contemporary Judaism. In addition, it is not fair to Jews to describe the exodus generation as representing such unbelief that made them unable to benefit from God's promises contrasted to the belief of the author's generation, which made them able to reach the rest of God instead of the Israelites.

It is also disparaging to the Levitical priesthood that at the same time as Jewish writers accepted the system as given by God, Hebrews presents it as earthly, contrasted to the heavenly and eternal status of Christ as a high priest. When the author of Hebrews dismisses the Levitical sacrificial system and its powerlessness to cleanse, he in fact invalidates its ability to sanctify and enable people to approach God. Furthermore, the author rejects the whole Mosaic law by stating that it has been changed and abrogated. This is a strong attack on the whole Jewish sacrificial system and the law, which were both regarded as given by God in Judaism. Furthermore, it is disparaging to define the covenant between Moses and God as obsolete and replaced by a better one in Christ. It is also remarkable that the descriptions of the Levitical sanctuary as a shadowy copy of the true one and "made by hand" could even

---

93. Attridge, *Hebrews*, 221. Therefore, it is surprising that Roloff (*Die Kirche im Neuen Testament*, 282–85) totally rejects the idea that the new covenant could replace the old one in Hebrews but interprets that it only describes side by side the situation of God's people during the old and the new covenants. It is noteworthy, however, that Roloff neglects to refer to Heb 7.

include the notion that the sanctuary is idolatrous, which would be a serious accusation against the whole Jewish religious system.

It is also remarkable that the overall impression given of the covenant between Moses and God is ludicrous: Moses is described as a prophet who did not have a position in his own right; the Levitical priesthood is based on the law of a fleshly commandment that made nothing perfect, and thus the commandment was abrogated; and the Levitical sanctuary is only a shadowy copy of the true one, is made by hand, and hence is only a human invention, and perhaps is even idolatrous. In addition, the author draws the conclusion that the entire covenant is obsolete. The author of Hebrews clearly uses the technique of ridiculing one's opponents, which was commonplace in ancient literature. This description resembles Paul's attitude toward his opponents in Phil 3:2–3 and Gal 5:12, which presents in a ridiculous light those who demanded that people be circumcised.[94]

Besides the ridiculous descriptions, the author of Hebrews uses several other techniques typical of ancient writers to vilify his opponents. The exodus generation is stereotypically described as a representative of nothing but bad, and the author uses the method of referring to disreputable people from the past in order to vilify people of his own time who do not share the same opinion as he, and emphasizes the contrast between good addressees and bad opponents. Furthermore, the author of Hebrews passes a judgment-threat on his opponents when emphasizing that only those of the author's generation who share the same belief in Christ as he are able to reach God's rest. Moreover, the writer defends his argumentation by referring to the authority of the Holy Scriptures: in Heb 7 Christ's priesthood is based on the priesthood of Melchizedek promised in Ps 110; and in Heb 8, Jer 31:31–34 is used to show that it was God himself who canceled the validity of the first covenant. The writer also projects his own animosity onto God: it was God who was unsatisfied with the first covenant, which the author wishes to disparage.

The writer of Hebrews also uses an insider-outsider dichotomy several times. The author and his readers are "we"—those who have the correct confession (Heb 3:1), who are God's house (3:6), who have believed (4:3), and who have thus the superior high priest (3:1; 7:27; 8:1)—while the others are outsiders. The purpose of the othering process is to demonstrate power. Those who do not share the opinion of the author are objectified, made the

---

94. See Hans Dieter Betz, *Galatians* (Hermeneia; Minneapolis: Fortress, 1979), 270, who calls Gal 2:15 a "bloody" joke. Referring to Phil 3:2–3; 2 Cor 11:5; 12:11; and Gal 5:12, du Toit ("Vilification as a Pragmatic Device," 410) enumerates the describing of one's opponents as ludicrous characters among the vilification methods used in early Christian literature.

"other," and their teachings are marginalized. The author of Hebrews thus invalidates the authority of Moses, the Levitical system and its sanctuary, the Mosaic law, and the covenant between God and Moses. The central parts of the Jewish religious system are thus marginalized. Nevertheless, it is unlikely that the juxtaposition between insiders and outsiders, "we" and the "others," refers to the contrast between Jews and Christians. As we have noticed, all Christians as such do not belong to the insiders (see the end of §2). Moreover, we have not found any reference to the total exclusion of Jews as such. Therefore, I suggest that the purpose of Hebrews is to warn the readers about Jewish Christians who in one way or another accepted the observance of Jewish habits. The problem inside his own religious tradition influenced the author to criticize the entire Jewish sacrificial system so sharply.[95] The strong dichotomy of insiders and outsiders indicates that Hebrews represents a rigorous sectarian group the social setting of which would be worth analyzing in detail.[96] This project is beyond the scope of this essay, however.

We have noticed that scholars sometimes completely ignore or try to diminish the animosity of Hebrews in their interpretations. Furthermore, the hostility in the New Testament is also occasionally invalidated by stating that the vilifying of opponents in the writings is just typical of ancient texts.[97] It is very likely true that in ancient texts "nobody expected an objective description" and that adversaries were generally presented as immoral

---

[95]. See in this volume Jeremy Punt, "Paul and the Others: Insiders, Outsiders, and Animosity," 149–52, followed by Leppä, "Animosity in Early Christian Debates," 2, who argues that religious animosity has been noticed to be especially strong when the threat occurs inside one's own religious tradition. Johnson ("Anti-Jewish Slander," 426) also emphasizes the tendency of the New Testament writers to turn the polemic inward to other early Christian groups.

[96]. Dunnill (*Covenant and Sacrifice*, 19) suggests that the emphasis on the difference between members and nonmembers in Hebrews resembles the characteristics of sects. Furthermore, following Bryan R. Wilson ("An Analysis of Sect Development," in *Patterns of Sectarianism: Organisation and Ideology in Social and Religious Movements* [ed. Bryan R. Wilson; London: Heinemann, 1967], 22–45, esp. 36–37), Dunnill states that such a contradiction necessitates animosity toward nonmembers.

[97]. As mentioned above, Johnson often criticizes the habit of scholars of censoring from the New Testament anti-Jewish, hostile, and other tendencies that offend our sensibilities. Yet he somehow invalidates his critique by suggesting that the way the writers of the New Testament wrote about Jews is exactly the same as all contemporary opponents wrote about each other ("Anti-Jewish Slander," 429) and then concludes that the "curses" laid on Jews in the New Testament books are commonplace in ancient fights and thus the polemic indicates simply who the opponents were ("Anti-Jewish Slander," 441).

persons in order to alienate readers from them.[98] Therefore, we do not know how intentionally the author of Hebrews wanted to blacken Judaism. We must not ignore this hostility by suggesting that blaming one's opponents was just an ancient habit of writing, however, since the descriptions of Judaism in Hebrews must have looked acrimonious in the eyes of a current Jew. It is noteworthy also that, unlike New Testament texts generally, Hebrews does not blacken single false teachers only but fiercely attacks central parts of the Jewish religious system: the Mosaic law and covenant, the Levitical priesthood and its sanctuary, as well as the role of Moses as a prophet. Therefore, Hebrews must be regarded as a hostile attack upon Judaism.

---

98. Thurén, "Hey Jude," 458. See du Toit, "Vilification as a Pragmatic Device," 411–12.

No Retaliation! An Ethical Analysis of the Exhortation in 1 Peter 3:9 Not to Repay Evil with Evil

Fika J. van Rensburg

1. Introduction

This study seeks to contribute toward research on the ethics and ethos in 1 Peter, delimiting (for the purposes of the present essay) the scope to 1 Pet 3:9, within its immediate textual context, 3:8–12.

The method according to which the text is analyzed ethically is described first, defining the four categories used in the analysis (§2). The first category, the life situation of the addressees, is constructed (§3). Then the argument of 1 Peter and the local argument of the pericope in question, 3:8–12, is argued (§4). Then the second category, the basis for the ethics, is constructed (§5), followed by the ethics (§6) and the ethos (§7) in 1 Pet 3:8–12. Finally, pointers for the response to evil in present-day life situations are given.

2. Analyzing a Text Ethically

To analyze 1 Pet 3:9 ethically, four categories proposed by van der Watt[1] are used: (1) the basis (or motivation) for the ethics; (2) the ethics, viewed as the "rules" or "universal principles" for a lifestyle; (3) ethos as the actual lifestyle; and (4) the interaction with the life situation of the addressees of 1 Peter.[2]

---

1. See Jan G. van der Watt, "Directives for the Ethics and Ethos Research Project" (paper presented at a meeting of a research team on ethics, ethos, and identity, August 2004, in Pretoria), 2–4. The leader of the research team was Jan G. van der Watt. A selection of the papers read at the meeting was published in Jan G. van der Watt, ed., *Identity, Ethics, and Ethos in the New Testament* (Berlin: de Gruyter, 2006).

2. Pheme Perkins ("Ethics: New Testament," *ABD* 2:652–65) mentions two approaches to New Testament ethics: a descriptive approach to New Testament ethics that traces the sources, particular themes, and dominant perspectives of individual New Testament writ-

For Christianity, the *basis* (or motivation) of ethics is the reality of God, and specifically his will to bring persons who find themselves estranged from God (the *ab quo* of their salvation) into a restored relationship with God (the *ad quem* of their salvation). This results in a social redefinition of the individuals involved, with the new status being described in forensic, familial, economic, and similar language. This is usually done in terms of a descriptive image. The new social reality becomes the basis for the formulation of the ethics, the universal principles.[3]

The *universal principles* (or ethics) do not exist independently from the basis; they emanate from the new identity. In this sense the ethics in 1 Peter are part of the broader description of the identity of the addressees of the letter. They set out the "rules" for this new community in terms of the descriptive imagery used as the basis. Ethics, therefore, indicate prescriptiveness, which has the basis as motivation. The connection between the basis and the rules is logical. The rules function in a prescriptive way because they are motivated by the basis.

Ethos is used as a behavioral category and refers to the behavior of the persons sharing the identity. Ethos is the way the specific community brings its ethics into practice. This behavior is based on the interpretation of the rules, the ethics. The ethos (praxis of the ethics) can vary relative to the situation, but there always is a logical, social, and/or historical relation between the ethics and the ethos. Two types of ethos are distinguished: (1) *projected ethos* refers to exhortations given by the author in which he gives his own interpretation of the rule for the specific situation; and (2) *real ethos* refers to the actual behavior of the addressees, exhibiting their interpretation of the ethics.[4] The real ethos of a community can, to a lesser or greater degree, be constructed from the epistle.

---

ers or schools; and an attempt to trace recurring themes in several strands of the New Testament. The approach I am following is a further development of the first one Perkins mentions and is in this essay focused on just one pericope—as a sample of 1 Peter.

3. I disagree with Eduard Lohse (*Theological Ethics of the New Testament* [trans. M. Eugene Boring; Minneapolis: Fortress, 1991], 181), who states that "in 1 Peter the imperative is not based on the previous declaration of the indicative, but in the reverse order: ethical exhortation stands first, and is then provided with a more specific grounding." He says that this is different from Pauline theology, where the moral claim is derived from the proclamation of salvation already announced. I also do not agree with J. Ramsey Michaels (*1 Peter* [WBC 49; Waco, Tex.: Word, 1988], lxxiv) when he argues that "salvation and ethics in 1 Peter finally add up to much the same thing." This equation does not do justice to the text, since salvation is clearly the basis (or motivation) for the ethics.

4. Van der Watt, "Directives," 3.

The ethos of a community results in a specific interaction with their *life situation*,⁵ which may result in a clash of ethos: the ethos of the Christian community versus the ethos of society in general. This interaction causes reinforcement, adaptation, or repositioning of the ethos, because of the dynamic social process.⁶ This theological structure can be represented as follows (the arrows between the four categories indicate a cyclical movement).⁷

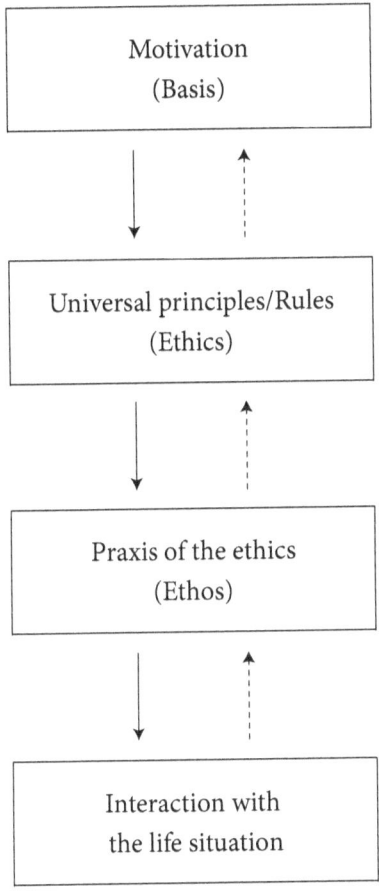

---

5. Perkins ("Ethics: New Testament") is right to argue that attempts to divorce New Testament ethics from their contexts and the particularities of the treatments of ethical topics usually result in generalities that fail to describe the data.

6. Lohse aptly writes in this regard that "one of the tasks of a New Testament ethics is to indicate how traditional content not only received a new grounding by being related to the gospel, but in essential parts also had its intrinsic meaning apprehended in a new way" (*Theological Ethics of the New Testament*, 4).

7. See van der Watt, "Directives," 2.

The basis motivates the ethics, which in turn is practiced as ethos, which receives approval and/or disapproval from society. This may result in the ethos being reconsidered in the light of the rules (ethics); the rules are in turn reconsidered in the light of the basis, and this either reinforces or reconstitutes specific behavior (ethos), and so on.

The focus of this essay is 1 Pet 3:9 and its immediate context, 3:8–12. In the ethical analysis the focus is on the second and third categories: the ethics and the ethos. The first category, basis, also receives attention, inasmuch as it provides the motivation for the ethics.[8] The fourth category, life situation, receives attention, since the ethos cannot be constructed without taking the life situation of the addressees into consideration.

The focus, however, is not so much on the ethos in itself, but the ethos is utilized to come to a clearer understanding of the ethics. The description of the ethos therefore has a heuristic function with regard to the ethics.

A subsidiary goal of the essay is to establish pointers for ethics for Christian response to animosity in present-day societies. This is done by constructing why and how the specific rules (ethics) in 1 Peter on the response to animosity lead to specific praxis of these rules (ethos) in 1 Pet 3:9. This may then provide analogical patterns (or, pointers) for ethical descriptions for the response to animosity in present-day life situations.

3. The Life Situation of the Addressees of 1 Peter

The method according to which the life situation of the addressees of the letter is constructed is the sociohistorical approach, enriched by the socioscientific approach.[9]

The goal of this construction of the sociohistoric context of the addressees of 1 Peter is to establish an interpretative framework for the ethical analysis of 1 Pet 3:9.

---

8. Perkins ("Ethics: New Testament") convincingly argues that early Christians were no more able to generate immediate and stable adhesion to virtue than their philosopher counterparts. What made them different is their religious understanding of salvation and divine judgment. This provides a more pressing call addressed to a wider range of persons than present among those converted to a philosophic life of virtue.

9. See Susan R. Garrett, "Sociology of Early Christianity," *ABD* 6:90. For a definition of this approach, see Fika J. van Rensburg, "Dekor of Konteks? Die verdiskontering van sosio-historiese gegewens in die interpretasie vir die prediking en pastoraat van 'n Nuwe Testamentteks, geïllustreer aan die hand van die 1 Peter-brief" [Decor or Context? The Utilization of Socio-historic Data in the Interpretation of a New Testament Text for Preaching and the Pastorate, Illustrated with 1 Peter], *Skrif en Kerk* (2000): 564–82.

3.1. 1 Peter as Letter

Together with quite a number of recent scholars, I view 1 Peter as a genuine letter, specifically a circular letter (like 2 Peter, Galatians, Ephesians, James, and Jude).[10] First Peter (as the other New Testament circular letters) also exhibits definite characteristics of the contemporary Jewish diaspora letter.[11]

There is quite a general consensus on the unity of 1 Peter. On the literary structure of the letter there is, however, no consensus.[12] There is also no consensus on the main theme of 1 Peter or on how the different motifs of the letter interrelate.

3.2. Dating 1 Peter

Research has given no persuasive arguments that Peter the apostle could not have written the letter, having dispatched it from Rome.[13] Therefore, I take the self-identification of the author as a matter of fact, as do a number of scholars.[14] This viewpoint implies that the letter must be dated before 70

---

10. See scholars such as Paul J. Achtemeier, *1 Peter: A Commentary on First Peter* (Hermeneia; Minneapolis: Fortress, 1996), 61–62; David E. Aune, *The New Testament and Its Literary Environment* (Philadelphia: Westminster, 1987), 159; Leonhard Goppelt, *Der erste Petrusbrief* (8th ed.; Göttingen: Vandenhoeck & Ruprecht, 1978), 45; Lauri Thurén, *Argument and Theology in 1 Peter: The Origins of Christian Paraenesis* (JSNTSup 114; Sheffield: Sheffield Academic Press, 1995), 93–94; John H. Elliott, "1 Peter, Its Situation and Strategy: A Discussion with David Balch," in *Perspectives on First Peter* (ed. Charles H. Talbert; Macon, Ga.: Mercer University Press, 1986), 61–78.

11. See Aune, *The New Testament*, 185. Thurén (*Argument and Theology*, 95) is, however, correct in cautioning that there is also an important difference between 1 Peter and the diaspora letter: 1 Peter's addressees are not just readers in general; they are specific persons in a specific (albeit wide) area.

12. See David W. Kendall, "The Literary and Theological Function of 1 Peter 1:3–12," in Talbert, *Perspectives on First Peter*, 103.

13. The origin of the letter is not disputed; scholars generally agree that it was sent from Rome. As an example, Willem C. van Unnik writes that the "place where 1 Peter was written may well have been Rome" ("The Redemption in 1 Peter i 18–19 and the Problem of the First Epistle of Peter," in *Sparsa Collecta: The Collected Essays of W. C. van Unnik* [3 vols.; Leiden: Brill, 1973–83], 2:81). Achtemeier concludes that "Rome remains … the most likely point of origin of 1 Peter" (*1 Peter*, 64).

14. E.g., Edward G. Selwyn, *The First Epistle of St. Peter* (London: Macmillan, 1947), 27–33; Thurén, *Argument and Theology*, 25–28. After an overview and evaluation of the different viewpoints, Thurén concludes: "Although not preferable to other solutions, an early date and Petrine authorship can certainly not be ruled out" (28). Van Unnik, at the end of his argument about the proselyte background of the addressees of the letter,

C.E.[15] The letter is not viewed as a mere appendix to the Pauline corpus and therefore a rephrasing of typical Pauline thoughts in a later era.[16]

---

says, "The situation which emerges from the epistle makes it difficult to argue *against* Peter's authorship. If anything, it argues *in favour* of it" ("Redemption in 1 Peter," 80). Donald Guthrie (*New Testament Theology* [Leicester: Inter-Varsity Press, 1981], 792–96), after having discussed a few other possibilities, comes to the same conclusion. Contra Achtemeier, *1 Peter*, 1–42, who gives an exhaustive overview of the scholarship on the authorship of 1 Peter and concludes that, "although authorship by Simon Peter continues to have its defenders, the evidence adduced for that position is weak enough and the evidence against it strong enough to make it apposite to reject that as a possibility and to assume pseudonymity."

15. The dating and authorship of 1 Peter are very much disputed. John H. Elliott (*A Home for the Homeless: A Sociological Exegesis of 1 Peter, Its Situation and Strategy* [Philadelphia: Fortress, 1981], 84) shows that there is "little scholarly consensus" even regarding the data that should be taken into consideration in the dating process. His own date for the letter is 73–92 C.E. (87), and he sees it as the product of either Peter himself or of a Petrine tradition transmitted by Petrine tradents of a Petrine circle (John H. Elliott, "The Rehabilitation of an Exegetical Step-Child: 1 Peter in Recent Research," *JBL* 95 [1976]: 248; idem, *Homeless*, 272–74). Jacques A. Rousseau ("A Multidimensional Approach towards the Communication of an Ancient Canonized Text: Towards the Thrust, Perspective and Strategy of 1 Peter" [Ph.D. diss., University of Pretoria, 1986], 18) characterizes the viewpoints as "a cacophony of opposing sounds." Three standard commentaries date the letter as follows: Selwyn, *The First Epistle of St. Peter*, 62: 63 C.E.; Goppelt, *Der erste Petrusbrief*, 64–65: 65–80 C.E.; Balch, *Let Wives Be Submissive: The Domestic Code in 1 Peter* (SBLMS 26; Chico, Calif.: Scholars Press, 1981), 138: 65–90 C.E. Others date the letter late in the first century and view it as pseudonymous: e.g., Aune, *The New Testament*, 218; Francis W. Beare, *The First Epistle of Peter* (3rd ed.; Oxford: Blackwell, 1970), 48; Achtemeier, *1 Peter*, 49–50; and Reinhard Feldmeier, *Die Christen als Fremde: Die Metapher der Fremde in der antiken Welt, im Urchristentum und im 1.Petrusbrief* (Tübingen: Mohr Siebeck, 1992), 199. Others have an earlier date but view it as pseudonymous anyway: e.g., Earl Richard, "The Functional Christology of First Peter," in Talbert, *Perspectives on First Peter*, 122. Van Unnik has no hesitation: "There can therefore be no doubt about the period to which this leads us: it must be *before the year 70*" ("Redemption in 1 Peter," 70).

16. Elliott ("1 Peter, Its Situation and Strategy," 7–8) argues persuasively against a dependence of 1 Peter on Paul. He acknowledges overlaps but ascribes it to the fact that both authors had access to the same tradition. The conclusion of Jens Herzer, *Petrus oder Paulus? Studien über das Verhältnis der Ersten Petrusbriefes zur paulinischen Tradition* (Tübingen: Mohr Siebeck, 1998) is essentially that of Elliott. Eduard Lohse ("Paränese und Kerygma im 1. Petrusbrief," *ZNW* 45 [1954]: 72) and Willem C. van Unnik ("The Teaching of Good Works in 1 Peter," in idem, *Sparsa Collecta*, 2:84, a reprint of a 1954 publication) have already concluded in the same direction.

3.3. Geography and Demography of the Identified Areas

Five areas are included in the address in 1 Pet 1:1: Pontus, Galatia, Cappadocia, Asia, and Bithynia (Πόντου, Γαλατίας, Καππαδοκίας, Ἀσίας καὶ Βιθυνίας). Achtemeier, after surveying the scholarship on the matter, convincingly concludes that "the best conjecture is that the intended readers of this epistle represented the broad spectrum of people living in northern Asia Minor."[17]

There is not enough data to allow full clarity on the number of Jews in these areas.[18] According to some estimates there were at least a quarter of a million Jews out of a total population of four million;[19] other estimations are as much as one million Jews from a total population of eight million.[20] These Jews, although fully participating in the Hellenistic culture and society,

---

17. Achtemeier, *1 Peter*, 57. The five areas mentioned in 1 Pet 1:1 cover about a quarter of a million square kilometers. A conservative estimate of the number of inhabitants during the last quarter of the first century is eight million. The topography of the area varies much, and it had different nations and a diversity of cultures, languages, faiths, and political histories (Elliott, *Home for the Homeless*, 60–61). There was little urbanization and military colonization (T. Robert S. Broughton, *Roman Asia Minor* [Baltimore: Johns Hopkins University Press, 1938], 734). There is evidence that cities in parts of Cappadocia never had more than a third of the surrounding area under their administration (Broughton, *Roman Asia Minor*, 738). One of the consequences was that most of the people lived in small, independent towns and villages. It furthermore seems as if the borders of urbanization were the borders of Hellenization as well.

18. H. Schaefer ("Paroikoi," PW 18.4:1701) gives evidence for about three hundred years earlier. Then there were about one thousand πάροικοι for every six thousand citizens. It seems legitimate to accept that the number of πάροικοι in these areas increased rather than decreased toward the first century C.E., so that the ratio could even have been higher than 1:6 by the second half of the first century C.E.

19. See Bo Reicke, *The Epistles of James, Peter and Jude* (AB 37; Garden City, N.Y.: Doubleday, 1964), 302–13.

20. Broughton, *Roman Asia Minor*, 815. The main source for information about Jewish communities in the Roman provinces in Asia Minor is epigraphic and archaeological material; see J. Cilliers Breytenbach, "Diaspora Judaism," in *The New Testament Milieu* (vol. 2 of *Guide to the New Testament*; ed. Andrie B. du Toit; Pretoria: NG Kerkboekhandel, 1998), 332. Emil Schürer, *The History of the Jewish People in the Age of Jesus Christ (175 B.C.–A.D. 135)* (trans. and ed. Geza Vermes, Fergus Millar, and Matthew Black; 3 vols.; Edinburgh: T&T Clark, 1973–86), 1:17–38, gives evidence from inscriptions and other documents that there were Diaspora Jews in all the areas mentioned in 1 Pet 1:1, as does Menahem Stern, "The Jewish Diaspora," in *The Jewish People in the First Century: Historical Geography, Political History, Social, Cultural and Religious Life and Institutions* (ed. Shemuel Safrai and Menahem Stern; CRINT 1.1; Assen: Van Gorcum, 1974), 153. Breytenbach ("Diaspora Judaism," 365), in his discussion of inscriptional evidence of the presence of Jews, proselytes, and God-fearers, mentions an inscription (CIJ I² 683a) from

viewed themselves as Jews living abroad.²¹ Frequent visits to Jerusalem, also by proselytes,²² witness to the fact that Judea was viewed as home. It is therefore quite possible that, also in these areas, Christianity moved into the world via the bridge of Hellenized Diaspora Judaism.²³

3.4. The Identity of the Addressees

The labeling of the addressees²⁴ as παρεπιδήμοις διασπορᾶς (resident foreigners of the Diaspora, 1:1; 2:11) and πάροικοι (visiting foreigners, 2:11) does not refer to a mere metaphorical figurative state of Christians being strangers in the world because they are citizens of heaven.²⁵ The addressees were, already before their conversion to the Christian faith, "visiting and resident foreigners" in the literal sociopolitical sense of the words.

There is, however, apart from being foreigners in the literal sociopolitical sense of the word, a second level on which they (or at least some of them) were παρεπίδημοι (διασπορᾶς) and πάροικοι, and that is the fact that they were, before their conversion, proselytes and God-fearers²⁶ (the φοβούμενοι and the σεβόμενοι τὸν θεόν), as argued convincingly by van Unnik.²⁷ Labeling the addressees as πάροικοι καὶ παρεπίδημοι (διασπορᾶς) therefore does not merely describe their social position; it indicates their previous status as "God-fearers" as well.

The author of 1 Peter links on to this sense of πάροικοι καὶ παρεπίδημοι (διασπορᾶς), transforming the (in some ways) abusive title to a proud self-identification by giving it a deeper and specific theologically positive sense. In a way it is part of the adoption of the honorific titles of the Old Testament

---

Panticapaeum at the Black Sea confirming that God-fearers were distinguished from Jews and proselytes; the inscription refers to the "synagogue of the Jews and the God-fearers."

21. See Shemuel Safrai, "Relations between the Diaspora and the Land of Israel," in Safrai and Stern, *The Jewish People in the First Century*, 185.

22. Safrai, "The Jewish Diaspora," 199–205.

23. Breytenbach, "Diaspora Judaism," 330.

24. Different scholars have adequately surveyed the scholarship on the identity and circumstances of the addressees of 1 Peter: Goppelt, *Der erste Petrusbrief*, 161–77; Achtemeier, *1 Peter*, 50–58; and especially Feldmeier, *Die Christen als Fremde*, being the most exhaustive.

25. Elliott (*Home for the Homeless*, 32) argues convincingly against such a spiritualization of πάροικοι in 1 Peter as being contra the social consciousness that is obvious from its use in early Christian and apocalyptic Jewish writings.

26. Contra Richard, "Functional Christology of First Peter," 123, who is of the opinion that the addressees were simply pagan Christians.

27. Van Unnik, "Redemption in 1 Peter," 72–74.

people of God, and in another way it has been transformed into a proud self-identification in its own right.[28]

3.5. THE CIRCUMSTANCES OF THE ADDRESSEES[29]

The addressees are identified as "resident and visiting foreigners" (1:1, 17; 2:11), but the letter does not give any explicit cause of this status of the addressees. It is improbable that official persecution was the cause.[30] The backdrop seems rather to be the sociopolitical status of the Christian groups in the diaspora, their daily relationships with Jews and other non-Christians, and the difficulties that they, as "resident and visiting foreigners,"[31] had to face daily. Their suffering, therefore, was not caused by official persecution but by spontaneous, local social ostracism.[32]

---

28. See Feldmeier, *Die Christen als Fremde*, 104.

29. Goppelt (*Der erste Petrusbrief*, 161–77) offers an extensive survey and evaluation of a variety of scholarly work on the circumstances of the addressees. Thurén (*Argument and Theology*, 29) also gives a valuable survey, as does Achtemeier (*1 Peter*, 51–58).

30. Contra Beare, *The First Epistle of Peter*, 188. For a good summary and rejection of the viewpoint that official persecution was the cause, see Elliott, "Rehabilitation of an Exegetical Step-Child," 251–52; Richard, "Functional Christology of First Peter," 126.

31. Having πάροικος-status in the first century C.E. already implied hardships. The πάροικοι had no political rights. Adolf Berger ("Peregrinus," in idem, *Encyclopedic Dictionary of Roman Law* [TAPS 64.2; Philadelphia: American Philosophical Society, 1953], 626) shows that this entailed restrictions such as the following: they were excluded from the *ekklesia*; they were excluded from military service; they could enter into a legitimate marriage only if the *ius conubii* was granted; they could not make a will in the same way Roman citizens could, and they could not act as a witness in these matters; they could not inherit from a Roman citizen; and they could enter into trade negotiations with a Roman citizen only after having been granted the *ius commercii*.

32. Breytenbach ("Diaspora Judaism," 341) shows that ostracization by the Jews was typical. They did not socialize with people who did not enter Judaism (Josephus, *C. Ap.* 2.210), and they viewed the Gentile nations as "lawless." The Jews were often accused of being "haters of people" (see Tacitus, *Hist.* 5.1 = Menahem Stern, ed., *Greek and Latin Authors on Jews and Judaism* [3 vols.; Jerusalem: Israel Academy of Sciences and Humanities, 1974–84], 2:281). Balch is very specific in his counterargument: "Rather, certain slaves and wives converted to Christianity; therefore, persons in Roman society reacted by accusing them of being immoral, perhaps seditious, and certainly insubordinate" (*Let Wives Be Submissive*, 95); see also Elliott, "Rehabilitation of an Exegetical Step-Child," 252; Elliott, "1 Peter, Its Situation and Strategy," 14; van Unnik says, "nowhere do we read that they suffered from the pagan authorities. … We think of the pagan surroundings and the persecution which might have arisen there, but we read nothing about that either. Is it not more obvious to think about persecution by the Synagogue? … That is why Christ, who himself underwent betrayal and death at the hands of the Jews, can be an example to them (chapter

The hardships were, by and large, experienced in the smaller circle of the household.³³ The *paterfamilias* had more or less full authority over his wife/wives, children, servants, and slaves. When the *paterfamilias* did not convert to the Christian faith when any member of the household did, it could result in severe discrimination against such a member.

What Philo writes about the hardships of persons who converted to Judaism may be used to construct the responses with which "new" Christians had to cope, since they were no longer "doing what the Gentiles like to do" (1 Pet 4:3; see also 1:18). See, as an example, their being labeled "deadly enemies" (Philo, *Spec.* 4.178).³⁴ Breaking with ancestral tradition was just not allowed.³⁵

These small windows on the social reality in which the addressees of 1 Peter typically had to cope offer evidence to the fact that spontaneous local ostracizing was the probable cause for their sufferings.

3.6. THE PURPOSE OF THE LETTER

The author uses the letter to persuade the addressees of their status before God as saved persons, of God's loving care for them, and of Christ's vicarious suffering and subsequent glory and supreme power. All of this is, however, not the purpose for writing; it serves as basis for the actual purpose: ethical

---

ii and iii). This too fits perfectly into the picture that we get in Acts of the earliest mission. There, again and again, it is the Jews who resist and slander Paul and his companions (see Acts xiii 50; xiv 19; xvii 5,13)" ("Redemption in 1 Peter," 79–80); see further Willem C. van Unnik, "Christianity according to 1 Peter," in idem, *Sparsa Collecta*, 2:113, 116; see also C. F. D. Moule, "The Nature and Purpose of First Peter," *NTS* 3 (1956–57): 1–11.

33. There is solid evidence that this situation changed soon, as evidenced by the letter (to be dated more or less 110 C.E.) of Pliny the Younger (*Ep.* 10.96) to Emperor Trajan and in Trajan's answer to Pliny (*Ep.* 10.97). From these letters the government's involvement in the persecution of Christians is evident.

34. These proselytes had to suffer many difficulties (Philo, *Somn.* 2.273; *Spec.* 1.51, 317; *Virt.* 102–103; *Praem.* 16–17; *Abr.* 17–26).

35. See Cicero, *Leg.* 2.7.19–27; Plutarch, *Amat.* 756 A–B, D; Josephus, *C. Ap.* 1.91, used this high regard for ancestral tradition in his apology for the Jewish faith. He argued that the Jews deserve honor because, even when in a foreign country, they never forsook their ancestral tradition. Change of religion would lead to the corruption of society, and if the gods were not honored in the "proper" way, they would retaliate against the whole of society (Horace, *Carm.* 3.6.5–8). There was the perception that change of religion would result in wives, children, and slaves no longer obeying their husbands, parents, and owners and that they would become isolated from society and despise other people (Tacitus, *Hist.* 5.5).

exhortations to have a good lifestyle (τὴν ἀναστροφὴν ὑμῶν ἐν τοῖς ἔθνεσιν ἔχοντες καλήν, 2:12) and to persevere in doing good (ἐν ἀγαθοποιΐᾳ, 4:19), even amidst, and in spite of, their own suffering.

3.7. Conclusion: The Animosity the Addressees of 1 Peter Suffered

The addressees lived in the districts comprising all of Asia Minor from the Cappadocian Mountains and the Anatolian Highlands down to the Black Sea in the north. They were visiting and resident foreigners, people who had formerly been pagans. Most of them had probably had an intermediate state as "God-fearers," having joined the synagogue. As foreigners they had no rights, and in a society where group identity and belonging to a group was so important, they were mere individuals.

When these foreigners became Christians, it had positive and negative social consequences. On the positive side, they became part of a Christian group and were no longer isolated individuals or small groups. Those who had been God-fearers and could not become full proselytes no longer were second-class members of the new Christian group.

The new Christians, however, also had to cope with negative consequences as a result of their new alliance. The unjust suffering that they had to endure as (political) foreigners became even more severe, since now one more dimension had been added to their "otherness": the fact that they aligned themselves with an obscure foreign sect. This resulted in further and more intense ostracizing and discrimination. The fact that they stopped participating in the general lifestyle of society (futile ways: living in licentiousness, passions, drunkenness, revels, carousing, and lawless idolatry, 4:3) caused them to be maligned as evildoers (2:12; 3:16; 4:4).[36]

As aliens and exiles, they were very vulnerable and easy prey for discrimination. They suffered various trials, testing them like fire and becoming a fiery ordeal (1 Pet 1:6; 4:12). Their suffering is likened to the devil prowling around like a roaring lion, looking for someone to devour. They were intimidated and suffered for doing what was right. One example of "suffering in the flesh" is household servants who had to endure unjustified beatings.[37] These

---

36. See Rudolf Schnackenburg, *The Moral Teaching of the New Testament* (Kent: Burns & Oates, 1982), 368.
37. John T. Fitzgerald, "Early Christian Missionary Practice and Pagan Reaction: 1 Peter and Domestic Violence against Slaves and Wives," in *Renewing Tradition: Studies in Honor of James W. Thompson* (ed. Mark W. Hamilton, Thomas H. Olbricht, and Jeffrey Peterson; Princeton Theological Monograph Series; Eugene, Ore.: Pickwick, 2007), 24–44.

circumstances forced them to either retaliate for the injustices, the "evil," they suffered or to forsake their new commitment to the Christian faith.

4. The Argument of 1 Peter and the Local Argument of 3:8–12

4.1. Some Methodological Considerations

My approach to constructing the argument[38] of 1 Peter has a functional dimension, namely, to establish what van Dijk calls "effectiveness in bringing about acceptance or attitude change by the recipient in some social setting."[39] This means that grammatical structures and styles or narrative structures are viewed as "theoretical abstractions of the kinds of structures, units, representations, schemata and rules or strategies used in verbal interaction."[40]

The macro-argument (the global coherence)[41] of 1 Peter that I propose controls the micro-connections and continuations. In the process of establishing and motivating the argument of 1 Peter, the intersentence relational particles and *asyndeta*[42] used to mark the relations between the different units of the letter are of importance.

---

38. In establishing the argument of 1 Peter, "argument" is viewed as the use of "language to justify or refute a standpoint, with the aim of securing agreement in views" (Frans H. van Eemeren, Rob Grootendorst, Sally Jackson, and Scott Jacobs, "Argumentation," in *Discourse as Structure and Process* [vol. 1 of *Discourse Studies: A Multidisciplinary Introduction*; ed. Teun A. van Dijk; London: Sage, 1997], 208). Argument is "the use of a statement in a logical process of argumentation to support or weaken another statement whose validity is questionable or contentious" (Josef Kopperschmidt, "An Analysis of Argumentation," in *Dimensions of Discourse* [vol. 2 of *Handbook of Discourse Analysis*; ed. Teun A. van Dijk; London: Academic Press, 1985], 159).

39. See Teun A. van Dijk, "Introduction: Levels and Dimensions of Discourse Analysis," in van Dijk, *Dimensions of Discourse*, 2.

40. Ibid., 5.

41. See Teun A. van Dijk, "Semantic Discourse Analysis," in van Dijk, *Dimensions of Discourse*, 115.

42. Greek can either express the interrelation of sentences explicitly by the use of particles or dispense with connection, using asyndeton (Friedrich Blass, Albert Debrunner, and Robert W. Funk, *A Greek Grammar of the New Testament and Other Early Christian Literature* [Chicago: University of Chicago Press, 1961], 225). Asyndeton refers to the phenomenon that Greek sentences sometimes do not have a relational particle. Asyndeton in itself, like a "zero" morpheme in linguistic theory (Vern S. Poythress, "The Use of the Intersentence Conjunctions 'de', 'oun', 'kai' and Asyndeton in the Gospel of John," *NovT* 26 [1984]: 318), actually then becomes the relation marker. This comes very close to what John D. Denniston (*The Greek Particles* [Oxford: Clarendon, 1934], xliii) calls formal (as distinct from stylistic) asyndeton.

4.2. The Macro-Argument of the Letter

I view the pericope 1:3–12 as the basis for the rest of the letter, with the key phrase the reassurance in 1:3 of the fact that God has begotten[43] the addressees anew: ὁ θεὸς καὶ πατὴρ τοῦ κυρίου ἡμῶν Ἰησοῦ Χριστοῦ ... ἀναγεννήσας ἡμᾶς.[44] The body of the letter is largely paraenetic, with the pericope 1:3–12 as the motivating basis for four inferential exhortations: 1:13–25; 2:1–10; 2:11–4:19;[45] and 5:1–11.

My view of the argument of 1 Peter can be presented in the following nutshell form. The *letter heading* (1:1–2) has the author, the addressees, and the greeting. By labeling the addressees as "the elect exiles of the Diaspora," the author already prepares them for his message. The *letter opening* is 1:3–12, and it takes the labeling of the addressees one step further: God has begotten them anew. The *letter body* (1:13–5:11) has four inferences (each of them an exhortation), with 1:3–12 as the basis.

- The exhortation in 1:13–25 is the first inference that has "God has begotten us anew" in 1:3 as the basis: the addressees are urged to set all their hope on the grace of God and to ensure that their lifestyle is holy, because they have been begotten anew by God.

---

43. The English equivalent "(God) who has begotten us anew" is used for Greek *participium* ἀναγεννήσας, to stay as close as possible to the reference of the verb ἀναγεννάω. The result of this "rebegetting" is a new birth (2:2; see Achtemeier, *1 Peter*, 91).

44. David W. Kendall ("The Literary and Theological Function of 1 Peter 1:3–12," in Talbert, *Perspectives on First Peter*, 104) has the same view of the function of 1:3–12. However, Kendall does not view the statement in 1:3 about God's initiative in begetting the addressees (ἀναγεννήσας) as having any special function in the argument.

45. The contribution of viewing the argument of 1 Peter in this way is especially the interpretation of the interrelations of the pericopes in 1:13–5:11 and more specifically the interrelations of the pericopes in 3:17–4:19, as well as the fact that no major break is signified between 4:11 and 4:12–19. Quite a number of scholars see a major break between 4:11 and 4:12. However, I agree with Balch (*Let Wives Be Submissive*, 127–28) that 4:12–19 is about the very same theme as the preceding. In spite of this statement, Balch (129) places 4:12–19 with 5:1–11 in his exposition of the argument of 1 Peter. Another scholar who does not propose a major break between 4:11 and 4:12 is Charles H. Talbert, "Once Again: The Plan of 1 Peter," in Talbert, *Perspectives on First Peter*, 143. However, he proposes a close link between 4:12–19 and the whole of 3:8–4:11, whereas I think the link is just with 3:13–4:11. For a broader motivation, see Fika J. van Rensburg, "Indikatief en paraklese in 1 Petrus en die implikasie daarvan vir die kerklike prediking vandag," *In die Skriflig* 24 (1990): 88–89.

- The exhortation in 2:1–10 is the second inference that has "God has begotten us anew" in 1:3 as the basis, expounding the two responsibilities of persons having been begotten anew by God: to ensure (1) individual spiritual growth and (2) communal spiritual growth.
- The exhortation in 2:11–4:19 is the third inference that has "God has begotten us anew" in 1:3 as the basis: it gives a code of conduct for "resident and visiting foreigners." First the basic exhortation is given: the addressees must always have a good lifestyle (2:11–12). This basic exhortation is then applied to the relationship with political authorities (2:13–17), with masters (2:18–25), with the marriage partner (3:1–7), with the neighbor in general (3:8–12), and, finally, in the attitude toward and the response to unjust suffering (3:13–4:19).
- The exhortation in 5:1–11 is the fourth inference that has "God has begotten us anew" in 1:3 as the basis: it gives a code for conduct within the church.

The *letter closing* (5:12–14) contains the purpose of the letter ("to encourage" [παρακαλῶν]), greetings are conveyed, and the letter ends with a blessing.

This view of the argument of 1 Peter, and specifically the coherence between the letter opening (1:3–12) and the body of the letter, can be represented as in the chart on the following page.

4.3. The Place and Function of 1 Peter 3:8–12 in the Argument

Since the pericope 3:8–12 is part of the third exhortation (2:11–4:19), it is necessary to explicate my view of the pericopes of 2:11–4:19 and the interrelations of these pericopes.

The exhortation in 2:11–12 ("Beloved, I urge you as visiting and resident foreigners to abstain from your natural inclination" [ἀγαπητοί, παρακαλῶ ὡς παροίκους καὶ παρεπιδήμους ἀπέχεσθαι τῶν σαρκικῶν ἐπιθυμιῶν]) functions as the principle for all the exhortations that follow, up to 4:19.[46] The principle is first applied on three societal structures: how the addressees should conduct themselves in their relationship with the political authorities (2:13–17), with their masters (2:18–25), and with their marriage partners (3:1–7). The

---

46. See van Unnik, "Teaching of Good Works," 100, who says about 2:11–12: "The sentences of ii 11–12 are the heading of the whole ethical part of the letter, in which the 'Haustafel' in part is incorporated."

Synopsis of the Argument of 1 Peter

LETTER HEADING

1:1–2: Author, addresses, and greeting.

LETTER OPENING

1:3–12: Praise be to God, the Father of our Lord Jesus Christ, who has begotten us anew.

> **FOUR INFERENTIAL EXHORTATIONS (basis "God has begotten us anew")**
>
> Exhortation 1   1:13–25: Set your hope fully on the grace and therefore be holy
> Exhortation 2   2:1–10: The obligation of a person having been given a new birth by God to grow spiritually, both personally and communally
> Exhortation 3   2:11–4:19: Code of conduct for foreigners
>   2:11–12:   The basic exhortation
>   2:13–17:   Relationship with political authorities
>   2:18–25:   Relationship with employers
>   3:1–7:   Relationship with the marriage partner
>   3:8–12:   Relationship with neighbors in general
>   3:13–4:19: Attitude toward and response to unjust sufferings
> Exhortation 4   5:1–11: Code of conduct within the church

LETTER CLOSING

5:12–14: Conclusion: Purpose, salutations, letter closing

principle is then applied to the relationship with the neighbor in general (3:8–12).[47]

In the next section (3:13ff.) the focus is no longer on the relationship with persons in specific societal structures (2:13–3:7) or outside of such structures

---

47. This fourth exhortation (3:8–12) is marked by the combination of δέ with τό τέλος in 3:8; see L&N 1:612. The section 3:8–12 summarizes the guidelines for relationships with other people. From 3:13 the topic shifts to the attitude toward and response to unjust suffering.

(3:8–12). From 3:13 (right through to 4:19) the topic shifts to the attitude toward and reaction to unjust suffering. Before making a construction of the local argument of 3:8–12, a representation of my view of the interrelationship of the subsections of 2:11–4:19 will bring further clarity:

The Third Exhortation as a Consequence of Having Been Begotten Anew by God

2:11–12:	Since you are visiting and resident foreigners, abstain from your natural inclination. Your lifestyle among the non-Christians must be good.

Applied to the relationship with political authorities

2:13–17:	Submit yourselves to every human authority, for God, who has ransomed you to be his slaves, demands this from you.

Applied to the relationship with employers

2:18–25:	Following the example Christ has set in his suffering, you as household servants must submit yourselves even to unreasonable employers, following in the footprints of the Shepherd to whom you have been returned.

Applied to the relationship with the marriage partner

3:1–7:	Even in a society where women are being discriminated against, God's exhortation to married persons stays valid.

Applied to the relationship with neighbors in general

3:8–12:	The key to true joy of life lies in the execution of God's exhortations regarding fellow human beings, especially those who malign and insult you.

Applied to the attitude toward and response to injustice

3:13–4:19:	Even if you should suffer for doing what is right, you must view it as commendable before God.

4.4. The Local Argument of 1 Peter 3:8–12

The pericope 3:8–12 lacks an explicit main verb. The imperative form of the copula (ἐστε) is supposed on the grounds of the content and the context. Verse 9 is linked to ἐστε in verse 8 by the juxtaposed *participia* ἀποδιδόντες … δὲ εὐλογοῦντες ("do not repay … but bless"), constituting a further explication of the code of conduct given in 3:8. Verses 10–11 give a double motivation for this code of conduct, the motivation being signaled by γὰρ … παυσάτω τὴν γλῶσσαν ἀπὸ κακοῦ … ἐκκλινάτω δὲ ἀπὸ κακοῦ ("for he must keep his tongue from evil … and he must turn from evil").

The following representation of my interpretation of the syntactic structure shows the interrelations on the micro-level:

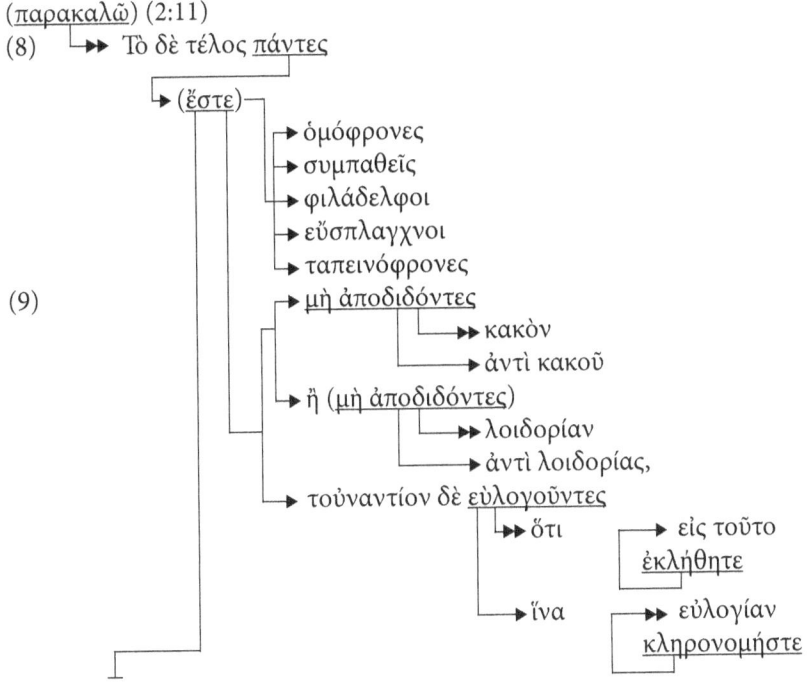

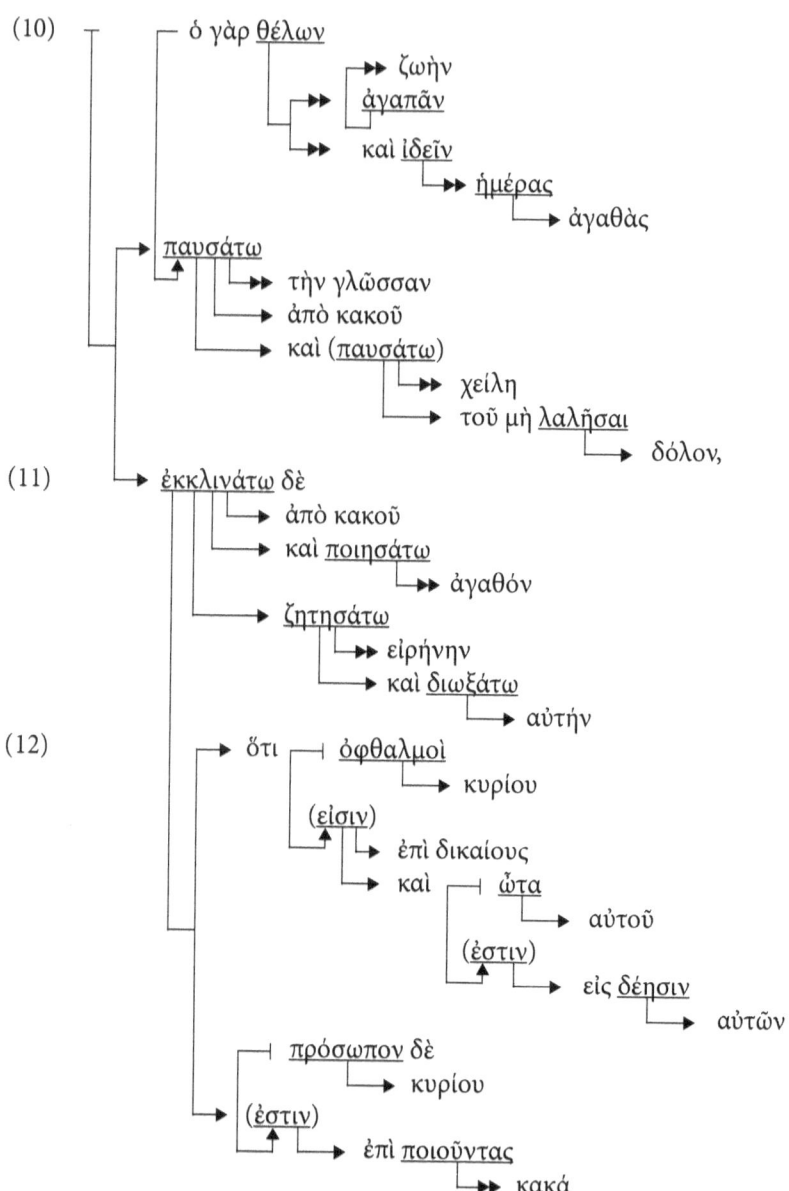

This means that I construct the local argument of 3:8–12 as follows. The pericope starts in 3:8 with an exhortation that the addressees must be persons who live in harmony with one another, who are sympathetic, who love as brothers, who are compassionate and humble (πάντες ὁμόφρονες, συμπαθεῖς, φιλάδελφοι, εὔσπλαγχνοι, ταπεινόφρονες). The juxtaposed participles in 3:9 (ἀποδιδόντες … δὲ εὐλογοῦντες) mark this verse as a further explanation of the exhortations in 3:8, adding two more exhortations ("do not repay … but bless"), delimiting the exhortations in 3:8. The exhortation to bless is motivated by: "because to this you were called" (ὅτι εἰς τοῦτο ἐκλήθητε), and the consequence of repaying evil with a blessing is stated: "so that you may inherit a blessing" (ἵνα εὐλογίαν κληρονομήσητε).

All of this is motivated[48] with a quotation from Ps 33:13–17 (LXX 34:12–16). This quotation, however, not only motivates the exhortations of 3:8–9 but repeats in 3:10–11 the essence of the exhortations of 3:8–9. Then, in 3:12 the quotation gives a motivation for the exhortation that doing good and seeking peace is the condition, if one wants to love life.

This construction of the local argument of 3:8–12 can be represented as in the chart on the following page.

---

48. The relation is marked by the γάρ in 3:10; see John Piper, "Hope as the Motivation of Love: 1 Peter 3:9–12," *NTS* 26 (1980): 226.

Exhortation for the Relationship with Neighbors in General[49]

> 3:8: **Finally, all of you:**
> - **live in harmony with one another**
> - **be sympathetic**
> - **love as brothers**
> - **be compassionate**
> - **and humble**

The code of conduct given in 3:8 narrowed down to: response to animosity

> 3:9a: Negative: **Do not repay evil with evil or insult with insult**
> 3:9b: Positive: **but with blessing,**

Motivation for the exhortation to repay evil and insult with blessing

> 3:9c: **because to this conduct you were called,**

The consequence when one repays evil with a blessing

> 3:9d: **so that you inherit a blessing.**

Motivation for this code of conduct, specifically for the response to animosity

> 3:10: **For, "whoever wants to love life and see good days**
> Negative: **must keep his tongue from evil**
> **and his lips from deceitful speech.**
> 3:11: **He must turn from evil**
> Positive: **He must do good;**
> **he must seek peace and pursue it.**

Motivation for the argument that, to love life, one must turn from evil, etc.

> 3:12a: Positive: **For the eyes of the Lord are on the righteous,**
> **and his ears are open to their prayer,**
> 3:12b: Negative: **but the face of the Lord is against those who do evil."**

---

49. As argued in §4.3 above, the pericope 3:8–12 is the fourth application of the basic exhortation in 2:11–12.

5. The Basis for the Ethics in 1 Peter

5.1. Introduction

It has been argued in §2 above that for Christianity the basis of ethics is the reality of God, specifically his will to bring persons who find themselves estranged from God (the *ab quo* of there salvation) into a restored relationship with God (the *ad quem* of their salvation). This results in a social redefinition of the individuals involved, with the new status being described in forensic, familial, economic, and similar language. This is usually done in terms of a descriptive image.[50] The new social reality then becomes the basis for the formulation of the ethics.[51]

Using this definition of the basis, the text of 1 Peter has been scrutinized to establish the different facets of the soteriology in this letter. The salvific utterances in 1 Peter can be categorized in different ways. Content-wise it seems logical to take the two subjects of the salvation as categorizing principle: God the Father (theological) and Jesus Christ (christological).

This categorization produces the following hierarchy of the salvific utterances:

Theological Salvific Utterances

1. Salvation as having been made part of the family of God
   1.1. Salvation as having been begotten anew by God the Father (1:3, 23; 2:2–3)
   1.2. Salvation as having become heirs in the household of God (1:4–5; 3:7, 9)
   1.3. Salvation as having been ransomed by God into his household (1:18–19; 2:16)
   1.4. Salvation as having become the house(hold) of God (4:17)

---

50. "Imagery" is understood as the total and coherent account (or mental picture) of objects, with corresponding actions and relations associatively (and thematically) belonging together; see Jan G. van der Watt, *Family of the King: Dynamics of Metaphor in the Gospel according to John* (BibInt 47; Leiden: Brill, 2000), 18.

51. Eduard Lohse ("Paränese und Kerygma im 1. Petrusbrief," ZNW 45 [1954]: 87) has aptly stated that the paraenesis finds its real anchor in being traced back to the kerygma. He states: "The last and real basis, however, that 1 Peter gives for the ethical exhortations is christological" (86, my trans.). Goppelt (*Der erste Petrusbrief*, 121) has also referred to the motivative function of the "christological units."

1.5. Salvation as having been transformed by God into his nation (2:9–10)
2. Salvation as having been elected (1:1–2; 2:9a; 5:13) and called (2:9b; 5:10b) by God
3. Salvation as having been the object of God's mercy (1:3; 2:10) and grace (1:10; 5:10a, 12)
4. Salvation as being endowed with a living hope (1:3)
5. Salvation as having been saved by God, with imminent full revelation (1:5, 9–10; 2:2; 4:18)

Christological Salvific Utterances

1. Salvation as having been healed by Christ's sufferings
   1.1. Salvation as having been the reason for Christ's suffering (2:21, 24a, 24b; 3:18)
   1.2. Salvation as having been brought to God by Christ through his suffering (3:18)
   1.3. Salvation as glory sequencing on Christ's suffering (1:11; 4:13; 5:1b)
2. Salvation as having been sprinkled by the blood of Christ (1:1–2)
3. Salvation as having become a living stone, because of Christ the living Stone (2:4–5)
4. Salvation as having been returned from being lost to Christ as Shepherd (2:25)
5. Salvation as being "in Christ" (3:16; 5:14)

Formulating the basis in terms of these categories proves to be more productive than the approach by Lohse. He identifies "for Christ also suffered" (3:18) as the "basis for ethical instruction derived from the kerygma" and says that it "is held fast throughout the letter to the very end (3:18–22; 4:1)."[52]

5.2. The Basis in Terms of Theological Salvific Utterances

Salvation as having been made part of the family of God. The author, right at the outset of his letter (1:3) and two more times (1:23; 2:2–3), uses the beget/birth-imagery to persuade his addressees that they are what they are because

---

52. Lohse, *Theological Ethics of the New Testament*, 185. I also disagree with Lohse (ibid., 181) when he states that in 1 Peter the imperative is not based on the previous declaration of the indicative. See n. 3 above (p. 200).

of God: God, in his great mercy and because of no other reason than his own will, took the initiative. He rebegot them, as if in a woman's womb, using the everlasting seed of his word. He effected their (re)birth, and as part of the beget/rebirth process, he provided them, as newborn babies, with the immediate sustenance they needed. In all of this God's mercy, his goodness, has become evident.

This status that they have before God as his children is therefore in no way at risk of being changed or neutralized by either their own weakness, trying circumstances, or evil persons. The fact that they, as part of their beget/birth-process, tasted (from the *colostrum*) that the Lord is good must motivate them to yearn for the undiluted milk of God's word. The more they digest this undiluted milk, the more their lifestyle will evidence their status as persons (re)begotten by God, their status as children of God. As children they have become heirs in the household of God, heirs of the gift of life (1:4; 3:7, 9).

The image of having become part of the family of God does not stop here but is expanded in two more ways: not only have the addressees been ransomed (as slaves) into the household of God (1:18–19; 2:16); they have actually become the house(hold) of God (4:17). The final image extends the household to the national level: they have been transformed by God to be his nation (2:9–10).

Salvation as having been elected and called by God. The author, in the very first sentence of his letter (1:1) and two more times (2:9a and 5:13), reminds his addressees that God has elected them. Closely related is his reference to the fact that God has called them: out of darkness to his wonderful light (2:9b) and to his eternal glory in Christ (5:10b).[53]

Salvation as having received God's mercy and grace. The fact that the addressees have been made the object of the mercy (1:3; 2:10) and the grace (1:10; 5:10a,12) of God is stressed several times.

Salvation as being endowed with a living hope (1:4). Part and parcel of having been begotten anew by God is being endowed with a living hope (1:3).

Salvation as having been saved by God, with imminent, full revelation. The author emphasizes that his addressees have already received their salvation (1:9–10; 4:18) and that its imminent, full revelation is guaranteed by God (1:5), although the believers have the responsibility to—through proper feeding—grow up in their salvation (2:2).

---

53. Michaels makes a useful distinction between being called ethically and eschatologically: "Ethically, Christians are called to holy conduct and nonretaliation (cf. 1:15; 2:21); eschatologically, they are called to God's 'marvellous light' (2:9) or 'eternal glory' (5:10)" (*1 Peter*, 178).

5.3. The Basis in Terms of Christological Salvific Utterances

Salvation as having been healed by Christ's sufferings. The author argues that the reason for Christ's suffering was the salvation of his addressees (2:21, 24a, 24b; 3:18). The outcome of Christ's suffering was that they were brought to God (3:18) and witness the revealing of Christ's glory (1:11; 4:13; 5:1b).

Salvation as having been sprinkled by the blood of Christ. The addressees have been chosen by God for sprinkling by the blood of Christ (1:1–2). This assures them that they are acceptable for God and ready to live in an intimate relationship with him.

Salvation as having become a living stone, because of Christ the living Stone. The status of the addressees is pictured as living stones, being built into a spiritual house. They are living stones because of Christ, the living Stone (2:4–5).

Salvation as having been returned from being lost to Christ as Shepherd. The addressees are pictured as sheep going astray but who have now been returned to the Shepherd and Guardian of their souls (2:25). This obligates them to follow in Christ's steps, the very steps that he has described in 2:22-23.

Salvation as being "in Christ." The author uses the formula "being in Christ" (3:16; 5:14) to image his addressees' saved status. In 3:16 this is directly linked to the responsibility they have to respond in a correct way when being maligned.

5.4. Conclusion

The analyses of the text of 1 Peter to establish the basis for its ethics have proved to be very effective and productive. Different images are used to emphasize the saved status of the addressees, each with an ethical implication:

	BASIS	ETHICAL IMPLICATION
1.	The addressees are children of God, having been begotten anew by him (1:3, 23; 2:2–3).	They have to live up to this status (by being obedient).
2.	As children they are heirs of God, and they are assured of the safekeeping of both themselves, as well as their inheritance (1:4–5; 3:7).	They must live assured that no circumstance or evildoers can rob them of their inheritance.

3.	They have been ransomed by God with the precious blood of Christ into his household (1:18–19; 2:16), actually becoming his household (4:17).	They are now "slaves of God" and must live in obedience.
4.	They have been transformed by God into his nation (2:9–10).	Their lifestyle must show that they have the Lord as King.
5.	They have been elected (1:1; 2:9a; 5:13) and called by God (2:9b; 5:10b).	They must live assured that no circumstance or evildoers can undo this state.
6.	God has shown them his mercy (1:3; 2:10) and grace (1:10, 13; 5:10a, 12).	They must know that their saved state is not because of something they deserved.
7.	As children of God they have been endowed with a living hope (1:3; 3:15).	This hope must enable them to accept only Christ as Lord by being willing to suffer for what is right.
8.	They have received the goal of their faith, the salvation of their souls (1:9–10; 2:2; 4:18), and its imminent full revelation is guaranteed by God (1:5).	They must be fearless when experiencing animosity.
9.	Christ suffered because of them (1:11; 2:21; 3:18), bearing their sins in his body (2:24a) and healing them through his wound (2:24b), bringing them to God (3:18), and revealing his glory (1:11; 4:13; 5:1).	They must follow in his steps (by not retaliating, even when experiencing bodily harm).
10.	They will share in Christ's glory (5:1).	Present suffering must not deter them from sharing in Christ's suffering.
11.	They have been sprinkled by the blood of Christ (1:1–2).	They can enter into an intimate relationship with God, since they have been purified.

12. They have been built into a spiritual house for God, having been made living stones through their contact with the living Stone (2:4–5).	They must perform the priestly duty of this spiritual house.
13. They have been returned to Christ as Shepherd and Overseer of their souls (2:25).	They must follow in his steps, willing to suffer evil without retaliating.
14. They are "in Christ" (3:16; 5:14).	Their lifestyle must evidence to this fact, especially when being abused.

This basis in different ways empowers the addressees to be ready for the ethics, the directives the author issues for their lifestyle.

6. The Ethics in 1 Peter 3:8–12

6.1. Introduction

It has been argued in §2 above that the ethics (or universal principles) emanate from the new identity. Ethics, therefore, indicate prescriptiveness, which has the basis as motivation. In this section the ethics of 3:8–12 are established.

6.2. The Universal Principle: No Retaliation, but Blessing

The universal principle stated in 3:9 is very clear: "do not repay evil with evil or insult with insult" (μὴ ἀποδιδόντες κακὸν ἀντὶ κακοῦ ἢ λοιδορίαν[54] ἀντὶ λοιδορίας), followed by its positive counterpart: "but with blessing" (τοὐαντίον δὲ εὐλογοῦντες).

The link with the core of Jesus' teaching on no retaliation is obvious.[55] According to Luke 6:27–28, Jesus said: "But I say to you who listen, Love your enemies, do good to those who hate you, bless those who curse you, pray for those who abuse you [Ἀλλὰ ὑμῖν λέγω τοῖς ἀκούουσιν, ἀγαπᾶτε τοὺς ἐχθροὺς ὑμῶν, καλῶς ποιεῖτε τοῖς μισοῦσιν ὑμᾶς, εὐλογεῖτε τοὺς καταρωμένους ὑμᾶς, προσεύχεσθε περὶ τῶν ἐπηρεαζόντων ὑμᾶς]." Most probably the wording μὴ

---

54. The noun λοιδορία is used only here and in 1 Tim 5:14 in the New Testament.
55. Michaels, *1 Peter*, 177; Piper, "Hope as the Motivation of Love," 221–22.

ἀποδιδόντες κακὸν ἀντὶ κακοῦ was taken from the early Christian paraenetic tradition that had adopted it from Hellenistic-Jewish tradition, as convincingly argued by Piper.[56]

The appeal implicitly made in 2:23 to imitate Jesus' no retaliation is made explicitly here in 3:9, marked by the fact that λοιδορέω of 2:23[57] is picked up in 3:9 with the noun λοιδορία.[58]

To "bless" someone is to extend to that person the prospect of salvation or the favor of God.[59] It corresponds to praying for someone (see Luke 6:28b).[60]

---

56. Piper, "Hope as the Motivation of Love," 220. The obvious parallel with Rom 12:14, 17 also points to such a common paraenetic tradition: "Bless those who persecute you; bless and do not curse them. ... Do not repay anyone evil for evil, but take thought for what is noble in the sight of all [εὐλογεῖτε τοὺς διώκοντας [ὑμᾶς], εὐλογεῖτε καὶ μὴ καταρᾶσθε. ... μηδενὶ κακὸν ἀντὶ κακοῦ ἀποδιδόντες, προνοούμενοι καλὰ ἐνώπιον πάντων ἀνθρώπων]." As does the parallel with 1 Thess 5:15: "See that none of you repays evil for evil, but always seek to do good to one another and to all [ὁρᾶτε μή τις κακὸν ἀντὶ κακοῦ τινι ἀποδῷ, ἀλλὰ πάντοτε τὸ ἀγαθὸν διώκετε [καὶ] εἰς ἀλλήλους καὶ εἰς πάντας]."

57. 1 Pet 2:23 reads: "When they hurled their insults at him, he did not retaliate; when he suffered, he made no threats [ὃς λοιδορούμενος οὐκ ἀντελοιδόρει, πάσχων οὐκ ἠπείλει]."

58. See Michaels, *1 Peter*, 178. The Stoics had reflected on this problem and in general admonished the true philosopher to endure reviling (λοιδορούμενος ἀνέχεσθαι [Epictetus, *Diatr.* 3.12.10; 21.5; *Ench.* 10]) and to treat the reviler with gentleness (ἀπὸ τούτων οὖν ὁρμώμενος πράως ἕξεις πρὸς τὸν λοιδοροῦντα [Epictetus, *Ench.* 42]). However, the motive was different: the key word "blessing" is missing. See Piper, "Hope as the Motivation of Love," 220.

59. BAGD, 322; I. Howard Marshall, *1 Peter* (IVP New Testament Commentary Series; Leicester: Inter-Varsity Press, 1991), 109. Except for 1 Pet 3:9 and 1 Cor 4:12, there are no other comparable uses of εὐλογέω in the New Testament; see Piper, "Hope as the Motivation of Love," 221.

60. Michaels, *1 Peter*, 178; Ernest Best, *1 Peter* (NCB; Grand Rapids: Eerdmans, 1971), 130. This agrees more or less with John Calvin: "To *bless* here means to pray. ... Peter teaches us a general principle that evils are to be overcome by acts of kindness. This is indeed very hard, but we ought to imitate our heavenly Father in this ... for when Christ said, 'Love your enemies,' He at the same time confirmed his teaching by saying, 'That ye might be the children of God'" (*Hebrews and I and II Peter* [trans. William B. Johnston; Grand Rapids: Eerdmans, 1963], 285). Calvin appropriately refers in this context to Matt 5:44-45: "But I say to you, Love your enemies and pray for those who persecute you, so that you may be children of your Father in heaven; for he makes his sun rise on the evil and on the good, and sends rain on the righteous and on the unrighteous."

6.3. The Universal Principle Motivated by Recapitulating the Basis

The second part of 3:9 motivates why the addressees must repay evil and insult with blessing: "because to this conduct they were called [ὅτι εἰς τοῦτο[61] ἐκλήθητε]." Immediately the consequence[62] of "repaying with blessing" is stated: "so that you inherit a blessing [ἵνα εὐλογίαν κληρονομήσητε]."[63]

It becomes evident that the addressees' attitude toward others is not to be determined by the attitude they adopt toward them but by their relationship toward God and their recollection of the kind of life to which he has called them.[64]

---

61. The τοῦτο refers back to the exhortations; see Michaels, *1 Peter*, 178; Wayne Grudem, *1 Peter* (TNTC; Grand Rapids: Eerdmans, 1988), 147; Best, *1 Peter*, 130, specifically blessing one's revilers; see also Piper, "Hope as the Motivation of Love," 228. It is not a reference forward to the ἵνα-clause, contra Goppelt, *Der erste Petrusbrief*, 228; Selwyn, *The First Epistle of St. Peter*, 190; Reicke, *The Epistles of James, Peter and Jude*, 105; J. N. D. Kelly, *A Commentary on the Epistles of Peter and Jude* (London: Black, 1969), 137; Charles Bigg, *A Critical and Exegetical Commentary on the Epistles of St. Peter and St. Jude* (ICC 42; Edinburgh: T&T Clark, 1910), 156; Peter H. Davids, *The First Epistle of Peter* (NICNT; Grand Rapids: Eerdmans, 1990), 127. Piper ("Hope as the Motivation of Love," 228) adds: "The way 1 Peter 3:9–12 motivates enemy-love is by showing that it is a condition for inheriting the eschatological blessing. Therefore the 'desire to enjoy (eternal) life' (3:10) should motivate a person to bless those who revile him." Piper acknowledges that this interpretation is inconsistent with the author pointing the readers to their accomplished redemption through "the precious blood of Christ" (1:18–19), but he states: "The writer apparently sees no inconsistency between pointing the reader *forward* toward the future of God's judgment (1:17; 3:12b) and *backward* in the next verse (1:18f) to their accomplished redemption through 'the precious blood of Christ'" (228). Piper adds that this behavior is a "means of inheriting the blessing of eternal life" (229). I, however, agree with van Unnik that "good works have no place in the process of salvation. The work Christ has done is the unshakable basis in the relation with God" ("Teaching of Good Works," 107). See also Grudem, *1 Peter*, 150: "Verses 8–12 as a whole should not be taken as evidence for final salvation by good works, for they are addressed to those who are already Christians and already have an imperishable 'inheritance' kept for them in heaven (1:4). Yet this passage does present a bold affirmation of the relation between righteous living and God's present blessing in this life."

62. Michaels (*1 Peter*, 179) convincingly argues that the future salvation is not the principal ground of the responsibility of Christians to bless those who insult them but that it is clearly the inevitable outcome of such behavior.

63. The εὐλογία, or "blessing," is God's final pronouncement (i.e., bestowal) of eternal well-being on his people at the last day; see Michaels, *1 Peter*, 179. However, Grudem (*1 Peter*, 149) is correct in pointing out that this pericope teaches that a motive for righteous living is the knowledge that such conduct will bring blessings from God *in this life*. This is especially clear from 3:10–12, as will be argued below.

64. See Francis W. Beare, *The First Epistle of Peter* (Oxford: Blackwell, 1958), 134.

The phrase "inherit a blessing" recalls the κληρονομία ("inheritance") of 1:4 and the συγκληρονόμοι of 3:7,[65] linking this blessing again to the basis of being made part of the family of God. To inherit a blessing "indicates goods received simply because of who one is and the generosity of the testator, not because of what one has earned. … it is a concomitant part of their calling, a calling that promises a blessing from God, that they likewise should give unmerited blessings to others."[66]

This means that the addressees will enter increasingly into the full enjoyment of the *blessing* of God's forgiveness and goodwill as they themselves extend similar forgiveness and goodwill to others (Matt 6:12, 14–15; 18:32–35).[67] The addressees should behave this way for the reason that their own enjoyment of the divine mercy demands it.

6.4. THE UNIVERSAL PRINCIPLE MOTIVATED (AND REPEATED) BY A QUOTATION FROM PSALM 34

In 3:9b the author motivated the universal principle by recapitulating the basis for the ethics. In 3:10–12 he again motivates the universal principle, this time with a quotation from Ps 33:13–17 (LXX 34:12–16).

This quotation,[68] however, not only motivates the exhortations of 3:9 but repeats[69] the essence of the exhortations of 3:9 in 3:10–11: The tongue must be kept from evil and the lips from deceitful speech; "he must turn from evil and do good; he must seek peace[70] and pursue it." Then, in 3:12, this section of the quotation gives a motivation for the exhortation in 3:10–11 that doing good and seeking peace is the condition if one wants to love life.

---

65. See Michaels, *1 Peter*, 179; Piper, "Hope as the Motivation of Love," 227.

66. Davids, *The First Epistle of Peter*, 127.

67. See Alan M. Stibbs, *The First Epistle General of Peter* (Leicester: Inter-Varsity Press, 1959), 131.

68. In the LXX Ps 33:13–17 reads: τίς ἐστιν ἄνθρωπος ὁ θέλων ζωὴν ἀγαπῶν ἡμέρας ἰδεῖν ἀγαθάς; παῦσον τὴν γλῶσσάν σου ἀπὸ κακοῦ καὶ χείλη σου τοῦ μὴ λαλῆσαι δόλον. ἔκκλινον ἀπὸ κακοῦ καὶ ποίησον ἀγαθόν, ζήτησον εἰρήνην καὶ δίωξον αὐτήν. ὀφθαλμοὶ κυρίου ἐπὶ δικαίους, καὶ ὦτα αὐτοῦ εἰς δέησιν αὐτῶν. πρόσωπον δὲ κυρίου ἐπὶ ποιοῦντας κακὰ τοῦ ἐξολεθρεῦσαι ἐκ γῆς τὸ μνημόσυνον αὐτῶν. The author's variation from the LXX is probably to be explained by a combination of two factors: (1) his own editorial activity; and (2) his apparent use of a different textual tradition. See Michaels, *1 Peter*, 180.

69. See ibid., 174.

70. Michaels (ibid., 180) agrees with Goppelt (*Der erste Petrusbrief*, 230) that, although "peace" is mentioned nowhere else in 1 Peter, the author sees in these words from Ps 34 the kernel of all he wants to say in 3:8–12. This may be correct.

I thus take the phrase ὁ θέλων ζωὴν ἀγαπᾶν καὶ ἰδεῖν ἡμέρας ἀγαθὰς[71] to mean: "whoever wants to love life and see good days," taking "life" not metaphorically of the world to come but as referring to the present earthly life.[72] Obeying this exhortation of no retaliation then neutralizes the vanity-call of Eccl 2:17: "So I hated life, because what is done under the sun was grievous to me; for all is vanity and a chasing after wind [καὶ ἐμίσησα σὺν τὴν ζωήν, ὅτι πονηρὸν ἐπ' ἐμὲ τὸ ποίημα τὸ πεποιημένον ὑπὸ τὸν ἥλιον, ὅτι τὰ πάντα ματαιότης καὶ προαίρεσις πνεύματος]."

6.5. Motivation for the Argument That, to Love Life, One Must Turn trom Evil

The final section of the quotation, 3:12, is a motivation for the argument that, to love life, one must turn from evil: "For the eyes of the Lord are on the righteous and his ears are attentive to their prayer, but the face of the Lord is against those who do evil [ὅτι ὀφθαλμοὶ κυρίου ἐπὶ δικαίους καὶ ὦτα αὐτοῦ εἰς δέησιν αὐτῶν, πρόσωπον δὲ κυρίου ἐπὶ ποιοῦντας κακά]." This does not mean that blessing those who revile is a condition to receive inheritance from the Lord but that it is a condition to love life.[73] Again, the blessings referred to in 3:12 relate to this life.[74]

6.6. Conclusion

The ethics of the pericope 1 Pet 3:8–12 on the response to animosity can be typified as an ethics of no retaliation. It is formulated both in the negative and in the positive:

---

71. Piper ("Hope as the Motivation of Love," 227) aptly says that "the entire Old Testament quotation is an expansion and restatement of the argumentation in 3:9."

72. Contra Michaels, *1 Peter*, 180, who argues that "the language of the Psalm is the language of this world, but Peter has made it metaphorical of the world to come." Quite a number of scholars share Michaels's view, e.g., Beare, *The First Epistle of Peter*, 135; Best, *1 Peter*, 131; Kelly, *Commentary on the Epistles*, 138; Piper, "Hope as the Motivation of Love," 226; and Davids, *The First Epistle of Peter*, 128. Bigg and Stibbs, however, agree with my view. Bigg says: "ζωή means this present earthly life ... made sweet and delectable by righteousness" (*Critical and Exegetical Commentary*, 157). Stibbs states that obeying this exhortation is "the way to enjoy true and satisfying life. ... It describes the man who wishes to live a life which he can love and find worth while" (*First Epistle General*, 131).

73. Piper has a different view: "The insertion of this ὅτι shows how 1 Peter intends the logic of 3:9: one must bless those who revile him *because* his inheritance from the Lord depends on it" ("Hope as the Motivation of Love," 227).

74. Grudem, *1 Peter*, 148.

Negative: Do not repay evil for evil or insult with insult (3:9a).
    Keep tongue from evil (3:10b).
    Keep lips from deceitful speech (3:10c).
    Turn from evil (3:11a).

Positive: Repay with blessing (3:9b).
    Do good (3:11b).
    Seek peace and pursue it (3:11c).

The fact that the consequence of practicing these ethics is the inheritance of a blessing recalls their status as children of God the Father. The universal principle that can be deduced is: children of God must not repay evil for evil or insult for insult; they must repay with blessing and do good, seeking peace. The basis is: because as children of God the Father (1:3), they are entitled to inherit, and their inheritance is a blessing—God's final bestowal of eternal well-being on his people at the last day.

This ethics of no retaliation has another basis in 1 Peter: the example of Christ's response to evil and insult, in whose steps they are exhorted to follow (2:21), like sheep following in the steps of their Shepherd (2:25).

7. The Ethos in 1 Peter 3:8–12

It was argued in §2 above that ethos is the praxis of the ethics, the way a specific community brings its ethics into practice. In the pericope 1 Pet 3:8–12 there is no ethos, neither projected nor real. However, in the rest of 1 Peter the praxis of the ethics of no retaliation is evident in three exhortations: the code for the relationship of household servant with their masters, of wives with their husbands, and in the response to threats.

> *Household servants:* Household servants, submit yourselves to your masters with all respect, not only to those who are good and considerate, but also to those who are harsh. For it is commendable if a man bears up under the pain of unjust suffering because he is conscious of God. But how is it to your credit if you receive a beating for doing wrong and endure it? But if you suffer for doing good and you endure it, this is commendable before God. (1 Pet 2:18–20)

> *Wives:* Wives, in the same way be submissive to your husbands so that, if any of them do not believe the word, they may be won over without words by the behavior of their wives, when they see the purity and reverence of your lives. Your beauty should not come from outward adornment, such as braided hair and the wearing of gold jewelry and fine clothes. Instead, it

should be that of your inner self, the unfading beauty of a gentle and quiet spirit, which is of great worth in God's sight. (1 Pet 3:1–4)

Threats: Do not fear their threats. But in your hearts set apart Christ as Lord. Always be prepared to give an answer to everyone who asks you to give the reason for the hope that you have. But do this with gentleness and respect, keeping a clear conscience, so that those who speak maliciously against your good behavior in Christ may be ashamed of their slander. (1 Pet 3:14–16)

8. Pointers for the Response to Evil in Present-Day Life Situations

From all of this it can be deduced that the ethics on the response to animosity in 3:8–12 is: Repay animosity with blessing! Keep on doing good! Seek peace and pursue it! This is what it means to follow in the steps of Jesus (2:21–22): to do the will of God, in spite of the suffering it causes.

The ethics in 1 Peter are universal principles, applicable for all times and circumstances. The ethos, however, is for a very specific life situation, where the believers, as resident and visiting aliens, had no political rights and were caught up in social structures of oppression (at least for the household servants and the wives). Their "kindness" to an "enemy" may win the person over, demonstrating the superiority of Christians to their enemies, since they are not implicated in the anger or the hostility of the relationship. They refuse to be persons who "return evil for evil," but by blessing, they continue to do good in response to animosity.

The ethos in present-day societies, where fundamental rights are accepted and respected, will have a different praxis of the ethics of 1 Peter. But the fundamental ethics of continuing to do good as the Christian response to animosity is universally and timelessly applicable—with the promise that the outcome of this ethics of no retaliation is that one loves life and enjoys good days!

Animosity in the Johannine Epistles: A Difference in the Interpretation of a Shared Tradition

Dirk G. van der Merwe

1. Introduction

During the first century c.e., differences in respect of doctrine and ethics led to traces of animosity within the church. This phenomenon resulted in divisions between certain early Christian communities, which necessitated the writing of some of New Testament books (e.g., 2 Corinthians, Galatians, 1 and 2 John). Although animosity is a negative phenomenon and discrepant to the nature of the church, which should be characterized by love, the need to address this problem in the various Christian communities where it occurred contributed positively to the formulation of the doctrine and ethics of the church. This was surely the case as far as the Johannine Epistles are concerned.

This chapter deals with animosity as addressed in the Johannine Epistles and focuses on only the first two epistles.[1] From 1 and 2 John, commonly accepted among scholars as originating from the same early Christian circles, it is clear that a serious internal crisis developed among these believers subsequent to the expulsion of Johannine Jewish Christians from the Jewish community. Throughout these epistles the situation is depicted as a schism that has already occurred in the community. Scholars dispute the specifics of this crisis but agree on two main points: (1) this was an internal crisis in

---

1. The other Johannine epistle (3 John) does not offer evidence of this crisis and is not so concerned with christological issues. "Hospitality" and "inhospitality" in the church seem to be the issues there. It may have been written in a different situation in the Johannine community. Therefore, it is not regarded as important and relevant to this discussion. For more on the dispute between the Elder and Diotrephes, consult the section "Hospitality and Inhospitality" in Abraham J. Malherbe, *Social Aspects of Early Christianity* (2nd ed.; Philadelphia: Fortress, 1983), 92–112.

which the key issue was Christology; (2) this dispute regarding beliefs rapidly led to social consequences. This was a painful schism in the history of the Johannine community,[2] which probably played a major role in its disintegration some years later.

The reference in the title regarding animosity to which the first two Johannine Epistles refer as "a difference in the interpretation of a shared tradition" indicates the essence of what led to the schism in this community. In investigating this schism, the interest will naturally focus on 1 John, the longest of the three epistles. As far as method is concerned, this research will be approached sociorhetorically. First we will look at the socioreligious situation in the Johannine community; second, we will investigate the setting within which animosity in this community is to be understood; third, we will scrutinize the nature of animosity in this community; fourth, we will probe how the Elder dealt with the problem of animosity; and, finally, we will provide some hermeneutical principles that are to be followed in order to manage animosity in the church today. The socioreligious situation of the Johannine community and the identities of their opponents will now be discussed.

---

2. The exact social description or label of the Johannine community is still a matter of debate. Is it a community (Raymond E. Brown, *The Community of the Beloved Disciple* [New York: Paulist, 1979]; John Painter, *1, 2, and 3 John* [Collegeville, Minn.: Liturgical Press, 2002], 75–76), a sect (Wayne A. Meeks, "The Man from Heaven in Johannine Sectarianism," *JBL* 91 [1972]: 44–72; see also John Bogart, *Orthodox and Heretical Perfectionism in the Johannine Community as Evident in the First Epistle of John* [SBLDS 33; Missoula, Mont.: Scholars Press, 1977], 136–41; Craig S. Keener, *The Gospel of John: A Commentary* [2 vols.; Peabody, Mass.: Hendrickson, 2003], 1:149; and Kåre S. Fuglseth, *Johannine Sectarianism in Perspective: A Sociological, Historical, and Comparative Analysis of Temple and Social Relationships in the Gospel of John, Philo, and Qumran* [NovTSup 119; Leiden: Brill, 2005], who argues against this community being a sect; see also on the definition of "sect" David Rensberger, *Johannine Faith and Liberating Community* [Philadelphia: Westminster, 1988], 136), a circle (Oscar Cullmann, *The Johannine Circle* [trans. John Bowden; Philadelphia: Westminster, 1976]; see also Painter, *1, 2, and 3 John*, 75–76), a "Konventikel" (Ernst Käsemann, *The Testament of Jesus* [trans. Gerhard Krodel; Philadelphia: Fortress, 1978]), a school (R. Alan Culpepper, *The Johannine School: An Evaluation of the Johannine School Hypothesis Based on an Investigation of the Nature of Ancient Schools* [SBLDS 26; Missoula, Mont.: Scholars Press, 1975]; Georg Strecker, *The Johannine Letters* [Hermeneia; Minneapolis: Fortress, 1996], xxxv), a group (Jan G. van der Watt, "Ethics and Ethos in the Gospel according to John," in *Identity, Ethics, and Ethos in the New Testament* [ed. Jan G. van der Watt; Berlin: de Gruyter, 2006], 121), or something else? Because of this uncertainty, the reference "Johannine community" will be used for the group of Johannine Christians. Such an indication tends to be more neutral.

2. The Socioreligious Situation in the Johannine Community

2.1. The Depiction of the Opponents and the Socioreligious Situation in the Community

Numerous attempts have been made to identify the "opponents" of the Elder.[3] They have been depicted as charismatics, Jewish Christians, Cerinthians, docetists, and gnostics.[4] While these opponents have some points (characteristics) in common with the proposed depictions, differences militate against a precise identification with any of these groups.[5] It can be taken for granted

---

3. In this essay it has been accepted, in agreement with the point of view of most scholars, that the three Johannine Epistles were written by the same person, referred to in 2 John 1 and 3 John 1 as the πρεσβύτερος; see Brown, *Community of the Beloved Disciple*, 398; R. Alan Culpepper, *The Gospel and Letters of John* (Nashville: Abingdon, 1998), 251; Garrett C. Kenney, *Leadership in John: An Analysis of the Situation and Strategy of the Gospel and the Epistles of John* (Lanham, Md.: University Press of America, 2000), 12; Painter, *1, 2, and 3 John*, 18; J. Christopher Thomas, *A Pentecostal Commentary on 1 John, 2 John, 3 John* (Cleveland: Pilgrim, 2004), 4. Therefore, the author will be referred to as "the Elder."

4. For a discussion of these depictions, see Floyd V. Filson, "First John: Purpose and Message," *Int* 23 (1969): 268ff.; Raymond E. Brown, *The Epistles of John* (AB 30; Garden City, N.Y.: Doubleday, 1982), 55ff.; Ruth B. Edwards, *The Johannine Epistles* (New Testament Guides; Sheffield: Sheffield Academic Press, 1996), 57ff.; Larry Hurtado, *Lord Jesus Christ: Devotion to Jesus in Earliest Christianity* (Grand Rapids: Eerdmans, 2003), 418; see also Culpepper, *Gospel and Letters*, 51. Brown, *The Epistles of John*, 55, also adds the Ebionites and libertines.

5. Any attempt to discover the precise nature of the crisis within the Johannine community is made more difficult because of the fact that there is so much disagreement about the interpretation of 1 John. A glance at some commentaries and other publications on 1 John illustrate just how divergent this interpretation is. See Filson, "First John," 268–69; Rudolf Bultmann, *The Gospel of John* (trans. G. R. Beasley-Murray; Oxford: Blackwell, 1971), 9; Pheme Perkins, *The Johannine Epistles* (Wilmington, Del.: Glazier, 1979), xviff.; Brown, *The Epistles of John*, 47ff.; Kenneth Grayston, *The Johannine Epistles* (Grand Rapids: Eerdmans, 1984), 12–13; Stephen S. Smalley, *1, 2, 3 John* (WBC 51; Dallas: Word, 1984), xxiii; Rudolf Schnackenburg, *The Johannine Epistles* (New York: Crossroad, 1992), 17; Dietmar Neufeld, *Reconceiving Texts as Speech Acts: An Analysis of 1 John* (BibInt 7; Leiden: Brill, 1994), 7–8; Edwards, *The Johannine Epistles*, 59ff.; Culpepper, *Gospel and Letters*, 51; Painter, *1, 2, and 3 John*, 88ff.; Dennis C. Duling, *The New Testament: History, Literature, and Context* (Belmont, Calif.: Wadsworth Thompson, 2003), 439; Hurtado, *Lord Jesus Christ*, 418ff. The most striking feature that emerges from the review of these publications is the great diversity in the interpretation of the various aspects concerning the opponents of the Elder in 1 and 2 John. Those who left the community were seen as either Gentile Christians or Jewish Christians or both. Their deception has been interpreted as either doctrinal or ethical or both. Grayston goes further and interprets it as the "exaggera-

that none of these identifications is absolutely convincing. Therefore, the identification of these opponents as such would not have been particularly enlightening; considering how little we know about these groups, it would be to explain *ignotum per ignotius* ([to explain] something not understood by one still less understood).[6] This does not mean that "opponents" did not exist, only that the precise historical situation is not known to us.

Within the framework of this investigation, these opponents can perhaps be best identified through a study of the three key passages: 1 John 2:18-27; 4:1-6; and 2 John 7-11. These passages delineate some aspects regarding the background of these opponents of the Elder:

2:18	ἀντίχριστοι πολλοὶ γεγόνασιν ...	ἐξ ἡμῶν ἐξῆλθαν
4:1	πολλοὶ **ψευδοπροφῆται**	ἐξεληλύθασιν εἰς τὸν κόσμον
2 John 7	πολλοὶ **πλάνοι** ...	ἐξῆλθον ...... εἰς τὸν κόσμον

In these texts the Elder refers to the fact that in the schism apparently *many* (πολλοί) had separated from him and his network of house churches.[7] It can be deduced that *many* people left the community. Since there is no inference that they left their environment, they could still have influenced the adherents of the Elder.

By *labeling his opponents* as ἀντίχριστοι, ψευδοπροφῆται, and πλάνοι, the Elder refers to unnamed people who had once been members of the Johannine group but had subsequently abandoned their association with this group (2:19). Other references in this passage to "lies" (2:21), "liars" (2:22), and "those who would deceive you" (τῶν πλανώντων ὑμᾶς, 2:26; see also 4:6) probably also refer to those who had left the Johannine community. They promoted a religious viewpoint that differed so much from "what they have heard from the beginning" (see 1:1; 2:7, 13, 14, 24) that the Elder regarded it as an unacceptable innovation.[8] The term "antichrist" is used in the singular and the plural (2:18). Where the singular form is used, the reference may be to the

---

tion of the role of the Spirit" (*The Johannine Epistles*, 19-20). Urban C. Von Wahlde (*The Johannine Commandments: 1 John and the Struggle for the Johannine Tradition* [New York: Paulist, 1990], 128 n. 17) points out that there are various ways of approaching the statements regarding the opponents.

6. Brown, *The Epistles of John*, 69ff.; and see also Schnackenburg, *The Johannine Epistles*, 17.

7. See Culpepper, *The Johannine School*; Cullmann, *The Johannine Circle*; Brown, *Community of the Beloved Disciple*; see also J. Louis Martyn, *History and Theology in the Fourth Gospel* (Nashville: Abingdon, 1979).

8. Hurtado, *Lord Jesus Christ*, 408f.

principal leader of the opponents. It is almost unthinkable that the schism did not involve a leadership struggle. While no leader is named, the fluidity of the one antichrist and the many antichrists suggests a leader and his schismatic followers. The names "deceiver," "liar," and "antichrist" seem to focus on the leader of the opponents. His followers are characterized in similar terms.[9] The reference in the plural form, made to the ἀντίχριστοι (2:18), ψευδοπροφῆται (4:1), and πλάνοι (2 John 7) should be understood in the light of the impact of the schism and the activities of those who were, according to the Elder, false teachers, false prophets, and deceivers.

That "they went out" (ἐξῆλθαν) implies that they were once part of the community and left of their own accord.[10] The phrase εἰς τὸν κόσμον (4:1; 2 John 7)[11] is merely another way of stating emphatically that they have left the community and characterizes them as opposing those in the community. They are of the world, while those in the community are of God (see 4:1–6).

Throughout 1 John the opponents are vehemently depicted and treated as existing outside the Johannine community[12] and are (1) labeled according to the deeds they committed at the ethical level, on account of which they are called murderers (ἀνθρωποκτόνος, 3:15; see also 3:12, ἔσφαξεν) who do not love a brother (4:20; see also 2:11; 3:15), and, at the doctrinal level, on account of which they are depicted as deceivers (2 John 7; also 1 John 2:26; 3:7), antichrists (2:18, 22; 4:3; 2 John 8), liars (1 John 2:22) and false prophets (4:1). (2) These deceivers are also described within specific relationships: concerning the devil they are seen "as children of the devil" (3:8, 10); in relation

---

9. Painter, *1, 2, and 3 John*, 203.

10. Ibid., 204.

11. Of the 23 occurrences of κόσμος in 1 and 2 John, only two (4:9, 17) refer to locality. In 4:1–6 κόσμος occurs six times. In all these cases it is used antithetically to God. The phrase "they have gone out into the world" (also 2 John 7) alludes to 2:19, where it is stated: "They went out from us," which implies that they were formerly part of the community but had severed all ties. See Schnakenburg, *Epistles*, 199, for a different interpretation. "They went out from us…" characterizes their appearance in public all over the world. The adherents of the Elder may come upon them anywhere.

12. Scholars refer to them differently. Painter, *1, 2, and 3 John*, 84, refers to them as "opponents." According to him, they could also be called "schismatics" or "heretics." An alternative nomenclature used by Brown, *The Epistles of John*, 69, 70, 70 n. 156; also Hurtado, *Lord Jesus Christ*, 409ff., is "secessionists"; Brown, *The Epistles of John*, 358, 415, 429, 574, 618, also refers to "adversaries," "opponents," "deceivers," and "propagandists." Schnackenburg calls them "heretical teachers" (*The Johannine Epistles*, 18). Each of these terms can be justified as representative of the Elder's point of view. For a brief discussion of why references to these secessionists as "docetists" or "gnostics" are unacceptable, see Hurtado, *Lord Jesus Christ*, 418.

to God they are depicted "as not from God" (3:10; 4:3, 6), "do not know him" (God) (3:1), and "do (not) have fellowship with him" (1:6); and, finally, they are seen as "to be in the world" (4:5). (3) Metaphorically speaking, in a reciprocal sense, it is said that "they walk in the darkness and do not know the way to go, because the darkness has brought on blindness" (2:11). (4) In probably the harshest description it is said that they "do not have life" (5:12; also 3:15) and "abide in death" (3:14). In most of these references the harsh depiction of these opponents is contrasted with the characteristics of the adherents of the Elder.[13]

2.2. CONCLUSION

The above analysis verifies the fact that these opponents of the Elder were once part of the Johannine community and that they had shared the same tradition. Differences in the interpretation of this tradition caused the schism. Many members of the community, and this is a relative indication, went astray but remained in the vicinity region. They were probably influenced by an influential leader, referred to as the antichrist. This is due to his contradictory confession regarding Jesus' identity. This historical event and the circumstances were reinterpreted by the Elder as an eschatological event: it is the "last hour" (ἐσχάτη ὥρα ἐστίν), and this hour is the hour of the coming of the antichrist(s).

Questions that arise are: Why did a difference in the interpretation of doctrine and ethics cause the Elder to react so strongly when he wrote these epistles? In what setting should the animosity be understood?

3. Fellowship in the *Familia Dei* as the Setting within Which Animosity Is to Be Understood

The Johannine community has been depicted, metaphorically, by the Elder as the family of God (*familia Dei*). The fellowship that existed in this family was torn apart by the deception of some of its members. This led to animosity in the community. In order to grasp these circumstances and consequences, it is necessary to understand what the Elder meant when he depicted the community as the *familia Dei* and what he understood under "fellowship in the family."

---

13. Dirk G. van der Merwe, "Understanding 'Sin' in the Johannine Epistles," *Verbum et Ecclesia* 26 (2005): 543–70.

3.1. The Johannine Community as the *Familia Dei*

In the ancient Mediterranean world, being part of a group was important and a matter of convention.[14] The in-group of the Johannine community and how the common life was lived within this group were what mattered to the Elder, and this was the focus of his doctrine and ethics.[15] By reminding his adherents of their fictive kinship, of their common identity (ἀδελφοί [2:9, 10; 3:10, 12 (bis), 13, 15, 17; 4:20 (bis), 21; 5:16], ἀλλήλους [1:7; 3:11, 14, 16, 23; 4:7, 11, 12; 2 John 5]) and the values, conduct, and doctrine that set them apart from other groups (e.g., their opponents) in their society, the Elder entrenched their identity as a group and served to continue to regulate social behavior in this group.

To this end, the Elder uses the most intimate social phenomenon in the ancient world, namely, "the family,"[16] to describe the existential reality of being and living as Christians in such a group. In doing so, he uses a coherent network of metaphors related to the social reality of first-century family life,[17]

---

14. Bruce J. Malina, "The Social Sciences in Biblical Interpretation," *Int* 37 (1982): 229–42; idem, *Christian Origins and Cultural Anthropology: Practical Models for Biblical Interpretation* (Atlanta: John Knox, 1986); idem, *The New Testament World* (Philadelphia: Fortress, 1993); idem, *The Social World of Jesus and the Gospels* (London: Routledge, 1996), 64; Vernon K. Robbins (*Exploring the Texture of Texts* [Valley Forge, Pa.: Trinity Press International, 1996], 101) points out how important group identity, real kinship, and fictive kinship relations were in the first-century Mediterranean world—it fully determined the identities of individuals. Since they were group-oriented, they were socially minded, attuned to the values, attitudes, and beliefs of their in-groups. Because these people were strongly embedded in a group, their behavior was controlled by strong social inhibitions along with a general lack of personal inhibition.

15. See J. Eugene Botha, "Simple Salvation, but Not a Straw ... Jacobean Soteriology," in *Salvation in the New Testament: Perspectives on Soteriology* (ed. Jan G. van der Watt; NovTSup 121; Leiden: Brill, 2005), 395–96.

16. Jan G. van der Watt, "Ethics in First John: A Literary and Socio-scientific Perspective," *CBQ* 61 (1999): 494. In the New Testament, Jesus groups are described from a strongly "group-embedded, collectivistic perspective," perceiving themselves as forming "the household of God" (*familia Dei*). Karl O. Sandnes points out "that in the family terms of the New Testament, old and new structures come together. There is a convergence of household and brotherhood structures. The New Testament bears evidence of the process by which new structures emerged from within the household structures" ("Equality within Partriarchal Structures: Some New Testament Perspectives on the Christian Fellowship as a Brother- or Sisterhood and a Family," in *Constructing Early Christian Families: Family as Social Reality and Metaphor* [ed. Halvor Moxnes; London: Routledge, 1997], 156).

17. Van der Watt, "Ethics in First John," 491; see also Eva M. Lassen, "The Roman Family: Ideal and Metaphor," in Moxnes, *Constructing Early Christian Families*, 103.

to provide an understanding of fundamental Christian concepts. He applies widely accepted conventions from everyday life to what happens in the community and uses generally accepted ideas about family life to explain what Christian life in the community comprises.[18] Therefore, the relevant social and family conventions of that time have to be considered for better understanding. In using these complex metaphors, developed in the text itself,[19] the Elder focuses only on specific central and widely accepted and relevant aspects[20] that serve his purpose. In this way he tries to activate in the minds of his adherents the social dynamic of the interrelatedness between a father and his child and between children mutually. Through all this he tries to redefine their position and relationship to one another. They constitute the family of God (*familia Dei*). This *familia Dei* is the sphere where Christian fellowship is constituted and experienced.

3.2. Fellowship in the Family

Contrary to his opponents, who claimed fellowship with God, the Elder wants his readers to be assured of the indwelling God through their abiding relationship with him (2:28; 5:13) and with one another. The attitude, teaching, and conduct of the opponents of the Elder annihilated this fellowship in the community. The Elder, therefore, wrote this epistle to encourage this kind of fellowship in the *familia Dei* and to promote the role and function of Jesus Christ in the constitution and realization of this fellowship in the community that had been abandoned by these opponents.

In 1:3 the Elder enunciates this objective. He desires his adherents to have fellowship with him and with his associates by sharing their experience of the manifested life (1:1, 2); fellowship with them meant simultaneous fellowship with the Father and his Son.[21]

---

18. Paul J. Achtemeier, Joel B. Green, and Marianne M. Thompson, *Introducing the New Testament: Its Literature and Theology* (Grand Rapids: Eerdmans, 2001), 547, assert that the family imagery may provide useful evidence regarding the internal structure and organization of the Johannine community.

19. See van der Watt, "Ethics in First John," 493.

20. Jan G. van der Watt, "Interpreting Imagery in John's Gospel: John 10 and 15 as Case Studies," in *Hupomnema: Feesbundel Opgedra aan J. P. Louw* (ed. J. H. Barkhuizen, H. F. Stander, and G. J. Swart; Pretoria: University of Pretoria Press, 1992), 272–79.

21. The opponents claim fellowship with God without fellowship with the Son and one another.

The noun κοινωνία ("fellowship") occurs twice in the *prooemium* (1:3) and twice more in the rest of chapter 1 (1:6–7) to create a chiastic pattern as indicated below:

A   ἵνα καὶ ὑμεῖς <u>κοινωνίαν</u> ἔχητε **μεθ' ἡμῶν** (1:3)
B   καὶ ἡ <u>κοινωνία</u> δὲ ἡ ἡμετέρα ... μετὰ τοῦ πατρὸς καὶ μετὰ τοῦ υἱοῦ αὐτοῦ Ἰησοῦ Χριστοῦ (1:3)
B' <u>κοινωνίαν</u> ἔχομεν ... μετ' αὐτοῦ καὶ ἐν τῷ σκότει περιπατῶμεν (1:6)
A' ἐὰν δὲ ἐν τῷ φωτὶ περιπατῶμεν ὡς αὐτός ἐστιν ἐν τῷ φωτί, <u>κοινωνίαν</u> ἔχομεν **μετ' ἀλλήλων** (1:7)

The κοινωνία statements in A-A' refer to the fellowship among believers, while the statements in B-B' refer to the corporate fellowship that believers experience with the Father and his Son Jesus Christ. The function of the chiastic structure is to emphasize the interrelatedness and interdependence of the fellowship among believers and their corporate fellowship with God. The one kind of fellowship demands and constitutes the other.[22] This would imply that the opponents cannot claim fellowship with God if they do not participate in fellowship with other Christians (ἀδελφοί and ἀλλήλους). The vertical fellowship is essential for true horizontal fellowship. The primary reference made by the Elder when he says "we have fellowship with one another" (1:7) is dependent on "you may have fellowship with us" (1:3), which opens up κοινωνία with the Father and his Son Jesus Christ.[23]

---

22. Although the reference to κοινωνία occurs explicitly only here, is it certainly implied throughout the epistle in other themes and concepts, e.g., the formulas of immanence: "knowing" (γινώσκειν, 1 John 2:3, 4, 13, 14; 3:6; 4:6–8), "having" (ἔχειν, 1 John 2:23; 2 John 9; see also 1 John 5:12), "being in" (εἶναι ἐν, 2:5; 5:20), and "abiding in" (μένειν ἐν, 2:6, 24; 3:24; 4:13, 15, 16). Methodologically speaking, within this purview the formulas of immanence should also include the "abiding" in other entities that are also closely connected to God, such as "truth" (1:8; 2:4; 2 John 2); "his word" (1 John 1:19; 2:14; see also 2:24; 5:10); his "anointing" (2:27); "his seed" (3:9); "eternal life" (3:15); "love" (4:12; see also 2:5; 3:17); the Spirit (3:24; 4:13); God (3:24 [bis]) abiding in the believer and reciprocally the abiding of the believer in the Son (2:6, 24, 28; 3:5, 24). Mutual abiding is referred to in 4:13, 15, 16 and 2 John 9.
23. See Painter, *1, 2, and 3 John*, 128; Dietrich Rusam, *Die Gemeinschaft der Kinder Gottes: Das Motiv der Gotteskindschaft und die Gemeinden der johanneischen Briefe* (Stuttgart: Kohlhammer, 1993), 182; Brooke F. Westcott, *The Epistles of St John: The Greek Text with Notes and Essays* (London: Macmillan, 1883; repr., Grand Rapids: Eerdmans, 1982), 11.

A high Christology is present in 1:3. Jesus is regarded as one with the Father, so that fellowship "with the Father" and participation in "his Son Jesus Christ" are treated as parallel and synonymous ideas (hence the Greek formulation μετὰ ... καὶ μετὰ ["with ... and with"]). Jesus revealed God; moreover (1:1–3, 7), he made fellowship with the Father possible. The Elder's use of the full title, "his Son Jesus Christ," nevertheless points to the humanity (Jesus), the divine status (Son), and the mission (Christ) of Jesus. He was, as typically in Johannine thought, one with humankind (Jesus, who was "heard, seen, observed, felt," 1:1–3) and is also one with God (his Son, the Messiah, who "from the beginning existed with the Father," 1:1–2). He is also the Christ who died (2:2; 4:10) an expiatory death.

This fellowship was broken because of the opponents' attitude of claiming true and vital knowledge through the Spirit for themselves, which led to their deviating Christology and conduct in the community. These three claims will now be discussed in order to provide the reader with a better understanding of the nature of the animosity and how it hampered fellowship in the community.

4. The Nature of Animosity

Even though references are scattered throughout the epistle, the Elder is quite thorough in his description of the claims of his opponents.[24] By studying the Elder's references to the opponents, it is possible to piece together their claims of true divine knowledge and the outlines of their doctrine and ethics.

4.1. A Pneumatological Issue: The Claim of True and Vital Divine Knowledge through The Spirit

Hurtado provides an apt summary of the situation in the Johannine community at the time 1 and 2 John were written.[25] According to him, a group arose in this community that based their christological assertions on professed revelatory experiences of the Spirit.[26] The opponents of the Elder claimed a special illumination by the Spirit (2:20, 27) that imparted to them true knowledge of God. This caused them to regard themselves as *the* children of God. They claimed that their christological views and their own spiritual

---

24. For an indication of all the possible views of the opponents contested by the Elder, see Grayston, *The Johannine Epistles*, 16ff.
25. Hurtado, *Lord Jesus Christ*, 415.
26. See also Grayston, *The Johannine Epistles*, 20.

status were superior.[27] It seems as if they believed that they had been given new and superior insight. They also may have claimed that they possessed (or had been given) fellowship with God that was superior to that enjoyed by other Johannine Christians and that their higher spiritual status justified the severing of ties. It seems as if they were so thoroughly persuaded of the superiority of their inspiration that they removed themselves from the circle of Johannine Christianity.[28] For them, their revelations validly superseded all previous understanding of Jesus and his significance. They drew upon Johannine traditions and even considered themselves the valid interpreters of those traditions. Nevertheless, in the opinion of the Elder they not only abandoned the ties of fellowship with other Johannine believers but also departed from traditional christological convictions. Their apparently volitional secession suggests that they were convinced that they had gone far beyond the level of understanding of those they abandoned.[29]

Their new insights regarding Christ amounted to a notably different stance from what the Elder continued to see as binding tradition. Therefore, the Elder contrasts the opponents' claim to knowledge with the knowledge that can come only from the Christian tradition (2:24)[30] and the Spirit of God (4:2; 5:6). The christological convictions of the opponents will now be discussed.

4.2. The Christological Issues

In order to understand the basic christological tenets of the opponents in 1 and 2 John, we need to look at the confessional formulas that are brought to bear against them (1 John 2:22; 4:2, 3, 15; 5:1, 5, 6, 10, 13; 2 John 7).[31] The

---

27. Hurtado, *Lord Jesus Christ*, 416.

28. Ibid., 424.

29. Hurtado, *Lord Jesus Christ*, 419; Kenney, *Leadership in John*, 101; see also Brown, *The Epistles of John*, 52; Judith Lieu, *The Second and Third Epistles of John* (Edinburgh: T&T Clark, 1986), 207.

30. See also Culpepper, *Gospel and Letters*, 49. The Elder does not surrender the Christian claim to true and vital knowledge. It is hardly by chance that he uses the verb γινώσκειν "to know" twenty-five times and οἶδεν "to know" fifteen times. He writes "we know" seventeen times and "you know," referring to the readers, twelve times. The Elder and his adherents are the people who really know the gospel to which the church must firmly hold (Filson, "First John," 268–69).

31. First John emphasizes certain tests that the adherents of the Elder are to apply to themselves to judge whether they are true or false Christians. One prominent phrase that highlights certain tests is ἐν τούτῳ (2:3, 5; 3:10, 16, 19, 24; 4:2, 6, 13; 5:2). Another pattern is the *if*-clause: ἐάν (1:6–7, 8ff.; 2:3, 15, 24, 29; 3:21; 4:12, 20; 5:15). In these *if*-clauses the

christological focus in 1 John is the historical intersection of the divine and the human in Jesus. This intersection is asserted in what the Elder urges his readers to believe and confess: (1) "Jesus is the Christ" (2:22; 5:1), "Jesus is the Son of God" (4:15; 5:5); (2) "Jesus Christ has [is] come in the flesh" (4:1–3; 2 John 7); and (3) "the one who came by water and blood, Jesus Christ" (1 John 1:7; 2:1–2; 4:2, 9, 10, 14 (15); 5:6; see also 3:16). These three creedal formulas reflect the basic christological tenets of the opponents.[32] This is verifiable from the negations (οὐκ [also ὁ ἀρνούμενος], 2:22; μή, 4:2; 2 John 7; οὐκ [μή], 1 John 5:6 [10]) that occur in all three of these references.

4.2.1. Ἰησοῦς ἐστιν ὁ Χριστός (2:22; 5:1) ... ὁ υἱὸς [τοῦ θεοῦ] (2:22–23; 4:15; 5:5)

Related texts with explicit doctrinal references depicting the first christological tenet of the opponents are:

2:22: Τίς ἐστιν ὁ ψεύστης εἰ μὴ ὁ ἀρνούμενος ὅτι Ἰησοῦς οὐκ ἐστιν ὁ Χριστός (negative)
5:1: Πᾶς ὁ πιστεύων ὅτι Ἰησοῦς ἐστιν ὁ Χριστός, ἐκ τοῦ θεοῦ γεγέννηται (positive)

These two texts form an antithetical parallelism and a chiasm. The contents of both concern the denial/belief that "Jesus is the Christ." The one contradicts the other. Both texts are without any elaboration to qualify any meaning. The only help here, although vague, comes from 2:22–23, which has a parallelism (2:22) followed by an antithetical parallelism (2:23).

2:22: Τίς ἐστιν ὁ ψεύστης εἰ μὴ ὁ ἀρνούμενος ὅτι Ἰησοῦς οὐκ ἔστιν ὁ Χριστός; οὗτός ἐστιν ὁ ἀντίχριστος, ὁ ἀρνούμενος τὸν πατέρα καὶ τὸν υἱόν.
2:23: πᾶς ὁ ἀρνούμενος τὸν υἱὸν οὐδὲ τὸν πατέρα ἔχει, ὁ ὁμολογῶν τὸν υἱὸν καὶ τὸν πατέρα ἔχει.

---

verb is used in the subjunctive mood, but 2:19 uses εἰ ("if") and the indicative mood in a contrary-to-fact condition, and 3:17 has ὃς δ' ἂν and the subjunctive in the conditional relative clause. Filson ("First John," 264 n. 7) points out that all these passages involve a condition. These clauses show how serious the Elder was to set up tests and conditions by which Christian thoughts and actions could be guided.

32. See Rondey A. Whitacre, *Johannine Polemic: The Role of Tradition and Theology* (SBLDS 67; Chico, Calif.: Scholars Press, 1982), 123; Schnackenburg, *The Johannine Epistles*, 18–19.

The confessions of Jesus as ὁ Χριστός and ὁ υἱός (τοῦ θεοῦ) are closely interrelated. They are virtually interchangeable. This is evident from 2:22–23 (cf. also 5:1 with 5:5).[33] To predicate one of them to Jesus is to be conscious of the other as well, and to deny one regarding Jesus is to deny the other as well.[34] According to this Christology, the Elder wants to point out that Jesus is "the Son [of God]" and "the Christ." Thus "the Son [of God]" and "the Christ" is the same person, namely, Jesus, or Jesus is "the Son [of God]" as well as "the Christ."[35]

The parallelism in 2:22 clearly illustrates that, if *Jesus* is the Christ, *he* is the Son of God. If *he* is denied to be the Christ, then *he* is not the Son, which implies that such a denial would also be a denial of the Father. This is explicitly stated in the antithetical parallelism in 2:23. The issue here, then, concerns *Jesus*. Thus the crux of the issue is not the predicate ὁ Χριστός but the subject Ἰησοῦς. It is not because the opponents thought someone else was the Christ (e.g., the false christs of Matt 24:5); the issue *"was whether the man Jesus could be the same person as the divine Christ."*[36]

It is difficult to determine from these verses what the opponents were affirming or denying about Jesus being ὁ Χριστός and ὁ υἱός (τοῦ θεοῦ). The following christological statement will give more clarity on this problem.[37]

---

33. 4:15: ὃς ἐὰν ὁμολογήσῃ ὅτι Ἰησοῦς ἐστιν ὁ υἱὸς τοῦ θεοῦ
    5:5: εἰ μὴ ὁ πιστεύων ὅτι Ἰησοῦς ἐστιν ὁ υἱὸς τοῦ θεοῦ
34. Whitacre, *Johannine Polemic*, 123; Schnackenburg, *The Johannine Epistles*, 145.
35. Marinus de Jonge, "Variety and Development in Johannine Christology," in idem, *Jesus: Stranger from Heaven and Son of God. Jesus Christ and the Christians in Johannine Perspective* (SBLSBS 11; Missoula, Mont.: Scholars Press, 1977), 200–205; also, Schnackenburg (*The Johannine Epistles*, 145) points out that this close relationship between ὁ Χριστός and ὁ υἱός (τοῦ θεοῦ) indicates that, whatever the background of ὁ Χριστός in Judaism, it is in Johannine thought first of all a Christian term molded by Christian experience in the Christian communities. In a comparison of the Fourth Gospel with 1 and 2 John, ὁ Χριστός has even less reference to Jewish expectations. Of the eleven occurrences of the term in 1 and 2 John, six are used in conjunction with Ἰησοῦς as Ἰησοῦς Χριστός (2:1, 22; 4:2; 5:1, 6; 2 John 7), of which two concern where it is denied (2:22) or believed (5:1) that "Jesus is the Christ." In four other texts (1 John 1:3; 3:23; 5:20; 2 John 3), Christ is used in conjunction with Jesus and Son as τοῦ υἱοῦ αὐτοῦ Ἰησοῦ Χριστοῦ. Only in 2 John 9 is it used in connection with the "teaching of Christ." This implies that the content of ὁ Χριστός in 1 John is influenced by that of Ἰησοῦς and ὁ υἱός (τοῦ θεοῦ).
36. Brown, *The Epistles of John*, 352.
37. See Whitacre, *Johannine Polemic*, 125.

4.2.2. Ἰησοῦν Χριστὸν ἐν σαρκὶ ἐληλυθότα (1 John 4:1-3; 2 John 7)

The second christological tenet of the opponents concerns the "coming of Jesus Christ in the flesh," which is referred to in 4:2 and 2 John 7:

4:2: **πᾶν πνεῦμα ὃ ὁμολογεῖ** Ἰησοῦν Χριστὸν ἐν σαρκὶ ἐληλυθότα ἐκ τοῦ θεοῦ ἐστιν (positive)

2 John 7: **οἱ μὴ ὁμολογοῦντες** Ἰησοῦν Χριστὸν ἐρχόμενον ἐν σαρκί· οὗτός ἐστιν ὁ πλάνος καὶ ὁ ἀντίχριστος (negative)

Here another antithetical parallelism occurs. The contents of both concern the confession or denial that "Jesus Christ has come in the flesh." The one confession is the opposite of the other; so also are the results of these confessions. The confession that Ἰησοῦν Χριστὸν ἐν σαρκὶ ἐληλυθότα (4:2) is contrasted with πᾶν πνεῦμα ὃ μὴ ὁμολογεῖ τὸν Ἰησοῦν ἐκ τοῦ θεοῦ οὐκ ἐστιν (4:3) and helps to clarify the issue here.

This issue here, already present in 2:22 and 5:1, also concerns *Jesus* (Χριστόν is omitted in 4:3). The issue is not whether Jesus has come in the flesh. This clause could refer only to confessing (or denying) that Jesus is "the Christ who came in the flesh," that the expected Messiah has arrived on earth and he is Jesus. With such a confession, 4:2 would make more specific the confession that Jesus is the Christ as stated in 2:22 and 5:1.[38] Hence, 4:2 is concerned with Jesus as ὁ Χριστός, thus the Elder's use of the double designation of Ἰησοῦν Χριστόν. Hence, the opponents are to be understood as representing a simple denial of Jesus as ὁ Χριστός. The problem here is not the σάρξ of Jesus but the σάρξ of ὁ Χριστός. This crucial distinction is confirmed and elucidated by the christological passage in 5:6 (Οὗτός ἐστιν ὁ ἐλθὼν δι' ὕδατος καὶ αἵματος, Ἰησοῦς Χριστός, οὐκ ἐν τῷ ὕδατι μόνον ἀλλ' ἐν τῷ ὕδατι καὶ ἐν τῷ αἵματι) and other related passages in 1 John (1:7; 2:1-2; 3:16; 4:9, 10, 14 [15]).

---

38. See Whitacre, *Johannine Polemic*, 127ff., for a valuable discussion on the Fourth Gospel's use of the noun σάρξ with reference to Jesus. He tries to point out that, e.g., for the Fourth Evangelist the point was never that the resurrected Jesus has a body but that the flesh and blood body standing in front of his disciples is the Jesus who was crucified. According to the Fourth Gospel, it was the death of Jesus that gives life to the world, and σάρξ is most likely an element in this motif.

4.2.3. Ἰησοῦς Χριστός, οὐκ ἐν τῷ ὕδατι μόνον ἀλλ' ἐν τῷ ὕδατι καὶ ἐν τῷ αἵματι (1 John 5:6)

This verse cryptically takes the nature of the false teaching of the opponents to a final point. In 1 John 5:6 the Elder indicates that the opponents, while accepting his baptism, deny the death of Jesus: Οὗτός ἐστιν ὁ ἐλθὼν δι' <u>ὕδατος</u> καὶ **αἵματος**, Ἰησοῦς Χριστός, οὐκ ἐν τῷ <u>ὕδατι</u> μόνον ἀλλ' ἐν τῷ ὕδατι καὶ ἐν τῷ **αἵματι**. Scholars agree that the noun ὕδατι ("water") refers to the baptism, whereas the noun αἵματι ("blood") refers to his death. The death of Christ plays a central role throughout the entire epistle. It is with the rejection of this death by the opponents that the Elder is most concerned.[39] It is through this death of Ἰησοῦς ὁ Χριστός that the love and forgiveness of God are revealed (4:9–10; see also 1:7; 2:1–2) and fellowship is constituted in the *familia Dei*. According to the Elder, to deny that Jesus died as the Christ is to deny the essence of Jesus' revelation (μαρτυρίαν) of the Father and his redemption (ζωήν) of those who believe in him (see 5:10–12). Whereas the σάρξ of ὁ Χριστός is denied in 4:2, the essential identity of Jesus as the Christ, his expiatory death, is denied in 5:6. Thus, the opponents denied that Jesus died as the Messiah. This is confirmed by all the other references in 1 John that support this conclusion.

4.2.4. Conclusion

Jesus and *Christ* occur and are related in all three of the christological tenets discussed above.

Ἰησοῦς ἐστιν ὁ Χριστός
Ἰησοῦς   Χριστὸν   ἐν σαρκὶ ἐληλυθότα
Ἰησοῦς   Χριστός, οὐκ ἐν τῷ ὕδατι μόνον ἀλλ' ἐν τῷ ὕδατι καὶ ἐν τῷ αἵματι

It has been pointed out that the christological problem is not the denial of the fact that Jesus has come in the flesh. It is the denial that Jesus is "the Christ (who is the Son of God) who came in the flesh" (4:2) and that he, as the

---

39. See all the references throughout 1 John to the death and crucifixion of Jesus: blood of Jesus (1:7); atoning sacrifice (2:2); he laid down his life for us (3:16); he sent his only Son into the world so that we might live through him (4:9), to be the atoning sacrifice for our sins (4:10), as Savior of the world (4:14); came by water and blood (5:6, 7). All the references to Jesus as (eternal) life also imply the cross event (1:1, 2; 2:25; 5:11–13, 20). Even the references "Jesus is the Christ" and "Jesus Christ" imply the death of Jesus.

Christ, through his death, revealed God par excellence and brought salvation for humankind. He constitutes *koinonia* in the *familia Dei*. Therefore, for the Elder, the denial of the "coming of Christ in the flesh" and the "atoning death of Christ" is the denial that "Jesus is the Christ."

For him such a denial is the denial of the very nature of Christianity. Due to the many direct and indirect references to the death of Jesus Christ[40] throughout 1 John, it seems as if the Elder, in his Christology, wants to focus on and emphasize the atoning death of Jesus as the Christ. With this doctrine the Elder tries to lead his adherents to understand why these opponents cannot enjoy fellowship with God and with one another and why they block their own way to salvation.[41] Serious ethical problems emanate from these doctrinal (pneumatological and christological) issues.

4.3. The Ethical Issues

Influenced by Schnackenburg's literary analysis, Painter recognizes "seven slogan-like" assertions that characterize the conduct of these opponents and strengthen the tension in the community.[42] These assertions seem to encapsulate their "true ethical claims." They are grouped in dictums introduced by quotation formulae. Six of these assertions occur in the first major section (1:5–2:28) of 1 John, while the seventh (4:20) is closely related to the sixth. These assertions are cyclically developed throughout the epistle.

4.3.1. The First Group of Assertions

Following the *prooemium* the Elder turns to one of the decisive issues. In 1:5, the beginning of the first major section of the epistle, the Elder states that God is light. The inference drawn from this affirmation was that, since there is no darkness in God, there can be no darkness in his followers. His opponents were denying that they were guilty of sinning. It seems that they thought that through their belief in Jesus they had become enlightened, could claim to be living in the light, and were free from sin.[43] While holding to the

---

40. See 1:7; 2:1–2; 3:16; 4:9, 10, 14 [15]. All these texts refer to the expiatory death of Christ.

41. See Schnackenburg, *The Johannine Epistles*, 145.

42. Ibid., 77; Whitacre, *Johannine Polemic*, 90, also 122; Thomas F. Johnson, *1, 2, and 3 John* (Peabody, Mass.: Hendrikson, 1993), 29, 39, 117; Culpepper, *Gospel and Letters*, 256ff.

43. Most of the references to sin are in the singular. This calls attention to the principle or fact of sin in human life (e.g., 1:8) rather than individual acts of sin.

same tradition, the Elder argues that those with such an understanding are badly deceived. He briefly discusses this in 1:5–2:2.

These verses (1:5–2:2), which form a subsection, are organized around a group of three assertions. Each concerns the place of sin in the life of the believer. They express conditions that are misguided and destructive (1:6, 8, 10). Since the three undesirable conditions each begin with the phrase ἐὰν εἴπωμεν ("if we say"), it is reasonable to assume that some members of the community were making these assertions and others were in danger of accepting these views.[44] These claims seem clearly to represent views advanced by the false teachers.[45]

The following table contains a synopsis of the opponents' false claims regarding sin:

	ASSERTIONS	CONDEMNATION	CONSEQUENCE
1:6	<u>ἐὰν εἴπωμεν ὅτι</u> κοινωνίαν ἔχομεν μετ' αὐτοῦ καὶ ἐν τῷ σκότει περιπατῶμεν **Denying the seriousness of sin**	ψευδόμεθα	καὶ <u>οὐ</u> ποιοῦμεν τὴν ἀλήθειαν
1:8	<u>ἐὰν εἴπωμεν ὅτι</u> ἁμαρτίαν <u>οὐκ</u> ἔχομεν **Denying human sinfulness**	ἑαυτοὺς πλανῶμεν	καὶ ἡ ἀλήθεια <u>οὐκ</u> ἔστιν ἐν ἡμῖν
1:10	<u>ἐὰν εἴπωμεν ὅτι</u> οὐκ ἡμαρτήκαμεν **Denying the practice of sin**	ψεύστην ποιοῦμεν αὐτὸν	καὶ ὁ λόγος αὐτοῦ <u>οὐκ</u> ἔστιν ἐν ἡμῖν

---

44. Three tests are laid down by him in the form of false claims introduced by the conditional clause "if we say" (ἐὰν εἴπωμεν ὅτι, 6a, 8a, 10a) in the protasis of these verses. Each of these three tests consists of two parts: the first positive and the second negative (see F. F. Bruce, *The Epistles of John* [London: Pickering & Inglis, 1970], 42. The first part contains a claim, the second a condemnation with a negative consequence. In the first two tests the correctives (introduced by a conditional particle ἐάν) are supplied in verses 7 and 9. In the third test (also ἐάν, 2:1–2), the Elder advances to a higher level. Instead of supplying another corrective, he moves over to the provision made to address the problem of sin.

45. D. Edmond Hiebert, "An Expositional Study of 1 John," *Bibliotheca Sacra* 145 (1988): 332; Culpepper, *Gospel and Letters*, 257; Hurtado, *Lord Jesus Christ*, 414.

In this subsection, the Elder starts the protasis of verses 6, 8, and 10 with "expectational" *claims*:[46] "If we say that…" (ἐὰν εἴπωμεν ὅτι…). The *first* claim in verse 6 marks a clear contradiction between the claim (κοινωνίαν ἔχομεν μετ' αὐτοῦ) and the conduct maintained (ἐν τῷ σκότει περιπατῶμεν). Verses 8 and 10 relate to verse 6 in the sense that it is as wrong to deny, as a way of conduct, both human sinfulness (1:8) and the practice of sin (1:10) in one's life.

In the apodosis of these verses (1:6, 8) the Elder pronounces a *condemnation* on this conduct by stating that "we lie" (ψευδόμεθα/ἑαυτοὺς πλανῶμεν). In his condemnation of these claims, the Elder announces a verdict. In verses 6 and 8 he describes it as falsehood on the part of humans. However, in verse 10 the Elder defines the condemnation even more strongly with reference to *God*. The claim of being without sin suggests falsehood on God's part; it "makes him out to be a liar" (ψεύστην).

The *consequences* of such claims are that they hamper fellowship with both God and other believers in the family (see 1:6, 7). Such a person walks in darkness: "we are not practicing the truth" (1:6); and "the truth has no place in us" (1:8). This proves that these opponents do not have God's word abiding in them.

4.3.2. The Second Group of Assertions

Like the previous subsection, 1 John 2:3–11 contains three allusions to the claims of the Elder's opponents. Rather than following the earlier patterns that relate these claims in conditional sentences, the Elder reports them using the formula ὁ λέγων ("he who says…" in 2:4, 6, 9). The following analysis of 2:3–11 spells out these assertions.

Assertions	Test	Consequence
4: ὁ λέγων … ὅτι ἔγνωκα αὐτὸν (focus on God [αὐτὸν])	καὶ τὰς ἐντολὰς αὐτοῦ *μὴ τηρῶν*,	*ψεύστης* ἐστὶν καὶ ἐν τούτῳ ἡ ἀλήθεια οὐκ ἔστιν
6: ὁ λέγων … ἐν αὐτῷ μένειν (focus on Jesus [καθὼς ἐκεῖνος])	<u>ὀφείλει καθὼς ἐκεῖνος περιεπάτησεν</u> καὶ αὐτὸ [οὕτως] περιπατεῖν	[ὀφείλει καθὼς ἐκεῖνος περιεπάτησεν <u>καὶ αὐτὸ [οὕτως] **περιπατεῖν**</u>]

---

46. Hiebert ("An Expositional Study of 1 John," 332) interprets all three claims in 1:6, 8, 10 as "hypothetical." To interpret them as "expectational" claims seems to be closer to the truth.

9: ὁ λέγων ... ἐν τῷ φωτὶ εἶναι (focus on brother [ἀδελφὸν])	<u>καὶ τὸν ἀδελφὸν αὐτοῦ **μισῶν**</u>	ἐν τῇ ***σκοτίᾳ*** ἐστὶν ἕως ἄρτι

This trio of *false claims* relate to being in a right relationship with God, Christ, or brother: *knowing* God (2:4); *abiding* in Christ (2:6); *being* in the light (2:9).[47] All three assertions have in common their emphasis on "the observance of the commandment of love for one another."[48]

The opponents were guilty of this. Their doctrine and ethics caused them to look down upon those who did not conform to their doctrine and ethics. Therefore, they could not announce the reality of these claims stated in 2:4, 6, 9.

These claims are not in themselves false or objectionable. The Elder might well make each of these claims with regard to himself and his adherents. His point is that those who make such claims must show through the way they live that they are speaking the truth. By implication it may be concluded that his opponents made precisely these claims but did not maintain a pattern of life consistent with their claims. Again the *ethical test* of love falsifies the claim made by the opponents. Their lack of love for their brothers (τὸν ἀδελφὸν αὐτοῦ) and sisters implies that they did not obey God's commandments and consequently did not live as Jesus lived. The *consequences*: they are accused by the Elder of being liars and therefore (ἕως ἄρτι) people living in darkness. It is only when such love is realized in the lives of God's children that it can be said that they have the truth in them and live as Jesus lived.

4.3.3. The Last Assertion

This group includes only one assertion (4:20), as indicated in the following analysis:

ASSERTION	TEST	CONSEQUENCE
ἐάν τις εἴπῃ ὅτι **ἀγαπῶ τὸν θεὸν**	καὶ τὸν ἀδελφὸν αὐτοῦ μισῇ,	**ψεύστης** ἐστίν

This assertion is introduced by the formula ἐάν τις εἴπῃ ("if anyone says," 4:20). The first four of the first six assertions are seemingly given in the words of the opponents. The quotation is signaled by the ὅτι-particle followed by the

---

47. No explicit references to God or Christ occur in this subsection. Even from the context it is not always clear to which person the personal pronouns or verbs refer.
48. See Johnson, *1, 2, and 3 John*, 39.

words quoted in the first person "I" or "we."[49] Here the formula "If anyone says" is followed by a ὅτι-*recitativum*. The assertion is "I love God." These are apparently the words of the opponents.

If the treatment of the sixth claim ends with the test of loving the brother, the seventh claim, "I love God" (4:20), is shown to be false by the absence of brotherly love. This can be seen in the parallel of these two statements:

2:9: ὁ λέγων ἐν τῷ φωτὶ εἶναι καὶ τὸν ἀδελφὸν αὐτοῦ μισῶν ἐν τῇ **σκοτίᾳ** ἐστὶν ἕως ἄρτι

4:20 ἐάν τις εἴπῃ ὅτι **ἀγαπῶ τὸν θεὸν** καὶ τὸν ἀδελφὸν αὐτοῦ μισῇ, ψεύστης ἐστίν

The parallel is created by the phrase καὶ τὸν ἀδελφὸν αὐτοῦ μισῶν, which occurs in both texts. According to this parallel, the statement "to walk in the light" is equivalent to "I love God." Even the consequences are the same, although they are stated differently. Hence, these opponents do not love God or walk in the light. They are liars and are still in darkness because they hate (do not love) some of their brothers in the community.[50] This absence of love is evident in the schism they caused, and according to 3:16–17 they showed no concern for the needs of others.

The Father is the source of love (4:8, 16), and love is defined in terms of his love for his children. But if a person hates his brother but claims to love God, the Elder says that he is a liar (ψεύστης). In the apodosis part of the verse, *hating* the brother is equated with "not loving his brother." For the Elder, not to love is to hate. The Elder states categorically that "those who do not love a brother whom they have seen cannot love God whom they have not seen." What is referred to here is not a single act but a way of being.[51]

---

49. William F. Arndt and F. Wilbur Gingrich, *A Greek-English Lexicon of the New Testament and Other Early Christian literatur* (Chicago: University of Chicago Press, 1957), 593 n. 2; BDAG, 732.

50. In these assertions the Elder portrays his opponents very negatively. In the seven assertions the noun ψεύστης ("liar," 1:10; 2:4; 4:20) occurs three times, the verb ψεύδομαι ("lie," 1:6) once, and the verb πλανάω ("deceive," 1:8) once. Two more negative consequences are also stated by the Elder: ἐν τούτῳ ἡ ἀλήθεια οὐκ ἔστιν ("in such a person the truth does not exist," 2:4); and ἐν τῇ σκοτίᾳ ἐστὶν ἕως ἄρτι ("is still in the darkness," 2:9). These references clearly characterize and refer to the conduct of the opponents. They harmed the fellowship in the *familia Dei*.

51. Painter, *1, 2, and 3 John*, 284–85.

4.3.4. Conclusion

The schism occurred because the group who separated themselves from the Johannine community claimed a form of spiritual illumination. This claim influenced their Christology to such an extent that, in the end, they did not believe that Jesus was the Christ who came in the flesh to reveal God as light, love, and righteous and constitute redemption for humankind through his life and expiatory death. Through this spiritual illumination, they also claimed to have attained a state beyond ordinary Christian morality in which they had no more sin and had already attained a form of moral behavior that would enable them to continue to resist sin. Because of this spiritual illumination, they discriminated against others in the *familia Dei* in a way that led to a lack of love and to animosity.

5. Dealing with the Problem of Animosity

Now that the circumstances of the schism, the setting within which animosity is to be understood, and the nature of the animosity have been discussed, it is necessary to investigate how the Elder managed to deal with this problem in the Johannine community. He addresses this problem by proposing critical action (*conduct*) against his opponents and in guiding the community through influential teaching (*doctrine/faith*).

5.1. Critical Action against the Opponents

5.1.1. Action against the Opponents from the Community

The Elder exhorts (present active imperative) his adherents to act against these opponents in the following ways: "do not receive [μὴ λαμβάνετε] into the house or welcome anyone who comes and does not bring this teaching" proclaimed by the Elder (2 John 10). Family metaphor helps one to understand this exhortation. The main social value in the Mediterranean region was honor. Accretions to the honor of one family member added to the honor rating of the whole family. On the other hand, when one family member was shamed, the whole family was shamed.[52] When a father was disobeyed, he would be dishonored or shamed, which comprised the loss of honor, repu-

---

52. Philip F. Esler, "'Keeping It in the Family': Culture, Kinship and Identity in 1 Thessalonians and Galatians," in *Families and Family Relations as Represented in Early Judaisms and Early Christianities: Texts and Fictions* (ed. Jan Willem van Henten and Athalya Brenner; Leiden: Deo, 2000), 152.

tation, and respect.⁵³ Disobedience was regarded as reprehensible because it destabilized relationships and fellowship within the family and dishonored the character of that family.

Compliance with the rules in the *familia Dei* was crucial for Christian fellowship, honor, and the identity of this family, which can be regarded as introversion in its preoccupation with its own holiness.⁵⁴ Anything that threatened this, such as false doctrine or related behavior, was severely frowned upon.

When a family member misbehaved, there was a possibility that the mistake could be corrected and the honor of the family restored⁵⁵ (1 John 1:9; 2:1). The harsh terms used by the Elder to describe his opponents (see §2.1), provide a clear indication that he had already accepted that they would not be able to correct their mistakes and could no longer be part of the *familia Dei* (2:19). Therefore, he labeled them as people who had been ejected from the Johannine community.

5.1.2. Conclusion

For the Elder, the situation is acute, which explains this harsh exhortation with which he intends to amputate these dangerous opponents from the community in order to end their influence and deception. Their conduct brings shame to the *familia Dei* and harms the fellowship within.

5.2. Influential Teaching to Guide the Community to Unity⁵⁶

The Elder uses a few related imperatives (present active), for example, μενέτω (2:24), μηδεὶς πλανάτω (3:7), μὴ πιστεύετε, and δοκιμάζετε (4:1), to exhort

---

53. Bruce J. Malina and Jerome H. Neyrey, "First-Century Personality: Dyadic, Not Individualistic," in *The Social World of Luke-Acts: Models for Interpretation* (ed. Jerome H. Neyrey; Peabody, Mass.: Hendrikson, 1993), 26, 27.

54. See Philip F. Esler, *The First Christians in Their Social World: Social-Scientific Approaches to New Testament Interpretation* (London: Routledge, 1994), 90.

55. See Plutarch, *Moralia* 483D, 488B–489B, 490F–491A (trans. W. C. Helmbold; LCL; Cambridge: Harvard University Press, 1957).

56. These two epistles are characterized by a stylistic duality. The duality occurs when the Elder moves between passages of polemical tone to those of pastoral concern. He wrote to oppose the opponents and to encourage his adherents (see Painter, *1, 2, and 3 John*, 78); hence, the multiple rhetorical character of the text. Painter (ibid.) explains that, although the polemical passages are directed against the opponents of the Elder, they are addressed to the Johannine community with a view to dissuading them from following these opponents into schism. The paraenetic material deals with this problem, but

his adherents not to be influenced by the opponents but to "abide in what they have heard from the beginning." Of relevance here are the two subsections 2:18–28 and 4:1–6, where the opponents are explicitly referred to as "antichrists," "false prophets" and "deceivers" (confirmed in 2 John 7).

5.2.1. Abide in What You Have Heard from the Beginning (2:24; 2 John 9)

Within the context of fighting false doctrine and undesirable conduct, the numerous reminders that the children of God have heard strongly suggest that the Elder is referring to the teaching (τῇ διδαχῇ) they had received in this community (2:24; 2 John 9).

2:24: ἐὰν ἐν ὑμῖν *μείνῃ* ὃ ἀπ' ἀρχῆς ἠκούσατε, καὶ ὑμεῖς ἐν τῷ υἱῷ καὶ ἐν τῷ πατρὶ μενεῖτε
2 John 9: ὁ *μένων* ἐν τῇ διδαχῇ (τοῦ Χριστοῦ), οὗτος καὶ τὸν πατέρα καὶ τὸν υἱὸν ἔχει

---

then only to encourage the adherents of the Elder in the face of the trauma caused by the schism. Although part of the strategy of the Elder was to deal with the position of the opponents in a polemical way, exposing the error, 1 and 2 John were not written to the opponents. It was written to the traumatized and disturbed community whose assurance of faith had been undermined. Painter correctly interprets the situation in the community after the schism: "Though the heretics had withdrawn, the community was in turmoil and continued to be threatened by the false teaching" (*John, Witness and Theologian* [London: SPCK, 1975], 116). The Elder wanted to restore that assurance and to place it on a solid basis; hence the many occurrences of the phrase ἐν τούτῳ γινώσκομεν (2:3, 5; 3:16, 19, 24; 4:2, 13; 5:2), which are also supported by the strong pastoral concerns of the two epistles and the numerous rhetorical devices that complement one another. In these epistles the following rhetorical devices can be distinguished: deliberative rhetoric (Hans-Josef Klauck, "Zur rhetorischen Analyse der Johannesbriefe," *ZNW* 81 [1990]: 205–24); dialectic rhetoric (antilanguage; Kenneth D. Tollefson, "Certainty within the Fellowship: Dialectical Discourse in 1 John," *BTB* 29 [1999]: 79–89); and epideictic rhetoric (Duane F. Watson, "1 John 2:12–14 as *Distributio, Conduplicatio,* and *Expolitio*: A Rhetorical Understanding," *JSNT* 35 [1989]: 97–110). The paradeigmatic rhetoric of Aristotle and Quintilian (Dirk G. van der Merwe, "Perseverance through Suffering: A Spirituality for Mission," *Missionalia* 33 [2005]: 348) can also be added here. An archetypal metaphor in rhetoric also occurs (family metaphoric; John Adams, "The Familial Image in Rhetoric," *CQ* 31 [1983]: 56–61). These rhetorical strategies must be understood as complementary to one another. They have been interwoven by the Elder and attempt to convince readers to believe in and act according to what they *have heard from the beginning*. This not only sets them against the opponents but also identifies them as *the* children of God.

In 2:24a the Elder uses the verb μενέτω (present imperative) to exhort his adherents to let the foundational message (ὃ ἠκούσατε ἀπ' ἀρχῆς)[57] abide in them.[58] The reference ὃ ἠκούσατε ἀπ' ἀρχῆς (2:7, 24; 3:11; 2 John 6; see also John 14:34) suggests that the Elder has in mind the earliest period of the Johannine community. The teaching that they heard in the beginning is the traditional and orthodox doctrine taught in the community—a doctrine based on the eyewitness testimony of those who associated closely with Jesus (1 John 1:1–3). For the Elder, this traditional doctrine is the revelatory word of Christ himself (2 John 9; see the parallelism with 2:24), the assurance of eternal life with God (John 8:51).

During this period the Beloved Disciple (one of the disciples who was with Jesus ἀπ' ἀρχῆς, John 15:27) and Paraclete taught the community, and the orthodox teaching of the community was established. It is to the authority of this teaching that the Elder appeals in 2:24 and 2 John 9.[59] The message they have heard should abide in them (see John 5:38; 1 John 2:14). This infers that they must abide "in the word of Christ" (see John 8:31; 15:7). They must adhere to it and let it abide in them, like the "anointing" (1 John 2:20) or "God's seed" (3:9). The Elder is concerned with purity of doctrine. That should saturate their minds, remain with them, and promote true fellowship.

In 4:1 the Elder exhorts his adherents with more related directives, "Beloved, *do not believe* every spirit, but *test* the spirits to see whether they are from God." The renewed warning by the Elder against the opponents in this verse arises from the concern that the children of God are not sensible enough to resist the seductive talk of the opponents. Despite all the assurances he communicated to them in 2:11–14 and in 2:20–27, namely, that they know the truth and have the guidance of the Holy Spirit, the Elder indicates that he thinks the danger is far from over. The danger confronting his adherents causes him to return once again to the opponents. Therefore, he again debates the pneumatological (4:1), christological (4:2, 15), and moral (4:8, 20) heresy in subsection 4:1–6.

A summary of the foundational doctrine and conduct in the *familia Dei* to which the children of God had to conform follows. Conformity to this doctrine and conduct will combat the opponents and strengthen fellowship within the *familia Dei*.

---

57. The phrase (ὃ ἠκούσατε) ἀπ' ἀρχῆς has been understood in a variety of ways. For Charles H. Dodd, it refers to "the fundamental content of the Gospel" (*The Johannine Epistles* [London: Hodder & Stoughton, 1953], 58). It is the message they heard when they initially became Christians.

58. Painter, *1, 2, and 3 John*, 207.

59. Schnackenburg, *The Johannine Epistles*, 158–59.

5.2.1.1. Johannine Pneumatology. The Elder attached great value to the presence of the Spirit in fellowship and in the experiencing of the *familia Dei*. Therefore, they could declare that the future blessings were already present. In opposition to the lies of the opponents, this Spirit is the Spirit of truth (5:6), which teaches the truth (see 2 John 1) in order to walk in the truth (2 John 4). The Spirit seems associated with the divine presence that results in the new life of the believer (4:13; 3:24). Through the Spirit, the Father guides and educates his children (2:27) in the *familia Dei* not only to experience his divine life "now" but also to prepare them for his future eschatological revelation and judgment.[60] The Spirit becomes the guiding influence in the lives of God's children (2:20–7; 5:7), influencing their conduct "to live as Jesus lived" (2:6) and sustaining the κοινωνία in the family. Therefore, the role of the Spirit in 1 John appears to relate to knowledge or knowing.[61]

5.2.1.2. Johannine Christology. First John contains no systemic exposition vis-à-vis the doctrine that the community has been taught from the beginning. The Elder deals with doctrinal beliefs as they arise, in no discernable order, but as it suits his rhetorical purpose. On the basis of 1:1–4, some aspects of Jesus' identity and his function in legitimizing fellowship between God and these believers can be pointed out: a unique relationship exists between the Father and his Son Jesus Christ (1:3). This Son of God has incarnated in the world so that through him people can come to know God. God's own life has been revealed to believers through his Son. Through Jesus Christ, a person can receive the life that exists within God because he himself, the Son of God, is the life (1 John 1:1–2; 5:11–12; see also John 1–4).

The unique *relationship between the Father and his Son Jesus Christ* (1:3) is evident throughout 1 John, where Jesus is mentioned in association with the Father, predominantly in the connotation of "the Father of Jesus Christ."[62] In these letters this title reflects the intimate, indissoluble unity between the Father and the Son.[63] The impression is created that in his total opposition to

---

60. Other functions of the Spirit are those of teacher (2:27), empowerer (3:24, in the context of obedience; 4:13, in the context of love), confessor (4:2), and witness (5:7–8; see Garrett C. Kenney, *The Relation of Christology to Ethics in the First Epistle of John* [Lanham, Md.: University Press of America, 2000], 47). The Spirit will give God's children knowledge (2:20). The Spirit witnesses the truth (5:6a) and will guide God's children in the truth (5:6; see also Von Wahlde, *The Johannine Commandments*, 126ff.).
61. Thomas, *A Pentecostal Commentary*, 13.
62. 1:2, 3; 2:1, 22–24; 4:14; 2 John 3, 9; see also 1 John 1:2; 4:2, 3, 10; 5:10.
63. J. C. Coetzee, "The Letters of John: Introduction and Theology," in *The Gospel of*

the false prophets (4:1), the Elder wishes to emphasize the intimate bond of love between the Father and Son and their essential unity (1:2).

When Jesus is referred to as "his Son" (τοῦ υἱοῦ αὐτοῦ, 1:3) or "only" (μονογενῆ, 4:9) or "the Son" (τὸν υἱόν, 2:23), it is in close conjunction with the Father (ὁ πατήρ, 2:23; see also 1:3; 4:14). A repeated parallelism occurs, effectively putting the Father and the Son at the same level (1:3; see also 2:23; 4:15; 5:11, 12).[64] The close bond between Jesus as Son and God as Father is expressed in terms that indicate that the experience of one carries with it experience of the other (2:24).[65]

For the Father to communicate himself to the world, the Son of God had to be incarnated. To prove the reality of his Incarnation, the Elder begins his epistle by emphasizing the physical dimension (ἀκηκόαμεν, ἑωράκαμεν, ἐθεασάμεθα, ἐψηλάφησαν) of the life of the Son Jesus Christ (1:1, 3).[66] He emphasizes his baptism and death (5:6, ἐλθὼν δι' ὕδατος καὶ αἵματος), his moral conduct (2:1, δίκαιον; 2:6, περιεπάτησεν; 3:3, ἁγνός; 3:5, ἁμαρτία ἐν αὐτῷ οὐκ ἔστιν), the willing sacrifice of his life (3:16, τὴν ψυχὴν αὐτοῦ ἔθηκεν), and his *parousia* (2:28; 4:17, παρουσίᾳ αὐτοῦ).[67]

The incarnation was the outcome of the sending of God's only Son into the world so that God's children might live through him. In 1 John 4:9 the Elder tells how God's love was conclusively revealed (ἐφανερώθη, 1:2) to the church and the world. This activity of God, also described in 4:10, 14, by which his love is manifested, is regarded as salvific in purpose: (a) the Son was "sent" into the world "so that we might live through him" (ἵνα ζήσωμεν δι' αὐτου, 4:9), as an "atoning sacrifice for our sins" (ἱλασμὸν περὶ τῶν ἁμαρτιῶν ἡμῶν, 4:10), and as the "Savior of the world" (σωτῆρα τοῦ κόσμου, 4:14). (b) In each verse it appears that God, the Father of Jesus Christ, is deeply involved in his world and has acted in history for the purpose of human salvation.[68] (c) The saving act of sending Jesus involved the serving life, as well as the death, of God's Son. This is implied in 4:9 (ζήσωμεν) by the parallels in 4:10 (Jesus as ἱλασμὸν) and 4:14 (Jesus as σωτῆρα). (d) Jesus is described in all three verses as the Son (4:9, τὸν υἱὸν αὐτοῦ τὸν μονογενῆ; 4:10, τὸν υἱὸν αὐτοῦ; 4:14, τὸν

John; *Hebrews to Revelation: Introduction and Theology* (vol. 6 of *Guide to the New Testament*; ed. Andrie B. du Toit; Halfway House: Kerkboekhandel, 1988), 219.

64. Edwards, *The Johannine Epistles*, 160.

65. Judith Lieu, *The Theology of the Johannine Epistles* (Cambridge: Cambridge University Press, 1991), 72.

66. See Hiebert, An Expositional Study of 1 John," 203.

67. See Kenney, *Relation of Christology to Ethics*, 49.

68. Dodd, *The Johannine Epistles*, 110–11.

υἱὸν), who was sent by God so that people could receive and participate in God's life.

The life that God has given to his children is in his Son Jesus who is the Christ. In 1 John 1:1–2 the Elder personifies "eternal life" in the person of Jesus Christ.[69] In 5:11–12 the Son (of God) is presented as the one who mediates this life given by God. Thus Jesus *is* life and *mediates* this life of God. This life, which originally existed with the Father (1:2), is perfectly manifested in God's Son (see 5:11b) who is the Christ.

5.2.1.3. Johannine Ethics. According to the assertions made by the opponents (1:6–2:11; 4:20), the following summarizes the Elder's ethical guidance of his adherents. It is not up to the children of God in the *familia Dei* to determine the paradigm and model of the "walk"; it is determined by God's nature. Because believers are now part of the *familia Dei*, they have to act according to their status and knowledge,[70] which must relate to the social conduct (rules and values) of the family into which they were born. This conduct in the family has been determined by the character of the Father and was embodied in the conduct of Jesus, as described in the following four texts in which the phrase καθὼς ἐκεῖνός ἐστιν occurs. These four texts can be compared as follows:[71]

2:6: ὁ λέγων ἐν αὐτῷ μένειν ὀφείλει **καθὼς ἐκεῖνος** περιεπάτησεν καὶ <u>αὐτὸς [οὕτως]</u> περιπατεῖν.

3:3: <u>ἁγνίζει ἑαυτόν</u> **καθὼς ἐκεῖνος** ἁγνός **ἐστιν**.

---

69. See further P. J. Du Plessis, *Die Briewe van Johannes* (Kaapstad: Kerk-Uitgewers, 1978), 20.

70. See 1 John 1:6, 7; 2:3–5, 9–10; 3:16; 4:11; 2 John 6, 9; see also 1 John 2:29; 3:6, 9–10, 18; 4:7.

71. This καθώς concept focuses, according to the Fourth Gospel, on the following basic aspects concerning the *imitatio Christi*: dependence ([5:19–15:5]; 6:57; 15:15; [12:49; 14:10–17:8]); mission (13:20; 17:18; 20:21); knowledge (10:14, 15); love in obedience ([15:9, 10; 13:34–35; see 15:12]; [5:20–14:12]; 17:23); unity (14:10–11; 14:20; [14:10–15:4]; 10:30; 17:11, 21–23); glory (15:8; 17:1–5, 22–24); obedience of Jesus' commands (15:10); and life (6:57); also 1 Cor 11:1. See Dirk G. van der Merwe, "*Imitatio Christi* in the Fourth Gospel," *Verbum et Ecclesia* 22 (2001): 131–48. Commentators almost without exception refer the demonstrative pronoun (ἐκεῖνος) to Christ. This is suggested by the parallel passages (2:6; 3:3, 7), which use a similar comparative construction to refer to Christ as an example. In these passages the use of the present tense of the verb ἐστιν shows that the model existence of Christ transcends time and space and is meant to be pertinent for the community in all ages (Strecker, *The Johannine Letters*, 166). The community's task will be to present itself in the world in the same way as Jesus did.

3:7: <u>δίκαιός ἐστιν</u>, **καθὼς ἐκεῖνος** δίκαιός **ἐστιν**·
4:17: <u>τετελείωται ἡ ἀγάπη</u> μεθ' ἡμῶν, ... ὅτι **καθὼς ἐκεῖνός ἐστιν** καὶ ἡμεῖς ἐσμεν ἐν τῷ κόσμῳ τούτῳ.

According to the Elder, Christ, the Son of God, is the template for the conduct of believers. In 1 John his example is both probative and illustrative. This is probably what the Elder had in mind in his two ὀφείλει ("ought to," 2:6; 3:16) references and four καθὼς ἐκεῖνος ("just as he," 2:6; 3:3, 7; 4:17) references to Christ. Through their active participation or sharing in the way Jesus lived, they have a "common" (κοινός) ground, which not only molds the character of the children of God but also constitutes the κοινωνία in the family. Because Jesus is the Christ, the Son of God, the Elder can exhort his adherents to imitate the life of Jesus, which comprises confession of sin, obedience of God's commands, and love for one another.

5.2.1.4. Conclusion. It has been pointed out that the Elder exhorted his adherents to abide in what they had heard from the beginning. This is spelled out in terms of pneumatology, Christology, and ethics and opposes the false doctrine and loveless ethical conduct of the opponents.

6. An Eschatological Perspective

From an eschatological perspective, the Elder rhetorically tries to persuade his adherents to realize that both their beliefs and conduct "now" have future implications.

The Elder views the schism in the community from an eschatological perspective by relating it to the *last hour*, the *parousia* of Jesus, and the *day of judgment* (2:18ff., 28; 3:2; 4:17). In these eschatological texts the Elder attends to the main issues of his opponents: the confession about Jesus Christ (2:18–28); the sin of the opponents (2:29–3:10); and love for one another and God (4:16–21).[72] Present belief and conduct have future implications and consequences.

The Elder interprets the emergence of these opponents as the coming of the antichrist(s), which marks the arrival of the "last hour."[73] If the last hour has brought the revelation (φανερωθῇ) of the antichrist, it will soon end in the

---

72. In the future eschatological texts the encouragement to imitate Christ closely relates to probably the three most important forms of conduct expected from God's children: to abide in Christ (2:28); to purify themselves, just as he is pure (3:3, do not sin); to love one another (4:17, 18).

73. Painter, *1, 2, and 3 John*, 203.

revelation of Christ (2:28b). Therefore, in these texts concerning the future eschatological events, the Elder exhorts his adherents to "prepare" themselves for the *parousia* and the *day of judgment*, so that "we may have confidence and not be put to shame before him at his coming" (2:28; 4:17), because "we will be like him, for we will see him as he is" (3:2). Such preparation would require people to live as Jesus lived (2:6, καθὼς ἐκεῖνος περιεπάτησεν): to live in the light in confessing their sins (3:3, καθὼς ἐκεῖνος ἁγνός ἐστιν); to obey God's commandments by living a life of righteousness (3:7, καθὼς ἐκεῖνος δίκαιός ἐστιν); and to love one another (4:17, τετελείωται ἡ ἀγάπη μεθ᾽ ἡμῶν, … ὅτι καθὼς ἐκεῖνος ἐστιν). Hence, what the opponents claim in their relationship with God can only be achieved through an *imitatio Christi* with a consummation at the *parousia*.

All three of these exhortations are associated with Jesus. On the day of judgment, faith in him as the Son of God, the Christ, God incarnate, and the example of his earthly life to which believers have to conform will be the standard (καθὼς ἐκεῖνος ἐστιν) according to which people will be judged. Because he and God are both righteous (2:1; 1:9 and 2:29), his judgment will be fair.

7. Conclusion

In response to a crisis in the Johannine community, the Elder wrote 1 John to *warn* the community of the dangers (dealing with the problem of animosity) of false teachings and improper conduct by his opponents, to *correct* (discussing the nature of animosity) this false teaching and improper conduct, and especially to *encourage* (seen from an eschatological perspective) those who remained faithful.

It seems that the controversy in the Johannine community was based on differences in the interpretation of a shared tradition.[74] Therefore, the Elder urged his readers: "do not believe every spirit, but test the spirits to see whether they are from God" (4:1). This implies that they were to measure the charismatic utterances of all so-called prophets according to the norm of sound, Christian tradition, at the center of which is the real incarnation and death of Christ.

There is ample evidence of exhortation and attempts to dissuade his adherents from following the opponents who left the community. The Elder reveals his concern in his exhortations and recalls his adherents to commit-

---

74. Brown, *The Epistles of John*, 69f; Von Wahlde, *The Johannine Commandments*, 108; Culpepper, *Gospel and Letters*, 256; Kenney, *Leadership in John*, 102.

ment to the common Johannine orthodoxy as the foundation of their *koinonia* (1:5–10) in the *familia Dei*.

The internal evidence of these two epistles reveals that the Johannine community was an embattled community in their experience of conflict—external conflict with the synagogue (according to the Fourth Gospel) and internal conflict and division resulting from different interpretations of the tradition. In time, the community withdrew further from the world and adhered to the teachings and new commandment of Christ, mediated to them by the Elder. The depiction of this community is ironic—the last references to the Johannine community depicts it as a community torn apart by dissension and struggling for survival. Wrecked by conflict, it collapsed. The adherents of the Elder were probably assimilated into other streams of Christianity during the early second century while the opponents of the Elder found their way into gnostic communities of the mid-second century.[75]

8. Some Hermeneutical Principles for Dealing with Animosity in the Church Today

From the above discussion the following hermeneutical principles can be claimed. (1) To prevent animosity in the church, Christian believers must *strive to achieve fellowship* among community members and with God. This should be attained, according to the Elder, through: (a) living in the light: the confession of sin toward God and one another; (b) living in righteousness: seek to comply with the will of God in obeying his commandments; and (c) living in love: love has to be the epithet of the Christian life.

(2) Christian believers always have to consider their identity in Christ. They constitute, metaphorically speaking, according to the Elder, the *family of God*. Relationships in such a family characteristically differ from the hostile relationships commonly found in the world outside.

(3) Christian believers must *abide in the creeds and tradition of the church* (2:24; 2 John 9). This has to be translated according to their idiom for a better comprehension of the biblical message; they must guard against being influenced by various fallacies[76] but must be open-minded with regard to the renewal of their understanding of the biblical message and its application in a postmodern society. A critical hermeneutical distinction must be

---

75. See Culpepper, *The Johannine School*, 287; idem, *Gospel and Letters*, 61.
76. Fundamentalism, liberalism, modernism, anachronism, ethnocentrism, postmodernism, literalism, allegorism, anthromorphism, rationalism, etc.

drawn between scopic and peripheric truths, authority and the doctrine of the Bible.

(4) The *harsh reference* in 2 John 10, "Do not receive into the house or welcome anyone who comes to you and does not bring this teaching," should not be interpreted literally. The principle that the Elder tries to communicate is an urgent appeal to refrain from conforming to teachings and conduct that annihilate the truth of the Christian doctrine and conduct and to reject it vehemently. The church must manage all forms of deception with critical solidarity.

(5) The discourse of the church in its opposition to deception and animosity can, according to the Elder, be complete only in its *paraenesis* regarding the *parousia* and the *day of judgment*. On the *day of judgment*, faith in him as the Son of God, the Christ, through whom God incarnated, and the example of his earthly life (καθὼς ἐκεῖνος ἐστιν) to which believers had to conform, will be the standard for judgment.

Hostility against the Wealth of Babylon: Revelation 17:1–19:10

Paul B. Decock

1. Introduction

According to Adela Yarbro Collins, "Revelation 18 is perhaps the passage that has most deeply offended the moral sensibilities of readers, Christian and non-Christian alike."[1] D. H. Lawrence saw it as a raw expression of envy against wealthy and luxurious Rome, while Collins reads the book as an attempt at cathartic expression of envy and aggression, dangerous feelings that need to be managed. However, calling on the work of Rollo May, she also recognizes the life-giving potential of anger and violence as a protest against the injustice of their current situation.[2] Elisabeth Schüssler Fiorenza and Richard Bauckham seem to focus precisely on the positive potential of these feelings of aggression against Rome as they situate this anger against the wealth and luxury of Rome in the context of an experience of hardship, oppression, violence, and persecution. Such anger can be seen as the spark of a potentially right, moral judgment and commitment.[3] Robert Royalty, on

---

1. Adela Yarbro Collins, "Persecution and Vengeance in the Book of Revelation," in *Apocalypticism in the Mediterranean World and the Near East: Proceedings of the International Colloquium on Apocalypticism, Uppsala, August 12-17, 1979* (ed. David Hellholm; Tübingen: Mohr Siebeck, 1983).

2. Adela Yarbro Collins, *Crisis and Catharsis: The Power of the Apocalypse* (Philadelphia: Westminster, 1984).

3. While feelings are still usually seen as irrational forces, some authors have stressed the crucial importance of emotions for moral judgment. According to Cosgrove, who draws especially on the work of Daniel Goleman, "Hence we can say that there are no 'mere' feelings, but only feelings and emotions that give us to understand something and make some assertion or disclose something about the situation from which they arise" (William Cosgrove, "The Emotions in the Moral Life," *Doctrine and Life* 55 [2005]:17). Against the radically negative views on anger inspired by Stoic writers, in *De ira Dei* Lactantius defends

the other hand, denies any genuine concern for justice in the Apocalypse and sees the whole argument, including the negative view on commercial wealth and the positive view on inherited wealth, as a means of vilifying and undermining John's rival prophets and boosting his own position.[4]

By drawing on the biblical tradition of Babylon to envision the Roman Empire, John could stir up dangerous feelings, as are found in Ps 137.[5] However, John seems to want to call forth these dangerous feelings of anger and envy in order to give direction to them by means of the symbolic universe that he evokes and within which he then challenges the churches to "conquer." As Schüssler Fiorenza puts it:

> In short, just as resistance poetry does, Revelation constructs a world of vision that challenges the symbolic discourse of Rome's hegemonic colonizing power. It does so by fashioning a rival symbolic discourse of power and empire that seeks to unmask the force of evil sustaining Rome's dominion in order to alienate its audience from the persuasive power of Rome's hegemonic vision.[6]

Instead of the feeling of being a mere victim of the power of Rome, a sense of dignity and hope for justice can be born out of the vision of sharing in God's empire.[7] Their anger at the injustice is channeled into an ardent

---

the view of divine anger as part of the biblical understanding of God's involvement in the history of the world; the God of the Bible is not an apathetic God but a God who loves what is good and hates what is evil. Even human anger "has been given as a necessary part of creation, but [God] forbids the continuation of anger" (Lactantius, *Ir.* 21); "that anger on the other hand, which has to do with the correction of vices ought not to be taken from man, nor can it be taken from God, because it is both useful and necessary for human affairs" (Lactantius, *Ir.* 17; trans. Mary Francis McDonald, *Lactantius: The Minor Works* [FC 54; Washington, D.C.: Catholic University of America Press, 1965], 109 and 102).

4. Robert M. Royalty, *The Streets of Heaven: The Ideology of Wealth in the Apocalypse of John* (Macon, Ga.: Mercer University Press, 1998).

5. On the image of Babylon in the Old Testament, see Ulrike Sals, *Die Biographie der "Hure Babylon": Studien zur Intertextualität der Babylon-Texte in der Bibel* (FAT 2/6; Tübingen: Mohr Siebeck, 2004), who studied Gen 11:1–9; Zech 5:5–11; Ps 137; Isa 13; 14; 21; 47; Jer 25; 50; 51. Royalty (*The Streets of Heaven*, 63–65) has highlighted how John developed the commercial wealth of his image of Babylon by drawing on prophecies against Tyre in Ezek 26–27 and Isa 23:1–18.

6. Elisabeth Schüssler Fiorenza, *Revelation: Vision of a Just World* (Edinburgh: T&T Clark, 1993), 124.

7. "The middle term *basileia*, which is usually translated as 'kingdom' or 'reign,' can refer to both the empire of Rome and to the empire of God. In Rev 1:5–6 John addresses the audience as those who were made a *basileia* and priests for God" (ibid., 119).

prayer for justice, which as priests of God they are able to present before God.[8] Above all, what is needed in the present is to fight and conquer by making a choice for God and turning away from Satan. The two options are put very starkly before the churches: they have a choice between God and the dragon, between the Lamb and the beast. The two outcomes are placed before them in vivid contrasts: Jerusalem and Babylon.

In this essay I will first consider the text of Rev 17:1–19:10, then highlight the response of the five authors mentioned above. After that I will examine four themes that fundamentally shaped John's work and that enable us to understand John's hostile way of presenting Rome and its wealth: the rhetorical device of the two ways, the theology of creation, the true meaning of battle and conquest, and the gift of understanding.

2. Revelation 17:1–19:10: Desire for, and Rejoicing Over, the Destruction of Babylon and Its Wealth

This unit, which is the pendant to the passage on the new Jerusalem (21:9–22:9), depicts the realization of the judgment for which the martyrs were praying under the heavenly altar (6:10).[9] As the story progresses, it becomes clear that the judgment involves both the fall of Babylon (14:10; 16:9) and the descent of the heavenly Jerusalem (19:7–8). Babylon and the old creation will be removed to make way for the new creation and the new Jerusalem. The theme of judgment is announced at the beginning of the unit as the *judgment of the great prostitute* (17:3), and its realization is celebrated toward the end, because God has *judged the great prostitute* (19:2). The judgment means the *destruction* of the great prostitute (17:16), the destruction of Babylon the great city (Rev 18). The ardent prayer of Rev 6:10 corresponds to the joyful hallelujah of 19:1–4. Finally, joy over the destruction of Babylon moves into

---

8. The opening of the fifth seal (6:9–11) reveals to John the prayer for justice of the martyrs, who are now at the heavenly altar. Their prayer is heard: they are given a white garment, but they are also told to rest for a while until the number of the martyrs fixed by God will be complete. Before the first series of plagues affects the earth, the trumpets, we are reminded that the prayer of all the saints is brought before the throne of God (8:3–4). The start of the series of plagues is linked to the offering of these prayers as the burning coals of the censer are poured out over the earth (8:5). The prayers of the saints symbolized by the golden bowls filled with incense were first mentioned at the decisive moment when the Lamb received the scroll from the hand of God in order to open it (5:8).

9. "From now on [6:10] we find the verb κρίνω a number of times: 11:18; 16:5; 18:8,20; 19:2, 11; 20:12, 13. The verb ἐκδικέω reappears only in 19:2 … in a hymn in which God is praised for having fulfilled his promise" (Paul B. Decock, "The Symbol of Blood in the Apocalypse of John," *Neot* 38 [2004]: 168–69).

joy over the wedding feast of the other woman, Jerusalem (19:5-8), and this links the Babylon unit once more to the Jerusalem unit. In Rev 18:6-7 there is a call for double punishment on Babylon because of her luxurious life and her foolish confidence in her own greatness, while in 18:20 there is an invitation for heaven, the saints, the apostles, and the prophets to exult because of God's judgment. This invitation to rejoice is dramatically situated immediately after the third lament over the great city (18:10, 16, 19) and concludes the section 18:4-20. Richard Bauckham has rightly pointed out that as 18:1-3 (A) relates to 18:4-20 (B), so does 18:21-24 (A') relate to 19:1-8 (B').[10] While the destruction of Babylon is a divine judgment,[11] the destruction is executed by the beast and the ten horns as unwitting instruments of God's judgment (17:16-17).

This prayer and call for judgment and this rejoicing over the destruction of Babylon are motivated by the evil of Babylon, in which wealth plays a special role. From the beginning (17:3-6), the wealth of Babylon is associated with her "prostitution" and her "murderous violence." Her wealth is highlighted by the fact that she is repeatedly called the great one: 17:1, 5, 18; 18:2, 10, 16, 18, 19, 21; 19:2. In 17:1, 18 we have an inclusion (the great prostitute), and in verse 18 the theme of greatness is developed by means of the reference to her "rule over the kings of the earth."

The theme of wealth is particularly emphasized in Rev 18:4-20, the whole of which should be seen as the content of the other voice from heaven mentioned in verse 4.[12] In verses 4-5 we have a call to God's people to come out of Babylon because the judgment is imminent. Verse 5 states the reasons for the judgment in general terms: ἁμαρτίαι ... ἀδικήματα. Verses 6-7 are a call for a double punishment; the agents of divine justice addressed here are left unspecified, but the sins of Babylon are more specific: luxury and foolish self-reliance (v. 7). Verse 8 proclaims the divine verdict: in one day Babylon will reach her end. Verses 9-19 develop this verdict by picturing the reaction of three groups of people to this sudden destruction: the kings of the earth (vv. 9-10); the traders (vv. 11-17a); the mariners and those associated with the trade by sea (vv. 17b-19). Each of these sections ends with "in one hour" (vv. 10, 17a, 19), recalling and intensifying the "in one day" of verse 8. It is

---

10. Richard Bauckham, "The Economic Critique of Rome in Revelation 18," in *The Climax of Prophecy: Studies on the Book of Revelation* (ed. Richard Bauckham; Edinburgh: T&T Clark, 1993), 340.

11. Rev 18:20 anticipates 19:2, and in both texts the judgment of God is highlighted; see also 14:7-8; 18:8.

12. See Antonius P. van Schaik, *De Openbaring van Johannes* (Roermond: Romen, 1971), 213; Bauckham, "Economic Critique of Rome," 340-41.

important for our purpose to note that each of these three groups refers to the great city (vv. 10, 16, 19) and to her wealth, power, or sensual living.[13] The middle group (vv. 11-17a, of the traders) develops and highlights the theme of wealth by means of the list of goods (vv. 12-13), through a description of the splendid appearance of the great city (v. 16), and by means of the inclusion οἱ πλουτήσαντες and πλοῦτος in verses 15 and 17. Verse 14, situated at the center of verses 11-17a, highlights the loss of so much wealth and glamour: καὶ παντά τὰ λιπαρὰ καὶ τὰ λαμπρὰ ἀπώλετο ἀπὸ σοῦ.

The Apocalypse aims at destroying the perception in the churches that Babylon's wealth and power will last forever. Babylon is repeatedly called the great one: 14:8; 16:19; 17:5; 18:2, 10 (and strong), 21, but each of these texts, except for 17:5, are proclamations or laments about the fall of Babylon the Great. The three woes of 18:10, 16, 19 highlight the contrast between the greatness, strength, and particularly the wealth of the city and her terrible fate.

The Apocalypse plays with the contrast between present and future,[14] which can shift to the contrast between appearance and reality, as we can see in Rev 2:9 and 3:17. The church in Laodicea seems to be a copy of Babylon[15] in their blind reliance on wealth (3:17). John points out that they have a false appreciation of themselves as being rich, while in fact they are wretched, pitiable, poor, blind, and naked ("poor" stands in the middle!). Christ counsels them to "buy" from him gold refined by fire against their poverty, white gar-

---

13. Στρηνιάω, στρῆνος occur only here in the whole of the New Testament: 18:3, 7, 9. Johannes P. Louw and Eugene A. Nida (L&N 1:769) associate these words with extravagant, intemperate living: "to live sensually by gratifying the senses with sexual immorality." Bauckham presses the economic dimension: "[it] may here refer to the sensual indulgence of the harlot's clients, but it will also suggest the luxury of material wealth" ("Economic Critique of Rome," 372).

14. Compare Mark 13:1-2, where the "Synoptic apocalypse" expands on the issue.

15. I take Babylon as a tensive symbol and not as a mere steno-symbol (a code name for Rome). The meaning of Babylon as symbol cannot be reduced to just "another name" for Rome. It says something about Rome, which can also be said about other entities or persons. Pieter de Villiers has shown the "serious problems in identifying the symbols of Revelation with people, institutions and events in the Roman Empire" (Pieter G. R. de Villiers, "Rome in the Historical Interpretation of Revelation," *Acta Patristica et Byzantina* 13 [2002]: 137). I think his argument is valid if one thinks in terms of steno-symbols, but not if one thinks in terms of tensive symbols. This is quite clear from the following remark: "In short, then, the attempts to find one clear meaning in the symbols of John and to relate that meaning to a particular historical situation, ignores and belittles the ambiguity and multifaceted nature of the symbols. It also overlooks the complexity of the symbols in the text" (128-29).

ments against their nakedness, ointment against their blindness. They seem to have been caught up in the market economy of the beast (13:17) instead of turning to Christ. On the other hand, the church of Smyrna *appears* to be in trouble and poverty, but they are *really* rich (2:9).[16]

The theme of wealth in Rev 17:1–19:10 therefore functions together with prostitution and violence as part of that contrast between the temporary greatness and ultimate annihilation. Babylon, riding the beast, is misled by the beast and the false prophet and copies their belief that they are invincible (13:4; 18:7). They worship the dragon because they expect all power from him (13:4), but they do not realize that the dragon has already been thrown down from heaven and that his time is short (12:12). For John, true wealth will be the fruit of the worship of God and not of the beast (Rev 13:16–17). In the present situation, the churches have to be prepared to give up even their lives to God in order to receive it from God: "they did not cling to life even in the face of death" (12:11; also 14:13).[17] The evil wealth of Babylon is interwoven with arrogance, violence, and idolatry. It is against this complex of evil that the Apocalypse announces God's judgment. John draws abundantly from the prophetic tradition of judgment against Babylon and Tyre: Isa 23; 13:1–14:23; 21:1–10; 47; Ezek 26–28; Jer 25:12–38; 50–51.[18] Nevertheless, the hostility and violence of the prayer for justice and the rejoicing at the prospect of Babylon's destruction are raising questions.

---

16. "In Revelation 18, it is implied that among the reasons for Rome's predicted destruction are her wealth (17:4; 18:16) and her role as a source of wealth for merchants (18:3, 15) and shipowners (18:19). The first reason for Babylon's demise given by the angel with the great stone is that her merchants were *hoi megistanes tes ges* (18:23). As was noted above, the messages to Pergamum and Thyatira oppose assimilation to the surrounding Greco-Roman culture. It is not improbable that the Christian faith and life-style as John understood them were incompatible with ordinary participation in the economic and social life of the cities of Asia Minor. Such a conclusion is supported by the fact that the Christians in Smyrna are portrayed as economically poor and threatened by persecution (2:8–11), but those of Laodicea as wealthy and apparently avoiding persecution (3:14–22)" (Collins, "Persecution and Vengeance," 745).

17. This corresponds to the contrast between the treasure in heaven and the treasure on earth: Mark 10:21 (and par. Matt 19:21; Luke 18:22); Luke 12:33–34 (and par. Matt 6:19–21).

18. Bauckham, "Economic Critique of Rome," 345.

3. D. H. Lawrence: Envy

In recent years several scholars have drawn attention to the work by D. H. Lawrence.[19] Collins, for instance, quotes the following passage:

> Only the great whore of Babylon rises rather splendid, sitting in her purple and scarlet upon her scarlet beast. She is the Magna Mater in malefic aspect, clothed in the colors of the angry sun, and throned upon the great red dragon of the angry cosmic power. Splendid she sits, and splendid is her Babylon. How the late apocalyptists love mouthing out all about the gold and silver and cinnamon of evil Babylon! How they want them all! How they envy Babylon her splendor, envy, envy! How they love destroying it all! The harlot sits magnificent with her golden cup of wine of sensual pleasure in her hand. How the apocalyptists would have loved to drink out of her cup! And since they couldn't: how they loved to smash it![20]

Royalty opens his work with a similar quote from Lawrence:

> By the time of Jesus, all the lowest classes and mediocre people had realized that never would they get a chance to be kings, never would they go in chariots, never would they drink wine from gold vessels. Very well then—they would have their revenge by destroying it all. "Babylon the great is fallen, is fallen, and is become the habitation of the devils"—how one hears the envy, the endless envy screeching through this song of triumph.[21]

Loubser views Lawrence's *Apocalypse* through the category of the "ordinary reader" and he calls him an "extra-ordinary" ordinary reader. Lawrence "deliberately chose for an intuitive reading";[22] almost ten years before *Apocalypse* he wrote: "We do not care, vitally, about theories of the Apocalypse: what the Apocalypse means. What we care about is the release of the imagination. A real release of the imagination renews our strength and our vitality, makes us feel stronger and happier."[23] The inspiration for his ordinary reading

---

19. Collins, "Persecution and Vengeance," 730–31; Royalty, *The Streets of Heaven*; J. A. (Bobby) Loubser, "D H Lawrence's Extra-ordinary 'Ordinary Reading' of the Apocalypse," *Neot* 38 (2004): 326–46. D. H. Lawrence, *Apocalypse* (Florence: Orioli, 1931). "As D. H. Lawrence was dying in 1929 he focused his attention to the value system that had informed his early development. The book *Apocalypse* was completed in January 1930, two months before his death" (Loubser, "D H Lawrence's Extra-ordinary," 326).

20. Collins, "Persecution and Vengeance," 730–31.
21. Royalty, *The Streets of Heaven*, 1.
22. Loubser, "D H Lawrence's Extra-ordinary," 331.
23. Ibid., 329.

is his reading for a cause: "Melvyn Bragg explains the cause as 'his acute and growing certainty that democracy, industry, technology and the Judaic religious inheritance had led men onto barren ground.'"[24] According to McGinn, he "felt compelled to write his own form of commentary to exorcise it from his mind."[25] The dominant horizon of this reading seems to be Lawrence's dissatisfaction with his own social and spiritual context and with his inherited reading of the Apocalypse. He therefore reads the work "against the grain," siding with Babylon against Jerusalem. Within this perspective the prayer for judgment and the rejoicing at the fall of Babylon are seen in a decidedly negative light, as an expression of envy and lust for vengeance. Such a reading has stimulated some commentators to take a closer look at these.

4. Adela Yarbro Collins: Aggression and Catharsis

For Collins, the reading of D. H. Lawrence makes the book "even more disturbing and challenging for the Christian who accepts Revelation as Scripture."[26] She observes that most commentators have tried to make the unacceptable desires of revenge and envy somewhat acceptable,[27] and she points to William Barclay, who admits in commenting on 18:1–3: "It may be that we are far from the Christian doctrine of forgiveness; but we are very close to the beating of the human heart"; on 18:20: "it is not the more excellent way which Jesus taught."[28] The element of vengeance is made acceptable by pointing out that vengeance is left to God in the faith that God does not abandon the faithful and that punishment is the natural consequence of evil behavior: "every man is working out his own judgment."[29] Barclay's horizon of reading is a firm commitment to the positive value of the Apocalypse as Scripture, although he concedes that, while the Apocalypse does not manifest the perfection of Jesus' teaching on nonviolence, the basics are nevertheless in place.

---

24. Ibid., 334.

25. Ibid., 327. "He responded to the vulgar manner in which Christian society of his time explained the Apocalypse and not to the way in which its original audiences received it" (336).

26. Collins, "Persecution and Vengeance," 730.

27. Ibid.: "Bishop Lilje thought that this was not just petty human revenge but holy joy! ... they are not animated by joy over destruction, but by certainty that God achieves his purpose, in spite of the arrogance of this secular power."

28. William Barclay, *The Revelation of John* (2nd ed.; 2 vols.; Edinburgh: Saint Andrews, 1960), 2:195 and 2:213–14.

29. Ibid., 2:198–99.

In her conclusion to *Crisis and Catharsis*, Collins briefly displays a more systematic way of dealing with the issues. With regard to *the world behind the text*, Collins rejects the view, which used to be widely accepted, of a vicious persecution against Christians by Domitian. Instead, she speaks of a *perceived crisis*: "The Apocalypse was indeed written in response to a crisis, but one which resulted from the clash between the expectations of John and like-minded Christians and the social reality within which they had to live."[30] With regard to *the world of the text*: "Much of the Apocalypse can be explained persuasively as literary means for dealing constructively with aggressive feelings aroused by the perceived crisis."[31] The most challenging task presents itself when we face *the world in front of the text*: "If we wish to move beyond pre-critical reaction to the text, we must assess critically the Apocalypse's means of resolving the tension."[32] The way forward is that of biblical hermeneutics.[33] Such an "attempt to interpret biblical texts in a responsible way" requires norms of responsibility.[34] Collins asserts that the authority of biblical norms cannot be assumed, taken for granted, or presupposed but must be conferred. "The only reliable guide in making judgments is the interpreter's or reader's own *critically interpreted* present experience."[35] In other words, only a reader able to reflect critically on who one is and where one stands in society will be able to recognize where authority is to be found in the biblical narrative. Collins points to the necessarily partial and imperfect success of such a task:

> The movement from a precritical to a critical reading of the Apocalypse involves the experience of its vision as a broken myth. The critical reader

---

30. Collins, *Crisis and Catharsis*, 165. "Some persecution had been experienced, more was expected; a disparity of wealth existed and economic survival was a problem" (Collins, "Persecution and Vengeance," 746). In such a situation feelings of anger, frustration, envy, and vengeance are to be expected: "It may not always be psychologically possible to love one's enemies or to rejoice in their good fortune" (747). Should people be encouraged to offer prayers for the destruction of their enemies? "Justice may seem to call for them at times, but there is also the very real danger of becoming like the oppressor in one's opposition" (747).

31. Collins, *Crisis and Catharsis*, 166.

32. Ibid.

33. Collins (ibid.) points to other criteria of assessment: the traditional approach is guided by the rule of faith; the historical-critical approach was able to show diversity within the biblical tradition on a number of questions and differences between the biblical perceptions and contemporary ways of assessing the issues.

34. Ibid. Various solutions have been put forward: among these solutions, that of a canon within the canon (e.g., the exodus, the historical Jesus, the Pauline gospel, …).

35. Collins, *Crisis and Catharsis*, 167.

can no longer simply live and move and have one's being within the "world" of the text. A critical reading also leads to an awareness of how the text is flawed by the darker side of the author's human nature, which we, like all the readers, share. In spite of, and perhaps because of, these insights, we can move to a personal reinvolvement with the text on a new level. A postcritical reading is one in which a partial, imperfect vision can still speak to our broken human condition.[36]

After these methodological questions, which are crucial and enlightening particularly for our topic, Collins proposes the values of humanization, justice, and love as the criteria for assessing the political stance and relational tone of the Apocalypse.[37] Her basic assessment is that "[t]he violent imagery was apparently intended to release aggressive feelings in a harmless way."[38] However, she raises the question about the long-term effectiveness of this means of reducing tension. The Apocalypse itself exhibits a failure of love in its dualist division of humanity (those with the mark of the beast and those with the mark of God) and in its dehumanization of Christian rivals and non-Christian opponents.[39] On the other hand, relying on the work of Rollo May, she recognizes the appropriateness of expressions of anger and violence against injustice: "Revelation serves the value of humanization insofar as it insists that the marginal, the relatively poor and powerless, must assert themselves to achieve their full humanity and dignity."[40] In the end, she points out that the achievement of the Apocalypse is *ambiguous* "insofar as aggressive feeling and violence can be destructive as well as constructive."[41]

---

36. Ibid., 172. In my view, the question of who one is and where one stands needs to be understood more holistically and more dynamically. Interaction with the subject matter of the text should invite us to move beyond "who we are" and "where we stand." The threefold conversion of Bernard Lonergan (intellectual, moral, religious) is helpful here (see Bernard Lonergan, *Method in Theology* [2nd ed.; London: Darton, Longman & Todd, 1973], *passim*).

37. Collins, *Crisis and Catharsis*, 167.

38. Ibid., 171.

39. Ibid., 170.

40. Ibid., 171.

41. Ibid., 172. "Revelation's call for vengeance and the possibility of the book's function as an outlet for envy give the book a tremendous potential for real psychological and social evil. Its dangerous power must be recognized and dealt with. At the same time, these elements have a relative and limited validity. It may not always be psychologically possible to love one's enemies or rejoice in their good fortune. At least Revelation limits vengeance and envy to the imagination and clearly rules out violent deeds" (Collins, "Persecution and Vengeance," 747).

5. Elisabeth Schüssler Fiorenza and Richard Bauckham: Protest against Economic Oppression

Schüssler Fiorenza understands the Apocalypse basically as a vision of liberation: "Oppressive powers, whether they be political, social, or religious, cannot coexist with the life-giving empire and power of God."[42] In order to be able to appreciate the Apocalypse, one needs to hunger and thirst for justice in a context in which one experiences oppression and exclusion.[43] Even in John's sociohistorical context there must have been people, and even Christians like those in Laodicea, who did not feel any oppression and experienced no thirst for justice.[44] Schüssler Fiorenza envisions the task of rhetorical analysis as understanding the interaction between the text and the sociohistorical context but in dialogue/argument with "conflicting symbolic universes and rhetorical struggles over values and status"; John's response is not the *only* one, "but *one* response among other competing voices."[45] She sees the real problem with John's symbolic vision in his image of God as an almighty ruler, fashioned after the rulers of that time.[46]

Schüssler Fiorenza questions the now popular view of those who "make a sharp distinction between the textualized rhetorical situation and the actual historical rhetorical situation, between ideal reality and material reality."[47] Even if there was no general persecution under Domitian or if he was not

---

42. Schüssler Fiorenza, *Revelation*, 128.

43. Referring to the South American anti-U.S. liberation theology rhetoric, Schüssler Fiorenza writes: "It might very well be that many will feel as helpless or resentful vis-à-vis such prophetic liberation rhetoric as they feel vis-à-vis the theology of Revelation" (ibid.).

44. It is a question of *how* one looks at the situation and particularly *from where* one looks, one's social location. "If Revelation stresses the economic exploitation and oppression perpetrated by Babylon/Rome's imperialist power, then it expresses an assessment of life in Asia Minor that was not necessarily shared by all Christians" (ibid., 127).

45. Ibid., 132.

46. "Not the theology of justice and judgment and its 'advocacy stance' for the oppressed and powerless, but its envisioning of God and Christ in analogy to the Oriental Great King and the Roman emperor seems to me the theological 'Achilles' heel' of the visionary rhetoric of Rev. that calls for theological evaluation. ... Since Rev. is not the only biblical writing that promotes the image of an Almighty Ruler-God, G. Kaufmann has called upon theologians to 'enter into the most radical deconstruction and reconstruction' of the central Christian symbols for God and Jesus Christ" (Elisabeth Schüssler Fiorenza, *The Book of Revelation: Justice and Judgment* [Philadelphia: Fortress, 1985], 9).

47. Schüssler Fiorenza, *Revelation*, 126. See Collins, *Crisis and Catharsis*, who introduced the idea of a "perceived crisis"; Royalty (*The Streets of Heaven*, 14) quotes Leonard L. Thompson, *The Book of Revelation: Apocalypse and Empire* (New York: Oxford University Press, 1990), 175: "the conflict and crisis in the Book of Revelation between Christian

worse than any other emperor, this does not mean that John's vision was not "developed in response to an actual sociotheological crisis."[48] The memory of the persecution and execution under Nero must still have been vivid in the communities.

Bauckham also continues to hold on to a context of economic oppression experienced in (most) of the churches.[49] He wants to highlight how in Rev 18 John, in continuity with the prophets, focuses on the economic dimension in his critique of Babylon.[50] However, John did not simply challenge Rome's exploitation and economic oppression but warned those in the Christian communities who were deeply involved with Rome to dissociate themselves from her: "It also required those who could share in her profits to side with her victims and become victims themselves."[51]

Bauckham does not focus on the issue of violence and coercion in the text. However, in his discussion of the conversion of the nations he argues that "John's central prophetic conviction about the coming of God's kingdom on earth: [is] that the sacrificial death of the Lamb and the prophetic witness of his followers are God's strategy for winning all the nations of the world from the dominion of the beast to his own kingdom."[52] Bauckham argues, from the contrast between Rev 11:13 and 9:20–21, that John goes beyond the Old Testament understanding of prophetic judgment:

> Thus the reason why the prophetic ministry of the two witnesses has an effect unparalleled by their Old Testament precedents lies in their participation in the victory of the Lamb. Jesus himself is the faithful witness (1:5;

---

commitment and the social order derive from John's perspective on Roman society rather than from significant hostilities in the social environment."

48. Schüssler Fiorenza, *Revelation*, 126.

49. Bauckham, "Economic Critique of Rome."

50. "The economic element in this critique is probably the one which has received the least attention in previous scholarship" (ibid., 350).

51. Ibid., 378. According to J. Nelson Kraybill, "Jews and Christians … usually avoided the military as a route for upward mobility. Now John of Patmos identifies commerce—the second main route for advancement—as equally infested with idolatrous influence" (*The Imperial Cult and Commerce in John's Apocalypse* [JSNTSup 132; Sheffield: Sheffield Academic Press, 1996], 110). However, "the point is not that John wrote Revelation because he was poor and socially marginalized. Rather, it is more likely he identified with the poor and marginalized because he believed Christians no longer could participate in an unjust commercial network thoroughly saturated with idolatrous patriotism. This study examines how commerce and the imperial cult blended in the first century Roman world, and how John of Patmos thought followers of Jesus should respond" (Kraybill, *Imperial Cult and Commerce*, 23).

52. Bauckham, "Economic Critique of Rome," 336.

3:14) because he maintained his witness even to the point of death, beyond which it was vindicated as true witness in his resurrection.[53]

6. Robert M. Royalty: An Aristocratic Attitude of Disdain for the Commercial Wealth of Rome, Instead of Protest Against Economic Oppression

Royalty holds that the real enemy for John is not Greco-Roman culture but the competing prophetic leaders in the churches. The attacks on Babylon/Rome are rhetorical devices to vilify his opponents in the churches and to legitimate his own power. Furthermore, he holds that his audience was more familiar with the Greco-Roman symbolic and ethical universe than with that of the Old Testament prophets. John clearly presents two kinds of wealth: that of Babylon, which is presented in very negative terms; and that of Jerusalem, which is excessive and nevertheless presented in very glowing terms. Royalty argues that in order to understand John's rhetoric we have to see how he evokes the aristocratic disdain for the commercial wealth of the *nouveaux riches* (Babylon) and the aristocratic status consciousness of the established classes. Although his language reflects that of the great prophets, his use of the theme of wealth does not in any way reflect the prophetic concern for the poor and for social justice.[54] On the contrary, John adopts the aristocratic views on wealth,[55] which could easily be accepted by the common people, in order to vilify Rome and his opponents and to win favor for him and those following his party. His attack on the wealth of Babylon is, therefore, not inspired by an alternative culture of justice but simply by a violent will to power:

---

53. Ibid., 280.

54. "There are no passages in Revelation that express special concern for the poor, widows, orphans, the traditional recipients of charity, to counterbalance the bias against the poor in Rev 6:6–6 [sic]. This absence is remarkable in the context of ancient Jewish and Christian literature. It is an absence all the more striking by the wealth of heaven and it is important to keep in mind when the forces of heaven destroy the wealthy city of Babylon" (Royalty, *The Streets of Heaven*, 183).

55. Royalty sees John more as a hypocritical aristocratic Stoic rather than a radical Cynic when it comes to the question of wealth. He finds the Stoics to be arm-chair philosophers who condemn reliance on wealth while justifying its enjoyment in their own lives. "Cynic philosophy propounded freedom from wealth, possessions, and social convention. Stoic philosophy emphasized freedom from reliance on *adiaphora*, such as wealth, as a way to happiness rather than seeking out poverty as a means to virtue and happiness" (ibid., 96).

The texts create a new culture of power that mimics the dominant ideology; only the names and labels are changed. Revelation replaces Rome with the new Jerusalem and Caesar's court with God's, but the underlying power structures are essentially the same. The point of this rhetoric is not redemption of the world or even of the Christian community but the establishment of a new theocratic empire.[56]

However, it is more likely that John's critique of his opponents in the churches is based on their different view of Greco-Roman culture and particularly of the imperial ideology. John's effort at recognition in the churches is based on his conviction that he proclaims the truth from God about the true status of the Roman Empire and the true status of those who follow his teaching in opposition to the Roman imperial ideology. John's desire for recognition and power in the churches is unlikely to be driven by a blind desire for power. He claims that it is based on insight, which he obtained by revelation from God and Jesus. In what follows I will attempt to understand that insight more fully.

7. Four Traditions That Contribute to a Fuller Understanding of John's Hostility against the Wealth of Rome

My aim is not to focus on the world in front of the text but to explore some aspects of the world of the text more fully in the hope of doing more justice to this world. This may spark off new insights for the world in front of the text.

7.1. The Pattern of the Two Ways

Royalty has rightly pointed out how the hostility against the wealth of Babylon cannot be understood apart from the favorable view of the wealth of Jerusalem. The two stand in antithetic parallelism to each other. This dualism of the Apocalypse has been widely recognized, but it has not been looked at in the light of the well-known device of the two ways.[57] However, I think that

---

56. Ibid., 246.

57. Scholars get involved in discussion on the kind of dualism. Adela Yarbro Collins writes: "Revelation certainly does not express an absolute dualism in which the power of Good and the power of Evil are both primordial. It lacks an ethical dualism of the deterministic type. Revelation seems to affirm the freedom of rational creatures to choose whether to obey or to disobey God. Nevertheless, there is what we may call a practical dualism" (review of Leonard L Thompson, *The Book of Revelation: Apocalypse and Empire*, JBL 110 [1991]: 750). Here she comes close to the idea of the two-ways tradition. In another work, however, she writes "The dualist division of humanity in Apocalypse is a

recognizing this device is most helpful in order to appreciate the kind of language we have in front of us. According to David Aune,[58] it was a widely used tradition that can be found in Egyptian, Greek, and Latin literature as well as in the Old Testament, Judaism, the New Testament, and early Christian literature.[59] Furthermore, it is important to remember here that the two-ways tradition was regularly used in connection with apocalyptic imagery of the end. In the Epistle of Barnabas the section on the two ways is followed by a conclusion that evokes the resurrection, the retribution, the day of judgment, the nearness of the Lord, and his reward (Barn. 21). Both the Didache and the Testament of Asher begin with the two ways and end by evoking apocalyptic images of the end.[60]

According to T. Ash. 1:3-4: "God has granted two ways to the sons of men, two mind-sets, two lines of action, two models, and two goals. Accordingly, everything is in pairs, the one against the other." We find these elements in the Apocalypse. The dual goal is prominent in the parallel scenes of Babylon and Jerusalem, which form the climax of the work. To this dual goal correspond two opposing lines of action: worship of God (4:10; 11:1; 14:7;

---

failure in love. ... It is an oversimplification that eliminates not only the possibility of neutrality but also the complexities of life in which there are always shades of gray. But most important, this dualism is destructive and dehumanizing" (Collins, *Crisis and Catharsis*, 170). According to Schüssler Fiorenza, "Revelation engages in a radical ethical dualism that places before the audience a either-or decision. Either one succumbs to the oppressive world power of Babylon/Rome and its religious legitimization or one engages in the struggle for God's qualitatively new *cosmopolis* that is free from all oppression and evil" (*Revelation*, 130).

58. David E. Aune, *The Westminster Dictionary of New Testament and Early Christian Literature and Rhetoric* (Louisville: Westminster John Knox, 2003), 478.

59. Old Testament: Deut 30:15; Jer 21:8; Ps 1; Prov 2:12-15. Judaism: Sir 15:11-17; 21:10; T. Ash. 1-6; 1QS 3:13-4:26; 2 En. 30:15. New Testament: Matt 7:13-14; 21:32. Early Christian literature: Did. 1-5; Barn. 18-21; Shepherd of Hermas, *Mand.* 6.1-2-5 and *Vis.* 3.7.1-2.

60. John S. Kloppenborg points out that the Didache "has eliminated both angels and eschatology" (the dualistic schema) from the two ways ("The Transformation of Moral Exhortation in *Didache* 1-5," in *The Didache in Context: Essays on Its Text, History, and Transmission* [ed. Clayton N. Jefford; Leiden: Brill, 1995], 97). The difference between the two ways in the Didache and Barnabas is "the lack of apocalyptic appeals" and "the marked shift to the authority of the Torah" (109). We have to ask whether there really is a connection between these two shifts. The Didache nevertheless ends with warnings about the coming of the world deceiver and the division of people into two categories, those who will perish and those who will be saved. Kloppenborg's view that an ethical strategy and an apocalyptic horizon are mutually exclusive (101) is not convincing. In the Didache as we now have it, they seem to support each other.

15:4; 19:10) and worship of the beast (9:20; 13:8, 12, 15; 14:9, 11; 16:2; 19:20). Furthermore, these two opposing lines of action are embedded in a conflict between two opposing spiritual forces, God and the dragon, who each have their agents, the Lamb and the prophets on the one hand, the two beasts on the other hand.[61] We find a contrast between the side of God (faithful and true: 3:7, 14; 6:10; 15:3; 16:7; 19:2; 19:9, 11; 21:5; 22:6) and the side of the devil (deceiving: 2:20; 12:9; 13:14; 20:3, 8, 10). Although the image of the *way* is not prominent in the Apocalypse (15:3; 16:12), the rhetorical use of opposing sets is a form of what is commonly called "the two ways."[62]

If we understand the contrast between Babylon and Jerusalem in the light of the two-ways tradition, the purpose of the contrast becomes clearer: the two different ways of life, guided by two different prophetic teachings, will have radically differing ends. The option before the churches is presented in the sharpest possible way in order to move them to commitment. This is not a philosophical discussion that details all the possible options and discusses the positive and negative points of each. It simply evokes good and evil, wisdom and foolishness. The emphasis is on choice and the consequences of this choice. As in Ps 1, we find contrasting images of a flourishing life and a hopeless end, the consequences of a choice to be made in the present. For rhetorical effect, Babylon is described in the worst possible way and Jerusalem in the most glorious way. Babylon is a whore, Jerusalem a faithful bride. The wealth of Babylon is about to disappear, while the wealth of Jerusalem will be everlasting. The wealth of Babylon is associated with arrogance and violence, while the wealth of Jerusalem is associated with the absence of pain, tears, or death (21:4). The wealth of Babylon is associated with idolatry and sorcery, while the wealth of Jerusalem is a gift from God (21:1–7) and reflects the glory of God (21:11).

The aim of the contrast between Babylon and Jerusalem is precisely to get people to make a choice and not to remain neutral. However, it is clear that this way of speaking can have negative effects and consequences: the judgments made in this way can collude with our absolutizing instinct: what we love is absolutely good; what we hate is absolutely evil. Rome and its supporters are seen as totally evil.

---

61. See 1QS 3:13–4:26, where the cosmic struggle between the two angels is replicated in the moral struggle within the human heart (Kloppenborg, "Transformation of Moral Exhortation," 94).

62. It is interesting that Ps 1 presents us with the two ways. Although the image of the way appears as an inclusion (vv. 1 and 6), it is not the only image used. What matters is the sets of opposition.

Seeing the contrast between Babylon and Jerusalem as part of the two-ways tradition helps us to see more clearly that the Apocalypse is not interested in announcing the end simply for its own sake; all this is part of, and subordinated to, a wider complex of instruction, exhortation, challenge, and encouragement for the present life.

7.2. The Roman Imperial Myth Countered by the Biblical Myth of God the Creator

For the articulation of his two-ways pattern John did not so much use the contrast between vice and virtue, as in the Didache or Barnabas. Instead, he drew on the imagery of the mythological pattern that Collins has called the combat myth.[63] Collins has reminded us that "The rule of Augustus was celebrated as a golden age and as the rule of Apollo. The Apollo myths and cult were made to function as political propaganda for the empire."[64] Friesen provides further evidence from archaeological remains from Miletos, Aphrodisias, and Ephesus.[65] Comparing this material with Rev 13, he concludes that both the imperial cults and John are mythologizing Rome.[66] The city of Rome becomes the goddess Roma, and its emperors are presented as divine figures. While the authorities in the Asian cities integrated both their local and the

---

63. Adela Yarbro Collins, *The Combat Myth in the Book of Revelation* (HDR 9; Missoula, Mont.: Scholars Press, 1976).

64. Ibid., 188.

65. Steven J. Friesen, "Myth and Symbolic Resistance in Revelation 13," *JBL* 123 (2004): 281–313. In fact, ever since the first emperor, Augustus, the idea that a new golden age had been reached through Augustus was propagated by a number of well-known writers of the period, such as Virgil and Horace. They claimed that the messianic peace, the *pax Romana*, had been established in the world through Augustus. Virgil's passage in the *Fourth Eclogue* about the birth of a boy (Augustus) was seen by Christians in later times as a pagan prophecy of the birth of Jesus: "Now the last age by Cumae's Sibyl sung / Has come and gone, and the majestic roll / of circling centuries begins anew; / Justice returns, returns old Saturn's reign, / with a new breed of men sent down from heaven. / Only do thou, at the boy's birth in whom / the iron shall cease, the golden age arise… / Apollo reigns. And in thy consulate / this glorious age, O Pollio, shall begin, / and the months enter on their mighty march." In 17 c.e. Horace wrote his *Carmen saeculare* for a religious festival that was meant to lend luster to the new political order inaugurated by Augustus. This text was known by many people, since it was inscribed on a marble pillar in the ancient center of Rome. Augustus had a special devotion to Apollo, the sun-god, and this song is addressed to him (also called Phoebus); see especially lines 57–65 to get a sense of the mythology. See Paul Barnett, "Polemical Parallelism: Some Further Reflections on the Apocalypse," *JSNT* 35 (1989): 111–20.

66. Friesen, "Myth and Symbolic Resistance," 308.

Pan-Hellenic myths into the mythology of the empire as an exercise of submission to, cooperation with, and glorification of the Roman Empire, John let his mythological tradition of the combat myth, that of God the creator,[67] interact with these traditions in order to undermine the claims of the empire by identifying Rome, the emperor, and the local Asian authorities as manifestations of the forces of chaos and death.[68] He achieves this by associating the Roman establishment with the great sea monsters, including Rahab, the dragon, and Leviathan.[69] John stood within an already established tradition of mythologizing the enemies. For instance, in Dan 7 the four beasts from the sea represent the four empires that troubled Israel: the Babylonians, the Medes, the Persians, and the Greeks.[70]

The hostility against the wealth of Rome is not simply human hostility; John places this hostility in the context of God's hostility against anything that threatens creation and life. In order to understand the imagery and emotion of this hostility and violence in the Apocalypse, we have to bear in mind that John is drawing on the biblical creation tradition with all its complexity.[71] First, God's work of creation is seen as a combat with the forces of chaos.[72]

---

67. John's interest in the theme of creation is quite evident in various ways: in Rev 4:11 and 10:6 God is called the creator; in 3:14 Jesus is the beginning of God's creation; in 5:13 all creatures in heaven and on earth and under the earth and in the sea honor God and the Lamb. The title παντοκράτωρ, which occurs nine times in the Apocalypse, also seems to evoke the image of the creator-victor: 1:4; 4:8: 11:17; 15:3; 16:7, 14; 19:6, 15; 21:22.

68. According to Rev 11:17–18, the reign of God will involve the destruction of those who destroy the earth; in 19:2 Babylon is the one who destroys the earth.

69. "The author of Revelation could thus draw on two Leviathan patterns to link chs. 12 and 13: Leviathan the mythic opponent shapes the dragon image of ch. 12, and the Leviathan-Behemoth pattern [from the sea and from the earth: 1 En. 60:7-9, 24; 2 Bar. 29:3-4] shapes ch. 13" (Friesen, "Myth and Symbolic Resistance," 307).

70. See also Ezek 29:3–5; 32:4: Egypt; Isa 51:9–10, which at least alludes to the exodus and Egypt; Isa 27:1 with verses 12–13, which link the beast with Egypt and Assyria.

71. For this I draw on the work of Walter Brueggemann, *Theology of the Old Testament: Testimony, Dispute, Advocacy* (Minneapolis: Fortress, 1997), 528–51. "On the one hand, the complete sovereignty of Yahweh, as Levenson has shown, never completely drives out what seems to be the autonomous force of chaos. On the other hand, the freedom assigned to Yahweh as Creator, in Israel's rhetoric, is never free from moral condition, in which Israel has brought negation upon itself; thus the act of negation is not a completely free act of Yahweh, but is at the same time an act required and mandated by covenant sanctions. Yahweh's sovereign freedom, according to Israel's testimony, must endlessly contend with these two qualifications" (Brueggemann, *Theology of the Old Testament*, 543).

72. "Yahweh so ordered the 'preexistent material substratum,' which was wild, disordered, destructive, and chaotic, to make an ordered reliable place of peaceableness and viability" (ibid., 529).

While God wants to bring life through order and blessing (Gen 1), the primordial forces of chaos are always there as a potential or even a real threat.[73] Even in the Apocalypse these forces have not yet been reduced to the metaphysical-theological *nihil*. They reveal John's experience of real disorder and evil in his world, but they are also constantly shown as being conquered by God (Rev 12; 17; 18; 19:19–20; 20:7–10). God's hostility is a struggle for life against primordial chaos. Second, God is presented as undoing creation in response to the lack of human cooperation (the flood; Jer 4:23–26).[74] God's anger is the expression of frustration at the human opposition to the project of creation.[75] A number of texts expect—in vain—the experience of God's destructive force to lead people to conversion (Amos 4:6–11), as in Rev 9:20–21; 16:9, 11, 21. Nevertheless, in spite of all of this, God's life-giving commitment is dominant. Brueggemann[76] sees this expressed first of all in stories of destruction where the extermination is not total and ultimate: the flood, Sodom, the plagues against Egypt, and Jer 4:23–27. This last text ends with the contrast: "the whole land will be a desolation … yet I will not make a full end." Finally, Brueggemann[77] points to texts like Hos 2:2–23; Isa 45:18–19; 62:3–5; and 65:17–25,[78] which open a perspective in which God, as it were in an ultimate surge, overcomes God's own anger, human disobedience, and the forces of chaos. In other words, there is hope for creation in spite of these three real threats.

In the Apocalypse we witness the drama of God's creative victory over the beasts and those that belong to them and the realization of the new creation. It is this drama of God the creator that shapes the polemical rhetoric of John's

---

73. "We may believe, moreover, that Israel rearticulated this claim in its own texts, not because Israel was a careless borrower of texts from its environment, but because these articulations are seen to be a faithful witness to a dimension of reality that Israel is not able or willing to deny" (ibid., 534).

74. Brueggemann (ibid., 537–43) also refers to a number of other texts; the plagues of Egypt, as another form of temporary and partial reduction to primeval chaos (or darkness), are particularly relevant for the Apocalypse.

75. "From our perspective, this is almost a grotesque articulation of Yahweh's relationship to the world. This view of Yahweh's potentially destructive capacity, however, is evidently a staple of Israel's sense of the world, for which Israel exhibits neither wonderment nor embarrassment" (ibid., 540). Even nature itself rebels against the evil and violence of humanity (Hos 4:1–3).

76. Ibid., 544–46.

77. Ibid., 546–49.

78. These last two texts are of course very prominent in the evocation of the new Jerusalem of the Apocalypse.

two ways and is the source of the violent imagery[79] and complex emotion. However, what are the churches called to do within such a vision?

7.3. Heavenly Prayer for Justice—Earthly Victory through Faithfulness unto Death

Revelation 6:10 reads: καὶ ἔκραξαν φωνῇ μεγάλῃ λέγοντες· ἕως πότε, ὁ δεσπότης ὁ ἅγιος καὶ ἀληθινός, οὐ κρίνεις καὶ ἐκδικεῖς τὸ αἷμα ἡμῶν ἐκ τῶν κατοικούντων ἐπὶ τῆς γῆς; Prayer for "vengeance" is an appeal to God the creator to remember creation and to act. Judgment and warfare (19:11) are the two main images for this divine action.[80] The unit on the destruction of Babylon (17:1–19:10) concludes in Rev 19:2 by recalling the prayer of Rev 6:10:

> ὅτι ἀληθιναὶ καὶ δίκαιαι αἱ κρίσεις αὐτοῦ·
> ὅτι ἔκρινεν τὴν πόρνην τὴν μεγάλην
> ἥτις ἔφθειρεν τὴν γῆν ἐν τῇ πορνείᾳ αὐτῆς,
> καὶ ἐξεδίκησεν τὸ αἷμα τῶν δούλων αὐτοῦ
> ἐκ χειρὸς αὐτῆς.

"Avenging" the blood of God's servants on Babylon is linked to Babylon's crime of destroying the earth. The prayer of the martyrs indeed does not remain a petty desire for personal revenge;[81] the anger is taken up in a cosmic

---

79. The blood on the robe of the rider in Rev 19:13 has to be seen primarily as part of the imagery of the divine warrior, inspired by exegetical traditions on the Messiah based on Isa 63:1–6; see David E. Aune, *Revelation 17–22* (WBC 52C; Nashville: Thomas Nelson, 1998), 1048–50, 1057, who fully recognizes the divine warrior motif (without paying attention to the connection with the creation motif). However, Aune accepts an inevitable shift from the primary image of the divine warrior to a reference to Jesus' atoning death. On the other hand, Heinz Giesen (*Die Offenbarung des Johannes* [RNT; Regensburg: Pustet, 1997], 422) sees the blood-stained cloak as symbolizing the dignity that Jesus has received from God as a result of his victory on the cross.

80. Κρίνειν:16:5; 18:8, 20; 19:2, 11; 20:12, 13; κρίσις: 14:7; 16:7; 18:10; 19:2; κρίμα: 17:1; 18:20; 20:4; δικαιώματα: 15:4; 19:8. The image of war is also common; the heavenly Jesus wages war with the sword of his mouth (2:16; 19:15), which seems to merge the image of warfare and judgment. In the final battle the satan is conquered by a fire from heaven (20:9).

81. In 18:6 the appeal for "double" punishment is based on the assumption that Babylon is a thief who according to Exod 22:1–2, 6–8 has to repay twice the value of the damage. The theme of a double punishment was widespread: while God had threatened with a sevenfold punishment (Lev 26:21, 24, 28), he is satisfied with a twofold punishment in Isa 40:2 (compare also Jer 16:18; 17:18); Zech 9:12 mentions a double compensation.

framework as an ardent desire for God's rule in the world (against Satan) and for the fertility and justice of the earth (against the destructive violence of Babylon). The song in Rev 19:6–9 therefore celebrates the reign of God and looks forward to the marriage of the Lamb with the Woman.

However, the churches are not only encouraged to join in these heavenly prayers and given a vision of God's destruction of Babylon, but the rhetoric of the two ways challenges them to take the side of the ultimate conqueror (the Lamb) and not the side of the ultimate victim (Babylon). As each letter ends with a promise to the one who conquers, the focus and emphasis are on the positive side of the two ways and hold out to the churches the prospect of sharing in the new creation and the heavenly Jerusalem. In the last letter (3:21), the victory of Jesus is presented as the model for the victory of each member of the churches. The theme of victory or conquest appears again as one of the elders introduces the one who is worthy to open the seals of the scroll: the Lion of the tribe of Judah, the root of David has conquered (5:5). Paradoxically, Jesus is victorious through his violent death (his blood), which is an expression of his love for his people even unto death (1:5–6; 5:9–10). Similarly, the conquering members of the churches may appear to be victims, but the true victory is won by resisting the demands of the beast and faithfulness to the Lamb unto death (12:11; 15:2).[82] Each of the seven letters gives more contextual indications on how to conquer. It is significant that repentance plays such a prominent role (Rev 2:5, 16, 21, 22; 3:3, 19). The churches should be careful not to take their victory for granted.[83] The first battleground is within themselves and among themselves. It is not a battle against Babylon in the form of an attack but in the form of disengagement (18:4). Babylon is the realm where Satan is accepted as ruler, where Satan is worshiped; she is riding on the beast, stained by her prostitution and her violence. Victory means rejecting her cup (17:2, 4).

The battle that destroys Babylon is a different one; it is the work of the beast and the ten horns (17:16), but according the divine plan (17:17). The beast and the ten horns first attack the Lamb, but they suffer defeat (17:12–14);

---

82. Rev 15:2 clearly refers back to chapter 13: the beast, the statue of the beast, and the number of its name. The faithful resist and believe (v. 10). See Paul Middleton, *Radical Martyrdom and Cosmic Conflict in Early Christianity* (Library of New Testament Studies 307; London: T&T Clark, 2006), who shows the link between martyrdom and the holy-war tradition in early Christianity: martyrdom was seen as sharing in the cosmic victory of Jesus over Satan.

83. The churches that did not receive a challenge to repent are nevertheless challenged to be "faithful until death" (2:10), "to do my works to the end" (2:26), to "hold fast to what you have, so that no one may seize your crown" (3:11).

they then turn against Babylon and destroy her.[84] We find the same pattern in Rev 2:20–23, where Jezebel is as it were the embodiment of Babylon within the church and an agent of Satan as one who leads people astray (12:9; 13:14; 20:3, 8, 10). The victory of the church consists in disengaging from her as one who leads astray. The battle, by which she will be punished with sickness and her children with death unless they repent, is entirely in God's hand.

Although the world of humans is divided between those who follow the beast and those who follow the Lamb, this division is not final.[85] In fact, repentance is a major concern in the Apocalypse and is in principle open to all. With regard to the churches the overall mood is optimistic; the letters end with a prospect of victory based, of course, on the hope that they will persevere or repent where needed. On the other hand, although the series of trumpets and bowls is meant to move to repentance people who do not have the seal of God on their forehead (9:4) or who bear the mark of the beast (16:2), they fail to have the desired effect (9:20–21; 16:9, 11, 21). However, there is a positive response to the ministry, death, resurrection, and ascension of the two witnesses in 11:11–13, and two categories of people who move from the one camp to the other are the ἔθνη and the kings of the earth.[86]

7.4. The Gift of Wisdom in Order to Overcome the Scandal and Deal with Envy

Royalty quotes Wayne Meeks: "the general strategy of the Apocalypse is to oppose to the ordinary view of reality, as anyone might experience it in Smyrna or Laodicea, a quite different picture of the world as seen from the standpoint of heaven."[87] What John is attempting to do is to shape his churches' perception of their situation. Some, like the church in Laodicea, live

---

84. Verse 17 resumes verse 13 to show that the alliance was really inspired by God; what was meant as the destruction of the Lamb turned out to be the destruction of Babylon.

85. In her *JBL* review of Thompson, Collins sounds too negative: "It is assumed likewise that the wrongdoers will continue to act wrongly and that the good will continue to act rightly (see 22:11). Of course the *possibility* of repentance is always open, but the seer does not expect it from outsiders" (750).

86. The ἔθνη are mentioned as participating in the new Jerusalem in 21:24, 26; 22:2; in 15:3–4 they are on the side of God, but they can be seduced by Babylon or Satan (14:8; 18:3, 23; 20:3, 8); they are hostile in 11:9, 18. The kings of the earth also feature in the new Jerusalem (21:24), although they too were seduced by Babylon (17:2, 18; 18:3); they were among the three categories of people lamenting the destruction of Babylon (18:9), and they are even seduced to fight on the side of the beast (19:19).

87. Royalty, *The Streets of Heaven*, 13.

in a false security; others experience a clash between their expectations and the social reality, or, "the tension between their common experience of tribulation and their common empire status."[88] What John is offering is the gift of heavenly wisdom and insight into their situation (13:18; 17:9). A similar experience of the gift of insight is found in Ps 73. The person who prays recognizes his envy at the prosperity of the wicked, until he enters the sanctuary and has an experience of enlightenment about their "end" (vv. 16–20). We have a similar struggle and enlightenment in 4 Ezra. The complaining and questioning attitude of the first part of the work is transformed through an experience of enlightenment when Ezra meets a woman mourning her only son and tries to console her (9:38ff.).[89] The Apocalypse must be situated in this tradition of revelatory experiences by which persons see their situation and the whole of reality in a new way, a heavenly way. John is sharing his experience with his audiences so that they may have a similar experience of enlightenment. The hymnic character of the book is meant to lead them to such a spiritual experience.

8. Conclusion

The desire for punishment and destruction of those who are believed to ruin God's world is part of the primary emotional response to whatever is experienced as evil and destructive. Such emotions are a sign of healthy moral sensitivity; the challenge, however, is how to manage these emotions in a constructive way. The Apocalypse evokes these emotions by means of the prophetic tradition of judgment on Babylon and other nations, but it steers these emotions away from violent action to another kind of warfare, namely, conquering Satan by responsible living in contrast with Babylon. The victors conquer not by allowing themselves to be seduced by Satan or Babylon but by allowing their lives to be shaped by the Lamb. The controversial issue in the churches for John is how to understand the empire and how to relate to it; the issue of "food offered to idols and prostitution" (2:14, 20) is an expression of this conflict. Although the empire claims divine status as the agent of creation, life, and peace, John wants his readers to see the empire as an agent of Satan, destroying God's creation, as can be seen in their violence against some members of the churches and in their arrogance based on a foolish overestimation of their military power and wealth. The rhetorical device of the two

---

88. Collins, *Crisis and Catharsis*, 165; Schüssler Fiorenza, *Revelation*, 119.
89. See Michael E. Stone, "A Reconsideration of Apocalyptic Visions," *HTR* 96 (2003): 167–80.

ways both invites and enables John to present Babylon and Jerusalem in a very stark contrast: the power and glory of Babylon are radically relativized, while the power and glory of God, who is to dwell in the new Jerusalem, is exalted. The hoped-for effect is that John's audience will experience the same gift of understanding as he himself has received so that fear of the destructive empire is calmed down and is transformed into prayer in which the relativized issue is transferred from human hands into God's hands. God, the creator, is a God of hope in the midst of primordial evil, human failure, and divine impatience and anger. Such hope enables people to live in this world in a way that enhances creation because they are able to cope with the fear of primordial evil, of human frailty, and even of God's anger.

Animosity and (Voluntary) Martyrdom: The Power of the Powerless

Henk Bakker

A couple of years ago the Portuguese-Canadian pop idol Nelly Furtado sang: "When you feel so powerless, what are you gonna do?" In her song Furtado sings of the sense of helplessness people can have when they look for power. Being without any power—really being powerless—hurts and feels like being worthless, like disappearing and vanishing from the earth. All people need at least some power to exist and to express themselves as strong and self-confident individuals. No one is able to survive society without availing a sound consciousness of power and a healthy self-esteem. This power the Hebrews called *kabôd*: the unique human capacity of self-empowerment.[1] One's *kabôd* is vital because it is full of reverence of life, and it shapes and forms human personality and identity. To take away power equals taking away honor and so willfully distorting someone's identity.

Now exactly this Christianity suffered during the first and second centuries C.E. Emerging Christianity was often rejected for proclaiming a hostile religion. Christians were being equated to "public enemies" (*publicos hostes*, Tertullian, *Apol.* 2.8), because they generally did not sympathize with Roman manners. Living life according to Roman style seemed to exclude authentic participation in Christian churches. The average citizen proved solidarity to the state by showing up at public festivities and rituals, annual ceremonies, and imperial birthdays. Christians refused to do so. The Carthaginian apologist Tertullian (ca. 160–220 C.E.), for example, could not imagine truly dedicated Christians visiting gladiatorial games (see Tertullian, *Spect.* 1–30). No one would see sincere Christian women using makeup or fancy clothes to dress themselves up (Tertullian, *Cult. fem.* 1.1–9; 2.1–13). Though Tertullian was a Montanist and a moralist who looked for a kind of "charismatic"

---

1. See C. John Collins, "כבד," *NIDOTTE* 2:577–87.

reformation of the Carthaginian mainstream church, still the average Christian lifestyle could certainly be taken as a provocation to the non-Christian. Moreover, Christian-watching non-Christians were by all means apt to think suspiciously of their Christian fellow citizens. They suspected quiet Christian people of subversive activities and secret conspiracy against the dominion of mighty Rome. As a matter of fact, Christian religion was in bad repute because it proposed bowing down to absolutely no images. It only venerated, like the Jews, one invisible God and propagated simplicity of life and mind. Nothing, in fact, to be ashamed of, but to the pagan mind invisibly and exclusively serving one God seemed to be offensive and was considered a sign of subversive Christian tendencies and an act of violence against state affairs. This is the main reason why Christians were sometimes hated and hunted down.

Why did not Christians worship their God in public as the Romans and so many others did? Why did most Christian families behave so shyly, timidly, and distractedly? Such questions crossed the mind of many a loyal citizen whose eyes fell by chance on a decent but also spiritually "vague" Christian. Minucius Felix, an unknown third-century Christian author of probably North-African origin, created a significant dialogue between the critical pagan thinker Caecilius Natalis and Octavius Ianuaris, a Christian. Walking along the fair beaches of Ostia with Minucius Felix himself (the story could be a creation, however), Caecilius Natalis accused the Christian community of banding together against the gods like a gang of desperados. Those creepy Christian believers met at night, in the dark, shunning light and transparency. Caecilius signaled: they were "silent in the open, but talkative in hid corners" (*in publicum muta, in angulis garrula*).[2] Despising every temple and spitting upon all the gods ordinary people normally respected, Christians jeered at Roman rites, Caecilius asserted.

To the ears of the Romanized Caecilius, many of the wild accusations hurled at Christians may have sounded false or superstitious (like committing incest and consecrating the head of a donkey or the private parts of their Christ[3]), yet nevertheless he objected:

> Why make such efforts to obscure and conceal whatever is the object of their worship, when things honorable always rejoice in publicity, while guilt loves

---

2. Minucius Felix, *Oct.* 8.4 (Rendall, LCL).

3. Christians were also accused of infanticide and cannibalism; see Minucius Felix, *Oct.* 8–9, 28, 30–31; Athenagoras, *Leg.* 3; Tertullian, *Apol.* 6.11–7.2; Tatian, *Oratio ad Graecos* 31.7–35; Theophilus of Antioch, *Autol.* 3.4–5; Eusebius, *Hist. eccl.* 4.7.9–11; Origen, *Cels.* 6.27.40.

secrecy? Why have they no altars, no temples, no recognized images? Why do they never speak in public, never meet in the open, if it be not that the object of their worship and their concealment is either criminal or shameful? (Minucius Felix, *Oct.* 10.2)

Critical questions provoked by Christian behavior itself. Christians worshiped differently, and they did not even twine blossoms for the head or perfume their bodies (Minucius Felix, *Oct.* 12.5–6). Their conduct seemed to incite hostile behavior toward Roman culture and customs.

Now in particular, Tertullian was disgusted by pagan symbols and rituals while walking on his way through the city. This clearly controversial church leader blessed Christians who for the sake of their faith were captured and captivated. After all, an imprisoned Christian *sub contrario* was a safe Christian—a still, bodily free Christian was yet in fact hampered by all kinds of pagan inconveniences that distracted him or her. Writing to a group of *morituri*, Tertullian heaped up these kinds of paradoxes for the sake of comforting the *confessores*. He declared:

> You have no occasion to look on strange gods, you do not run into their images; you have no part in heather holidays, even by mere bodily mingling in them; you are not annoyed by the foul fumes of idolatrous solemnities; you are not pained by the noise of public shows, nor by the atrocity or madness or immodesty of their celebrants; your eyes do not fall on stews and brothels; you are free from causes of offence, from temptations, from unholy reminiscences; you are free now from persecution too. The prison does the same service for the Christian which the desert did for the prophet.[4]

For Tertullian, the prison doors gracefully closed the world outside of the eyes and minds of shackled Christians (therefore Christians should never flee when persecuted, according to Tertullian). Though jailed, the Christians were not captivated—indeed, paganism disappeared behind bars: a bizarre reversal of facts but very true to the radical North-African Christian mindset in the late second century C.E.[5]

The church of Jesus the Christ differed thoroughly from the world of unregenerated humans. Both spiritual hemispheres separated completely. Famous are Tertullian's words: "What indeed has Athens to do with Jerusalem? What concord is there between the academy and the church?"[6] Jesus and

---

4. Tertullian, *Mart.* 2 (Thelwall, *ANF* 3:694).
5. See Henk Bakker, *"Ze hebben lief, maar worden vervolgd": Radicaal christendom in de tweede eeuw en nu* (Zoetermeer: Het Boekencentrum, 2005).
6. Tertullian, *Praescr.* 7.9 (Holmes, *ANF* 3:246).

pagan philosophy, indeed Jesus and Plato or sophisticated religious systems, should not be confused. Doing so would be detrimental to the Christian faith, according to Tertullianists.

So far we could detect an inclination toward concealment or detraction among Christians and a wrinkle of animosity toward worldly institutions and ethics in certain early Christian writings. Tacitus in his *Yearbooks* surmises and compresses down to only a few simple words the negative impression Christians generally suffered. They were badly stigmatized with the label "haters of the human race."[7] Of course this excessive qualification was untrue, but this is what Christianity was all about for most ordinary people.

In such bad reputation the *Christiani* sometimes had to flee or die a gruesome death. If, for example, disasters such as earthquakes or starvation happened, the first to be blamed were the Christians or the Jews or both. Tertullian writes: "If the Tiber reaches the walls, if the Nile does not rise to the fields, if the sky doesn't move or the earth does, if there is famine, if there is plague, the cry is at once: 'The Christians to the lion!'" (Tertullian, *Apol.* 40.2). Such absurdity—but these situations adequately inform us about the vulnerability and instability of Christian social existence. If any catastrophe took place, people turned their forefingers to a socially isolated and obstinate group of people who seemed to break up the peace with the Roman gods. These freaky Christian atheists dared disturbing the *pax deorum* and thereby threatened the very *pax Romana*.

Now it would be very wrong to consider Christians to be persecuted everywhere and all the time. Moreover, most emperors of the first three centuries advocated tolerance and were too clever and important to busy themselves with a minority of religious fanatics hidden somewhere in the endless empire. In fact, most Roman governors were not keen on chasing Christians and killing them. No imperial decree concerning the illegitimacy of Christianity was ever drawn up by any emperor during the first and second centuries. Trajan in his well-known epistolary response to Pliny the Younger deems it impossible and unnecessary to promulgate a conclusive law against Christianity. The imperial letter says: "For it is not possible to lay down any general rule to serve as a kind of fixed standard. They [Christians] are not to be sought out; if they are denounced and proved guilty, they are to be pun-

---

7. Tacitus, *Ann.* 15.44: *igitur primum correpti qui fatebantur, deinde indicio eorum multitudo ingens haud proinde in crimine incendii quam odio humani generis convicti sunt* ("Accordingly, an arrest was first made of all who pleaded guilty; then, upon their information, an immense multitude was convicted, not so much of the crime of firing the city, as of hatred against mankind").

ished."[8] So Christians were not to be chased after or systematically hunted down or persecuted. When at random they were found, justice was to be exercised. It can be definitely assumed that Trajan's epistolary response was gradually used in other provinces. These indications of Trajan were adopted by most emperors and governors of the second century.

It turned out to be exactly this vagueness of legislation that caused Christians so much harm.[9] Fed by negative public opinion, witch hunts could easily be instigated against the Christians. When vague complaints against Christians were reported, the governor saw the need to investigate them seriously in order to maintain the civic order. Whenever and wherever social equilibrium was disturbed, local authorities could act as they wanted. Even without normal legal proceedings, simply because of the name, Christians could be prosecuted and executed. An investigation *extra ordinem* should suffice to condemn those who confessed to be Christians and persevered in their refusal to offer to the genie (*genius*) of Caesar.[10] A legal investigation did not have to be based on a broad preliminary inquiry. The governor had sufficient authority to consent to legal proceedings *extra ordinem* (an investigation and trial without a judge [*iudex privatus*]).[11] The jurisdiction then lay entirely in his hands, and a judge need not be assigned to the case. If he was dealing with Christians, then this fact became apparent during the interrogation, and they were condemned simply because they bore this title. For a legal basis on which to find them guilty, reference could always be made to the prohibition against practicing a superstition that was ultimately hostile to the state. So,

---

8. Pliny, *Ep.* 10.97 (ed. Trisoglio, Opere di Plinio Cecilio Secundo, 2:1098: *Neque enim in universum aliquid, quod quasi certam formam habeat, constitui potest. Conquirendi non sunt; si deferantur et arguantur, puniendi sunt, ita tamen ut, qui negaverit se Christianum esse idque re ipsa manifestum fecerit, id est supplicando dis nostris, quamvis suspectus in praeteritum, veniam ex paenitentia impetret*).

9. The rescript from Trajan did offer some protection but was, according to Eusebius, vague enough to allow all those wanting to harm Christians the opportunity to do so. See Eusebius, *Hist. eccl.* 3.33.2.

10. See A. N. Sherwin-White, "The Early Persecutions and Roman Law Again," *JTS* 3 (1952): 199–213; Antonie Wlosok, "Die Rechtsgrundlagen der Christenverfolgungen der ersten zwei Jahrhunderte," *Gymnasium* 66 (1959): 14–32; G. E. M. de Sainte Croix, "Why Were the Early Christians Persecuted?" *Past and Present* 26 (1963): 6–38; C. Paulus, "Cognitio," *DNP* 3:59–60; Dieter Flach, "Die römischen Christenverfolgungen: Gründe und Hintergründe," *Historia* 48 (1999): 442–64.

11. A *cognitio* is a legal investigation. Proceedings against Christians were, in general, *cognitiones* (*cognitio extraordinaria*). The fact that they were, to a certain extent, arbitrary cannot be denied.

not officially by law but at a more semiofficial level Christian existence was illegal (*Non licet esse vos*).[12]

The unswerving pertinacity and stubborn obstinacy of certain Christians during many horrific interrogations and tortures was proverbial[13] and eventually produced a new style of literature, the *passio* or *martyrium*, a precious early hagiographic phenomenon in Christian history. Often these popular and favorite texts display a special interest in the very gory details of the last moments of the deceased martyrs, especially if they were women.[14] For example, the repulsive sufferings of Blandina, Perpetua, and Potamiaena have been described with meticulous precision. In the *Martyrium Lugdunensium* we read about a severe persecution of the Christian church in the cities of Lyons and Vienne in southern France (around 177 C.E.).[15] One of the unfortunates was Blandina, who was so brutally tormented that even the mad crowds acknowledged "no woman had ever suffered so much in their experience."[16] Of course, one should be critical regarding the historical reliability of these texts. The somewhat theatrical event and heroic characters in the story make up a kind of public drama that is easily embellished with legendary fiction.[17]

The fragile Christian slave Blandina had to suffer much bodily infliction. Executioners mutilating her in every possible way from dawn to dusk grew weary and exhausted, while Blandina remained strong and refused to renounce her faith.[18] In the amphitheater she was hung on a post in the form of a cross to be torn to pieces by the wild animals. Because the beasts did not touch her, Blandina had to appear again. After subjecting her again to every atrocity and torture, they scourged her, made her sit on a hot griddle, and at last crammed her into a net to be thrown to a bull, which indicated total sexual humiliation. Eventually, after being tossed around by the bull for a

---

12. Tertullian, *Apol.* 4.4: "Your existence is illegal!"

13. See *Passio Sanctorum Scilitanorum* 14 (*obstinanter perseveraverunt*) and Pliny the Younger, *Ep.* 10.96.3 (*pertinacia et inflexibilis obstinatio*).

14. See Kathleen M. Coleman, "Fatal Charades: Roman Executions Staged as Mythological Enactments," *JRS* 80 (1990): 44–73.

15. See Aideen M. Hartney, *Gruesome Deaths and Celibate Lives: Christian Martyrs and Ascetics* (Exeter: Bristol Phoenix, 2005): 44–47.

16. *Martyrium Lugdunensium* 56.

17. See, for classification, Johannes Quasten, *Patrology* (3 vols.; Westminster, Md.: Newman, 1950–60), 1:176–85. See also Hans Reinhard Seeliger, "Märtyrerakten," in *Lexikon der antiken christlichen Literatur* (ed. Siegmar Döpp and Wilhelm Geerlings; 2nd ed.; Freiburg im Breisgau: Herder, 1999), 411–19. Trial records were kept in archives (*commentarii, acta*) and used by Christians; see Gary A. Bisbee, *Pre-Decian Acts of Martyrs and Commentarii* (HDR 22; Philadelphia: Fortress, 1988).

18. *Martyrium Lugdunensium* 18.

while, the brave Christian woman was, like many other Christians, sacrificed to the idols. Such was the anger and hatred of the people of Lyons and Vienne against the Christian population, and consequently they cheered at the utter destruction of these martyrs.[19] Every group or individual infected by lethal rage so forceful and dangerous tries to exercise full control over its victims.

Now let us turn for a moment to the young Carthaginian Christian woman Perpetua. She died a martyr's death in 203 C.E. Brought to the amphitheater the fresh *catechumen* Perpetua and her servant Felicitas were stripped naked, pushed into nets to be crushed by a mad heifer. In the arena the crowds initially were appalled at the sight of these two young ladies. The text says: "one was a delicate young girl and the other was a woman fresh from childbirth with the milk still dripping from her breasts."[20] Immediately thereafter both women were called back and dressed in unbelted tunics. Exposed to the mad heifer, the animal tossed Perpetua on her back. Then she sat up and pulled down her dress to cover her thighs. Next the modest Perpetua took a pin to tidy her hair (*Passio Perpetuae et Felicitatis* 20.4). After helping Felicitas get up from the ground, the two celebrated Christian martyrs were led back to the Porta Sanavivaria to be slaughtered only a moment later in the open, together with other helpless survivors.

Early Christian martyrological texts appear to have a strange and altogether improper and unexpected fascination for cruel detail. Why? Many of these martyr stories would nowadays be classified as unfit to be told at home to our children. Personally, I certainly would not read the *passio Potamiaenae* to our youth at church for spiritual edification. The picture Eusebius in his *Ecclesiastical History* draws of the extreme sufferings of the Alexandrian Christian Potamiaena is absolutely outrageous (Eusebius, *Hist. eccl.* 6.5). In my own words: "The sexual sadism inflicted on her is more than disgusting, and more than a storyteller could bear. Twice her entire body (stripped we suppose) was tortured and defiled. She was threatened by rape at the hands of gladiators, insulted, and finally destroyed inch by inch."[21] Indeed, for all her assailants Potamiaena was reduced to a lump of flesh, an object of hate. One

---

19. *Martyrium Lugdunensium* 17: "the wrath of the mob, the prefect and the soldiers"; 39: "they continued to rage"; 57: "their madness"; 58: "their bestial anger … undeserved hate"; 60: "Some men raged and ground their teeth at these bodies."

20. *Passio Perpetuae et Felicitatis* 20.2 (Herbert Musurillo, *Acts of Christian Martyrs* [2 vols.; Oxford: Clarendon, 1972], 2:129).

21. See Henk Bakker, "Potamiaena: Some Observations about Martyrdom and Gender in Ancient Alexandria," in *The Wisdom of Egypt: Jewish, Early Christian and Gnostic Essays in Honour of Gerard P. Luttikhuizen* (ed. Anthony Hilhorst and George H. van Kooten; Leiden: Brill, 2005), 349–50.

could wonder why no Christian redactor ever intervened to stop this androcentric tradition of violence and eroticizing exhibitionism.

Here I believe the notion of the "power of the powerless" comes in. Most of the martyrs we read about gladly died for their convictions. Under no circumstances did they ever feel or behave like victims. Their fellow Christians saw them as "athletes," on course to conquer the adversary. The ugliness of martyrdom only enhanced the envisioned victory, and the more suffering a martyr endured the more God's vindication and rehabilitation was to be expected. Martyrs such as Ignatius of Antioch died "freely" for God (Ignatius, *Rom.* 4.1). Ignatius himself longed for the wild beasts—yes, he yearned for death.[22] Christians were often voluntary victims, and after Ignatius we read about more examples of this kind of martyrdom in early Christian literature.[23] Sometimes Christians took the initiative and even delivered themselves to the authorities.[24] Voluntary deaths might have cost more Christian lives than involuntary ones.[25]

---

22. Ignatius, *Rom.* 5.2; 7.2. For Ignatius's martyrology, see Henk Bakker, "*Exemplar Domini*: Ignatius of Antioch and His Martyrological Self-Concept" (Ph.D. diss., University of Groningen, 2003).

23. See Agathonice (ca. 165 C.E.; *Martyrium Carpi* 44), a group of Christians (185 C.E.; Tertullian, *Scap.* 5), Pionius and others (middle of the third century; *Passio Pionii* 18.2), Apollonia (middle of the third century; Eusebius, *Hist. eccl.* 6.41.7), Anthimus and the circle around him (at the end of the third century; Eusebius, *Hist. eccl.* 8.6.6), Euplus (29 April 304 C.E.; *Acta Eupli* 1). Not all details of these *acta* are historically reliable.

24. See previous note, but here I would like to make mention of the young girl Eulalia (twelve years old, Merida [Spain], beginning of the fourth century), who heard about Diocletian's edict regarding sacrificing to the imperial gods and walked to Merida in order to confront the governor and reproach him. After refusing to perform the required sacrifice, Eulalia was tortured and killed (Prudentius, *Peristephanon* 3.1-200).

25. Arthur J. Droge and James D. Tabor, *A Noble Death: Suicide and Martyrdom among Christians and Jews in Antiquity* (San Francisco: HarperCollins, 1992), 140, 154, 156. The motives for such morbid desires were, however, diverse and are not of concern here. They might briefly be described as follows: (1) to inspire others to confess their faith: see *Passio Sanctorum Mariani et Iacobi* 3.5 and 9.2-4; Lucius (between 150 and 160 C.E.) in *Martyrium Ptolemaei* 11-20 (Justin Martyr, *2 Apol.* 2.1-20); *Acta Cypriani* 5.1 (14 September 258 C.E.); Eusebius, *Hist. eccl.* 8.9.5 (at the beginning of the fourth century); see also Eusebius, *Mart. Pal.* 3.2-4; (2) penitential reasons: Eusebius, *Hist. eccl.* 7.12.1; (3) to take care of the imprisoned confessors: see Vettius Epagathus in the *Martyrium Lugdunensium* (177 C.E.); Eusebius, *Hist. eccl.* 5.1.9-10; Alexander in Eusebius, *Hist. eccl.* 5.1.49-50; Saturus in the *Passio Perpetuae* 4.5 (203 C.E.); *Passio Phileae* (recensio Latina) 7.1-3 (see Eusebius, *Hist. eccl.* 8.9.7). See also Robin Lane Fox, *Pagans and Christians in the Mediterranean World from the Second Century AD to the Conversion of Constantine* (London: Penguin, 1986), 441-45.

These martyrs reckoned all the way with God's flaming justice. Animosity, persecution, imprisonment in gloomy dark places, the breaking of bones, fire, the teeth of the lion, the hooks of the hangman—all this weird sickness only stirred up the Christian sense of vindication and rehabilitation. God could not neglect exposure to this kind of evil.[26] He certainly would bring enemies to justice who fry Christians on red-heated chairs or cut off noses or breasts. Martyrdom was in every way a power encounter event. The forces of good and evil, of light and darkness stood confronted. Powerless martyrs knew they had God on their side. The mighty tyrant was definitely supposed to lose in the end.

Christian churches strongly anticipated the coming justice by writing sacred texts that extensively testify to the urgency of public rehabilitation of the martyrs. In Rev 6 we meet the souls of deceased martyrs who cry out to God: "How long, O Lord, holy and true, dost thou not judge and avenge our blood on them that dwell on the earth?" (6:10).[27] Powerless martyrs plead their causes *coram Deo* ("please Lord, avenge our blood!"), bringing all their grievances to him, even expecting to see the destruction of the enemy with their very own eyes. Seeing and watching and gazing in apocalyptic literature is very important. It heals the wounded soul. Those who were struck by oppressive anger shall see Jesus coming and trampling the tyrants of the earth. Jesus the Messiah will then be clothed with a vesture dripping from

---

26. See As. Mos. 9.6–7 (probably dating from first-century C.E. Palestina). The Levite Taxo under suppressive circumstances said to his seven sons: "Here is what we shall do. We shall fast for a three-day period and on the fourth day we will go into a cave, which is in the open country. There let us die rather than transgress the commandments of the Lord of Lords, the God of our fathers. For if we do this, and do die, our blood will be avenged before the Lord" (J. Priest, "Testament of Moses," OTP 1:931). See also Johannes Tromp, *The Assumption of Moses: A Critical Edition with Commentary* (SVTP 10; Leiden: Brill, 1993). See Norbert J. Hofmann, *Die Assumptio Mosis: Studien zur Rezeption massgültiger Überlieferung* (JSJSup 67; Leiden: Brill, 2000).

27. Nota bene, the cry is negative: "How long dost thou *not*!?" See also 4 Ezra 4:35 ("Did not the souls of the righteous in their chambers ask about the matters, saying, 'How long are we to remain here? And when will come the harvest of our reward?'" [this verse is non-Christian]; Bruce M. Metzger, "The Fourth Book of Ezra," OTP 1:531); 1 En. 9:3 ("the souls of people are putting their case before you pleading, 'Bring our judgment before the Most High'") and 10 ("and those who have died will bring their suit up to the gate of heaven. Their groaning has ascended"); 47:2 ("Their prayers shall not stop from exhaustion before the Lord of the Spirits—neither will they relax forever—[until] judgment is executed for them"), 104:3 ("Cry for judgment, and it shall appear for you; for all your tribulations shall be [demanded] for investigation from the [responsible] authorities—from everyone who assisted those who plundered you"; see also Luke 18:1–7; quotations from 1 Enoch from E. Isaac, OTP 1:13–89); Ascen. Isa. 9.24–27.

hostile blood.[28] The oppressors, utterly helpless in turn, shall see their victims ascend to heaven.[29] Vindication and rehabilitation acted out by God mean stripping the powerful of his or her might and openly showing the treatment of disgrace to the meek and lowly. God dramatically chooses the side of the abused, hurt, and scandalously treated, so they will feel safe.[30]

The powerful has to fully succumb to God and feel powerless. This is a most essential dimension of the κρίμα the Christian martyrs in Rev 20 finally and happily receive.[31] They will be comforted and glad. Tertullian really exults in the prospective sight of the enemy biting the bullet. Almost ecstatically he cheers at the idea of doomsday. In his exposition about Christians visiting theaters and games, Tertullian lauds the only uproar Christians may attend: the spectacle of the *eschaton*, the final end of time, when Jesus enters the secular scene. The church leader writes:

> Yes, and there are still to come other spectacles—that last, that eternal Day of judgment, that Day which the Gentiles never believed would come, that Day they laughed at, when this old world and all its generations shall be consumed in one fire. How vast the spectacle that day, and how wide! What sight shall wake my wonder, what my laughter, my joy and exultation? As I see all those kings, those great kings, welcomed (we were told) in heaven, along with Jove, along with those who told of their ascent, groaning in the depths of darkness! And the magistrates who persecuted the name of Jesus, liquefying in fiercer flames than they kindled in their rage against the Christians![32]

Tertullian, quite unnecessarily, draws a horrific, almost Dante-like picture of the eschatological end. Interesting to our subject is the complete turning of facts announced in early Christian (and Jewish) texts concerning martyrs and martyrdom. A voluntary Christian martyr was not defeated at all. According to the martyr's perception, one sacrificed oneself, giving Satan and his pomp

---

28. Rev 19:13; see also Isa 63:3. Note God's vehemence in searching the blood of the martyrs. He breaks the murderous city Babylon into three pieces (Rev 16:19) and finds the blood of all those who were slaughtered in her (Rev 18:23). The city was drunk on the holy blood of the innocent (Rev 17:6). Those who will be rejected by God deserve their fate (Rev 16:6: ἄξιοί εἰσιν). Because of their bloodshed, God gives them blood to drink (Rev 16:6).

29. Rev 11:11; see also Ps 23:5; Luke 16:19–31; 1 En. 108:14, 15.

30. See Judith Lewis Herman, *Trauma and Recovery: The Aftermath of Violence—From Domestic Abuse to Political Terror* (New York: Basic Books, 1992).

31. Rev 20:4; see also 17:1 and 18:20 (see also Dan 7:9, 27; Luke 22:30; 1 Cor 6:2).

32. Tertullian, *Spect.* 30 (Glover, LCL).

a deathblow, crushing diabolical heads under foot. I call this phenomenon a mysterious early Christian enigma—it is the paradox of the power of the seemingly pathetic martyr. Brutality, anger, and hostility toward martyrs did not affect their power, because Christian power in the torture chambers was spiritualized into a prognostic kind of fantasy vision.[33] Animosity in the end will fly back and explode in the intruders' own faces. Their future is portrayed in terms of fear and pain and darkness and blood and constant remorse. Here I think we clearly notice remains of sublimated Christian rage, at least: not of God's fury and hostility.

"When you feel so powerless, what are you gonna do?" We should not sacrifice ourselves in an act of blind hatred, supposing God to rehabilitate us. Self-sacrifice is the ultimate weapon in the hands of the powerless, but it is a dangerous weapon. We all know that. We ought to rethink voluntary martyrdom, Christian martyrdom as well, because of the devastating consequences it can have at home, in the church, but also in culture and society. Suicidal terror is a wrong though powerful way of saying "I am powerless." The principal answer to this usually religious problem is to give back power to sincere and wise powerless people and to show certain respect to the identity of the devotees of other systems. A little respect betwixt differing populations in multiethnic society helps to maintain social balance.

---

33. See Ernest G. Bormann, "Fantasy and Rhetorical Vision: The Rhetorical Criticism of Social Reality," *Quarterly Journal of Speech* 58 (1972): 396–407; idem, "Fantasy and Rhetorical Vision: Ten Years Later," *Quarterly Journal of Speech* 68 (1982): 288–305; idem, "A Fantasy Theme Analysis of the Television Coverage of the Hostage Release and the Reagan Inaugural," *Quarterly Journal of Speech* 68 (1982): 133–45.

Assessment—Animosity, the Bible, and Us: A Few Tentative Remarks

Herrie F. van Rooy

At the end of his volume, it is fitting to look back at a process that started late in 2003, with a final result in this volume. The project brought together scholars from different continents and countries, all interested in the problem of animosity. We live in a world where animosity and violence have become endemic. One can only look at the dire situation in Iraq, the never-ending (so it seems) circle of violence in Israel and the Palestinian territories, the many conflicts in Africa and elsewhere in the world to recognize the truth of this statement. The aim of this project was to look at what the Bible has to say in this regard. Only some of the papers read at three conferences were selected for inclusion in this volume. This volume cannot claim to have spoken the final word in this regard. We will have to struggle with this problem in our time, and the struggle will undoubtedly continue for years to come.

However, this volume hopes to make a contribution to understanding the problem better and, in some small way, to contribute toward finding solutions. It is clear from the studies presented here that this problem has been with humankind from early on. Animosity is reflected in the writings contained in the Bible, as well as in writings from the world of the Bible, as can be seen from the contribution of Eben Scheffler as well as in most of the other contributions. In the first book of the Bible, the first murder is described, as discussed by Eric Peels. Testimonies to enemies occur even in the headings of that very old collection of songs, the book of Psalms. References to animosity and enemies abound in all the genres of the Bible. Marius Nel refers to apocalyptic literature, Herrie van Rooy to the Psalms, Eveline van Staalduine-Sulman to targumic literature, Rainer Reuter to the Acts of the Apostles, Jeremy Punt to the Letters of Paul in general, Fritz Krüger to the Letter to the Colossians, Outi Leppä to Hebrews, Fika J. van Rensburg to 1 Peter, Dirk van der Merwe to the Johannine Epistles, and Paul Decock to Revelation. Animosity occurred in the households, as discussed by John T. Fitzgerald, and the early church had to struggle with this problem as well, as indicated by Henk Bakker.

Many books and specific passages are, however, not covered by this volume. Other papers read at various meetings of the research group are not included in this volume. Many of them will be published elsewhere, testifying to the work done by a greater group than those whose contributions are included. It was impossible to include all the contributions in one volume. The editors want to express their gratitude to all the participants, whose contributions made the three meetings unforgettable. In the end, we had to make a choice, deciding inter alia not to include more than one paper of any single participant. Some scholars read two or three papers with valuable insights, but the restrictions of space made the selection inevitable.

Work in this field will continue, looking at texts and hermeneutics. Our hope is that this volume will be a stimulus for further research and discussions. Especially the implications of these studies for our world and our time need further exploration. May we indeed experience more universal peace in our time.

Bibliography

Aalen, Sverre. " 'Reign' and 'House' in the Kingdom of God: Supplement: 'Kingdom' and 'House' in Pre-Christian Judaism." *NTS* 8 (1961): 215–40.

Achenbach, Reinhard. "Das Heiligkeitsgesetz und die sakralen Ordnungen des Numeribuches." Paper presented at the Colloquium Biblicum Lovaniense. Louvain, August 2006.

———. *Die Vollendung der Tora. Studien zur Redaktionsgeschichte des Numeribuches im Kontext von Hexateuch und Pentateuch.* Wiesbaden: Harrassowitz, 2003.

Achtemeier, Paul J. *1 Peter: A Commentary on First Peter.* Hermeneia. Minneapolis: Fortress, 1996.

Achtemeier, Paul J., Joel B. Green, and Marianne M. Thompson. *Introducing the New Testament: Its Literature and Theology.* Grand Rapids: Eerdmans, 2001.

Acta Divi Augusti. Rome: Ex officina typographica R. Academiae italicae, 1945.

Adams, John. "The Familial Image in Rhetoric." *CQ* 31 (1983): 56–61.

Aland, Barbara, Kurt Aland, Johannes Karavidopoulos, Carlo M. Martini, and Bruce M. Metzger, eds. *The Greek New Testament.* 4th ed. Stuttgart: Deutsche Bibelgesellschaft, 1993.

Amidon, Philip R., trans. *Philostorgius: Church History.* SBLWGRW 23. Atlanta: Society of Biblical Literature, 2007.

Anderson, Arnold A. *The Book of Psalms.* 2 vols. NCB. London: Oliphants, 1972.

Anderson, George W. "Enemies and Evildoers in the Book of Psalms." *BJRL* 48 (1965–66): 18–29.

Anderson, Robert A. *Signs and Wonders: A Commentary on the Book of Daniel.* ITC. Grand Rapids: Eerdmans, 1984.

Argall, Randal A., Beverly Bow, and Rodney Alan Werline, eds. *For a Later Generation: The Transformation of Tradition in Israel, Early Judaism, and Early Christianity.* Harrisburg, Pa.: Trinity Press International, 2000.

Ariarajah, S. Wesley. *The Bible and People of Other Faiths.* RISK book series. Geneva: World Council of Churches, 1985.

Arndt, William F., and F. Wilbur Gingrich. *A Greek-English Lexicon of the New Testament and Other Early Christian Literature.* Chicago: University of Chicago Press, 1957.

Arnold, Clinton E. *The Colossian Syncretism: The Interface between Christianity and Folk Belief at Colossae.* Tübingen: Mohr Siebeck, 1995.

———. *Ephesians, Power and Magic: The Concept of Power in Ephesians in the Light of Its Historical Setting.* SNTSMS 63. Cambridge: Cambridge University Press, 1989.

Asad, Talal. *Genealogies of Religion: Discipline and Reasons of Power in Christianity and Islam.* Baltimore: Johns Hopkins University Press, 1993.
Astour, Michael C. "Melchizedek (Person)." *ABD* 4:684–86.
Attridge, Harold W. *The Epistle to the Hebrews: A Commentary on the Epistle to the Hebrews.* Hermeneia. Philadelphia: Fortress, 1989.
———. "Hebrews, Epistle to the." *ABD* 3:97–105.
———. "On Becoming an Angel: Rival Baptismal Theologies at Colossae." Pages 481–89 in *Religious Propaganda and Missionary Competition in the New Testament World: Essays Honouring Dieter Georgi.* Edited by Lukas Bormann, Kelly Del Tredici, and Angela Standhartinger. Leiden: Brill, 1994.
Attridge, Harold W., John J. Collins, and Thomas Tobin, eds. *Of Scribes and Scrolls: Studies on the Hebrew Bible, Intertestamental Judaism and Christian Origins.* Lanham, Md.: University Press of America, 1990.
Aune, David E. *The New Testament and Its Literary Environment.* Philadelphia: Westminster, 1987.
———. *Revelation 1–5.* WBC 52A. Dallas: Word, 1997.
———. *Revelation 17–22.* WBC 52C. Dallas: Word, 1998.
———. *The Westminster Dictionary of New Testament and Early Christian Literature and Rhetoric.* Louisville: Westminster John Knox, 2003.
Azevedo, Joaquim. "At the Door of Paradise: A Contextual Interpretation of Gen 4:7." *BN* 100 (1999): 45–59.
Bakel, Hendrik Anthonie van. "Het Credo van Wulfila." Pages 86–113 in idem, *Circa Sacra: Historische Studiën.* Haarlem: Willink, 1935.
Bakker, Henk. "*Exemplar Domini:* Ignatius of Antioch and His Martyrological Self-Concept." Ph.D. diss., University of Groningen, 2003.
———. "Potamiaena: Some Observations about Martyrdom and Gender in Ancient Alexandria." Pages 331–50 in *The Wisdom of Egypt: Jewish, Early Christian and Gnostic Essays in Honour of Gerard P. Luttikhuizen.* Edited by Anthony Hilhorst and George H. van Kooten. Leiden: Brill, 2005.
———. *"Ze hebben lief, maar worden vervolgd": Radicaal christendom in de tweede eeuw en nu.* Zoetermeer: Het Boekencentrum, 2005.
Balch, David L. *Let Wives Be Submissive: The Domestic Code in 1 Peter.* SBLMS 26. Chico, Calif.: Scholars Press, 1981.
Balla, Peter. *The Child-Parent Relationship in the New Testament and Its Environment.* WUNT 155. Tübingen: Mohr Siebeck, 2003.
Ballhorn, Egbert. "'Um deines Knechtes David willen' (Ps 132,1): Die Gestalt Davids im Psalter." *BN* 76 (1995): 16–31.
Barclay, William. *The Revelation of John.* 2nd ed. 2 vols. Edinburgh: Saint Andrews, 1960.
Barmash, Pamela. *Homicide in the Biblical World.* New York: Cambridge University Press, 2005.
Barnett, Paul. "Polemical Parallelism: Some Further Reflections on the Apocalypse." *JSNT* 35 (1989): 111–20.
Barrett, Charles K. *A Critical and Exegetical Commentary on the Acts of the Apostles.* 2 vols. ICC. Edinburgh: T&T Clark, 1994–98.

———. "Light on the Holy Spirit from Simon Magus (Acts 8,4–25)." Pages 281–95 in *Les Actes des Apôtres: Traditions, rédaction, théologie*. Edited by Jacob Kremer. BETL 48. Leuven: Leuven University Press, 1979.
Bauckham, Richard. *The Bible in Politics: How to Read the Bible Politically*. London: SPCK, 1989.
———. "The Economic Critique of Rome in Revelation 18." Pages 338–83 in *The Climax of Prophecy: Studies on the Book of Revelation*. Edited by Richard Bauckham. Edinburgh: T&T Clark, 1993.
Bauer, Walter, Barbara Aland, and Kurt Aland. *Griechisch-deutsches Wörterbuch zu den Schriften des Neuen Testaments und der frühchristlichen Literatur*. 6th ed. Berlin: de Gruyter, 1988.
Bauernfeind, Otto. *Die Apostelgeschichte*. THKNT 5. Leipzig: Deichert, 1939.
Bauman, Clarence. *Gewaltlosigkeit im Täufertum: Eine Untersuchung zur theologischen Ethik des oberdeutschen Täufertums der Reformationszeit*. Leiden: Brill, 1968.
Beare, Francis Wright. *The First Epistle of Peter*. Oxford: Blackwell, 1958. 3rd ed. Oxford: Blackwell, 1970.
Beck, Norman A. *Mature Christianity in the 21st Century: The Recognition and Repudiation of the Anti-Jewish Polemic in the New Testament*. Rev. ed. Shared Ground among Jews and Christians 5. New York: Crossroad, 1994.
Becking, Bob. "Abel הבל." *DDD*, 3–4.
———. "Cain קין." *DDD*, 343–44.
Bedke, Michael A. Foreword to American Bar Association Commission on Domestic Violence, *A Guide for Employers: Domestic Violence in the Workplace*. Washington, D.C.: American Bar Association, 1999.
Bekkenkamp, Jonneke, and Yvonne Sherwood, eds. *Sanctified Aggression: Legacies of Biblical and Post-biblical Vocabularies of Violence*. JSOTSup 400. Bible in the Twenty-First Century 3. London: T&T Clark, 2003.
Berger, Adolf. "Peregrinus." Pages 626–27 in idem, *Encyclopedic Dictionary of Roman Law*. TAPS 64.2. Philadelphia: American Philosophical Society, 1953.
Best, Ernest. *1 Peter*. NCB. Grand Rapids: Eerdmans, 1971.
Betz, Hans Dieter. "De Fraterno Amore (Moralia 478A–492D)." Pages 231–63 in *Plutarch's Ethical Writings and Early Christian Literature*. Edited by Hans Dieter Betz. SCHNT 4. Leiden: Brill, 1978.
———. *Galatians*. Hermeneia. Minneapolis: Fortress, 1979.
Bidez, Joseph. *Philostorgius Kirchengeschichte*. Leipzig: Hinrich, 1913.
Bigg, Charles. *A Critical and Exegetical Commentary on the Epistles of St. Peter and St. Jude*. ICC. Edinburgh: T&T Clark, 1910.
Birkeland, Harris. *The Evildoers in the Book of Psalms*. Avhandliger utgitt ar Det Norske Videnskaps-Akademi i Oslo. II. Hist.-Filos. Klasse. 1955. No. 2. Oslo: Dybwad, 1955.
Bisbee, Gary A. *Pre-Decian Acts of Martyrs and Commentarii*. HDR 22. Philadelphia: Fortress, 1988.
Black, Matthew. *The Book of Enoch or 1 Enoch: A New English Edition with Commentary and Textual Notes*. SVTP 7. Leiden: Brill, 1985.
Blass, Friedrich, Albert Debrunner, and Robert W. Funk. *A Greek Grammar of the*

New Testament and Other Early Christian Literature. Chicago: University of Chicago Press, 1961.
Blenkinsopp, Joseph. "A Post-exilic Lay Source in Genesis 1–11." Pages 49–61 in *Abschied vom Jahwisten: Die Komposition des Hexateuch in der jüngsten Diskussion*. Edited by Jan Christian Gertz, Konrad Schmid, and Markus Witte. BZAW 315. Berlin: de Gruyter, 2002.
Bloemendaal, W. *The Headings of the Psalms in the East Syrian Church*. Leiden: Brill, 1960.
Boccaccini, Gabriele. *Beyond the Essene Hypothesis: The Partings of the Ways between Qumran and Enochic Judaism*. Grand Rapids: Eerdmans, 1998.
———. *Middle Judaism: Jewish Thought, 300 BCE to 200 CE*. Minneapolis: Fortress, 1991.
———. *Roots of Rabbinic Judaism*. Grand Rapids: Eerdmans, 2002.
———, ed. *Enoch and Qumran Origins: New Light on a Forgotten Connection*. Grand Rapids: Eerdmans, 2005.
Bogart, John. *Orthodox and Heretical Perfectionism in the Johannine Community as Evident in the First Epistle of John*. SBLDS 33. Missoula, Mont.: Scholars Press, 1977.
Bormann, Ernest G. "Fantasy and Rhetorical Vision: Ten Years Later." *Quarterly Journal of Speech* 68 (1982): 288–305.
———. "Fantasy and Rhetorical Vision: The Rhetorical Criticism of Social Reality." *Quarterly Journal of Speech* 58 (1972): 396–407.
———. "A Fantasy Theme Analysis of the Television Coverage of the Hostage Release and the Reagan Inaugural." *Quarterly Journal of Speech* 68 (1982): 133–45.
Boshoff, Willem S., Eben H. Scheffler, and Izak Spangenberg. *Ancient Israelite Literature in Context*. Pretoria: Protea, 2000.
Botha, J. Eugene. "Simple Salvation, but Not a Straw Jacobean Soteriology." Pages 389–408 in *Salvation in the New Testament: Perspectives on Soteriology*. Edited by Jan G. van der Watt. NovTSup 121. Leiden: Brill, 2005.
Botha, Pieter J. J. "Submission and Violence: Exploring Gender Relations in the First-Century World." *Neot* 34 (2000): 1–38.
Botterweck, G. Johannes, and Helmer Ringgren, eds. *Theologisches Wörterbuch zum Alten Testament*. Stuttgart: Kohlhammer, 1970–.
Bovon, François. "The Child and the Beast: Fighting Violence in Ancient Christianity." *HTR* 92 (1999): 369–92.
Bowker, J. W. "Cosmology, Religion and Society." *Zygon* 25 (1990): 7–23.
Brenner, Athalya. "Some Reflections on Violence against Women and the Image of the Hebrew God: The Prophetic Books Revisited." Pages 69–81 in *On the Cutting Edge: The Study of Women in Biblical Worlds: Essays in Honor of Elisabeth Schüssler Fiorenza*. Edited by Jane Schaberg, Alice Bach, and Esther Fuchs. New York: Continuum, 2003.
Breytenbach, J. Cilliers. "Facets of Diaspora Judaism." Pages 327–74 in *The New Testament Milieu*. Vol. 2 of *Guide to the New Testament*. Edited by Andrie B. du Toit. Pretoria: Kerkboekhandel, 1998.
Briggs, Charles A. *The Book of Psalms*. 2 vols. ICC. Edinburgh: T&T Clark, 1906–7.
Bright, John. *The Authority of the Old Testament*. Grand Rapids: Baker, 1975.

Brock, Sebastian P. *Catalogue of Syriac Fragments (New Finds) in the Library of the Monastery of Saint Catherine, Mount Sinai*. Athens: Mount Sinai Foundation, 1995.
Brongers, Hendrik A. "Die Rache- und Fluchpsalmen im Alten Testament." Pages 21–42 in *Studies on Psalms*. Edited by P. A. H. de Boer. OtSt 13. Leiden: Brill, 1963.
Brooks, Walter Edward. "The Perpetuity of Christ's Sacrifice in the Epistle to the Hebrews." *JBL* 89 (1970): 205–14.
Broughton, T. Robert S. *Roman Asia Minor*. Baltimore: Johns Hopkins University Press, 1938.
Brown, Raymond E. *The Community of the Beloved Disciple: The Life, Loves and Hates of an Individual Church in New Testament Times*. London: Chapman, 1979.
———. *The Epistles of John*. AB 30. Garden City, N.Y.: Doubleday, 1982.
Bruce, F. F. *The Epistles of John*. London: Pickering & Inglis, 1970.
Brueggemann, Walter. *Genesis*. Interpretation. Atlanta: John Knox, 1982.
———. *Theology of the Old Testament. Testimony, Dispute, Advocacy*. Minneapolis: Fortress, 1997.
Buchanan, George Wesley. *To the Hebrews: Translation, Comment and Conclusions*. AB 36. Garden City, N.Y.: Doubleday, 1972.
Bultmann, Rudolf. *The Gospel of John*. Translated by G. R. Beasley-Murray. Oxford: Blackwell, 1971.
Burns, J. Patout, ed. *War and Its Discontents: Pacifism and Quietism in the Abrahamic Traditions*. Washington, D.C.: Georgetown University Press, 1996.
Cadbury, Henry James. *The Making of Luke-Acts*. London: SPCK, 1968.
Caldwell, Richard. *The Origin of the Gods: A Psychoanalytical Study of Greek Theogonic Myth*. New York: Oxford University Press, 1989.
Calvin, John. *Hebrews and I and II Peter*. Translated by William B. Johnston. Grand Rapids: Eerdmans, 1963.
Campbell, David A. *Greek Lyric Poetry: A Selection of Early Greek Lyric, Elegiac and Iambic Poetry*. London: Macmillan, 1967.
Cassuto, Umberto. *From Adam to Noah: Genesis I–VI 8*. Vol. 1 of *A Commentary on the Book of Genesis*. Jerusalem: Magnes, 1961.
Castelli, Elizabeth A. *Imitating Paul: A Discourse of Power*. LCBI. Louisville: Westminster John Knox, 1991.
Chadwick, Henry, trans. *Saint Augustine: Confessions*. New York: Oxford University Press, 1991.
Charlesworth, James H., ed. *The Old Testament Pseudepigrapha*. 2 vols. New York: Doubleday, 1983–85.
Chazon, Esther G., and Michael E. Stone, eds. *Pseudepigraphic Perspectives: The Apocrypha and Pseudepigrapha in Light of the Dead Sea Scrolls*. STDJ 31. Leiden: Brill, 1999.
Childs, Brevard S. *Introduction to the Old Testament as Scripture*. London: SCM, 1979.
———. "Psalm Titles and Midrashic Exegesis." *JSS* 16 (1971): 137–50.
Chopra, Deepak. *Peace Is the Way: Bringing War and Violence to an End*. London: Rider, 2005.

Clark, Patricia. "Women, Slaves, and the Hierarchies of Domestic Violence: The Family of St. Augustine." Pages 109–29 in *Women and Slaves in Greco-Roman Culture: Differential Equations*. Edited by Sandra R. Joshel and Sheila Murnaghan. London: Routledge, 1998.

Clarke, Ernest G. *Targum Pseudo-Jonathan: Deuteronomy*. ArBib 5B. Edinburgh: T&T Clark, 1998.

Coetzee, J. C. "The Letters of John." Pages 201–226 in *The Gospel of John; Hebrews to Revelation: Introduction and Theology*. Vol. 6 of *Guide to the New Testament*. Edited by Andrie B. du Toit. Halfway House: Kerkboekhandel, 1993.

Cohen, Shaye J. D., ed. *The Jewish Family in Antiquity*. BJS 289. Atlanta: Scholars Press, 1993.

Coleman, Kathleen M. "Fatal Charades: Roman Executions Staged as Mythological Enactments," *JRS* 80 (1990): 44–73.

Collins, Adela Yarbro. "Apocalyptic Themes in Biblical Literature." *Int* 53 (1999): 117–30.

———. *The Combat Myth in the Book of Revelation*. HDR 9. Missoula, Mont.: Scholars Press, 1976.

———. *Crisis and Catharsis: The Power of the Apocalypse*. Philadelphia: Westminster, 1984.

———. "Persecution and Vengeance in the Book of Revelation." Pages 729–49 in *Apocalypticism in the Mediterranean World and the Near East: Proceedings of the International Colloquium on Apocalypticism, Uppsala, August 12–17, 1979*. Edited by David Hellholm. Tübingen: Mohr Siebeck, 1983.

———. Review of Leonard L. Thompson. *The Book of Revelation: Apocalypse and Empire*. *JBL* 110 (1991): 748–50.

Collins, C. John. "כבד." *NIDOTTE* 2:577–87.

Collins, John J. *The Apocalyptic Imagination: An Introduction to the Jewish Matrix of Christianity*. New York: Crossroad, 1984. 2nd ed. Grand Rapids: Eerdmans, 1998.

———. *Apocalypticism in the Dead Sea Scrolls*. London: Routledge, 1997.

———. "Cosmos and Salvation: Jewish Wisdom and Apocalyptic in the Hellenistic Age." *HR* 17 (1977): 121–42.

———. "From Prophecy to Apocalypticism: The Expectation of the End." Pages 64–88 in *The Continuum History of Apocalypticism*. Edited by Bernard J. McGinn, John J. Collins, and Stephen J. Stein. New York: Continuum, 2003.

———. "The Meaning of 'The End' in the Book of Daniel." Pages 91–98 in *Of Scribes and Scrolls: Studies in the Hebrew Bible, Intertestamental Judaism and Christian Origins*. Edited by Harold W. Attridge, John J. Collins, and Thomas H. Tobin. Lanham, Md.: University Press of America, 1990.

———. "Pseudepigraphy and Group Formation in Second Temple Judaism." Pages 43–58 in *Pseudepigraphic Perspectives: The Apocrypha and Pseudepigrapha in Light of the Dead Sea Scrolls*. Edited by Esther G. Chazon and Michael E. Stone. STDJ 31. Leiden: Brill, 1999.

———. "Response: The Apocalyptic Worldview of Daniel." Pages 59–66 in *Enoch and Qumran Origins: New Light on a Forgotten Connection*. Edited by Gabriele Boccaccini. Grand Rapids: Eerdmans, 2005.

———. *Seers, Sybils and Sages in Hellenistic-Roman Judaism.* JSJSup 54. Leiden: Brill, 1997.
Collins John J., and Peter W. Flint, eds. *The Book of Daniel. Composition and Reception.* 2 vols. Boston: Brill, 2001.
Conzelmann, Hans. *Die Apostelgeschichte.* 2nd ed. HNT 7. Tübingen: Mohr Siebeck, 1972.
Cook, Philip W. *Abused Men: The Hidden Side of Domestic Violence.* Westport, Conn.: Praeger, 1997.
Cosgrove, William. "The Emotions in the Moral Life," *Doctrine and Life* 55 (2005): 12–20.
Craig, Kenneth M. "Questions outside Eden (Genesis 4.1–16): Yahweh, Cain and Their Rhetorical Interchange." *JSOT* 86 (1999): 107–28.
Craigie, Peter C. *Psalms 1–50.* WBC 19. Waco, Tex.: Word, 1982.
Cross, Frank M. *The Ancient Library at Qumrân and Modern Biblical Studies.* Rev. ed. Garden City, N.Y.: Doubleday, 1961.
Cullmann, Oscar. *The Johannine Circle.* Translated by John Bowden. London: SCM, 1976.
Culpepper, R. Allan. *The Gospel and Letters of John.* Nashville: Abingdon, 1998.
———. *The Johannine School: An Evaluation of the Johannine School Hypothesis Based on an Investigation of the Nature of Ancient Schools.* SBLDS 26. Missoula, Mont.: Scholars Press, 1975.
Cupitt, Don. *The Sea of Faith: Christianity in Change.* London: BBC, 1984.
D'Angelo, Mary Rose. *Moses in the Letter to the Hebrews.* SBLDS 42. Missoula, Mont.: Scholars Press, 1976.
Dahl, Nils A. *Studies in Paul. Theology for the Early Christian Mission.* Minneapolis: Augsburg, 1977.
Dahood, Mitchell. *Psalms: Introduction, Translation, and Notes.* 3 vols. AB 16–17A. Garden City, N.Y.: Doubleday, 1966–70.
Danker, Frederick W., ed. *Greek English Lexicon of the New Testament and Other Early Christian Literature.* 3rd ed. Chicago: University of Chicago Press, 2000.
Davids, Peter H. *The First Epistle of Peter.* NICNT. Grand Rapids: Eerdmans, 1990.
Dawkins, Richard. *The God Delusion.* London: Bantam, 2006.
Decock, Paul B. "The Symbol of Blood in the Apocalypse of John." *Neot* 38 (2004): 157–82.
Deist, Ferdinand E. *Die Noodlottige Band: Kerk en Staat in Oud-Israel.* Kaapstad: Tafelberg, 1975.
Delitzsch, Franz. *Biblische Kommentar über die Psalmen.* Leipzig: Dörffling & Franke, 1894.
Delling, Gerhard. "μάγος, μαγεία, μαγεύω." *TDNT* 4:356–59.
Denniston, John D. *The Greek Particles.* Oxford: Clarendon, 1934.
deSilva, David A. "Despising Shame: A Cultural-Anthropological Investigation of the Epistle to the Hebrews." *JBL* 113 (1994): 439–61.
Desjardins, Michel R. *Peace, Violence and the New Testament.* Biblical Seminar 46. Sheffield: Sheffield Academic Press, 1997.
Deurloo, Karel. *Genesis.* Kampen: Kok, 1998.

———. *Kain en Abel. Onderzoek naar exegetische methode inzake een 'kleine literaire eenheid' in de Tenakh*. Amsterdam: Ten Have, 1967.
———. *De mens als raadsel en geheim: Verhalende antropologie in Genesis 2–4*. Baarn: Ten Have, 1988.
Devreesse, Robert. *Le Commentaire de Théodore de Mopsueste sur les Psaumes (I–LXXX)*. Studi e Testi 93. Cittádel Vaticana: Biblioteca Apostolica Vaticana, 1939.
Dibelius, Martin. *Aufsätze zur Apostelgeschichte*, FRLANT 42. Göttingen: Vandenhoeck & Ruprecht, 1968.
Dietrich, Walter. "'Wo ist dein Bruder?' Zu Tradition und Intention von Genesis 4." Pages 94–111 in *Beiträge zur Alttestamentlichen Theologie: Festschrift für Walther Zimmerli zum 70. Geburtstag*. Edited by Herbert Donner, Robert Hanhart, and Rudolf Smend. Göttingen: Vandenhoeck & Ruprecht, 1977.
Díez Merino, Luis. "Exculpación-Inculpación: Principio de exegesis Targúmica desconocido en la hermenéutica judia oficial." Pages 441–76 in *III Simposio Bíblico Español (I Luso-Espanhol)*. Edited by J. Carreira das Neves et al. Valencia-Lisboa: Fundación Bíblica Española, 1991.
———. "Translation of Proper Names: A Targumic Method of Hermeneutics in Targum Esther." Pages 203–23 in *Targum and Scripture: Studies in Aramaic Translations and Interpretation in Memory of Ernest G. Clarke*. Edited by Paul V. M. Flesher. SAIS 2. Leiden: Brill, 2002.
Dijk, Teun A. van. "Introduction: Levels and Dimensions of Discourse Analysis." Pages 1–12 in *Dimensions of Discourse*. Vol. 2 of *Handbook of Discourse Analysis*. Edited by Teun A. Van Dijk. London: Academic Press, 1985.
———. "Semantic Discourse Analysis." Pages 103–36 in *Dimensions of Discourse*. Vol. 2 of *Handbook of Discourse Analysis*. Edited by Teun A. Van Dijk. London: Academic Press, 1985.
Dixon, Suzanne. *The Roman Family*. Baltimore: Johns Hopkins University Press, 1992.
Dodd, Charles H. *The Johannine Epistles*. London: Hodder & Stoughton, 1953.
Dodds, Eric R. *Pagan and Christian in an Age of Anxiety*. Cambridge: Cambridge University Press, 1965.
Doran, Robert. *Birth of a Worldview: Early Christianity in its Jewish and Pagan Context*. Boulder, Colo.: Westview, 1995.
Dozeman, Thomas B., and Konrad Schmid, eds. *A Farewell to the Yahwist? The Composition of the Pentateuch in Recent European Interpretation*. SBLSymS 34. Atlanta: Society of Biblical Literature, 2006.
Droge, Arthur J., and James D. Tabor, *A Noble Death: Suicide and Martyrdom Among Christians and Jews in Antiquity*. San Francisco: HarperCollins, 1992.
Du Plessis, P. J. *Die Briewe van Johannes*. Kaapstad: Kerk-Uitgewers, 1978.
Du Toit, Andrie B. "Vilification as a Pragmatic Device in Early Christian Epistolography." *Bib* 75 (1994): 403–12.
Du Toit, Cornel W., ed., *Violence, Truth and Prophetic Silence*. Pretoria: Research Institute for Theology and Religion, Unisa, 1999.
Duling, Dennis C. *The New Testament: History, Literature, and Context*. Belmont, Calif.: Wadsworth Thompson, 2003.

Dunn, James D. G. *The Epistle to the Galatians*. BNTC. Peabody, Mass.: Hendrickson, 1993.
Dunnill, John. *Covenant and Sacrifice in the Letter to the Hebrews*. SNTSMS 75. Cambridge: Cambridge University Press, 1992.
Dyk, Peet van. "Violence and the Old Testament." *OTE* 16 (2003): 96–112.
Edwards, Ruth B. *The Johannine Epistles*. New Testament Guides. Sheffield: Sheffield Academic Press, 1996.
Eemeren, Frans H. van, Rob Grootendorst, Sally Jackson, and Scott Jacobs. "Argumentation." Pages 208–29 in *Discourse as Structure and Process*. Vol. 1 of *Discourse Studies: A Multidisciplinary Introduction*. Edited by Teun A. van Dijk. London: Sage, 1997.
Einstein, Albert. *Über den Frieden: Weltordnung oder Weltuntergang*. Edited by Otto Nathan and Heinz Norden. Neu Isenburg: Melzer, 2004.
Eliade, Mircea. *Cosmos and History: The Myth of the Eternal Return*. Translated by Willard R. Trask. Princeton: Princeton University Press, 1965.
Elliott, John H. "1 Peter, Its Situation and Strategy: A Discussion with David Balch." Pages 61–78 in *Perspectives on First Peter*. Edited by Charles H. Talbert. Macon, Ga.: Mercer University Press, 1986.
———. *A Home for the Homeless: A Sociological Exegesis of 1 Peter, Its Situation and Strategy*. Philadelphia: Fortress, 1981.
———. "The Rehabilitation of an Exegetical Step-Child: 1 Peter in Recent Research." *JBL* 95 (1976): 243–54.
Elliott, Neil. "Paul and the Politics of Empire: Problems and Prospects." Pages 17–39 in *Paul and Politics: Ekklesia, Israel, Imperium: Essays in Honor of Krister Stendahl*. Edited by Richard A. Horsley. Harrisburg, Pa.: Trinity Press International, 2000.
Esler, Philip F. *The First Christians in Their Social World: Social-Scientific Approaches to New Testament Interpretation*. London: Routledge, 1994.
———. "'Keeping It in the Family': Culture, Kinship and Identity in 1 Thessalonians and Galatians." Pages 145–84 in *Families and Family Relations as Represented in Early Judaisms and Early Christianities: Texts and Fictions*. Edited by Jan Willem van Henten and Athalya Brenner. Leiden: Deo, 2000.
Eusebius. *Ecclesiastical History*. Translated by Kirsopp Lake and John E. L. Oulton. 2 vols. LCL. Cambridge: Harvard University Press, 1980.
Evans, Craig A. "The Colossian Mystics." *Bib* 63 (1982): 188–205.
Fagles, Robert., trans. *Homer, The Iliad*. New York: Penguin, 1990.
Family Violence Prevention Fund. "Get the Facts." Online: http://endabuse.org.
Feldmeier, Reinhard. *Die Christen als Fremde: Die Metapher der Fremde in der antiken Welt, im Urchristentum und im 1.Petrusbrief*. Tübingen: Mohr Siebeck, 1992.
Ferguson, Everett. *Backgrounds of Early Christianity*. Grand Rapids: Eerdmans, 1987. 3rd ed., 2003.
Festinger, Leon, Henry W. Riecken, and Stanley Schachter. *When Prophecy Fails: A Social and Psychological Study of a Modern Group That Predicted the Destruction of the World*. New York: Harper, 1956.
Filson, Floyd V. "First John: Purpose and Message." *Int* 23 (1969): 259–76.

———. *'Yesterday': A Study of Hebrews in the Light of Chapter 13*. SBT 2/4. London: SCM, 1967.

Fitzgerald, Allan D. "Thagaste." Pages 824–25 in *Augustine through the Ages: An Encyclopedia*. Edited by Allan D. Fitzgerald. Grand Rapids: Eerdmans, 1999.

Fitzgerald, John T. "Early Christian Missionary Practice and Pagan Reaction: 1 Peter and Domestic Violence against Slaves and Wives." Pages 24–44 in *Renewing Tradition: Studies in Honor of James W. Thompson*. Edited by Mark W. Hamilton, Thomas H. Olbricht, and Jeffrey Peterson. Princeton Theological Monograph Series; Eugene, Ore.: Pickwick, 2007.

———. "Proverbs 3:11–12, Hebrews 12:5–6, and the Tradition of Corporal Punishment." Pages 291–317 in *Scripture and Traditions: Essays on Early Judaism and Christianity in Honor of Carl R. Holladay*. Edited by P. Gray and G. R. O'Day. NovTSup 129. Leiden: Brill, 2008.

Flach, Dieter. "Die römischen Christenverfolgungen: Gründe und Hintergründe." *Historia* 48 (1999): 442–64.

Flesher, Paul V. M., and R. Torry, "Filming Jesus: Between Authority and Heresy." *SBL Forum*. Online: http://www.sbl-site.org/Article.aspx?ArticleId=226.

Fox, E. "Stalking The Younger Brother: Some Models for Understanding a Biblical Motif." *JSOT* 60 (1993): 45–68.

Francis, Fred O. "The Background of *Embateuein* (Col 2:18) in Legal Papyri and Oracle Inscriptions." Pages 197–207 in *Conflict at Colossae: A Problem in the Interpretation of Early Christianity Illustrated by Selected Modern Studies*. Edited by Fred O. Francis and Wayne A. Meeks. SBLSBS 4. Missoula, Mont.: Scholars Press, 1975.

Fredrickson, David E. "Παρρησία in the Pauline Epistles." Pages 163–83 in *Friendship, Flattery, and Frankness of Speech*. Edited by John T. Fitzgerald. NovTSup 82. Leiden: Brill, 1996.

Friedman, Mordechai A. "Tamar, A Symbol of Life: The 'Killer Wife' Superstition in the Bible and Jewish Tradition." *AJSR* 15 (1990): 23–61.

Friesen, Steven J. "Myth and Symbolic Resistance in Revelation 13." *JBL* 123 (2004): 281–313.

Gantz, Timothy. *Early Greek Myth: A Guide to Literary and Artistic Sources*. Baltimore: Johns Hopkins University Press, 1993.

García Martínez, Florentino. "Apocalypticism in the Dead Sea Scrolls." Pages 89–111 in *The Continuum History of Apocalypticism*. Edited by Bernard J. McGinn, John J. Collins, and Stephen J. Stein. New York, London: Continuum, 2003.

Garrett, Susan R. *The Demise of the Devil. Magic and Demonic in Luke's Writings*. Minneapolis: Fortress, 1989.

———. "Sociology of Early Christianity." *ABD* 6:89–99.

Geertz, Clifford. *The Interpretation of Cultures*. London: Hutchinson, 1973.

Georgi, Dieter. *Theocracy in Paul's Praxis and Theology*. Translated by David E. Green. Minneapolis: Fortress, 1991.

Gerber, Douglas E., ed. and trans. *Greek Elegiac Poetry: From the Seventh to the Fifth Centuries BC*. LCL 258. Cambridge: Harvard University Press, 1999.

———, ed. and trans. *Greek Iambic Poetry: From the Seventh to the Fifth Centuries BC*. LCL 259. Cambridge: Harvard University Press, 1999.
Gerleman, Gillis. "*slm*, genug haben." *ThWAT* 2:919–35.
Gerstenberger, Erhard S. *Psalms, Part 2, and Lamentations*. FOTL 15. Grand Rapids: Eerdmans, 2001.
Ghandi, Mohandas Karamchand. *An Autobiography: The Story of My Experiments with Truth*. Boston: Beacon, 1993.
Giesen, Heinz. *Die Offenbarung des Johannes*. RNT. Regensburg: Pustet, 1997.
Goleman, Daniel. *Emotional Intelligence: Why It Can Matter More Than IQ*. London: Bloomsbury, 1996.
———. *Working with Emotional Intelligence*. London: Bloomsbury, 1999.
Golka, Friedemann W. "Keine Gnade für Kain." Pages 58–73 in *Werden und Wirken des Alten Testaments: Festschrift für Claus Westermann zum 70. Geburtstag*. Edited by Rainer Albertz et al. Göttingen: Vandenhoeck & Ruprecht; Neukirchen-Vluyn: Neukirchener, 1980.
Goold, G. P., ed. and trans. *Chariton: Callirhoe*. LCL 481. Cambridge: Harvard University Press, 1995.
Goosen, L. *Van Abraham tot Zacharia: Thema's uit het Oude Testament in religie, beeldende kunst, literatuur, muziek en theater*. Nijmegen: SUN, 1990.
Goppelt, Leonhard. *Der erste Peterbrief*. 8th ed. Göttingen: Vandenhoeck & Ruprecht, 1978.
Gordon, Robert. *Holy Land, Holy City: Sacred Geography and the Interpretation of the Bible*. Carlisle: Paternoster, 2004.
Görg, Manfred. "Kain und das 'Land Nod.'" *BN* 71 (1994): 5–12.
Gowan, Donald E. *From Eden to Babel: A Commentary on the Book of Genesis 1–11*. ITC. Grand Rapids: Eerdmans, 1988.
Grabbe, Lester L. *Judaic Religion in Second Temple Judaism*. London: Routledge, 2000.
Graetz, Naomi. "Rejection: A Rabbinic Response to Wife Beating." Pages 13–23 in *Gender and Judaism: The Transformation of Tradition*. Edited by Tamar M. Rudavsky. New York: New York University Press, 1995.
———. *Silence Is Deadly: Judaism Confronts Wifebeating*. Northvale, N.J.: Aronson, 1998.
Graf, Fritz. "Ephesia Grammata." *DNP* 3:1076–77.
Grant, Frederick C. *Roman Hellenism and the New Testament*. Edinburgh: Oliver & Boyd, 1962.
Grayston, Kenneth. *The Johannine Epistles*. NCBC. Grand Rapids: Eerdmans, 1984.
Green, William S. "Otherness Within: Towards a Theory of Difference in Rabbinic Judaism." Pages 49–69 in *To See Ourselves as Others See Us. Christians, Jews, "Others" in Late Antiquity*. Edited by Jacob Neusner, Ernest S. Frerichs, and Caroline McCracken-Flesher. Chico, Calif.: Scholars, 1985.
Gruber, Mayer I. "Was Cain Angry or Depressed?" *BAR* 6.6 (1980): 35–36.
Grudem, Wayne. *1 Peter*. TNTC. Grand Rapids: Eerdmans, 1988.
Gunkel, Herrman. *Genesis*. HKAT. Göttingen: Vandenhoeck & Ruprecht, 1902.

———. *Schöpfung und Chaos im Urzeit und Endzeit*. Göttingen: Vandenhoeck & Ruprecht, 1895.
Guthrie, Donald. *New Testament Theology*. Leicester: Inter-Varsity Press, 1981.
Hackett, JoAnn. "Violence and Women's Lives in the Book of Judges." *Int* 58 (2004): 356–64.
Haenchen, Ernst. *Die Apostelgeschichte*. 7th ed. KEK 3. Göttingen: Vandenhoeck & Ruprecht, 1977.
Hallett, Judith P. *Fathers and Daughters in Roman Society: Women and the Elite Family*. Princeton: Princeton University Press, 1984.
Hamilton, Victor. *The Book of Genesis. Chapters 1–17*. NICOT. Grand Rapids: Eerdmans, 1990.
Hanson, Paul D. "War and Peace in the Hebrew Bible." *Int* 38 (1984): 341–62.
Harnack, Adolf von. *Marcion: Das Evangelium vom fremden Gott*. 2nd ed. Leipzig: Hinrichs, 1924. Repr., Darmstadt: Wissenschaftliche Buchgesellschaft, 1960.
Harrington, Daniel J., and Anthony J. Saldarini. *Targum Jonathan of the Former Prophets: Introduction, Translation and Notes*. ArBib 10. Edinburgh: T&T Clark, 1987.
Harris, William V. *Restraining Rage: The Ideology of Anger Control in Classical Antiquity*. Cambridge: Harvard University Press, 2001.
———. "The Roman Father's Power of Life and Death." Pages 81–95 in *Studies in Roman Law in Memory of A. Arthur Schiller*. Edited by Roger. S. Bagnall and William V. Harris. Columbia Studies in the Classical Tradition 13. Leiden: Brill, 1986.
Hartney, Aideen M. *Gruesome Deaths and Celibate Lives: Christian Martyrs and Ascetics*. Exeter: Bristol Phoenix, 2005.
Hauser, Alan J. "Linguistic and Thematic Links between Genesis 4:1–16 and Genesis 2–3." *JETS* 23 (1980): 297–305.
Hays, Richard B. *The Moral Vision of the New Testament: A Contemporary Introduction to New Testament Ethics*. San Francisco: HarperSanFrancisco, 1996.
Hayward, C. T. R. "Inconsistencies and Contradictions in Targum Pseudo-Jonathan: The Case of Eliezer and Nimrod." *JSS* 37 (1992): 31–55.
———. "A Portrait of the Wicked Esau in the Targum of Codex Neofiti 1." Pages 291–309 in *The Aramaic Bible: Targums in Their Historical Context*. Edited by D. R. G. Beattie and Martin J. McNamara. JSOTSup 166. Sheffield: JSOT Press, 1994.
Hellholm, David. "The Problem of Apocalyptic Genre and the Apocalypse of John." *Semeia* 36 (1986): 13–64.
Hendel, Ronald S. "When Gods Act Immorally." Pages 16–25 and 310–11 in *Approaches to the Bible: The Best of Bible Review*. Edited by Harvey Minkoff. Washington, D.C.: Biblical Archeology Society, 1995.
Hengel, Martin. *Judaism and Hellenism: Studies in Their Encounter in Palestine during the Early Hellenistic Period*. 2 vols. Philadelphia: Fortress, 1974.
Herion, Gary A. "Why God Rejected Cain's Offering: The Obvious Answer." Pages 52–65 in *Fortunate the Eyes That See: Essays in Honor of David Noel Freedman in Celebration of His Seventieth Birthday*. Edited by Astrid B. Beck et al. Grand Rapids: Eerdmans, 1995.
Herzer, Jens. *Petrus oder Paulus? Studien über das Verhältnis der Ersten Petrusbriefes zur paulinischen Tradition*. Tübingen: Mohr Siebeck, 1998.

Hesse, Hermann. *Lektüre für Minuten I.* Frankfurt am Main: Suhrkamp, 1971.
———. *Lektüre für Minuten: Neue Folge.* Frankfurt am Main: Suhrkamp, 1976.
Hiebert, D. Edmond. "An Expositional Study of 1 John." *Bibliotheca Sacra* 145 (1988): 329–42.
Hill, Robert C., trans. *Theodore of Mopsuestia: Commentary on Psalms 1–81.* SBLW-GRW 5. Atlanta: Society of Biblical Literature, 2006.
Hoffecker, W. Andrew. "Preface: Perspective and Method in Building a World View." Pages ix–xvi in *God, Man and Knowledge.* Vol. 1 of *Building a Christian World View.* Edited by W. Andrew Hoffecker. Phillipsburg: Presbyterian & Reformed, 1986.
Hofmann, Norbert J. *Die Assumptio Mosis: Studien zur Rezeption massgültiger Überlieferung.* JSJSup 67. Leiden: Brill, 2000.
Horrell, David G. *Solidarity and Difference: A Contemporary Reading of Paul's Ethics.* London: T&T Clark, 2005.
Horsley, Richard A. "Social Relations and Social Conflict in the *Epistle of Enoch*." Pages 100–115 in *For a Later Generation: The Transformation of Tradition in Israel, Early Judaism, and Early Christianity.* Edited by Randal A. Argall, Beverly Bow, and Rodney Alan Werline. Harrisburg, Pa.: Trinity Press International, 2000.
Houtman, Alberdina. "Doom and Promise in the Targum of Isaiah," *JJS* 49 (1998): 17–23.
———. "Sin and Illness in the Targum of the Prophets." Pages 195–206 in *Purity and Holiness: The Heritage of Leviticus.* Edited by Marcel J. H. M. Poorthuis and Joshua Schwartz. Leiden: Brill, 1999.
Houtman, Alberdina, and Eveline van Staalduine-Sulman. "Joden, christenen en hun Targum." Pages 147–60 in *Joden, christenen en hun Schrift: Een bundel opstellen aangeboden bij het afscheid van C. J. den Heyer.* Edited by C. Houtman and L. J. Lietaert Peerbolte. Baarn: Ten Have, 2001.
Hubbard, Thomas K. "Elemental Psychology and the Date of Semonides of Amorgos." *AJP* 115 (1994): 175–97.
Hughes, Philip Edgcumbe. *A Commentary on the Epistle to the Hebrews.* Grand Rapids: Eerdmans, 1977.
Hunter, Virginia J. *Policing Athens: Social Control in the Attic Lawsuits, 420–320 B.C.* Princeton: Princeton University Press, 1994.
Hurst, Lincoln D. *The Epistle to the Hebrews: Its Background of Thought.* SNTSMS 65. Cambridge: Cambridge University Press, 1990.
Hurtado, Larry. *Lord Jesus Christ: Devotion to Jesus in Earliest Christianity.* Grand Rapids: Eerdmans, 2003.
Isaac, E., trans. "1 Enoch." *OTP* 1:13–89.
Jacob, Benno. *Das Buch Genesis.* Berlin: Schocken, 1934. Repr., Stuttgart: Calwer, 2000.
Janowski, Bernd. "Jenseits von Eden: Gen 4,1–16 und die nichtpriesterliche Urgeschichte." Pages 137–59 in *Die Dämonen Demons: Die Dämonologie der israelitisch-jüdischen und frühchristlichen Literatur im Kontext ihrer Umwelt.* Edited by Armin Lange, Hermann Lichtenberger, and Diethard Römheld. Tübingen: Mohr Siebeck, 2003.

Jaubert, Annie. "Le calendrier des Jubilés et de la secte de Qumrân: Ses origenes bibliques." *VT* (1953): 250–64.
Jervell, Jacob. *Die Apostelgeschichte.* KEK 3. Göttingen: Vandenhoeck & Ruprecht, 1998.
Jewett, Robert. "Response: Exegetical Support from Romans and Other Letters. Pages 58–71 in *Paul and Politics: Ekklesia, Israel, Imperium, Interpretation: Essays in Honor of Krister Stendahl.* Edited by Richard A. Horsley. Harrisburg: Trinity Press International, 2000.
Johnson, Luke Timothy. "The New Testament's Anti-Jewish Slander and the Conventions of Ancient Polemic." *JBL* 108 (1989): 419–41.
———. *The Writings of the New Testament. An Interpretation.* Minneapolis: Fortress, 1986. 2nd ed., 1999.
Johnson, Thomas F. *1, 2, and 3 John.* NIBC. Peabody, Mass.: Hendrikson, 1993.
Jones, Amos, Jr. *Paul's Message of Freedom: What Does It Mean to the Black Church?* Valley Forge, Pa.: Judson, 1984.
Jonge, Marinus de. "Variety and Development in Johannine Christology." Pages 193–213 in idem, *Jesus: Stranger from Heaven and Son of God: Jesus Christ and the Christians in Johannine Perspective.* SBLSBS 11. Missoula, Mont.: Scholars Press, 1977.
Justin Martyr. *Second Apology.* ANF 1:188–93.
Kant, Immanuel. *Perpetual Peace, and Other Essays on Politics, History and Moral Practice.* Indianapolis: Hackett, 1983.
Käsemann, Ernst. *The Testament of Jesus.* Translated by Gerhard Krodel. Philadelphia: Fortress, 1978.
Kasher, Rimon. *Toseftot of the Targum to the Prophets.* SSJC 2. Jerusalem: World Union of Jewish Studies, 1996.
Keel, Othmar. *Feinde und Gottesleugner: Studien zum Image der Widersacher in den Individualpsalmen.* SBM 7. Stuttgart: Verlag Katholisches Bibelwerk, 1969.
Keener, Craig S. *The Gospel of John: A Commentary.* 2 vols. Peabody, Mass.: Hendrickson, 2003.
Kelly, J. N. D. *A Commentary on the Epistles of Peter and Jude.* London: Black, 1969.
Kendall, David W. "The Literary and Theological Function of 1 Peter 1:3–12." Pages 103–20 in *Perspectives on First Peter.* Edited by Charles H. Talbert. Macon, Ga.: Mercer University Press, 1986.
Kennedy, George A., trans. *Invention and Method: Two Rhetorical Treatises from the Hermogenic Corpus.* SBLWGRW 15. Atlanta: Society of Biblical Literature, 2005.
Kenney, Garrett C. *Leadership in John. An Analysis of the Situation and Strategy of the Gospel and the Epistles of John.* Lanham, Md.: University Press of America, 2000.
———. *The Relation of Christology to Ethics in the First Epistle of John.* Lanham, Md.: University Press of America, 2000.
Kerényi, Carl [Karl]. *Zeus and Hera: Archetypal Image of Father, Husband, and Wife.* Bollingen Series 65:5. Princeton: Princeton University Press, 1975.
Kittel, Gerhard, and Gerhard Friedrich, eds. *Theological Dictionary of the New Testament.* Translated by Geoffrey W. Bromiley. 10 vols. Grand Rapids: Eerdmans, 1964–76.

Klauck, Hans-Josef. *Magie und Heidentum in der Apostelgeschichte des Lukas*. SBS 167. Stuttgart: Katholisches Bibelwerk, 1996.
———. "Zur rhetorischen Analyse der Johannesbriefe," *ZNW* 81 (1990): 205–24.
Kloppenborg, John S. "The Transformation of Moral Exhortation in *Didache* 1–5." Pages 88–109 in *The Didache in Context: Essays on Its Text, History, and Transmission*. Edited by Clayton N. Jefford. Leiden: Brill, 1995.
Klopper, Frances. "Doodstraf in Ou-Testamentiese Perspektief." M.A. thesis, University of Port Elizabeth, 1988.
Knibb, Michael A., trans. "Martyrdom and Ascension of Isaiah." *OTP* 2:156–76.
Koch, Dietrich Alex. "Geistbesitz und Wundermacht: Erwägungen zur Tradition und zur lukanischen Redaktion in Acts 8,5–25." *ZNW* 77 (1986): 64–82.
Koch, Klaus. "עוז." *ThWAT* 5:1160–77.
Koester, Craig R. *Hebrews: A New Translation with Introduction and Commentary*. AB 36. New York: Doubleday, 2001.
Koester, Helmut. *History, Culture and Religion of the Hellenistic Age*. New York: de Gruyter, 1995.
———. "'Outside the Camp': Hebrews 13.9–14." *HTR* 55 (1962): 299–315.
Kopperschmidt, Josef. "An Analysis of Argumentation." Pages 159–68 in *Dimensions of Discourse*. Vol. 2 of *Handbook of Discourse Analysis*. Edited by Teun A. van Dijk. London: Academic Press, 1985.
Kraus, Hans-Joachim. "Krieg im AT." *RGG* 4:64–65.
———. *Psalm 1–59*. Vol. 1 of *Psalmen*. 5th ed. BKAT 15.1. Neukirchen-Vluyn: Neukirchener, 1978.
———. *Theologie der Psalmen*. Neukirchen-Vluyn: Neukirchener, 2003.
Kraybill, J. Nelson. *The Imperial Cult and Commerce in John's Apocalypse*. JSNTSup 132. Sheffield: Sheffield Academic Press, 1996.
Krijger, Ph. L. *De tragiek van de schepping: Het geding rondom Marcion in de Nederlandse theologie van de twintigste eeuw*. Zoetermeer: Boekencentrum, 2005.
Kruijf, G. G. de. "Give Place unto Wrath!" Pages 115–29 in vol. 2 of *Christian Faith and Violence*. Studies in Reformed Theology 11. Edited by Dirk van Keulen and Martien Brinkman. Zoetermeer: Meinema, 2006.
LaCocque, Andre. *The Book of Daniel*. Translated by David Pellauer. London: SPCK, 1979.
Lake, Kirsopp, and Henry J. Cadbury. *English Translation and Commentary*. Vol. 4 of *The Acts of the Apostles*, part 1 of *The Beginnings of Christianity*. Edited by F. J. Foakes Jackson and Kirsopp Lake. London: McMillan, 1933.
Lane, William L. *Hebrews 1–8*. WBC 47A. Dallas: Word, 1991.
Lane Fox, Robin. *Pagans and Christians in the Mediterranean World from the Second Century AD to the Conversion of Constantine*. London: Penguin, 1986.
Lang, Carl, ed. *Cornuti theologiae graecae compendium*. Bibliotheca scriptorum Graecorum et Romanorum Teubneriana. Leipzig: Teubner, 1881.
Lange, Armin. "Dream Visions and Apocalyptic Milieus." Pages 27–34 in *Enoch and Qumran Origins: New Light on a Forgotten Connection*. Edited by Gabriele Boccaccini. Grand Rapids: Eerdmans, 2005.
Lassen, Eva M. "The Roman Family: Ideal and Metaphor." Pages 103–20 in *Construct-

ing Early Christian Families: Family as Social Reality and Metaphor. Edited by Halvor Moxnes. London: Routledge, 1997.

Laurence, Richard, trans. *The Book of Enoch the Prophet.* Oxford: Parker, 1821; 2nd ed., 1833; 3rd ed., 1838.

———, ed., *Libri Enoch prophetae versio aethiopica.* Oxford: Typis Academicis, 1838.

Lawrence, D. H. *Apocalypse.* Florence: Orioli, 1931.

Lee, Samuel. *Vetus Testamentum Syriace.* London: Bible Society, 1823.

Lehne, Susanne. *The New Covenant in Hebrews.* JSNTSup 44. Sheffield: JSOT Press, 1990.

Lehrman, S. M., trans. *Exodus.* Vol. 3 of *Midrash Rabbah.* Edited by H. Freedman and M. Simon. 3rd ed. 10 vols. London: Soncino, 1983.

Lepelley, Claude. *Les cités de l'Afrique romaine au bas-empire.* 2 vols. Paris: Études Augustiniennes, 1979–81.

Leppä, Outi. "Animosity in Early Christian Debates about the Jewish Food Rules." Paper presented at the European Association of Biblical Studies Annual Meeting, Dresden, 8 August 2005.

———. *The Making of Colossians: A Study on the Formation and Purpose of a Deutero-Pauline Letter.* Publications of the Finnish Exegetical Society 86. Helsinki: Finnish Exegetical Society; Göttingen: Vandenhoeck & Ruprecht, 2003.

Levine, Étan. *The Aramaic Version of the Bible: Contents and Context.* BZAW 174. Berlin: de Gruyter, 1988.

Lewis Herman, Judith. *Trauma and Recovery: The Aftermath of Violence—From Domestic Abuse to Political Terror.* New York: Basic Books, 1992.

Liedke, Gerhard. *Gestalt und Bezeichnung alttestamentlicher Rechtssätze. Eine formgeschichtlich–terminologische Studie.* WMANT 39. Neukirchen-Vluyn: Neukirchener, 1971.

Lieu, Judith. *The Second and Third Epistles of John: History and Background.* Studies of the New Testament and Its World. Edinburgh: T&T Clark, 1986.

———. *The Theology of the Johannine Epistles.* Cambridge: Cambridge University Press, 1991.

Lindars, Barnabas. *The Theology of the Letter to the Hebrews.* New Testament Theology. Cambridge: Cambridge University Press, 1991.

Lindberg, Gertrud. "Hera in Homer to Ancient and Modern Eyes: The Nagging Wife, the Evil Seductress, or the Forceful Goddess in the Struggle for Power?" Pages 65–80 in *Greek and Latin Studies in Memory of Cajus Fabricius.* Edited by Sven-Tage Teodorsson. Göteborg: Acta Universitatis Gothoburgensis, 1990.

Lindgård, Fredrik. *Paul's Line of Thought in 2 Corinthians 4:16–5:10.* WUNT 2/189. Tübingen: Mohr Siebeck, 2005.

Lintott, Andrew. *Violence, Civil Strife and Revolution in the Classical City: 750–330 BC.* London: Croom Helm, 1982.

———. *Violence in Republican Rome.* 2nd ed. Oxford: Oxford University Press, 1999.

Lipiński, Edward. "קנה." *ThWAT* 7:63–71.

Lloyd-Jones, Hugh. *Females of the Species: Semonides on Women.* London: Duckworth, 1975.

Loader, James A. "Was Isaiah a Quietist?" *OTWSA* 22–23 (1979–80): 130–42.

Lohse, Eduard. *Colossians and Philemon: A Commentary on the Epistles to the Colossians and to Philemon.* Translated by William R. Poehlmann and Robert J. Karris. Hermeneia. Philadelphia: Fortress, 1971.

———. *The New Testament Environment.* Nashville: Abingdon, 1976.

———. "Paränese und Kerygma im 1. Petrusbrief." *ZNW* 45 (1954): 68–89.

———. *Theological Ethics of the New Testament.* Translated by M. Eugene Boring. Minneapolis: Fortress, 1991.

Lonergan, Bernard. *Method in Theology.* 2nd ed. London: Darton, Longman & Todd, 1973.

Loseke, Donileen R., and Demie Kurz. "Men's Violence toward Women Is the Serious Social Problem." Pages 79–95 in *Current Controversies on Family Violence.* Edited by Donileen R. Loseke, Richard J. Gelles, and Mary M. Cavanaugh. 2nd ed. Thousand Oaks, Calif.: Sage, 2005.

Loubser, J. A. (Bobby). "D H Lawrence's Extra-ordinary 'Ordinary Reading' of the Apocalypse." *Neot* 38 (2004): 326–46.

Louw, Johannes P., and Eugene A. Nida, eds. *Greek-English Lexicon of the New Testament Based on Semantic Domains.* 2nd ed. 2 vols. New York: United Bible Societies, 1989.

Lüdemann, Gerd. *Das frühe Christentum nach den Traditionen der Apostelgeschichte: Ein Kommentar.* Göttingen: Vandenhoeck & Ruprecht, 1987.

Luz, Ulrich. "Der alte und der neue Bund bei Paulus und im Hebräerbrief." *EvT* 27 (1967): 318–36.

MacDonald, Margaret Y. *Colossians and Ephesians.* Sacra Pagina 17. Collegeville, Minn.: Liturgical Press, 2000.

Maguire, Katie. "Hellenism and the Jewish Afterlife." Online: http://classes.maxwell.syr.edu/his301-001/hellenistic_effects_on_judaic_li.htm.

Maher, M. *Targum Pseudo-Jonathan: Genesis.* ArBib 1B. Edinburgh: T&T Clark, 1992.

Malherbe, Abraham J. *Social Aspects of Early Christianity.* 2nd ed. Philadelphia: Fortress, 1983.

Malina, Bruce J. *Christian Origins and Cultural Anthropology: Practical Models for Biblical Interpretation.* Atlanta: John Knox, 1986.

———. *The New Testament World.* Philadelphia: Fortress, 1993.

———. "The Social Sciences in Biblical Interpretation." *Int* 37 (1982): 229–42.

———. *The Social World of Jesus and the Gospels.* London: Routledge, 1996.

Malina, Bruce J., and Jerome H Neyrey. "First-Century Personality: Dyadic, Not Individualistic." Pages 67–96 in *The Social World of Luke-Acts: Models for Interpretation.* Edited by Jerome H. Neyrey. Peabody, Mass.: Hendrickson, 1993.

Marshall, I. Howard. *1 Peter.* IVP New Testament Commentary Series. Leicester: Inter-Varsity Press.

Marti, Karl. *Das Buch Daniel.* HKAT 18. Tübingen: Mohr Siebeck, 1901.

Martin, Luther H. "The Anti-individualistic Ideology of Hellenistic Culture." *Numen* 41 (1994): 117–40.

Martyn, J. Louis. *History and Theology in the Fourth Gospel.* Nashville: Abingdon, 1979.

Marxsen, Willi. *New Testament Foundations for Ethics.* Minneapolis: Fortress, 1993.

Mathews, Kenneth A. *Genesis 1–11*. NAC. Nashville: Broadman & Holman, 2001.
Matthews, Shelly, and E. Leigh Gibson, eds. *Violence in the New Testament*. London: T&T Clark, 2005.
Mayor, Federico. "The Human Right to Peace." *Bulletin* 4 (1997): 1–2.
Mays, James L. "The David of the Psalms." *Int* 40 (1986): 143–55.
McCann, J. Clinton, ed. *The Shape and Shaping of the Psalter*. JSOTSup 159. Sheffield: Sheffield Academic Press, 1993.
McDonald, Mary Francis. *Lactantius: The Minor Works*. FC 54. Washington, D.C.: Catholic University of America Press, 1965.
McEntire, Mark H. *The Blood of Abel: The Violent Plot in the Hebrew Bible*. Macon, Ga.: Mercer University Press, 1999.
McGinn, Bernard J., John J. Collins, and Stephen J. Stein, eds. *The Continuum History of Apocalypticism*. New York: Continuum, 2003.
Meeks, Wayne A. "The Man from Heaven in Johannine Sectarianism," *JBL* 91 (1972): 44–72.
———. *The Moral World of the First Christians*. LEC. Louisville: Westminster John Knox, 1986.
Mellinkoff, Ruth. *The Mark of Cain*. Berkeley and Los Angeles: University of California Press, 1981.
Merwe, Dirk G. van der. "*Imitatio Christi* in the Fourth Gospel." *Verbum et Ecclesia* 22 (2001): 131–48.
———. "Perseverance through Suffering: A Spirituality for Mission." *Missionalia* 33 (2005): 329–54.
———. "Understanding 'Sin' in the Johannine Epistles." *Verbum et Ecclesia* 26 (2005): 543–70.
Metzger, Bruce M., trans. "The Fourth Book of Ezra." *OTP* 1:525–59.
Michaels, J. Ramsey. *1 Peter*. WBC 49. Waco, Tex.: Word, 1988.
Michel, Andreas. *Gott und Gewalt gegen Kinder im Alten Testament*. FAT 37. Tübingen: Mohr Siebeck, 2003.
Middleton, Paul. *Radical Martyrdom and Cosmic Conflict in Early Christianity*. Library of New Testament Studies 307. London: T&T Clark, 2006.
Milik, J. T. *The Books of Enoch: Aramaic Fragments of Qumran, Cave 4*. Oxford: Clarendon, 1976.
Millard, Matthias. *Die Komposition des Psalters: Ein formgeschichtliche Ansatz*. FAT 9. Tübingen: Mohr Siebeck, 1994.
Miller, James Maxwell, and John H. Hayes. *A History of Ancient Israel and Judah*. Philadelphia: Westminster, 1986.
Minucius Felix. *Octavius*. Translated by G. H. Rendall. LCL. Cambridge: Harvard University Press, 1931.
Moffatt, James. *A Critical and Exegetical Commentary on the Epistle to the Hebrews*. ICC. Edinburgh: T&T Clark, 1986.
Montefiore, Hugh. *A Commentary on the Epistle to the Hebrews*. BNTC. London: Black, 1964.
Moor, Johannes de. "The Sacrifice Which Is an Abomination to The Lord." Pages 211–26 in *Loven en geloven: Opstellen van Collega's en Medewerkers aangeboden*

aan Prof. Dr. Nic. H. Ridderbos. Edited by H. M. van Es et al. Amsterdam: Bolland, 1975.
Moore, Michael. *Will They Ever Trust Us Again? Letters from the War Zone*. London: Penguin, 2004.
Moule, C. F. D. "The Nature and Purpose of First Peter." *NTS* 3 (1956–57): 1–11.
Mowinckel, Sigmund. *Awän und die individuellen Klagepsalmen*. Vol. 1 of *Psalmenstudien*. Christiana: Dybwad, 1921.
Mukenge, André Kabasele. "Relecture de Gn 4,1–16 dans le contexte africain." Pages 421–41 in *Lectures et relectures de la Bible: Festschrift P.-M. Bogaert*. Edited by André Wénin and Jean-Marie Auwers. Leuven: Leuven University Press; Peeters, 1999.
Murray, A. T., trans. *Homer: The Odyssey*. 2 vols. LCL. London: Heinemann, 1919.
Musurillo, Herbert. *Acts of Christian Martyrs*. 2 vols. Oxford: Clarendon, 1972.
National Coalition against Domestic Violence. "Alabama Domestic Violence Facts." Online: http://www.ncadv.org/files/Alabama.pdf.
———. "Domestic Violence Facts: National Facts." Online: http://www.ncadv.org/files/DomesticViolenceFactSheet(National).pdf.
Nelson-Pallmeyer, Jack. *Is Religion Killing Us? Violence in the Bible and the Quran*. Harrisburg, Pa.: Trinity Press International, 2003.
Neufeld, Dietmar. *Reconceiving Texts as Speech Acts: An Analysis of 1 John*. BibInt 7. Leiden: Brill, 1994.
Neusner, Jacob. *Bavli Tractate Megillah*. Vol. 10 of *The Talmud of Babylonia: An Academic Commentary*. Atlanta: Scholars Press, 1995.
Nickelsburg, George W. E. *1 Enoch: A Commentary on the Book of 1 Enoch, Chapters 1–36; 81–108*. Hermeneia. Minneapolis: Fortress, 2001.
———. *Ancient Judaism and Christian Origins: Diversity, Continuity, and Transformation*. Minneapolis: Fortress, 2003.
Niditch, Susan. *War in the Hebrew Bible*. New York: Oxford University Press, 1993.
Nock, Arthur Darby. "Paul and the Magus." Pages 164–88 in *Additional Notes to the Commentary*. Vol. 5 of *The Acts of the Apostles*, part 1 of *The Beginnings of Christianity*. Edited by F. J. Foakes Jackson and Kirsopp Lake. London: McMillan, 1933.
O'Brien, Peter Thomas. *Colossians, Philemon*. WBC 44. Waco, Tex.: Word, 1982.
O'Meara, John J. *The Young Augustine: The Growth of St. Augustine's Mind up to His Conversion*. 2nd ed. New York: Alba House, 2001.
Oden, Robert A. "Cosmogony, Cosmology." *ABD* 1:1162–71.
Olson, Daniel. *Enoch: A New Translation*. North Richland Hills, Tex.: BIBAL, 2004.
Olson, S. Douglas. "The Return of the Father." Pages 161–83 in idem, *Blood and Iron: Stories and Storytelling in Homer's Odyssey*. Mnemosyne. Leiden: Brill, 1995.
Osiek, Carolyn. "Female Slaves, *Porneia*, and the Limits of Obedience." Pages 255–74 in *Early Christian Families in Context: An Interdisciplinary Dialogue*. Edited by Carolyn Osiek and David L. Balch. Religion, Marriage, and Family. Grand Rapids: Eerdmans, 2003.
Osiek, Carolyn, and David L. Balch. *Families in the New Testament World*. The Family, Religion, and Culture. Louisville: Westminster John Knox, 1997.

———, eds. *Early Christian Families in Context: An Interdisciplinary Dialogue.* Religion, Marriage, and Family. Grand Rapids: Eerdmans, 2003.
Otto, Eckart. *Krieg und Frieden in der Hebräischen Bibel und im Alten Orient: Aspekte für eine Friedensordnung in der Moderne.* Stuttgart: Kolhammer, 1999.
———. "שׁבע." *ThWAT* 7:1013–15.
Painter, John. *1, 2, and 3 John.* Collegeville, Minn.: Liturgical Press, 2002.
———. *John, Witness and Theologian.* London: SPCK, 1975.
Park, Eung Chun. *Either Jew or Gentile: Paul's Unfolding Theology of Inclusivity.* Louisville: Westminster John Knox, 2003.
Pathfinder on Domestic Violence in the United States. New York: Center on Crime, Communities & Culture, 1997.
Patte, Daniel. *Early Jewish Hermeneutic in Palestine.* SBLDS 22. Missoula Mont.: Scholars Press, 1975.
Paulus, C. "Cognitio." *DNP* 3:59–60.
Peels, Eric. *The Vengeance of God: The Meaning of the Root NQM and the Function of the NQM-Texts in the Context of Divine Revelation in the Old Testament.* OtSt 31. Leiden: Brill, 1995.
Pellizer, Ezio, and Gennaro Tedeschi, eds. *Semonides: Testimonia et Fragmenta.* Lyricorum Graecorum quae exstant 9. Rome: Edizioni dell'Ateneo, 1990.
Penner, Todd, and Caroline Vander Stichele. "Gendering Violence: Patterns of Power and Constructs of Masculinity in the Acts of the Apostles." Pages 193–209 in *A Feminist Companion to the Acts of the Apostles.* Edited by Amy-Jill Levine. FCNTECW 9. London: T&T Clark, 2004.
Perdue, Leo G., Joseph Blenkinsopp, John J. Collins, and Carol Meyers. *Families in Ancient Israel.* The Family, Religion, and Culture. Louisville: Westminster John Knox, 1997.
Perkins, Pheme. "Ethics: New Testament." *ABD* 2:652–65.
———. *The Johannine Epistles.* Wilmington, Del.: Glazier, 1979.
Perrett, Bryan. *The Taste of Battle: Front Line Action 1914–1991.* London: Cassel, 2000.
Peshitta Institute. *List of Old Testament Peshitta Manuscripts (Preliminary Issue).* Leiden: Brill, 1961.
Petersen, David L. "Genesis and Family Values." *JBL* 124 (2005): 5–23.
Petersen, Norman R. *Rediscovering Paul: Philemon and the Sociology of Paul's Narrative World.* Philadelphia: Fortress, 1978.
Pfitzner, Victor C. *Hebrews.* ANTC. Nashville: Abingdon, 1997.
Philo. Translated by F. H. Colson, G. H. Whitaker, J. W. Earp, and Ralph Marcus. 12 vols. LCL. London: Heinemann: 1929–61.
Pietersma, Albert. "David in the Greek Psalter." *VT* 30 (1980): 213–26.
Pilch, John J. "'Beat His Ribs While He Is Young' (Sir 30:12): A Window on the Mediterranean World." *BTB* 23 (1993): 101–13.
Piper, John. "Hope as the Motivation of Love: 1 Peter 3:9–12." *NTS* 26 (1980): 212–31.
Pippin, Tina. *Death and Desire: The Rhetoric of Gender in the Apocalypse of John.* LCBI. Louisville: Westminster John Knox, 1992.

Plummer, Alfred. *A Critical and Exegetical Commentary on the Second Epistle of St. Paul to the Corinthians.* ICC. Edinburgh: T&T Clark, 1915.
Plutarch. *Moralia.* Translated by F. C. Babbitt et al. 16 vols. in 15. LCL. London: Heinemann, 1927–76.
Polaski, Sandra Hack. *Paul and the Discourse of Power.* Gender, Culture, Theory 8. Sheffield: Sheffield Academic Press, 1999.
Pomeroy, Sarah B. *Families in Classical and Hellenistic Greece: Representations and Realities.* Oxford: Clarendon, 1997.
Porteous, Norman W. *Daniel: A Commentary.* 2nd ed. OTL. London: SCM, 1979.
Povinelli, Elizabeth A. "The State of Shame: Australian Multiculturalism and the Crisis of Indigenous Citizenship." *Critical Inquiry* 24 (1998): 575–610.
Poythress, Vern S. "The Use of the Intersentence Conjunctions 'de', 'oun', 'kai' and Asyndeton in the Gospel of John." *NovT* 26 (1984): 312–40.
Preuss, Horst D. *Israels Weg mit JHWH* Vol. 2 of *Theologie des Alten Testaments.* Stuttgart: Kohlhammer, 1992.
——— . "Die Psalmenüberschriften in Targum and Midrasch." *ZAW* 71 (1959): 44–54.
Priest, J., trans. "Testament of Moses." *OTP* 1:927–34.
Pritchard, James B., ed. *Ancient Near Eastern Texts Relating to the Old Testament.* Princeton: Princeton University Press, 1969.
Procksch, Otto. *Die Genesis.* Leipzig: Deichert, 1913.
Pulleyn, Simon. *Homer, Iliad, Book One.* New York: Oxford University Press, 2000.
Punt, Jeremy. "Enscripturalised Identity: Scripture and Identity in Christian Communities." *NGTT* 43 (2002): 83–93.
——— . "Paul and the Others: Insiders, Outsiders and Animosity." Paper presented at the annual meeting of the European Association of Biblical Studies, Budapest, August 2006.
——— . "Peace, Conflict and Religion in South Africa: Biblical Problems, Possibilities and Prospects." *Missionalia* 27 (1999): 263–98.
——— . "A Politics of Difference in the New Testament: Identity and the Others in Paul." Pages 199–225 in *The New Testament Interpreted: Essays in Honour of Bernard C. Lategan.* Edited by Cilliers Breytenbach, Johan C. Thom, and Jeremy Punt. NovTSup 124. Leiden: Brill, 2006.
Puukko, A. Filemon. "Die Feind in den alttestamentliche Psalmen." *OtSt* 8 (1950): 47–65.
Quasten, Johannes. *Patrology.* 3 vols. Westminster, Md.: Newman, 1950–60.
Quinones, Ricardo J. *The Changes of Cain: Violence and the Lost Brother in Cain and Abel Literature.* Princeton: Princeton University Press, 1991.
Rad, Gerhard von. *Der Heilige Krieg im alten Israel.* Zürich: Theologischer Verlag, 1951. ET: *Holy War in Ancient Israel.* Translated and edited by Marva J. Dawn. Grand Rapids: Eerdmans, 1991.
——— . *Die Theologie der geschichtlichen Überlieferungen Israels.* Vol. 1 of *Theologie des Alten Testaments.* Munich: Kaiser, 1961.
Rahlfs, Alfred. *Psalmi cum Odis.* 3rd ed. Vetus Testamentum Graecum 10. Göttingen: Vandenhoeck & Ruprecht, 1979.

Räisänen, Heikki. *Jesus, Paul and Torah: Collected Essays.* Translated by David E. Orton. JSNTSup 43. Sheffield: JSOT Press, 1992.

———. *Paul and the Law.* Philadelphia: Fortress, 1986.

Ramose, M. B. "Wisdom in War and Peace." Pages 151–78 in *After September 11: Globalisation, War and Peace.* Edited by Cornel W. du Toit and G. J. A Lubbe. Pretoria: Research Institute for Theology and Religion, Unisa, 2002.

Reicke, Bo. *The Epistles of James, Peter and Jude.* AB 37. Garden City, N.Y: Doubleday, 1964.

Reiser, Marius. "Numismatik und Neues Testament." *Bib* 81 (2000): 457–88.

Rensberger, David. *Johannine Faith and Liberating Community.* Philadelphia: Westminster, 1988.

Rensburg, Fika J. van. "Dekor of Konteks? Die verdiskontering van sosio-historiese gegewens in die interpretasie vir die prediking en pastoraat van 'n Nuwe Testamentteks, geïllustreer aan die hand van die 1 Peter-brief." *Skrif en Kerk* (2000): 564–82.

———. "Indikatief en paraklese in 1 Petrus en die implikasie daarvan vir die kerklike prediking vandag." *In die Skriflig* 24 (1990): 71–101.

Richard, Earl. "The Functional Christology of First Peter." Pages 121–39 in *Perspectives on First Peter.* Edited by Charles H. Talbert. Macon, Ga.: Mercer University Press, 1986.

Ridderbos, Herman N. *Aan de Kolossenzen.* Commentaar op het Nieuwe Testament. Kampen: Kok, 1960.

Ridderbos, Nicolaas H. *De Psalmen I.* KV. Kampen: Kok, 1962.

Riessen, Hendrik van. *Wijsbegeerte.* Kampen: Kok, 1970.

Robbins, Vernon K. *Exploring the Texture of Texts: A Guide to Socio-rhetorical Interpretation.* Valley Forge, Pa.: Trinity Press International, 1996.

Roberts, J. H. "Jewish Mystical Experience in the Early Christian Era as Background to Understanding Colossians." *Neot* 32 (1998): 161–89.

Rogerson, John W. "The Enemy in the Old Testament." Pages 284–93 in *Understanding Poets and Prophets: Essays in Honour of George Wishart Anderson.* JSOTSup 152. Edited by A. Graeme Auld. Sheffield: Sheffield Academic Press, 1993.

Roloff, Jürgen. *Die Apostelgeschichte.* 2nd ed. NTD 5. Göttingen: Vandenhoeck & Ruprecht, 1988.

———. *Die Kirche im Neuen Testament.* NTD, Ergänzungsreihe 10. Göttingen: Vandenhoeck & Ruprecht, 1993.

Rooy, Herrie F. van. "The Headings of the Psalms in the Dead Sea Scrolls." *JNSL* 28 (2002): 127–41.

———. "The Headings of the Psalms in the Two Syriac Versions of the Commentary of Athanasius." *OTE* 17 (2004): 659–77.

———. *Studies on the Syriac Apocryphal Psalms.* Journal of Semitic Studies Supplement 7. London: Oxford University Press, 1999.

Rosemond, John. "Proper Socialization Requires Powerful Love and Equally Powerful Discipline." Pages 131–36 *Current Controversies on Family Violence.* Edited by Donileen R. Loseke, Richard J. Gelles, and Mary M. Cavanaugh. 2nd ed. Thousand Oaks, Calif.: Sage, 2005.

Ross, Allen P. *Creation and Blessing: A Guide to the Study and Exposition of the Book of Genesis.* Grand Rapids: Baker, 1988.

Rousseau, Jacques A. "A Multidimensional Approach towards the Communication of an Ancient Canonized Text: Towards the Thrust, Perspective and Strategy of 1 Peter." Ph.D. diss., University of Pretoria, 1986.

Royalty, Robert M. *The Streets of Heaven: The Ideology of Wealth in the Apocalypse of John.* Macon, Ga.: Mercer University Press, 1998.

Ruppert, Lothar. *Gen 1,11–11,26.* Vol. 1 of *Genesis: Ein kritischer und theologischer Kommentar.* FB 70. Würzburg: Echter, 1992.

Rusam, Dietrich. *Die Gemeinschaft der Kinder Gottes: Das Motiv der Gotteskindschaft und die Gemeinden der johanneischen Briefe.* Stuttgart: Kohlhammer, 1993.

Russell, Donald A., and David Konstan, eds. and trans. *Heraclitus: Homeric Problems.* SBLWGRW 14. Atlanta: Society of Biblical Literature, 2005.

Sacchi, Paolo. *History of the Second Temple Period.* JSOTSup 285. Sheffield: Sheffield Academic Press, 2000.

Safrai, Shemuel. "Relations between the Diaspora and the Land of Israel." Pages 184–215 in *The Jewish People in the First Century: Historical Geography, Political History, Social, Cultural and Religious Life and Institutions.* Edited by Shemuel Safrai and Menahem Stern. CRINT 1.1. Assen: Van Gorcum, 1974.

Sainte Croix, G. E. M. de. "Why Were the Early Christians Persecuted?" *Past and Present* 26 (1963): 6–38.

Salisbury, Eve, Georgiana Donavin, and Merrall Llewelyn Price, eds. *Domestic Violence in Medieval Texts.* Gainesville: University of Florida Press, 2002.

Sals, Ulrike. *Die Biographie der "Hure Babylon": Studien zur Intertextualität der Babylon-Texte in der Bibel.* FAT 2/6. Tübingen: Mohr Siebeck, 2004.

Sanders, Jack T. *Schismatics, Sectarians, Dissidents, Deviants: The First One Hundred Years of Jewish-Christian Relations.* London: SCM, 1993.

Sandnes, Karl O. "Equality within Partriarchal Structures: Some New Testament Perspectives on the Christian Fellowship as a Brother- or Sisterhood and a Family." Pages 150–65 in *Constructing Early Christian Families: Family as Social Reality and Metaphor.* Edited by Halvor Moxnes. London: Routledge, 1997.

Sappington, Thomas J. *Revelation and Redemption at Colossae.* JSNTSup 53. Sheffield: JSOT Press, 1991.

Sarna, Nahum M. *Genesis.* JPS Torah Commentary. Philadelphia: Jewish Publication Society, 1989.

Schaefer, H. "Paroikoi." "Paroikoi," PW 18.4:1695–1707.

Schaik, Antonius P. van. *De Openbaring van Johannes.* Roermond: Romen, 1971.

Scharbert, Josef. *Genesis 1–11.* Würzburg: Echter, 1983.

Scheepers, Coenie, and Eben H. Scheffler. *From Dan to Beersheba: An Archaeological Tour through Ancient Israel.* Pretoria: Biblia, 2000.

Scheffler, Eben H. *Fascinating Discoveries from the Biblical World.* Pretoria: Biblia, 2000.

———. "Die Kommunikasie van die Gelykenis van die Barmhartige Samaritaan in Konteks." *HvTSt* (2001): 318–43.

———. Die nie al te wyse Salomo. *HvTSt* 60 (2004): 769–89.

———. *Politics in Ancient Israel*. Pretoria: Biblia, 2001.
———. "Saving Saul from the Deuteronomist." Pages 263–71 in *Past, Present and Future: The Deuteronomistic History and the Prophets*. Edited by Johannes C. de Moor and Herrie F. van Rooy. Leiden: Brill, 2000.
———. *Suffering in Luke's Gospel*. Zürich: Theologischer Verlag, 1993.
Schille, Gottfried. *Die Apostelgeschichte des Lukas*. THKNT 5. Berlin: Evangelische Verlagsanstalt, 1983.
Schlueter, Carol J. *Filling Up the Measure: Polemical Hyperbole in 1 Thessalonians 2.14–16*. JSNTSup 98. Sheffield: JSOT Press, 1994.
Schmithals, Walter. *Die Apostelgeschichte des Lukas*. ZBK 3.2. Zürich: Theologischer Verlag Zürich, 1982.
Schnackenburg, Rudolf. *The Johannine Epistles*. New York: Crossroad, 1992.
———. *The Moral Teaching of the New Testament*. Kent: Burns & Oates, 1982.
Schneider, Gerhard. *Die Apostelgeschichte*. 2 vols. HTKNT 5.1–2. Freiburg: Herder, 1980–82.
Schoedel, William R. "Ignatius, Epistles of." *ABD* 3:383–87.
Scholem, Gershom G. *Major Trends in Jewish Mysticism*. New York: Schocken, 1964.
Schroeder, Joy A. "John Chrysostom's Critique of Spousal Violence." *JECS* 12 (2004): 413–42.
Schulz, Siegfried. *Die Mitte der Schrift: Der Frühkatholizismus im Neuen Testament als Herausforderung an den Protestantismus*. Stuttgart: Kreuz, 1976.
Schunack, Gerd. *Der Hebräerbrief*. ZBNT 14. Zürich: Theologische Verlag, 2002.
Schürer, Emil. *The History of the Jewish People in the Age of Jesus Christ (175 B.C.–A.D. 135)*. Translated and edited by Geza Vermes, Fergus Millar, and Matthew Black. 3 vols. Edinburgh: T&T Clark, 1973–86.
Schüssler Fiorenza, Elisabeth. *The Book of Revelation: Justice and Judgment*. Philadelphia: Fortress, 1985.
———. "Paul and the Politics of Interpretation." Pages 40–57 in *Paul and Politics: Ekklesia, Israel, Imperium, Interpretation: Essays in Honor of Krister Stendahl*. Edited by Richard A. Horsley. Harrisburg: Trinity Press International, 2000.
———. *Revelation: Vision of a Just World*. Edinburgh: T&T Clark, 1993.
Schwager, Raymund. *Brauchen wir einen Sündenbock? Gewalt und Erlösung in den biblischen Schriften*. München: Kösel, 1978.
Schweizer, Eduard. "Das hellenistische Weltbild als Produkt der Weltangst." Pages 15–27 in *Neotestamentica: Deutsche und englische Aufsätze 1951–1963*. Edited by Eduard Schweizer. Zürich: Zwingli, 1963.
———. "σάρξ, σαρκικός, σάρκινος." *TDNT* 7:98–151.
———. σῶμα. *TDNT* 7:1024–94.
Seebass, Horst. *Urgeschichte (1,1–11,26)*. Vol. 1 of *Genesis*. Neukirchen-Vluyn: Neukirchener, 1996.
Seeliger, Hans Reinhard. "Märtyrerakten." Pages 411–19 in *Lexikon der antiken christlichen Literatur*. Edited by Siegmar Döpp and Wilhelm Geerlings. 2nd ed. Freiburg im Breisgau: Herder, 1999.
Seesemann, Heinrich. "πάλαι, παλαιός, παλαιότης, παλαιόω." *TDNT* 5:717–20.
Segal, Alan F. "Response: Some Aspects of Conversion and Identity Formation in the

Christian Community of Paul's Time." Pages 184-90 in *Paul and Politics: Ekklesia, Israel, Imperium, Interpretation: Essays in Honor of Krister Stendahl*. Edited by Richard A. Horsley. Harrisburg: Trinity Press International, 2000.

Selengut, Charles. *Sacred Fury: Understanding Religious Violence*. Walnut Creek, Calif.: AltaMira, 2003.

Selwyn, Edward G. *The First Epistle of St. Peter*. London: Macmillan, 1947.

Shaw, Brent D. "The Family in Late Antiquity: The Experience of Augustine." *Past and Present* 115 (1987): 3-51.

Shelton, Jo-Ann. *As the Romans Did: A Sourcebook in Roman Social History*. 2nd ed. New York: Oxford University Press, 1998.

Sherwin-White, A. N. "The Early Persecutions and Roman Law Again." *JTS* 3 (1952): 199-213.

Simon, Bennett. *Tragic Drama and the Family: Psychoanalytic Studies from Aeschylus to Beckett*. New Haven: Yale University Press, 1988.

Sizgorich, Thomas. "'Not Easily Were Stones Joined by the Strongest Bonds Pulled Asunder': Religious Violence and Imperial Order in the Later Roman World." *JECS* 15 (2007): 75-101.

Slater, Philip E. *The Glory of Hera: Greek Mythology and the Greek Family*. Boston: Beacon, 1968.

Smalley, Stephen S. *1, 2, 3 John*. WBC 51. Dallas: Word, 1984.

Smelik, Klaas. *Een tijd van oorlog, een tijd van vrede: Bezetting en bevrijding in de Bijbel*. Zoetermeer: Boekencentrum, 2005.

Smelik, Willem F. *The Targum of Judges*. OtSt 36. Leiden: Brill, 1996.

Smith, Jonathan Z. *Map Is Not Territory: Studies in the History of Religions*. SJLA 23. Leiden: Brill, 1978.

Smolar, Leivy, and Moses Aberbach. *Studies in Targum Jonathan to the Prophets*. New York: Ktav, 1978.

Snijders, Lambertus A. *Jesaja: Deel I*. Nijkerk: Callenbach, 1969.

Spina, Frank A. "The 'Ground' for Cain's Rejection (Gen 4): *'adāmāh* in the Context of Gen 1-11." *ZAW* 104 (1992): 317-32.

Staalduine-Sulman, Eveline van. "Reward and Punishment in the Messianic Age (Targ. 2 Sam. 23.1-8)." *JAB* 1 (1999): 273-96.

———. *The Targum of Samuel*. SAIS 1. Leiden: Brill, 2002.

Stählin, Gustav. *Die Apostelgeschichte*. 7th ed. NTD 5. Göttingen: Vandenhoeck & Ruprecht, 1980.

Standhartinger, Angela. *Studien zur Entstehungsgeschichte und Intention des Kolosserbriefs*. NovTSup 94. Leiden: Brill, 1999.

Steinrück, Martin. *Regards sur la femme: Analyse rythmique et interprétation de Sémonide fr. 7 Pellizer-Tedeschi*. Biblioteca di quaderni urbinati di cultura classica 6. Rome: Gruppo Editoriale Internazionale, 1994.

Stern, M. "The Jewish Diaspora." Pages 117-83 in *The Jewish People in the First Century: Historical Geography, Political History, Social, Cultural and Religious Life and Institutions*. Edited by Shemuel Safrai and Menahem Stern. CRINT 1.1. Assen: Van Gorcum, 1974.

Stibbs, Alan M. *The First Epistle General of Peter*. Leicester: Inter-Varsity Press, 1959.

Stone, Michael E. "A Reconsideration of Apocalyptic Visions." *HTR* 96 (2003): 167–80.
Strack, Hermann L., and Paul Billerbeck. *Die Briefe des Neuen Testaments und die Offenbarung Johannis*. Vol. 3 of *Kommentar zum Neuen Testament aus Talmud und Midrasch*. 8th ed. Munich: Beck, 1985.
———. *Exkurse zu einzelnen Stellen des Neuen Testaments: Abhandlungen zur Neutestamentlichen Theologie und Archäologie*. Vol 4. of *Kommentar zum Neuen Testament aus Talmud und Midrasch*. 2nd ed. 2 vols. Munich: Beck, 1966.
Straus, Murray A. "Children Should Never, Ever, Be Spanked No Matter What the Circumstances." Pages 137–57 in *Current Controversies on Family Violence*. Edited by Donileen R. Loseke, Richard J. Gelles, and Mary M. Cavanaugh. 2nd ed. Thousand Oaks, Calif.: Sage, 2005.
———. "Women's Violence toward Men Is a Serious Social Problem." Pages 55–77 in *Current Controversies on Family Violence*. Edited by Donileen R. Loseke, Richard J. Gelles, and Mary M. Cavanaugh. 2nd ed. Thousand Oaks, Calif.: Sage, 2005.
Strecker, Georg. *The Johannine Letters: A Commentary on 1, 2, and 3 John*. Hermeneia. Minneapolis: Fortress, 1996.
Summers, Randal W., and Allan M. Hoffmann, eds. *Domestic Violence: A Global View*. Westport, Conn.: Greenwood, 2002.
Surburg, Raymond F. *Introduction to the Intertestamental Period*. London: St Louis, 1975.
Synodinou, Katerina. "The Threats of Physical Abuse of Hera by Zeus in the Iliad." *Wiener Studien* 100 (1987): 13–22.
Syrén, R. "Ishmael and Esau in *Jubilees* and Targum Pseudo-Jonathan." Pages 310–15 in *The Aramaic Bible: Targums in Their Historical Context*. Edited by D. R. G. Beattie and Martin J. McNamara. JSOTSup 166. Sheffield: JSOT Press, 1994.
Sysling, H. *Techiyyat ha-Metim: De opstanding van de doden in de Palestijnse Targumim op de Pentateuch en overeenkomstige tradities in de klassieke rabbijnse bronnen*. Zutphen: Terra, 1991.
Tacitus. *Jaarboeken*. Translation and commentary by J. W. Meijer. Baarn: Ambo, 1990.
Talbert, Charles H. "Once Again: The Plan of 1 Peter." Pages 141–51 in *Perspectives on First Peter*. Edited by Charles H. Talbert. Macon, Ga.: Mercer University Press, 1986.
Tamarkin Reis, P. "What Cain Said: A Note on Genesis 4.8." *JSOT* 27 (2002): 107–13.
Tate, Marvin E. *Psalms 51–100*. WBC 20. Waco, Tex.: Word, 1990.
Taves, Ann, ed. *Religion and Domestic Violence in Early New England: The Memoirs of Abigail Abbot Bailey*. Religion in North America. Bloomington: Indiana University Press, 1989.
Taylor, James E. "Seleucid Rule in Palestine." Ph.D. diss., Duke University, 1979.
Taylor, Nicholas H. "Conflict as Context for Defining Identity: A Study of Apostleship in the Galatian and Corinthian letters." *HvTSt* 59 (2003): 915–45.
Tertullian. *Ad martyras*. Translated by S. Thelwall. *ANF* 3:693–96.
———. *Apology. De spectaculis*. Translated by T. R. Glover. LCL. Cambridge: Harvard University Press, 1931.
———. *De cultu feminarum*. Translation and commentary by W. Kok. Ph.D. diss., Free University, Amsterdam, 1934.

———. *The Prescription against Heretics*. Translated by P. Holmes. *ANF* 3:243–65.
———. *To Scapula*. Translated by S. Thelwell. *ANF* 3:105–8.
Theissen, Gerd. *Sociology of Early Palestinian Christianity*. Translated by John Bowden. Philadelphia: Fortress, 1978.
Thielecke, Helmut. *Ethik des Politischen*. Tübingen: Mohr Siebeck, 1958.
Thimmes, Pamela. "Women Reading Women in the Apocalypse: Reading Scenario 1, the Letter to Thyatira (Rev. 2.18–29)." *CurBR* 2 (2003): 128–44.
Thomas, J. Christopher. *A Pentecostal Commentary on 1 John, 2 John, 3 John*. Cleveland: Pilgrim, 2004.
Thompson, Leonard L. *The Book of Revelation: Apocalypse and Empire*. New York: Oxford University Press, 1990.
Thrall, Margaret E. *A Critical and Exegetical Commentary on the Second Epistle to the Corinthians*. 2 vols. ICC. Edinburgh: T&T Clark: 1994.
Thurén, Lauri. *Argument and Theology in 1 Peter: The Origins of Christian Paraenesis*. JSNTSup 114. Sheffield: Sheffield Academic Press, 1995.
———. "Hey Jude! Asking for the Original Situation and Message of a Catholic Epistle." *NTS* 43 (1997): 451–65.
Tiller, Patrick A. *A Commentary on the Animal Apocalypse of 1 Enoch*. SBLEJL 4. Atlanta: Scholars Press, 1993.
———. "The Sociological Context of the Dream Visions of Daniel and 1 Enoch." Pages 23–26 in *Enoch and Qumran Origins: New Light on a Forgotten Connection*. Edited by Gabriele Boccaccini. Grand Rapids: Eerdmans, 2005.
Tolbert, Mary Ann. "Afterwords. The Politics and Poetics of Location." Pages 305–17 in *Social Location and Biblical Interpretation in the United States*. Vol. 1 of *Reading from this Place*. Edited by Fernando F. Segovia and Mary Ann Tolbert. Minneapolis: Fortress, 1995.
Tollefson, Kenneth D. "Certainty within the Fellowship: Dialectical Discourse in 1 John." *BTB* 29 (1999): 79–89.
Trible, Phyllis. *Texts of Terror: Literary-Feminist Readings of Biblical Narratives*. OBT 13. Philadelphia: Fortress, 1984.
Trisoglio, F., ed. *Opere di Plinio Cecilio Secundo*. Vol. 2. Torino: Tipografia Torinese, 1973.
Tromp, Johannes. *The Assumption of Moses: A Critical Edition with Commentary*. SVTP 10. Leiden: Brill, 1993.
Tur-Sinai, N. Harry. "The Literary Character of the Psalms." *OtSt* 8 (1950): 263–81.
Twerski, Abraham J. *The Shame Borne in Silence: Spouse Abuse in the Jewish Community*. Pittsburgh: Mirkov, 1996.
Uitman, J. E. *De brief van Paulus aan de Colossenzen*. De prediking van het Nieuwe Testament. Nijkerk: Callenbach, 1972.
Unnik, W. C. van. "Christianity according to 1 Peter." Pages 111–20 in vol. 2 of *Sparsa Collecta: The Collected Essays of W. C. van Unnik*. Leiden: Brill, 1980.
———. "The Redemption in 1 Peter i 18–19 and the Problem of the First Epistle of Peter." Pages 3–82 in vol. 2 of *Sparsa Collecta: The Collected Essays of W. C. van Unnik*. Leiden: Brill, 1980.

———. "The Teaching of Good Works in 1 Peter." Pages 83–105 in vol. 2 of *Sparsa Collecta: The Collected Essays of W. C. van Unnik*. Leiden: Brill, 1980.

Ussishkin, David. *The Conquest of Lachish by Sennacherib*. Tel Aviv: Institute of Archaeology of Tel Aviv University, 1982.

VanderKam, James C. "2 Maccabees 6:7a and Calendrical Change in Jerusalem." *JSJ* 12 (1981): 52–74.

———. *Calendars in the Dead Sea Scrolls*. London: Routledge, 1998.

———. *Enoch: A Man for All Generations*. Columbia: University of South Carolina Press, 1995.

———. *Enoch and the Growth of an Apocalyptic Tradition*. CBQMS 16. Washington, D.C.: Catholic Biblical Association of America, 1984.

———. *An Introduction to Early Judaism*. Grand Rapids: Eerdmans, 2001.

———. "The Origin, Character, and Early History of the 364-Day Calendar: A Reassessment of Jaubert's Hypotheses." *CBQ* 41 (1979): 390–411

VanderKam, James C., and Peter Flint. *The Meaning of the Dead Sea Scrolls*. New York: HarperSanFrancisco, 2002.

Vaux, Roland de. *Ancient Israel: Its Life and Institutions*. London: Darton, Longman & Todd, 1961.

Vergeer, W. C. "ΣΚΙΑ and ΣΩΜΑ: The Strategy of Contextualization in Colossians 2:17: A Contribution to the Quest for a Legitimate Contextual Theology Today." *Neot* 28 (1994): 413–42.

Villiers, J. L. de. "Philosophical Trends in the Graeco-Roman World." Pages 169–90 in *The New Testament Environment*. Vol. 2 of *Guide to the New Testament*. Edited by Andrie B. du Toit. Halfway House: Orion, 1998.

———. "Religious Life." Pages 191–214 in *The New Testament Environment*. Vol. 2 of *Guide to the New Testament*. Edited by Andrie B. du Toit. Halfway House: Orion, 1998.

Villiers, Pieter G. R. de. "Rome in the Historical Interpretation of Revelation." *Acta Patristica et Byzantina* 13 (2002): 120–42.

Volf, Miroslav. *Exclusion and Embrace: A Theological Exploration of Identity, Otherness, and Reconciliation*. Nashville: Abingdon, 1996.

Vriezen, Th. C. *Hoofdlijnen der Theologie van het Oude Testament*. Wageningen: Veenman en Zonen, 1974.

Wahlde, Urban C. von. *The Johannine Commandments: 1 John and the Struggle for the Johannine Tradition*. New York: Paulist, 1990.

Watson, Duane F. "1 John 2:12–14 as *Distributio, Conduplicatio,* and *Expolitio*: A Rhetorical Understanding." *JSNT* 35 (1989): 97–110.

Watt, Jan G. van der. "Directives for the Ethics and Ethos Research Project." Paper presented during a meeting of the research team on ethics, ethos, and identity, August 2004, in Pretoria.

———. "Ethics and Ethos in the Gospel according to John." Pages 107–33 in *Identity, Ethics, and Ethos in the New Testament*. Edited by Jan G. van der Watt. Berlin: de Gruyter, 2006.

———. "Ethics in First John: A Literary and Socio-Scientific Perspective." *CBQ* 61 (1999): 491–511.

———. *Family of the King: Dynamics of Metaphor in the Gospel according to John.* BibInt 47. Leiden: Brill, 2000.

———. "Interpreting Imagery in John's Gospel: John 10 and 15 as Case Studies." Pages 272–82 in *Hupomnema: Feesbundel Opgedra aan J.P. Louw.* Edited by J. H. Barkhuizen, H. F. Stander, and G. J. Swart. Pretoria: University of Pretoria Press, 1992.

———, ed. *Identity, Ethics, and Ethos in the New Testament.* Berlin: de Gruyter, 2006.

Weems, Renita J. *Battered Love: Marriage, Sex, and Violence in the Hebrew Prophets.* OBT. Minneapolis: Fortress, 1995.

Weiser, Alfons. *Die Apostelgeschichte.* 2 vols. ÖTK 5.1–2. Gütersloh: Mohn; Würzburg: Echter, 1985.

Wenham, Gordon J. *Genesis 1–15.* WBC 1. Waco, Tex.: Word, 1987.

West, M. L. *Greek Lyric Poetry.* Oxford: Clarendon, 1993.

———. "Semonides." *OCD,* 1383.

Westcott, Brooke F. *The Epistles of St John. The Greek Text with Notes and Essays.* London: Macmillan, 1883. Repr., Grand Rapids: Eerdmans, 1982.

Westermann, Claus. *Genesis 1–11.* BKAT 1.1. Neukirchen-Vluyn: Neukirchener, 1974.

———. *Theologie des Alten Testaments in Grundzügen.* Göttingen: Vandenhoek & Ruprecht, 1978.

Whitacre, Rondey A. *Johannine Polemic: The Role of Tradition and Theology.* SBLDS 67. Chico, Calif.: Scholars Press, 1982.

Williams, Charles S. C. *A Commentary on the Acts of the Apostles.* HNTC. New York: Harper, 1957.

Williamson, Ronald. "Platonism and Hebrews." *SJT* 16 (1963): 415–24.

Wils, Jean-Pierre. *Sacraal geweld.* Assen: Van Gorcum, 2004.

Wilson, Bryan R. "An Analysis of Sect Development." Pages 22–45 in *Patterns of Sectarianism: Organisation and Ideology in Social and Religious Movements.* Edited by Bryan R. Wilson. London: Heinemann, 1967.

Wilson, Gerald H. *The Editing of the Hebrew Psalter.* SBLDS 76. Chico, Calif.: Scholars Press, 1985.

Wilson, Walter T. *The Hope of Glory: Education and Exhortation in the Epistle to the Colossians.* NovTSup 88. Leiden: Brill, 1997.

Wlosok, Antonie. "Die Rechtsgrundlagen der Christenverfolgungen der ersten zwei Jahrhunderte." *Gymnasium* 66 (1959): 14–32.

Wolde, Ellen van. "The Story of Cain and Abel: A Narrative Study." *JSOT* 52 (1991): 25–41.

Wolters, Albert M. *Creation Regained: A Biblical Basis for a Reformational Worldview.* Grand Rapids: Eerdmans, 1985.

Wright, Benjamin G., III. "Fear the Lord and Honor the Priest: Ben Sira as Defender of the Jerusalem Priesthood." Pages 189–222 in *The Book of Ben Sira in Modern Research: Proceedings of the First International Ben Sira Conference.* Edited by Pancratius C. Beentjes. BZAW 255. Berlin: de Gruyter, 1997.

Wright, Christopher J. H. *Old Testament Ethics for the People of God.* Downers Grove, Ill.: InterVarsity Press, 2004.

Wright, N. T. *The New Testament and the People of God.* Vol. 1 of *Christian Origins and the Question of God.* Minneapolis: Fortress, 1992.
Yoder, John H. *The Politics of Jesus.* Grand Rapids: Eerdmans, 1972.
Zeitlin, S. "Notes relatives au calendrier juif." *Revue de études juives* (1930): 349–54.
Zenger, Erich. *Ein Gott der Rache? Feindpsalmen verstehen.* Freiburg: Herder, 1998.
———. "Psalmenforschung nach Hermann Gunkel und Sigmund Mowinckel." Pages 399–435 in *Congress Volume: Oslo, 1998.* Edited by André Lemaire and Magne Sæbø. VTSup 80. Leiden: Brill, 2000.
Zerbe, Gordon M. *Non-retaliation in Early Jewish and New Testament Texts: Ethical Themes in Social Contexts.* JSPSup13. Sheffield: JSOT Press, 1993.
Zimmerli, Walter. *Grundriss der alttestamentlichen Theologie.* Stuttgart: Kohlhammer, 1978.
———. *Die Weltlichkeit des Alten Testamets.* Göttingen: Vandenhoeck & Ruprecht, 1971.
Žižek, Slavoj. "Multiculturalism, Or, the Cultural Logic of Multinational Capitalism." *New Left Review* 225 (1997): 28–51.
Zuurmond, Rochus. "Het oordeel over Kain in de oud-joodse traditie." *Amsterdamse cahiers voor exegese en Bijbelse theologie* 3 (1982): 107–17.

Contributors

Henk Bakker (Ph.D., Early Christian Literature, University of Groningen) teaches Theology and Historical Theology at Ede University, at the Dutch Baptist Seminary, Barneveld (The Netherlands), and at the Center of Evangelical and Reformation Theology, Free University, Amsterdam (The Netherlands). He is also a member of the Center of Patristic Research (Free University, Amsterdam, and Catholic University of Tilburg). His research interests include early Christian martyrs, such as Ignatius (the subject of his doctoral dissertation) and Potamiaena, on whom he has recently contributed the article "Potamiaena: Some Observations about Martyrdom and Gender in Ancient Alexandria," in *The Wisdom of Egypt* (ed. A. Hilhorst and G. H. van Kooten; Brill, 2005).

Paul B. Decock is a Lecturer in Biblical Studies and Early Christian Exegesis at St. Joseph's Theological Institute and Honorary Research Fellow of the University of KwaZulu-Natal (both at Pietermaritzburg, South Africa). Recent and forthcoming publications include "The Works of God, of Christ, and of the Faithful in the Apocalypse of John," *Neot* 41(2007): 37–66, and "The Reception of the Letter to Philemon in the Early Church: Origen, Jerome, Chrysostom, and Augustine," which is scheduled to appear shortly in a volume on Philemon that will be published in the monograph series of *ZNW*.

John T. Fitzgerald is Professor of Religious Studies at the University of Miami in Coral Gables, Florida (U.S.A.), and Professor Extraordinary at North-West University in Potchefstroom (South Africa). His recent volumes include *The Writings of St. Paul* (co-edited with Wayne A. Meeks; Norton, 2007) and *Passions and Moral Progress in Greco-Roman Thought* (Routledge, 2008).

J. J. Fritz Krüger currently serves as a missionary in Nqutu, northern KwaZulu-Natal (South Africa) for the Netherlands Reformed Church of Leerdam (The Netherlands). He is also extraordinary senior lecturer in Missiology at North-West University, Potchefstroom (South Africa). His research interests include Colossians (the subject of his doctoral dissertation), the interface between ecclesiology, ethics, and missiology, urban mission and church planting, and theological contextualization in dealing with AIDS and extreme poverty.

Outi Leppä is a researcher at the University of Helsinki. Her research interests include the Pauline heritage and early Christian conflicts. Her recent publications include *The Making of Colossians: A Study on the Formation and Purpose of a Deutero-Pauline Letter* (Vandenhoeck & Ruprecht, 2003), and "Debates within the New Testament Canon," in *The Formation of the Early Church* (ed. J. Ådna; Mohr Siebeck, 2005).

Dirk G. van der Merwe is Associate Professor at the University of South Africa (UNISA) in the Department of New Testament and Early Christian Studies. His main field of current interest is early Christian living, with a focus on spirituality, discipleship, and Christ devotion. Recent publications include "Salvation in the Johannine Epistles," in *Salvation in the New Testament* (ed. J. G. van der Watt; Brill, 2005), and "'A Matter of Having Fellowship': Ethics in the Johannine Epistles," in *Identity, Ethics, and Ethos in the New Testament* (ed. J. G. Van der Watt; de Gruyter, 2006).

Marius Nel has earned one doctorate from the University of South Africa and two doctorates from the University of Pretoria. He is a pastor and lecturer, and associate professor in the Faculty of Theology at North-West University, Potchefstroom (South Africa). His research focuses on apocalyptic and the wisdom literature of the Hebrew Bible/Old Testament. He is the author or co-author of thirty publications and thirty-five scholarly articles.

Eric Peels is Professor of Old Testament Studies at Apeldoorn Theological University (The Netherlands), and Research Associate in the Department of Old Testament Studies, University of the Free State (South Africa). His main field of interest is Old Testament theology and exegesis, and his recent major publications include *The Vengeance of God* (Brill, 1995) and *Shadow Sides: God in the Old Testament* (Paternoster, 2003). He is currently preparing a commentary on the book of Jeremiah for the Historical Commentary on the Old Testament (HCOT) series.

Jeremy Punt is Associate Professor of New Testament in the Faculty of Theology, University of Stellenbosch (South Africa). His research interests include Pauline studies and biblical hermeneutics, including postcolonial theory. Recent publications include "A Politics of Difference in the New Testament: Identity and the Others in Paul," in *The New Testament Interpreted: Essays in Honour of Bernard C. Lategan* (ed. C. Breytenbach, J. Thom, and J. Punt; Brill, 2006), and "Paul and Postcolonial Hermeneutics: Marginality and/in Early Biblical Interpretation," in *As It Is Written: Studying Paul's Use of Scripture* (ed. S. P. Porter and C. D. Stanley; SBLSymS 50; Atlanta: Society of Biblical Literature, 2008).

Fika J. van Rensburg is Professor of New Testament in the Faculty of Theology at North-West University, Potchefstroom (South Africa). His research interests are the sociohistorical study of the New Testament (presently focusing on the early church and the ancient economy), 1 Peter (presently focusing on the soteriology of 1 Peter), developing tools for the interpretation and translation of the Bible, and the interpretation of the New Testament for present-day preaching. His recent publications include

Making a Sermon: A Guide for Reformed Exegesis and Preaching (Potchefstroom Theological Publications, 2005), and "Metaphors in the Soteriology in 1 Peter: Identifying and Interpreting the Salvific Imageries," in *Salvation in the New Testament* (ed. J. G. van der Watt; Brill, 2005).

Rainer G. H. Reuter earned his doctorate at the University of Göttingen (Germany), with his dissertation published as *Textvergleichende und synoptische Arbeit an den Briefen des Neuen Testaments: Geschichte-Methodik-Praxis; Textvergleich Kolosser- und Philemonbrief* (Lang, 2003). He was pastor in the Evangelical-Lutheran congregation of Paderborn, Germany, from 1990 to 2002 and was Professor of Biblical Theology at the Theological Seminary of the Evangelical Lutheran Church of Russia and Other States in Novosaratovka, Saint Petersburg, Russia, from 2002 to 2006. While maintaining an academic affiliation with the Novosaratovka Seminary, he is once again serving primarily as a pastor.

Herrie F. van Rooy is Professor of Old Testament in the Faculty of Theology at North-West University, Potchefstroom (South Africa). His research focuses on the ancient versions of the Old Testament, especially the Peshitta. He has published a book on the Syriac apocryphal psalms and is currently working on a critical edition of the East Syriac psalm headings.

Eben Scheffler is Professor of Old Testament and Biblical Archaeology at the University of South Africa in Pretoria (South Africa). His research interests include ancient Israelite historiography, pentateuchal criticism, psychological exegesis, hermeneutics, the historical Jesus, and Luke's Gospel. His publications include *Suffering in Luke's Gospel* (Theologischer Verlag, 1993), *Fascinating Discoveries from the Biblical World* (Biblia, 2000), and *Politics in Ancient Israel* (Biblia, 2001).

Eveline van Staalduine-Sulman is an Old Testament lecturer at the Vrije Universiteit in Amsterdam (The Netherlands) and researcher within the project "A Jewish Targum in a Christian World" in cooperation with the Protestant Theological University (The Netherlands) and the Evangelical Theological Faculty (Louvain, Belgium). She is the author of *The Targum of Samuel* (Brill, 2002) and the editor of three Samuel volumes in *A Bilingual Concordance to the Targum of the Prophets* (Brill, 1996).

Index of Ancient Authors and Texts

Citations and abbreviations for ancient authors and texts generally follow the SBL guidelines as published in *The SBL Handbook of Style* (Peabody, Mass.: Hendrickson, 1999). Where no abbreviation has been recommended by the SBL, preference in citing ancient texts is given to the abbreviations used by the *OCD* and by lexicons such as LSJ and *OLD*.

1. Hebrew Bible/Old Testament
2. Biblical Versions
3. Apocrypha and Pseudepigrapha
4. Dead Sea Scrolls and Related Texts
5. Josephus and Philo
6. Talmud and Midrashim
7. Targumic Texts
8. New Testament
9. Noncanonical Early Christian Literature
10. Other Ancient Authors and Texts
11. Papyri and Epigraphica

1. Hebrew Bible/Old Testament

Genesis
1	21
1–2	163, 165
1–11	21n, 23–25n, 28–33n, 37n, 116n
1–15	21n, 25n, 27–28n, 30–31n, 38n
1–17	25n
1:1–2:3	21
1:11–11:26	21n
2	21
2–3	21n
2–4	21, 28
2–11	38
2:4	20n
2:4–4:26	21, 116n
2:15	36n
2:17	27
2:24	30
3	21, 28, 31
3:1–24	116n
3:5	27
3:17–19	24
3:21	31
3:22	27
3:23	24
4	20–24, 28, 30, 33–35, 37–39
4:1–5	23–24
4:1–6	12, 19–20, 22, 30
4:1–16	12, 19–22, 25–26n, 30, 32–33, 36, 116
4:3–5	36
4:6–7	25
4:7	25n
4:8	25–26n

Genesis (cont.)

Reference	Page
4:9–15a	27
4:15	29n, 32, 36n
4:15b	30
4:15b–16	29
5	21, 63–64
5:1	20n
5:21–24	61, 64
5:22	64n
5:23–24	62
6:1–4	67
6:9	20n
7:11	74
7:24	74
8:3–4	74
9:16	31
10:1	20n
11:1–9	264n
11:10	20n
11:27	20n
19:11	125n
24:33	95
25:12	20n
25:19	20n
25:27	96
27:41–42	116
34:7	25n
36:1	20n
36:9	20n
37	36n
37:2	20n
37:20	116

Exodus

Reference	Page
4:10	181
12:41	2
14:4	2
14:31	181
15	viii
15:3	2
15:14	4
20:13	12
22:1–2	282n
22:6–8	282n
23:4–5	14, 47
23:9	14, 47
23:27	4

Leviticus

Reference	Page
19:17–18	13, 47
24:14–16	94
26:21	282n
26:24	282n
26:28	282n

Numbers

Reference	Page
11:11	181
12:7–8	179–80
20:2	181
21:14	2, 4

Deuteronomy

Reference	Page
1:30	2
3:24	181
17	12
17:16	11
19:11	27
20	4
20:10–14	46
21:1–4	14
22:25	27
23:9	4
30:15	277n
33:11	95

Joshua

Reference	Page
1:2	181
2:24	4
3:5	4
6:2	4
6:18	4
10:14	2
17:4	132n

Judges

Reference	Page
4–5	6
4:14	4
5:11	4
5:13	4
6	6

INDEX OF ANCIENT AUTHORS AND TEXTS

6:4	4	8:14			2, 4
6:12	9	8:15			9
13–15	6	12:14			90
19	1	12:31b			89
20:2	4	15–18			49
20:23	4	16:19			92
20:27	4	17:8			9
		22			50

1 Samuel

2:5	93	**1 Kings**	
4:3	2	2	11
5:9	4, 125n	9:15–22	11
7:13	131n	10:26	2
10:27	88	22	4, 9
13:9	4	22:17	10
14:22	9		
15	4	**2 Kings**	
15:23	90n	9–10	12
15:26	90n	9:14–10:36	7
16:1	90n	10:30	12
16:7	90n	19:32–34	8
16:18	9	19:35	8
17	6, 94	23:2	125n
18:8	25n	23:27	10
18:12	90n	24:3	10
18:17	2	24:20	10
21:6	4	25:26	125n
23:22	9		
24–26	48	**1 Chronicles**	
24:9	9	11:11–14	179
24:14	92	16:40	181
25:28	90	18:1–17	9
28:15	90n	18:6	11
28:16	90n, 91	18:18	11
30:2	4, 125n	20:4–8	11
30:19	4, 125n	21	11
30:26	90	22:8	11

2 Samuel

1:23–25	9	**2 Chronicles**	
5:6	90	28:12–15	13, 14
5:8	90		
7:14	179	**Nehemiah**	
8	11	4:1	25n
8:1–16	9		

Job		44	2, 41, 44, 55–56
15:22–23	28	45	55
18:18–21	28	46	55
30:3–8	28	47	55
		48	55
Psalms		52	55
1	277–78	53	55
2	46, 55–57	54	48, 55
3	43, 48–49, 54–55	56	56
5	41, 43–44	58	56
6	41, 43	62	56
7	41, 43–44, 50, 55	63	48
8	55	64	55
9	41, 55	66	2
9–10	44	69	56
10	41, 43, 56	70	55
11	43, 55	73	285
12	43	74	41, 44, 56
12:7	29n, 48	75	55
13	41	77	55
14	43, 55–56	79	41, 44, 56
15	55	79:12	29n
16	54, 56	80	41
17	43–44, 55	83	41, 56
18	43, 50, 53	86	55
20	43, 55	87	55
21	43, 55	91	55
22	41, 55–56	92	52, 55
23:5	15n, 296n	93	52
26	43	95	52
27	41, 55	95:7	183
28	43, 56	95:11	183
29	55	96	52
30	53	104	52
31	43–44	109	44, 56
33	43, 52	110	55, 178, 187, 193, 195
33:13–17	217, 227	110:4	185
34	43, 53	117	56
35	43, 55	123	56
36	55	124	56
37	43	126	56
38	43	127:5	43
39	43, 55	133	44
40	43	137	46, 48, 264
41	43, 56	139	55

INDEX OF ANCIENT AUTHORS AND TEXTS

140	44	65:17–25	281
141	44		
143	44, 54, 56	Jeremiah	
149	56	3:12	25
		4:3	10
Proverbs		4:6	10
2:12–15	277n	4:23–26	281
6:31	29n	6:13	125n
8:22–32	163	7	11
25:21–22	14	16:18	282n
		17:18	282n
Ecclesiastes		21:5	10
2:17	228	21:8	277n
		25	264n
Isaiah		25:12–38	268
1:1–14:23	268	31	193
2:2–4	10	31:31–34	192, 195
7	4	34:22	10
7:4	2	38:34	125n
9:1–7	10	49:1	125n
13	3, 264n	49:8	125n
14	264n	50	264n
18:1	2	50–51	268
21	264n	51	264n
21:1–10	268	51:12	125n
21:9–10	280n		
22:5	125n	Ezekiel	
22:24	125n	9:4	30
23	268	26–27	264n
27:1	280n	26–28	268
27:12–13	280n	29:3–5	280n
29:13	190	30	3
30:1	2	32:4	280n
30:5–16	4		
30:15–16	4, 10	Daniel	
31:1	2	1	77
31:4	2	2	128n
34	3	3:19	29n
40:2	282n	5	128n
42:18–19	90n	6:8(7)	73
45:18–19	281	6:13(12)	73
47	264n, 268	7	76, 81n, 280
62:3–5	281	7:9	296n
63:1–6	282n	7:25	72, 75
63:3	296n	7:27	296n

Daniel (cont.)
8	76
8:14	73, 75
9:27	75
10–12	76
10:4	73
12:1–2	73
12:5–13	73
12:7	75
12:11–12	73, 75

Hosea
2:2–23	281
4:1–3	281n

Joel
3:10	14

Amos
4:6–11	281

Micah
4:3	14

Zephaniah
1:7	3

Zechariah
4:6	2
5:5–11	264n
9:12	282n

2. Biblical Versions

Peshitta	48, 51–54, 333
Septuagint	vii, 48, 51–52, 57, 61–62, 125n, 131–32n, 191–92, 217, 227

3. Apocrypha and Pseudepigrapha

Apocalypse of Abraham	68
Ascension of Isaiah. *See* Martyrdom and Ascension of Isaiah	
Astronomical Book. *See* 1 Enoch 72–82	

Assumption of Moses
1.14	181
9.6–7	295n

2 Baruch	68
29:3–4	280

Ben Sira. *See* Sirach

Book of the Heavenly Luminaries. *See* 1 Enoch 72–82

1 Enoch	60–69, 71, 74–85, 162–63, 295
1–36	64
1:1	166
1:2	170
3	164
6–16	67n
7–8	164
9:3	295
9:13–14	166
10	167, 170–71
12:5–7	167
13–14	167
14	168
17–18	65, 168
17–36	65
19:3	168
24	171
25–26	171
33–35	168
36:4–5	171
37–71	64
37:1–2	168
38	170–71
39	168, 171
41	168
45:3–5	170
46	170–71
48	165, 170
50:1	170
52–53	171
52:6–7	171

INDEX OF ANCIENT AUTHORS AND TEXTS 341

55:1	170	Jubilees	60, 62, 68, 69n, 72–74, 76–78, 83–85, 98n
56:3	171	5:17	78
56:5	171	6:23	77
58	170	6:24	77
59	168	6:28–29	77
60:7–9	280n	6:31–32	77
60:11	170	6:32–38	78
60:24	280n	29:16	78
61	165, 170–71		
63–74	165	Judith	
68	164, 170	8:18	191
70	167–68, 170	13:4	125n
72	70, 76n, 77	13:13	125n
72–82	63–64, 68–69n, 69–72, 77–79, 165	13:14	132n
73–74	70	Life of Adam and Eve	68
74:11–12	71		
74:13–17	71	1 Maccabees	
75:1	71	1:54	75
75:2	71, 78	4:52–54	75
75:3	71	5:45	125n
79	63, 164	5:62	132n
81:1–82:3	64–65		
81:5–10	64n	2 Maccabees	
82:5	78	4:40	80
83–90	64–65	6:7a	68n, 72n, 77n
85–90	65		
91	64	Martyrdom and Ascension of Isaiah	
91:11–17	65	9.24–27	295n
92–105	64, 81		
93:1–10	65	Sirach (Ben Sira)	80–81, 106
106–107	64	15:11–17	277n
108	64–65	21:10	277n
108:14–15	296	28:17	106
		30:12	110n
2 Enoch	68–69, 71	31:30	vii
13:3–4	69		
30:15	277n	Testament of Asher	
72–77	71	1–6	277n
75:2	72	1:3–4	277
82	71–72		
		Testament of Benjamin	
4 Ezra	68, 285	9:1	68
4:35	295n		

Testament of Dan		Ant.	
5:6	68	7.161	89
		8.45–47	133n
Testament of Jude		12.138–144	80
18:1	68	12.239–240	80
		12.320	77
Testament of Levi		18.21	83n
10:5	68	20.142	130n
14:1	68	C. Ap.	
16:1	68	1.91	208n
		2.210	207n
Testament of Moses	68, 295		
		Philo	59, 83n, 180–81, 186, 189, 208, 232n
Testament of Naphtali		Abr.	
4:1	68	17–26	208n
		Leg.	
Testament of Reuben		2.67	180
5:1–6	68	3.228	180
		Mos.	
Testament of Simeon		2.166	181
5:4	68	Plant.	
		68	180
Testament of Zebulon		Praem.	
3:4	68	16–17	208n
		Prob.	
Wisdom of Solomon		75	83n
6–9	163, 165	Sacr.	
12:6	132n	132	186
14:8	191	Somn.	
		2.273	208n
		Spec.	
4. Dead Sea Scrolls and Related Texts		1.51	208n
		1.317	208n
Qumran	50–52, 59–62, 65–66, 68–70, 72–73, 78–79, 81–85, 87, 232n	4.178	208
		Virt.	
1QS		102–103	208n
3:13–4:26	277, 278n		
		6. Talmud and Midrashim	
4Q180	85n		
		Babylonian Talmud	
5. Josephus and Philo		Meg. 10b	viiin
Josephus	59n, 77, 80–83n, 89, 130n, 133n, 186, 207, 208n	Midrash Rabbah	
		Exod 23:7	viiin

7. Targumic Texts

7.1. Targumim of the Torah

Palestinian Targumim to the Pentateuch
93–94

Targum Neofiti	96–97
Gen 25:27	96
Targum Onqelos	91n, 97n
Exod 20:5	91n
Deut 1:27	91n
Deut 7:10	91n
Targum Pseudo-Jonathan	94–98
Gen 24:31	97n
Gen 24:33	97n
Gen 25:29	95
Deut 33:11	94–95

7.2. Targumim of the Prophets

Targum Jonathan to the Prophets	87–92, 94, 97
Targum of Samuel	88–90, 90n, 92–93, 93n, 98, 333
1 Sam 2:5	93
1 Sam 2:8–9	92n
1 Sam 10:27	88
1 Sam 24:14	92
1 Sam 28:16	90–91
2 Sam 5:8	90
2 Sam 12:31b	89
2 Sam 16:9	92
2 Sam 22:26–27	97n
2 Sam 22:29	92n
2 Sam 23:1–8	89
2 Sam 23:4	92n

7.3. Targumim of the Writings and Tosefta-Targumim

Targum of 1 Chronicles	
1 Chr 11:11	89
Targum of Job	87
Tosefta-Targumim	93, 94n

8. New Testament

Matthew	
3:7	185
5:43–44	13
5:44–45	225n
6:12	227
6:14–15	227
6:19–21	268n
7:13–14	277n
12:27	133n
12:43–45	133n
15:9	190
18:32–35	227
19:21	268n
21:32	277n
24:5	243
26:61	191
Mark	
4:11	143
5:7	133
5:27	132n
6:2	132n
7:7	190
9:38–41	134n
10:21	268n
13:1–2	267n
14:58	191
Luke	
3:7	185
4	137
6:27–28	224
6:28b	225

Luke (cont.)		8:4–25	124
8:27	125n	8:5–8	124
8:29	133	8:5–13	124n
8:44	132n	8:6	125
9:49–50	134n	8:6–7	126
11:19	133	8:9	124n, 125
11:24–26	133n	8:10	125
12:33–34	268n	8:11	124n, 125–26
16:19–31	296n	8:12–13	126
18:1–7	295n	8:13b	127
18:22	268n	8:14	126n
20:9	125n	8:14–17	124n, 127
22:30	296n	8:14–25	124n
23:8	125n	8:18–24	124n, 127
24:49	128	8:20	128
		8:21	128
John		8:24	128
1–4	255	11:30	132n
1:11	142n	13:2	129
5:16	141	13:4–12	129
5:38	254	13:6	124n
8:31	254	13:7a	130
8:51	254	13:8	124n
8:57–59	141	13:8–9	130
14:34	254	13:10	131n
15:7	254	13:11b	131
15:27	254	14:3	125n, 127n, 132n
18:12	141	14:11–12	125
19:10	141	15:12	127n
		15:23	132n
Acts		16:16	124n
1:8	128	16:19	124n
2:22	127	17:24	192
2:23	132n	19:11	132n
2:43	127n	19:11–20	132
3:4	130n	19:12	134
4:30	127n	19:13	124n, 133
5:12	127n, 132n	19:13–17	134
5:15	132n	19:14	134
6:5	124	19:15	134
6:8	127	19:17	135
7:25	132n	19:18–19	135
7:36	127n	19:26	132n
7:42–50	191–92	26:22	125n
8	130–31	27:9	125n

INDEX OF ANCIENT AUTHORS AND TEXTS

Romans		Ephesians	
1:14	142, 144	1:22	142n
1:18	185	4:15	142n
2:5	185		
7:6	188	Philippians	
7:12	187	3:2–3	195
7:14	187		
8	185	Colossians	
9:4	193	1:1–3	161
12:3–5	142	1:2	168
12:3–8	144	1:5	170
12:19	185	1:9–10	169
13:1–14	142	1:11	169
13:14	175	1:12	170
15:7–13	144	1:13	161, 166
		1:13–14	168
1 Corinthians		1:14	167
4:12	225n	1:15	165
5:12	143	1:15–20	164
5:13	143	1:16	165
6:2	296n	1:17	165
6:9–11	143	1:18	142n, 156n, 167–68
10–12	142	1:19	164, 166
12:12–13	142	1:20	154, 166–67
		1:22	166–67, 170
2 Corinthians	231	1:27	167
3:6–7	188	1:28	170
3:7–11	181	2:2	169
4:16	143n	2:6	174
5:1	191	2:7	170
9–12	137	2:8	159–60, 166
10–13	147	2:9	164
11:2–3	147	2:9–10	169
11:15	185	2:11	191
		2:11–13	168
Galatians	231	2:14	166–67
3:21	193	2:14–15	163
3:27–28	142	2:15	166–67, 169
3:28	144	2:16–17	190
4:19	147n	2:19	168, 170
4:26	143	2:20	166
5:10	185	2:21	166
5:12	195	2:22	190
		2:22–23	166
		3:1	167

Colossians (cont.)

3:2	174	3:2	180
3:3	170	3:5	180–81
3:4	170	3:6	195
3:5	174	3:7	184, 192n
3:5–9	166	3:7–19	184
3:5–17	173	3:15	192n
3:6	166, 170	4:1–3	183–84
3:7	174	4:3	192n, 195
3:8	174	4:7	184, 192n
3:9–11	142	5:1–10	177
3:10	169, 174	5:9	188
3:11	169, 175	6:14	192n
3:12	168, 174	7:8	193
3:12–14	175	7:11	188, 193
3:12–15	169	7:11–28	185
3:15	168, 175	7:12	187
3:16–17	169	7:14	186
3:17	175	7:16	186
3:18–4:1	169	7:17–18	187
3:24	170	7:26–27	187, 190
3:25	170	7:27	195
4:2–6	169	8:1	195
4:5	143	8:1–2	189–90
4:5–6	160	8:5	189
		8:6	181, 193
		8:6–13	194
1 Thessalonians		8:7	192
2:7–8	142	8:7–13	177
2:14–16	184	8:8	192n
4:8	185	8:8–12	192
4:12	143	8:13	192
5:15	225n	9:1	189
		9:1–14	177
1 Timothy		9:9–10	186
5:14	224n	9:11	190–92
		9:13	186
Hebrews		9:15	181
1:13–14	177	9:15–22	177
2:3	178n	9:20	192n
2:6	192n	9:24	190–92
2:10	188	10:1	189–91
2:12	192n	10:5	192n
3–4	184	10:15	192n
3:1	195	11	92n
3:1–6	177, 179, 181–82, 190	11:4	38n

11:23–29	181	2:25	220, 222, 224, 229
12:5	192n	3:1–4	230
12:24	177, 181	3:1–7	214
12:26	192n	3:7	219, 221–22, 227
13:22	ix, 178	3:8–9	217–18
		3:8–12	199, 202, 210, 212, 214–15, 217, 224, 228–30
1 Peter		3:9	ix, 199, 219, 221–22, 224–29
1:1	6, 205, 207, 221	3:9–12	226n
1:1–2	213, 220, 223	3:10	226n, 229
1:3	212, 219–23, 229	3:10–11	217–18
1:3–12	203n, 211–13	3:10–12	226n, 227
1:4	221, 226–27	3:11	229
1:4–5	219, 222	3:12	217–18, 226n, 228
1:5	220–21, 223	3:13–4:19	214
1:6	209	3:14–16	230
1:9–10	220–23	3:15	223
1:10	220–21, 223	3:16	209, 220, 222, 224
1:11	220, 222–23	3:17–4:19	211n
1:13–25	211, 213	3:18	220, 222–23
1:15	221n	3:18–22	220
1:17	207, 226n	4:1	220
1:18	208, 223	4:3	209
1:18–19	219, 221, 223, 226n	4:4	209
1:23	219–20, 222	4:11	211n
2:1–10	211–13	4:12	209
2:2	220–23	4:12–19	211n
2:2–3	219–20, 222	4:13	220, 222
2:4–5	220, 222, 224	4:17	219, 221, 223
2:9	220–23	4:18	208, 220–21, 223
2:9–10	220–21, 223	4:19	209
2:10	220–21, 223	5:1	220, 222–23
2:11	6, 207, 215	5:1–11	211–13
2:11–12	214	5:10	220–23
2:11–4:19	211–14	5:12	220–21, 223
2:12	209	5:12–14	212–13
2:13–17	214	5:13	220–21, 223
2:16	219, 221, 223	5:14	220, 222, 224
2:18–20	229		
2:18–25	214	2 Peter	
2:18–3:6	121n	2:3–22	185
2:21	220–23, 229	3:16	185
2:21–22	230		
2:22–23	222	1 John	231, 233n
2:23	225	1:1	234, 238, 240, 245n, 256–57
2:24	220, 222		

1 John (cont.)

Reference	Pages
1:1–2	255
1:1–3	240, 254
1:1–4	255
1:2	238, 240, 245n, 255n, 256–57
1:3	238–40, 243n, 255–56
1:5	246
1:5–10	260
1:5–2:2	247
1:5–2:28	246
1:6	247, 250n, 257n
1:6–7	239, 241n, 248
1:6–2:11	257
1:7	237, 240, 242, 244–45, 257n
1:8	239n, 241n, 246–48, 250n
1:9	252, 259
1:10	247–48, 250n
1:19	239n
1:20	254
2:1	252, 255–56, 259
2:1–2	242, 244–45, 247n
2:2	240, 245n
2:3	239n, 241n, 253n
2:3–5	257n
2:3–11	248
2:4	239n, 241n, 248–49, 250n, 253n
2:5	239n
2:6	239n, 248–49, 255, 256, 258–59
2:7	234, 254
2:9	237, 248–49, 250n, 254
2:9–10	257n
2:10	237
2:11	235–36
2:11–14	254
2:13	234, 239n
2:14	234, 239n, 254
2:15	241n
2:18	234–35, 258
2:18–27	234
2:18–28	253, 258
2:19	234, 235n, 252
2:20	240, 254
2:20–27	255
2:21	234
2:22	234–35, 241–42, 244
2:22–23	242–43
2:22–24	255n
2:23	239n, 256
2:24	234, 239n, 241, 252, 254, 256, 260
2:25	245n
2:26	234–35
2:27	239–40, 254–55
2:28	238–239n, 256, 258–59
2:29	241n, 257n, 259
2:29–3:10	258
3:1	236
3:2	258–59
3:3	256, 258–59
3:5	239n
3:6	239n, 256–57n
3:7	235, 252, 258–59
3:8	235
3:9	239n, 254
3:9–10	257n
3:10	235–37, 241n, 253n
3:11	237, 254
3:11–12	38
3:12	235, 237
3:13	237
3:14	236–37
3:15	235–37, 239n
3:16	237, 241n, 245n, 253n, 256–58
3:16–17	250
3:17	237, 239n
3:18	257n
3:19	241n, 253n
3:21	241n
3:23	237, 243n
3:24	239n, 241n, 253n, 255
4:1	235, 252, 254, 256, 259
4:1–3	242, 244
4:1–6	234–35, 253–54
4:2	241–42, 244–45, 253–255n
4:3	236, 241, 244, 255n
4:5	236
4:6	234, 236, 241n, 253n
4:6–8	239n
4:7	237, 257n
4:8	250, 254

4:9	235n, 242, 244, 256	3 John	142n, 231n
4:9–10	245	1	233n
4:10	240, 242, 244, 255–56		
4:11	237, 257n	Jude	67
4:12	237, 239n, 241	4–16	185
4:13	239n, 241n, 253n, 255	5–11	184
4:14	242, 244–45n, 255–56	11	38
4:15	239n, 241–44, 254, 256		
4:16	239n, 250	Revelation	
4:16–21	258	1:4	280n
4:17	235n, 256, 258–59	1:5	274
4:18	258n	1:5–6	264n, 283
4:20	235, 237, 241n, 246, 249–50, 250n, 254, 257	2:5	283
		2:8–11	268n
4:21	237	2:9	267–68
5:1	241–42, 244	2:10	283n
5:2	241n, 253n	2:14	184, 285
5:5	241–42, 243	2:16	282n, 283
5:6	241–42, 244–56	2:20	184, 278, 285
5:7	245n, 255	2:20–23	284
5:10	239n, 241, 255n	2:21	283
5:10–12	245	2:22	283
5:11	256	3:3	283
5:11–12	255, 257	3:7	278
5:11–13	245n	3:11	283n
5:12	236, 239n, 256	3:14	275, 278
5:13	238, 241	3:14–22	268n
5:15	241n	3:17	267
5:16	237	3:19	283
5:20	243n, 245n	3:21	283
		4:8	280n
2 John	142n, 231	4:10	277
1	233n, 255	4:11	280n
2	239n	5:5	283
3	243n, 255n	5:8	265n
4	255	5:9–10	283
5	237	5:13	280n
6	254, 257n	6:6	275n
7	235, 241–44, 253	6:9–11	265n
7–11	234	6:10	265, 278, 282, 295
8	235	7:9	30
9	239n, 243n, 253–55, 255n, 257n, 260	8:3–4	265n
		8:5	265n
10	251, 261	9:4	284
		9:20	278

Revelation (cont.)

Reference	Pages
9:20–21	274, 281, 284
10:6	280n
11:1	277
11:2	73
11:3	74
11:9	284n
11:11	296n
11:11–13	284
11:13	274
11:17–18	280n
11:18	265n, 284n
12	281
12:6	74
12:9	278, 284
12:11	268
12:12	268
12:14	74
13	279
13:4	268
13:5	73
13:7	268
13:8	278
13:12	278
13:14	278, 284
13:15	278
13:16–17	268
13:18	285
14:7	277, 282n
14:7–8	266n
14:8	267, 284n
14:9	278
14:10	265
14:11	278
14:13	268
15:2	283n
15:3	278, 280n
15:3–4	284n
15:4	278, 282n
16:2	278, 284
16:5	265n, 282n
16:6	296n
16:7	278, 280n, 282n
16:9	265, 281, 284
16:11	281, 284
16:12	278
16:14	280n
16:19	267, 296n
16:21	281, 284
17	281
17:1	266, 281n, 296n
17:1–19:10	263, 265, 268, 282
17:2	283–84, 284n
17:3	265
17:3–6	266
17:4	268n, 283
17:5	266–67
17:6	296n
17:12–14	283
17:16–17	265–66, 283
17:18	266, 284n
17:19	285
18	265, 274, 281
18:1–3	266, 270
18:2	266
18:3	267–68, 268n, 284n
18:4	283
18:4–20	266
18:6	282n
18:6–7	266
18:7	267–68
18:8	266n, 282n
18:8–20	265n
18:9	267n, 284n
18:10	266–67, 282n
18:15	268n
18:16	266–68, 268n
18:18	266
18:19	266–68, 268n
18:20	266, 270, 281–82, 282n, 296n
18:21–24	266
18:23	268n, 284n, 296n
19:1–4	265
19:1–8	266
19:2	265–66, 266n, 278, 280n, 282
19:5–8	266
19:6	280n
19:6–9	283
19:7–8	265

INDEX OF ANCIENT AUTHORS AND TEXTS

19:8	282n	9.11.28	105n
19:9	278, 284n		
19:10	278	Barnabas	277, 279
19:11	265n, 278, 282n	1:4	125n
19:13	282n, 296n	4:3	68
19:15	280n, 282n	16:5–6	68
19:19–20	281	18–21	277n
19:20	278	21	277
20:3	281n, 284n		
20:4	296n	Clement of Alexandria	68n
20:7–10	281		
20:8	278, 284	2 Clement	
20:9	282n	10:5	185
20:10	278, 284		
20:12	265n, 282n	Didache	277, 279
20:13	265n, 282n	1–5	277n
21–22	142n		
21:1–7	278	Eusebius	288n, 291n, 293–94
21:4	278	*Hist. eccl.*	
21:5	278	3.33.2	291n
21:9–22:9	265	4.7.9–11	288n
21:11	278	5.1.9–10	294n
21:22	280n	5.1.49–50	294n
21:24	284n	6.5	293
21:26	284n	6.41.7	294n
22:2	284n	7.12.1	294n
22:6	278	8.9.5	294n
		8.9.7	294n
9. Noncanonical Early Christian Literature		8.66	294n
		Mart. Pal.	
		3.2–4	294n
Acta Cypriani			
5.1	294n	Hermas. *See* Shepherd of Hermas	
Acta Eupli		Ignatius	185n, 294, 331
1	294n	*Phld.*	
		6:1	185n
Athenagoras		*Magn.*	
Leg.		8:1	185n
3	288n	*Rom.*	
		4:1	294
Augustine	61n, 105n, 113–15, 115n, 121, 331	5:2	294n
		7:2	294n
Conf.	113		
9.9.19	105n, 114–15		

Irenaeus
   Haer.
      1.23.1   125n
      4   68n

Justin Martyr   68n, 125n, 133n, 294n
   Apol.
      1.26.3   125n
   2 Apol.
      2.1–20   294n
   Dial.
      85   133n

Marcion   2, 13–14, 19

Martyrium Carpi
   44   294n

Martyrium Lugdunensium
   17   293n
   18   292n
   39   293n
   56   292n
   57   293n
   58   293n
   60   293n

Martyrium Ptolemaei
   11–20   294n

Minucius Felix   288
   Oct.
      8–9   288n
      8.4   288n
      10.2   289
      12.5–6   289
      28   288n
      30–31   288n

Origen   68n, 288n, 331
   Cels.
      6.27.40   288n

Passio Perpetuae et Felicitatis
   20.2   293n
   20.4   293

Passio Phileae
   7.1–3   294n

Passio Pionii
   18.2   294n

Passio Sanctorum Mariani et Iacobi
   3.5   294n
   9.2–4   294n

Passio Sanctorum Scilitanorum
   14   292n

Philostorgius
   Church History
      2.5   88n

Prudentius
   Peristephanon
      3.1–200   294n

Shepherd of Hermas
   Mand.
      6.1–2–5   277n
   Vis.
      3.7.1–2   277n

Tatian
   Oratio ad Graecos
      31.7–35   288n

Theophilus of Antioch
   Autol.
      3.4–5   288n

Tertullian   68n, 287–90, 292n, 294n, 296
   Apol.
      2.8   287
      4.4   292n
      6.11–7.2   288n
      40.2   290
   Cult. fem.
      1.1–9   287

2.1–13	287	Demosthenes	
Mart.		*Andr.*	
2	289n	55	120
Praescr.		*Mid.*	
11.9.1	289n	78–79	107–8, 108n
Scap.			
5	294n	Dio of Prusa (Dio Chrysostom)	59
Spect.			
1–30	287	Diodorus Siculus	
30	296	20.17.1	130n
Theodore of Mopsuestia	56–58	Dionysius of Halicarnassus	
		Ant. rom.	
10. OTHER ANCIENT TEXTS AND AUTHORS		2.26–27	109n
		Heraclitus	
Acta Divi Augusti		*Hom. Prob.*	
113–116	108n	21–25	120n
123	108n	22.1	119n
126	108n	25.12	119n
		26.1–16	119n
Aelian		40.1–12	119n
Nat. an.			
16.24	111n	Hesiod	113n, 116–17
		Theog.	
Aelius Aristides		155–156	117
Platonic Discourses		156–159	117
307.10	186n	178–181	117
		459–460	117
Aeschylus	116–17n	589–602	113n
Seven against Thebes	116n	717–733	117
		Works and Days	116n
Athenaeus			
Deipn.		Hermogenes. *See* Pseudo-Hermogenes	
5.179d	111n		
		Homer	
Chariton		*Il.*	
Chaer.		1.399–406	120n
1.4.10	108n	1.565–567	117–18
2.7.3	115n	1.586–588	120
		1.590–594	118
Cicero		6.490	120
Leg.		8.1–27	118
2.7.19–27	208n	8.406–408	118
		8.415–424	118

Homer, Il. (cont.)		Am. prol.	105
14.256–261	118	Amat.	
15.16–17	118	756a–b, d	208n
15.18–21	118	Cohib. ira	
15.22–24	118	455b	107n
18.394–399	118n	455d	107n
19.126–131	118	455f	107n
21.479–488	119n	459a	106n
Ody.		459d	106n
14.29–38	113n	459f–460a	106n
14.32	113n	460c	106n
14.35–36	113n	460e–f	107n
14.37–38	113n	460f	106n
18.26–29	113n	461b–c	106n
		462a	106–7n
Horace		462e	106n
Carm.		463a–b	106n
3.6.5–8	208n	464a	107n
Saec.		Frat. amor.	105, 116n
57–65	279n	478a–492d	116n
		483d	252n
Lysias		488b–489b	252n
Or.		490f–491a	252n
1.30–31	108n	Pseudo-Hermogenes	
Philostratus		On Invention	
Vit. Ap.		95	109n
4.20	130n	96	109n
		99–100	109n
Phocylides		108	109n
Fragmenta		125	109n
2	111n	136–137	109n
		155–156	109n
Pliny the Elder	59	163	109n
Nat.		206	109n
30.2	129n	210	109n
		425	109n
Pliny the Younger	290		
Ep.		Semonides of Amorgos	111–13, 115
10.96	208n	Fragmenta	
10.96.3	292n	7	111n
10.97	208n, 291n	7.1	112n
		7.7	112n
Plutarch	105, 106–7, 107n, 116n,	7.12–20	112
	208n, 252n	7.71–72	112

INDEX OF ANCIENT AUTHORS AND TEXTS

7.83–84	112	5.5	208n
7.92–93	112		
7.96–97	111–12	Xenophon	
7.100	112	*Hier.*	
7.104–105	112	3.3	108n

Seneca
  Ira
    2.25.1–4   106n
    3.5.4   106n
  [*Oct.*]
    728–739   108n

Tacitus   109, 207–8n, 290
  Ann.
    15.44   290n
  Dial.
    35   109n
  Hist.
    5.1   207n

11. Papyri and Epigraphica

Black Obelisk of Shalmaneser III	7
Israel Stela of Merneptah	6
Moabite Stone	5
PGM	
4:3019–20	133n
Taylor Prism (Sennacherib)	8

Index of Modern Scholars

Aalen, S.   179n
Aberbach, M.   88n
Achenbach, R.   14n
Achtemeier, P. J.   203–7n, 211n, 238n
Adams, J.   253n
Aland, B.   132n
Aland, K.   132n
Albertz, R.   32n
Amidon, P. R.   88n
Anderson, A. A.   49n
Anderson, G. W.   41n, 44n, 46n
Anderson, R. A.   75n
Argall, R. A.   82n
Ariarajah, S. W.   151n
Arndt, W. F.   250n
Arnold, C. E.   157n, 162n
Asad, T.   150n
Astour, M. C.   185n
Attridge, H. W.   72n, 160n, 177–78n, 181–83n, 185–90n, 194n
Auld, A. G.   41n
Aune, D. E.   184n, 203–4n, 277n, 282n
Auwers, J.-M.   33n
Azevedo, J.   25n

Bagnall, R. S.   109n
Bakel, H. A. van   88n
Bakker, H.   vi, ix, 287–301, 289n, 293–94n, 331
Balch, D. L.   104n, 106n, 203–4n, 207n, 211n
Balla, P.   104n
Ballhorn, E.   53
Barclay, W.   270
Barkhuizen, J. H.   238n

Barmash, P.   104n
Barnett, P.   279n
Barrett, C. K.   125–35n
Bauckham, R.   263, 266–68n, 273–74
Bauer, W.   xi, 132n
Bauernfeind, O.   128n
Bauman, C.   17n
Beare, F. W.   204n, 207n, 226n, 228n
Beattie, D. R. G.   96n, 98n
Beck, A. B.   37n
Beck, N. A.   179n, 188
Becking, B.   xii, 24n
Bedke, M. A.   102n
Beentjes, P. C.   81n
Bekkenkamp, J.   103n
Berger, A.   207n
Best, E.   225–26n, 228n
Betz, H. D.   116n, 195n
Bidez, J.   88n
Bigg, C. A.   226n, 228n
Billerbeck, P.   133n, 180n
Birkeland, H.   43–44
Bisbee, G. A.   292n
Black, M.   63–64n, 69n, 205n
Blass, F.   210n
Blenkinsopp, J.   104n, 116n
Bloemendaal, W.   52, 54–55n
Boccaccini, G.   59–62n, 66–67n, 73–75n, 77–79n, 83–85n
Bogart, J.   232n
Bormann, E. G.   160n, 297n
Boshoff, W. S.   8n
Botha, J. E.   237n
Botha, P. J. J.   140n
Botterweck, G.   xv

INDEX OF MODERN SCHOLARS

Bovon, F.   103n
Bow, B.   82n
Bowker, J. W.   154n, 159n
Brenner, A.   104, 251n
Breytenbach, C.   152n, 205–7n, 332
Briggs, C. A.   48–49
Bright, J.   2n
Brinkman, M.   36n
Brock, S. P.   54n
Bromiley, G. W.   xiv–xv
Brongers, H. A.   44, 47n
Brooks, W. E.   178n, 185n, 187n
Broughton, T. R. S.   205n
Brown, R. E.   xi, 232–35n, 241n, 243n, 259n
Bruce, F. F.   247n
Bruce, J.   62n
Brueggemann, W.   27n, 36n, 280–81n
Buchanan, G. W.   178–80n, 182–83n, 186–87n, 189n, 192n
Bultmann, R.   233n
Burns, J. P.   15n

Cadbury, H. J.   129–30n, 132n, 135n
Caldwell, R.   117
Calvin, J.   225n
Campbell, D. A.   111–12n
Cassuto, U.   22, 23n
Castelli, E. A.   139n
Cavanaugh, M. M.   102n, 110n
Chadwick, H.   115n
Charlesworth, J. H.   xiv, 62–63n, 66n, 68n, 81n
Chazon, E. G.   83n
Childs, B. S.   21n, 48–51n
Chopra, D.   16n
Clark, P.   115n
Clarke, E. G.   95–96n
Coetzee, J. C.   255n
Cohen, S. J. D.   104n
Coleman, K. M.   292n
Collins, A. Y.   263n, 268–73n, 276–77n, 279, 284–85n
Collins, C. J.   287n
Collins, J. J.   60–61n, 63n, 65–66n, 68n, 72–73n, 75–77n, 79n, 81–86n, 104n, 157–58n
Conzelmann, H.   125–26n, 128–33n
Cook, P. W.   102n
Cosgrove, W.   263n
Craig, K. M.   25n, 27n, 37n
Craigie, P. C.   47n
Cross, F. M.   61n, 69n, 78n
Cullmann, O.   232n, 234n
Culpepper, R. A.   232–34n, 241n, 246–47n, 259–60n
Cupitt, D.   14n

D'Angelo, M. R.   179–80n
Dahl, N. A.   138–39n
Dahood, M.   49n
Danker, F. W.   xi
Davids, P. H.   226–28n
Dawkins, R.   16n
Dawn, M. J.   2n
Debrunner, A.   210n
Decock, P. B.   vi, ix, 263–86n, 265n, 299, 331
Deist, F. E.   10n
Delitzsch, F.   48n
Delling, G.   129n
Denniston, J. D.   210n
deSilva, D. A.   178n, 181–82n
Desjardins, M. R.   140n
Deurloo, K.   20–21n, 24n, 26n, 28n, 30n, 37n
Devreesse, R.   57n
Dibelius, M.   134n
Dietrich, W.   22n
Díez Merino, L.   95–97n
Dijk, T. A. van   210n
Dixon, S.   104n
Dodd, C. H.   254n, 256n
Dodds, E. R.   162n
Donavin, G.   103n
Donner, H.   22n
Döpp, S.   292n
Doran, R.   157n
Dozeman, T. B.   116n
Droge, A. J.   294n

Du Plessis, P. J. 257n
Du Toit, A. B. 162n, 179n, 184–85n, 195n, 197n, 205n, 256n
Du Toit, C. W. 16n
Duling, D. C. 233n
Dunn, J. D. G. 143n
Dunnill, J. 178n, 180n, 185n, 190n, 196n
Dyk, P. van 1n, 14n, 16n

Edwards, R. B. 233n, 256n
Eemeren, F. H. van 210n
Einstein, A. 16n
Eliade, M. 158n
Elliott, J. H. 203–7n
Elliott, N. 149n
Es, H. M. van 38n
Esler, P. F. 251–52n
Evans, C. A. 156n

Fagles, R. 118n
Feldmeier, R. 204n, 206–7n
Ferguson, E. 124n, 135n, 162n
Festinger, L. 75n
Filson, F. V. 177–78n, 233n, 241–42n
Fitzgerald, A. D. 114n
Fitzgerald, J. T. vii–x, 101–22, 106n, 110n, 115n, 209n, 299, 331
Flach, D. 291n
Flesher, P. V. M. 87n, 93n, 96n
Flint, P. W. 73n, 82n
Foakes Jackson, F. J. 129n
Fox, E. 37n
Francis, F. O. 156n
Fredrickson, D. E. 115n
Freedman, D. N. xi
Freedman, H. viii
Frerichs, E. S. 152n
Friedman, M. A. 107n
Friedrich, G. xiv
Friesen, S. J. 279–80n
Funk, R. W. 210n

Gantz, T. 118n
García Martínez, F. 60n, 66n, 83n, 85n
Garrett, S. R. 125–29n, 132–34n, 202n

Geerlings, W. 292n
Geertz, C. 154n
Gelles, R. J. 102n, 110n
Georgi, D. 138n, 160n
Gerber, D. E. 111–12n
Gerleman, G. 16n
Gerstenberger, E. 48n
Ghandi, M. K. 16
Gibson, E. L. 103n
Giesen, H. 282n
Gingrich, F. W. 250n
Glover, T. R. 296n
Goleman, D. 263n
Golka, F. W. 32n, 36n
Goold, G. P. 115n
Goosen, L. 22n
Goppelt, L. 203–4n, 207n, 219n, 226–27n
Gordon, R. 30n
Görg, M. 30n
Gowan, D. E. 23n, 28n
Grabbe, L. L. 66n, 82n
Graetz, N. 110n
Graf, F. 135n
Grant, F. C. 162n
Grayston, K. 233n, 240n
Green, J. B. 238n
Green, W. S. 152n
Grootendorst, R. 210n
Gruber, M. I. 25n
Grudem, W. 226n, 228n
Gunkel, H. 28n, 36n, 51n, 74n
Guthrie, D. 204n

Hackett, J. 103n
Haenchen, E. 127–28n, 130n, 134n
Hallett, J. P. 105n
Hamilton, M. W. 106n, 209n
Hamilton, V. 25n, 28n, 37n
Hanhardt, R. 22n
Hanson, P. D. 16n
Harnack, A. von 2n
Harrington, D. J. 88n
Harris, W. V. 44n, 109n, 185n
Hartney, A. M. 292n

INDEX OF MODERN SCHOLARS

Hauser, A. J.   21n
Hayes, J. H.   10n, 12n
Hays, R. B.   138n
Hayward, C. T. R.   96–97n
Hellholm, D.   61n, 263n
Helmbold, W. C.   252n
Hendel, R. S.   36n
Hengel, M.   83n
Herion, G. A.   37n
Herzer, J.   204n
Hesse, H.   17n
Hiebert, D. E.   247–48n, 256n
Hill, R. C.   57n
Hoffecker, W. A.   155n
Hoffmann, A. M.   102n
Hofmann, N. J.   295n
Holmes, P.   289n
Horrell, D. G.   152n
Horsley, R. A.   81n, 98n, 138–39n, 144n, 149n, 182n
Houtman, A.   90n, 92n, 94n
Houtman, C.   94n
Hubbard, T. K.   101n, 111–12n
Hughes, P. E.   179n, 181–85n, 187–88n, 190n, 192–93n
Hunter, V. J.   106n
Hurst, L. D.   189n
Hurtado, L.   233–35n, 240–41n, 247n

Isaac, E.   62n, 71n, 295n

Jackson, S.   210n
Jacob, B.   20n, 29n, 31–32n
Jacobs, S.   210n
Janowski, B.   26n
Jaubert, A.   72–74n, 78n
Jefford, C. N.   277n
Jervell, J.   124–26n, 128n, 130n, 132–35n
Jewett, R.   144n, 149n
Johnson, L. T.   150n, 158–59n, 162n, 181n, 184n, 186n, 188n, 196n
Johnson, T. F.   246n, 249n
Jones, A., Jr.   137n
Jonge, M. de   243n

Kant, I.   16
Käsemann, E.   232n
Kasher, R.   94n
Keel, O.   45n
Keener, C. S.   232n
Kelly, J. N. D.   226n, 228n
Kendall, D. W.   203n, 211n
Kennedy, G. A.   109n
Kenney, G. C.   233n, 241n, 255–56n, 259n
Kerényi, C.   117n
Keulen, D. van   36n
Kittel, G.   xiv
Klauck, H. J.   128n, 130n, 132–35n, 253n
Kloppenborg, J. S.   277–78n
Klopper, F.   1n
Knibb, M. A.   66n
Koch, D. A.   124n
Koch, K.   28n, 66n
Koester, C. R.   177–78n, 180–83n, 186–89n, 191–93n
Koester, H.   162n, 178n
Konstan, D.   119n
Kopperschmidt, J.   210n
Kraus, H.-J.   1–2n, 42n, 45n, 49n
Kraybill, J. N.   274n
Krijger, Ph. L.   19n
Kruijf, G. G. de   36n
Kurz, D.   102n

LaCocque, A.   76n
Lake, K.   129n, 132n, 135n
Lane, W. L.   177–79n, 181–82n, 187n, 189n, 192–93n
Lane Fox, R.   294n
Lang, C.   120n, 333
Lange, A.   26n, 84
Lassen, E. M.   237n
Laurence, R.   62n, 68n
Lawrence, D. H.   263n, 269n, 270
Lee, S.   51n, 54
Lehne, S.   178n, 180n, 183n, 187n, 190n, 193n
Lehrman, S. M.   viii

Lemaire, A.   51n
Lepelley, C.   114n
Leppä, O.   iv, xi, 177–197, 182n, 184n, 190n, 196n, 299, 332
Levine, A.-J.   103n
Levine, É.   88n
Lewis Herman, J.   296n
Lichtenberger, H.   26n
Liedke, G.   29n
Lietaert Peerbolte, L. J.   94n
Lieu, J.   142n, 241n, 256n
Lindars, B.   177–78n, 187n
Lindberg, G.   120n
Lindgård, F.   191n
Lintott, A.   103n
Lipiński, E.   23n
Lloyd-Jones, H.   111–12n
Loader, J. A.   10n
Lohse, E.   162n, 174–75n, 190n, 200–201n, 204n, 219–20n
Lonergan, B.   272n
Loseke, D. R.   102n, 110n
Loubser, J. A.   269n
Louw, J. P.   xiii, 153n, 238n, 267n
Lubbe, G. J. A.   16n
Lüdemann, G.   126n, 130–31n
Luz, U.   188n, 190n

MacDonald, M. Y.   175n
Maguire, K.   91n
Maher, M.   96n
Malherbe, A. J.   231n
Malina, B. J.   237n, 252n
Marshall, I. H.   225n
Marti, K.   74n
Martin, L. H.   138n
Martyn, J. L.   234n
Marxsen, W.   153n
Mathews, K. A.   23n, 28n, 33n
Matthews, S.   103n
Mayor, F.   137n, 145n, 150n
Mays, J. L.   50n, 52–53n
McCann, J. C.   50n
McCracken-Flesher, C.   152n
McDonald, M. F.   264n

McEntire, M. H.   20n, 27n, 36n, 103n
McGinn, B.   60–61n, 270
McNamara, M. J.   96n, 98n
Meeks, W. A.   146n, 156n, 232n, 284, 331
Mellinkoff, R.   30n
Merwe, D. G. van der.   vi, ix, 231–62, 236n, 253n, 257n, 299, 332
Metzger, B. M.   295n
Meyers, C.   104n
Michaels, J. R.   200n, 221n, 224–28n
Michel, A.   104n
Middleton, P.   283n
Milik, J. T.   62–63n, 70n, 79n
Millar, F.   205n
Millard, M.   49–51n
Miller, J. M.   10n, 12n
Minkoff, H.   36n
Moffatt, J.   180–81n
Montefiore, H.   178–82n, 184n, 187–88n, 192n
Moor, J. de   8n, 38n
Moor, M.   17n
Moule, C. F. D.   208n
Mowinckel, S.   42–44, 51n
Moxnes, H.   237n
Mukenge, A. K.   33n
Murray, A. T.   113n
Musurillo, H.   293n

Nelson-Pallmeyer, J.   103n
Neufeld, D.   233n
Neusner, J.   viii, 152n
Neves, J. Carreira das   95n
Neyrey, J. H.   252n
Nickelsburg, G. W. E.   60, 62–63n, 65–68n, 82–84n
Nida, E. A.   xiii, 153n, 267n
Niditch, S.   1n, 14n, 16n
Nock, A. D.   129–30n

O'Brien, P. T.   190n
O'Meara, J. J.   114n
Oden, R. A.   155n, 158n
Olbricht, T. H.   106n, 209n

Olson, D. 62n
Olson, S. D. 117n
Osiek, C. 104n, 106n
Otto, E. 12n, 16n, 29n

Painter, J. 232–33n, 235n, 239n, 246, 250n, 252n, 253–54n, 258n
Park, E. C. 143n
Patte, D. 92n
Paulus, C. 291n
Peels, E. viii, 1n, 12n, 19–40, 27–29n, 299, 332
Pellizer, E. 111–12n
Penner, T. 103n
Perdue, L. G. 104n
Perkins, P. 199–202n, 233n
Perrett, B. 17n
Petersen, D. L. 50n, 116n
Petersen, N. R. 156n
Peterson, J. 106n, 209n
Pfitzner, V. C. 177–80n, 182–83n, 185n, 187–89n
Pietersma, A. 52n
Pilch, J. J. 110n
Piper, J. 217n, 224–28n
Pippin, T. 142n
Plummer, A. 191n
Polaski, S. H. 144n, 146n, 152n
Pomeroy, S. B. 104n
Poorthuis, J. H. M. 90n
Porteous, N. W. 74–75n
Povinelli, E. A. 150n
Poythress, V. S. 210n
Preuss, H. D. 32n, 48n, 51n
Price, M. L. 103n
Priest, J. 295n
Pritchard, J. B. xi
Procksch, O. 31n
Pulleyn, S. 118n, 120n
Punt, J. ix, 137–52, 151–52n, 196n, 299, 332
Puukko, A. 43–44

Quasten, J. 292n
Quinones, R. J. 22n

Rad, G. von 2–4, 21n, 32–33n, 36, 38n
Rahlfs, A. 52n
Räisänen, H. 187–88n, 192–93n
Ramose, M. B. 16n
Reicke, B. 205n, 226n
Reiser, M. 135n
Rendall, G. H. 288n
Rensberger, D. 232n
Rensburg, F. J. van vi–vii, ix, 199–230, 202n, 211n, 299, 332
Richard, E. 204n, 206–7n
Ridderbos, H. N. 164n
Ridderbos, N. H. 38n, 41–43n
Riecken, H. W. 75n
Riessen, H. van 160n
Ringgren, H. xv
Robbins, V. K. 237n
Roberts, J. H. 160n
Rogerson, J. W. 41n, 46–47n
Roloff, J. 125–28n, 131–35n, 182–83n, 194n
Römheld, D. 26n
Rooy, H. F. van vi–viii, x, 8n, 41–58, 52n, 54n, 56n, 299–300, 333
Rosemond, J. 110n
Ross, A. P. 38n
Rousseau, J. A. 204n
Royalty, R. M. 263–64n, 269n, 273n, 275–76n, 284n
Rudavsky, T. M. 110n
Ruppert, L. 21n
Rusam, D. 239n
Russell, D. A. 119n

Sacchi, P. 66n, 71n
Sæbø, M. 51n
Safrai, S. 205–6n
Sainte Croix, G. E. M. de 291n
Saldarini, A. J. 88n
Salisbury, E. 103n
Sals, U. 264n
Sanders, J. T. 191n
Sandnes, K. O. 237n
Sappington, T. J. 160n, 164n
Sarna, N. M. 29n

Schachter, S.   75n
Schaefer, H.   205n
Schaik, A. P. van   266n
Scharbert, J.   31n
Scheepers, C.   7n
Scheffler, E. H.   viii, 1–18, 2n, 5–8n, 10–13n, 299, 333
Schille, G.   130–35n
Schlueter, C. J.   179n, 184–85n
Schmid, K.   116n
Schmithals, W.   132n
Schnackenburg, R.   209n, 233–35n, 242–43n, 246n, 254n
Schneider, G.   128n, 135n
Schneider, H.   xii
Schoedel, W. R.   185n
Scholem, G. G.   162n, 164n
Schroeder, J. A.   121n
Schulz, S.   178n, 188n
Schunack, G.   178n
Schürer, E.   205n
Schüssler Fiorenza, E.   98–99n, 104n, 139n, 146–47n, 149n, 182n, 263–64n, 273–74n, 277n, 285n
Schwager, R.   19n
Schwartz, J.   90n
Schweizer, E.   154n, 156n, 160n, 162–63n, 186n
Seebass, H.   14n, 22n, 30n
Seeliger, H. R.   292n
Seesemann, H.   193n
Segal, A. F.   138–39n, 143n
Segovia, F. F.   150n
Selengut, C.   145n, 150–51n
Selwyn, E. G.   203–4n, 226n
Shaw, B. D.   105n, 115n
Shelton, J.-A.   109n
Sherwin-White, A. N.   291n
Sherwood, Y.   103n
Simon, B.   117n
Simon, M.   viii
Sizgorich, T.   103n
Slater, P. E.   117n
Smalley, S. S.   233n
Smelik, K.   34n

Smelik, W. F.   87n
Smend, R.   22n
Smith, D.   146n
Smith, J. Z.   82n
Smolar, L.   88n
Snijders, L. A.   10n
Spangenberg, I.   8n
Spina, F. A.   28n, 37n
Staalduine-Sulman, E. van   ix, 87–100, 89–90n, 92–94n, 299, 333
Stählin, G.   128–29n, 131n
Stander, H. F.   238n
Standhartinger, A.   160n
Stein, S. J.   60–61n
Steinrück, M.   111–12n
Stern, M.   205–7n
Stibbs, A. M.   227–28n
Stone, M. E.   66n, 83n, 285n
Strack, H. L.   133n, 180n
Straus, M. A.   102n, 110n
Strecker, G.   232n, 257n
Summers, R. W.   102n
Surburg, R. F.   84n
Swart, G. J.   238n
Synodinou, K.   119n
Syrén, R.   98n
Sysling, H.   95n, 98n

Tabor, J. D.   294n
Talbert, C. H.   203–4n, 211n
Tamarkin Reis, P.   26n
Tate, M. E.   41–42n, 46n
Taves, A.   103n
Taylor, J. E.   80n
Taylor, N. H.   143n
Tedeschi, G.   111–12n
Teodorsson, S.-T.   120n
Theissen, G.   192n
Thielecke, H.   13n
Thimmes, P.   182n
Thom, J. C.   152n, 332
Thomas, J. C.   233n, 255n
Thompson, L. L.   273n, 276n, 284n
Thompson, M. M.   238n
Thrall, M. E.   191n

Thurén, L.   179n, 184n, 197n, 203n, 207n
Tiller, P. A.   79–82n
Tobin, T.   72n
Tolbert, M. A.   150n
Tollefson, K. D.   253n
Torry, R.   87n, 93n
Trible, P.   103n
Trisoglio, F.   291n
Tromp, J.   295n
Tur-Sinai, N. H.   48n
Twerski, A. J.   110n

Uitman, J. E.   174n
Unnik, W. C. van   203–4n, 206–8n, 212n, 226n
Ussishkin, D.   7n

Vander Stichele, C.   103n
VanderKam, J. C.   61–64n, 66n, 68–70n, 72n, 77n, 82n, 85n
Vaux, R. de   3n, 4–5, 11n
Vergeer, W. C.   163n
Vermes, G.   205n
Villiers, J. L. de   162n
Villiers, P. G. R. de   267n
Volf, M.   137n, 151n
Vriezen, Th. C.   38n

Wahlde, U. C. von.   234n, 255n, 259n
Watson, D. F.   253n
Watt, J. G. van der   199–201n, 219n, 232n, 237–38n, 332–33

Weems, R. J.   104n
Weiser, A.   130n, 134–35n
Wenham, G. J.   21n, 25n, 27–28n, 30–31n, 38n
Wénin, A.   33n
Werline, R. A.   82n
West, M. L.   111–13n
Westcott, B. F.   239n
Westermann, C.   21–25n, 27–30n, 32n, 36–37n
Whitacre, R. A.   242–44n, 246n
Williams, C. S. C.   126n, 131n, 134n
Williamson, R.   189n
Wils, J.-P.   19n
Wilson, B. R.   196n
Wilson, G. H.   50–51, 50–52n
Wilson, W. T.   154–57n, 159–60n
Wlosok, A.   291n
Wolde, E. van   23n, 26–27n, 37n
Wolters, A. M.   155n
Wright, B. G., III   81n
Wright, C. J. H.   20n
Wright, N. T.   155n

Yoder, J. H.   17n

Zeitlin, S.   76n
Zenger, E.   41n, 46–47n, 51n
Zerbe, G. M.   141n
Zimmerli, W.   4, 15n, 21–22n, 36
Žižek, S.   150n
Zuurmond, R.   22n